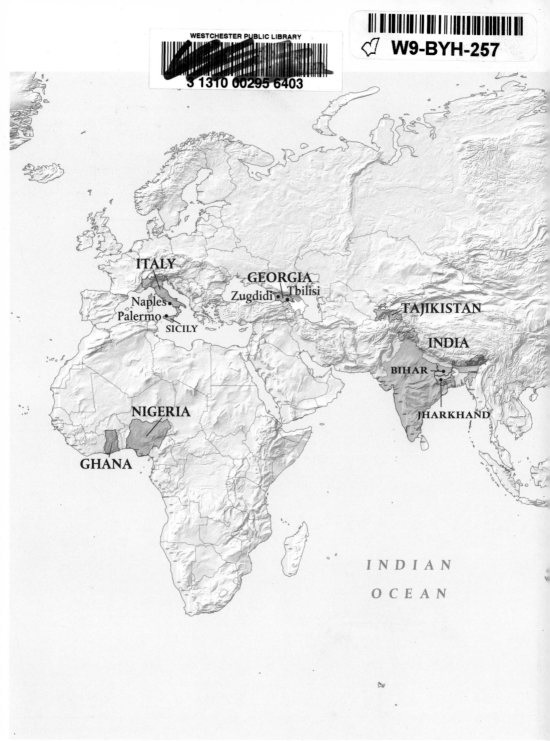

ITALY

GEORGIA
Zugdidi• •Tbilisi

TAJIKISTAN

Naples•

INDIA

Palermo•

BIHAR •

SICILY

NIGERIA

JHARKHAND

GHANA

INDIAN

OCEAN

A SAVAGE ORDER

A SAVAGE ORDER

HOW THE WORLD'S

DEADLIEST

COUNTRIES

CAN FORGE A PATH

TO SECURITY

RACHEL KLEINFELD

PANTHEON BOOKS, NEW YORK

Grateful acknowledgment is made to the Carnegie Endowment for
International Peace for providing the graphs that appear in this book.

The map on page 55 is reproduced courtesy of The Map Company,
copyright © Kappa Map Group LLC. Used with permission.

Endpaper map by Mapping Specialists, Ltd.

Library of Congress Cataloging-in-Publication Data
Name: Kleinfeld, Rachel, author.
Title: A savage order : how the world's deadliest countries can forge a path
to security / Rachel Kleinfeld.
Description: First edition. New York : Pantheon Books, 2018. Includes
bibliographical references and index.
Identifiers: LCCN 2018014527. ISBN 9781101871997 (hardcover : alk. paper).
ISBN 9781524746872 (ebook).
Subjects: LCSH: Internal security—Cross-cultural studies. Human security—
Cross-cultural studies. National security—Cross-cultural studies. Violence—
Prevention. Violence—Government policy.
Classification: LCC HV6419 .K54 2018 | DDC 363.32/17—dc23 |
LC record available at lccn.loc.gov/2018014527

www.pantheonbooks.com

Jacket design by Janet Hansen

Printed in the United States of America
First Edition

2   4   6   8   9   7   5   3   1

For all those striving for the security,
justice, and dignity of humanity,

may your efforts be rewarded.

CONTENTS

A SAVAGE ORDER

INTRODUCTION

It is impossible to move tons of cocaine, launder thousands of millions of dollars, and maintain a clandestine organization of several hundred armed persons without a system of political and police protection.

—YOLANDA FIGUEROA, A JOURNALIST MURDERED ALONG
WITH HER HUSBAND AND THREE CHILDREN IN MEXICO,
DECEMBER 1996[1]

Ebed Yanes knew better than to leave the house at night. He was a diligent student, the kind of teenager who washed his father's car every Sunday before church. But he was also fifteen, and it was an early summer Saturday. A girl he knew from Facebook had suggested a rendezvous. After his parents had gone to bed, Ebed snuck out and drove off on his father's motorcycle. He followed the roads for a while looking for the girl. He couldn't find her. He sent her a text message telling her that he had to return home.

The next morning, his father noticed the car was unwashed. He called the guard booth at the entrance to their gated community. The guard said that Ebed had left around midnight and hadn't returned. Ebed's parents tried to stay calm. They checked the children's hospital, then the jail. Next, they stopped at the police homicide division. Ebed's parents finally found their only son in the morgue, with a broken jaw and a bullet wound near his mouth.[2]

In Honduras, one of the most violent countries on earth, Ebed's

killers might have been members of a gang or a drug cartel. The police
mentioned they could have been at a party near where the body had
been found: in a country with so much impunity, small arguments
mixed with alcohol often led to death. As Ebed's father walked the
street where his son had last been alive, a neighbor poked out his
head. He had heard shots the night before, he explained, and saw soldiers prodding a splayed body with their rifles. The neighbor handed
Ebed's father the empty bullet cases he had collected after the soldiers
had left.[3] "The problem isn't that [security agencies] are overwhelmed
by crime," explained Julieta Castellanos, the president of the National
Autonomous University of Honduras, whose own son had been murdered by police the year before. "The problem is that they are working
with the criminals."[4]

As a senior fellow at a Washington think tank, I advise governments
and philanthropists on how major social change occurs in democracies, particularly how to build security, improve governance, and
deepen justice in badly governed countries. My desk is cluttered with
studies analyzing terrorism, fragile states, insurgencies, and war. But
the dirty secret is that we know surprisingly little about how to solve
these problems. Policies often simply mimic the strategies used in
functional countries. We had no proof, for instance, that the program
used to train Germany's police would be effective in Afghanistan. But
that was the policy Europe and America decided would mend the
warring country after the United States and allied forces invaded in
2001.[5] It's the sort of idea that gets trotted out again and again.

Nearly all the research we have about violence offers insight into
countries at war. Today, however, most violent death looks like Ebed's
murder in Honduras. Since the end of the Cold War, wars between
countries and civil wars have plummeted.[6] While all the statistics
should be treated with caution, about 83 percent of all violent death
now occurs outside conflict zones.[7] In 2015, more people died violently in Brazil than in Syria's civil war.[8]

VIOLENCE ISN'T JUST WAR

Three kinds of carnage kill four times as many people as the battle deaths in all current wars put together.[9] The greatest killer in most years is homicide.[10] Next comes governments killing their own people.[11] Rwanda's genocide, for instance, precipitated the largest spike in violent death since the end of the Cold War. If Nigeria included police and military killings in its murder statistics, its reported homicides in 2008 would have jumped by 40 percent.[12] The third, rising cause is murder between gangs, Mafias, drug cartels, and other groups of organized, armed civilians. Mexico had more violent death from 2007 to 2014 than the combined civilian death toll in Iraq and Afghanistan over those years.[13]

VIOLENT DEATHS IN 2016 BY CAUSE[14]

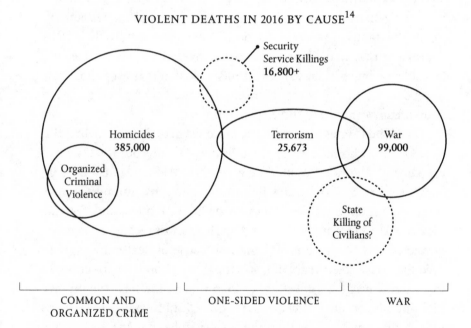

(Dotted lines indicate severely underreported statistics.)

With a handful of exceptions, the most violent countries in the world today are not at war but are buckling under a maelstrom of gang warfare, organized crime, state brutality, and murders by paramilitaries, death squads, and ordinary people.[15] This is the violence devastating Central America, the cocktail that has made Venezuela the most deadly country in the world. It adds to the death toll in some countries formally in conflict like Afghanistan and creates fertile soil for terrorists like ISIS. War grabs the headlines. But the security problem of our time is boiling over from countries caught in a vortex of internal violence.

Violence devastates lives and destroys countries. Its effects can last for generations. In Central America, children get recruited to join gangs or are raped by gang members starting at around age thirteen.[16] In Mexico, 90,000 married men were murdered between 2000 and 2009, meaning that around 180,000 kids are growing up without fathers and often without their primary breadwinners.[17] Scientists are now exploring the theory that children who experience violence suffer epigenetic changes. Early exposure to violence may switch off a gene that tamps down overreaction. These alterations to their DNA expression may make kids more easily stressed and aggressive, and less able to control their violent impulses, so that they are more likely to repeat violent behaviors themselves as adults.[18] Altered genes, of course, can be passed to future generations.

The United States has a particular interest in this problem. In 2011, New Orleans's homicide rate (the number of deaths per 100,000) was on par with the rate for all violent death in Afghanistan.[19] Detroit, New Orleans, St. Louis, and Baltimore now rank among the fifty most violent cities on the planet. Medellín, Colombia, and Tijuana, Mexico, are safer.[20] In 1994, after America's most recent crime wave, homicide was the third most common cause of death among children five to fourteen years old, and the rate of homicide for children in America was five times higher than that of the next twenty-five high-income countries *combined*.[21] The U.S. homicide rate remains four to five times higher than that of Australia, Canada, or Europe. Americans like to imagine that our gang warfare, police brutality, and inner-city predation stand apart from the problems faced by "developing" countries. But they are far more similar than we like to admit.

———

Violence feels like an intractable problem. That sense of hopeless-
ness has altered global politics. Over half a century ago, creative
leaders forged the European Union to unite a continent where two
world wars had killed millions; now, the idea of European world war
is unimaginable. Fifty years ago, the United States sent men to the
moon. Today, we send women and children back to countries where
they are being hunted by gangs.[22]

"Every country for itself," demands the new Western zeitgeist. Refugees fleeing violence, from Central America to the Middle East, are
igniting political backlash on both sides of the Atlantic. In the United
States, neither the more militaristic policies of President George W.
Bush nor the lighter touch of Barack Obama have been able to stanch
the bleeding around the globe. Indeed, both tactics poured fuel on
the conflagration. Europe's leaders have done no better. Crowded
schools, strained public services, and fears about immigration and
Islam have fueled movements to shut down borders. Britain's Brexit
is a nostalgic demand for a return to a little England that hasn't existed
for decades. The leader of the rising Alternative for Germany party
declared that border guards might need to aim their guns on illegal
frontier crossers.[23] Austria's Freedom Party, which campaigned under
the slogan "Austria First," is part of the governing coalition in charge
of the Defense, Interior, and Foreign Ministries. It demands tighter
borders just as America's president calls for higher walls.

WE CAN FIGHT VIOLENCE

Yet understanding today's violence is crucial precisely because reducing it is well within our grasp. The media portrays violence as constant and overwhelming, and politicians profit from stoking fear. But
the world is actually vastly less dangerous than it has ever been. Violent deaths of every kind have fallen across the globe since the Middle
Ages and fell again after the Cold War's end.[24]

Today, wars are less frequent, and those that do occur are less
deadly. One thousand deaths a year is the traditional line used to
demarcate "war" from other struggles. In the 1950s, the average international war such as France's war in Indochina or the Korean War
killed over twenty-one thousand people a year. Today, wars between

states no longer entail battalions of troops. Instead, they look more like the messy urban fighting in Ukraine between Ukrainian soldiers and local rebels supplemented by Russian militiamen, where ten or twelve troops may be killed in a firefight, instead of tens of thousands slaughtered in a single engagement.[25] The change from large battles to smaller-scale warfare means that the average conflict between countries today kills fewer than three thousand people annually.[26]

Meanwhile, since 1989, 80–90 percent of all wars have been civil wars.[27] Their numbers have also fallen: many had been kept alive by proxy fighting between the United States and the Soviet Union and petered out a few years after the Cold War ended.[28] Modern civil wars are generally less deadly than they were in the twentieth century.[29] In part, that is because the vast majority of twenty-first-century civil wars are new outbreaks of past conflicts in places such as Somalia and Sudan that happen to have fairly small populations.[30]

Since 1989, there has been a 70 percent decline in all wars, and the average conflict today inflicts 90 percent fewer deaths in battle than in the 1950s.[31] Despite the horrors of Syria, Yemen, and Ukraine, conflict deaths are still dropping today.[32]

GLOBAL DEATH RATE IN BATTLE PER 100,000 PEOPLE, 1946–2013[33]

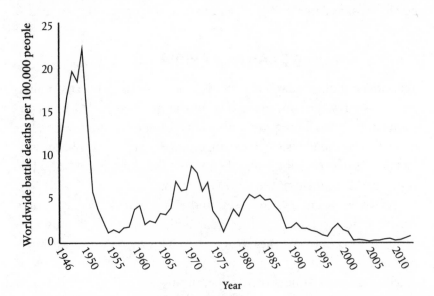

It's not just war. These numbers, like the rest of the statistics in this book, don't include rapes, shootings, and other violence short of death, because their different definitions and levels of reporting make them incomparable across countries. Yet all types of violence have been dropping.[34] Homicide rates have been falling for centuries.

HOMICIDE RATES IN WESTERN EUROPE, 1300–2010[35]

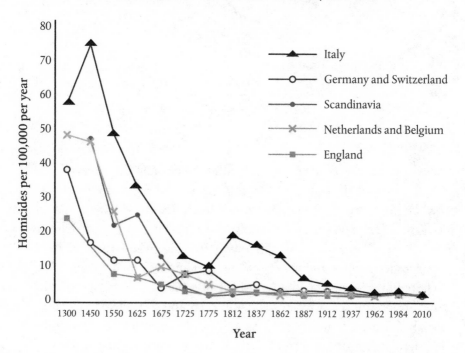

The trend continues in the modern era. Across all high-income countries globally, murders fell by 57 percent from 1995 to 2011.[36] In the United States, violence is near an all-time low. Despite a slight uptick in the year or two before this book was published, the country has not been so safe since the 1950s, the decade with the lowest homicide rate until today.[37]

There will always be violence in the world. But it is eminently conceivable that fewer people could suffer from it. Wars are less deadly today in part because we have learned what works to reduce their carnage. When powerful countries want to reduce conflict, they succeed more often than in years past. The number of wars that were ended

HOMICIDE RATE IN THE UNITED STATES, 1920–2015[38]

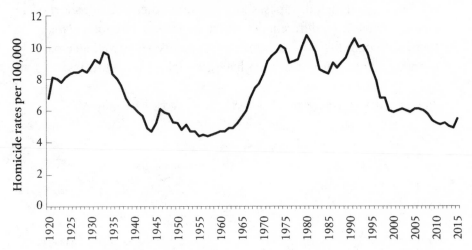

by peace treaties rose in the 1990s after the cessation of superpower-imposed global gridlock.[39] Negotiators gained a stronger sense of what made these agreements more likely to last.[40] Policy makers learned that it was hard for countries to trust each other enough to maintain agreements on their own. Warring groups needed third parties to mediate and verify that agreements were being kept.[41] The United States, the UN, the Catholic Church, and a bevy of "friends" groups composed of interested nations sprang up to help make deals stick. Scholars found that peace agreements were more likely to be sustained if women and organizations that represented a diverse range of people gained seats at the table, and policy makers followed suit.[42] Gradually, peace agreements lasted longer, and peacekeeping efforts got better at reducing violence during conflicts and limiting the spread of war to neighboring countries.[43]

No one is going to send UN peacekeepers to patrol the streets of Venezuela or deploy NATO to fight crime in South Africa. Yet there are ways to reduce the kinds of violence that afflict these countries.

STUDYING SUCCESS

The solutions lie in places like Colombia; the Republic of Georgia; Bihar, India; and Sicily that faced extreme violence and emerged, if not at peace, then far safer than before. After two decades spent studying countries mired in violence, I traveled through these places that had revived, as well as similar countries that failed to improve, interviewing politicians and police, journalists and activists, and militia leaders and businessmen to understand what had made some places successful while others remained mired in violence. My findings form the basis of this book, which first seeks to explain why some modern democracies have become so extraordinarily violent, and then explores what people can do to help countries pull themselves out of carnage.

Consider Colombia, where 200,000 people were murdered in the late 1940s and early 1950s in a civil war so senseless and vicious it is known simply as *La Violencia*. The ensuing years of carnage caused the biggest crisis of internally displaced people in the world until Syria's civil war in 2011.[44] Guerrilla terror simmered in pockets of the country through the 1960s and 1970s. Then violence skyrocketed again in the 1980s and 1990s as insurgents, paramilitaries, drug cartels, and gangs fought, yielding the greatest homicide rate on earth. To match Medellín's peak murder rate of 381 killings per 100,000 people, New York City's 2017 homicide rate would have had to grow over a thousandfold.[45]

And then something miraculous happened. Twenty-five years later, Medellín is a tourist destination. The *New York Times* travel section suggests visitors try paragliding, visit discos, and tour the former drug kingpin Pablo Escobar's favorite haunts.[46]

Colombia is not alone in achieving a spectacular recovery. In the early 1990s, the Republic of Georgia was torn apart by civil war and militias, not unlike Libya after Qaddafi's fall. Less than two decades later, Georgia was a place where women could walk alone at night in safety. In the same era, Sicily's Mafia assassinated generals, politicians, and prosecutors and bombed Florence, Milan, and Rome. The Sicilian mob has since been decimated. In Bihar, India, in the year 2000, armed men drove down the streets of the capital with guns sticking out of windows.[47] Restaurants and businesses shuttered at dark.[48] By 2015, nightlife was flourishing. These places are far from perfect, but all have become safer by orders of magnitude.

What could their recoveries teach us about countries buckling under similar violence today? The idea of studying success has led to breakthroughs in other fields. Jim Collins's best-selling business book *Good to Great* examines outliers, or "positive deviants," among high-performing companies. Similar approaches have yielded surprising and important findings in fields from fighting malnutrition to treating veterans with post-traumatic stress.[49] Studying success, however, is prey to a universal danger. Look at a group of peaceful countries, and it's easy to conclude that approaches they all share could reduce violence. But what if places that had failed had also taken the same steps? To guard against this pitfall, for each case of success I found a case of failure as similar as possible, ideally as close to a naturally occurring experiment as I could find.[50] Policies that were the same in cases of failure and success were unlikely to be effective, or could point to a missing link needed to make the ingredients work together.[51] For instance, during the 1990s, both Naples and Sicily had the same laws, prosecutors, and national government. Both had impressive local mayors committed to urban renewal, but only one had a citizenry that organized itself to fight the Mafia.

Thus I delved into why Naples remained Mafia-ridden while Sicily's mob was cowed. I contrasted Colombia with Mexico to understand why the latter remained rent by bloodshed while the former was able to end the world's longest-running war. Why could Bihar quell Maoist insurgents, militias, and criminal gangs while Jharkhand, its neighboring state, could not? In the United States, the "Wild West" became safe a few decades after the Civil War. Why did the South become more violent as war receded, and why is it still the most violent part of the United States today? The former Soviet Republic of Georgia emerged from near anarchy into democracy, while nearby Tajikistan devolved into a dictatorship. What did they do differently? Nigeria has been roiled by rebels, terrorists, and war for decades, while Ghana never faced significant bloodshed, despite multiple coups, even after its government nearly failed in the 1970s. Why not?

While each of these places had high levels of violence for their regions, they differed substantially in degree. I was looking not for an absolute amount of violence but for pervasiveness that created high rates for a country's level of wealth and region. While Italy in the 1970s was clearly not Colombia in the 1990s, both faced political terrorism, left- and right-wing armed groups, and endemic organized crime that made them among the most violent places in Europe and South America, respectively. There was a fractal nature to the violence afflicting these democracies. The same pattern kept recurring, whether death rates were just extraordinary for a region or among the highest in the world.

FOXES GUARDING THE HENHOUSE

When democracies face significant violence, policy makers often blame state weakness. After all, if an elected government isn't protecting its voters, it must be unable to fight effectively. To help these governments provide security, the United States and European countries often support their police and military forces with training and equipment. Domestically, politicians facing rising crime call for more police on the streets. Law-enforcement experts suggest proven policing strategies, such as targeting "hot spots" where crime most frequently occurs. All these efforts can be effective, but only if local politicians and security agencies are committed to stopping violent groups.

In the world's deadliest democracies, that assumption is frequently wrong. In Venezuela, where the murder rate soared to be the world's highest in 2016, the vice president and the minister of interior and justice are believed to be drug kingpins, while the U.S. Drug Enforcement Administration (DEA) caught the first lady's nephews running a major drug-trafficking operation. The Venezuelan government hires armed gangs known as *colectivos* to assist with drug distribution and intimidate regime opponents.[52] During the heights of Colombia's violence in the 1990s, its air force was known as the "blue cartel" after military jets were caught trying to smuggle cocaine into the United States.[53] At least in these countries, the government is in control. In some Mexican states, drug cartels assassinate politicians who don't follow their orders. Elsewhere, politicians or security agencies and criminals are one and the same: in 2009–2010 in Bihar, 168 candidates running for state parliament had been charged with attempted murder.[54] Sixty percent of Brazil's Congress either had been convicted of a crime or were under investigation in 2016 for charges ranging from

corruption to homicide.[55] About 600 police and former police running extortion rings in Brazil were jailed in 2011, until the judge who
prosecuted them was shot by six military-police officers.[56] In Sicily,
the scholars Peter and Jane Schneider describe a situation of *intreccio*,
which "signifies more than a simple reciprocity between the Mafia
and the State; it points to a vast gray area where it is impossible to
determine where one leaves off and the other begins."[57] Governments
or security services that are supporting violent groups are unlikely to
implement even the most tested of technical solutions to stop them.

What can be done when the parts of government that are supposed to protect people are, instead, fueling bloodshed? That is the
problem this book sets out to solve.

FIVE GUIDING IDEAS

A Savage Order journeys through crumbling, corrupt countries that
have faced some of the most crushing violence in the world and
were then reborn. Part 1 describes what makes some democracies
so violent, why current explanations are wanting, and why common
"solutions" backfire. Part 2, which makes up the bulk of the book,
describes the steps that successful democracies followed to achieve
greater security. Each country's story is woven throughout the chapters, because their steps are not linear. Nearly every democracy must
take measures that appear to lead backward in order to progress, just
as hikers must often descend into a canyon to eventually reach a sum-
mit. Upward momentum is not inevitable. Societies lurch forward,
then make mistakes and fall back into new pathologies. Part 3 discusses the implications of this new way of understanding violence
and what governments, businesses, philanthropists, and regular people can do to help.

Five ideas serve as guides.

1. **Violence as a Governing Strategy:** Democracies become engulfed by violence in two situations. As common wisdom suggests, one cause is when states are too weak to enforce order. The
   second arises when politicians abdicate the monopoly of force and
   collude with violent groups to maintain power. The latter situa-

tion I call Privilege Violence because it occurs in highly unequal, politically polarized societies governed by political and economic elites who twist the law to their benefit to monopolize exorbitant state resources. This idea is new, and so it has never before been the focus of policy. Yet complicit states are far more common than those that are merely weak, and require a different solution.

2. **Societies Decivilize and Recivilize:** Ubiquitous violence changes society. Even in Mafia-riddled Sicily and insurgent-scarred Colombia, organized gangs, professional criminals, militias, and guerrillas accounted for only a portion of the bloodshed. Ordinary people contributed, too. When people lose trust in their government and antagonism deepens toward fellow citizens, violence increases, and impunity grows. Ordinary people's inhibitions to using force fall. Businessmen murder rivals; neighbors extort neighbors. As predatory elites allow violence to rise, societies polarize into two camps: those who seek a return to law and order even at the cost of government repression, and those who demand a more just government. In each faction, most people simply become apologists for the violence emanating from "their" side. But some join gangs claiming to protect their neighborhoods, support guerrillas, or donate to paramilitaries. This is called the "decivilizing process," and it can happen in any culture, from Bloody Kansas on the eve of the U.S. Civil War, to Michoacán, Mexico. These places look pathological. But any society can decivilize when governments abandon ordinary people to fend for themselves.

3. **The Middle Class Is the Fulcrum of Change:** Policy makers fighting violence tend to focus solutions on perpetrators or victims. They propose peace treaties with rebels or suggest grassroots programs to deter people from joining gangs or terrorist groups. Yet Privilege Violence is rooted in the way a state is governed. Change begins when the middle class, the people with enough voice and power to change the system, mobilize. In these democracies, politicians depend on the middle class for votes and ensure that they are rarely touched by violence. In highly unequal societies, the lives of those shattered by murder are so remote from most middle-

class families that the problem can be ignored for a long time. The middle class rouses only when its sense of invulnerability breaks. Then whether they organize to change the system perpetuating violence or double down by supporting repression determines whether a country takes a step toward security or deepens its devastation. It takes social leaders to organize the middle class into movements that are focused on effective goals, strong enough to overcome entrenched interests, and broad and nonpartisan enough to achieve success in highly polarized countries.

4. **Governments Need Dirty Deals, Centralization, and Surveillance:** Countries that have fallen prey to Privilege Violence have bureaucrats and politicians who are helping criminals and insurgents. To fight this enemy within, politicians must centralize power and use dangerous tools such as surveillance and asset seizure. When a state's police, military, and courts have been hollowed out by corruption and criminality, pragmatic leaders must make peace treaties and offer amnesties to the worst violent groups to buy the bureaucracy time to repair. Those agreements are essential, but they also make the job of rebuilding a just and trustworthy state more difficult. A skilled politician can wield these tools without becoming authoritarian. But often the scalpel slips. Politicians lauded as reformers become more dictatorial. Societies must choose whether to allow their countries to descend into authoritarianism or rise up again and demand that their newspapers report the truth, their courts convict government wrongdoers, and their police walk the thin, difficult line of justice.

5. **States and Societies Recivilize Together:** Like the sand and the sea, states and societies function in tight relationship. Societies decivilize when states abandon the monopoly on violence. They recivilize when people decide to trust one another and follow the law. Yet communities cannot start that process alone. Reform-minded politicians must first prove that the state is governing for all of its people and enforcing the laws equally. But in a broken state, political leaders have few tools to start this process. It takes

savvy politicians using all their political skills to get the state working before a government has a strong bureaucracy and security services. Throughout the process of descent and rebirth, states and societies pass the baton back and forth, spurring each other toward vicious cycles of increasing violence or virtuous cycles of renewal.

I began studying violence twenty years ago, on the streets of New Haven, Connecticut, and in the villages of northern India. The strategy I've uncovered is morally murky. It requires difficult ethical choices that will make many people on both the Left and Right as uncomfortable as they have made me in the years that I have grappled with these findings. The path out of bloodshed is measured not in years but in generations. There is nothing inevitable about success. Once a democracy descends into extreme violence, it is always more vulnerable to backsliding. The fault lines that split citizens into polarized camps and the temptation of repression are ever present. The struggle to escape doesn't end.

But to say that the story is never over does not deny the reality of success. Some of the places I will describe faced total collapse and anarchy. In most, death sentences emanated from the mouths of the most powerful. Today, each is at a different point along the path toward recovery. They remain flawed, but all are much safer societies than in years past. They have become places where people have far greater chances to educate their children, build productive lives without fear, and grow old among those they love. Over 1.5 billion people, and 1 in 6 children, live in countries beset by serious conflict and crime.[58] For them and for those lucky enough to live in more stable societies, this book provides more than hope. It offers a blueprint for action.

PART I

THE PROBLEM

1

VIOLENCE TODAY

We know of oppression and torture,
We know of extortion and violence,
Destitution, disease,
The old without fire in winter,
The child without milk in summer,
Our labour taken away from us,
Our sins made heavier upon us.
We have seen the young man mutilated,
The torn girl trembling by the mill-stream.
And meanwhile we have gone on living,
Living and partly living.

—T. S. ELIOT, *MURDER IN THE CATHEDRAL*[1]

Consider a map of countries struck by high levels of violence such as the one on page 22, which shows total deaths around the world from war, homicide, terrorism, and government murder.[2]

You'll see a few places like Iraq, Afghanistan, and Libya that are decimated by international or civil wars (categories that often blend together today).[3]

Take these few away, and you are left with a set of countries mired in largely internal violence. A handful of these places have governments that barely function, such as Somalia. These are states so weak that they are often considered to have failed.

VIOLENT DEATH RATES PER 100,000 POPULATION,
ANNUAL AVERAGE FROM 2010 TO 2015[4]

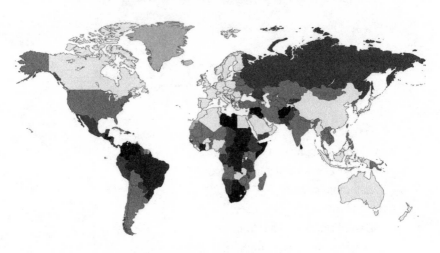

Number of violent deaths per 100,000 population

■ 30 or over   ■ 10.0–19.9   ☐ <3
■ 20.0–29.9   ■ 3.0–9.9   ■ No Data

Created with mapchart.net ©

But for a multitude of other places, it is harder to understand why they are so bloody. In absolute numbers, Brazil, India, Syria, Nigeria, Venezuela, South Africa, Afghanistan, Mexico, Iraq, and Pakistan are the most deadly countries in the world. Adjusting for population, Syria, unsurprisingly, tops the list of countries with the highest rates of violent death in 2016, followed by El Salvador, Venezuela, Honduras, Afghanistan, Jamaica, Iraq, Libya, Somalia, and South Sudan.[5] Lesotho, a kingdom within South Africa, stands at number 15 because tiny populations skew the numbers—a few deaths in a place with few people translate into a very high rate. Large countries skew in the other direction. Brazil is sixteenth on the list, because, although it had more violent deaths than any country in the world, including Syria, it also has a large population, creating a lower per capita rate.[6]

These states cross ethnicities, religions, and most regions of the globe. None of them are rich, but many are middle income, and some—such as Brazil and South Africa—have the highest GDPs in their regions.[7] If state weakness is causing death tolls to rise, then *why* are these states so weak when they seem to have enough funds to build industry, opera houses, and world-class cities? A variation of that question applies to clearly weak states such as Afghanistan. Why has violence *worsened* there since 2001, when the United States and allies first entered, despite the billions of dollars poured into the country for nearly two decades to rebuild the military, police, and government?

Not only does the data show high levels of violence in a number of unexpectedly wealthy states, but it also reveals that violence is concentrating. Since 2004, the number of countries reporting violent death rates of more than 10 per 100,000 (the World Health Organization's threshold for when violence becomes epidemic) has been decreasing, while the average rate of violent death in the most violent countries has been increasing.[8] In 2016, 71 percent of all terrorist attacks occurred in just five countries: Iraq, Afghanistan, Syria, Somalia, and Nigeria, all of which were also experiencing violence from warfare.[9] (Developed Western nations were the target of only 1 percent of global terror.)[10] That year, just twenty-three countries, with only 7 percent of the world's population, accounted for 44 percent of violent death worldwide.[11]

What is causing such massive violence in places as disparate as Jamaica and Afghanistan?

The question seems ridiculous. Jamaica's violence stems from rampant crime. Afghanistan's emanates from insurgency and war. The two appear to have nothing in common. Different kinds of violent groups have different motives, which means they use force according to different strategies to accomplish their goals and require different methods to counter. Thus, experts spend their careers focused on just one kind of violence: civil war, gangs, terrorism, or organized crime. A map like the one at the beginning of this chapter conflates apples and oranges. That is the dominant thinking in my profession, and it was once mine, too.

Yet when I began to study the most violent democracies in the world today, I found that separating each kind of violence obscured what was actually happening on the ground. Terms like "war," "crime," and "state violence" were far tidier than the truth.[12] The Taliban guerrillas were at war, struggling to overthrow Afghanistan's government. But they were also criminals locked in violent competition with parts of the government over control of drug-smuggling routes.[13] In Jamaica, criminal gangs were also perpetrating political violence by suppressing the vote for politicians during campaign season.[14] In Mexico, security forces, ostensibly perpetrating violence for the state, moonlight for drug cartels, sometimes while in uniform. The notorious Colombian paramilitary commander Don Berna started his career as a Marxist insurgent, then switched to a life of crime in Pablo Escobar's drug cartel before eventually becoming the leader of a right-wing paramilitary that had support from parts of the government for its criminal and political violence.

Meanwhile, the world's most violent democracies usually face multiple types of violent groups, many of which cross lines between political and criminal, state and private violence.[15] Since 1989, 88 percent of all terrorist attacks have occurred in countries at war.[16] Warring parties often finance their efforts through violent crimes such as kidnapping, extortion, and trafficking.[17] As General Stanley McChrystal, the commander of the international war effort in Afghanistan, wrote, "There are no clear lines separating insurgent groups, criminal networks (including the narcotics networks), and corrupt GIROA [Government of the Islamic Republic of Afghanistan] officials."[18]

Scholars working in silos miss the relationships between these types of violence, as well as the connections between governments and private groups. Looking across categories uncovered a common cause that was enabling so many forms of bloodshed to root in the same places, and unveiled a common solution.

WHAT CAUSES VIOLENCE?

Popular theories for violence blame pathological religions, ethnicities, and cultures. Policy makers point at states that are too weak and overwhelmed to fight due to a dearth of effective policing and deterrence. I am going to argue that the main reason some democracies face so many kinds of violence today is something else entirely: a particularly pernicious form of state power in which political and economic leaders on both the Left and the Right consciously enable violent groups to proliferate in order to protect their perks and maintain control. I call this Privilege Violence, and understanding why it emerges and how it works is essential to making violent democracies safer.

States engulfed in Privilege Violence are usually weak, but the weakness is not born from poverty or inability. It emanates from governments that have deliberately chosen to hobble state institutions and politicize their police and security services to better manipulate them. These societies often develop cultures of violence. But the culture isn't ancient. It's a recent shift spurred by governments that have chosen to abandon law enforcement in some of their territories to concentrate resources in wealthier neighborhoods. Different racial, ethnic, or religious groups may harbor hate, but those emotions are allowed to devolve into mob murder because politicians provide immunity for the perpetrators.

Islam: A Red Herring

In *The Clash of Civilizations and the Remaking of World Order*, one of the most influential works of foreign policy in the twentieth century, the Harvard scholar Samuel Huntington claims, "The underlying problem for the West is not Islamic fundamentalism. It is Islam."[19] This is a popular view in a world where countless people have been killed by those who claim a purer form of the Muslim faith as their motive. Islamic radicals have murdered thousands of Syrians and Iraqis. Their terror has infiltrated the United States, France, Britain, Belgium, Turkey, and a seemingly endless list of other countries. Radical jihadists are killing Nigerians under the flag of Boko Haram, and they are attacking in neighboring Chad, Cameroon, and Niger as well. The majority of countries facing civil war today are Islamic.[20] Ignoring such a reality would be naïve.

But there are three problems with arguing that Islam is causing most violence in the world. First, the world's most populous Islamic country is Indonesia, which has been notably peaceful over the last decade after facing growing pains during its transition to democracy. Its murder rate of 1 per 100,000 is on par with Europe, and it has contributed few fighters to global jihad. India's massive Muslim citizenry

has been equally quiet on the jihadist front. With two countries housing the biggest Muslim populations in the world as outliers, it is hard
to pin violence on the religion itself.[21]

Second, the religion of Islam hasn't changed greatly over the last
few centuries. So why wasn't it a major cause of violence in the 1990s
or 1890s? In fact, the latest wave of global violence pales in comparison to previous eras of bloodletting, which had nothing to do with
Islam. Christianity was the dominant cause cited for most violence
when Montesquieu noted in 1721 that "no kingdom has ever existed
with as many civil wars as occur in the kingdom of Christ."[22] The
Thirty Years' War, fought between Catholics and Protestants in the
seventeenth century, killed more than a third of Germany and devastated European populations. Genghis Khan's Mongols likely killed
between thirty and fifty million people in the thirteenth century.[23]
They were mostly animist nature worshippers. In the twentieth century, Mao and Stalin killed tens of millions in the name of atheistic
Communism. Even Buddhism is not immune from violence, as the
bloody civil war in Sri Lanka and the monk-led ethnic cleansing of
Rohingya Muslims in Myanmar have demonstrated.

The third reason Islam is suspect as a cause of violence is the lack
of Islamic knowledge among many terrorists. While the earliest generation of political Islamists in the 1950s were steeped in theology,
recent suicide bombers have been caught reading *Islam for Dummies.*[24]
Scholars who study modern terrorism have come to the conclusion
that religion is at most a rationalization for the current generation of
terrorists.

These facts have led many to adopt the more nuanced argument,
contra Huntington, that the problem isn't Islam but its more funda-
mentalist, political form. It is undeniably true that a politicized version of Islam has been used to justify much violence in the world
today. But it's the first half of "political Islam" that is doing much of
the work. The anthropologist Scott Atran, who has interviewed ISIS
fighters and young people in European neighborhoods supporting
jihad, found they share a twisted, but real, "mission to change and
save the world."[25] Like Communism, Fascism, and nationalism, political Islam is the latest rationale to rally young people dreaming of taking part in a heroic struggle against systems they see as unjust and

corrupt.[26] In the West, radical leaders have been recruiting from jails, enabling the already criminally minded to subsume violent impulses in a grander justification.[27] Most Islamist terrorists emerge from the Middle East and Central Asia. Barbara Walter, one of the foremost scholars of civil war, has explained that radical leaders are finding it easy to gain recruits from so many Muslim countries because these states are among the most repressive in the world, not because they are Islamic.[28] Repression, not religion, unites countries that spawn terrorist violence with distinctly non-Islamic countries plagued by endemic bloodshed such as Venezuela and Brazil.

Ancient Ethnic and Religious Hatreds? Not Alone.

In the 1990s, many blamed primordial hatreds for the violence that seemed to be exploding around the globe. The media plumped stories about civil wars in Yugoslavia, the Congo, Nepal, Algeria, and Sierra Leone, the implosion of Somalia, and the constant conflict eating away the edges of the former Soviet Union. The journalist Robert Kaplan wrote an article in 1994 titled "The Coming Anarchy," in which he describes a "crowded planet of skinhead Cossacks and juju warriors, influenced by the worst refuse of Western pop culture and ancient tribal hatreds . . . battling over scraps of overused earth in guerrilla conflicts that ripple across continents and intersect in no discernible pattern."[29] Kaplan suggested that when dictatorial rulers were swept away with the fall of the Soviet Union, ancient ethnic tensions and cultural identities were unleashed to deadly effect. The new twenty-four-hour cable news channels beamed graphic violence into peaceful living rooms. The "CNN effect" combined with fearmongering journalism known politely as "if it bleeds, it leads" made the world feel particularly chaotic.[30]

In 1993, Paul Collier, an economist who studies conflict and international development, compiled cases of civil war dating back to 1965. He expected to find ethnic hatred at the root of most fighting. Instead, he found little evidence of ethnic causation. Rather, he discovered many so-called political rebels seeking economic gains from diamonds, oil, mineral wealth, smuggling routes, and wartime economies.[31] A debate arose between Collier, who believed that greed lay at the root of modern civil wars, and field-based researchers who believed that conflict was rooted in grievances against inequality and unequal treatment by the state.[32] But either way, both saw supposedly ethnic hatred as a smoke screen for fights over power and wealth. The violence scholar Ted Robert Gurr, who had suggested in 1994 that the growth of new democracies was stoking ethnic tension, wrote in 2000 that ethnic conflict, had it ever been a real cause, had waned by the early 1990s.[33]

In fact, not only was ancient group hatred not a main cause of warfare, but wars of all kinds were dropping in frequency in the wake of the Cold War. Other than the conflicts in the former Yugoslavia, the terrible genocide in Rwanda, and the related conflict in the neighboring Democratic Republic of the Congo (DRC), the decade's violence affected relatively few people.[34] Instead of an era of anarchy, the 1990s are now seen as one of the safest periods in human history.

Violent Culture? Not Exactly.

In the 1890s, the historian John F. Baddeley wrote about the culture of crime he witnessed while traveling through the Republic of Georgia and the Caucasus Mountains. "Cattle-lifting, highway robbery, and murder were, in this strange code, counted deeds of honour . . . these, together with fighting against any foe, but especially the hated Russian, were the only pursuits deemed worthy of a grown man."[35] A century later in the 1990s, a scholar of the region wrote,

> The people's orientation remained toward family, relatives and friends at the expense of public or civic life. Two centuries of living under an alien state, and the absence of a modern nation-state mentality, were synthesized in a habituated psychological attitude—distrust or indifference toward the state and a complacent perception of corruption. . . . In other words, everything which was outside the private realm belonged to the Soviet or post-Soviet state, i.e. to nobody. It was nobody's and everybody's, so people were welcome to it, if they needed it.[36]

This sounds quite convincing to anyone who has spent time in formerly Communist countries. Together, the two quotations suggest an endemic criminal culture over a century old. Yet despite its history, the Republic of Georgia eradicated its so-called culture of corruption and radically diminished violence in a single generation in the early years of the twenty-first century.

The most salient problem with blaming violence on culture is explaining change such as Georgia's. How does the culture of violence often ascribed to Colombia, for example, account for a country that was viciously bloody in the 1940s and 1950s, then fairly peaceful in the 1960s and 1970s, before facing a tsunami of murder in the 1980s and 1990s?[37] This problem dogs even nuanced renderings of the cultural hypothesis. For instance, many antiviolence programs target the culture of machismo in Latin America.[38] Yet in the past three decades, Colombia's death rate has fallen while neighboring Venezuela's has ballooned, though neither has exhibited significant change to its culture of masculinity.[39]

Culture *does* matter. There are subcultures, from inner-city gangs in the United States to political Islamists, that glorify violence.[40] Professional cultures are fiendishly hard to change and play an important role in explaining why some police or military forces are more brutal than others. As the management guru Peter Drucker purportedly claimed, "Culture eats strategy for breakfast," and I agree.[41] Shifts in culture, which I term "decivilizing" and "recivilizing," play a crucial role in this story. I'm not denying its explanatory power.

But culture is shaped by other forces, particularly governments. In the 1990s, a tribe of economists known as the New Institutionalists led by the Nobel Prize–winning Douglass North claimed that institutions had the power to shape behaviors and thus cultures. Schools, the media, businesses, and religious congregations are among the many institutions that spell out the subtle, informal rules regarding what behaviors are right and wrong, how feelings are appropriately expressed, and how status is bestowed. As the father of comparative politics, Barrington Moore, wrote, "To maintain and transmit a value system, human beings are punched, bullied, sent to jail, thrown into concentration camps, cajoled, bribed, made into heroes, encouraged to read newspapers, stood up against a wall and shot, and sometimes even taught sociology."[42]

Or, as was memorably described to me by Temuri Yakobashvili, Georgia's former ambassador to Washington, in 2015, "What we proved was that corruption as a cultural issue was bullshit. Corruption in Georgia was institutional." Enforcing laws, especially laws that are supported by much of society, is a particularly potent means of altering culture. When Georgia's government started arresting and jailing people for crimes, behavior changed quickly.

The United States, for instance, is often critiqued for its culture of violence.[43] Nearly 150 years ago, the *Chicago Tribune* wrote, "There is no people so prone as the American to take the law into their own hands when the sanctity of human life is threatened and the rights of property invaded in a manner that cannot be adequately reached and punished by the tortuous course of the law. Judge Lynch is an American by birth and character."[44] In 1925, the *Los Angeles Times* described two men who had hunted down a mugger and killed him. The paper noted approvingly that the police didn't bother arresting them, because they were doing a public good.[45] After the United States government began to prosecute cases where private citizens enacted vigilante justice, such as Bernhard Goetz's shooting of four muggers in the New York subway in 1984, these instances became rare and subject to massive, nationwide moral debate.[46] Conversely, when the government reduces penalties on private violence, as with the "Stand Your Ground" laws now in twenty-three states, homicide rates rise.[47] America still carries some forms of violence deep in its DNA.[48] But altering institutions (in this case, the government's willingness to arrest and convict people who undertake vigilante justice) changes behavior and culture over time.

Weak, Poor Governments: Yes, but Why?

So it's no surprise that in the years after the terrorist attacks of September 11, 2001, policy makers tried to improve global security by strengthening institutions such as police forces and courts within violent countries. Policy makers in the United States, Britain, and Europe began to believe that weak states—governments whose militaries and police were incompetent and underequipped, whose writ didn't extend across their entire territories, whose bureaucracies were understaffed and untrained—enabled terrorist activity. In 2002, George W. Bush wrote an introduction to the U.S. National Security Strategy that read, "The events of September 11, 2001, taught us that weak states, like Afghanistan, can pose as great a danger to our national interests as strong states. Poverty does not make poor people into terrorists and murderers. Yet poverty, weak institutions, and corruption can make weak states vulnerable to terrorist networks and drug cartels within their borders."[49]

The idea that weak governments with weak institutions engender violence has a storied pedigree. In 1651, Thomas Hobbes published his classic book, *Leviathan*. The volume appeared just months after the end of the English Civil War, three years after the Thirty Years' War, and in the midst of the general interpersonal murder and mayhem of the era. To overcome a "war of all against all" and a life that was "nasty, brutish, and short," Hobbes argued for a state strong enough to overawe all challengers and establish a monopoly on violence. While today's Western policy makers disagree with Hobbes's endorsement of absolute monarchy, his insight into the importance of a strong state to maintain stability and peace remains central. The Stanford political scientist Francis Fukuyama's *Political Order and Political Decay* describes how the institutions of a strong state build order and reduce violence. Quantitative researchers such as the Stanford professors James Fearon and David Laitin have found that weak states that lack strong police and military capabilities invite challengers.[50] Few people would envision getting together a few dozen armed followers to oust the U.S. government, but multiple successful coups in Ghana took place with that level of manpower. Like a skinny kid with a fistful of lunch money, a weak state offers an easy target for those willing to use force to get what they want.[51]

The United States and Europe have spent two decades developing security and aid programs based on a simple rendering of this "weak state" thesis. The theory ran, basically, "We need to strengthen weak states." But *why* were these states weak? The answer appeared so obvious that few bothered with the question. In Albania, I visited judges who worked in the dark because the electricity failed constantly.

Police officers in Honduras complained that they had no budget for gas and needed to ask crime victims for fuel money to start their investigations. Western governments assumed these countries were simply too poor to purchase equipment for their law enforcement and military and too unskilled to train their security services, lawyers, and judges.

Based on the idea that state weakness was caused by poverty and ignorance, the United States, European countries, and international organizations like the World Bank began to pour funds into scores of so-called weak and fragile states from Nigeria to El Salvador in the first decade of the twenty-first century.[52] By 2016, the United States was spending over $18 billion a year offering security sector assistance to more than two-thirds of the world's countries.[53] That was two to three times more than what the United States spent on military equipment and training to other countries two decades before. The effort to shore up weak states to prevent threats from spilling over at times merged with a new strategy to keep American troops out of harm's way by fighting potential threats "by, with, and through" foreign militaries that were often in countries deemed too weak and incapable to fight effectively without help.[54] The European Union spent a quarter of a billion euros on security reform in 2016, while the United Nations spends around $100 million each year.[55] In addition to training security personnel and ensuring an adequate supply of prisons and police academies, additional funds are spent trying to build efficient tax collection, meritocratic civil services, and improved courts to strengthen states.[56]

These programs have been bedeviled by failure.[57] After a decade of war in Afghanistan and millions of dollars spent aiding the Afghan National Police, the international-law-enforcement expert Robert Perito found that "in many communities . . . officers were viewed as predatory and a greater threat to security than the Taliban. For many Afghans, the police were identified with demands for bribes, illegal taxes, and various kinds of human rights violations. They were also known to use house searches as an opportunity to shake down occupants and steal their possessions."[58]

The United States spent over a decade training the military in

Iraq, but in 2011 Iraq's army failed to fight small groups of ISIS fighters traveling the country in pickup trucks. In 2014, insurgents who were outnumbered nearly thirty to one routed Iraq's military and took control of the country's second-largest city.[59] Despite decades of American training and aid, military officers staged a coup in Honduras in 2009. In Mali, after four years of partnership with the United States, officers did the same in 2012. European governments and the United Nations trained police forces in Burundi for a decade before the country's leading politicians used them to assassinate opponents in 2016. The Zetas, Mexico's most violent drug cartel, began as U.S.-trained members of the Mexican military's special forces.[60]

The repeated failures led the U.S. Congress to commission its internal research service to determine what the United States was doing and how much it was spending on these programs.[61] Separately, RAND, an independent think tank that commonly undertakes research for the government, assessed their effectiveness. Their studies found that training and capacity-building programs were effective only in the small number of cases where countries wanted to improve, independent of foreign help. In the majority of cases, aid and training were ineffectual in helping fragile states secure themselves.[62]

Poverty was not the problem. True, poor countries are correlated with more civil war.[63] But war makes countries poorer, so the direction of causation is murky.[64] Meanwhile, war is not the main cause of violent death, and countries with middling incomes like Honduras and Brazil, not the poorest states, have the highest homicide rates.[65] Many Islamic terrorists come from wealthy Gulf states and have middle- to upper-middle-class backgrounds.[66] International terrorism is correlated with government repression, not poverty.[67]

Some argue that the issue is economic decline, rather than poverty per se, but that also doesn't hold up to the evidence. With the exception of domestic violence, most violent crime does not correlate with economic downturns.[68] Few people kill because they are broke. In fact, in his study of murder rates in New York City from the colonial period to the present, the violence historian Eric Monkkonen notes that "in some of New York City's most miserable periods, murder rates were at their lowest."[69] The Great Depression caused no spike in homicides. The two most recent peaks of U.S. violence, in the late 1960s and early 1990s, coincided with periods of economic growth. The biggest period of Mafia expansion in Sicily occurred during the years of "extraordinary intervention" in the 1950s and 1960s when the central government poured funds into the poor South. Colombia was also at its most violent during its economic boom in the 1980s. That should come as no surprise: mafiosi thrive in flush times when organized criminals can skim more off the top.[70]

But if the issue isn't money, why do so many democratic countries seem unable to fight the violence that is harming their voters?

WEAK STATES V. COMPLICIT GOVERNMENTS

To gain a better understanding of the role of state weakness in endemic violence, Elena Barham, my research assistant, and I tried a simple test. We graphed democracies by how well they could deliver water, electricity, and other public goods to their citizens and by their successful implementation of World Bank programs. Presumably, countries that could do both of these activities well, those in the upper-right quadrant of the graph, were not particularly weak.[71] We then mapped numbers of murdered journalists onto these graphs.

KNOWN MURDERED JOURNALISTS AND STATE CAPACITY

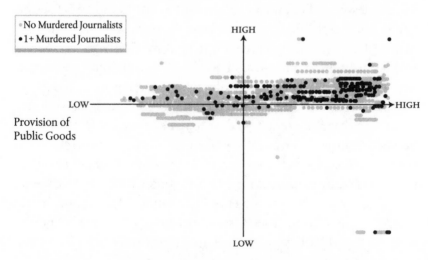

World Bank Government Performance Evaluations

A few murders were occurring in the weakest states. But the strongest countries in the upper-right-hand quadrant were most prone to reporters dying violently. Why? And why did these otherwise capacious states show a consistent pattern of journalist homicides over multiple years?[72]

We then took the same graph of state strength and mapped atop it countries that violently repressed at least one peaceful minority group or moderately repressed multiple peaceful groups.[73]

GOVERNMENT CAPACITY AND VIOLENCE
AGAINST MINORITY GROUPS

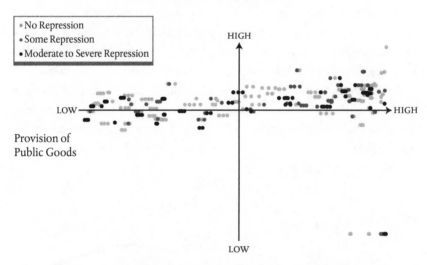

World Bank Government Performance Evaluations

A number of weak states faced pogroms and used state violence, but so did a cluster of countries that were able to provide 85 to 99 percent of their populations with public services and achieve excellent marks executing World Bank projects.[74] Why were countries that were clearly capable in many other realms unable to protect their peaceful minorities?

IS THE PROBLEM DEMOCRACY?

Some policy makers worried that democracy itself, or at least the transition to democracy, was responsible for increasing violence.[75]

James Fearon, a Stanford political scientist, found that weak democracies with corruption and bad governance had the highest murder rates among all countries on the globe.[76] Barbara Walter, one of the foremost scholars of civil wars worldwide, found that all else being equal, democracies where it was hard for outsiders to enter politics and where the rule of law was weak were two to ten times as likely to face recurring civil wars.[77] Monty Marshall, director of a leading political database, found that countries that mixed democratic and authoritarian elements, such as Nigeria, were about six times more likely than consolidated democracies and two and a half times more likely than autocracies to implode into new wars.[78] A consortium of violence scholars working with the U.S. government's intelligence agencies tried to predict which countries were most likely to fail, face violent regime change, or descend into genocide. The most predictive variable was the level of polarization in democracies. Instability is thirty times higher in countries with highly polarized politics than in those with less.[79] These findings mean that if I map rates of violence by regime type, I get a graph in which consolidated democracies are by far the least violent form of government, but countries in the middle are worse than the most autocratic states.

VIOLENCE BY REGIME TYPE

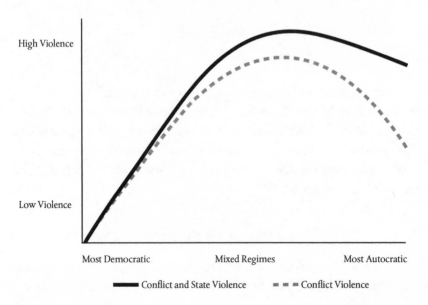

I suggest using the top line, which modifies the normal graph of violence derived from the studies previously described, because research tends to undercount autocratic deaths. Most conflict databases don't count killings of civilians by the state, and autocracies, which control the press, often manipulate self-reported statistics. China, whose data covers a seventh of humanity, hides deaths from forced labor camps and extrajudicial execution, though it is believed to be the largest executioner in the world.[80] Russia may be undercounting its murders by a third.[81] Homicides are not included in the graph, because while they are believed to be highest for mixed regimes, African dictatorships don't provide homicide statistics at all, and numbers from multiple Middle Eastern autocracies are suspect.[82] Autocracies are thus likely to be more violent than the studies suggest. But even the modified graph doesn't explain why mixed regimes were more likely than autocracies to engage in civil war, face insurgency, or simply collapse.

What was going on in these semi-democracies?

POWER STRUCTURE, NOT IDEOLOGY

"Kto kovo?" asked Lenin. "Who will rule over whom?" In the twentieth century, states were defined by their ideologies. Those ideologies were supposed to indicate the power structure—who had authority, how they obtained it, how decisions were made. The century's wars were fought by a progression of anarchists, Fascists, Communists, and democrats who had different answers to Lenin's question.

When a wave of democracy swept the world, beginning in 1974 with Portugal and Spain, moving through Latin America, Taiwan, and South Korea, and toppling the Soviet Union fifteen years after it began, Francis Fukuyama, who had just left the State Department's Policy Planning Staff, wrote that it was the "end of history," the finale of a long and bloody era of ideological conflict. Democracy, he claimed, where power was held by the people and delegated to elected officials to serve the interests of the broad mass of voters, had won. From just 46 democracies in 1974, the world had around 119 by 2007, out of 192 countries in the world.[83]

But many of these new democracies soon faltered.[84] While only eight faced coups after 1980, nearly three dozen faced incremental,

rising authoritarianism that pushed them into that middling territory by 1995.[85] These countries continued to hold elections, but
politicians were increasingly skilled at manipulating them. Incum-
bents might gain control of the media, then forbid negative coverage
of the government. They might harass opposition groups' donors
or ban popular candidates on a variety of pretexts. An overlapping
group of new democracies were struggling with violence. As crime
and homicide rose across these countries that were teetering between
their authoritarian pasts and democratic futures, violence from the
state seemed to have swapped places with greater, and less predict-
able, violence from fellow citizens.[86] By 2015, only 37 percent of
Latin Americans—whose region had become the most violent on the
planet—were satisfied with their governments, even though indicators of civil liberties and freedom were all better than under previous authoritarian regimes.[87] There was no language to describe what
was happening in the most violent among over fifty countries from
Cambodia to Nigeria that found themselves stranded in global indi-
ces between authoritarianism and consolidated democracy, a group
that had nearly doubled between 1989 and 2013.[88] The semantic gap
pointed to the need for a paradigm shift to understand the twenty-
first century: scholars and policy makers were still looking at ideologies, but these obscured real power structures.

For a decade, I ran a political organization that worked to improve
U.S. national security policies. That meant I spent a great deal of time
raising money from the same billionaires who gave the maximum
allowable amounts to congressional candidates and political parties,
then donated more to so-called super PACs. Many nonprofit execu-
tives hate fund-raising, but I found it useful. If I wanted to influence
a particular policy, talking to these wealthy men and women was
often the most effective way to get my organization's views into the
minds of elected officials. When members of Congress called me to
get a briefing on an issue like going to war with Iran, they would often
have just twenty or thirty minutes in between fund-raising calls to
dash out of the phone-booth-sized cubicle in their political party
offices, meet me at the bad Mexican restaurant across the street, and

talk foreign policy before a twenty-three-year-old aide would yank them back to the phones.[89] Our donors, meanwhile, spent hours with the leaders of crucial congressional committees, who came to their homes on speaking tours when they needed to raise funds.

Many of the people who supported my organization were smart, self-made businessmen and professional women. I liked them. But I was also aware of how fundamentally undemocratic it was for the wealthy to have such outsized access and influence. The problem wasn't crude money-for-legislation corruption. With campaigns so expensive and the Supreme Court issuing rulings since 1976 that money equated to speech and therefore could not be controlled without undermining the First Amendment, politicians were forced to spend vast quantities of time fund-raising.[90] That also meant they spent most of their waking hours with wealthy individuals whose concerns, interests, and ways of looking at the world had little to do with the problems faced by the majority of Americans. The philosopher Michael Walzer argued that justice lies in keeping different "spheres of power," such as wealth and political influence, separate.[91] America is a democracy, but clearly its power structure is failing Walzer's test.

Scorecards from groups like Freedom House that measured the civil and political liberties that delineate democracy from autocracy did not count variables that would illuminate peccadilloes within power structures, such as corruption, crime, and changing concentrations of wealth. Using a twentieth-century ideological ruler to measure the line between freedom and tyranny, scholars and policy makers simply found that a number of countries were stagnating in the middle. Academics called these countries "anocracies," "competitive authoritarian regimes," or "semi-competitive democracies."[92] Policy makers referred to them as "weak," "incomplete," or "in transition," treating them as if they had been pulled from the oven half-cooked and needed extra time and assistance to finish evolving into functional political systems.

Many of these countries, however, aren't "transitioning" anywhere. The regimes of countries like Nigeria and the Philippines have lasted over two decades. They are fully baked. These violent semi-democracies are oligarchies in the raw—places ruled by the few to maintain their privilege, and willing to use violence to keep things that way.

Aristotle was the first to delve deeply into oligarchies, and he defined them not as rule by the few, but as rule by the wealthy.[93] Thus, "democracy may change into an oligarchy, if the wealthy class are stronger than the people."[94] This pattern of governance was so common that oligarchy had been the dominant form of government across the globe until World War I, when Theodore Roosevelt wrote that Gilded Age America was flawed for "attempting to combine political democracy with industrial autocracy."[95] But in the great clashes of ideas in the twentieth century, oligarchy didn't fit. It was a power structure, not an ideology. Oligarchies backed by violence can be authoritarian, as in Russia today; democratic, as in Nigeria; left-wing; right-wing; or anywhere in between. Ideology and democratic institutions are façades used to obscure the fact that material wealth and privilege are overwhelmingly concentrated in a few hands and muscle is used to keep a grip on power.

Not all oligarchies are violent. Polarized politics that create a viable challenge make some democracies more bloody. When Barham and I analyzed the statistics, we found that the violent democracies we had graphed shared a broader pattern of governance. They had more corruption in executive branch bureaucracies than other democracies. Their courts were less independent, and their governments frequently attacked their judiciaries.[96] While they could deliver public goods, rural populations were significantly underserved compared with urbanites or rural citizens of less violent democracies. In places where minorities were being harmed, political terrorism was also higher, and terrorism increased even more in countries facing journalistic homicides as well, suggesting that some people had deep anger at their government.[97]

To understand how oligarchy and violence function within a democratic carapace, consider Mexico's recent history. For over seventy years, Mexico was a one-party state governed by the Partido Revolucionario Institucional (PRI). The party appointed all governors and mayors, fixed elections, and ran corruption rackets that stretched from the president to the policeman on the street.[98] As drug use grew in the 1970s, the PRI decided to regulate the business rather than try to halt shipments between growers in South America and the world's biggest drug market, the United States. The party negotiated exclusive trafficking routes to reduce fighting between cartels and would regulate the market if turf wars grew too hot.[99] The regime encouraged cartels to form alliances and share profits with PRI politicians and each other.[100] By the 1980s, the Mexican intelligence agency, the Dirección Federal de Seguridad (DFS), had become active in the drug trade, providing protection to traffickers and even giving some cartel leaders DFS badges.[101] In 1985, DFS agents and cartel leaders jointly kidnapped, tortured, and murdered Kiki Camarena, a U.S. DEA agent. When the United States pressured the Mexican government to disband the DFS, some of its former leaders simply became drug kingpins.[102] Collusion with the cartels was so great that from 1990 to 1994 (and possibly before) government officials sent airplanes to collect money and gifts offered as tribute from the criminals to their political protectors.[103] The PRI also encouraged the military to traffic in drugs and make money from smuggling and prostitution.[104] A weak, rich, happy military was unlikely to unleash a coup.[105]

Violence grew under autocratic protection, particularly as this centralized system broke down. From 1991 to 1997, Mexican crime rates might have nearly doubled (the statistics are problematic), and crime became increasingly aggressive and organized, particularly in hot spots like Tijuana.[106] Hundreds of women were raped, tortured, and murdered in Ciudad Juárez near the U.S. border. In Mexico City, President Ernesto Zedillo fired over five thousand police officers accused of corruption and placed military troops on the streets in 1994. But in a state with no accountability, many of the ousted police turned to crime full-time. A Mexican Interior Ministry report estimated that by 1995 Mexico had nine hundred armed criminal bands, over half of which were composed of active or retired law enforcement.[107] In 1997, there were 240 assaults, robberies, or murders in Mexico City each hour according to the legislature's Committee on Public Security.[108]

While bloodshed grew under corrupt, collusive one-party rule, it was contained. People with a little money could stay out of certain neighborhoods, take private cars instead of dangerous taxis, and avoid the worst of it. The PRI autocracy organized the system of crime and violence to fund its party and fill politicians' pockets. But working with the cartels also required corrupting and deliberately weakening state security agencies and allowing violence to simmer at a high rate.

When Mexico officially became a democracy and ended seven decades of one-party rule in 2000, violence exploded. But the problem was more decentralization than democratization.[109] With more political players, there were more deals to be made between politicians and drug traffickers at the state and local levels.[110] More alliances meant more possibilities for broken promises, ensuring more reprisals and murders to improve negotiating positions. Because one party could profit electorally if its region was less violent than another, local officials would make deals with criminals and outsource turf wars to other states, especially if those states were run by a different party.[111] Violence became endemic, and with a freer press, corruption was more exposed. In 2015, only 26 percent of Mexicans felt that their elections were clean, just 17 percent felt represented by their own elected congressional members, and unsurprisingly only 19 percent were satisfied with their government, the lowest satisfaction rate of any country in Latin America. Their disillusion was so great that only 48 percent supported democracy as a whole.[112]

But was this democracy? Transitioning from a one-party to a multiparty system was heralded as a massive success for freedom. But it didn't really change Mexico's underlying power structure. A team of interviewers from New York University's Wagner School working with me in Mexico City and Monterrey in 2017 kept hearing the same thing: despite Mexico's supposed democratic system, everyone interviewed insisted that the government was uninterested in the views of most of its citizens.[113] Without altering the economy and other power structures, legalizing multiple political parties didn't bring power to regular people.[114] It only expanded the ladders to power available for the elites. Regardless of which party won, the same small group of families came out ahead. Regular citizens had a vote, but they didn't have a voice in the most important issues affecting their lives, the way they were supposed to in a democracy.[115]

Hobbes and the "weak state" scholars and policy pundits are right. Countries with weak institutions *are* the ones most afflicted by violence. The problem lies in drawing the simple conclusion that weakness is caused by poverty, lack of equipment, or inadequate training. Instead, we need to understand why these government institutions are so weak and what makes them impervious to growing stronger.

Countries face massive internal violence for two reasons. In a few cases, the government really is too poor and its bureaucracy too scant or unqualified to enforce order. If these weak states are willing, they are amenable to being improved with money and training. The vast majority of democracies that face serious internal violence, however, are not too weak to fight back, as conventional wisdom holds. They are, instead, complicit. They are specifically organized to enable corruption, privilege, and impunity for a few while allowing the rest of society to fester. To understand the difference, Americans can look to our own backyard.

2

PRIVILEGE VIOLENCE

It is not mere imperfection, not corruption in low quarters, not occasional severity . . . it is incessant, systematic, deliberate violation of the law by the Power appointed to watch over and maintain it.

—WILLIAM GLADSTONE, FUTURE BRITISH PRIME MINISTER,
DESCRIBING NAPLES IN 1851[1]

On a cold February morning in 1866, not quite a year after the end of the Civil War, ten horsemen in long blue overcoats appeared on the main street of Liberty, Missouri. Whooping and shouting, the men galloped up and down the dusty roads. Then they started shooting.

Students at William Jewell College ran into classrooms for cover. Shopkeepers pulled their customers inside and closed the shades. The horsemen wheeled to a stop in front of the bank. They locked the cashier and his son in the vault, swept the money into a grain sack, and careened away. At that moment, an unlucky college boy was walking to class. Four shots hit him as he dove for cover.[2]

This was Jesse James's first bank heist. His James-Younger Gang was one of many groups of criminals, guerrillas, and murderers terrorizing the country in the years after the Civil War. America's western frontier and postwar South were both wild, but there was a fundamental difference. The West was a classic weak state. The South was complicit in what I call Privilege Violence.

THE WILD WEST: A WEAK STATE

Squint at a picture of America's western frontier in the 1870s, and it looks like parts of the Democratic Republic of the Congo today. Former soldiers demobilized from a bloody civil war had regrouped into criminal gangs. Guerrilla raids terrified communities who had settled on Indian lands. A long, porous border allowed violent groups to escape and reorganize within Mexico's even less functional state. The federal government could barely protect its rural hinterlands: in 1866, the United States had just eleven thousand volunteer soldiers thanks to speedy postwar demobilization. The military beefed up for a decade but shrank to just twenty-eight thousand troops by 1877.[3] Government barely reached most of the West, and what existed was riddled with corruption.

Unlike European countries that built strong bureaucracies and militaries before they expanded the vote, the United States, unique among today's wealthy countries but similar to many developing nations, established a new state and a democracy at the same time.[4] The result was massive pressure for patronage jobs in exchange for votes. Governors were asked to hire donors' family members. Party hacks filled police forces. When Abraham Lincoln first took office in 1861, he spent hours each day dealing with menial job seekers demanding patronage posts in return for their election help. As one of his aides wrote,

> The Executive Mansion was a curious study during many days and weeks following the inauguration. Its halls and offices were literally packed with human beings. There were days when the throng of eager applicants for office filled the broad staircase to its lower steps; the corridors of the first floor; the famous East Room; the private parlors; while anxious groups and individuals paraded up and down the outer porch, the walks, and the Avenue.[5]

The result was a bloated and ineffectual bureaucracy, riddled with corruption that undermined the military and made it hard to provide security.[6]

Like the thinly governed territories of all weak states, the American West was ravaged by a multitude of groups. The territory that is now Oklahoma, one of Jesse James's hideouts, was among the most violent parts of the country. Between the Civil War and 1907, it was Indian Territory, governed by laws made specifically for Native American tribes that had a special sovereignty unto themselves. But in a significant loophole, white wrongdoers could not be tried by Indian courts. One judge was in charge of maintaining the federal laws that bound Anglos across the entire region. The workload was too massive to try all the wrongdoers. Word got out, and the most notorious white criminals from around the country infested the territory. It was "the rendezvous of the vile and wicked from everywhere," declared the editor of Fort Smith's *Western Independent*.[7] As this semi-anarchy festered in the middle of America, sixty-five of the region's two hundred deputy marshals were murdered between 1875 and 1896.[8]

Violence also exploded in what were known as cow towns. A cattle blockade intended to starve the South of money during the Civil War had created a glut of longhorns stuck in Texas. After the war, ranchers could sell their animals for $2 or $3 nearby. But if they could get them on a railway headed to a northern meatpacking plant, they could make $30 or $40 a head. The railroads, fast-tracked by Lincoln to win the war, didn't extend into the South. So in 1866, cowboys began taking herds of cattle north to railheads to sell. At the trail's end, they would spend their windfall on whiskey, sex, and gambling, get into fights, and shoot each other over petty squabbles.[9]

Meanwhile, from New Mexico north across the High Plains, battles broke out between farmers and ranchers. The federal government, trying to settle the West, had offered free land to homesteaders willing to prove up their property.[10] The new and often poor farmers and sheep ranchers clashed with wealthy cattlemen needing open range to graze their cows. The cattlemen claimed that the homesteaders were stealing their cows and hired private security. Small ranchers and suspected cattle thieves started to turn up dead.[11] Kate and Jim Averell had the temerity to build their homesteads on pastureland near the Sweetwater River, where cows previously watered. In 1889, cattlemen lynched the couple, leaving them hanging in the July heat for days—a warning to other smallholders who crossed the powerful ranching interests.[12] When homesteaders formed an organization to protect themselves, the cattlemen hired a fifty-man militia. In the spring of 1892, this private army set out from Cheyenne, cutting telegraph lines along the way to prevent the homesteaders from sounding the alarm. They killed the head of the homesteaders' association, then laid siege to the cabins of suspected rustlers. The governor sent the Sixth Calvary when he received news of the murders. The cattlemen faced trial. But witnesses disappeared. Intimidated townspeople declined to serve on the jury. The violence continued unabated for a decade.[13]

Texas cowboys were often southern Confederates just out of uniform, trying to make a living outside the impoverished South. The few sheriffs and lawmen who patrolled the West were often former Union soldiers.[14] The animosity between the two abetted the criminal killings, drunken murders, and economic assassinations.

But in a weak state, the government is just too far away or underresourced to exact repercussions. In the freezing winter of 1883, a young Theodore Roosevelt was raising cattle on his ranch in South Dakota. He also served as the local volunteer sheriff. When three men stole his boat, Roosevelt built a raft and organized a few of his neighbors into a posse. They traveled the river for three days through a blizzard until they found the thieves. After arresting the men, the posse spent two weeks traveling the frozen river. When they hit land, Roosevelt's neighbors hightailed it home, leaving him to hike over thirty miles by foot and wagon over rough land to get his three prisoners to the nearest jail.[15] Then he had to get back. Most westerners, unsurprisingly, preferred a swift citizen hanging to such arduous justice. Often it was even simpler to let criminals go free.

Unchecked, violence reigned. Homicide rates were 165 per 100,000 in Dodge City, Kansas, from 1876 to 1885, higher than in Bogotá at the peak of Colombia's drug violence. They were 105 per 100,000 in the mining boomtown of Leadville, Colorado, in 1880; 116 per 100,000 from 1878 to 1882, when the gold boom reached Bodie, California. They hit over 150 per 100,000 in Gila, Arizona, and 250 per 100,000 in New Mexico.[16] Sometimes small populations skew statistics, but in the 1860s and 1870s even Los Angeles had murder rates of 198 per 100,000.[17]

Yet by the time Buffalo Bill founded his touring show with Sitting Bull, Annie Oakley, and other western celebrities in 1883, the talent was available because the Wild West was already growing tamer. In California, for instance, homicides fell from gold rush highs of 100–200 per 100,000 in the 1850s, to just 5–15 per 100,000 by 1890.[18] This is an astounding decline.

Some very specific problems resolved naturally. Meatpacking plants spread as more towns were connected by railroads, making cattle drives to railheads unnecessary. The new invention of barbed wire reduced the practice of grazing across the open plains, and the long drives largely disappeared after a particularly devastating winter in 1886–1887 killed over 80 percent of all open-range cattle in the upper Great Plains.[19] The overabundance of unattached young men—the most violence-prone demographic of any population—diminished as itinerant adventurers settled and married. Women and children turned tent camps into towns. America was lucky that the West was seen as a place of opportunity. Rural Colombia; Bihar, India; and other violent places today rarely attract high-quality police, lawyers, and teachers to live in villages where medical care is poor, schools are bad, and friends won't come to visit. But the American West was viewed as a place of adventure for ambitious, educated people.

As families settled into towns, governments followed. The federal government was splitting funds between rebuilding the war-torn South, financing a series of wars against Indian tribes, and serving the settled population in the East. But established politicians and businesspeople were excited about the prospects of the West and were willing to share government resources to see the frontier succeed, rather than starving rural hinterlands of funds, as often occurs in violent countries with more self-serving elites. Corruption skimmed some money off the top. But not enough was stolen to stop public schoolteachers, judges, and postmen from spreading throughout the West. The story of the Wyoming cattlemen was indicative. They set aside vigilante violence and started a lobbying group. They won control of the range by getting tough laws passed against cattle stealing.

THE POST-CIVIL WAR SOUTH: PRIVILEGE VIOLENCE

Violence in the West ended fairly quickly as government arrived. Yet southern violence worsened over the same years as government consolidated, because it was stoked by the politicians themselves.

The aftermath of the Civil War turned the southern social order upside down. Its great farms lay in ashes. Plantations were without hands. Demobilized soldiers had no money. It was a land of dead and maimed young men. In 1866, Mississippi spent a fifth of its budget on artificial limbs.[20] The cream of the white Confederate military and political leadership was legally disenfranchised. Over 150,000 remained unable to vote or hold office until 1872.[21]

Black Americans, meanwhile, had the vote. Five years after the war's end, 15 percent of all southern elected officials were black.[22] By 1877, two thousand African Americans had held elected and appointed office.[23] The Raleigh *Daily Sentinel* wrote about "a dinner party attended by three former governors, a former justice of the state supreme court, one or two former members of Congress, and several other distinguished men. The only person in this august gathering who could vote was the black man waiting on the tables."[24] The *New-York Tribune* channeled the views of many southerners that "the most intelligent, the influential, the educated, the really useful men of the South, [were] deprived of all political power . . . taxed and swindled by a horde of rascally foreign adventurers, and by the ignorant class, which only yesterday hoed the fields and served in the kitchen."[25]

Without work or money, men gathered in drinking clubs where they nattered about a likely black insurrection. On Christmas Eve 1865 in Pulaski, Tennessee, one such club formed the Ku Klux Klan. The Klan was one of many armed gangs of "night riders" across the South. Under cover of darkness, the White League, the Red Shirts, the Swamp Fox Rangers, Innocents, Seymour Knights, Hancock Guards, and the Knights of the White Camellia terrorized newly freed blacks.[26] The gangs saved particular ire for African American community leaders, such as schoolteachers and pastors. Another target were people of either race who supported the Republicans, the hated party of Lincoln, to which freed blacks had understandably flocked.[27] In Claiborne Parish, Louisiana, night riders murdered a literate former slave who had served in the Constitutional Convention. They grabbed another black leader in his home, shot him, then cut off his head. A white schoolteacher trying to hire more teachers for the black school in Chickasaw County, Mississippi, was pulled into the woods, whipped, and escaped a noose on a nearby tree only by overpowering the Klansmen. For weeks, he slept in the woods and taught school with a gun slung over his shoulder.[28] Gangs would set fire to former slave cabins, pull blacks into the road to be whipped, and shoot at them for sport.[29]

This kind of rioting is called "communal violence" or "pogroms" when it happens in poor, faraway places. Journalists often depict such sprees as the unleashing of ancient ethnic hatreds. But many people harbor prejudice and don't attempt or get away with murder. The resentments are real, but governments permit killing sprees to continue by granting impunity to murderers. Violence runs rampant when it is allowed to.

Violence had been an electoral tactic in the South before the Civil War. James Madison Wells, the pro-Union governor thrust on Louisiana under federal rule, explained to the president, "A branch of the Know-Nothing party [a nativist, anti-immigrant party], known and called from their practices 'thugs,' were accustomed before every election to go, painted and otherwise disguised, into the poorer quarters of the city and shoot down innocent and inoffensive citizens, and repeat their assassination if these atrocious and diabolical outrages failed."[30]

After the war, election violence became a common strategy for southern Democrats, known as Dixiecrats, to regain lost power. Freed blacks "organized a seemingly unending series of mass meetings, parades, and petitions demanding civil equality and . . . suffrage."[31] Those opposed organized their bullets and whips. In Arkansas, a mob assassinated a black Republican congressman.[32] They disemboweled a Republican leader in front of his wife in Monroe County, Mississippi. In Meridian, Mississippi, a mob came into a courtroom in the midst of a trial and shot at a Republican judge and a group of black spectators, threw a defendant from the roof, shot another, and rampaged through the streets for days. The riot killed nearly twenty-five blacks and ended Republican control of the town.[33]

In the months before elections, the violence of the night riders rose. The governor of Louisiana wrote to President Andrew Johnson to tell him that in the six weeks from mid-June to August, 150 people had been killed in political violence; an investigator later told him that the number was actually double that. The next month, as elections loomed, another 150 to 200 African Americans were murdered in the parishes surrounding Shreveport.[34]

Most of the killings sprang from racial hatred and personal animosities. But they served southern Confederate politicians by driving potential Republican voters out of their districts while deterring those who stayed from voting.[35] So Dixiecrats nudged the violence along. "We hold this to be a Government of White People, made and to be perpetuated for the exclusive political benefit of the White Race," asserted the Louisiana Democratic Party's platform in 1865.[36] On July 30, 1866, they made good on their promise with force. That Monday morning, a Constitutional Convention was scheduled to meet in New Orleans to approve voting equality and other policies mandated by the North. Policemen left their assigned beats and gathered at their station houses with pistols, knives, clubs, and revolvers lent to them by local gun shops. They moved to prearranged assembly points surrounding the convention hall and awaited the signal of the city fire bell. Meanwhile, Sheriff Harry Hays organized a brigade of firemen, members of secret rebel societies, and assorted citizens and thugs, also armed.

The plan was well known. The son of a member of the Constitutional Convention asked his dad "why they were going to kill all the Union men and negroes in the city on Monday" because it was all anyone was talking about at school.[37] As a procession of black delegates made their way to the convention hall around eleven, fights broke out. The parade ran into the hall. Hays's brigade and the mob were close behind, shooting through the windows of the building. The police broke the doors and ran inside. Black delegates jumped from windows and tried to escape into the surrounding streets. Armed white men dragged them back from streetcars and shops, pummeling them to death with guns and fists. The riot stopped when federal troops summoned by the governor finally arrived late that afternoon, but only after forty-six were killed and sixty more severely wounded.[38]

To keep order as similar riots spread, Congress separated the South into five military districts, placed a northern general and troops in charge of each, and allocated funds to hire more than fifty thousand soldiers by 1867.[39] The show of force helped, though it didn't completely stop local politicians determined to regain power through party-sponsored mobs. In April 1867, the Ku Klux Klan held a conference in Tennessee at the Maxwell House Hotel in Nashville. Their gathering perfectly coincided in time and place with the state Democratic Party's nomination convention.[40] The event elevated the group from a club to an organized militia. The next year at election time, white supremacist paramilitaries murdered over 200 people in Arkansas, 336 in Georgia, and hundreds of others in Louisiana and surrounding states.[41] On Election Day 1868, twenty-seven thousand fewer Republicans turned out to the polls. Across sixteen Louisiana parishes, a grand total of just nineteen people were willing to cast a Republican ballot.[42]

Because this violence was carried out by private citizens, Dixie-cratic politicians avoided blame. But violence in the South didn't stem from demographics or government weakness. Unlike the West's testosterone-heavy population, the South had an unusually small percentage of young men after the war.[43] Southern states reconstituted functioning courts, educated judges, and hired full police departments within a year of the Civil War's completion. Democratic politicians were enabling private violence to claw their way back into power.

In Republican areas, local officials and citizens worked together to ward off mobs and foiled a third of the attempted lynchings.[44] In Arkansas, the pro-Union governor, Powell Clayton, declared martial law from 1868 to 1869 and raised a local militia that temporarily curbed the Klan. Under Edmund Jackson Davis, a Republican former Union officer who governed Texas from 1870 to 1874, the state even built an integrated black and white police force and state militia. They arrested a thousand of the most wanted criminals across the state in just two years.[45] For the first and only time in Texas history, black and white citizens were imprisoned at rates commensurate with their populations. The *Texas Star Gazette* fretted that the police force "never trouble themselves in pursuing real offenders . . . but devote all their precious time and talents in hunting up imaginary Ku Klux Klans."[46] When Dixiecrats regained control, they slashed the police force so white tax dollars wouldn't go to empowering black communities, and unsurprisingly violence rose.[47] Across the South, violence was strongest where Democrats were in power.[48] The South's Democratic politicians weren't powerless to stop the night riders or curb the interpersonal violence that beset their states. They were collusive.

Of course, the U.S. federal system should have been able to rein in the violence. For a time, it tried. President Johnson, who took office after Lincoln's assassination, was a lifelong southerner who tried to undo his predecessor's work.[49] But Congress fought back. In 1866, legislators passed the Civil Rights Act to force states to recognize the rights of all citizens.[50] By 1867, northern-appointed governors could call on newly rebuilt federal military forces for support. In 1869, the Union war hero Ulysses Grant became president and aided congressional Republicans. In 1870, they passed the Enforcement Act, which allowed federal troops to protect the right to vote. Because southern courts wouldn't convict whites for black murders, in 1871 the Ku Klux Klan Act made racist terror a federal crime.[51] From 1869 to 1900, Congress voided election results over thirty times and ordered opposition congressmen seated twenty-six times when it concluded that voters had been excluded due to violence or fraud.[52]

But as the night riders swung elections, the House and the Senate repopulated with Confederates. Dixiecrats regained national power and fought laws that would have punished the violent gangs that helped them win their offices. Meanwhile, Congress needed to pass legislation to govern the rest of the country. Endless fights over the South were precluding other business. In 1872, Congress passed the Amnesty Act, restoring the right to vote and hold office to all but five hundred former Confederates.[53] Congress withdrew federal troops from the South to fight Indian wars in the West until just six thousand soldiers remained to patrol the 790,000 square miles of the former Confederacy.[54] That same year, Congress shuttered the Freedmen's Bureau that Lincoln had established to help former slaves realize their rights. On Inauguration Day 1873, just eight years after the end of the

Civil War, eight of the eleven states that had seceded were back in the hands of Confederates. The following year, Democrats regained control of the House thanks to the solid Dixiecratic bloc.

The Supreme Court, meanwhile, overrode Republicans in Congress to ensure white southern impunity. In 1873, over 130 blacks were murdered on the eve of a Louisiana election.[55] A federal court convicted some of the murderers. On appeal, the Supreme Court ruled in *United States v. Cruikshank* (1876) that murder was a state crime and the federal government had no jurisdiction.[56] The killers walked free, and attacks increased. A series of ensuing decisions deepened the doctrine of states' rights, forming a legal wall of impunity that empowered Dixiecrats.

The violence was effective, so candidates stoked it, and once in office, politicians allowed it to continue. A Senate committee investigating the 1875 election in Mississippi reported that Democrats had won "by acts of violence, fraud, and murder, fraught with more than all the horrors of open war."[57] Before the next election, Democratic parties in multiple states drew up semiofficial strategies such as South Carolina's Edgefield Plan to use organized, armed private militias to suppress opposition voting.[58] In 1876, in what was the most disputed presidential election in American history, Samuel Tilden, the Democratic candidate for president, won the popular vote and the vote of the Electoral College by a small margin. But the Republican Party contested, claiming that ballot stuffing and intimidation by night riders, particularly in South Carolina, Florida, and Louisiana, had scared blacks and other Republican voters away from the polls.[59] Democrats agreed to concede the presidency to the Republican candidate, Rutherford Hayes. In exchange, they wanted an end to Reconstruction. By 1877, all federal troops had left the South, ending the last vestiges of protection offered to newly freed slaves and white southern Republicans.

FROM LYNCHINGS TO JIM CROW, 1880s–1890s

Night-rider violence didn't, on the face of it, look political. Neither did lynching, which rose rapidly in the South after federal troops left. By 1892, a quarter century after the end of the Civil War, someone was

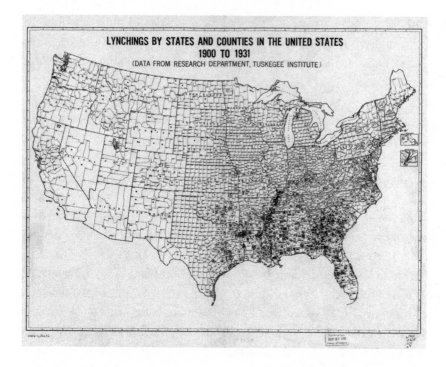

LYNCHINGS BY STATES AND COUNTIES IN THE UNITED STATES
1900 TO 1931
(DATA FROM RESEARCH DEPARTMENT, TUSKEGEE INSTITUTE)

lynched in America every thirty-six hours.[60] Yet both were forms of
Privilege Violence.

Unlike earlier western lynchings, southern lynchings had nothing to do with weak institutions and rural impediments to justice
of the sort faced by the young Roosevelt.[61] Instead, mobs often took
their quarry straight out of jail cells, unwilling to have them tried
and perhaps acquitted in the courts. While some sheriffs would fight
jailhouse mobs and plead to "let the law take its course," Janus-faced
politicians often claimed the state should have the monopoly on violence, while encouraging the mob with a wink and a nod.[62] As James
Vardaman, eventual governor, then senator, of Mississippi, said during his gubernatorial race, "If I was Sheriff and a mob came to the jail,
I would run it off. If I was Governor and the Sheriff called for troops, I
would send troops. But if I was neither Sheriff nor Governor, I would
lead the crowd that would take him out and hang him."[63]

The proximate cause of most lynchings was personal. Murders
were often justified as fair punishment for what was viewed as the
most heinous crime—a black man having sex with a white woman.

Others stemmed from a variety of local squabbles mixed with racial animus. Around 10 percent of lynching victims were white—often Jews, immigrants, labor organizers, or teachers working to help black Americans.[64]

Violence was often used to maintain white economic dominance. Stewart Tolnay and E. M. Beck, sociologists who compiled one of the largest data sets of the phenomena, found that lynchings were more frequent when pay was due in years that cotton prices had fallen. White planters might have thought that a murder or two might deter the remaining pickers from asking for fair wages.[65] Terror was also used to steal successful blacks' property and businesses. In May 1871, for instance, nine men visited Samuel and Hannah Tutson, former slaves who had bought and homesteaded 163 acres in Clay County, Florida. They demanded the couple give up their land. Samuel and Hannah refused. In the middle of the night, a group of men dragged Samuel out of the house and took him away. A deputy sheriff yanked Hannah's baby from her arms and threw it across the room, then pulled Hannah out of the house and tied her to a tree. Separated in the pitch black, Samuel and Hannah were both stripped and beaten with saddle girths. The deputy sheriff raped Hannah, then left them both for dead. But the couple lived, and after searching all night, they found their children hiding in a field. When Hannah reported the attack, she was arrested and fined for filing a false report.[66]

Above all, lynchings looked like racial hatred run rampant. But when Brad Epperly and a group of scholars analyzed lynchings at the county level in eleven southern states, they found a telling pattern.[67] Lynchings increased before elections.[68]

Stoking terror and then allowing impunity to participants helped southern politicians hide a political agenda amid mob violence. Thus, lynchings exploded in the 1890s when southern Democrats faced a new threat: Populist politicians.[69] The Populists were gaining ground in the Midwest, which was racked by agricultural depression, by calling on farmers to unite against rich industrialists and East Coast plutocrats. In the South, they tried to unite poor white and black sharecroppers against the southern planter class.

So Dixiecrats encouraged highly public, symbolic murders. The pageant helped convince poor whites that they were united to the planters by their superior skin color and bore no common cause with poor blacks.[70] The purposeful solidarity was one reason why lynchings were often premeditated public spectacles rather than furtive and spontaneous crimes. In 1893, a man accused of raping and killing a four-year-old white girl was placed on a carnival float through a crowd ten thousand strong.[71] The mayor declared a public holiday rather than try to stop the murder. For other lynchings, schools were let out, and railroads ran special excursion trains. So many lynching postcards circulated through the mail that the United States' post office passed a law banning them in 1908, though the South failed to enforce it.[72]

Epperly's team found that lynchings fell when politicians found a less violent way to eradicate challengers.[73] Between 1890 and 1908, ten of the eleven states of the former Confederacy amended their constitutions. Most required a "poll tax" to vote that former slaves could rarely afford. States legislated a host of other provisions that made voting impossible for blacks and for many of the poor whites the Populists were recruiting.[74] Funding for schools was slashed; then literacy was made a prerequisite for voting.[75] Because jurors in America are drawn from the rolls of qualified voters, those who lost the ability to vote also couldn't expect justice in the courts.

"Mississippi's constitutional convention of 1890 was held for no other purpose than to eliminate the nigger from politics," declared James Vardaman, who helped frame that constitution. "When that device fails, we will resort to something else." Vardaman finished this thought during his gubernatorial candidacy: "If it is necessary, every Negro in the state will be lynched."[76]

It was not necessary, because the new Jim Crow laws worked as intended. Black Americans had embraced voting after the Civil War. By the early 1870s, over a million black Americans were registered to vote.[77] The feat had been accomplished thanks to scores of northern organizers who joined locals in 1867 to register new voters in what was known as the "Republican summer."[78] In 1880, two-thirds of eligible black men voted for president.[79]

As Jim Crow laws passed in state after state, these gains were erased. Alabama had 181,471 registered black voters in 1900, and only 3,000 after its new constitution took effect. Virginia and North Carolina had no black voters at all in the presidential election of 1904.[80] In Texas, where around 100,000 black men voted in the 1890s, turnout was just 5,000 by 1906.[81] In Louisiana, over 130,000 black voters were registered in 1896, but after Jim Crow laws took effect, the state contained only 1,342 black voters.[82] By 1910, more than half of the state's parishes had only 1 black voter or none at all.[83] By 1912, across the former Confederacy, black turnout had fallen to just 1.8 percent.[84]

One of the more robust findings in behavioral science is that positive human relationships across groups reduce extreme political polarization.[85] Segregation made normal relationships impossible. Laws legally separated whites from blacks in churches, restaurants, restrooms, hotels, schools, cemeteries, swimming pools, orphanages, libraries, funeral homes, morgues, and, of course, buses and public transportation, among other locales. In Birmingham, Alabama, a law passed in 1930 prohibited interracial dominoes and checkers.[86] This made it nearly impossible to build the political alliances between the few remaining black voters and the lower-class whites that the Populist Party needed to win office. The Dixiecrats' de facto one-party state, whose laws were backed with the threat of violence, had staying power. In 1954, across seven Mississippi counties where blacks composed more than 60 percent of the population, African Americans cast only two votes.[87]

Jim Crow laws gave the Dixiecrats the electorate they needed to maintain an oligarchic regime ruled by the rich planter class.[88] Southern politicians no longer required public lynchings, and so politicians began to intervene more frequently to stop mobs from succeeding.[89] Lynchings began declining around 1894. They took a long time to disappear, because by then southern society had decivilized and normalized the brutality. But the timing of those that occurred was no longer tied to the election cycle.[90]

"We have done our level best," proclaimed "Pitchfork Ben" Tillman, South Carolina's former governor turned senator, on the Senate floor. "We have scratched our heads to find out how we could eliminate every last one of them. We stuffed ballot boxes. We shot them. We are not ashamed of it."[91]

LYNCHINGS IN ELEVEN SOUTHERN STATES
AS JIM CROW LAWS PASSED[92]

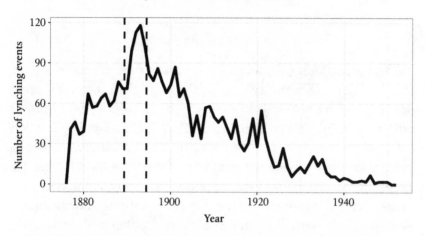

The first dashed line is 1889, the year the first Jim Crow voter suppression law was introduced, averaged across states; the second line, in 1894, depicts when two such laws were in effect, averaged across states.

Privilege Violence: The Three-Headed Hydra

Privilege Violence begins with an economic and political elite who run the state for their benefit. They manipulate budgets and taxes so that government resources are spent extravagantly on their neighborhoods, tribes, or racial groups, and they often benefit from corruption or the cozy cronyism that emerges from any small, intertwined elite. Political leaders court the middle class for their votes, but leave the marginalized to their own devices, secure in the knowledge that most won't vote due to disinterest with the limited options, or disenfranchisement.

Such relatively peaceful oligarchies exist the world over. Endemic violence emerges when these states undertake a trio of steps. First, elites face competition and turn to private violent groups to maintain their political and economic control. Then politicians politicize and weaken state security forces until they grow inept and brutal. Finally, faced with a violent or absent state they cannot trust to protect them, marginalized citizens turn to vigilantes, militias, rebels, and criminals for security, while the middle class hires private guards. By the end, violence that began with the state saturates society.

Above-the-Law Elites

Political leaders in a democracy who face viable competition and fear that they lack majority support thanks to their own corruption or rapacious monopoly on privilege can try to hold on to power through peaceful or violent means. They can manipulate election rules—for instance, by passing laws that disenfranchise likely opposition voters or by making it impossible for independent candidates to get on the ballot. But if these methods are too blatant, they may earn international opprobrium. If they are not strong enough, opponents may still manage to win. Alternatively, politicians can use violence to shape the voting environment. Sitting politicians could, of course, use state security for such purposes, but private groups can often offer campaign funding or bribes as well as votes. They are also helpful to muddy the waters of culpability. Research across countries has found that governments that collude with private militias also use greater state repression. The inability to clearly assign guilt allows politicians to evade accountability.[93] It can even create a supportive constituency, because voters ironically often support state repression to fight private violence.[94] So using private groups whose interests align with politicians' goals is a low-cost, high-reward strategy for power maintenance.[95]

Support for these private militias takes many forms. In Pakistan, the intelligence service, the ISI, provides radical Islamist groups with money and sometimes arms, then directs them against political opponents. Meanwhile, the ISI uses the threat of Islamic terror to maintain its position and budget. As the Pakistan expert Frédéric Grare wrote, the ISI "took some steps against sectarian organizations, but the objective of the ISI was to maintain violence at an 'acceptable' level, not to eliminate the groups. . . . This cannot be overemphasized."[96] Similarly, in Nigeria, Kenya, Bangladesh, and many countries that suffer from Privilege Violence today, political parties hire gangs at election time to scare opposition voters away from the polls, then protect those violent groups between campaigns.[97]

Political and military leaders may provide logistics, money, arms, or simply offer impunity to support private militias that will fight dirty wars while avoiding direct culpability.[98] A declassified cable from the then U.S. secretary of state, Madeleine Albright, to the U.S. ambassador to Colombia notes concern over "persistent reports that the 24th Brigade, and the 31st Counterinsurgency Battalion in particular, has been cooperating with illegal paramilitary groups." As the United States pressured Colombia to improve its human rights record, researchers found that paramilitary violence rose at the same times and places as military abuses declined.[99] As with the night riders in the South, these militias often arise independently of governments and have their own motivations for fighting that simply align with the goals of a political party.

Political parties also cooperate with violent groups for their money, implicitly providing freedom from prosecution if organized criminals can help pay for elections. In the early years of the twenty-first century, a third of Colombia's parliament had their campaigns financed by paramilitary groups, who provided both money and muscle to elect their preferred candidates.[100]

When the violent seek office for themselves, politics and violence fuse. Political parties may be unable to prevent criminals from running, but in some cases they actively recruit lawbreakers. A 2004 study by Samuel Paul and M. Vivekananda looked at the criminal records of Indian candidates for the Lok Sabha, the lower house of parliament, and found that the richer candidates committed the most serious offenses.[101] These wealthy warlords and criminals fund their own campaigns and fill the coffers of other party candidates, making them attractive to cash-strapped parties. In the state of Bihar, the treasurer of one political party explained, "All parties claim to shun criminality ... but the reality is different. ... Parties select people who can win by *saam daam dhand bhed* [by hook or by crook] and the most important criterion is financial assets."[102]

Politicians who rule through Privilege Violence often share the privilege of private militias and state-supported brutality with economic elites. The mutual use of private violence to cement their privileged positions binds economic and political leaders and increases the concentration of wealth. Business leaders often quite legitimately begin asking for self-protection because the state is too weak to protect them and they are targets for kidnapping and extortion. But their militias nearly always transmute into a means of maintaining wealth. Private armies were legalized in Colombia, Bihar, and Sicily, and in each case landlords used them both to fight guerrillas and to suppress wages.[103] In Chiapas, Guerrero, and Oaxaca, three Mexican states facing insurgency in the 1990s, the army served as an armed wing of local caciques, elite families who controlled social, political, and economic life.[104] In return, the wealthy help fund political campaigns. Sometimes, as in Bihar, they round up their workers to vote en masse for a preferred candidate.

Of course, even in countries in the grip of this governing strategy, many people with wealth, privilege, or government positions reject violent groups. But they lack enough power to alter the system.[105] Meanwhile, as criminals and rebels strengthen, they use threats in addition to bribery, offering the choice of *plomo o plata* (bullet or silver) to gain protection within police, courts, parliaments, and other government agencies.

POLITICIZED, BRUTAL SECURITY

The word "privilege" comes from the Latin *privus*, meaning "private," and *legis*, or "law." Because violence and corruption are usually illegal, politicians must create a form of private law to evade justice. They therefore politicize and weaken security agencies and courts so that they answer to political leaders, not any higher law. Sometimes privileged groups put people of their own social class, caste, ethnicity, or religion in charge of security to ensure a common interest in upholding the status quo, as with the Shia military of modern Iraq or the all-white police forces in the segregated South.[106] In every case, budgets and career success hinge on the whims of politicians, not meritocratic policies.

It may seem as if politicized police, militaries, courts, and jails could function normally, except for a few high-profile cases. Yet such forces become holistically ineffective at maintaining order. A report by India's National Police Commission from 1980 provides a graphic description of how politicization rots an entire force. "We were repeatedly told by different sections of the public about police malpractices that were becoming increasingly oppressive and extortionist in character," the report reads. It then describes a long list of crimes, from fabricating false evidence to smuggling. The report continues,

> The reward and punishment mechanism of the system has become totally ineffective because of increasing political interference and, therefore, the senior officers, however determined and committed they might be to the cause of anticorruption work, find themselves unable to deal with corrupt officers who have political contacts and are able to draw political intervention on their behalf whenever anything is attempted to be done to discipline them. The patent inability of a superior officer to deal with a known corrupt subordinate immediately lowers his prestige in the department and induces other subordinates also to seek and develop political contacts as a protective cover to escape punishment for their malpractices. . . . The problem of police corruption cannot, therefore, be satisfactorily tackled unless these [political] links are broken.[107]

Politicized security agencies filled with patronage appointees thus become unable to provide security even in routine cases.

Corruption deepens the ineptitude. In Nigeria, the former national security adviser purportedly pocketed up to U.S.$2 billion while his soldiers went without equipment and pay.[108] Parts of the military have been accused of selling firearms, mortars, combat vehicles, and grenades to Boko Haram insurgents.[109] In Afghanistan, "Malign actors within [the government] support insurgent groups directly, support criminal networks that are linked to insurgents, and support corruption that helps feed the insurgency," wrote General McChrystal, commander of the NATO war there.[110]

Politicized, corrupted security services soon become brutal. Some violence emerges from a frustrated sense of professionalism. Used as holding pens for patronage appointees and lacking adequate resources for real police or military work, some officers who are unable to arrest or fight people they know are culpable turn to violence out of a perverse sense of duty.[111] In Uttar Pradesh, India, the state next door to Bihar, a policeman known for his extrajudicial killings explained,

> I do not kill for personal gain, but for the greater good. . . . [The people] queued up by the thousands at the station to thank me for doing what the courts could not . . . this man had been arrested and charged and acquitted dozens of times, because he could pay off the judges and police! This time he was not acquitted. . . . The really bad criminals, they cannot be disciplined. And the legal system has completely degenerated, so it cannot stop them. But they must be stopped.[112]

High levels of law-enforcement brutality are only possible, however, when politicians incentivize repression. Under the banner of improving security, political and security leaders in countries governed through Privilege Violence encourage repressive policing practices. "A good criminal is a dead criminal," stated a popular congressman from Rio de Janeiro, and unsurprisingly, one-fifth of all homicides in that city are killings by state security.[113] One officer there explained, "My initial experience of policing was to kill criminals. Killing was required as good performance by my supervisors."[114] In the 1990s, government incentives to kill Maoists in Bihar led to hundreds of so-called encounter killings, in which suspects and many innocent low-caste villagers were shot during engineered extrajudicial "encounters." In 2015, the vice president of El Salvador told police that they could kill gang members "without any fear of suffering consequences."[115]

This kind of state repression is more easily deniable when politicians use the proliferation of gang, cartel, or paramilitary murders to obscure violence that is committed—or commissioned—by political and economic leaders. In Central America, for instance, the risk for reporters covering state violence is so great that covering drug traffickers and gang members is, ironically, less dangerous. Thus, governments get away with blaming the gangs for most murders, although in Honduras the independent Violence Observatory at the National University could attribute only 5 percent of homicides in 2015 to gangs, a percentage similar to previous years.[116] A 2017 analysis of violence in Guatemala could attribute only 28 percent of the country's murders to cartels in the major drug-trafficking corridor.[117] Even in the neighborhoods most renowned for gang violence, nearly 60 percent of murders were unconnected to the gangs.[118] Gang violence in these countries is real and horrific, but it also obscures government and business collusion with private violence, such as the murders of over 120 Honduran environmental activists between 2009 and 2017. Their deaths have been blamed on general lawlessness, but urban gangs rarely murder rural community leaders.[119] Similarly, Mexico is currently the deadliest country in the world for journalists. But contrary to popular perception, the most frequently murdered reporters are not those who cover the cartels but local journalists investigating government corruption. Government security services are responsible for three times as much journalist harassment as any other group, but journalists are most often killed by criminals, suggesting a possible division of labor.[120] Or, as Rodrigo Duterte, president of the Philippines, blatantly declared in 2016, "Just because you're a journalist, you are not exempted from assassination if you're a son of a bitch."[121]

Secure in the knowledge that they won't be prosecuted, it is a small step for some security personnel to run extortion rings, serve as contract assassins, or collude with violent groups to enrich themselves.[122] In Honduras, the former deputy drug czar Gustavo Alfredo Landaverde gave an interview in December 2011 describing how the Honduran National Police killed on behalf of the cartels. He cited a military intelligence officer who explained, "You write a report, give it to your boss and then realize it was him who was committing the crimes. . . . It's the police, the army, the security ministry . . . even prosecutors."[123] Two weeks after the interview, assassins pulled a motorbike alongside Landaverde's car and murdered him.

The violence, ineptitude, and corruption of security services is mirrored in the prison system. The head of Barrio 18, one of Honduras's most brutal gangs, was allowed out of prison two days a week to visit girlfriends and conduct drug business in exchange for handing a cut of his profits to the prison warden. On the day of his release, he was shot by the prison police. The warden wanted to keep their deal a secret.[124]

The prisons of Honduras and other Central American countries that marry ruthlessness with insecurity are not an anomaly. A criminal justice system that is built to maintain privilege rather than fight crime makes prison more dangerous for prisoners and the public. Prisoners kept in appalling but poorly controlled conditions are more likely to riot or escape. In the Reconstruction South, rather than increase taxes to pay for secure prisons, states leased convicts out for hard labor.[125] Bureaucrats picked a small circle of men allowed to lease from the state. They in turn subleased the prisoners, creating a tidy circle of kickbacks profitable to all involved. Joseph Brown, a Georgia governor and state supreme court chief justice, founded Dade Coal Company, one of the South's largest convict-fueled operations. Congressmen Edwin and Andrew Ewing, two brothers who represented Tennessee's Eighth District at different times, founded Tennessee's Coal, Iron, and Railroad Company with a convict workforce.[126] Nathan Bedford Forrest, a founder of the Ku Klux Klan, built a railway fortune with convict labor.[127]

The horrific conditions of the leasing system meant that the penalty for minor crimes like loitering or stealing food was often, de facto, death.[128] Between the late 1880s and 1918, four thousand convicts died in Andrew Carnegie's Tennessee coal mines.[129] In Mississippi, 15 percent of all working convicts died in 1877. Of the prisoners leased to railroad companies between 1877 and 1879, 25 percent died in Arkansas and a stunning 45 percent in South Carolina, where the G&A Railroad "lost" 128 of 285 prisoners to accidents, disease, and murder by the guards.[130] Nearly all working convicts were black, thanks to selective enforcement of new laws passed under Reconstruction.[131] So for decades, their plight attracted little public concern.

But the bloodcurdling conditions of labor sites also imperiled the public, because work sites were dangerously insecure. In just two years, thirty-nine prisoners escaped from G&A Railroad camps.[132] In Tennessee in 1895, coal miners set prisoners free in mines where convict labor was depressing wages.[133] Around 10 percent of southern inmates escaped each year from their poorly guarded work sites.[134]

VIGILANTES AND ROBIN HOOD

As the state brutalizes, citizens stop distinguishing between security services and criminals.[135] When a prominent Mexican journalist facing a death threat tried to confirm who was trying to kill him, his source in the cartel network explained, "It's the government you should be concerned about." But, she hastened to explain, "there's not much difference between the cartels and the government."[136] In Sicily, just before being found dead in jail with strychnine swirling in his coffee, a mafioso claimed that "bandits, police and mafia are one and the same, like Father, Son and Holy Ghost."[137]

Why should a vicious, corrupt state have any greater claim to its people's allegiance than criminals and insurgents? The Stanford political scientist Margaret Levi, who has spent decades investigating why citizens trust their governments, explained, "When citizens believe government actors promote immoral policies, have ignored their interests, or have actually betrayed them, citizens are unlikely to feel obliged to comply with the laws."[138] When law enforcement is brutal or simply absent, as often occurs in marginalized areas starved of state support, space opens for criminals and insurgents to compete with the state for citizen loyalty.

Vigilante violence for self-protection grows.[139] In Nigeria, where vigilantism is rampant, the public-safety expert Innocent Chukwuma explains that "the feeling is that by handing [a supposed criminal] over to the police, the police will release them and collect money from them," so it is better to extract immediate, do-it-yourself justice.[140] While superheroes appear heroic in comic books, real-life vigilantes look more like the Ku Klux Klan, whose founding documents claimed, "This is an institution of chivalry, humanity, mercy, and patriotism . . . to protect the weak, the innocent, and the defenseless from the indignities, wrongs, and outrages of the lawless, the violent, and the brutal."[141] In nearly every case, even vigilantes that begin with noble intentions and public support become violent thugs.[142] Gangs often claim to be vigilantes protecting their abandoned neighborhoods.[143] "We police our own," said a gang member in Southeast Los Angeles. "Why are we called gangsters," when "soldiers are heroes"?[144]

As the ethical line between criminality and do-it-yourself justice blurs, Mafias such as Sicily's Cosa Nostra and Georgia's thieves-in-law compete with the government by offering more honest, effective, and swift justice than the nation's corrupt court systems.[145] Afghanistan's Taliban does the same, gaining support from people who do not share its ideology but who appreciate its ability to resolve disputes more cheaply, swiftly, and honestly than the state courts.[146]

The idea that people willingly choose to be governed by vicious criminals and terrorists rather than by their governments seems absurd. Of course, most people do not make such a choice willingly. The KKK threatened reluctant Klansmen with whippings, and those who wanted to quit feared they would be killed. "There was no way to get out of it," explained one Klansman who rode on three raids. "Worms would have been eating me now, I suppose, if I hadn't gone to the meeting."[147] Once violent groups gain a foothold, they often resort to deadly coercion to force people to stay in their fold.

But violent groups don't survive because of repressive tactics alone. They don't have to be morally pure or even halfway palatable to gain a following. They simply have to be better than the alternative.[148] When the government is corrupt, predatory, or simply absent, that is a low bar. Boko Haram, for instance, is commonly seen as a vicious terrorist group. It began, however, as a movement of middle-class young men who rejected northern Nigeria's deeply corrupt religious leadership.[149] They formed to fight a degenerate elite, the same issues that inflamed the supporters of Bernie Sanders, Donald Trump, and anticorruption movements globally. Boko Haram further appealed to recruits by covering its members' wedding costs, helping many young men to marry.[150] Of course, Boko Haram is a brutal terrorist organization that uses children as suicide bombers. But to locals, the relevant comparison is to the alternative—the Nigerian government.

In 2014, Boko Haram burned down a series of towns in northern Nigeria. But the year before, the military had razed the same towns in retaliation against a Boko Haram attack. Boko Haram killed more than sixty-five hundred people in 2014. But over seven thousand died that year in Nigeria's military prisons from starvation, torture, and neglect, while twelve hundred more were executed by the military without trial.[151] An additional twenty thousand men and boys were arrested and sometimes tortured while in prison, but lived. To many northern Nigerians, their government was the greater threat.[152]

The only people who benefit from this maelstrom are criminals. By posing as noble outlaws against an ignoble power structure, they gain legitimacy that societies would never extend under normal circumstances. That's why violent individuals in places of Privilege Violence frequently adopt a Robin Hood persona. Colombia's drug lord Pablo Escobar set off bombs at a bookstore full of schoolchildren. But he also built soccer fields and constructed an entire neighborhood of low-income housing. Many saw his war on the state as another form of protest against an unjust system. "We are 100 percent with Pablo—he fought a lot for the people," exclaimed a young man at his funeral. *The New York Times* quoted a twenty-nine-year-old engineering student saying, "In the future, people will go to his tomb to pray, the way they would to a saint."[153]

Because they gain from Privilege Violence, organized criminals accelerate its progression by supporting policies that concentrate privilege. Then they dispense largesse to enhance their own reputations.[154] In Chicago during the gangster years of Prohibition, a newspaperman wrote, "The Boss gives $100 to charity, but accepts $1,000 for voting against an ordinance for better housing. He pays the funeral expenses of the man who died because the boss killed the law to safeguard the machinery on which he worked. He helps the widow, whose suit for damages was blocked under a system he paid to perpetuate."[155]

Criminals, outlaws, and insurgents know the value of public relations. Escobar owned a newspaper and a television program that publicized his good works and criticized "corrupt" and "lazy" politicians. Other Colombian cartel leaders funded over two dozen radio stations and added print journalists to their payroll to ensure friendly press.[156] The Japanese *yakuza* Mafia invested in the Japanese film industry to buttress its reputation.[157] The Georgian Mafia built churches, Sicily's Mafia courted the Catholic hierarchy, and even the brutal Mexican drug gang La Familia Michoacana distributed its own version of the Bible.[158] Jesse James worked with the pro-Confederate editor of *The Kansas City Times* to burnish his image as a heroic outlaw fighting corrupt northern banks and railroads on behalf of the poor and, most important, the South. A popular song, covered by Bruce Springsteen, ran, "Jesse was a man / A friend to the poor / He'd never rob a mother or a child." The popular image brought James useful friends. When the Missouri governor vowed to capture his gang, Missouri's Confederate-sympathizing legislature tried to sabotage the attempt by capping the ransom money the state could offer.[159]

Gangs, vigilantes, and Mafias obscure the governing origins of Privilege Violence. They are responsible for jaw-dropping cruelty. But they metastasize as an effect, not a cause, of a state whose elites enable lawlessness for their own benefit.[160]

THE MIDDLE CLASS TURNS A BLIND EYE

So long as members of the middle class don't become activists who agitate for change or investigative journalists who threaten the elites, they remain fairly safe from this spreading terror. In democracies governed through Privilege Violence, politicians depend on the middle class for votes and for the democratic façade they offer to the international community. So elites spend state resources on streetlights and police in middle-class neighborhoods and allow the middle class to vote unfettered, so long as elections don't raise issues that would undermine the basic power structure.

Armed groups, especially those in collusion with parts of the government, understand that bloodshed will be ignored among the marginalized, but murders that touch the middle class will be met with a government response. So the middle class is generally off-limits, with the exception of activists, the occasional mistake, and cases in which an armed group is using violence as a means of bargaining with the government.[161] Violent organizations that fail to accept the implicit bargain face crackdowns. The Zeta cartel in Mexico tried to terrorize rivals through its sheer ruthlessness, but its indiscriminate carnage led the Mexican government to cooperate with the United States to fight back. The effect was not to bring law and order but to hand the

Zetas' trafficking routes to other cartels, particularly the Sinaloans, who played by the rules.[162]

The middle class thus generally keeps out of politics, other than voting at election time. To address the crimes that do affect them, such as extortion and kidnapping, they hire private security.[163] As Mexico faced a surge in kidnappings in the 1990s, private security companies proliferated. By 1997, Mexico City alone had 587 such companies employing tens of thousands of guards. In El Salvador by 2001, private security agents hired by the middle class and business owners outnumbered police by seventy thousand to twenty thousand.[164] In fact, in all six Spanish-speaking Central American countries, private security officers outnumber the police.[165] Many of these private guards are just criminals in different uniforms, protected and enriched by the wages of the middle class.

Privilege Violence starts with the state. Yet it ends in a society that normalizes violence. As force becomes accepted as a way to solve problems and impunity becomes nearly absolute (Mexico's unsolved murder rate is 90 percent; in Guatemala, El Salvador, and Honduras, over 95 percent of homicides don't result in punishment), the ability to resolve disputes through force tempts otherwise ordinary people.[166] The majority of society remains law-abiding, but some use the cover of political and criminal violence to settle long-standing arguments with neighbors, business partners, and family members at gunpoint. The ubiquity of bloodshed changes society itself. As Michael Fellman, a historian of political violence in the United States, wrote about Bloody Kansas and Missouri on the eve of the Civil War, "Normal expectations collapsed, to be replaced by frightening and bewildering personal and cultural chaos. The normal route by which people solved problems and channeled behavior had been destroyed. The base for their prior values—their 'moral structure'—underwent frontal attack."[167] This is decivilization, and when it has taken hold, the sickness unleashed by Privilege Violence has spread from the government to the people.

3

DECIVILIZATION

Each man feels an impulse to kill his neighbor, lest he be first killed by him. Revenge and retaliation follow. . . . Murders for old grudges, and murders for [ill-gotten gains] proceed under any cloak that will bear cover for the occasion.[1]

—ABRAHAM LINCOLN, WRITING ABOUT
BLOODY MISSOURI AND KANSAS, 1863

On a spring morning in 1948, world leaders from the Conference of American States met in a convention hall in downtown Bogotá. Hours later, Jorge Eliécer Gaitán, the beloved left-wing presidential candidate of Colombia's Liberal Party, was dead. To this day, no one knows who was behind the bullet. A mob immediately seized the man holding the gun and beat him to death. Many of Colombia's poor had seen Gaitán as their savior, and the capital exploded with riots. For three days, Bogotá was in flames. Pro-Gaitán police, many from the lower classes themselves, joined the mob. Pro-government soldiers shot their weapons directly into the crowds.[2] In three days, two thousand people were killed in Bogotá—more than the number of U.S. troops who have died in battle in Afghanistan since 2001.[3]

Then the carnage moved to the countryside. For years, the sitting Conservative government had used the army to intimidate peasants and deepen its grip on rural areas. After the assassination, the Liberal Party teamed up with bandits and private militias to fight back. For the next nine years, liberals and conservatives murdered each other with medieval viciousness. Perpetrators created techniques so wide-spread they were given names: *Picar para tamal* was when a person was carved into pieces while still alive. *Bocachiquiar* meant puncturing a body with hundreds of tiny wounds until the person bled to death. Families used the strife to settle scores with neighbors, relatives, and bosses, cloaking their personal vendettas within the political violence.[4] The era was known simply as *La Violencia*, and by the end of the decade nearly 200,000 Colombians were dead, while a million more had been forced from their homes to seek shelter in slums on the outskirts of Colombia's cities.

Decivilization occurs when violence is normalized across a society, as it was during *La Violencia*. It can happen anywhere, as Abraham Lincoln and Michael Fellman noted regarding Missouri and Kansas during the Civil War. Its origins lie not in a naturally barbaric society or a pathological culture, despite how obvious those causes appear, but in choices by the state. Across cultures, governments that can't or won't enforce order, give up the monopoly on violence, and resort to repression create "emergent behavior." What materializes is a process in which ordinary people become impulsive, quicker to anger, more ready to see violence as normal. As countries decivilize, people polarize into warring camps, dehumanize those who were once fellow citizens, and excuse previously unthinkable brutality. The ubiquity of violence among regular people obscures the political roots of the disorder. It also alters the nature of the problem itself. Once society has normalized violence, a government can no longer restore security on its own.

PRIVILEGE ENTRENCHES: COLOMBIA, 1957–1960

To understand how Colombia descended into Privilege Violence, the decivilization that ensued, and how it then saved itself, I traveled to Bogotá in the winter of 2015. Set on a mountain plateau eighty-six hundred feet above sea level, Bogotá is a sprawling capital anchored by tall glass office towers in its far west. The city center bustles with universities. Posh apartments climb steep hillsides. Dog walkers pour out each morning with their furry charges. In the grimy, historic downtown, government workers sit in the cobblestoned plaza eating arepas and drinking tropical juices. On my first day in town, I rode buses to the end of multiple lines, visiting the outskirts of the city, where passengers had more tattoos, graffiti covered the stations, trash piled up, and teenage boys held boom boxes aloft. It felt a lot like New York in the 1990s, with better fruit.

One of Colombia's many charms is that hot chocolate is considered an acceptable drink for adults. I spent the next afternoon in a downtown Bogotá *pastelería*, nursing a cocoa to ward off the winter chill while talking with Álvaro Balcázar, the bureaucrat in charge of bringing government to guerrilla-held territories under President Álvaro Uribe in the first decade of the twenty-first century. "There was a lot of empty space that lacked governmental presence," he began, "they could not guarantee rights—no health, no education, no justice, no security . . . so the FARC could exploit that." But as we talked, he revealed that the problem wasn't just a lack of state presence.

Colombia's political elites ended *La Violencia* with a deal. The rival liberals and conservatives met in Spain in 1957 and forged an agreement to share power. They rewrote election rules to block new parties; then, regardless of who won elections, the two parties split governmentally appointed positions from national ministries to local mayors evenly. That way, both parties could constantly benefit from state power and patronage.[5] For decades, this unified National Front government, as it was known, ran Colombia. Regular elections allowed the country to claim the title of one of the longest-running democracies in Latin America, but it was a democracy in name only. Votes meant little when power was handed back and forth among the same cozy elite.

"It was never in the government's interest to have a strong judicial system, strong police," Balcázar explained. "The elite powers did not think it was important for them and their businesses in the short term."[6] Instead, they wanted to keep taxes low and ensure that what government there was maintained the roads in their neighborhoods and built schools for their children, leaving scraps for the poor and rural parts of the country. Low taxes meant there was little money for a strong judiciary, police, or military. But this was not considered a problem. General Fernando Landazábal Reyes, a former Colombian general and head of the army, shared Balcázar's assessment. The agreement to end *La Violencia* occurred after a military coup had forced both parties out of power from 1953 to 1957. Despite the long-running guerrilla war, "the politicians don't let the armed forces grow because they don't trust them," General Landazábal grumbled in the late 1990s. "They're afraid of a coup."[7]

GIVING UP THE MONOPOLY ON FORCE

By the late 1950s, although the worst of *La Violencia* was over, unrest burbled throughout the countryside. Hardened criminals gained support by claiming they were stealing from rich, right-wing landowners on behalf of the poor and fighting the *pájaros*, assassins who evicted and killed peasants on behalf of the Conservative Party.[8]

Raising the specter of global Communism (the CIA had blamed Communists for the riots after Gaitán's death), Colombia's government appealed to the United States for help. President Eisenhower sent an assessment team out in October 1959. The team suggested that the new government needed to restore honesty to the administration, depoliticize the police, rebuild state institutions, and restore moral values that had been "outraged and even warped" by the years of murder and impunity.[9]

That was not the path Colombia's government chose. Instead, when landlords sought protection from the highwaymen, the government allowed them to employ private armies, officially legalizing these militias in 1965.[10]

Giving up the monopoly on force is a common tactic used by elites who are trying to fight violence while keeping state institutions, particularly security services, weak. It is a mistake. Private armed groups exacerbate the descent into Privilege Violence and its attendant decivilization. In 1919, the political theorist Max Weber wrote that having the legitimate and exclusive right to use, threaten, or authorize force against citizens was the attribute that defined a government.[11] Across most of Europe, England, Japan, and other modern democracies with low rates of violence, states fought for decades to gain such total control. While lords and ladies are much romanticized, when transposed to Afghanistan today, these wealthy families with their private armies look like what they were: warlords. To quell the threat these warlords posed, kings and emperors centralized power. The Tudors curbed the rights of England's noblemen; in France, Louis XIII condemned dueling and private armies and Louis XIV created a centralized surveillance state; Japan disarmed its feudal lords and their armies.[12]

The centralization of power, however, is a double-edged sword. In 1215, nearly three centuries before the Tudors reined in England's armed lords, noblemen rallied their armies and forced the king to sign the Magna Carta at bow point. The charter enshrined the rights of citizens, ended impunity for the monarchy, and began England's famed rule of law. If power is centralized before laws and traditions recognize more fundamental rights, a country can become dictatorial. Yet if a country fails to ever centralize power and establish a strong state with a monopoly on force, pervasive violence makes life nasty, brutish, and short, as Hobbes observed four hundred years ago.

Some places get the balance right. Powerful parts of society use the threat of violence to establish a nascent rule of law that hems in the government's power, and only then do rulers create a strong state with a monopoly on violence that can enforce these rules among citizens. The results, in the U.K., Japan, most European countries, and some former British dominions like Canada and Australia, are some of the least violent, most secure societies the world has ever known.

The United States took a different path. After the Revolutionary War, citizen militiamen who helped win independence weren't interested in disarming. The scrawny central government was too weak to force the issue, and some statesmen concerned about an overly strong centralized government, such as Thomas Jefferson, did not want it to.[13] The states couldn't offer enough protection to their populations to make disarmament a reasonable proposition, particularly on the frontier.

Crucially, those frontiersmen had the vote. The United States is unique among developed nations for having a democracy before a strong state. So unlike in much of Europe, an authoritarian monarchy couldn't simply enforce its will. The U.S. Constitution's Second Amendment, the right to bear arms, was the product of a government too weak to protect its people and too democratic to take away their right to protect themselves.

I was raised in Alaska where I grew up shooting .22s with my father, so this is not a statement on gun rights, which would require a separate book.[14] But there's no getting around the fact that the Second Amendment is a particularly formal declaration that a state is not going to fully centralize power. Instead, the United States shares the legitimate use of force with its citizens.

ROBIN HOOD CRIMINALS AND GUERRILLAS: COLOMBIA, 1960s

In most countries, relinquishment of the legitimate use of force is more haphazard and more tilted toward elites. In Colombia, landlords, not any citizen, were allowed private armies to fight the bandits left over from *La Violencia*. But those highwaymen were becoming more powerful in the 1960s because of a conundrum of the landlords' own making. They were enclosing vast common lands for ranching. The pastures, however, weren't theirs. An old piece of English doggerel explains the problem, which also occurred in seventeenth-century England:[15]

> *The law locks up the man or woman*
> *Who steals the goose from off the common*
> *But lets the greater felon loose*
> *Who steals the common from off the goose.*

The political thinker George Orwell wrote about that period of English history in words applicable to Colombia in the mid-twentieth century:

Stop to consider how the so-called owners of the land got hold of it. They simply seized it by force, afterwards hiring lawyers to provide them with title-deeds. In the case of the enclosure of the common lands, which was going on from about 1600 to 1850, the land-grabbers did not even have the excuse of being foreign conquerors; they were quite frankly taking the heritage

of their own countrymen, upon no sort of pretext except that
they had the power to do so.[16]

In 1960s Colombia, land that had been considered common property or owned by peasants without legal title was seized by the
wealthy. Landholders called on the army to evict problematic peasants, employed politically connected assassins, and used their legalized private militias to ensure their writ held. Peasants were driven
off farms their families had lived on for generations. Some joined the
masses in the urban slums. Others cast their lot with the small guerrilla movements forming in the jungles. They created eleven independent citadels in Colombia's rural interior. Within these statelets,
peasants governed and protected themselves with their own armed
citizen militias.

Worried about Communist unrest, Colombia again appealed to
the United States, and America provided intelligence training to Colombia's military and sent helicopters and small arms to equip an
anti-guerrilla unit. In 1962, an American team spent twelve days assessing the country, then recommended a program that came to be
called Plan Lazo.[17] Under the plan, the United States trained Colombian forces in intelligence, counterinsurgency, and propaganda to
combat the bandits and around two thousand guerrillas active in
the eleven self-declared "independent republics" in the jungles. The
United States also funded the Colombian military to construct roads
and health centers in guerrilla-rich areas to increase economic opportunity and demonstrate that the government cared about its people.[18]

The program was considered quite progressive for its time. In fact,
the policies the United States has attempted in Afghanistan since 2001
follow the same logic (and have faced similar problems).[19] In practice, Plan Lazo strengthened the security services that supported the
existing, oligarchic power structure. Despite providing the roads and
health care, the strategy didn't give Colombia's poor any more voice
in their supposed democracy. A small coterie of elites still monopo-
lized power and resources. Security forces were still politicized, brutal, and partial to the landlords. Unsurprisingly, Plan Lazo backfired.

In 1964, the newly trained and equipped Colombian military
reconquered all eleven guerrilla republics and destroyed about half

the bandit gangs. Only a few hundred insurgents remained. But the military success was Pyrrhic. The remaining guerrillas regrouped and declared themselves "victims of the policy of fire and sword proclaimed and carried out by the oligarchic usurpers of power." They formed the Revolutionary Armed Forces of Colombia (FARC) and began one of the longest-running wars in modern times. Before the conflict ended in 2017, the FARC would field tens of thousands of troops and control territory within Colombia the size of Switzerland.[20]

From the mid-1960s through the early 1980s, multiple guerrilla groups formed in response to the Privilege Violence born from the nefarious relationship between Colombian elites, private militias, and state repression. They catered to different demographics: The stolid, rural, Stalinist FARC attracted peasants in the jungle. The hip, urban M-19 declared that "the revolution is a party" and specialized in an outrageous mix of audaciousness and terror to attract college students, such as tunneling under a military cache in central Bogotá and making off with forty-two hundred military weapons.[21]

"When I was in the university, there were, like, nine offers a day to join different guerrillas," Nacho, a renowned Colombian investigative journalist, told me. He had agreed to meet in his fourth-floor walk-up apartment in a nondescript neighborhood of Bogotá to discuss the ties between politicians, cartels, and paramilitaries. Smoking a chain of cigarettes, he kept a constant eye on the bank of dirty windows behind him. Nacho's journalism had already spawned twenty assassination attempts by nearly every violent faction in the country— guerrillas, gangs, paramilitaries, retired paramilitary criminal bands, and drug cartels, as well as Colombia's intelligence agency and military. On the day of our interview, his bodyguard, who was supposed to be keeping watch, was missing, a pattern common to many state-sponsored assassinations. His teenage daughter, all long legs and long black hair, fussed in the kitchen a few feet away. I sat, six months pregnant, on the small, worn couch in their tiny living room and considered the strength of the many padlocks on the door.

Nacho kept his distance, but in the 1970s and 1980s many Colombian students and intellectuals started supporting violent insurgents. They despaired at the falsity of their democracy and the force used to suppress anyone protesting the Privilege Violence that upheld the oligarchic order. The Colombian government had tried to end *La Violencia* in 1950 by banning public meetings, using the army to close Congress, outlawing independent labor unions, censoring the press, and taking over the courts. The effort failed, but over the ensuing decades Colombia's governments continued to declare states of emergency and suspend civil rights to fight the guerrilla threat. As other South American countries descended into military dictatorship, Colombia's president, Julio Turbay, passed the 1978 Security Statute. It let the military operate in Colombia's cities and granted it the right to detain and try supposed guerrillas in military tribunals, as well as perpetrators of illegal strikes and so-called social crimes. Union members, human rights activists, Catholics fighting poverty, and other left-wing groups were tried in military courts and jailed. The Right's support for blanket repression against peaceful help for the poor created a self-fulfilling prophecy: left-wing activists began excusing Marxist murder.

REPRESSION BREEDS MORE VIOLENCE

A vast trove of research into rebel and terrorist movements worldwide finds that government repression is the turning point that transforms citizens with moderate grievances into violent insurgents.[22] A recent study of Islamist terrorists across Africa, for example, found that for 71 percent of the nearly five hundred interviewed, the trigger that led them to join a terrorist group was government violence or the arrest of a family member or friend.[23] As James Fearon, the Stanford political scientist, has written, growing human rights abuse "is a *very* bad sign for a government: major civil conflict is much more likely to begin."[24]

Poverty is often cited as a root cause of insurgency. But as Jeff Goodwin, a sociologist at New York University who has studied rebel movements around the world, has found, plenty of impoverished people dislike their governments and don't resort to violence. It is true that most civil wars occur in poor states.[25] But many more poor countries do *not* devolve into warfare. Instead, they look more like Ghana.

Ghana was the first African country to gain its independence, in 1957. Once the embarkation point for many of America's slaves, Martin Luther King Jr. declared that "the birth of this new nation will give impetus to oppressed peoples all over the world."[26]

The promise wouldn't last. For the next thirty-five years, every Ghanian government ended in a coup; no president served out a term. Inept, rapacious leaders destroyed the economy.[27] Poverty was so extreme that in the 1970s, city dwellers begged rural family members for food. The poor resorted to eating grass. Ghana had deep divisions between its ethnicities. Its impoverished North was more Muslim, its richer South deeply Christian. It had all of the ingredients that had sparked civil wars in Liberia, Nigeria, and other nearby countries.

But while feckless and corrupt, Ghana's government was not brutal. It never used violence against its citizens. Politicians did not try to gain voters by deepening hatred between groups.[28] So unlike many nearby nations, the country never decivilized. Ghana's strong chiefs, imams, and churches upheld social norms of propriety, right, and wrong, even as the economy and government disintegrated.[29] Eventually, a multitude of lawyers' associations, professional groups, and churches came together in 1992 to demand democracy and an end to coups and dictatorships.

In countries where societies are healthy, moderate organizations and leaders try to address problems through normal politics and protest. It is only when states show themselves impervious to this sort of peaceful change that political moderates begin to look impotent and inconsequential.[30] The more brutal and less discriminating government repression is against nonviolent groups, the easier it is for violent fringes to recruit members.[31] Armed rebellion grows and so does backlash.

DRUG CARTELS AND VIGILANTES: COLOMBIA, 1970s–1980s

In Colombia, drugs set the tinder aflame. As demand for drugs grew in the 1970s, Carlos Lehder, son of a Colombian mother and a German father with Nazi sympathies, pioneered the new Colombian industry. He learned the marijuana trade from a cellmate while imprisoned in

Danbury, Connecticut, for car theft. He bought small planes to move his inventory, then purchased a Caribbean peninsula two hundred miles off Miami and transformed it into an armed garrison for his drug operation. He was one of the more successful Colombians taking advantage of the U.S. demand for drugs. Colombia's government initially shrugged off concerns about the new business. Colombia was a poor country in the 1970s, and marijuana smuggling didn't seem threatening. Desperate for hard currency, its central bank opened what was known as the "wicked window" in 1975, allowing drug money to enter the country with no tax repercussions. Tax amnesties passed in 1976 and 1978 allowed early traffickers to legalize their windfall profits.[32]

Marijuana was bulky, and the profit margin was modest. Cocaine, however, was easier to ship and more profitable. When a raid forced Lehder back to Colombia, he concocted a plan to carry cocaine into the States by the planeload.[33] He invited Pablo Escobar and other dealers to buy enough of the white powder to fill larger and larger planes heading north. The joint shipping arrangements led to increased collaboration among independent dealers and eventually birthed the cartels—drug-fueled corporations run out of Medellín and Cali. By 1984, cocaine money constituted about 10 percent of Colombia's GDP.[34]

At first, some Colombians viewed the cartel leaders as entrepreneurs. Two brothers and a friend who all hailed from elite local families formed the Cali cartel. Their compound filled a city block, enclosing a swimming pool, tennis court, and half a soccer field. One wing held their living quarters; another featured marble-floored rooms paneled with dark wood and furnished in leather. The leaders' taste and backgrounds eased their entrée into respectable Cali society. The cartel gained control of a major bank and put local notables on the board, offering loans and favors to the business community for their studied ignorance.[35] Businessmen looked to the cartel for capital, treating its leaders like successful CEOs. It was a plausible fiction, since the cartel laundered profits through a chain of 150 pharmacies that it owned. Cali's politicians ignored the fact that their city's building boom was fueled by drug money.[36]

Pablo Escobar, born in the slums in 1949, was too rough for such a makeover. Medellín's elite turned him down from their El Poblado country club when he applied.[37] So he cultivated a Robin Hood image by claiming that his first killing was one of the hated landlord class, a textile mill owner who was laying off workers.[38] Escobar paid his workers well and donated funds for roads, electricity, and soccer fields. By 1978, he was popular enough to win election as a substitute city councilman in Medellín. In 1982, he was elected to a seat in Colombia's national parliament.

Throughout the 1970s and early 1980s, drug dealers cooperated with each other and with Marxist guerrillas. Violence was low, but by allowing the cartels to take root, the government enabled the further weakening of the state. The Cali cartel created a "support your local police" program that funded police stations and held parties to build relationships between drug dealers, officers, and beat cops.[39] Cartel fixers hung around courts carrying briefcases full of pesos to bribe judges and clerks.[40] Where Cali lured with honey, Escobar's Medellín cartel preferred death threats to ensure cooperative relationships. Between 1982 and 1992, 2,834 police were killed in the line of duty.[41] Meanwhile, cartels paid taxes to the guerrillas for the right to grow and process drugs in guerrilla-held territory. The insurgents used this income to increase their arsenals and manpower.[42] By the time the government saw the threat, the guerrillas and cartels were stronger than the deliberately weakened and corrupted state security services.

Cozy relationships among violent business partners rarely endure. By the mid-1980s, drug cartels began fighting over profits and turf. At the same time, the guerrillas and cartels began to clash as the insurgents angled for more funds from the wealthy traffickers. The M-19 guerrillas kidnapped Martha Nieves Ochoa, the sister of three brothers high up in the Medellín cartel, and demanded $15 million in ransom money. The cartel formed a vigilante group called Muerte a Secuestradores (MAS), or "Death to Kidnappers." To deter further extortion, other drug traffickers pitched in with money and manpower to murder the guerrillas. Martha was returned alive, but the cartel's vigilantes discovered a new business niche: renting themselves out to landlords in need of protection.

Meanwhile, drug lords bought ranches throughout the Colombian countryside, especially the verdant Antioquian region around

Medellín. Cattle ranches were a status symbol, part of the leisure life-style of old-money Colombians. They were also a convenient cover to launder drug money. Now that they were also rural landlords who needed protection from guerrillas, cartels bulked up their own private armies and funded the existing militias started by other ranchers.[43] These paramilitary forces fought Communist guerrillas, but by the mid-1990s, under cover of guerrilla skirmishes, they also started ousting peasants who happened to be on desirable land. Their violence caused property values to plummet. Drug lords could simply steal suddenly vacant fields or buy prime real estate for fire-sale prices.[44]

The paramilitaries could get away with this economic coercion because they also had a sideline in helping Colombia's security forces and providing cover for extrajudicial executions. A Colombian government investigation into MAS found that by 1983, fifty-nine of the murders attributed to MAS had actually been committed by police and military officers on duty.[45] A U.S. government cable noted that hundreds of murders were taking place in the Antioquian region under the control of General Landazábal, the man who would later become the national minister of defense. The cable explained that "the reign of terror has proceeded largely unimpeded because the security forces in the region deliberately have not interfered with the vigilante bands."[46] Vigilante violence gave the drug lords a stronger negotiating position with guerrillas over turf and taxes and built strong, positive relationships with Colombia's state security services by carrying out their dirty work.[47] It was a win-win for the drug kingpins.

Ousted peasants fled to the outskirts of cities like Medellín, where they joined earlier exiles from La Violencia in slums perched precariously along the mountainsides. Poor and often darker-skinned than the surrounding population, the peasants were just as marginalized in the cities as in the country. Medellín's police didn't enter their illegal settlements, built on land they didn't own. Peasant women could find work cleaning houses, but the men, skilled in farm labor but barely educated, had trouble finding urban jobs. Domestic violence grew. With no state to enforce the laws, kids formed gangs. Guerrillas erected "peace camps" to recruit and train. Paramilitaries followed, winning the blessing of small-business owners and other respectable members of the community by "cleansing" the slums of petty thieves, the homeless, street kids, and drug addicts who scared customers after smoking *bazuco,* the paste left at the bottom of barrels of cocaine.[48] In 1980, Medellín's murder rate was 43 per 100,000, more than four times epidemic levels. By 1984, it had jumped to 101 per 100,000.[49]

COLOMBIA'S MURDER RATE, 1975–1993

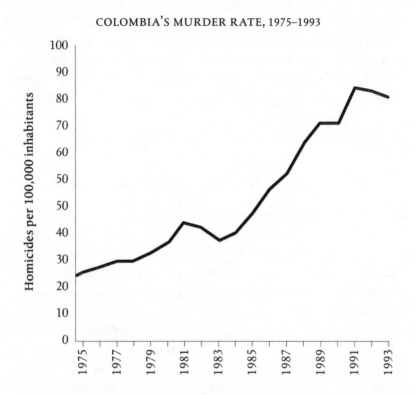

The government decided the time had come to crack down. But it had allowed the institutions of the state to rot for too long. The system of Privilege Violence had corrupted the security services, whose members worked with, not against, the paramilitaries, which were themselves connected to the cartels. State brutality had deepened social support for guerrillas and criminals. The only way to fight was to let the United States help, by extraditing the worst criminals north.

It was the one thing the cartels feared. They could bribe and intimidate poorly paid Colombian judges to evade charges. They could run their businesses from insecure Colombian prisons. But they couldn't function within the high-security lockups of the United States. On November 6, 1985, the M-19 guerrillas stormed the Supreme Court on the day it was due to rule on extradition. Many suspect that the guerrillas were hired by the drug cartels, though it hasn't been proven.[50] They seized four hundred hostages, including all of the members of the Supreme Court. Colombia's military supposedly came to their relief but bungled the twenty-eight-hour siege. The building was set on fire, all the incriminating material on the traffickers was burned beyond use, and one hundred people, including nine Supreme Court justices, died. In an after-action report, the remaining Supreme Court judges hinted at military collusion in the attack, noting that the judges' military-supplied bodyguards had all failed to show up for work on that particular day.[51] The surviving members of the court knew they were unprotected. They voted to end extradition soon after.

THE DECIVILIZING PROCESS

In normal circumstances, an attack on an august institution of the state such as the Supreme Court would have a rally-round-the-flag effect. But by the mid-1980s, Colombian society was polarized. A chasm had opened between citizens demanding a more full democracy and those willing to excuse government repression to regain law and order.

Jorge Humberto Botero, a leading Colombian businessman, provided insight into Colombia's split personality in those years. Tall, thin, and urbane like the glass high-rise office in which we met in central Bogotá, he cocked his head to the side as he reflected on that era. "For the intellectual elite, who were connected with the Left in this country and many others—the sympathy and tolerance for the violence exercised by the guerrilla was a generalized attitude in those years," though, he hastened to add, not in the twenty-first century. "But at the same time that the guerrillas . . . became more and more powerful, this sense of lack of security and protection created the climate for the development of paramilitaries. And those elites on the right tended to support, implicitly at least, the paramilitaries."

In 1985, a poll found that if elections had been held that year, the M-19 guerrillas would have won 36.7 percent of the vote.[52] As I drove around Bogotá, faded hammer-and-sickle graffiti still showed on university walls where students and professors rationalized the murders and kidnappings by balaclava-clad Stalinists as the only hope for justice for the poor. Meanwhile, at cocktail parties in weekend homes in the Bogotá hills, business elites defended the war crimes of paramilitary vigilantes that killed and tortured in the jungles. In the late 1980s, violence that was once unthinkable had become excusable. Colombian society was in the grip of decivilization.

The idea that societies can decivilize was first broached in 1939, when Norbert Elias, a German Jew, published his book *The Civilizing Process* just as Adolf Hitler prophesied his "final annihilation of the Jewish race in Europe." Elias fled to London, and his work languished. In 1969, the volume was published in English and discovered by American researchers trying to understand the assassinations, riots, and domestic terrorism that were then roiling the United States. Elias sought to explain the long decline in European violence that began after the Middle Ages. He suggested a very unusual theory.

Criminologists today know that poor impulse control in individuals is highly correlated with a propensity for violent crime. People with damaged prefrontal cortices or disorders that harm the genes that regulate self-control are both more impulsive and more prone to violence.

Elias depicted the Middle Ages as a time when poor impulse control was ubiquitous, state punishment was nearly nonexistent, and violence was, therefore, constant. Impulsive peasants could switch from joking to stabbing one another within seconds over a perceived slight.[53] He suggested that over centuries Europeans gained self-control and thereby also reduced violence.

How does an entire society increase self-control? Elias described a social transformation that happened in tandem with changes to the nature of the state, beginning in the early Middle Ages. As described by Achille Luchaire, a historian of thirteenth-century France,

At that time the country had disintegrated into provinces. . . . The provinces were in turn divided into a multitude of feudal estates whose owners fought each other incessantly. Not only the great lords, the barons, but also the smaller lords of the manor lived in desolate isolation and were uninterruptedly occupied in waging war against their "sovereigns," their equals or their subjects. In addition, there was constant rivalry between town and town, village and village, valley and valley, and constant wars between neighbors.[54]

In a period when states were weak and violence common, the people quickest to reach for a sword were the most likely to survive. "Across most of human history and cultures, violence against other groups was considered a moral virtue," claims the anthropologist Scott Atran.[55] Villages not only tolerated violent peasants and lords, they needed them for collective protection, even if the price was an occasional murder or rape within the community.

When kings began jockeying for greater power a few centuries later, they needed to control their nobles and knights in order to gain a monopoly on the use of force. Religious crusades and wartime inflation unintentionally abetted Europe's centralizing process by impoverishing the nobles. In Japan and France, cunning emperors and kings forced their noblemen to spend vast amounts of time at court with their retinues. The nobles bled cash to maintain multiple households and traveling retainers.[56]

Medieval etiquette books proliferated to help these rural lords. Elias describes the excruciating detail with which these books cataloged a new regimen of self-control required for court life. Lords needed to improve their table manners, have sex in private, and stop defecating in closets. Under the watchful eyes of their king, rural big men had to abandon fights at dinner and peeing in stairwells. In 1661, Louis XIV opened a virtual school of etiquette for his noblemen that taught, for instance, the proper way to knock on a door (with one pinkie) and fold a napkin.[57] A nearly professional ballet dancer, the Sun King hosted regular dances performed by the nobles at court. Because those who were better dancers got to sit closer to the king, noblemen spent hours a day at intensive ballet classes.[58] Those who relied on force rather than manners to achieve power disappeared from the king's gaze; he would pretend not to see them. As these noblemen learned to inhibit their physical impulses, Elias argued, they learned to inhibit other impulses as well.

According to Elias, the court also fundamentally changed nobles' feelings toward others. Previously, violence wasn't just normal, it was justifiable. Peasants were seen as a different, less fully human caste. Nobles felt little sympathy, much less empathy, for peasants' lives. But in the new world of the court, brute force didn't bring power: Rural lords needed to pay attention to subtle hierarchies, body language, and relationships to get ahead. Growing social understanding increased empathy more generally. Together, higher levels of impulse control and emotional intelligence helped people check themselves before resorting to violence.

The strengthening of the state changed broader social norms. Court manners spilled into other realms of life, trickling down from the nobility to those making a bid for social status. A burgher's wife might admire the way a lady held herself, how she refrained from spitting in public, how her husband didn't fart, fondle barmaids, or drink himself into a murderous rage. With a stronger state offering more protection against capricious noblemen and knights, the rest of society was less willing to accept everyday violence from village strongmen as the price for their protection. Behavior that would have seemed normal in the early Middle Ages, such as raping a woman as she bent over to work the fields or killing a man over an insult, began to be seen as low class and, eventually, unacceptable.[59] Over time, the state and society civilized together. And gradually, violence in everyday life became less prevalent.

Modern brain science adds to our understanding of Elias's inhibitory theory. The Nobel Prize–winning psychologist Daniel Kahneman has shown that the brain functions at two speeds. The prefrontal cortex, an area associated with emotion, makes quick, automatic decisions. This process is known as "hot cognition" and happens before rational thought has kicked in, such as ducking when a ball is coming at you, or the split-second judgment of whether someone is friend or foe. A slower form of "cold" cognition controls rational thought, the kind of logical decision making that considers the consequences of various actions.[60] Cold cognition takes a lot of energy. So the brain defaults to hot cognition to save time and preserve precious power. Hot cognition, however, is more likely to cause missteps, particularly when a person's energy is depleted. People whose cold cognition is overwhelmed because of stress or fatigue, for instance, make more mistakes in a shoot/don't shoot game.[61]

Psychologists used to believe that moral choices were made by a rational cold cognition process that weighed the pros and cons and came to a decision based on facts.[62] We now know that's not true. Researchers such as Jonathan Haidt who study both the physical brain and the subjective mind believe that ethical choices are far more intuitive, automatic, and "hot," or at least a combination of both hot and cold.[63] The kind of decision making that leads to most social violence—particularly when someone is angry, drunk, or tired— takes place in the prefrontal cortex, the impulsive brain area associated with hot cognition and emotion.[64]

Elias's insights suggest that on a civilizational level greater inhibitions alter what people are willing to do impulsively, when under the influence of hot cognition. Hot cognition still overwhelms cold, and impulse control still diminishes, but from a much higher point, so people swear, but literally do not even think of stabbing. Violent people, of course, exist in all societies. But in civilized societies, these individuals are seen as pathological deviants, not heroic warriors or desirable spouses.

A number of scholars found Elias's theory worked to explain modern violence. Manuel Eisner, a violence historian, tracked homicide in the British Isles and found that as industrialization progressed from one shire to another, murder rates declined. He speculated that working in factories, where workers had to show up at a set time, eat at a particular hour, and perform actions in a specific way, reduced impulsive behavior, which then reduced violent behavior outside the workplace.[65] Roger Lane, an expert on American violence, suggested that the drop in homicides in the early twentieth century in the United States might have been helped by jobs moving from farms—where there was little regimentation—toward factories, bureaucracies, and even public schools that trained people to inhibit behavior.[66]

While explaining how violence had fallen following the European Middle Ages, Elias also noted that "these trends can go at any time into reverse gear."[67] Randolph Roth, a leading historian of violence, offers some ideas for how that occurs. In *American Homicide*, he pieced together homicide trends across the United States from the country's founding to the modern day. He found that Americans had begun civilizing in the eighteenth century, as measured by habits such as using individual cups and plates instead of communal implements, defecating in chamber pots, and acquiring better manners. Yet while homicide was on a long-term decline, the country was still struck by occasional spikes in violence.[68] He found that the historical U.S. homicide rate tracks quite closely with two variables: the percent of the population who trust and feel connected to one another, and the percent of the population who "trust the government to do what is right most of the time." When polarization between parts of the population grows and people believe that "quite a few people running the government are crooked," homicide rates rise.[69] He found similar correlations over four centuries in western Europe.[70] Independently, Eisner and a series of other violence historians reached the same conclusion.[71]

Roth has spent decades poring over long-buried homicide records. Yet his and other violence historians' careful research leads to a radical conclusion. Murder is often impulsive. But when unrelated adults kill one another, the choices those individuals are making in the heat of the moment are affected by the general zeitgeist, the feelings of polarization and trust among citizens and between citizens and their governments that pervade a society.

These theories together explain what I call decivilization. Elias claims that the state's increasing monopoly on force jump-starts self-control and self-policing. Thus, the converse should also hold: violence will grow as the state relinquishes its monopoly on force, particularly if it encourages repression and private violence. A government at turns absent and predatory loses trust. For many more marginalized citizens, laws twisted in the service of privilege begin to be seen as unjust, illegitimate, and eventually, optional. Meanwhile, pathological individuals who would normally be ostracized are tolerated when they are needed to protect one's neighborhood, racial, or ethnic group. Language coarsens, lowering inhibitions to violence. With everyone protecting his own, empathy and connection decline among social groups. People dehumanize the "other." A scholar who studied European terrorism during the 1960s quoted one German militant: "What I liked in [the violence] was the fact that it was possible, in some moments, to overcome the inhibitory restraints. . . . Even today, I do not feel any general scruple concerning a murder, because I cannot see some creatures—such as, for instance, Richard Nixon—as human beings."[72]

QUANTIFYING DECIVILIZATION: COLOMBIA

Colombia has been violent for so long that it has spawned a field of scholarship called violentology. Violentologists in universities and think tanks have been collecting meticulous statistics for decades, and so in Colombia it is uniquely possible to quantify decivilization. To do just that, I traveled to Medellín, the epicenter of murder, where the homicide rate had skyrocketed to 381 per 100,000 in 1991.

Known as the City of Eternal Spring for its lovely climate, Medellín sits in a river valley surrounded by lush green mountains. Its downtown of malls and office towers gives way to middle-class homes in the hills enclosing tropical gardens. But its Gini coefficient, which measures inequality, is worse than the Colombian average, which itself is one of the worst in the world.[73] "The city is like Switzerland surrounded by Bangladesh," one Colombian told me. On the lush campus of EAFIT, Medellín's MIT, some of the country's best students milled around open-air food courts and sprawled on grassy fields. I walked to one of the low-slung departments and met with a violentologist named Jorge Giraldo Ramírez in his corner office.

Medellín, he explained, happened to undergo a natural experiment that showed the magnitude of the city's decivilization. For years, a man named Don Berna controlled the national consortium of paramilitary groups, as well as Medellín's main drug cartel and most of the organized crime in the city. In 2003, he cut a deal with the government to demobilize the paramilitaries in return for significant impunity. "The incentive was not to kill . . . because they were negotiating the peace process and were trying to get some benefits," Jorge explained. Public outrage at the lenient terms of the demobilization agreement provided additional pressure for Don Berna to keep violence down. Almost overnight, Medellín's drug cartels, gangs, and paramilitaries put down their guns.

MEDELLÍN HOMICIDE RATE[74]

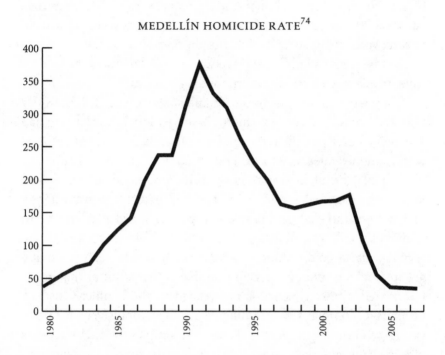

Violence plummeted. But it did not disappear. In 2002, the homicide rate in Medellín was 177 per 100,000. The year of the deal it fell to 107 per 100,000. As the paramilitaries demobilized, drug kingpins landed in jail, and the government fought guerrillas, the rate fell to around 35 per 100,000 in 2007.[75] That's a miraculous drop. But 35 per 100,000 is still one of the higher homicide rates in the world. It is seven times as high as America's current homicide rate, which itself is four or five times higher than the 0 to 1 per 100,000 in Europe.

Jorge hypothesized that from 2003 to 2015, when we met, murder rates at two to three times epidemic levels had become the rate of social violence in Medellín after so many years of normalizing killing. "In 2002, homicide was in the *comunas* [the vertiginous slums often controlled by paramilitaries, guerrillas, and gangs], but in this time of 2003–2008 the homicides were in the plains around the river. What's there? The airport, the industrial markets, two bus terminals, discos, casinos," he explained. "The most dangerous time was nights between Friday and Sunday morning; these are regular people killing." A decade earlier, the mayor of Cali, Rodrigo Guerrero, had found the same thing. Though the city was averaging 120 murders per 100,000 when he took office in 1992, when he gathered the data, he discovered to his surprise that most homicides were happening on weekends—particularly payday weekends—and many of the victims were drunk, not a normal pattern for drug killings.[76]

As cartel, guerrilla, paramilitary, and state violence fell, the story repeated across the country. In 2017, the national murder rate had declined to 22.1 per 100,000, low for Colombia, but still among the world's higher rates.[77] "At most, direct conflict violence is about 12 percent of all violent deaths now," a Bogotá-based violentologist, Jorge Restrepo, told me in 2015. The real percentage was slightly higher, he acknowledged, because many of the murders attributed to criminals—killings connected to "prostitution, drug running, illegal logging, illegal gold mining"—were actually conducted by warring groups making money through criminal activity. But at this point, he insisted, "most violence is not related to the conflict." Instead, ordinary Colombians were killing each other impulsively, for petty causes, while hiding under the cloak of impunity provided by decades of war, crime, and repression. This murder rate, more than twice epidemic levels, was the aftermath of decades of decivilization.

While decivilization can be reversed, its effects never fully leave a population. Still, 22.1 per 100,000 is an immense improvement, a reduction that cut Colombia's homicides by three-quarters from its peak, and yielded a level of safety last seen in the mid-1970s, before drugs and paramilitary warfare.[78] The story of how Colombia came so far is in the chapters ahead.

THE BANALITY OF EVIL

Like a carnival-mirror version of Silicon Valley's uniquely fecund start-up ecosystem, countries that have decivilized have created a fertile market for violence. Lawyers and other professionals are willing to work for violent clients. Experienced accountants understand how to launder money. Arms dealers know how to move illegal guns. The many violent groups create a job market that attracts a talent pool of

hangers-on who loiter around doing dirty work in hopes of climb-
ing the ladder.[79] In Colombia, criminal groups known as *oficinas* act
like an illicit FedEx, moving drugs, guns, people, and whatever illegal
goods are wanted to where they are needed. Hugo Acero Velásquez,
a wiry, intense Colombian security consultant, told me, "Today, you
can find a grandfather, father, and son being paid killers in Medellín—
more than forty years of assassins." The market for violence and the
relationships between armed groups in countries of Privilege Violence compounds bloodshed. It grows both when they cooperate and
enrich each other, as Colombia's guerrillas and drug cartels did in
the 1970s, and when they compete and fight each other in retaliatory
spirals.

Decivilization's deepest damage, however, is wrought not by professional killers but by ordinary people normalizing violence. In the
decades after the Civil War, outsiders commented on the impulsive-
ness, frequency, and triviality of southern murders.[80] "The heart is
sickened," described one northerner, "with the frequency of life
taken suddenly and by violence. Two neighbors, life-long friends,
perhaps members of the same church, have a slight difference; high
words pass; instead of giving reason sway, or referring the subject
to the courts, or to friends, one rushes for his pistol or shot gun."[81]
Duels, feuds, and homicides were all higher in the South than in any
other part of the country, which remains the most violent region in
the United States today.[82] The journalist Jill Leovy observed similar
patterns of killing in inner-city Los Angeles. The Centers for Disease
Control found that less than 5 percent of gang homicides in Los Angeles and Long Beach in the early years of the twenty-first century were
drug related.[83] Instead, "petty arguments, insults, and women seemed
to drive a lot of gang violence," Leovy wrote.[84] In a world that has lost
its inhibitions and where the state has abdicated protection, murder
occurs over the slightest of causes.[85]

Once a society has decivilized, countries are changed forever.
They can heal, but the wound remains. These societies live on fault
lines that can erupt under pressure. They will always be more violent than similar countries, quicker to fissure and take up arms again.
In 1974, the U.S. murder rate was forty times higher than Britain's,
and throughout most of the modern era it has been around ten times

as high.[86] Armchair pundits and even some scholars have blamed America's violence on the circumstances of the country's founding. They point to the honor-bound, retributive Scotch-Irish culture of the Appalachians and the South and the unique history of frontier justice.[87] But Eric Monkkonen, a violence historian, found that from 1776 until the 1850s America's rate of violence was only slightly higher than England's.[88] The United States was not unduly violent from birth. Nor is it uniformly violent across its territory: New England's homicide rates look European.[89] Instead, the decades surrounding the Civil War marked the time when society decivilized, and higher rates of violence have stuck with the South ever since.

The U.S. and other governments have long erred in treating countries fighting endemic violence in binary terms. But countries beset by Privilege Violence don't have white-hatted governments fighting black-hatted evildoers. Arming one faction or conquering another can't stop the violence, because there are not two sides to the equation; there are three. In countries where the government has proven unwilling to protect its citizens or complicit in violence itself, citizens also choose sides. While most people remain peaceful, in decivilized societies the number of otherwise ordinary people willing to consider or excuse violent behavior grows. Instead of a society composed of victims, perpetrators, and a mass of innocent bystanders, there are a hundred shades of gray: informers, supporters, propagandists, apologists, accomplices, suppliers, those coerced and intimidated into violence, those who lead the way, and every hue in between. Once Privilege Violence and its attendant decivilization have ravaged a country, neither the state nor society can stop the carnage alone. Instead, each side must propel the other, in steps that may move backward and sideways as often as forward. That staggering path toward security is the topic of part 2.

PART II

THE SOLUTION

4

DIRTY DEALS

[President] Felipe Calderon, With due respect, poison can only be fought with the same poison. Once we finish with [the Zeta cartel], you can continue [your work]. Withdraw the military.

—BANNERS HUNG ACROSS MEXICO BY THE "FUSION MEXICAN CARTEL UNITED AGAINST THE ZETAS," 2010[1]

How can a country find security, when politicians and police are criminal and criminals have gained the trust of some parts of society? How can a state rebuild on such a swampy foundation?

BUILDING A FUNCTIONAL STATE: THE THEORIES

Some of the smartest social scientists of the twentieth century have tried to answer these questions in a field known as state building. Charles Tilly studied how European states developed during the Middle Ages. These nascent governments of various duchies and fiefs led by warlords were not so unlike the violent, bureaucratically weak states of today. In his seminal work, "War Making and State Making as Organized Crime," Tilly argued that nobles of the early Middle Ages basically ran protection rackets, extorting serfs in exchange for defending them, often against the lords' own predation.[2] But when other nobles threatened their land, they needed to actually protect their peasants and territory. Gaining more wealth, meanwhile, required conquering other nobles' land. So these proto-states built roads to move armies. Paying for armies and roads required taxes, so they crafted bureaucracies to collect them. Tax revenue demands subjects with some wealth, so commerce was allowed to expand, along with laws to protect it. Thus, Tilly argued, feudal Europe built the institutions we associate with strong states and modern bureaucracies.

The economist Mancur Olson's theoretical models led to a similar insight. He posited that stateless, roving bandits collected less money than the lords who controlled territory.[3] These latter "stationary bandits," as he called them, were just as rapacious and self-interested as their highwaymen brethren. But because they controlled land, they were incentivized to help the people on their land grow wealthier. They could earn more profit with less risk through taxation (with its requirements of infrastructure and government institutions) rather than explicit theft.

Olson's and Tilly's theories, however, apply only in circumstances where a single leader has gained control of a portion of land and the people on it. How do governments—even protection-racket governments led by stationary bandits—form when multiple factions are still fighting for control over the same bit of territory? The Nobel Prize–winning economist Douglass North, with his co-authors John Wallis and Barry Weingast, looked at historical cases from ancient Greece and the Italian Renaissance to nineteenth-century America. In their book *Violence and Social Orders*, they theorized that in countries where privilege and wealth are limited to a small elite, states buy their way out of violence. Elites offer warlords an economic stake in a more peaceful system. Roving bandits, in other words, agree to become stationary in exchange for impunity for past violence, safety, and a cut of the money that comes from running an extractive government.[4]

These are pretty grim views of human progress. But for anyone who has looked under the hoods of states subsumed by violence, they are apt. As I carried out my research in country after country, North, Wallis, and Weingast's theory was confirmed to me over and over again. When a state is weak, even if it has been deliberately weakened, bargains are the first step on the path out of violence. Without a series of quick side steps, however, they can also be where that path dead-ends.

This chapter will explain why agreements with violent groups are crucial to a state's recovery. It will also argue, however, that they don't last. Instead, they usually herald an era of false peace, a limbo period when violence is latent but lurking. Though a country appears calm, the deal itself furthers the state's rot. When a government is forced to buy off violent groups, corruption becomes pervasive, creating a habitat that attracts organized crime the way stagnant water breeds mosquitoes. Over time, corruption further weakens the state, while impunity stokes anger.

When I mentioned to Barry Weingast that the security bought by making deals with those wielding weapons didn't last for long, he pulled me aside over a conference dinner, nodding vigorously. "Yes," he said. "We found the same thing. On average, we found the peace lasts about eight years."

Dirty deals don't buy peace. They purchase time. In the midst of immense violence, they give governments the opportunity to rebuild a more just, inclusive state, rather than one in which power is maintained through Privilege Violence. Governments that use this breathing room to fight corruption, rebuild state strength, and gain the trust of their people can continue their upward trajectory. Eventually, after multiple missteps, this is the path Colombia and Georgia chose.

DIRTY DEALS IN COLOMBIA, 1989-1993

In late November 1989, Avianca airline's Boeing 727 was leaving Bogotá on a short commuter flight to Cali. It exploded shortly after takeoff. Pablo Escobar was attempting to assassinate an antidrug presidential candidate he thought was on the plane. Instead, 107 innocent Colombians died.

The sitting president declared a state of siege, suspended civil rights, and reinstated extradition to the United States. The repressive strategy, tried off and on by a succession of Colombian governments since the 1970s, had always failed. This time, it failed spectacularly.

Four years earlier, the drug lords likely supported M-19's assault on the Supreme Court to end the threat of extradition. This time, the cartels banded together under the moniker the Extraditables. Then the bloodbath began. They assassinated three presidential candidates, a minister of justice, and high-ranking military officers. Escobar offered a bounty of $4,000 for every dead police officer. In 1990 alone, four hundred were killed.[5] Bombs began exploding in shopping malls and in front of the state intelligence building.

The United States grew concerned that Colombia's violence posed a national security threat. America spent approximately $700 million from 1989 to 1992 providing Colombia with helicopters, military and cargo jets, assault boats, antitank weapons, and other gear. American Special Forces ran training missions and began a high-tech intelligence operation from the air to suck up cartel communication and enable Colombian police to target the ringleaders.[6] It did little good, at first.[7] Colombian law enforcement on the cartel payroll kept leaking details of raids and other intelligence to the drug lords.[8]

The Extraditables offered a way out—the way ranchers offer cows a single exit from the corral to the branding iron. They opened up shop in a building near where a historic constitutional assembly was meeting. They bribed assembly members, offering to end the violence in exchange for a deal. They got what they paid for. When the new constitution was unveiled on July 4, 1991, it banned extradition.

In a pre-orchestrated arrangement, Escobar turned himself in the next day. Along with some of his trusted cartel associates, the drug lord was sent to a prison known as La Catedral that he had conveniently built himself. Set on the side of a mountain with stunning views (and chosen for the pattern of fog that would block air assaults from the government and the rival Cali cartel), it had manicured gardens, a hot tub, private apartments, and guards Escobar had chosen. It was more of a luxury office park than a cell block, and it functioned as one, because Escobar continued running his enterprise from inside. But on the streets, violence began an immediate decline. It would never again rise to such heights.

A year later in July 1992, the deputy justice minister and the head of Colombia's prison system tried to move Escobar to a more secure prison. Three of Escobar's men trained submachine guns on them when they arrived. As an army unit tried to rescue the hostages, a guard employed by Escobar turned off the prison lights. The drug lord managed to escape through a tunnel he had constructed for just such an eventuality.[9]

A shadowy group formed calling itself Los Pepes, a Spanish-language acronym for "People Wronged by Pablo Escobar." It was no normal collection of aggrieved citizens. Los Pepes were members of the Medellín cartel who hated Escobar, joined by army and police officers moonlighting with the criminals while off duty.[10]

The Colombian government made a second, implicit deal. Real-time government intelligence on the whereabouts of various members of the Medellín cartel somehow made its way from the U.S. surveillance program to the Colombian government into the hands of Los Pepes.[11] Unlike the leaky security services, Los Pepes used the information to deadly effect, killing anyone loyal to Escobar, from assassins to accountants. After U.S. intelligence traced Escobar's cell phone while he spoke to his son from the roof of an apartment building, they closed in. To this day, it's unclear who pulled the final trigger. It might have been the Colombian military troops who posed in a photograph with the bloody corpse, the elite Colombian police unit working with U.S. Special Forces and intelligence agencies who tracked the call, Los Pepes' leader Don Berna, or even a suicidal bullet from the cornered drug lord himself. On December 2, 1993, sixteen months and millions of dollars after Escobar's escape from La Catedral, a soldier yelled into his radio, "Viva Colombia! We have just killed Pablo Escobar!"[12]

Colombia's initial deal with Escobar and its later bargain with Los Pepes were unjust. They were agreements with drug dealers and murderers. Yet each caused violence to plummet. For a time.

To understand more about why these bargains worked and why they unraveled, I traveled in 2014 to the Republic of Georgia, a squidge of land on the edge of the former Soviet Union sandwiched between the Caucasus Mountains and the Black Sea. In the 1990s, the Georgian government had cut a series of dirty deals that proved exceptionally effective. In a little over a decade, a country whose violence was as dire in the 1990s as Libya's is today had transformed itself into a tourist attraction, as safe as the United States.[13]

DIRTY DEALS IN THE REPUBLIC OF GEORGIA, 1989–1995

"Even in the daytime you could see people with RPGs and machine guns in the subways," General Vladimer Chachibaia told me. It was a crisp fall afternoon in 2014, and we were sitting on the top floor of a military complex overlooking Tbilisi's sinuous river. The silver-haired general's office was full of pictures of him crouching with global military leaders in combat fatigues in the Iraqi desert and shaking hands in NATO headquarters. Outside the window, Tbilisi, with its pitched red roofs jostling up hillsides, gray stone castle crowning the skyline, cobbled streets, and turrets, looked as if it had been pulled from the pages of a medieval fairy tale. In the early 1990s, its violence was medieval, too.

As the winter snows melted in 1989, Georgians demanded independence from the Soviet Union. They stood on the gray stone steps of the parliament building and marched along Rustaveli Avenue in the center of the capital carrying placards and waving Georgian flags. In a sign of what was to come, the protests had divisive origins: a few weeks earlier, about thirty thousand people from Abkhazia, a region in the far west, had demanded independence from Georgia. Georgians blamed the Soviets for planting separatism in the hearts of their citizens and Georgian demands for sovereignty were intertwined with a fierce nationalism.[14]

But the Berlin Wall had not yet fallen, and the U.S.S.R. was not prepared to dismantle its empire. On April 8, Moscow sent police armed with poison gas and sharpened shovels into the protesting crowds. They killed at least nineteen demonstrators, most of them young women.[15] Fleeing protesters littered the sidewalks with bags and posters as tanks rolled over the empty streets. But as Soviet violence ebbed, protests swelled. Hundreds of thousands of Georgians again took up their placards to demand freedom, sometimes led by powerful Orthodox priests in their long cassocks, sometimes headed by demonstrators who linked their arms in solidarity in front of the sea of people.[16] A poll found that 89 percent of Georgians wanted independence.[17] By April 1991, on the second anniversary of the massacre, the U.S.S.R. was disintegrating. Georgia's parliament declared its liberation. The new country elected Zviad Gamsakhurdia president.

An independence hero, he was also an autocratic Georgian nationalist dismissive of the country's many ethnic groups. By December,
the country had descended into a civil war so terrible that one local
academic called it "the Afghanistan period."[18]

On my second day in Tbilisi, I was biding time before a meeting with
a member of parliament, gazing at a relief map of Georgia on the wall.
I noticed the bullet holes just as Tedo Japaridze, the parliamentarian,
walked in. "Those are from the National Guard after they holed up
in the hotel across the street in '91 and started shelling the government," he said. After two years facing a president who denied their
cultural existence, the Georgian regions of Abkhazia and South Ossetia declared themselves autonomous. They formed bumps on the
border with Russia where lawlessness could fester. Young Georgian
men formed gangs to regain the breakaway regions. Former countrymen turned weapons against each other. Terrorists nestled in a deep
gorge near Dagestan, an area just across the border that would later
become famous as the homeland of the Boston Marathon bombers.
Georgia was awash in armaments abandoned or sold by Soviet troops
and now in the hands of gangs and paramilitaries. "Everyone was robbing, extorting, kidnapping," General Chachibaia explained.

Two warlords recognized the opportunity. Tengiz Kitovani was
a meaty former sculptor with prison time behind him. He had be-
friended President Gamsakhurdia and built up a national guard for
the new state. The more aristocratic Jaba Ioseliani favored silk cravats
tucked into suit jackets. He had worked as a theater director before
rising to the top of the Georgian Mafia. In the chaos of independence,
Ioseliani walked out of the prison cell where he was serving twenty-
five years for armed robbery and started a private militia called the
Mkhedrioni, or "Horsemen." In deeply Christian Georgia, the name
was meant to recall the chivalrous knights of the Middle Ages. To
many, they evoked the Horsemen of the Apocalypse.

As the president grew more autocratic and unpopular, Kitovani
turned the national guard against the government in December 1991,
beginning the civil war. President Gamsakhurdia was forced into hiding. In a power grab, the prime minister wanted to be sure he was

gone for good. Under his charge, parliament declared an amnesty for imprisoned criminals willing to join the militias and hunt the routed president.[19] The soldiers of Kitovani's and Ioseliani's militias had no salaries; they survived on theft and looting as they fought to subdue the western half of the country, which remained loyal to Gamsakhurdia.

Under the cover of the political chaos, gangs and criminals proliferated.[20] An eighteen-year-old kid could don a leather jacket and a snarl and pass for a militia member, then make a living extorting passersby at makeshift checkpoints throughout the country. Driving into the suburbs became dangerous.[21] The capital was owned by armed gangs. Nights filled with the sounds of screeching tires and gunfire.[22] With the government fallen and electricity failing, people in the capital began heating water on wood fires in the streets to carry up to their apartments for baths.[23] Tbilisians—whose city had been renowned as the Paris of the Caucasus for its theater, dance, and opera, its wide tree-lined boulevards, its fine food and wine—closed their businesses, stayed indoors, or fled.[24]

Kitovani and Ioseliani, the two Georgian warlords, along with the former prime minister decided they could make more money running the country rather than pillaging it. Perhaps they had read Mancur Olson. On January 6, 1992, they allowed President Gamsakhurdia to escape from the fallout shelter where he had been hiding. They would chase him to a suicidal death two years later.[25] Meanwhile, they asked Eduard Shevardnadze to act as their figurehead president.[26] Shevardnadze was a former Georgian politician who had served as the foreign minister to the Soviet president Gorbachev. He was the perfect puppet. His presence gave Georgia an internationally respected leader and opened the purse strings of foreign aid, but he had no army or power base with which to challenge the warlords. He couldn't even move into a government office, because the buildings had all been destroyed in the street fighting.[27] When he made a brief foray out of the capital, supporters of the ousted president, Gamsakhurdia, grabbed control of Tbilisi's television station.[28] To the extent that anyone was in control, it was Kitovani and Ioseliani. They installed themselves as heads of various security services and ran their smuggling and extortion operations from within the government, where options for enrichment were vast.[29]

A former associate recalled "the daily ritual of humiliation and extortion" as the president was forced to oversee the looting of his state. Ioseliani "or one of his lieutenants walked in every day with a bunch of papers for [Shevardnadze] to sign—usually documents of ownership or deeds and titles to houses and apartment flats. . . . There were arrest warrants [for political enemies] as well. They didn't walk in with guns, but . . . there were guns in the building. He had to sign them. He had to sign them all."[30] Yet Shevardnadze's political wiles had long ago earned him the nickname the Silver Fox. He clawed back.

I caught an overnight train to Zugdidi, a post-Soviet town in the far west that had been the heart of the country's civil war. Once this was the gateway to Georgia's beach resorts along the Black Sea. The cream of the Soviet power elite would sprawl on the sand, enjoying fine Georgian cuisine beneath shoddy Communist cabanas. By 2014, Zugdidi was the edge of no-man's-land. Beyond lay a military checkpoint guarding the armed border of Abkhazia, the breakaway statelet now protected by Russia. In the early dawn half-light, I walked from the empty one-room train station to the office of an organization that used art therapy and education to help children recover from wartime trauma. A few hours later, I was sitting in a small children's chair across from Tsatsa, a former militia leader who had fought in the civil war, on the losing side. Fake leather jacket puffing out his chest and gold teeth glistening from both sides of his mouth, Tsatsa recalled war stories about the heroism of his makeshift militia. Loyal to the ousted president, Gamsakhurdia, ragtag groups like his had kidnapped twelve state council members, including the minister of internal affairs and one of Shevardnadze's national security advisers. Throughout the spring of 1992, they bombed bridges, railways, and pipelines across the west of the country.[31] Kitovani and Ioseliani were fighting loyalists like Tsatsa for control of Georgia, but in the fall of 1992 Kitovani continued the fight across the border into Abkhazia—putting him on the same side as Tsatsa's gang against Abkhaz separatists.[32]

The kaleidoscope of changing enemies made life in the west precarious. A chance encounter with a drunk militiaman might lead to rape or death. Tsatsa was speaking in Mingrelian, the language of Georgia's far west, and as he began describing battles that shaded into war crimes, my translator—a young kindergarten teacher whose father had been killed by Ioseliani's Mkhedrioni in those years—went pale.

"When did you know the war was over? That it was time to give up?" I asked him. "When we saw the Black Sea Fleet," he immediately replied. "People saw that the Russians were on that side and the airplanes were on that side, and we did not have anything to fight against them." I separately posed the same question to each militia leader I interviewed. Each had the same answer. When they saw Russia's warships parked in their port in November 1993 with guns pointed toward the coast, they knew Shevardnadze had reached an agreement to gain Russia's support. They could fight the weak government of Georgia but not Russia too.

Some believed that Shevardnadze had cut a deal with the head of the Black Sea Fleet to create the illusion that he had Russia's backing. Rumor had it that the admiral had moved his ships in exchange for a suitcase full of cash and two cases of Armenian cognac—a plausible claim in those years, when the Russian government barely controlled its own military.[33] But Tedo Japaridze, the parliamentarian with the bullet hole in his wall map, told me he had traveled with Shevardnadze to Moscow that fall. Russia's foreign minister walked into their meeting with a pre-written agreement for Georgia to join Russia's CIS, a loose confederation of states meant to help Russia regain its former Soviet stature.[34] Not long after, Georgia had a defense minister sent directly from Moscow to keep tabs on its government. Georgia gave up some sovereignty to its powerful neighbor to the north in exchange for ending the civil war.[35] It worked, just as a deal made earlier that year had ended the border conflict with South Ossetia, and a deal in July 1993 would end the war with Abkhazia, though low-level skirmishes would continue for years.[36]

War was over, but violence continued. Ioseliani's and Kitovani's men still formed the country's security services, and their troops were still terrorizing Georgians. Their smuggling rings fought in the streets, internal disputes led the Ministry of Defense to bomb the Ministry of Security, someone assassinated the deputy minister of defense, and

Tbilisi's police chief led an invasion of parliament.[37] Georgia wouldn't have security until Shevardnadze tamed the warlords.

To understand the president's next steps, I met with David Usupashvili. He was chairman of parliament when we met in 2014, but during the chaotic early 1990s he was a newly minted twenty-five-year-old law graduate working his first big job as the government's legal adviser. Usupashvili recalled a meeting of the National Security Council in those years. Someone had handed a note to Shevardnadze. He glanced at it, then looked at the group. "It says here that your guys in the security services and the Interior Ministry are shooting each other half a kilometer from here. I'm stopping this meeting until you can stop them." Then Shevardnadze picked up some papers and theatrically began to read while the heads of the security services and Interior Ministry left the room. Everyone else waited until they returned two hours later and the meeting resumed. When I asked Usupashvili when the meeting happened, he said, "Probably 1993, but maybe 1992, or it could have been 1994. Until 1995, the situation was pretty much the same."[38]

What happened in 1995? Checkbook peacekeeping. Shevardnadze worked methodically, buying loyalty from different segments of the small country's elites. He "gave properties, regions, authorities, and state agencies away," Usupashvili explained. "He used corruption to keep the balance of power." Business leaders, Mafia bosses, and intellectuals were given personal economic stakes in Shevardnadze's government. Much of the money came from abroad. Where once Georgia's elite had milked Moscow for funds, now "they started milking Brussels and Washington for humanitarian assistance," explained a Georgian anticorruption expert.[39]

Shevardnadze also cut side deals with Ioseliani's and Kitovani's underlings.[40] He gave them fiefdoms so that they could provide patronage to their men. The Ministry of Interior and the army became a hodgepodge of such personal patronage networks.[41] They were corrupt, inefficient, and often brutal, but they owed their positions to President Shevardnadze, not their former warlord leaders. At the same time, the president installed loyal friends and former colleagues from the KGB in powerful positions throughout the security services. Within a year, President Shevardnadze had sidelined Kitovani, the less astute of the two warlords. Then he told Ioseliani to disarm his Horsemen.

In August 1995, Ioseliani and the defense minister sent from Moscow planted a car bomb outside parliament. It missed Shevardnadze by seconds. The president ran up the steps, burst into the legislative chamber, and accused the two conspirators. They were finished. Too many of their men now answered to the president. And too many elites in the country owed their wealth to Shevardnadze to let him be killed. Within hours, the minister of defense was on a plane back to Russia. Ioseliani's former Horsemen rushed to arrest their onetime leader and prove their loyalty to President Shevardnadze, now the undisputed leader of Georgia.[42]

To those who lived through the violent years, it was a miracle. Almost overnight, roadblocks came down. The militias and gangs stopped shooting. It became safe to travel again. In three short years, Shevardnadze had transformed a state in almost complete anarchy into one with a government that controlled (most of) the monopoly on violence.

FORGING A DIRTY DEAL THAT LASTS

Scholars call the deals Shevardnadze made with the Russians, the warlords, the warlords' underlings, and the Tbilisi elite "elite bargains." They can be formal international peace agreements or informal understandings between governments and criminal groups, such as Colombia's unwritten agreement with Los Pepes. I prefer to call such arrangements what they are: dirty deals.

When a state is weak, even if it has been deliberately weakened as in Colombia, political leaders don't have effective militaries and police with which to conquer violent groups. Governments need to use dirty deals to buy time in which to rebuild state power. These agreements often seem magical. When a deal has been made, violence that seemed intractable disappears almost overnight. Journalists gushed at the "Medellín miracle" and the "Bihar miracle," dirty deals I'll describe in chapter 7. These miracles, however, are products of elite bargains, so named by scholars because they are made among the people who wield power through money, politics, and especially violence. Whether or not a state works for all of its people doesn't affect whether bloodshed stops in the immediate term.[43] Yet a large body of scholarship shows that over the long term, settlements that exclude portions of the population often lead to a re-outbreak of violence.[44] There is thus an inherent tension between getting an agreement that violent groups will sign and getting a deal that lasts.[45]

Agreements that give different groups of elites a stake in the system—like those Shevardnadze made with the warlords, their underlings, the intelligentsia, and the former Soviet bureaucrats— tend to be strongest.[46] They ensure that every group that could potentially take up arms and spoil the agreement personally benefits from a peaceful state. That makes peace more likely to stick. "Better the wolf in your living room, where you can hope to tame him, than hungry in the yard outside," runs a Georgian proverb. But they also spread corruption among larger numbers of people. Deals that offer too little profit for one armed faction may lead to a return to war if that side feels undercompensated.[47] Agreements that force rivals to share power tend to work for a time, but because they generally paper over differences, they can collapse quickly if those disagreements resurface.[48]

PITFALLS TO DIRTY DEALS

Dirty deals are necessary. But they have inherent flaws, bubbles in the glass that cause cracks over time.

First, while these deals can create order, they may first intensify violence. In Georgia, the prospect of a deal caused violent groups to fight harder to gain more power at the negotiating table.[49] Militias jockeyed for position by adding firepower so that Shevardnadze's government would have to take them into account as it doled out positions.[50]

Second, they are inherently unjust. Georgia's civil war ended in 1993, but brutal men guilty of war crimes, rapes, and murders ran the country. Violence fell further in 1995, but corruption blossomed. Left unaddressed, these injustices can inflame a country until violence recurs.

Finally, each deal sets a precedent. Countries caught in Privilege

Violence have, by definition, many violent groups, and those groups watch each other. When Colombia negotiated a disarmament agreement with its paramilitaries in 2003, those militias based their demands on the peace agreement Colombia had forged in 1989 with the M-19 guerrillas. If a country isn't careful, injustices built into one deal expand as later groups demand the same treatment, regardless of the extent of their depravity or battlefield strength.

The quick success of a dirty deal can make the price of peace without justice look cheap at first. But if a government doesn't use the breathing room to build effective institutions and govern inclusively, the injustices eat away at the insides of a state until the line between government and criminal is almost erased. Governments that continue to hoard wealth and keep their institutions weak often return their countries to violence.

In Nigeria, for instance, the government sponsored a deal in 2009 with rebels in its oil delta. In protest at the wealth being taken from their region by kleptocratic officials and foreign oil companies, the rebels—who fell somewhere between freedom fighters and thieves—had been stealing vast quantities of oil and bombing oil platforms, costing the government $1 billion a month in lost revenue.[51] The government brokered a cease-fire, and the rebels handed over their weapons in exchange for amnesty for past crimes, vocational training, and a monthly stipend. But the Nigerian government did nothing to bring jobs or environmental improvements to the impoverished delta. After five years, rebels returned to bombing pipelines, and new insurgent groups arose to seek deals for themselves through violence.[52]

CHECKBOOK PEACEKEEPING
AND THE RISE OF FALSE PEACE

Dirty deals are negotiations. Both sides have to give something. Those wielding violence agree to disband their militias. That's a big offer, rendering them defenseless and able to be jailed or killed by the government. What can the other side give in return?

Some kind of impunity for past crimes is nearly always on offer. In addition, the opportunity to trade war making for moneymaking can make peace much more attractive. This often takes the form of demanding control of various ministries that are desirable for their moneymaking opportunities. Thus, of the eighty-three civil war peace agreements made between 1989 and 2004, seventy of them included some form of political power sharing that granted each side positions in government.[53] Scholars claim that such political power sharing is a way of ensuring that the other side doesn't renege on its side of the deal, and that may be true. But it is also a lucrative way to reward warlords and their followers. Thus, government largesse such as Shevardnadze's generosity in Georgia often plays a role in making these deals stick. Such checkbook peacekeeping is an old tactic. During Mexico's rebellion of 1923, for instance, the then president, Álvaro Obregón, suddenly created fifty-four new generalships to purchase loyalty and gave 25,000 to 50,000 pesos, cars, and other bounty to potential dissidents.[54]

So is corruption a positive force for peace? That depends on what one means by peace.

Dirty deals put criminals in control of the pace of violence. After a successful agreement, violence plummets. Numbers, however, can be deceiving. Ensuing years tend to follow a pattern of lulls punctuated by spikes.[55] In El Salvador in 2012, homicide dropped by nearly two-thirds after political leaders brokered a truce between the gangs.[56] But when the truce faltered, the killings returned, and by 2015, El Salvador had one of the highest homicide rates in the world.[57] This pattern is one reason it is foolish to gauge a country's safety and stability through statistics alone.

While violence is usually latent, other crimes hint at the extent of criminal power. During El Salvador's gang truce, homicides fell, but extortion rose.[58] Extortion, of course, requires a plausible threat of violence. But it doesn't show up in murder statistics. In fact, it is rarely reported to police, because victims worry that law enforcement may be in on the action.[59] Is a country where homicide has fallen but extortion has risen actually safer?

Fear is even harder to quantify. For instance, in the early years of the twenty-first century, Colombia's paramilitaries, drug cartels, and guerrillas fought to control the Montes de María. For years, villages would be invaded by marauding guerrillas. In retaliation for "supporting insurgents," paramilitaries murdered thirty-eight villagers in a three-day orgy of depravity in the public square of El Salado, beat fifteen peasants to death in nearby Macayepo, and, in the next village's central plaza, crushed the heads of twenty-four avocado farmers with sledgehammers and stones.[60]

Uribe's peace agreement disarmed the militias in 2003, but between 2000 and 2001 all their vigilante forces remained in the region. They would drink beer in the town square or take slow drives in front of the homes of village activists. They needed no corpses; a letter or even a whispered threat was enough to send families fleeing. Though Colombia's homicides continued to diminish through the mid-2000s, its internal refugee population rose. By 2008, Colombia's death toll was greatly reduced under President Uribe. Yet more careful observation suggested that sustainable improvements would require new leadership, because the country had over 150,000 more newly displaced people than in 2006.[61]

Locals also intuit something statistics hide: the corruption of the false peace augments death, without violence. In Tbilisi, an older man described to me the agonizing tick of the clock as he waited after a heart attack for EMTs to hike up the stairs to his high-rise apartment. Corruption had left the city without electricity, and the elevator was out of service.[62] In Sicily, the Mafia had infiltrated all three of the large public hospitals by the early 1990s. Jobs were doled out by patronage, not merit. Hospitals were unable to afford essential medical supplies because they were forced to buy redundant and defective equipment, such as a hundred ambulances that went unused for years, to direct money to favored contractors.[63] In Naples in 1991, patients went on hunger strike to protest food infested with cockroaches, thanks to the Mafia, which held the hospital's cleaning contract.[64] In 2016, 231 people died when an earthquake toppled the hillside Italian village of Amatrice. Five elementary school children whose school collapsed atop them were among the dead. Just three years earlier, a Mafia-connected construction firm had been hired to carry out a €700,000 seismic retrofit of the school. The construction firm skipped the work and pocketed the money, while the local inspector rubber-stamped the effort in return for his cut.[65] Those children's deaths are not counted as homicides. And yet they are a form of violence caused by the corruption of false peace.

It is partially because of the built-in injustice within these agreements that 90 percent of civil wars recur. Often, however, countries stagnating in false peace trade one form of violence for another. In Guatemala, between 3,509 and 5,800 people were killed each year during a thirty-six-year civil war. A major international effort brokered a peace treaty in 1996. Yet the economic and political elites—whiter, taller, and vastly richer than most Guatemalans—refused to open up the economy to poor, rural areas. Tax codes and political rules reinstated the old cronyistic, corrupt political system. After a short interregnum, homicides began to climb. By 2009, there were 6,498 violent deaths, more than during any year of the war.[66] But while war is considered an international problem, murder is treated as a domestic issue and a lesser evil.

Claiming that corruption buys security is myopic. It considers only a pinhole view of a larger picture. Dirty deals are necessary beginnings, but they must be unraveled quickly. Allowing injustice and corruption to fester is what brings violence back.

CORRUPTION CHANGES CULTURE
AND WEAKENS THE STATE

In Tbilisi by the late 1990s, a bitter joke made the rounds: "What did Georgians have before candles? Electricity." The prime minister under Shevardnadze was popularly known as Mr. 25 Percent for the cut he took on state contracts.[67] With no money for wages, Shevardnadze's government paid civil servants little and expected less. The World Bank estimated that nearly half of all customs inspectors, 40 percent of tax inspectors and police, and more than a third of judges, investigators, and prosecutors bought their positions and planned to make back their investments. A job with the police cost anywhere from $2,000 to $20,000 depending on the bribery opportunities the beat offered.[68]

Some scholars claimed that corruption was rooted deep in the Georgian psyche. They argued that years living under foreign rule had led Georgians to view their government as alien and stealing from it as patriotic.[69] But despite an enormously different history, corruption was similarly rife in New York during the Gilded Age, when a U.S.

Senate seat could be bought for about $60,000.[70] A group of about thirty state legislators known as the Black Horse Cavalry cast their votes in return for bribes.[71] The construction of a single new courthouse in New York cost twice as much as the purchase of Alaska from Russia.[72] The going cost to become a New York City police captain was $12,000, a sum that could be made back only by extorting the criminals on your beat.[73]

All too often, the West claims countries with these pathologies aren't fit for democracy or that their cultures are congenitally corrupt and violent. But widespread corruption can alter any culture. It is a tipping-point phenomenon. When it's rare, the consequences of being caught are grave. Once it becomes rife, participation is necessary to survive—sometimes literally.[74]

In 2003, José Luis Montoya, a police supervisor in Mexico's Baja peninsula, took command of twenty officers and tried to fight drug trafficking. His own commanding officer warned him about the state police. "They are complicit and will plant drugs on you," he was told. Another superior officer working with the cartels ordered him to stop. Montoya persisted. Then the local cartel leader, Jazan Manuel Torres Garcia, showed up at his home. "I have lots of friends in your agency," he explained. "They have given me your address and phone number."[75] The kingpin wanted to make a deal. He would pay Montoya $2,000 a week—three times a normal police salary—if the officer ignored Garcia's crimes. To sweeten the offer, Garcia promised intelligence that would enable Montoya to catch rivals in other cartels, giving him the kind of arrest numbers that would allow him to become a star on the force. Montoya arrested Garcia instead.

The next morning, Montoya's house was set on fire. A funeral bouquet arrived at his door. A childhood friend who had been his informant was beaten and shot, then strangled to death. Two state agents told Montoya they had been offered $25,000 to kill him. "I have practically seen my own death in my dreams," he said. "It will be when I am getting in or out of the car, and it will be right here in the head."[76] He left the police force and went public with the story in an effort to protect his wife and son. Eventually, he returned to the force, but he was given a low-level post patrolling with cadets he once taught.[77]

When corruption becomes the norm, it gets woven into bureaucratic and political life. Political parties exist not to advance different policy ideas but to distribute spoils to different groups.[78] Police forces often function like pyramid schemes, with an expectation that corruption passes from the lower-level patrol cops to the top.

While often compared to cancer, corruption is much more like an epidemic. It is infectious: the more people think others are corrupt, the more corrupt they themselves become.[79] This "culture of corruption" is real, but it is not born from any national, religious, or ethnic predilection.[80] It is caused by a particular configuration of power in which those who follow the rules look like fools, while success comes through connections and taking what you can get when you are in a position to get it.[81] When corruption is systemic, it can't be solved by removing a few bad apples. Many of those who are corrupt are not bad apples at all; they work within institutions where they cannot do their jobs and be honest.[82] These systems function through corruption, not in spite of it. Corruption is not an occasional violation of the rules or a bug in the code. It is the operating system.[83] For lasting change, small reforms aren't enough. The system must be pushed into an entirely new equilibrium by overturning the way that power and money are distributed.

THE FALSE PEACE DEEPENS STATE ILLEGITIMACY: GEORGIA, 1995–2003

Scholars and surveys looking across Africa, India, and the former Soviet Union have shown that even in places where corruption is endemic, people believe it is wrong.[84] "Shevardnadze traded bandits with guns for bandits with ties," declared a Georgian in the 1990s.[85] A Neapolitan whose city council was riddled with Mafia-connected criminal politicians explained, "You vote for them, but you hate them."[86] People dislike feeling dirty just to live their lives. They resent seeing people who gained power through corruption or violence get ahead. As Theodore Roosevelt put it, "Every time a big moneyed offender, who naturally excites interest and sympathy, and who has many friends, is excused from serving a sentence which a man of less prominence and fewer friends would have to serve, justice is discredited in the eyes of plain people."[87] Mafia politicians and warlord businessmen, their well-coiffed wives, and their princeling children become symbols of the illegitimacy of elites in general. As the sense of injustice grows and the memory of mass violence recedes, popular anger increases, and people lose trust in the state.

The desire for fairness is one of the most basic, cross-cultural traits of humanity. Experiments repeated hundreds of times around the world and across nearly every conceivable culture suggest that extremely inequitable delivery of public goods—from roads to security—delegitimizes governments.[88] The desire for equity is so strong that in studies repeated around the world, people—and even chimpanzees—will reject offers to share a pot of money if the offer is less than around a seventy-thirty split, even if the rejection means they receive nothing.[89] This demand for equity has serious repercussions. Quintan Wiktorowicz, a former White House national security staffer, conducted a focus group in the Middle East in which a teenager praised ISIS: "They are the only ones fighting corruption."[90] In Afghanistan, polls taken from 2010 to 2012 found that corruption was one of the top three reasons why some Afghans were supporting the Taliban and other insurgent groups.[91] Anger over corruption has felled the national leadership of ten countries this decade alone, making it the greatest single cause of instability worldwide.[92]

In Georgia, by the turn of the millennium, corruption had made daily life unendurable. Pensions went unpaid for months because postal employees embezzled funds.[93] Sudden power outages left city dwellers stuck in the metro hiking their way out of the dark tunnels. Drinking water was no longer safe. Elementary schools crumbled.[94] Flights came rarely and at odd hours thanks to high tariffs established by corrupt aviation administrators with close ties to the president.[95] In a country that once prided itself on its education and culture, university admissions and grades were determined by the size of the bribe. Entry into a prestigious department like law or international affairs could cost $20,000.[96] Medicine was scarce, and doctors who had bought their degrees couldn't be trusted.

The U.S. and other foreign governments provided aid to develop

the army, strengthen borders, and create functioning institutions.[97]
The United States gave Georgia $1.4 billion from 1991 to 2005, the
World Bank lent and invested over $1 billion, the EU provided over
$300 million from 1992 to 2003, and individual European countries
together kicked in well over $1 billion during the years Shevardnadze
was in charge—in a country with just under 4.5 million people.[98]
Georgia signed the Council of Europe's conventions against corruption, created a series of governmental anticorruption bodies, and
passed the largest number of anticorruption measures in the former
Soviet Union.[99]

But it was window dressing. Corruption was the foundation of Shevardnadze's economic and political structure, painstakingly crafted
to ward off war. While not personally corrupt, Shevardnadze believed
that giving every powerful entity a personal stake in his government
was holding the state together.[100] He was right in 1995, when his dirty
deals saved Georgia from anarchy. He was probably still correct three
years later, when a skirmish on the border of Abkhazia broke out,
killing hundreds and forcing thirty to forty thousand Georgians to
flee their homes.

But eventually, the corruption intended to save Georgia began
causing the state to fray. Three army mutinies between 1998 and
2003 began over anger at stolen wages and food.[101] In the wealthy
Vake neighborhood of Tbilisi, people blocked traffic with burning
tires during the winter of 2000–2001 to protest electricity failures.[102]
A warlord controlled a chunk of the tiny country's territory wedged
between the Black Sea and Turkey, taking all the customs' revenue
and forcing Georgians to pay a "visa fee" to cross into his fiefdom.[103]
The country's porous borders nurtured smugglers and bandits. In
breakaway South Ossetia, Russian plutonium was smuggled through
at least once.[104] Islamic terrorists captured foreign aid workers in the
Pankisi Gorge; UN workers were repeatedly kidnapped in the Kodori
Gorge.[105] The country's Mafia, famed since Soviet times for its size
and acumen, owned whole sectors of the economy and was growing. Banks sprang into existence solely to launder money; one bank
laundered $1 billion for international criminals and corrupt offi-
cials.[106] Unemployed soldiers high on drugs with a reputation for
rapaciousness roamed the capital.[107] The anarchy of the early 1990s

was gone, but corrupt cops and the shabby smuggling of the army were omnipresent.

Georgians didn't think their government was weak. They knew it was criminal. The Ministry of Interior, swelled by the many militias it was forced to take in, had nearly thirty thousand personnel by 1995. Crime wasn't their side occupation; it was the primary enterprise of the police. They were recruited not to enforce the law but to smuggle cigarettes, drugs, and gasoline to make money for higher-ups.[108]

Anger at the criminal state allowed organized criminals to gain legitimacy. In the early 1990s, members of Georgia's Mafia made use of the popular disgust with government to portray themselves as men of honor. Sure, one of their peons might have stolen your car, but they could also get it back for you, quickly, politely, and for only a small fee. The police would make you wait, treat you rudely, ask for a bribe, and in the end your car would still be stolen. A 1995 poll found that 25 percent of schoolchildren wanted to be mafiosi when they grew up.[109]

This was Georgia's reality at the turn of the millennium. The country was at peace, but violent groups that had become part of the government controlled the pace of violence and whether it would recur. Like many Georgians, David Usupashvili, then in his thirties and still advising President Shevardnadze, had seen enough. "I wrote the president a very frank letter," he told me. It said, "There is nothing left for you to do. You are not able to do anything for this country unless you fight against corruption, against the system of government you yourself introduced. You were using it, but now it is eroding everything." Like a good staffer, he tried to make it easier for the president. "Go campaign to the people," he said. He even wrote a possible speech. "Tell them, 'My people, I served you as much as I could, but I see now that these people [I brought in] are bad. I won't rely anymore on police and judges for my support. I will rely on you, my people, and that requires your support.'"[110] But it was too much to ask. From within his presidential suite, Shevardnadze was like an aging Citizen Kane, watching the world he had built disintegrate around him.

Dirty deals are an essential first step out of massive violence, when a state needs to incentivize violent groups to disarm but lacks effective tools of coercion and has no trust from its citizenry. The moment of purchased peace provides a window of opportunity. When guns aren't firing, the government can choose to rebuild the social contract, proving that it will serve all its people equally and with justice. Yet even the best of these agreements is inherently flawed. By enabling impunity and often corruption, dirty deals usher in an era of false peace in which an unjust power structure can ooze throughout the state until it changes the nature of society itself. If the government fails to seize its moment, the state will rot. Yet dirty deals can lock politicians into relationships with violent and criminal characters that make it hard for even reform-minded leaders to change the rules and build a trustworthy state. The next step out of violence must be taken by society.

5

THE MIDDLE CLASS

Look, I'm not going to die of cancer.

—ITALIAN ANTI-MAFIA PROSECUTOR GIOVANNI FALCONE,
TO A FRIEND CRITICIZING HIS SMOKING[1]

In Sicily, the moment of redemption arrived in May 1992, when a five-hundred-kilogram bomb exploded on the main road from Palermo's airport. It killed Giovanni Falcone, a dogged anti-Mafia prosecutor, his wife, their bodyguard, and eight police escorts. A few months later, Falcone's childhood friend and fellow prosecutor, Paolo Borsellino, was murdered as he rang the bell to his aged mother's house.

Sicily had weathered multiple Mafia wars by the early 1990s. There had been a string of what were known as "excellent cadavers": the famous general Carlo Alberto Dalla Chiesa, who quelled Italy's terrorist violence of the 1970s, heroic police officers, a priest who spoke against the mob, the labor organizer and parliamentarian Pio La Torre. Each time, politicians would mouth pieties and pass a piece of anti-Mafia legislation that had been left to molder on a back shelf for years. Then business would return to normal.

In 1992, something changed. Falcone and Borsellino became martyrs, secular saints. A quarter century later, their portraits are sold by street vendors on magnets and hung on the walls of government offices. After years of quiescence, the murders of Falcone and Borsellino galvanized society. But why those two men, and why then?

International relations and development experts cite the importance of "critical junctures," major historical moments such as the death of a dictator or the fall of the Soviet Union that create the possibility for change. But there is nothing inevitable about society seizing such a moment of opportunity, and nothing linear about progress afterward.[2] History sets the stage, but actual people need to put on the play. Outside forces can assist, but what transforms a window of opportunity into a moment of reform is a middle class that mobilizes against entrenched interests.

Since Aristotle, scholars have recognized that the middle class plays an important role in upholding a well-governed state.[3] There is some disagreement, however, on who fits this coveted classification. Economists focus on income and consumption to group together a portion of the population with enough wealth to provide a sense of economic security and some cushion against misfortune.[4] Democracy scholars generally include other markers, such as educational credentials, autonomy in work, and, as per Aristotle's original thesis, a particular set of aspirational, "middle-class" values.[5] I use the term in this second manner. In countries facing Privilege Violence, a middle class can play its moderating role only if it has both a cushion of income and economic independence from the state. That independence emerges from education, a job that allows freedom from state interference, and aspirational values that lead the middle class to make demands on their governments. In countries governed through Privilege Violence, the middle class is the only group with enough voice and power to change the system, and the incentive to do so, because they are not overly co-opted by privilege or cowed by violence.

The middle class, however, is hard to rouse. Falcone's and Borsellino's deaths galvanized a movement because they were ordinary professionals, the kinds of people with whom others in the middle class could identify. Only when personal fear begins to affect members of the middle class themselves, when criminals, guerrillas, and terrorists threaten individuals who previously thought they could opt out of their countries' failures, does this part of society demand change.

Change, however, is not always a good thing. The middle class may demand justice, or they may press for a more repressive state that protects their families at the cost of deepening violence for other parts of society. Repression is the simpler path, and the temptation is strong. It takes leadership (and, sometimes, historical precedent) to move a country toward a better solution.

THE MIDDLE CLASS TOLERATES
VIOLENCE AGAINST OTHERS

It is surprisingly easy for middle-class professionals to ignore violence. Homicide rarely touches the middle class, even in the most murder-racked countries. In 2014, when I supervised a research team trying to help the U.S. government address violence in Honduras, we found that even in what was then the homicide capital of the world, our interviewees were more concerned with extortion. Homicide rates that looked massive by the percentage of the population still affected relatively few people, especially among the professionals we met.

To outsiders, a country may appear impossibly dangerous. But high crime rates hide immense demographic discrepancies. In 1993, whites in Los Angeles County were dying at a rate of 7 per 100,000. For African Americans, the proportion was 71 per 100,000.[6] Among young black men, the chances of meeting a violent death were 368 per 100,000—a percentage akin to U.S. soldiers deployed to Iraq a decade later, and similar to Medellín at the height of its drug violence.[7] Obvious differences between groups also create a sense of safety. Deaths are easier to ignore if they happen to people who live in other parts of town, are poorer, darker, or of a different religion. A jury foreman at a Los Angeles trial regarding the murder of a black policeman's son explained, "There is a perception that blacks are doing it to blacks, and if I'm white, it doesn't affect me."[8] Conversely, when violence befalls public figures, ordinary people rationalize that if they keep their heads down and live nonpolitical lives, they can remain safe. The middle class may feel sadness, anger, or pity, but not personal fear.

Epidemiological theories of crime suggest that murder travels in groups. Knowing someone who has been either a homicide victim or a killer is the greatest predictor of being killed oneself. In Chicago, where the studies have been conducted, murder travels like a disease within connected social groups. Researchers found that 40 percent of the city's gun-related homicides occurred within a network of just

4 percent of the population.[9] A later study by an overlapping group of researchers found that between 2006 and 2014 social networks explained nearly two-thirds of Chicago's homicides by firearms.[10] Victims who ended up in the wrong place at the wrong time were often innocent, but they were rarely random. Family relationships, friendships, and poverty compelled victims to spend time in parts of town where the chances of death were high.

In countries facing Privilege Violence, this statistical trend is augmented by the power structure. Governments and armed actors know they can get away with murder in certain parts of town, because as long as violence affects only marginalized groups—lower classes, castes, ethnic minorities, and so on—portions of the population with greater political efficacy and voice can distance themselves. As Paulo Sérgio Pinheiro, a Brazilian political scientist who served on the Inter-American Commission on Human Rights, wrote, "Police and other institutions of the criminal justice system tend to act as 'border guards' protecting the elites from the poor. Police violence remains cloaked in impunity because it is largely directed against these 'dangerous classes' and rarely affects the lives of the privileged."[11]

It is particularly easy for the middle class in unequal countries to ignore the problem because murders of the marginalized are so expected that they rarely make the news, and so aren't even known. The *Los Angeles Times* ran a banner headline the weekend after a bomb in Beirut "killed six people," recounted one L.A. detective. "We had nine murders that weekend, and not one of them made the paper. Not one."[12] The journalist Jill Leovy, author of *Ghettoside*, a searing account of those years, recounted a mother crying to a reporter the day after her son was murdered. "Nothing on the news!" she said, weeping. "*Please* write about it! *Please!*"[13]

A common method of psychological distancing occurs when members of the middle class write off victims of crime as being part of the problem. Even at the height of southern lynchings in the late nineteenth century, many in the black middle class accepted the common belief that the murders were rough justice meted out to rapists and other criminals.[14] In Los Angeles during the crime wave of the 1990s, police officers often claimed that "there are no victims here," assuming that homicides were tied to gangs or drugs and the dead "had it coming."[15] Police in Bogotá and Cali felt the same way; the perception that violence was just criminals killing criminals kept them from pursuing murderers with zeal, even though statistics later showed that many victims were entirely innocent.[16]

"In Mexico, they kill you twice," wrote a prominent journalist of the cartel killings. "First, with a bullet, an ax to your head or a bath full of acid. Then they spread rumors about you."[17] When murder rates skyrocketed in the first decade of the twenty-first century, President Felipe Calderón's administration claimed that 90 percent of those killed in the drug war were criminals.[18] Despite more than twenty thousand murders that year, many middle-class Mexicans felt similarly. They would frequently tut-tut a murder with "algo tenía que ver" or "sólo se matan entre ellos." They believed the dead were "people involved in the business," explained a man whose brother was murdered.[19] Only when the violence swelled beyond the marginalized did victims' movements organize. The most recent such movement began in 2009 after fifteen middle-class teenagers were murdered at a birthday party. They were celebrating at home, ironically, because their parents thought it would be safer than going to a nightclub. The shooting was a horrific case of a mistaken address, but President Calderón's first reaction was to publicly call the teenagers "gangsters."[20] Only when the parents' protests forced the president to apologize did the middle class begin to consider that violence was also their problem.

The father of one of the victims started the Movement for Peace and Justice with Dignity, an effort that was part of a pattern. All but one of the major Mexican movements against violence formed after the murder of someone in the upper or middle class. Such murders were still rare enough to spark outrage. In 1997, Mexico United Against Crime formed when a young engineer and director of a wealthy banana company was kidnapped and killed. Stop the Kidnapping began in 2005 after the same fate befell the thirty-one-year-old son of a wealthy family. In 2008, the Sistema de Observación para la Seguridad Ciudadana (known as S.O.S.) started when a successful businessman's fourteen-year-old boy was kidnapped and killed. Hundreds of poor women had been raped and murdered in the desert border near Ciudad Juárez and El Paso for over a decade before a spike in violence in middle-class neighborhoods galvanized advocacy groups to link the middle-class homicides to those affecting the poor.[21]

INTERNAL STRESS CAUSES
VIOLENT GROUPS TO OVERSTEP

The quiescence of the middle class enables insurgents and criminals to use immense violence. Why would they risk retribution by rousing this potentially powerful group?

In Sicily, the answer lurked in Corleone, the small Sicilian town in the hills above Palermo whose mob had killed the prosecutors Falcone and Borsellino and inadvertently launched the movement that would destroy Cosa Nostra. I took a bus for hours through the driving rain to speak to Dino Paternostro, a historian of the Mafia who lived in the heart of the Corleone empire.

Unlike the bucolic village featured in the Godfather films, Corleone has no quaint cobbled streets, no piazza. The town center is simply a circle of grass where the bus pulls up, a dark pub sticky with beer, and a nondescript coffee shop. Like most places under the control of organized crime, the town is grimy and poor. Any charm it once held had been destroyed by the shoddy strip malls and apartments built by mob-owned construction firms. The Corleone "family" had been intertwined with local church leaders and politicians for over a century.[22] A letter written in 1902 to the archbishop asked him to stop Corleone's priests from carrying guns.[23] But within Cosa Nostra, the Corleones had been provincial small fry. Their war in the early 1990s to run the Sicilian mob and its lucrative heroin routes was a hillbilly takeover of the big money in the city. The Corleones wanted to make a splash to frighten urbane families. They killed with grandiosity and little regard for who was a "civilian" and who was fair game. The ruthless show of force and bravado was intended to send a message to the other families written, literally, in blood. Internal dynamics within the Mafia drove the violence that finally pushed Italy's middle class into action.

A similar phenomenon occurred in the Republic of Georgia, where the Mafia was known as the "thieves-in-law" for the genteel code, or "law," they followed. But the anarchy of the early 1990s threatened their ranks. The lions of the underworld suddenly found themselves in the unthinkable position of prey to young upstart gangs with big weapons. The thieves-in-law loosened recruiting standards to keep their enemies close. But the new recruits' intemperate violence cost the organization its carefully cultivated reputation as men of honor.

Internal stressors also lead guerrillas and terrorists to commit too much violence.[24] Splashy acts of horror prove to recruits that a terror group is the place to go if you want to have the biggest impact.[25] When multiple groups are competing for talent, however, excess violence can turn local populations against them.[26] Colombia's FARC increased its kidnappings when it lost funding after the fall of the Soviet Union. Their "fishing expeditions" for kidnapping victims in the hills surrounding Bogotá alienated left-wing apologists in the capital's universities.

Not all violent groups, however, alienate their hosts.

NAPLES V. SICILY: A NATURAL EXPERIMENT

Naples's Camorra is responsible for more deaths than Sicily's Cosa Nostra, the Irish Republican Army (IRA), and the Basque separatists of Spain's terrorist ETA.[27] In just one Mafia war in the early 1980s, they murdered two mayors, a former mayor, and five city councillors.[28] But other than such public figures, the Camorra restricts most of its violence to other criminals. Innocents in poor, Camorra-controlled neighborhoods get caught in the cross fire, but their deaths occur far from the parts of town frequented by middle-class Neapolitans. Meanwhile, the Camorra is generous with its patronage jobs.[29] After the 1980 earthquake flooded the city with reconstruction money, the mob grew fat on construction contracts, and Naples's middle class became entangled with organized crime.[30]

During the years when Sicilians retook their island from the mob, Neapolitans enjoyed the same tough Italian laws used to destroy Cosa Nostra.[31] Some of the same prosecutors moved from Sicily to Naples to continue the fight. Naples had an effective, charismatic mayor, Antonio Bassolino, who employed every technique described in the following chapters to revive the city.[32] He rewarded merit, hired for excellence over loyalty, held his people to account, reclaimed public spaces, and used the media to trumpet his city's triumphs.[33] For seven years, he was called "Super Mayor," and for the following ten he served as president of the province—plenty of time to make his changes stick. The national government helped, dissolving more than seventy-five city councils in the Campania region in which Naples is located, fourteen of them twice, to help fight bought politicians.[34]

But Bassolino was not able to destroy the mob, because Naples's middle class never supported the effort.[35] They wanted him to jumpstart their city's economy and make their town more pleasant and functional. But they continued to knowingly vote for Mafia-ridden city councils. Anti-Mafia organizations published lists of dirty politicians, but Naples's chief prosecutor complained, "These lists have had no effect, nobody has been removed from office," because the population preferred politicians whose Mafia ties allowed them to dispense patronage and other favors.[36] An unemployed man summed up Bassolino's conundrum: "The old mayor, a Christian Democrat, was a thief—but he helped everyone. He stole but he gave us welfare cheques, cheese as well—he never made us pay for water or electricity. Now there's a new communist mayor and he has reported us to the police because we don't pay our bills."[37] A poll of young people taken in 1994 found that the Camorra's approval rating of 14.6 percent was low, but still higher than the average political party's 13.7 percent.[38]

So during the years that Sicily fought Cosa Nostra, the Camorra in Naples retained political protection. In 1993, Italy's Parliamentary Anti-Mafia Commission described the Camorra as having "merged" with Naples's local administration.[39] Over six hundred police remained on the Camorra payroll.[40] And the violence continued. By 2005, Naples's homicide rate was thirteen times the national average.[41]

THE GROWTH OF THE MAFIA AND
THE ANTI-MAFIA IN SICILY, 1870–1992

Sicily's movement against the Mafia began with the birth of the Mafia itself. As Dino Paternostro explained, "In Sicily, the anti-Mafia and Mafia grew up together for over a hundred years."[42]

Cosa Nostra's origins are shrouded in a mythical history. There are tarot-card-like initiation rituals, pious connections to the Roman Catholic Church, and incantations of *omertà*—the code of silence followed by so-called men of honor. Long after America's Mafia trials of the 1970s and a bevy of hit movies cast a floodlight on the criminal conspiracy behind the mob in the United States, many Sicilians clung to the idea that the Mafia was not an organization at all but a culture—a manly tradition of silence and self-defense born on an island that didn't trust any government after being conquered and reconquered by so many foreign forces over the centuries.[43]

Reality is far less romantic. Cosa Nostra emerged from the wealthy suburbs of Palermo in the mid-nineteenth century. A lemon boom was flourishing in the hills, an area known as the Conca d'Oro, or "Golden Bowl."[44] In 1834, Sicily exported 400,000 cases of lemons to New York and London. By the mid-1880s, Palermo was sending New York alone nearly 2.5 million cases of fruit, and Sicily's lemon groves had become among the most profitable agricultural land in Europe.[45]

It was a violent era. From about 1848 to 1870, Italy consolidated from a series of city-states, separate kingdoms, and bits of the French Bourbon empire into a single country. From 1816, when France founded the Kingdom of the Two Sicilies, until 1861, when Sicily became part of the new, united kingdom of Italy, the island was torn by repeated insurrections for independence and French reconquests.[46] Brigands and murderers flourished in the chaos.[47]

An economic boom and a weak government were a fatal combination. The fall of the Bourbon empire ended the king's control of all land and ushered in private property.[48] In 1867, the new united Italian government started expropriating and selling off church land, which covered 10 percent of the island.[49] Demand for lemons coincided with this newly available property. So the rich grew richer as landholders bought more, planted more, and became more powerful.[50] Large numbers of peasant families were moved to make way for citrus. Without homes or livelihoods, some turned to theft and violence to survive, joining the highwaymen and criminal gangs.

The new Italian state was too weak to offer the landlords protection.[51] So the government outsourced its monopoly on force. Landholders hired guards. But the easiest way to avoid theft was to know the criminals, so the most effective guards built networks among the thieves and crafted reputations for violent reprisal if crossed. They used these resources to protect their manors and do some business on the side for themselves.[52] These violent private security services with government connections formed the beginnings of Sicily's Cosa Nostra.

A weak Italian state enabled criminality to begin. It took a complicit state to embed Privilege Violence for over a century.[53] The guards cozied up to political parties forming in Italy's new democracy, which is why the mob flourished around the financial and political capital of Palermo rather than the poor, rural mountains where the government couldn't reach.[54] During election time, the guards and their gangs would help politicians get out the vote while deterring opposition voters. Landlords backed winning politicians, who in turn provided police help to landlords, a relationship that lasted until the 1920s.[55] When peasants organized to demand better wages, landlords turned their guards on the workers, confident that politicians wouldn't arrest the forces that helped them win elections.[56] The result was a death rate fourteen times as high in Sicily as in Italy's northern province of Lombardy. By 1875, nearly one in every three thousand Sicilians could expect to die violently—three times the rate considered an epidemic.[57]

In 1898, Palermo's chief of police wrote to the city's chief prosecutor, providing details on the mob's initiation rituals and business methods. His descriptions of how Cosa Nostra scared witnesses, paid off politicians, forged money, centralized funds to support the families of men in prison, and worked together across smaller units known as "families" were buried for a century because of a hitch the police chief foresaw in his poignant preface. "I need your support in dealings with the government. That is because, regrettably, the mafia's bosses act under the safeguard of Senators, MPs, and other influential figures who protect them and defend them and who are, in their turn, protected and defended by the *mafiosi*."[58]

An English traveler to Corleone in the 1890s found a town of "pale, anaemic women, hollow-eyed men, ragged weird children who begged for bread, croaking in hoarse accents like weary old people tired of the world."[59] "I am fifty years old," one Corleone peasant explained to a journalist in 1893, "and I have never eaten meat."[60] The government wasn't willing to fight these conditions, but some of Sicily's people were. As the landlords and their Mafia grew more repressive, peasants inspired by Communism organized to fight the island's endemic corruption backed by force. Landlords and the state repeatedly crushed their efforts. On January 3, 1894, fifty thousand troops shot into a crowd of peasants who were asking the government to dissolve corrupt local councils, killing eighty-three people.[61]

Until the 1990s, the relationship among politicians, economic elites, and the mob faced one serious challenge—the Fascists. Rumor has it that Benito Mussolini made a campaign stop in Sicily and was greeted by a Mafia don. "Why had Il Duce brought so much personal security?" he wanted to know, "You're under my protection."[62] But Mussolini didn't want a rival power center. He appointed General Cesare Mori to eradicate Sicily's Cosa Nostra. Fascist troops rounded up villages known for Mafia ties and placed their entire populations in jail, holding women and children hostage.[63] The Fascists jailed thousands of Mafia foot soldiers and used torture to extract confessions. Murder rates decreased temporarily, but Mussolini failed to break the political and economic relationships that sustained Cosa Nostra. Top dons escaped punishment, often by fleeing to the United States. After the war, the mob would return even stronger, thanks to about five hundred Italian mafiosi who forged transatlantic ties during the lucrative Prohibition era. Mori eventually lost his political support in Rome, and Mussolini ended the campaign in June 1929.[64]

When World War II ended, Allied forces found themselves in charge of Sicily. They needed local leaders who weren't Fascist or Communist. Mafiosi were local big men who had been hunted by the Fascists and whose Catholicism and long ties to leading businessmen cemented their anti-Communist credentials. The Allies, perhaps unwittingly, installed many in positions of power.[65] The Mafia surged back, first by exploiting the postwar black market and then by enriching themselves on government contracts meant to rebuild the devastated island. They continued to protect the landed elite's interests and occasionally murdered left-wing leaders.[66] On Labor Day 1947, mafiosi shot into a crowd of laborers celebrating the holiday, killing eleven workers as they picnicked and protested for better working conditions.

The battle lines were drawn. In the restored democracy, peasants cast their lot with the Communist Party, which became the country's anti-Mafia standard-bearer. The moderate Left distanced itself from the Communists, and the formidable Italian Roman Catholic Church sided with the right-wing Christian Democrats against the "godless" Communists.

Thanks in part to these origins, Italy's Communist Party soon became one of the largest in Western Europe. The United States and other Western democracies were concerned: the party was closely connected to the Soviet Comintern and received significant Soviet funding.[67] The West didn't want to pour Marshall Plan aid into rebuilding Italy only to have the country align with the Soviets.[68] It supported the right-leaning Christian Democrats.

Thus began what Francesco Renda, a historian of Sicily, called "that wicked deal."[69] The Communist Party would be permitted to take part in governing coalitions and share at the trough of patronage but would never be allowed enough votes to form a government on the island.[70] Parties heaped vitriol upon each other in public, but behind the scenes they collaborated in dividing up the spoils of the state.[71] All were corrupt, all controlled their own media outlets, all had their patronage employees, and so all maintained the power structure.[72]

In Sicily, volatile Italian politics masked constant rule by the Christian Democrats. They controlled the island for nearly half a century with the help of the Mafia, who added muscle to the Christian Democrats' electoral machine.[73] The mob could ensure 75,000 to 100,000 votes in the province of Palermo alone.[74] In exchange for these votes, the Mafia received relative immunity from law enforcement and was first to dip into government contracts. With more contracts, the Mafia could employ more people in labor-heavy sectors like construction and could thus deliver more votes.

Meanwhile, violence spread. In the 1960s, as left-wing student movements burgeoned around the globe, Italian police reverted to riot-control tactics unreformed after Fascism.[75] When leftist terrorists and anarchists set off bombs in the late 1960s, police placed agents provocateurs within their marches to incite violence while quietly assisting right-wing militants.[76] The 1970s are known in Italy as the "years of lead" for the armed violence between the left-wing Red Brigades and the neo-Fascist squads of the Right.[77] While all of Europe and North America faced an angry generation, Italy's violence was deeper and lasted longer. Between 1969 and 1982, the country better known for its pasta and hilltop villages suffered nearly four thousand bombings, over a thousand riots, and 164 deaths from political clashes.[78] Under cover of this political violence, southern Italy's Mafias killed around 2,600 people between 1979 and 1983, about a third more than the IRA killed in the entire history of the Northern Irish conflict.[79] A number of their murders were framed to look political, so their criminal violence deepened political polarization.[80]

Communists continued to protest Mafia violence and political connections in their newspapers and television stations. But the Mafia mustered its own apologists among respected politicians and intellectuals to argue that these claims were mere partisanship.[81] If Communists linked a particular political figure with the Mafia, the Catholic Church, guests at elite dinner parties, and Christian Democratic politicians would claim that the fight against the Mafia was an effort of the Soviet Internationale to undermine Sicily's local culture. Among Italians, you were born into a party. Political identity was passed down through generations. Political polarization meant that no one was investigated and nothing was done.

THE END OF THE COLD WAR INSPIRES MIDDLE CLASSES

Sicily's turning point came in 1992, just after the fall of the Soviet Union. Fear of Soviet-funded Communism receded, and the epithet leveled at anti-Mafia activists lost its punch. Italians (and foreign governments) were no longer willing to back the Christian Democrats at all costs. At the same time, a major scandal engulfed mainland Italy. A group of magistrates, known as the "clean hands" judges, were outing Italy's entire political class for corruption. Trials played out each evening on the news to rapt audiences. The judges brought down all the existing parties. Freed from the rigid political identities of the Cold

War, with the venality of their political class on nightly display, a generation of Italians demanded change.

Nearly all of the contemporary success stories I could find start after the end of the Cold War—excepting the United States, where the geopolitical dynamics played out differently. When the Soviet Union fell, a world polarized into two camps was freed. The ropes that rigidly bound political systems loosened, and a moment of opportunity opened throughout the world. In some places like Georgia and Tajikistan, wars broke out over new borders and new leaders. Elsewhere, democracies were born.

International relations scholars debate what ended the Soviet Union. They argue over the roles played by economic mismanagement, Ronald Reagan's arms race, the Soviet's Afghan war, and Gorbachev's perestroika. But people around the world watched on their television sets as Germans and Hungarians chopped off graffitied chunks of the Berlin Wall and danced on the concrete barricades in the autumn of 1989. Many drew a clear conclusion. Ordinary people had brought down the totalitarian empire. Young people wanting to wear jeans and listen to rock and roll, families wanting more for their children's futures, and apparatchiks who could no longer believe in the crushing gray system they served ended an evil regime. You did not need to be a superhero to change history. You did not need to be a politician. Peaceful protest could make a difference.

This realization was first voiced five hundred years earlier. In the mid-sixteenth century, a French student, Étienne de La Boétie, friend to the philosopher Michel de Montaigne, wrote one of the seminal books on resistance to repression. *The Discourse on Voluntary Servitude* articulated the revolutionary view that dictatorial repression relied on voluntary obedience. La Boétie looked at the jeweled carriages of the French court and the starvation of the peasantry and argued that although the state wielded weapons, prisons, torture chambers, and armies, it was still impossible to coerce an entire people into quiescence. The systems that tyrants built to maintain control could be felled if subjects cast doubt on their legitimacy. La Boétie was the first to understand that the nonviolent organizing of many people could be a powerful tool against a power structure maintained through violence.

La Boétie's revelation has recently been demonstrated statistically. Erica Chenoweth, a professor at the University of Denver, and Maria Stephan, a foreign policy expert, created a database of every case of challenge to a regime, whether successful or not, from 1900 to 2006. They found that not only did peaceful resistance work more than half the time but its track record was more than twice as successful as violent rebellion in changing entrenched power structures.[82]

People watching the U.S.S.R. collapse on their television sets in the early 1990s didn't need statistics to feel the power of ordinary people peacefully defeating a broken system. It was galvanizing. Sicilians too wanted to tear down the social and political walls of silence and violence and sleaze that corrupted their society. The energy lives on today. As my colleagues Tom Carothers and Richard Youngs have found, from 2000 to 2015 protests grew in every region of the world and under every type of regime, most of them sparked by a desire to fight corruption and other governance failures.[83]

Cosa Nostra's alignment with the landed class meant that Sicily's "anti-Mafia was a class movement," the historian Dino Paternostro told me. But from its peasant origins, Paternostro explained, "after the deaths of Falcone and Borsellino, the anti-Mafia . . . became part of the middle class as well." With the fall of the Soviet Union, the middle class that had reluctantly backed the Christian Democrats could join the fight against the mob without the fear of being tainted as Communist. So when Falcone and Borsellino were killed in 1992 and a few took to the streets, others followed.

On a raw February afternoon, I met Father Don Cosimo Scordato at his church in the heart of Palermo. Its stone walls jutted suddenly upward from a maze of alleys in what had been a Mafia-riddled slum just a few decades before. "Borsellino came often to our church on Sunday to pray, privately," Father Scordato said quietly as we sat in a small stone room off the nave. "When he was killed, we began a procession. I went through the streets with a megaphone. We started with thirty or forty, and by the end we were almost three hundred people because, slowly, the people came down and joined us."[84] The same happened across the city. By the end of the week, tens of thousands of people were marching, hanging bedsheets filled with anti-Mafia slogans out their windows, and leaving flowers at makeshift sites honoring their fallen heroes. Just days earlier, any one of these protests could have made someone a Mafia target. But average people, many of whose children had been forced to study in schools crammed into shoddy, Mafia-owned apartments and whose beautiful piazzas had been overtaken by Mafia-controlled parking lots, took courage from numbers.[85] The trickle became a wave. The mass outpouring broke society's paralysis and heralded the beginning of the end of the Sicilian Mafia as a major power on the island.

COLOMBIA'S MIDDLE CLASS ROUSES— AND HEADS BACKWARD, 1989-1991

Colombia's middle class awoke a few years earlier, but instead of pulling themselves out of violence, they took a step forward, then back. In January 1988, violence began to hit the middle class when a fight erupted between the Cali and the Medellín cartels over who controlled drug-trafficking turf in New York City. Soon bombs were going off at Colombian shopping malls, government buildings, and the chain of drugstores owned by the Cali cartel but frequented by ordinary Colombians.[86] Then, on August 18, 1989, Escobar assassinated Luis Carlos Galán, a leading presidential candidate with an anti-drug platform, as he walked to the stage of a campaign rally in front of ten thousand supporters. The drug lord wasn't working alone, but was helped by the former director of Colombia's intelligence agency and Alberto Santofimio, a former justice minister and congressman. Both would eventually be sentenced to decades in jail for collusion in the assassination.[87]

Colombian students took to the streets, inspired by striking shipyard workers in Poland who were forcing their government to negotiate half a world away.[88] Recognizing that their country's endemic violence stemmed from rot at the heart of the government, the students demanded a new constitution.

Only parliament, however, could call a constitutional referendum, and legislators weren't interested in ending their cozy system.

So Fernando Carrillo, a twenty-seven-year-old Colombian law

professor recently graduated from Harvard, called for an unofficial referendum to express the popular will. Carrillo's idea broke the "pro-guerrilla" or "pro-government" frame that had polarized Colombia's politics into a decades-long death spiral. Voters didn't have to pick sides to admit that their country's government wasn't working.

It was an election year, and as the protests grew, presidential candidates declared their support. On March 11, 1990, more than two million Colombians cast the unofficial ballots printed up by the country's main newspaper in support of a new constitution.[89] It wasn't binding, but the outcry forced the new president to hold an official plebiscite. On May 27, 1990, five million people, or 88 percent of those voting, approved a constitutional assembly.[90] Parliament still wouldn't budge. The Supreme Court bypassed the legislators and approved the assembly.[91]

What followed was like nothing in Colombia's history. Since the 1950s, decision making had been confined to a handful of elites trading power among themselves. In 1990, the government, assisted with funding from the United Nations and various European countries, as well as volunteers from civic groups across the country, held 1,580 working groups to solicit constitutional opinions from rural jungles, school classrooms, and urban slums.[92] The government held a national vote to choose the members of the constitutional assembly, and for the first time there were private voting booths, official ballots instead of party-distributed papers, and public financing.[93] The ensuing assembly was full of Afro-Colombians from the coast, peasants from the jungles, indigenous tribesmen, even recently demobilized urban Marxist guerrillas. It was the first time a political body resembled all of Colombia.[94]

In a country that had not had a bill of rights, the new constitution enshrined civil rights protections and created the Constitutional Court. Twenty years later, that court would save Colombian democracy by breaking open the scandalous relationships between parliamentarians and the paramilitaries. It enabled taxes to be collected and kept by municipalities so mayors had the wherewithal to act, and it allowed direct elections for mayors and better citizen oversight, so local officials could also be held responsible for getting things done. It also opened up politics to independent candidates, breaking the duopoly of the two main parties and paving the way for President Álvaro Uribe and mayors in Bogotá, Cali, and Medellín who were crucial to ending Colombia's decades of violence.[95]

Crucially, the constitution also convinced Colombia's Left that it no longer had to support guerrilla violence to achieve change. On November 20, 1992, leading left-wing intellectuals such as the Nobel laureate Gabriel García Márquez penned a public letter to the Simón Bolívar Guerrilla Coordinating Board, the umbrella group for the country's multitude of guerrilla outfits. In loose translation, the biggest voices on Colombia's Left wrote,

> Our condition as convinced democrats who stand against violence and authoritarianism gives us the moral right to question the legitimacy and effectiveness of the action you have sustained for years. We are against this form of struggle at the present time. We believe that instead of fostering social justice, as seemed possible at the beginning, it has generated all kinds of extremism.

The letter declared that terror, kidnapping, forced labor, and the murder of innocents were no longer acceptable methods for achieving liberal ends. The new constitution gave the poor and marginalized a chance to get real representation, something years of violence had failed to achieve.

But many Colombians were disgusted. Recently demobilized guerrilla murderers were helping to write the country's constitution. The FARC had formed a popular political party they saw as an insurgent front. Drug cartels who had bribed constitutional assembly members to ban extradition had gotten their wish. To some Colombians on the Right, the constitution was no step forward but a dangerous precedent.

A plurality of the middle class renewed their support for the paramilitary dirty war and government repression. Over the next few years, the FARC's entire political party would be murdered—by the paramilitaries, the military; no one knew for sure.[96] The killings strengthened guerrilla hard-liners who had argued that politics was a dangerous diversion from winning on the battlefield.[97] Over the next twelve years, paramilitary and guerrilla warfare would grow. The constitutional moment was a watershed, but Colombia would return to years of bloodshed before the country could reap its rewards.

THE TEMPTATION OF REPRESSION

Repression can look awfully tempting to much of the middle class. While a strong, solid democracy is the least violent form of government, moving a broken state to a consolidated democracy can seem herculean. Governments using Privilege Violence, meanwhile, try to protect their middle-class voters. Give the state a little more room to use any means necessary against its enemies, and the middle class is likely to be safer.

Politicians who want to maintain their power and perks while answering voter concerns about violence often try to sell repressive, tough-on-crime policies. When crime or corruption is high, these measures are popular with voters around the world.[98] In 1979 and 1980, the police in a particularly crime-ridden part of Bihar known as Bhagalpur gouged out the eyes of thirty-three young men who had been jailed but not yet convicted of theft, and poured acid into their eye sockets. When the case became public, residents protested and struck—in support of the police.[99] Law-abiding Biharis were convinced there was no other way to control rampant crime. They wanted the police to protect them, whatever it took. El Salvador's voters have long supported *mano dura* and mass incarceration, often accompanied by the military's taking over everyday policing.[100] So-called tough-on-crime policies are equally attractive to citizens of long-standing democracies when violence grows. In Spain, the majority of citizens favored the use of government death squads to kill the Basque ETA terrorists bombing the North; Northern Irish unionists similarly favored repression of the Irish Republican Army during the "Troubles."[101] In the late 1980s and early 1990s as America was in the throes of a crime wave, voters approved a slew of mandatory sentencing laws, "three strikes and you're out" provisions, and zero-tolerance policies. After the brutal rape and near murder of a white investment banker with degrees from Wellesley and Yale out for a jog in Central Park in the spring of 1989, Donald Trump (then a New York real estate developer) took out ads in all major New York newspapers at the time calling for the death penalty for the teens convicted of the attack.[102] The five teenagers initially jailed for the crime were later found innocent (a serial rapist turned out to be guilty), but Trump's knee-jerk response was shared by many others.

IS REPRESSION EFFECTIVE?

It is morally simple to claim that human rights abuse is always wrong, but if repression saves vastly more lives than it takes, it is immoral not to consider the option. A glance around the globe and at the graph on page 36 showing violence across regime types suggests that where repression is high, chaos is low. Thus, a group of foreign policy thinkers known as "realists" frequently advocate repression to fight violence. There's an "easy and reliable way of defeating all insurgencies everywhere," wrote Edward Luttwak, a defense intellectual who advises governments and businesses around the world. "Out-terrorize the insurgents, so that the fear of reprisals outweighs the [citizens'] desire to help the insurgents."[103]

Repressive authoritarianism can bring order. In Tajikistan, a country that crouches atop Afghanistan, chaos erupted in 1992 when the country was thrust out of the Soviet Union. The hopes of the vast army of people the Soviets had forced to pick cotton in the country's valleys were dashed when the post-Soviet bureaucrats suddenly in control refused to share power and wealth. Rural mobs looted former Soviet armories. The cities were soon engulfed by a Georgian-like civil war mixed with urban gang warfare. Rape and torture became common, village clans used the political chaos to settle old feuds, entire towns were burned, and desperate Tajiks fled into Afghanistan for safety.

Eventually, as in nearby Georgia, the warlords with the most muscle in the streets took positions of power in the government. In November 1992, twenty-four commanders of different militias met as a self-appointed "parliament" to represent their regions.[104] They elected a puppet president, a man few had heard of named Emomali Rahmonov, who later changed his name to the less Russified Rahmon. Rahmon's only previous experience of leadership was running a collective farm. Militia leaders fought in the streets for control of the ministries with the best opportunities for large-scale theft, the lucrative tax and passport authorities, and the smuggling routes that brought Afghan heroin north into Russia. As they sorted out their pecking order and established themselves in government positions, violence declined.

The international community had been fruitlessly trying to broker peace in Tajikistan for years. When the Taliban took over Afghanistan's capital in the fall of 1996, the situation grew more urgent. The UN, the United States, and Russia strong-armed Tajikistan's various factions into signing a peace treaty in 1997 that solidified the warlords' positions. Two years later, Rahmon was reelected in a dirty campaign with 97.6 percent of the vote. He shored up his position with Russia's support; until 2005, Russian troops guarded Tajikistan's 870-mile border with Afghanistan to keep Afghan violence from spreading north.[105] In 2001, when the United States went to war in Afghanistan, Rahmon extorted similar assistance in exchange for allowing the United States overland access into Afghanistan. In 2014, the United States was still paying Rahmon over $34 million a year, or 21 percent of Tajikistan's entire security budget.[106]

Tajikistan has been at peace for two decades. But it is a kleptocracy that extorts foreign countries to keep a lid on violence and survives on drug smuggling, which makes up 20–30 percent of its GDP.[107] The violence between armed factions over profits and power rumbles under the surface. In September 2015, a shoot-out in the middle of the capital between security forces and the country's deputy defense minister left twenty-six people dead. In 2015, the parliament voted to grant Rahmon constitutional immunity from all criminal charges in perpetuity. After the president suppressed all media and political dissent, 94.5 percent of the population elected him president for life in May 2016.[108] Rahmon's family controls the entire economy and has made his country the poorest in central Asia—a place where children are pulled out of school each year to pick cotton by hand.[109] With a tightly controlled press, it is impossible to know how much violence the state uses on its people.

REPRESSION ALTERS VIOLENCE

Repressive regimes like Tajikistan's often alter the form violence takes, rather than eliminating it. In Tajikistan, violence is down, but repression has radicalized parts of the population, spreading violence to other countries. In May 2015, a colonel in the police forces who received training from both the United States and Russia defected to ISIS, joining about four hundred other Tajiks. In 2016, Tajiks made up the greatest number of ISIS suicide bombers by nationality.[110] It is a common pattern: Alberto Abadie, then a Harvard professor, found that terrorism was highly correlated with a country's level of autocracy.[111] According to the Global Terrorism Index, 92 percent of countries that experienced terrorist attacks used high levels of political violence against their citizens.[112] Most of this terror remains domestically focused, but some slips across borders.

Rwanda is a similar case of repression succeeding spectacularly at quelling internal violence, only to export it in more virulent form. The country is justifiably lauded for ending its massive genocide in which perhaps 800,000 people were killed in just a hundred days in 1994.[113] For over two decades under Paul Kagame, the militia leader who quelled the fighting, Rwanda has been free from bloodshed as well as corruption and even plastic bags, which were banned in 2008.[114] Tight authoritarian rule means opposition leaders and regime defectors often end up jailed or dead, with government forces chasing them as far as England, Sweden, or South Africa to keep them quiet.[115] Yet after years of civil war and the 1994 genocide, Rwanda has been peaceful for nearly a quarter century.

Its much larger neighbor, the Democratic Republic of the Congo (DRC), however, has seen some of the worst violence of any country since World War II, partially because Kagame has outsourced Rwanda's troubles. In the aftermath of the genocide, Kagame murdered 100,000 civilians as they walked toward refugee camps in the DRC because genocidal militia members were hiding among their ranks.[116] Rwandan forces fought within the DRC to continue eradicating *génocidaires*. They also supported a horrifically violent rebel group within the DRC known as M23.[117] In addition to fighting Kagame's enemies, M23 rebels enriched his regime with the diamonds, gold, and minerals they smuggled out of their landlocked country through Rwanda (few of Rwanda's supporters ask why a country with no natural resources has become a major exporter of mineral wealth).[118] Rwanda has thus fueled one of the bloodiest conflicts since World War II. The millions of deaths in the DRC dwarf Rwanda's own genocide.[119]

Most commonly, however, authoritarian regimes substitute violence by the state for violence between citizens that looks more chaotic and is therefore more likely to make the news. It is also more likely to appear in international statistics. While homicides are counted by the United Nations, for instance, state violence against unarmed citizens is not. The latter is justified by reasons of sovereignty, national defense, or crime control.[120] Moreover, states rarely maintain accurate statistics on their own repression. Even a rough count, however, suggests that state repression is far more deadly than other forms of violence.

Compare an estimate of deaths from civil wars and murder from the beginning of the twentieth century to the present with similar numbers for state killings.[121] According to the most widely used data set kept at Uppsala University in Sweden, all civil and colonial wars from 1946 to 2008 have killed just under 6 million people.[122] But this data set notoriously undercounts non-English-speaking countries, so to be conservative, we'll double that number.[123] To capture earlier civil war deaths, add in high estimates for the Chinese and Russian Communist revolutions and ensuing civil wars, and about a dozen sizable conflicts such as the Spanish Civil War, and it appears that fewer than 50 million people have been killed by civil wars in the twentieth century.[124] Today, homicides kill far more than wars, causing around half a million deaths each year.[125] A very rough extrapolation thus suggests that the world suffered 50 million homicides over the twentieth century. Because homicides have been on the decline, let's increase that by 20 percent, to be conservative. That leads to a very rough toll of about 120 million people killed in the twentieth century by civil war and murder, the kinds of deaths repressive governments are supposedly good at preventing.

But state repression has been far bloodier. Rudolph Rummel, a scholar of democide, has found that governments killed approximately 264 million of their own people during the same time period.[126] The current war in Syria follows the same pattern. Heinous as ISIS is, it has killed approximately 4,882 Syrian civilians of the 103,490 killed since 2011, according to the Syrian Observatory for Human Rights, the most trusted source for statistics. Meanwhile, Syria's government under Bashar al-Assad and militias supported by the regime have murdered 66,394.[127]

REPRESSIVE POLICING BACKFIRES

Moreover, repression often backfires, so it not only yields more state violence but also increases other bloodshed. When the RAND Corporation, a nonprofit think tank, undertook an in-depth analysis of thirty different insurgencies, it found that although repression was a common tactic, it successfully reduced guerrilla warfare in only two cases, and then only alongside other strategies that also legitimized the government with the population.[128] Scholars who have studied rebellions from the Philippines to Latin America find that when grievances are met with repression, it strengthens violent groups.[129] State violence reinforces the moral justification for rebel violence.[130] It also increases rebel recruitment, because government violence leads people to abandon moderate, nonviolent efforts for organizations that espouse the same cause but offer some safety.

Similar effects occur with criminal violence. So-called tough-on-crime policing measures, often known as iron-fist or zero-tolerance policies, drive offenders into the arms of more organized violent groups while increasing those groups' virulence.[131] Thus, repressive policing increases criminal and law-enforcement violence. In El Salvador, for instance, after the government started its *mano dura* policy, fifteen times as many gang members were shot by government forces, while murder also doubled over the same period.[132]

When tough-on-crime regimes are announced, there are rarely empty prisons just waiting in the wings. But these policies imprison a lot of people, quickly. So it becomes overcrowded behind bars. There are fewer places to sleep, cells get hot, smelly, noisy, toilets back up, showers stop working. Prisoners get angry and fight more frequently. In prisons the world over, including in the United States, gangs rather than guards police violence (as well as granting access to coveted contraband and moving messages to loved ones).[133] As prison grows more dangerous for inmates, people who were only loosely connected to gangs or not connected at all are incentivized to align with the criminal leaders who control their fate.[134]

Meanwhile, as their foot soldiers are placed behind bars, organized criminals still have businesses to maintain. So they start pushing crime down to hangers-on who are below the age of criminal responsibility and thus can't be given long sentences. In Naples, under such a regime, the Camorra mob recruited younger and younger children. The percent of minors charged with crimes doubled in the 1980s and then jumped again by 28 percent between 1990 and 1992. The biggest increase was in kids under fourteen. By 1993, Naples's region of Campania, though only 10 percent of the population, composed more than a third of the young people arrested for violent robbery and nearly a quarter of those arrested for attempted murder across the country.[135] A study that looked across ten nations, including the United States, Colombia, and Nigeria, found the average age for joining a gang was thirteen and a half.[136] To address precisely this problem, the Republic of Georgia lowered its age of criminal responsibility to twelve for a short time, until the international outcry at the prospect of twelve-year-old kids serving prison time with hardened adult offenders forced the president to abandon the experiment.

Not only do mass arrests of twelve-year-olds seem inhumane, but jailing young people for minor offenses creates more hardened criminals.[137] Some people believe that juvenile delinquents are headed for a life of crime anyway and that a stint in jail might scare them straight. After all, most adult criminals begin offending at young ages. But if you trace the lives of teen delinquents forward, it turns out that while many stay on a criminal path, about as many—between 40 and 60 percent—become law-abiding on their own.[138] That's even more true of teens who commit minor offenses, like vandalism, car theft, or shoplifting. Most kids simply grow out of crime between eighteen and twenty-five as their brains mature, impulse control grows, and they are less influenced by their peers and more able to reflect on the consequences of their actions.[139] Yet research in the United States suggests that jailing young people who commit minor crimes sends them in the other direction.[140] After analyzing twenty-nine U.S.-

based studies over a thirty-five-year period looking at 7,304 juveniles, the majority of researchers agree that simply being arrested and processed in the criminal justice system increased kids' tendency to commit crimes. Those who end up in adult jails were a third more likely to become career criminals.[141]

That may be because mass imprisonment transforms prisons into schools of violence, a phenomenon researchers have found is particularly true for young adults, who are most prone to violent crime.[142] In Mexico, Honduras, Guatemala, and El Salvador, a bevy of researchers have shown that iron-fist policies that arrested people for wearing gang clothes or low-level criminal behavior strengthened gangs as they learned techniques from the more sophisticated organized criminals they met in jail. Criminality matured and complexified as different criminal groups connected.[143] Researchers who studied the trajectory of the Irish Republican Army after increased British arrests and the terrorist cells that emerged from Abu Ghraib prison in Iraq have found that a similar phenomenon happens with political insurgents, who harden and deepen their affiliations when placed together behind bars.[144]

From a violence-reduction perspective, perhaps the most significant problem with mass arrests for low-level infractions is that by casting such a broad net, law enforcement can't focus on the worst offenders. One well-researched fact about violent crime is that most of it is committed by a very few people, in a very few places. Proven policing techniques make use of this knowledge. Hot-spot policing maps where crime is occurring and sends cops to those places.[145] By addressing the problems that matter to the community, problem-oriented policing gains the community's trust, which helps officers get the information they need to build cases that put the most violent ringleaders in jail.[146] Phoenix and Washington, D.C., have experimented with repeat offender units that focus on the top twenty-five most frequently re-offending violent criminals, monitoring them so that when they commit a new offense, they are off the streets faster and in prison for longer.[147] Problem-oriented, highly focused policing techniques have a strong, well-studied history of success in the United States and are likely one of the causes behind the fall in crime the country has enjoyed since the early 1990s.[148]

———

The popularity of repressive measures to combat violence, combined with their tendency to backfire, presents a real problem for democracies. Awakening the middle class is essential to beginning the process of reform. When violence touches the middle class, people who had normalized violence that happened to others often arise from their half sleep and demand change. Unfortunately, a society angered at the status quo can turn to a strongman as easily as to a statesman. Military repression and tough-on-crime policing are tempting to members of the middle class. Yet by lumping together minor and major lawbreakers, and by building spirals of retaliation between armed groups and the state, they augment violence and push a country backward. So while Sicily's and Colombia's middle classes both demanded change, only one country would continue on a straightforward path out of violence.

In states governed through Privilege Violence, most of the increase in murder, insurgency, and state violence falls on the poor and marginalized. So the middle class may keep voting for failed policies for years, unaware of their costs and, ironically, believing them to be evermore necessary as violence rises. Even when portions of the middle class turn their backs on repression and instead demand justice, well-meaning people can dissipate their energy on matching T-shirts and markered placards. It takes social leaders to combat the popularity of repression and channel the desire for change into effective goals that lead society forward.

6

POLITICAL MOVEMENTS

We are not afraid, we are not afraid
We are not afraid today
Oh, deep in my heart, I do believe
We are not afraid, today.

—VERSE OF THE CIVIL RIGHTS ANTHEM
"WE SHALL OVERCOME"

Of the nearly thirty-five hundred black Americans who had been lynched since the 1880s, Emmett Till's murder was the first to galvanize a movement.[1] It was not because of his age or the cruelty of his killers: two fourteen-year-old boys caught hanging out on a bridge with a white girl had been murdered even more viciously in 1942.[2] It wasn't just that the time was ripe: two weeks earlier, a sixty-three-year-old black man walking out of a Mississippi courthouse with voting papers had been killed within sight of the sheriff. His murder barely made the papers.[3]

Till's death changed the country because his mother, desperate to ensure that her son's death had meaning, happened to be a gifted social organizer. Her efforts were made possible because they tapped into an organizing infrastructure that had been crafted over decades. These venerable organizations succeeded by attracting a broad new generation of middle-class activists across races who were pragmatic enough to channel their anger into political reform.

No event, no matter how horrible, incites change by itself. The timing must be right, but smart leaders create moments of opportunity; they don't just wait for them to arise. Leaders decide whether to aim a movement at effective levers of power or waste energy on feel-good symbols. The first half of this chapter describes the civil rights movement in the United States, one of the more effective efforts to overturn a violent social order, and the five essential lessons it embodies for struggles against violent social orders today: the importance of (1) seeking legitimacy within the current social rules, (2) winning over mainstream public opinion, (3) turning supporters into activists, (4) gaining a broad-based following across social groups, and (5) being political while remaining nonpartisan. These techniques can break a power structure built on Privilege Violence.

Yet even more skill is required to erect something more just and effective in its place. Social leaders also affect whether a movement can make the delicate leap from street protest to backing a politician who can take power. The second half of this chapter considers the ways movements propel a leader into a position to make change.

AN EFFECTIVE MOVEMENT:
THE U.S. CIVIL RIGHTS STRUGGLE, 1930-1965

Because most southern blacks were barred from voting, the ballot box was not going to yield improvements to a Jim Crow democracy that was bounded by the color of one's skin and held in place by an underlying threat of violence. The National Association for the Advancement of Colored People (NAACP) instead focused on the courts to establish the legitimacy of its cause. Its campaign slowly altered society's sense of what was acceptable, laying the foundations for the massive reforms to come.[4]

Starting in the 1930s, the NAACP mounted a narrow legal challenge to the doctrine of separate but equal. Rather than fight the Supreme Court ruling head-on, it claimed that black facilities were not equal and so violated the law. The NAACP won victories in 1936 to desegregate the University of Maryland Law School and in 1938 to admit a black student to the University of Missouri. It successfully fought laws in Texas and Oklahoma that segregated graduate schools (*Sweatt v. Painter* [1950] and *McLaurin v. Oklahoma* [1950]).[5] In the 1940s, Thurgood Marshall, the NAACP's special counsel, ended all-white primary elections (*Smith v. Allwright* [1944]). He also stopped segregation on interstate buses and trains (*Morgan v. Virginia* [1946]) and ended restrictions on blacks buying homes in white neighborhoods (*Shelley v. Kraemer* [1948]).

By this time, black servicemen had returned from World War II. The irony of fighting for freedom abroad and being denied it at home was sharp, and demand for change was strong. Having built an edifice of precedent, the NAACP had laid the foundations that would let them take advantage of a moment of opportunity. When the Supreme Court chief justice Earl Warren was elevated, the window opened. Unlike justices earlier in the century, Warren believed the court's role was to uphold constitutionally protected rights, even in the face of social disapproval.[6] On May 17, 1954, the NAACP won the landmark *Brown v. Board of Education* case, in which the Supreme Court declared that schools could no longer be segregated.[7]

After a win as significant as *Brown v. Board*, successful movements need to prepare for the fight over implementation and the inevitable backlash from threatened, entrenched interests. The judicial rulings determined what was legal, but not whether laws were obeyed. Segregation on interstate buses continued unabated. Blacks were still prevented from buying homes in certain neighborhoods.[8] Regardless of the law, only seventeen local school systems had been desegregated across the entire South by 1960.[9] A decade after *Brown v. Board*, only 1 percent of the South's black children were attending school with whites.[10] To avoid integration, Prince Edward County, Virginia, closed its entire school system from 1959 to 1964, funneling money to private academies to help the white students.[11] As Justice Oliver Wendell Holmes Jr. of the Supreme Court had predicted in 1904, if "the great mass of the white population intends to keep the blacks from voting . . . a piece of paper won't defeat them." Court rulings could determine the law, but they couldn't make people follow it.[12]

Meanwhile, the Court's ruling ignited a firestorm of pushback. In 1956, North Carolina's senator Sam Ervin Jr. drafted the "Southern Manifesto," promising to maintain Jim Crow by all legal means. He got 101 members of Congress to sign on to his cause, while a spate of fifty new Jim Crow laws were passed across five southern states. Lynchings had become rare in the years before the landmark case. After the Court decision, a new wave of violence swept the South, much of it conducted by the Ku Klux Klan but supported by clubs of leading white businesspeople known as Citizens' Councils.[13] Till's murder a year after the Court's ruling was part of this backlash.

Modern studies regarding successful movements echo the words Abraham Lincoln spoke in his first debate about slavery: "With public sentiment, nothing can fail, without it, nothing can succeed."[14] The civil rights movement had legal legitimacy, but the next field of battle was to win over the mainstream public. Emmett Till's mother mobilized popular opinion. From the moment she heard her son was missing after visiting his uncle down in Mississippi, she worked the media. She got press to come to the train station to see her boy's body, which had been beaten almost beyond recognition. She insisted on having an open-casket funeral in their hometown of Chicago and rallied 100,000 northern blacks to attend. That open casket made the travails of the South real and personal to people who wanted to believe they had escaped such darkness.[15] She convinced nearly a hundred journalists and thirty photographers from around the world to cover her son's trial, garnering coverage from Italy to Indonesia that made many in the United States feel ashamed.[16] She gave speeches across the country to fill the coffers of the NAACP. On December 1, 1955, four days after listening to a speech about the recent acquittals of Emmett Till's killers, Rosa Parks famously refused to move to the back of a crowded bus in Montgomery, Alabama.[17]

Parks's choice to stay seated was not, as is so often mythologized, a spontaneous decision born of aching feet. Like the cases that built up to *Brown v. Board*, Rosa Parks's act was the culmination of decades of patient organizing. Parks had joined her local NAACP chapter in 1943. She had spent twelve years learning with the NAACP, and had attended a ten-day workshop on nonviolent action run by the Highlander Folk School in Tennessee the summer before her sit-in. She was taking part in a small, planned protest and was one of multiple black women arrested that day.[18]

Civil rights organizers employed many concrete actions to garner public attention. Sit-ins were the most famous. They began in

1960, when Joseph McNeil was denied a spot on a Greyhound bus while trying to return to college in Greensboro, North Carolina, after Christmas break. When he finally got to his dorm, he convened three of his best friends to talk about what they could do to fight the racism that assaulted their daily dignity. A relative of one of the boys had told him about a sit-in—probably one of the sporadic protests organized since the 1940s by the Congress of Racial Equality (CORE), one of the early civil rights organizations. McNeil and his friends decided to give it a try. On February 1, 1960, they bought some items from the local Woolworths, then went to the dining area and ordered coffee. They were refused service and asked to leave. Instead, they sat at the lunch counter until the store closed. The next day, twenty students came. They sat in their white shirts, dark slacks, and ties, reading books and studying while being refused food.

Sit-in leaders consciously appealed to the middle class by asking students to dress well and act respectably. The studied tactics were intended to elicit mainstream sympathy while garnering media attention, and they succeeded. The sit-ins provided great pictures, so the media kept the cause in the spotlight. The third day, over sixty people came. On the fourth day, there were three hundred. More media outlets arrived. A week later, the sit-ins were taken up across North Carolina. Sit-ins were simple enough to spread, and within a month students were organizing similar protests in Richmond, Virginia; Nashville, Tennessee; Lexington, Kentucky; and about forty other southern cities.

Leaders made common cause with college-educated, middle-class northerners who could galvanize national attention in the mainstream media, not just the black press.[19] Newspaper coverage of the quiet efforts of these neat, orderly students was nonthreatening to both black and white middle classes, and built support. Black and white students protested in northern college towns like Boston; Ann Arbor, Michigan; and Madison, Wisconsin. On March 16, President Eisenhower expressed his deep sympathy for groups fighting for constitutional equality.[20] After seven months of protests and the loss of about a third of their sales income, the store manager at the Greensboro Woolworths told three black employees to take off their work uniforms and order a meal.[21] The sit-ins had worked. Protest-

ers began wade-ins at segregated swimming pools, read-ins at libraries, and stand-ins at parks, museums, and other public spaces as
blacks insisted that services paid for with tax dollars be open to all
taxpayers.[22]

Some lower-class black Americans claimed that the civil rights
movement was a middle-class effort that left them out. In some ways,
they were correct.[23] Self-appointed leaders chose to recruit the core of
the movement from students and professionals, because they knew
those were the images that would let them succeed. Pictures of quiet,
calm, college-going young men and women facing brutality, beamed
into nearly every American home in the age of television, moved
middle-class public opinion.

Today, mass protests often galvanize hundreds of thousands of
people to come into the streets, sometimes for months. But eventually, even the most avid protesters peter out. The organizations behind
the civil rights movement knew they needed to turn protesters willing to hold a placard on a sunny day into committed activists. In 1966,
researchers discovered that asking people to do something relatively
easy can lead to greater commitment over time, a finding that has
since been replicated repeatedly.[24] People who agreed to sign a peti-
tion encouraging safe driving, for instance, were later more willing to
place a large, ugly sign in their yards urging careful driving. The sit-
ins and other simple ways of getting involved in civil rights brought
in mass numbers of supporters who had to be led down this path of
greater commitment.[25] Arrests, ironically, helped: twenty thousand
peaceful protesters landed in southern jails between the fall of 1961
and the spring of 1963, bringing together activists who would not
otherwise have met and deepening their belief in the cause.[26] Meanwhile, civil rights organizers engaged in massive, organized trainings
to draw well-wishers into deeper and more serious commitments
until they had built an army of activists who understood that they
were engaged in a sustained campaign that would require years of
effort before it bore fruit.

Leaders painstakingly trained members to stay peaceful even as
people beat them and spit in their faces. Protesters were attacked, not
only by police and Klansmen, but also by ordinary citizens spurred
to violent rage by the threat to the social order as they had known it.

In Nashville, a restaurant manager turned on a fumigation machine and filled his restaurant with insecticide to gas the black students as they sat.[27] But movement leaders intuited what research by Erica Chenoweth and Maria Stephan would later prove: remaining nonviolent in the face of violent reprisal was essential to maintaining broad popular support.[28]

As they had after the civil war, southern police turned to private violence. One of the more committed ways to get engaged in the struggle was to take a "freedom ride," first attempted by the Congress of Racial Equality on May 4, 1961. Thirteen white and black riders boarded Greyhound and Trailways buses in Washington, D.C., with tickets to New Orleans to make good on the Supreme Court's desegregation decision fifteen years before. The riders, whose ranks included a retired navy captain and a white stockbroker, not just folksingers and students, faced few problems at first.[29] But Bull Connor, an Alabama police commissioner, was determined to stop their journey.

Connor met with the local Klan chapter, one of the most brutal in the country, to enlist its help. As the first bus tried to leave the station in the small army town of Anniston, Alabama, a mob descended, slashing its tires. People smashed the windows with brass knuckles and threw rocks at the windows. A man cocked a pistol and pointed it at one of the riders for a few minutes, locking eyes before moving on.[30] As the destroyed bus crawled out of town, a caravan of pickups and cars filled with screaming Klan members followed until, on a deserted section of road, one pulled in front of the bus and forced it to slow. The bus driver ran to a nearby grocery and called a garage to fix the tires, while a teenager with a crowbar smashed a bus window. An undercover officer who had been on the bus to keep tabs on activists the government considered suspect locked the bus door from the inside. The mob began rocking the bus to force it over. Then a man threw a flaming bundle of rags inside. Smoke filled the air and flames devoured the seats. The riders thought they would be burned to death.

When a fuel tank exploded, the mob stepped back, and the riders took advantage of the moment to flee. As one crawled away, gasping for air, a man in the crowd asked, "Are you all okay?" When the boy looked up, he saw the man's face twist into an ironic sneer just as he hit the boy with a baseball bat. A little white girl, just twelve years old, brought water to the beaten riders. Her family was so terrorized afterward that they were forced to move out of town.[31] A highway patrolman shot his gun in the air to prevent a lynching, and the mob scattered. The freedom riders, beaten, bloody, and still coughing smoke, made their way to a local hospital. At first, the nurses and doctors refused treatment to the black riders; then they asked all the patients to leave in the middle of the night as a new mob formed outside.

A second bus in the freedom riders' convoy had been boarded by Klansmen in Georgia. They beat one man nearly to death, leaving his middle-aged body stretched in the aisle as a warning. When the bus reached Birmingham, Alabama, the police colluded with another local Klan, promising it fifteen minutes to assault the riders before officers arrived. When police came at the appointed time, the violent mob had disappeared, and smirking officers refused to help bloody riders.[32] The freedom riders escaped to a church and abandoned the mission when it became clear they could all be killed. Another bus, however, started from Nashville, Tennessee, two weeks later. Despite the danger, more than sixty Freedom Rides crossed the South that year.

A factionalized society can make nearly any action to change the social order debatable. While most Americans claimed to support desegregation—a Gallup poll in the early summer of 1961 found 66 percent supported the Supreme Court's ruling ending racial segregation on trains and buses—only 24 percent approved of the freedom riders.[33] In the polarized Cold War era, those fighting for black rights had to work constantly to keep mainstream opinion on their side. Soft supporters, such as those admonished by Martin Luther King Jr. in his "Letter from a Birmingham Jail," painted activists as extremists who were pushing society too fast. Opponents sidelined them as Communist agitators. Before his assassination canonized him as a political saint, John F. Kennedy and his brother Robert, then attorney general, were decidedly lukewarm on civil rights. They asked the freedom riders to stop, arguing that the rides were calling attention to America's racial fissures and thus providing propaganda for the Soviet Union.[34] "I may have to send the Alabama National Guard to

Berlin tomorrow," Kennedy explained, "and I don't want to have to do it in the middle of a revolution at home."[35]

The country teetered between commitment to constitutional rights and concerns about Communism and law and order. If protesters could be dismissed as disorderly or unpatriotic, they would lose. Organizers needed to drive a wedge between real racists and the lukewarm middle class. Voting was the ideal cause. Few Americans could openly argue that the right of all American citizens to vote was a Communist plot. At the same time, gaining the vote wasn't just symbolic. The ability to vote would give real power to southern blacks.[36] In 1964, the Student Nonviolent Coordinating Committee (SNCC), a newer pillar of the civil rights movement, recruited hundreds of white students from the North to undertake a voter drive in Mississippi.

Freedom Summer, as the Mississippi voter drive was called, in an echo of its predecessor nearly a century before, was a turning point.[37] There had been a string of black church bombings in Mississippi, and three volunteers—two white and one black—had gone to visit the remains of a Mount Zion sanctuary on June 21, 1964. When a deputy sheriff, Cecil Price, noticed their station wagon with the insignia of CORE, the civil rights group, he pulled them over for speeding and took all three to the county jail. Just after releasing them at ten that night, Price called a friend in the local Ku Klux Klan. The three volunteers disappeared. CORE staff alerted the FBI. Two days later, the station wagon was found, still smoldering. But there were no bodies in the car. Every national news network began to cover the investigation as navy divers combed the swamps and FBI agents hacked through the woods. They found eight additional corpses—two were black college students reported missing that May, another wore a CORE T-shirt, and the final five were beyond identification. None were the three young men.

"Let this session of Congress be known as the session which did more for civil rights than the last hundred sessions combined," President Johnson thundered in his first State of the Union address.[38] On July 2, 1964, the Mississippi manhunts were still making the nightly news (the bodies of the three young volunteers would not be found until August 4, when they were discovered buried in an earthen dam).[39] Over the longest Senate filibuster in history—a sixty-day oration led by southerners within Johnson's own party, including a fourteen-hour speech by Senator Robert Byrd of West Virginia, a former member of the Ku Klux Klan—Johnson used the mainstream disgust to pass his legislation.[40] The 1964 Civil Rights Act banned segregation in public places and forbade employment discrimination. The next year, Johnson proposed a voting rights act that would force southern states to allow all citizens to participate in elections. In March 1965, with the Voting Rights Act in the balance, the movement created another opportunity. Martin Luther King Jr. marched with six hundred peaceful demonstrators through Selma, Alabama, to protest the intimidation and discrimination that kept the city's black population—half the city—from voting. Television crews caught local police beating the protesters with billy clubs and spraying tear gas. The middle class winced, and a century after the Civil War's end black Americans regained the vote.

The story of the civil rights movement reads as a moral fairy tale of reform. But the fine print is more ethically complex. As president, Lyndon Johnson spearheaded the civil rights laws of 1964, 1965, and 1968, allegedly declaring as he signed his first Civil Rights Act into law, "We have lost the South for a generation." He was right—but too modest. The South has never again elected a Democratic president, to date. Yet Johnson was not necessarily acting from moral righteousness against the interests of his party, which is how the story is usually told. By 1964, voters already associated Democrats with civil rights. Southern Dixiecrats had begun leaving for the Republican Party, which was by that time their more natural ideological base. By loudly declaring his fealty to civil rights, Johnson let go of a South that was already slipping away to cement political gains in the North.[41]

Civil rights leaders who chose to work with Johnson had to be equally pragmatic. For twenty years as a member of Congress from Texas, Lyndon Johnson had opposed every civil rights bill that appeared before him. He voted for Jim Crow legislation, refused to criminalize lynching, and had criticized his own party's president, Harry Truman, for desegregating the armed services.[42] Civil rights leaders had to let such a flawed vessel take credit for their success.

They were also careful not to amalgamate too many controversial causes under the same umbrella. They partnered with Johnson despite his escalation of the Vietnam War, for example, an issue that inflamed many of their supporters. In fact, despite many members' antipathy toward the war, civil rights leaders made common cause with cold warriors. As early as the Truman administration, Secretary of State Dean Acheson declared that racial discrimination was a national embarrassment that cost the country overseas power. In the early 1960s, African diplomats from newly decolonized countries found themselves victims of Jim Crow segregation while driving between Washington, D.C., and UN headquarters in New York.[43] The Soviet premier Nikita Khrushchev tried to use their anger to build an anti-U.S. bloc in the United Nations. National security leaders pressured Maryland to end segregation in hotels and restaurants along the highway the diplomats traveled.[44] The U.S. Justice Department sent briefs to the Supreme Court on how southern racism was costing the country potential allies in the fight against Communism.[45]

Rather than narrowing support to people who were fully behind every part of their cause, movement leaders sought allies who supported their goal, whatever their motives. Leaders of Freedom Summer consciously chose to recruit northern whites to keep their movement broad. White liberals naturally gravitated to civil rights, but unions were crucial to building support among the blue-collar Left. The Highlander Folk School, where Rosa Parks trained, had begun as a training center for union organizing. "We Shall Overcome" was a 1930s union song before the Highlander Folk School rewrote it for the civil rights movement.[46] While not all joined the cause, unions like the AFL and the United Packinghouse Workers of America were essential.[47] These unions tried to build worker solidarity, but many members had mixed views on race. Civil rights leaders were willing to accept more self-interested motives. Blacks who couldn't get any other jobs were frequently used as strikebreakers. They had so few options that they kept wages depressed. Justice for black workers meant more power for the unions. And southern violence was directed against unions as well. The civil rights movement succeeded through such unlikely allies. They could not achieve their goals by being too pure for political compromise.

Finally, a credo against the "politics of respectability" makes some modern activists abjure appeals to the middle class, consciously foreclosing a central lever of change.[48] It may not be fair to have to cajole a dominant order that is inherently unjust. But scare the middle class with too many challenges at once, and movements will fail.[49] Morally pure, psychologically obtuse reform efforts are profoundly misguided. Activists can remain untainted by compromise, or they can win.

MOVEMENTS MUST BE POLITICAL

At the height of Medellín's bloodshed in the early 1990s, a group of citizens from the Right and the Left formed an organization known as Compromiso Ciudadano. They spent years forging a plan for urban renewal that could save their city.[50] But when they presented their carefully crafted blueprint, the corrupt city council rejected it with barely a glance. The group realized that their effort was no techno-cratic exercise. Changing power structures requires taking power, and in a democracy that means elected politics. The reformers united behind Sergio Fajardo, an academic who was part of their group and could appeal to both sides of a polarized public. "We realized that we could work, talk, dream," Fajardo told *Newsweek*, "but to really do anything we had to go into politics, because politicians are the ones who have power."[51]

Since I began writing this book, friends have sent me a steady stream of articles on places that have fought violence. I keep them in a folder titled "Happy Stories." They are inspiring, and all follow a pattern. This country was among the most violent in the world. This neighborhood was a shooting gallery. Every family on this street has a child who is dead or in jail. Then someone started a church with a gang outreach program, or an after-school martial arts program for kids, or a nighttime soccer league. Police began a community out-reach program, holding spaghetti dinners to rebuild trust with the people living in violent neighborhoods. In each account, ordinary but heroic people, in the face of immense danger, take it upon themselves to do something positive that offers a real alternative to violence. These programs, if well executed, can make a dent in local violence.

They can keep kids out of gangs or move insurgents to other locales.[52] Such community efforts are critical in reasserting social norms and recivilizing once a government is in place that wants to improve. But they don't have the ability to change an entrenched power structure that governs through violence.

That doesn't mean they are worthless. In their study *Violence and Social Orders*, which looked at how countries moved from predatory to inclusive governments since ancient times, Douglass North, John Wallis, and Barry Weingast estimate that it takes an average of fifty years for countries to form the rule of law.[53] The World Bank and other studies estimate similar time spans, and so does my own research.[54] That's far too long to put off helping people while fighting for long-term solutions. So even if they just address symptoms, social programs are critical.

Social efforts can also teach people how to work together and can serve as academies for social leaders to find their voice and cause. In the United States, middle-class women who wanted to improve the lives of the immigrant poor volunteered at the settlement houses that grew in many cities during the 1880s. Inspired by similar programs in England, settlement houses offered health care, education, and job training for the poor. By 1895, they had spread to thirty-two states. Yet the problems besetting poor immigrant families in Gilded Age America were endless. Over time, many volunteers began to see that charity wasn't enough: the poverty would continue until the corrupt political machines were broken. From these settlement house origins, the Progressive movement's leadership grew as elements within both the Republican and Democratic parties. It eventually became one of the more successful efforts to open a country's power structure from a corrupt elite to a more fully realized democracy.[55]

The move from the morally clear path of service to politics, however, is a difficult leap. In countries where politicians are venal, corrupt, and violent, it can be hard to attract good people into electoral politics.[56] When I met with an Indian anticorruption activist who became a candidate to fight for honest government, she mentioned that she was embarrassed to share her career with old schoolmates. Her previous human rights work was seen as a worthy cause, while politicians were considered the lowest of the low.

Politics can also be anathema to the non-hierarchical style and leaderless culture that many modern movements prefer. While a number of protest movements in Italy, Spain, and Hong Kong have transformed themselves into political parties, others refuse to name leaders at all, much less support politicians with a real chance of winning elections.[57] This antipolitical, leaderless form of protest fails. A recent study by the Initiative for Policy Dialogue in Germany found that only about a third of recent protests achieved any success at all between 2006 and 2013.[58] Erica Chenoweth, co-author of *Why Civil Resistance Works*, also finds that leaderless movements today are less effective than previous nonviolent movements. While nearly 70 percent of campaigns to improve governance succeeded in the 1990s, only 30 percent have been effective since 2010.[59] Part of the challenge such movements face is that the environment for protest is becoming more difficult as authoritarian regimes learn from each other and democracies make it increasingly hard for civil society groups to function.[60] But this tougher landscape gives movements every reason to learn what can work and become more strategic and effective. Ineffectual politics-by-protest can take a generation of citizens who are the most willing to put their energy into reform and leave them cynical and unwilling to try again.

BROAD-BASED, NONPARTISAN MOVEMENTS

In a polarized society, movements have to walk a careful tightrope. They must be political while avoiding partisanship. Because Privilege Violence polarizes populations, hewing to one side of the political spectrum is a sure path to being dismissed by at least half the electorate.

There is a great deal of research on the mental shortcuts our brains make when issues become ideological. We filter out information that contradicts beliefs we already hold—a psychological trait known as confirmation bias.[61] Facts don't change minds. Instead, when confronted with facts intended to clarify divisive issues, people cling more tightly to their political ideologies. The neuroscientist Drew Westen carried out a series of fMRI experiments and found that when political partisans listened to points that challenged them, then heard information that confirmed their preexisting biases, they got a dopamine hit in the pleasure center of their brains—the same effect that occurs when people take a dose of heroin or cocaine. In other words, confirming one's political beliefs after hearing potentially undermining facts is addictive and rewarding.[62] "Wishful seeing," in which people literally spot facts and other things that they wish to see and hear more quickly than less desired information, is a fairly accepted finding in psychology.[63] It's part of an entire field known as motivated cognition, which studies the tendency of people to perceive the world as they want it to be and to seek out information that confirms what they already believe.[64] When people are afraid, as they often are when confronted with violence, they become even less tolerant of ideas and people different from them.[65]

Meanwhile, when politics are highly partisan, ideology becomes personal. People perceive their political party as a part of their identity, like being Christian or Jewish, Chinese or Indian. When party becomes so important to one's sense of self, people choose their policy positions based on their party, rather than the other way around.[66] Hence, in today's world of highly polarized identity politics, a U.S. voter who cares a great deal about abortion will also develop strong opinions on whether human action is affecting the climate and on economic regulation. Though little unites policies on childbirth, the environment, and taxation, they become linked as part of one's identity.[67] This trend is so strong that researchers have found that even when people hold moderate views on an issue they see as unimportant, they will rise to intense anger if challenged.[68]

These tendencies suggest that when issues connected to power structures, corruption, and violence are aligned with one party in a highly polarized atmosphere, they become intractable. Both sides become energized by refuting opponents rather than seeking a solution.[69]

People wishing to change a power structure defined by such polarization must engage in a particular form of jujitsu. They must address the political nature of Privilege Violence. But they must shun partisan arguments to avoid being ignored by half the electorate. In Medellín, for example, Sergio Fajardo, the candidate of Compromiso Ciudadano, refused to classify himself as right-wing or left-wing while running for mayor. He walked the barrios in the sandals of the poor and donned suits for meetings with the city's power brokers. The curls of his salt and pepper hair reached well down his neck, a sure sign of a liberal academic, but he came from an upper-crust family with old ties to conservative elites. His policies also crossed traditional partisan lines. He lobbied for more police, but also better education for the poor. He sought to improve the business climate, but also to increase tax collection. As a mathematician, he referred interlocutors to the numbers when challenged to pick a side, claiming to base his decisions on evidence rather than ideology. The posture let him avoid getting pigeonholed and dismissed.

In fact, even if a cause can galvanize a voting majority to win a particular policy along partisan lines, nonpartisanship is crucial to enacting broader social change. Chenoweth and Stephan's book, *Why Civil Resistance Works,* showed that a major reason why nonviolent social movements were twice as effective as violent ones stemmed from the fact that nonviolent movements could gain support from a broader swath of society.[70] Breadth often includes heft, of course. Numbers matter when making a show of force against entrenched power.[71] Yet sheer mass isn't enough. Uniting people across traditional boundaries allows broad-based movements to overcome the polarization endemic to societies split by Privilege Violence.

BRINGING A POLITICIAN TO POWER

"In a revolution, as in a novel, the most difficult part to invent is the end," wrote Alexis de Tocqueville, after watching France's revolutionary generation of 1848 miscarry following yet another uprising.[72] When the opening salvos of reform are successful, they tend to breed counterreform efforts that push back, often viciously. Movements that get people into the streets but fail to make pragmatic political change can therefore yield governments worse than those previously in place. Thus, when a regime is ousted, the most frequent replacement is another rotten regime. "Tyranny often changes into tyranny," Aristotle warned.[73]

Protesters can occupy Wall Street, huddle in the cold of Kiev's Maidan, and hold placards in Egypt's Tahrir Square. But unless they can unite behind a politician who can take the reins of power, policies and platforms will fail to be enacted—or worse, be stolen, co-opted, or turned against them. Knowing how to tear down governments without considering who will govern and how they will take power is profoundly counterproductive and often dangerous.

Movements must therefore use their heft to propel politicians into power, while avoiding polarizing partisanship. There are various ways successful movements navigate these shoals. First, they can reframe issues in ways that break the usual political gridlock, then make clear policy demands that force existing politicians to compete for their votes. At the turn of the last century, progressives in the United States reframed highly partisan issues in ways that made them sound technical and above the partisan fray. Efforts to aid destitute immigrants and slum dwellers became problems of sanitation and public health, not points of class conflict. The fight against corruption was recast as a positive effort to create a civil service. Civil service exams and laws would end mass patronage, thereby cutting off the fuel that kept the political machines running. But the language was not politically charged, so it was harder to dismiss. By forming large blocs within both the Republican and the Democratic Parties, progressives forced both sides of the aisle to compete for their allegiance.

Another method is to support independent candidates or create alternate parties unaligned with polarizing forces.[74] This was the strategy that propelled Sergio Fajardo to the mayorship of Medellín in 2003, after he refused an offer to join the ticket of an existing party. It was also the strategy eventually adopted by many progressive candidates in the United States.

Sometimes causality can reverse, and independent politicians facing cozy, closed politics choose to build their own social movements. That is what happened in the Republic of Georgia.

POLITICIANS CREATE THEIR OWN MOVEMENTS: GEORGIA, 2000–2003

By the early years of the twenty-first century, Georgians were desperate for change. Talented young people were emigrating to other countries, where they didn't have to pay bribes for their education. David

Usupashvili, once Shevardnadze's young legal staffer, had started the Georgian Young Lawyers' Association, which became the hub for returned, Western-educated Georgian professionals committed to reform. A woman named Tina Khidasheli joined the group the following year. Soon after, she and David married.

The newlyweds were among a small group of reformers who had also served in government. Zurab Zhvania, the most prominent among them, was in his mid-thirties, which made him an éminence grise in Georgian politics. It was commonly assumed that he would succeed President Shevardnadze. Trying to balance competing interests, the president had apparently tasked Zhvania to bring in smart, energetic political talent without ties to the old Communist elite.[75] Zhvania had chosen two young politicians to mentor. The first was a reform-minded parliamentarian named Nino Burjanadze. The second, Mikheil Saakashvili, had left Georgia to attend Columbia University Law School in New York. He had joined a U.S. law firm and started work on a Ph.D. by the time Zhvania asked him to come home and help with the country's judicial reform. Saakashvili consulted his dissertation adviser. "Go home," the adviser told him. "You don't have to write this thesis. Change your country and call it 'The Making of a New Country.' It will be much more interesting."[76]

When Saakashvili returned to Tbilisi in 1995, he stood out among the gray Soviet apparatchiks in Shevardnadze's cabinet. Brash, young, and smart, he had an American style Georgians wanted to emulate. He ran for parliament the year he came home. By 1997, a panel of Georgian journalists and organizations had named him "Man of the Year." A year later, foreign diplomats spoke of him as a future president.[77] Shevardnadze named Saakashvili minister of justice, the kind of appointment he often used to co-opt reformers and balance them with the old guard. Saakashvili, however, refused to play along. In August 2001, he plunged into a cabinet meeting brandishing photographs of the luxury mansions and summer dachas owned by cabinet members and ruling elites. The act was explosive. People knew about the corruption, but no one spoke of it publicly. Saakashvili brought reporters with him, throwing a bomb into the cozy world of the country's power brokers and destroying the walls of silence that kept the population from discussing the depth of their country's failure.

Saakashvili sought a bigger platform, and just a few months later the moment of opportunity seemed to have arrived. Police raids shut down Rustavi 2, the country's hard-hitting independent television station. Earlier that summer, Giorgi Sanaia, a twenty-six-year-old raven-haired television reporter whose investigations into government corruption had made him the station's most famous anchorman, had been found dead in his apartment, shot by an unknown assailant. Georgians blamed the government and poured into the streets.

Shevardnadze declared the protests a coup attempt. But they continued. The president threatened to quit, a scare tactic that had effectively ended past crises. This time, it failed. Rattled, Shevardnadze fired his entire cabinet to placate the protesters.

On the streets, many believed that the government would fall. Yet Zhvania and Burjanadze had agreed that Saakashvili was the most charismatic among them and thus the most likely to be elected president. But he was not yet thirty-five, the legal age required for the job. A brutal minister of the interior, Kakha Targamadze, also held sway over the security services. He might order troops to shoot into a crowd. Instead of riding the popular tide, the reformers trusted that they could create another wave when timing was in their favor. They began laying the foundations that would allow them to take power so that they would have control of the transition when it occurred.

CREATING A WINDOW OF OPPORTUNITY

Many scholars write about change becoming possible when a critical juncture, a historical moment of flux and opportunity, occurs.[78] "Never let a good crisis go to waste," claim political hacks when a scandal erupts. But Georgia's future leaders didn't wait for the right moment to come along. They created it. Everyone knew that the upcoming parliamentary elections were likely to be stolen. A poll conducted in August 2003 by Gallup found that only 11 percent of the population thought the elections would be fair. But that didn't mean they would do anything about it. Georgians felt little sense of personal efficacy. The same poll found that 87 percent of the population thought the average person had no say in the government's actions.[79] Moreover, many Georgians feared a return to the anarchy of just a decade before. They wouldn't risk making change unless they believed a better alternative was possible. A stolen election wasn't a moment of opportunity until an organized movement made it one.

Saakashvili quit his job as minister of justice and created the United National Movement, a proto–political party.[80] In parallel, a variety of student groups and activists organized around the country.[81] They weren't working with Saakashvili, but their mission often overlapped in practice. The Open Society Institute sponsored visits between these activists and the Otpor! movement, which helped end Milošević's rule in Serbia. One organizer explained that he had once seen a documentary about Poland's Solidarity movement in which the mobilizers were belittled for being "generals without armies." The words stuck in his mind. He needed to engage the majority of Georgians. He and his fellow organizers talked to teachers, pensioners, and people from across the country to "preheat society" and break the assumption that nothing anyone did could make their lives better.[82]

Students formed a group known as Kmara, or "Enough!"[83] They wanted to force people into having a political opinion. Their brash tactics—lying down in streets, painting graffiti on buildings, yelling in public—broke taboos in conservative Georgia. Apathy and neutrality were no longer options. Gradually, the campaigners started to use the media. A commercial appeared on television showing crumbling buildings and destitute citizens, followed by the words "Enough of Failing!" The cryptic message got people talking. After the commercial ran for some time, the words were changed to "Enough of Shevardnadze."[84]

One parliamentarian who traveled to Germany on business learned that the German government was giving significant aid to rebuild Georgia's energy infrastructure. "I lost my mind," he said. "What?! What money? When I returned, I wanted to know who had eaten that money."[85] Meanwhile, the IMF and the World Bank declared that they would stop sending aid to Georgia because of the rampant corruption, stoking more anger.[86]

On November 4, 2003, when Georgians went to the polls, ballot boxes were broken and stuffed. Dead people's names remained on voter lists, while living voters had been erased from the databases.[87]

The blatant fraud angered Georgians and insulted their dignity. The United States, the European Union, and the Open Society Institute sponsored election monitoring, which supported the popular impression. A day after voting, Georgians were back in the streets in Freedom Square, the block near parliament where Soviets had crushed the country's independence protests nearly fifteen years before. Saakashvili asked the protesters to return three days later. On November 8, police placed trucks on the highways to stop United National Movement allies from getting into the capital and arrested incoming supporters of Saakashvili for "drunk driving."[88] But tens of thousands of people gathered to hear Zhvania, Burjanadze, and Saakashvili speak.[89]

While a diverse group of organizations formed the movement that would later be called the Rose Revolution, Zhvania, Burjanadze, and Saakashvili were the architects of the smooth transition of power. In regimes ruling through Privilege Violence, ensuring the support of the security services is key to peaceful change.[90] General Vladimer Chachibaia recalled that one of the revolutionary leaders "called me a few times and asked me to come and show up at the demonstration. We were the only brigade in the country that was real. . . . I responded that if I did that, it would involve myself in politics, so I couldn't do that, but I promised that the military was not going to take part against them."[91] For three weeks in the cold winter rain, protesters gathered, sometimes just 100 sleeping overnight in the square, sometimes 100,000.[92] They handed food and flowers to the police, knowing the poorly paid officers were victims of the corrupt order, not just perpetrators. Meanwhile, Saakashvili used fiery rhetoric in the streets, but he and the rest of the trio were quietly meeting with Shevardnadze to discuss how to end the standoff.[93]

On November 20, Shevardnadze inaugurated the new parliament, but instead of playing along, Tedo Japaridze, the parliamentarian with the bullet hole in his map who at this time led the National Security Council, announced that there had been election fraud. Shevardnadze bused armed supporters from the provinces into the capital. Saakashvili called for another day of peaceful protest.

On November 22, both groups were in the city. Protesters broke past police and into the government offices. Guards trained by the

CIA didn't shoot.[94] Shevardnadze wasn't in his office. Saakashvili asked some supporters to remain behind and led another group to the parliament just a block away. They entered the legislative chamber and locked arms in front of the windows to prevent armed pro-government supporters from entering. Saakashvili held up a rose to Shevardnadze. "Resign," he demanded. The president's bodyguards hustled Shevardnadze out of the chamber. Saakashvili picked up the former president's abandoned glass of tea and drank.[95]

Throughout that evening and into the early morning dawn, Saakashvili and Shevardnadze met. Protesters waited nervously outside the presidential residence. On November 23, 2003, after less than three weeks of protests, Shevardnadze announced his resignation. "I'm going home now," he said.[96]

No vacuum of power ensued because the revolutionaries were ready. Organizers had been working throughout the countryside for years. They easily transitioned into a get-out-the-vote movement behind Saakashvili, whose role during the protests had been carefully orchestrated for positive media coverage. The revolutionaries weren't exactly united; Burjanadze and Saakashvili would fall out a few years later, and Zhvania would die suspiciously in 2005 of carbon monoxide poisoning.[97] But they were able to put aside differences at this critical moment. Nino Burjanadze, who was head of the parliament, became acting president and declared elections in forty-five days. On January 4, 2004, Saakashvili became president in an imperfect but vastly improved election with 96 percent of the vote.[98] The overwhelming mandate gave his new political party the popular support it needed to push aside entrenched interests and change the system, top to bottom.

Social movements are crucial when the political leaders who benefit from the system are the only ones with the power to change it. Movements form a source of internal pressure that, if large and focused enough, can force the hands of elected politicians.

Movements continue to matter after their preferred politician is elected. Public sentiment acts like the wind in a politician's sails, allowing a leader to blow past powerful, entrenched opposition.

When I asked Georgian political insiders how Saakashvili persuaded parliament mere weeks after his election to pass major constitutional changes that reduced their own power, they explained that no politician could stand against a man who had won 96 percent of the vote. Mayor Fajardo of Medellín came into office with a 72 percent approval rating that eventually grew to 95 percent.[99] As one aide explained, "Openly confronting . . . his enormous popularity would have been like political suicide."[100] Lyndon Johnson won his 1964 election in a landslide, gaining 486 electoral votes to his opponent's 52, numbers that enabled his historic Voting Rights Act the following year. Mayor Leoluca Orlando of Palermo gained 75 percent of the vote in his second term. "I did not have to balance political forces because, in some way, I was the political force."[101] Even violent criminals and warlords must bide their time against these levels of popularity.

Major social reform in a democracy requires a broad popular base; it can't happen with a single "Great Man." Yet movements also fail without particular talented individuals. Skilled social leaders translate anger and unrest toward positive change and away from repression. They determine whether movements are broad and unite society across partisan divides or are narrow and divisive. By joining with politicians, social leaders can wrest control away from entrenched interests. Where a country goes next depends on the character and ability of canny political operators.

7

POLITICIANS

I'm proud that I'm a politician. A politician is a man who under-stands government, and it takes a politician to run government. A statesman is a politician who has been dead ten or fifteen years.

—HARRY S. TRUMAN[1]

It's invigorating to imagine honest crusaders cresting to power on waves of massive public support. Yet those who succeeded at pulling their countries out of violence were not lily-white reformers. It takes people with political savvy and immense ego to decide they can save their failing countries. These qualities have a dark side. Mikheil Saakashvili skated dangerously close to repression and authoritarianism in Georgia, while Álvaro Uribe, president of Colombia from 2002 to 2010, presided over a spike in extrajudicial killings and other scandals. Nitish Kumar, chief minister of Bihar, avoided repression but kept adding criminals to his party roster so that he could win elections. Repression wasn't necessary for change; in fact it was harmful. Mayors like Sergio Fajardo of Medellín, Antanas Mockus of Bogotá, and Leoluca Orlando of Palermo, Sicily, avoided these excesses. But the former two benefited from bargains made by the more political, less ethnically pure President Uribe.

The task of governing requires politicians, not idealists. Effective politicians need vision, a commitment to reform, and strong management skills to hire and support talented technocrats, give them the room to succeed, and demand accountability. But they also need political skills, including the moral flexibility to undertake a new round of dirty deals to fight violence—this time, disarming all parties at the same time to fight cycles of retaliation. And before a strong state exists to institutionalize change, they must rely on their personal energy and direct accountability to rebuild a government that earns its citizens' trust.

THE RIGHT PERSON FOR THE JOB

All of the politicians who led their countries out of violence had to take a deliberately weakened state and make it work well enough to enforce the laws. With the normal tools of government broken, they needed to rely on political acumen—the ability to co-opt and convince with words, wiles, and charisma alone. That is likely why in each case I found except for the mayors in Colombia, the politicians who succeeded at fighting violence were not crusading outsiders but longtime political insiders who campaigned as mavericks promising fundamental change.

President Uribe of Colombia had spent his life in politics, serving as mayor of Medellín and governor of Antioquia, a region particularly infested with drug cartels and paramilitaries, before breaking free from the major parties to run for president as an independent. Mikheil Saakashvili had served multiple terms in parliament and was minister of justice by his mid-thirties. Nitish Kumar of Bihar and Mayor Orlando of Palermo entered politics in their twenties. President Lyndon Johnson began his career as a twenty-two-year-old campaign aide.

LBJ's personal character was typical of the successful reformers I found in other countries. Described by contemporaries and historians as ambitious and self-serving, he was known for his hunger for raw power and his willingness to use others to achieve it.[2] Such qualities can make effective politicians unappealing to more idealistic activists. But when states are broken, reformers, though they must have vision, must also be politically astute. Knowing how to fashion a good bargain, build support, and outwit challengers are political skills that require professional apprenticeship and a certain personality to learn.

WHY REFORMERS SO OFTEN FAIL TO DELIVER

Political novices who do get elected to fight Privilege Violence face a common problem: they often fail to deliver. Corrupt systems are built on a web of relationships. *You scratch my back, I'll scratch yours* is how things get accomplished. When reformers attempt to construct a government built on merit and institutions instead of patronage and personalities, they threaten these cozy relationships of reciprocal favors and directly challenge the power of politicians who are needed to implement legislation, pass budgets, and approve programs.[3] When a new administration stops greasing palms, they can close into fists. In countries governed through Privilege Violence, powerful legislators pose an ongoing challenge to reform.

The three Colombian mayors were the only novice politicians I found who succeeded in reducing violence. When a city council member asked Antanas Mockus, mayor of Bogotá, for patronage, he explained that he would look at his petitioner "as if he had vomited. . . . I just used body language [as if] I was wondering how to collect back his vomit from the carpet."[4] Mockus kept his administration clean, but council members had no interest in helping him. Instead, they disabled his attempts at substantive change. Mockus had the good fortune to follow a particularly adept mayor, Jaime Castro, a lifelong politician who had taken unpopular, tough measures such as improving tax collection that allowed Mockus to focus on more media-friendly initiatives. Yet even with such an auspicious introduction, Mockus relied on executive action and other policies he could enact on his own during his first term in office, because he could pass so few laws through the city council.[5] Many of his changes were thus undone by later mayors.

Sergio Fajardo, the academic mathematician who ran as an independent backed by a civic group of left- and right-wing professionals, faced the same problems. After becoming mayor of Medellín in 2004, he had to govern through a corrupt city council. He gradually learned to give councilmen credit for his reforms in exchange for support, so long as his administration was allowed to implement programs honestly.[6] The compromise allowed Fajardo to get the funding he needed to improve public spaces and connect slums to public transit, but it didn't stop councilmen from launching vindictive lawsuits against many of his aides, nearly bankrupting some and driving others out of politics.[7] In Cali, Dr. Rodrigo Guerrero, an epidemiologist who served as mayor from 1992 to 1994, pioneered the tactics to reduce violence that Mockus and Fajardo would later use in Bogotá and Medellín. But Guerrero couldn't institutionalize his changes in Cali. His immense success in fighting bloodshed didn't last beyond his two-year term. When he was reelected twenty years later, he was forced to start over.[8]

Such problems are common to reformers who are new to politics. They want to change the system, but they don't have years of favors that can be called in to pass legislation. They lack the political history to understand the psychology, pressure points, and weaknesses of legislators. They don't have networks to gather political intelligence. An unskilled political reformer can be like a duck bobbing along the surface of the water, unable to control or affect the dynamics underneath. Voters are often left with a choice between a functional but corrupt system and an honest but ineffective one.[9]

A POLITICIAN WIELDS POWER: COLOMBIA, 2002–2008

Mortar shells hit Bogotá on August 7, 2002, as Álvaro Uribe was being sworn in as president. The bombs made a low, rumbling sound inside the congressional building where he was taking the oath of office. They landed near the presidential palace, killing three children and eleven adults in the surrounding barrio.[10] "Many analysts thought that FARC was almost at the point of victory. Bogotá was surrounded at all angles," Álvaro Balcázar, the man in charge of rebuilding the government in former guerrilla areas, told me fourteen years later.[11]

Colombia's violence had declined after Escobar's death in 1993. But with parts of the population and government supporting paramilitaries, and the guerrillas focused on war rather than politics, it ticked upward. Both sides financed their efforts with drug trafficking, smuggling, and other forms of organized crime, so homicides ballooned in tandem with civil war deaths.[12] From 1997 to 2002, murders rose 40 percent. While still well below the heights of Escobar's deadly reign in the early 1990s, it was a bad trend.[13] Rafael Pardo, a former Colombian minister of defense, wrote an article in 2000 summarizing the carnage that had beset the country since the mid-1980s:

> In the last 15 years, 200 bombs (half of them as large as the one used in Oklahoma City) have blown up in Colombia's cities; an entire democratic leftist political party was eliminated by right-wing paramilitaries; 4 presidential candidates, 200 judges and investigators, half the Supreme Court's justices, 1,200 police officers, 151 journalists, and more than 300,000 ordinary Colombians have been murdered.[14]

Meanwhile, as Uribe swore his oath of office, "the country at the time was bankrupt. No one officially knew that," Andrés Felipe Arias, Uribe's director of macroeconomic policy in the Ministry of Finance, explained. One of Arias's first tasks after being appointed that inauguration day was to sell government bonds to the United States. "But no one wanted to buy Colombian bonds. It was 2002, and Colombia was seen as a failed state."[15]

Washington policy makers credit Colombia's rebirth to a massive influx of U.S. aid and military equipment under the $9.4 billion Plan Colombia program.[16] By helping President Uribe, a tough politician who had run on a platform of security, many policy makers in the United States believe that they enabled a leader with the will to decimate the FARC. Plan Colombia, which began under Uribe's predecessor, certainly played a role in Colombia's recovery. By the late 1990s, Colombia's professional military contained only about 22,000 men, supplemented by low-ability conscripts.[17] The guerrillas could put 23,000 soldiers in the field and regularly recruited (and kidnapped) more. By the early 2000s, the paramilitaries wielded around 30,000 troops.[18] In the four years before Uribe took office, the United States helped Colombia's government expand its armed forces by 60 percent, to 132,000, about 55,000 of whom were professional soldiers. By the end of Uribe's two terms, the military had grown to 283,000 and the National Police to 159,000.[19] More important than numbers was American assistance in helping Colombia's security services forge joint commands so that its army, air force, and navy could collect and analyze intelligence, then coordinate complex operations together.[20] The police officers and military consultants I interviewed all described the importance of Plan Colombia. While the money and equipment helped, they emphasized the managerial expertise and the psychological support the Americans offered as they tried to fight against overwhelming odds.[21] The aid also assisted Colombian efforts to rebuild courts, police, and a more legitimate state.

But Plan Colombia was successful only because it came when the government and society were united. U.S. military aid under Plan Lazo in the 1960s nearly eliminated a far smaller guerrilla threat, only to birth the FARC. In the late 1980s, the United States gave $700 million in aid to help Colombia's National Police fight Pablo Escobar, only to have other drug cartels, paramilitaries, and guerrillas step into the vacuum.[22] Two things had changed. First, Colombia ratified its new constitution in 1991, legitimating the government in the eyes of many on the Left. Second, Colombian society wanted to fight. Uribe's predecessor, Andrés Pastrana, had tried to forge peace by offering FARC nearly every concession it desired, including territory the size of Switzerland in which to operate during negotiations.[23] The guerrillas used the time to rearm, revealing themselves to be mere drug dealers and kidnappers masquerading as freedom fighters.[24] Betrayed, less than 1 percent of Colombia's population backed the FARC by April 2002.[25]

For the first time in Colombian history, Uribe wielded military force with the support of his people, with approval ratings that remained at over 70 percent for most of his two terms in office.[26] He began an all-out military assault on the guerrillas. Between 2002 and 2009, over twelve thousand FARC guerrillas were killed, and another twelve thousand were captured. By 2012, over seventeen thousand had demobilized.[27] The police had abandoned 200 municipalities to the guerrillas when Uribe took office. Four years later, after military operations in 377 municipalities, the government was a presence throughout the country.[28] By 2008, the FARC could muster few attacks with more than a dozen fighters, where once they could pull together fifteen hundred soldiers for a single battle.[29] Kidnapping rates also fell, because guerrillas in retreat couldn't hold prisoners.[30]

DEMOBILIZING PARAMILITARIES
WHILE FIGHTING GUERRILLAS

Military force had brought violence down before, only to have it boomerang back. The same problem was recurring in 2008 as Uribe's military campaign began to stall. By 2012, FARC was regrouping, with nine thousand fighters and a renewed ability to execute complex operations that let them contest 142 areas across the country.[31] Uribe's success depended on combining military force with politics, in the form of dirty deals to buy the peace of one violent group while fighting another. Unlike previous deals, this pincer allowed Uribe to focus militarily on one problem at a time while simultaneously addressing multiple violent groups to end retaliatory cycles between them.

For his first battle, months into his term in mid-October 2002, Uribe ousted Marxist guerrillas from Comuna 13, a neighborhood of Medellín that had become the epicenter of the city's insurgency and crime. The location was symbolic. The year before, President Pastrana had sent troops to retake control of the same neighborhood and had botched the effort. Guerrillas remained while government troops killed innocent people, embittering locals. But where his predecessor had failed, Uribe succeeded. Medellín would never again hit such peaks of violence.

To learn what Uribe did differently, I met with M——, an investigative journalist, high in the hills of Medellín. I sat in his garden, where flowers scented the humid afternoon air as his black cat wove in and out of the lawn furniture. "I was covering this in real time," M—— said, pacing back and forth. "During the famous Operation Orion, Don Berna [the paramilitary leader] was believed to have General Montoya of the Fourth Army Brigade on his payroll, as well as the chief of police of Medellín.... At night, after police finished operations [Don Berna's paramilitary] would drive through the streets with guerrilla deserters in their trucks. The deserters would point out guerrillas, and Berna's boys would snatch them off the streets and often kill them—most still haven't been found.... So the paramilitaries were acting as death squads for the police and army."[32] The payoff happened swiftly. The government let Don Berna control the paramilitary, organized crime, and street crime in Medellín. "This was the height of Berna's power. By December 2003, he controlled Medellín more thoroughly than Escobar ever did," M—— explained. His account was backed by many others, including the Inter-American Commission on Human Rights, which condemned the Colombian state for abuse, excessive force, and the assassination of a human rights defender during the incursion.[33]

Uribe had executed a classic dirty deal, trading impunity for peace by placing criminals in charge.[34] Unlike more self-serving politicians, Uribe used the breathing room well. In December 2002, just weeks after Operation Orion, Don Berna's paramilitary consortium declared a unilateral cease-fire after weeks of secret disarmament negotiations brokered through the Catholic Church. If they put down their arms permanently, Uribe offered them near impunity, just five to eight years in jail with no threat of extradition to the United States.[35] For the mass murderers, drug dealers, and election fixers that the United States desperately wanted to get its hands on, this was an amazing deal. The day before the September 11, 2001, attacks on the United States, the State Department had listed Don Berna's paramilitary coalition as a foreign terrorist organization. A year later, the U.S. Department of Justice had asked Colombia to extradite two top paramilitary leaders.[36] Uribe's offer provided these named terrorists and drug kingpins with a way to escape America's grip and gave foot soldiers a means to return to normal life.[37] Crucially, paramilitaries trusted Uribe to keep the bargain. He was a right-wing leader, so they shared an ideology, and Uribe had dealt with the paramilitaries for years as governor of Antioquia.[38]

Colombia's paramilitary militias had pillaged the countryside. They had massacred peasant men and raped women. They had sent hundreds of thousands of Colombians fleeing from their homes to urban slums. They doubled as drug dealers, making money on the side taxing go-fast boats carrying cocaine off the Caribbean coast. Their violence was often sadistic and frequently had nothing to do with guerrillas; in one village, their youngest victim was a six-year-old girl.[39]

In 2003, Uribe's bargain permitted many of these murderers and rapists to walk free or serve minimal sentences. Government funds were allocated to help them reintegrate into society. Human rights groups were incensed. Paramilitaries were faking disarmament and regrouping into criminal gangs, they claimed. They were right. Paramilitary leaders hired peasants to wear fatigues for at least one disarmament ceremony so that real militiamen could keep their weapons.[40] Around a quarter of the amnestied paramilitaries rejoined their old units and shifted to organized crime.[41] Yet this was a recidivism rate that would be enviable in the United States, where more than 70 percent of violent prisoners are rearrested within five years of their release.[42] Despite the injustice of the deal and the many imperfections of the disarmament and amnesty process, murder rates plummeted by 16 percent and assault rates by 15 percent.[43]

Locals rejoiced. The percentage of Medellín's citizens who told surveyors their city was getting better rose from 27 percent before Uribe's election to 79 percent after Operation Orion.[44] But responsibility for keeping violence from recurring fell to another man. Mayor Fajardo was elected in 2003, and it was Fajardo who rebuilt trust and reintegrated the marginalized and poor *comunas* to solve the underlying problems fueling Privilege Violence. By 2007, when Mayor Fajardo stepped down, Medellín's murder rate was half that of New Orleans and lower than that of St. Louis, Baltimore, and Detroit today.[45] His story is for the next chapter.

HOMICIDE IN COLOMBIA, 1975–2015[46]

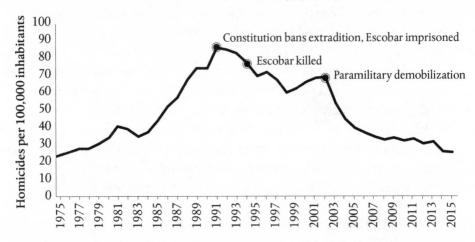

BIHAR: POLITICAL ACUMEN, TECHNOCRATIC MANAGEMENT

Colombia looked hopeless in 2002, but Bihar, India, faced even worse odds when Nitish Kumar became chief minister—a role equivalent to a state governor—in 2005. Bihar's population at the time was larger than Germany's, but its per capita income was on par with Eritrea's, the fifth-poorest nation on earth. Only 13 percent of households in Bihar had electricity in 2000. Less than 1 percent had a telephone.[47] Ninety percent of the population was rural, and 81 percent worked in agriculture.[48] In the dust along the roads sat men so poor they wore only loincloths. Those a little better off still plowed the fields with oxen. In the villages, families slept in mud barns in the hay alongside their cow or goat, their only valuable possession. Illiterate and innumerate, "we are no better than these animals," one man told me in 2000, weeping.

The poverty would have been daunting even for a more functional state. But when Kumar held his first press conference as chief minister and pledged to establish the rule of law, the audience laughed.[49] Kidnapping for ransom was Bihar's one growth industry, fueled by politicians who provided political cover to criminal gangs. An efficient supply chain distributed a cut of the proceeds to all: "a politician or a group to provide protection, a gangster to mastermind the activity, a group of people to carry out the abduction, another group to hide the victim, another set to arrange the transfer of money." The business was so established that "specialized abductors worked on credit."[50] Between 1992 and 2005, Biharis reported thirty thousand kidnappings.[51] People with moderate wealth traveled with bodyguards and were convinced that if they went to a dealer to buy a car or applied for a permit to build a house, they would receive an extortion note by the end of the day. Investment stagnated.[52] Bihar contained 8 percent of India's population in 2000, but its dusty provincial capital, Patna, accounted for 40 percent of all murders with firearms in all cities across India.[53] The author of a book on Indian democracy reflected that "if Bihar were an independent country, such conditions of breakdown would by now have precipitated a military coup, or external intervention, or some combination of the two."[54]

Bihar's problems had begun under British rule. Colonial Britain governed India with only a thin presence on the ground. Under the zamindar system it established, local landholders in northern India were granted the power to levy taxes that would be passed on to the colonists. Like southern plantation owners and Colombian ranchers, the landholders were empowered to act as judge, jury, and sometimes executioner of those under their sway.[55]

When India gained independence in 1947, Bihar's poor had been promised equal rights and the chance to own land. The poor were numerous, which should have given them voting power in a democracy. But with few possible jobs other than working the local landlords' fields, Bihar's low-caste poor relied on the landlords for survival, creating a near-feudal relationship sanctioned by centuries of history and religious tradition. Landowners rounded up workers tied to their land and forced them to vote for Congress, the landlords' preferred party. Collusion between the economic and the political leaders of the state enriched both. After independence, landowners stole fields and paid corrupt, upper-caste bureaucrats to fake new land titles and legalize the theft.[56] The national government set maximum limits on landownership to legislate fairer distribution, but in Bihar the effort largely failed. In the early 2000s, when researchers looked at Bihari landholdings far above government maximums, they often found politicians listed as owners.[57] Meanwhile, Bihar was ruled as a one-party state from independence until 1990. With the exception of one tumultuous year following 1975–1977 when voters threw out the Congress Party, disgusted with Prime Minister Indira Gandhi's suspension of democracy and instatement of emergency rule, Congress was always in control.[58]

Colombia and Sicily were divided by class, the U.S. South by race, and Bihar by caste. Each person was born into a divinely sanctioned status. Escape was nearly impossible.[59] Singles ads among India's urban upper class still advertise caste status today. Dalits were so far down the caste ladder they weren't even on a rung. In rural areas, many Dalits were still thought of by their previous name: "untouchables," so unclean they couldn't walk on the same roads as higher castes, who had to undertake a ritual cleansing if a Dalit's shadow crossed their own. In the 1980s, Dalits were occasionally turned away from buses or police stations if members of the upper castes were inside.[60] Many Dalits were stuck in debt bondage.[61] They borrowed money from their local landlord for sudden illnesses, burials, weddings, and from that moment onward they functioned as indentured servants.

Eric Monkkonen, a historian of U.S. violence, argued that "the South had a deliberately weak state. . . . Eschewing things such as penitentiaries in favor of local, personal violence."[62] His words echoed as I read a report on Bihar, India, titled "State Incapacity by Design."[63] In Bihar, the authors argued, the state's weakness was exacerbated by a deliberate electoral strategy designed by Lalu Yadav, who was first elected chief minister in 1990 and effectively ran Bihar for the next fifteen years.

Lalu was a Yadav, a member of a low-ranking cowherd caste. That status was the defining fact of his life. Yadavs were just a rung or two above Dalits. As a boy, young Lalu had been roughed up by upper-caste kids for combing his hair and carrying books—a display of cleanliness and learning that they felt should be reserved for members of the upper castes.

Lalu campaigned on the promise of lower-caste dignity. He became a symbol of righting a long-unjust system. Bihari villagers sported Lalu cigarettes; people sang Lalu hymns and asked barbers for Lalu-style haircuts.[64] Jovial and round-faced, he was armed with stinging quips that low-caste voters relished to show he could stick it to the elites. When upper-caste businessmen pressed Lalu to improve the roads to help his poor state's economy, he would ask, "Where are the cars?"[65] While businessmen stared agog at his lack of vision, Bihar's poor, who could rarely afford bicycles, loved him.

Lalu won thanks in part to excellent timing. The two years of repressive emergency rule from 1975 to 1977 had discredited the Congress Party. Over the next decade, lower castes organized to break the control of landlords over votes. Then, in 1989, massive pogroms against Muslims killed twelve hundred Biharis across 250 villages.[66] Massacres had been common in Bihar in the decades after independence, because leaders knew they needn't fear conviction.[67] But on the eve of the twenty-first century, Muslims revolted against a Congress Party that consistently failed to prosecute any pogrom leaders. For the first time in independent India, lower-caste Hindus and Muslims combined votes to break one-party rule and make Lalu Yadav chief minister.

Lalu inherited a state long weakened by Privilege Violence. By 1967, Bihar accounted for a fifth of all electoral bloodshed in India.[68] In 1969, a political analysis explained that to win a seat in the legislature, "the ballot must be backed with the bullet."[69] Some of the violent gang leaders grew tired of being used as middlemen and ran for office. For his seminal study on criminality in Indian politics, my colleague Milan Vaishnav spoke to one such former criminal-politician who explained,

> Politicians make use of us for capturing the polling booths and for bullying the weaker sections.... But after the elections they earn the social status and power and we are treated as criminals.... Why should we help them when we ourselves can contest the elections, capture the booths, and become MLAs [parliamentarians] and enjoy social status, prestige, and power? So I stopped helping the politicians and decided to contest the elections.[70]

Soon Bihar had the largest percentage of *bahubalis,* literally "strong-arms" or musclemen, in India. Rajesh Ranjan, known as Pappu Yadav, for instance, was a small-time teenage criminal who rose through the ranks to become a Mafia don. In 1990, when he was just twenty-three years old, he was elected to the state legislature. He has served in the assembly ever since, with the exception of a five-year stint in prison after he was convicted of murdering a fellow legislator.

By the late 1960s, Bihar's lower castes and poor had grown tired of fighting to make their voices heard through the supposedly "democratic" system. Around the world, university students were turning to Marxism for answers to the inequality and misery that surrounded them. They organized poor northern Indian villages, using Communist consciousness-raising sessions to teach peasant day laborers that they had rights, that there was a minimum wage in India, and that landlords were not allowed to rape Dalit women. Poverty-stricken Indians began to train as Maoist guerrillas. Known locally as Naxals for the birthplace of the Maoist movement in Naxalbari village, the guerrillas organized laborers to murder their landlords. India was soon engulfed by terrorist violence, crime, and political agitation. Maoist terror declined during emergency rule, but the repression backfired, and Naxals returned even stronger after it ended.

The government then made the classic mistake of relinquishing its monopoly on force. After a wave of Maoist attacks, magistrates were sent to violent districts to issue landholders with gun licenses on the spot.[71] The rural lords formed private armies to defend themselves. As in Colombia, the landlords also used their armies to uphold their system of wealth and power. In 1971, for instance, fourteen Dalits were murdered and their village utterly destroyed after a group of laborers asked to receive the minimum wage for their work.[72] With landlords in control of hundreds of votes, politicians shrugged off the use of militias to control peasants. Moreover, political parties also relied on the militias for help around election time.[73] A well-known party activist with the Bharatiya Janata Party (BJP) even moonlighted as the head of the Ranvir Sena, an umbrella militia.[74] While the state ignored militia violence, it cracked down on the guerrilla menace. Security forces targeted tribal and Dalit communities believed to be sympathetic to the guerrillas. Extrajudicial executions and torture of accused Naxalites, often innocent villagers, became common.

With the deadly triangle of Privilege Violence complete, savagery intensified. Between 2001 and 2005, Bihar had 1,309 Naxalite-related violent incidents, 760 civilian deaths, and 141 "armed encounters" in which security forces were responsible for killing. Retaliatory violence escalated between the Maoists and the militias. "We kill children because they will grow up to become Naxalites," explained one Ranvir Sena leader. "We kill women because they will give birth to Naxalites."[75]

———

In 2005, the ascension of Lalu Yadav offered hope that Bihar could become a more complete democracy and end the violence. Instead, Lalu simply switched the beneficiaries from the upper castes to his own, using Privilege Violence to help the Left and disempower the Right.[76] It was an exchange of tyranny for tyranny. Having inherited a weak state, he deliberately broke it further. He humiliated the bureaucracy, 83 percent of whom were from upper castes.[77] These white-collar clerks with easy office jobs had long made lower-caste Biharis grovel to attain the basic rights of citizenship. Lalu embarrassed them and broke their power. Then he created a patronage network, rendering Biharis who needed something from the government beholden to him, personally.[78] The patronage jobs didn't pay much, and in return no one was expected to work. In health-care centers, absent staff gave Bihar the worst health outcomes in the nation. A quarter of elementary schoolteachers didn't show up to school—the third-worst rate in the country.[79] Police positions went unfilled if no lower-caste members could pass the tests. Bihar became woefully under-policed, but what did Lalu's supporters care? Higher-caste Indians, usually the only ones who could pass the police civil service exam, often refused to take reports without a bribe. When Dalits were victims, police routinely refused to open investigations.[80]

Breaking the state to inflame political polarization was good politics. But the government wasn't too weak to fight violence when Lalu wanted it to. For instance, he needed to protect Muslims, who were a key part of his voting base. While Bihar had a long history of religious pogroms, during the fifteen years that Lalu held power, there were no riots against Muslims. Lalu ensured that incendiary Hindu-nationalist politicians couldn't rile up the state as they had in the past.[81] But despite this stunning success against religious violence long viewed as intractable, the Maoist-militia carnage continued. Many suspected he was willfully playing both sides: he didn't want to alienate the Dalits, who were crucial to his voting base, nor did he want to stop the militias, because grief and anger stoked the politics of caste grievance on which he had built his career.[82]

After seven years in office, Lalu was caught stealing millions of dollars of federal subsidies meant to purchase livestock fodder for his poorest constituents. His guilt was clear. He had diverted the money into his bank account. Other kickbacks were exposed, from a bitumen scandal in the roads department to the petty corruption of his patronage hires. Yet his constituents forgave him. Upper castes had been stealing from them for years. At least Lalu granted them dignity, even if he didn't give them their grain.[83] Though the conviction barred Lalu from office, he successfully ran his wife, Rabri Devi, for the chief minister's seat in 1997. She won despite being illiterate and evincing no interest in politics. Lalu controlled the state for eight more years.[84]

With this kind of support, people of Lalu's Yadav caste could get away with murder—and they did. His political cronies hung out at police stations, ensuring that the police didn't arrest any Yadav.[85] In that era, explained one police officer, "you couldn't do anything. Everybody had some political connection. We were constantly getting orders not to file charge sheets against this person or that person."[86] Yadavs formed the first kidnapping rings that became the scourge of the state. Yadav landholders operated their own militias and cracked down particularly hard on Dalits, one of the few groups lower on the social ladder than themselves.

The Yadavs' militias and higher-caste armies grew, and their deadly sprees continued. Two years after Lalu took office, Maoists massacred thirty-four landlords. The Ranvir Sena militia retaliated by raping over two hundred Dalit women, from six-year-old girls to seventy-year-old grandmothers.[87] Between 1995 and 1999, the Ranvir Sena killed more than four hundred Dalits.[88] Maoists fought back, and the death toll escalated throughout Lalu's rule.[89]

As in other places with Privilege Violence, ordinary Biharis also started using force. A rash of kidnappings afflicted marriageable, educated young men whose families demanded too much in dowry payments. Brides' families would haul boys off and force them to marry at gunpoint.[90] Landlords would employ Maoists to kill rival landholders and make the deaths appear political.[91] The headmaster of a popular school had a bomb thrown at his house by competitors.[92]

This was the state that Nitish Kumar inherited when he won the chief ministership in 2005. He crafted a turnaround so spectacular it was called the Bihar miracle. Articles touted Kumar's technocratic rule after decades of divisive caste politics. But while serious, dogged, and uncharismatic, Kumar was more than a technocrat. He had grown up in politics. His father had served in the Indian National Congress, and Kumar got involved with student politics at university. While committed to reform, Kumar was also a career politician, and it was his political skill that gave him the power he needed to realize his technocratic improvements.

Kumar squeaked into the chief ministership on a fluke. After a close, fraudulent, violent voting season in February 2005 led to a hung parliament that failed to form a state government, the federal government took over. It called for a by-election to be held in eight months, then turned to India's powerful national Election Commission to ensure a clean vote.

The Election Commission was politically independent, well funded, and highly empowered by India's courts.[93] Commission staff worked with the assistant director general of Bihar's police, Abhyanand, to remove two million fake voters from Bihar's fifty-million-person voter rolls.[94] They instituted electronic voting systems to deter fraud. They used algorithms to determine which voting booths were most likely to be stolen, and brought in police from across the nation as well as throughout the state to protect polls from armed gangs. During the campaign itself, the commission directed its own paramilitary forces to gather arms for safekeeping across Bihar. A fair election held in November 2005 gave Kumar's party the plurality of the parliament with 88 seats, and together his coalition held a strong majority of 143 out of 243.

CO-OPTING THE CRIMINAL POLITICIANS

It took more than a fair election, however, to enable Kumar's victory. In 2005, Kumar campaigned for chief minister on three planks: "governance, governance, governance." But too many people profited from the state's rampant criminality for an easy win. Criminal politicians were actually quite popular. In many districts of Bihar, when a *bahubali* ran against an honest politician, the crime lord won not in spite of his criminal record but because of it.[95]

Jeffrey Witsoe, an anthropologist who spent years conducting fieldwork in Bihar, asked one group of villagers from the high Rajput caste how they felt about the local crime lord and his henchmen. An older farmer "pointed to the distance and explained, 'The Bhumihars [a rival caste] reside just over there' ... without people like the strongman and his local muscle, 'Bhumihar goondas would prey on the village. He protects the village, protects the Rajputs, that's why we tolerate him.'"[96] Such feelings were replicated across Bihar. My colleague Milan Vaishnav found that voters weren't ignorant of candidates' criminality. As in many places where Privilege Violence forced people to fend for themselves, they hoped that their criminal-politicians would use muscle to protect them and look after their caste interests.[97] Meanwhile, seeing a tall, strong crime lord and his muscled entourage tramp through a village of poor stunted men and their families was enough to intimidate unprotected castes into voting for the local *bahubalis*.[98] "There are certain compulsions in politics," Kumar admitted, meaning that to win, he needed some of these *bahubalis* on his side.[99]

Kumar offered some crime lords a spot on his party's list.[100] By the time of the fall 2005 elections, 22 percent of the legislative candidates from Kumar's party faced criminal charges.[101] Anant Singh was one of the most notorious. A big man who favored dark sunglasses and leather jackets, Singh kept a pet python, an elephant, and an arsenal in his home. While he hadn't been convicted of a crime, allegations were legion. The first murder credited to him happened after Maoist rebels killed his older brother, a well-known landlord. Singh spent months tracking his brother's killers to a boat in the Ganges, then swam across the river and killed the alleged murderer. A video caught him dancing with AK-47s. When police raided his compound in 2004, his men started a shoot-out that forced the police to leave. When rumors spread that he had raped and murdered a young woman, Singh and his henchmen beat up the journalists who came to his home to inquire.[102]

How could Kumar run a law-and-order government after recruiting men like this to his party? He allegedly made a dirty deal. In return for a place on the ticket, *bahubalis* had to forswear future violence. He sweetened the offer. Kumar was about to use federal money to build highways across the state. *Bahubalis* could transform their gangs into construction crews, make money, and build the needed infrastructure.[103] But Kumar also threatened: any *bahubali* who used violence, particularly kidnapping for ransom, would be jailed.

This was the context for one of Kumar's most lauded anticrime reforms. Nitish Kumar knew that personnel mattered. He recruited talent, and one of his earliest appointments was Abhyanand, the police administrator who helped ensure Kumar's fair election.[104] Kumar asked him to serve as chief of police, arguably one of the most important and sensitive jobs in the administration. The two men had never met. In addition to taking on a man known to be a strong personality with his own ideas, Kumar disrupted the police hierarchy by hiring someone at a rung or two below the most senior leaders. When they first met, Kumar asked, "What do you need from me? Money, laws?" Abhyanand recounted. He retorted that he needed neither; they weren't building bridges.[105] He wanted freedom, support, and the chance to do his job without resorting to extrajudicial repression. Kumar agreed.

Abhyanand pioneered the key reforms that improved Bihar's security under Kumar's leadership. India's overwhelmed courts were so slow that criminals often spent years free on bail before their cases were tried. They poured money into lawyers' fees and bribes to win an endless number of delays. For a little pocket change, clerks happily "lost" files, and lawyers paid by the day profited if witnesses didn't materialize or cases were postponed on technicalities. Abhyanand worked to get police officers, prosecutors, and judges to develop a more efficient process so that justice could be delivered swiftly, and Kumar assisted by holding an unusual conference with all of these agencies present to show that ensuring swift justice was a personal priority of his administration.

Abhyanand turned to an old gun violations law to prosecute a vast array of violent crimes. While registered guns were legal, the Small Arms Act made it illegal to commit a crime with a gun, so if police could prove a gun was at a crime scene, a case could move quickly. Small Arms Act convictions didn't require witnesses—a crucial element because criminals could threaten witnesses and their families, and between such intimidation and the difficulty of traveling in Bihar, the failure of witnesses to show up in court was a major cause of delays.

Abhyanand trained the police in how to use the act, then brought thousands of cases over just a few months so the process became familiar to police, prosecutors, and judges. Bihar soon averaged a thousand small-arms trial convictions a month. Within three years, nearly twenty-five thousand criminals had been convicted under the act.[106] The crackdown didn't require any new laws, new institutions, or money, just a dedicated, creative leader who forced accountability through the system and systematically removed the bottlenecks that had previously been used as opportunities for corruption.[107]

On its own, the criminal convictions under the Small Arms Act wouldn't have been game changing. Most of those convicted were low-level trigger pullers. But combined with Kumar's implicit bargain, the act hooked enough big players to scare the remainder into accepting Kumar's dirty deal rather than risk a few years behind bars. Like the arrest of Al Capone on tax evasion, Small Arms Act convictions sometimes meant that murderers were sentenced to two years for illegal gun possession. But they would be convicted swiftly and would actually face jail time, rather than remaining free for decades through endless appeals. At times, the courts handed down longer sentences. And because felons couldn't run for office, a felony conviction, however short, was dire for the *bahubalis*.

To ensure the threat was dissuasive, Kumar made an example of a few crime lords. Anand Mohan Singh, who founded a Rajput militia and who was part of Kumar's coalition, was sentenced to death in 2007. The sentence was later commuted to life in prison, the same term handed to Mohammad Shahabuddin, a *bahubali* from the Muslim community with a Robin Hood reputation along with a record for murder, kidnapping, and inciting armed riots in 2007.[108] In 2008, Pappu Yadav received a life sentence. While the courts would eventually commute these sentences, years and sometimes over a decade of jail time for people once seen as invincible demonstrated Kumar's resolve to put major criminals behind bars and even sacrifice his own legislators if they refused to follow the law.

Police were accused of planting guns on suspects and giving false testimony to gain convictions. It was likely true. Such police behavior had occurred in India long before the Small Arms Act. But there is no evidence that the use of the act exacerbated the problem. Instead, Kumar and Abhyanand pushed for greater lawfulness and insisted that extrajudicial killings stop. Throughout Kumar's term, police brutality numbers fell, while accountability within the police rose.[109]

FIGHTING MAOISTS AND MILITIAS WITH POLITICS

A second set of dirty deals heralded the end of Maoist and militia violence. The success of Kumar's strategy is clear thanks to a fortuitous natural experiment. In 2000, five years before Kumar came to power, India's national government split Bihar into two states. Jharkhand, the southern half, inherited slightly more Maoists but also gained more infrastructure, industrial wealth, and the state's only police academy. India's national government augmented security budgets across the country, and Jharkhand received about four times the amount of assistance as Bihar.[110] Similar to the rest of Bihar in most respects, but with more infrastructure, money, and muscle, Jharkhand should have been able to bring about peace faster than its former northern half.

But Jharkhand chose to double down on force to maintain its privileged power structure. The government set its police loose to fight Maoists, but villagers didn't trust the officers. Police occupied their children's schools, ostensibly using them as temporary bases from which to fight Maoists, but really lounging outside in their underwear, drinking beer. The schools carried on in unoccupied rooms, but parents kept their little girls at home for their own safety. So despite being brutalized by the Maoists, who extorted exorbitant sums and kidnapped their children if they didn't pay, villagers didn't share information with the government.[111]

Police operating without intelligence faced heavy losses, so Jharkhand made a fatal mistake. It gave up the monopoly on force. The Maoists were constantly splintering into different factions over ideological disagreements, and the government supported some of these Maoist splinter groups that were willing to fight former comrades. "There can be no strategy better than to let the groups fight among themselves," proclaimed Gopinath Ghosh, a researcher at the Jharkhand-based Bindrai Institution for Research, Study, and Action. Let the criminals kill the criminals, in other words.

But, Ghosh acknowledged, the strategy expanded violence. The rebels "may have started as Maoist splinter groups, but with time they have reduced themselves to mere organised criminal groups whose main source of earning is abduction and extortion in and around coal mines with political patronage from local MLAs."[112] Other Maoists, instead of extorting the companies, worked for them. A coal mine employed one group to intimidate villagers. "If a local doesn't agree to give away land, the armed groups . . . threaten with a gun," explained a local near the mines.[113] Political candidates also found the Maoists helpful for affecting voters' preferences. One study found that Maoists could influence elections in fifty-four of Jharkhand's eighty-one constituencies.[114] In 2015, a community activist, Sunil Pandey, filed a request in the local court demanding an investigation into the collusion between senior police, politicians, and Maoist militias. In the middle of a bright December day, he was killed by masked bikers. His older brother commented to a journalist, "The truth is, police are growing one snake to kill the other. All these snakes are biting people."[115]

Maoism has declined throughout India in the last few years, thanks largely to economic improvements and a stronger national focus on countering the insurgency. In Jharkhand, the effort was costlier, and improvements were slower and less robust than anywhere else in the country. From 2011 to 2013, Jharkhand had the greatest number of deaths from Maoism of any state in India, more than double the rate of civilian casualties of any other Maoist-affected state.[116] Meanwhile, of the 519 civilians killed in the insurgency between 2009 and 2014, nearly half were killed by police, vigilantes, and state-supported Maoist splinter groups, not by Maoists themselves. The next year, militias, vigilantes, and splinter groups were responsible for more than 75 percent of civilian killings. So even as Maoist murders declined, proliferating state-sanctioned violence caused overall levels to remain about the same.[117]

Meanwhile, in Bihar, Kumar succeeded in fighting Maoist terror by applying the astute blend of dirty deals, technocratic policies, and force that had worked to fight the *bahubalis* criminal gangs. Initial conditions were hardly auspicious. During the 2005 elections that made Kumar chief minister, Maoists had staged a massive jailbreak in Jehanabad, thirty miles from Bihar's capital city.[118] After detonating a bomb and cutting electricity to the town, they attacked the police station and the jail.[119] When police regained control late in the morning of the following day, they found over half of the 650 inmates gone, including over 100 jailed Maoist comrades and 20 members of the Ranvir Sena, the upper-caste militia. Many of the latter were soon found dead.

Yet by 2005, the Maoists had lost the support of the Dalits they depended upon. They were extorting egregious amounts of money from the poor and brutally punishing internal infractions. Many rural Dalits would be happy to help crush them—if a savvy politician could gain the community's trust.

Like Uribe's simultaneous use of force against the FARC while demobilizing the paramilitaries, Kumar used a two-part strategy to stop the Maoists, realizing that he could not end their insurgency unless he also quelled the militias whose tit-for-tat retaliatory cycles fueled both groups. He started by offering the upper castes a dirty deal: impunity for past crimes. In 1998, after the Ranvir Sena had massacred fifty-eight Dalits, activists persuaded the Indian government to establish a commission to investigate ties between the upper-caste militias and political parties in rural Bihar. The massacre had been particularly horrific. One night in December, upper-caste militiamen crossed the river separating the upper- and lower-caste parts of the village. They broke into Dalit homes and shot at sleeping men, women, and children. Their youngest victim was a one-year-old baby. The killings were supposedly reprisal for the Maoist murder of thirty-seven upper-caste landlords six years before, but the victims had no connection to those killings.[120] Just a few weeks after his election, Kumar ended the truth commission for taking too long to investigate.[121] He also sidelined a land reform effort long cherished by social justice advocates, a measure he had supported on the campaign trail.

Bihar's upper castes rejoiced. After long, embattled years fighting for their interests against Lalu Yadav, they believed they had a supporter in office and didn't need militias. As Ashwini Kumar, a professor of development studies and no relation to Nitish, explained, "When Nitish Kumar came into power, these *senas* [militias] disappeared. The Ranvir Sena lost its appeal completely. [High castes] said, 'We are in power. Why do we need the Senas?'"[122] Meanwhile, the thousands of Small Arms Act cases meant that Nitish Kumar also wielded the threat of swift, certain jail sentences for anyone who committed a crime with a gun. The upper castes demobilized their armies.

Stopping here would probably have brought a temporary drop in killings at the price of increasing state illegitimacy and, eventually, a return to violence. But Kumar wanted sustainable peace. With the militias gone, the Maoists could no longer justify their assaults as a means of protecting Dalits. Kumar had the chance to win Dalits to his side.

In Bihar's caste-ridden world, politicians relied on their caste group for votes. But Kumar hailed from the Kurmi caste, which was too small to help electorally. Instead, he won with a coalition of upper-caste voters tired of Lalu Yadav's polarizing politics and Dalit voters he courted through promises of affirmative action, Bihar's perennial wedge issue. Since independence, the "reservations" system offered people from traditionally disadvantaged caste and tribal backgrounds a quota of reserved seats in universities, bureaucratic jobs, and other public offices. Which group got how many seats was a constant political battle.

Caste and class overlap significantly in India, but not completely. Some Dalits and low-caste members were able to amass wealth and education. These richer, better-connected individuals within each caste or tribe, the "creamy layer," as an Indian Supreme Court decision described them, reaped the greatest rewards from the affirmative action system.[123]

After his 2005 election, Kumar began channeling government aid and social programs to the poorest of the poor within the lowest castes, a group he called the Mahadalits. Suddenly land for the homeless, self-help groups for women, schools for children who had to work to support their families, and other government assistance started to reach the most needy Biharis, rather than being siphoned off by the rapacious "creamy layer."[124] Before the 2007 elections, Kumar created the Mahadalit Commission to recommend measures for "economic, social, cultural, and educational upliftment."[125] Then he forged new political quotas requiring villages on a rotating basis to elect half of their leaders from the Mahadalits.[126]

Next, Kumar empowered local governments to hire new teachers on short-term contracts so that they wouldn't have to be recruited through public exams only upper castes generally passed. He argued that the exam system would take too much time and children needed teachers immediately. State spending on education grew to 20–25 percent of the budget as local governments hired over 200,000 teachers and built ten thousand additional classrooms.[127] In practice, these simultaneous policy changes meant that after requiring many villages to elect poor Dalits, local Dalit leaders gained the ability to distribute patronage posts, building their political and economic power vis-à-vis the other castes.

The services Kumar's social programs provided had a mixed record. Enrollment increased to over 95 percent, and literacy rates rose by 17 percent by 2011.[128] Locally chosen teachers, however, were often unqualified. Enrollment was high, but school attendance was low (likely because many continued to treat their jobs as patronage posts and didn't show up to teach).[129] In Kumar's second term, he inaugurated new programs to improve teacher training.[130]

Although the educational effects of Kumar's policies were mediocre, the political ramifications were huge.[131] Kumar established a voter base for himself while focusing government resources on the most needy Biharis. His alliance with the BJP, which represented largely upper-caste Hindus, enabled him to unite the top and bottom of society to make fundamental reforms to Bihar's power structure. Meanwhile, Bihar's Dalits gained power and money, which gave them the ability to demand services, true police protection, and other rights as citizens. Crucially, these gains came from Dalits voting, not fighting.[132]

Dalits began providing intelligence to law-enforcement officers, enabling security forces to better target Maoist guerrillas. Kumar had been left with a thin police force after years of attrition under Lalu Yadav, who also hadn't rebuilt a new police training facility after losing Bihar's to Jharkhand when the states split. Kumar created a program to hire retired military men on a temporary basis. To avoid militarized policing, he forbade troops from patrolling the streets, instead assigning them to fight guerrilla insurgents. To enable military travel to Maoist areas, Kumar's administration laid thousands of miles of road, which also connected rural and urban Biharis and improved the economy.

Where Jharkhand's repression had failed, Kumar's vision, political prowess, and technocratic hires succeeded. Bihar's Maoist policies were among the cheapest in India, and its improvements came faster. With the guerrillas on the run, the paramilitary militias had no excuse to regroup. Less violence enabled security forces to focus on the worst offenders, reducing impunity for regular crime. By 2010, just five years after Kumar took power as chief minister, violent incidents across the state had more than halved, while Maoist arrests had grown by a third and civilian deaths dropped by two-thirds.[133] The state was strengthening. The forces of violence were beginning to yield.

THE MANAGEMENT HABITS OF STATE BUILDERS

Many pundits have tried to parse whether Kumar was a true reformer or just playing caste politics to gain power. He was doing both, and that is precisely what made him capable of instigating change. Kumar's and Uribe's mix of political and technocratic skills is shared among politicians who lead their countries out of violence. They are often career politicians with a particular combination of managerial habits: They have vision and decisively authorize major undertakings but hire able technocrats to take care of the details. They pick the best people regardless of loyalty, and they empower their staff to act. Their energy levels are enormous, and they expect the same work ethic from their hires. By upholding clear, tough, personal accountability, they get the state working immediately, long before government institutions can be improved. They also master the media to let the public know that change is afoot.

Empowering Technocrats

Saakashvili's government in Georgia saw itself as revolutionary. Its members wanted to deliver huge changes, fast. After determining that inept, corrupt law-enforcement officers, many of whom had been former warlords' underlings, were worse than no police at all, one of the administration's earliest acts was to fire the country's entire traffic police force, soon followed by the firing of thousands of corrupt bureaucrats and school administrators. For a month, Georgia went unpoliced. The Rose Revolutionaries held competitive exams and hired new college graduates, filling the streets with overeducated, under-trained officers. What they lacked in skills, however, they made up for in a customer service mentality consciously inculcated by the government. They were given new uniforms, new cars, and most important a sense that they really mattered.

Countries often purchase new equipment in an attempt to improve their police, and it rarely has much effect, by itself. It makes a difference when it is part of wholesale change in the state's attitude, a means of conveying status and professionalism. Saakashvili personally participated in the entry exams to inspire and lend cachet to the young recruits. David Bakradze, a leader of the new government, explained, "We had this message that this is now the most important thing to the state—so you young guys coming to the police, you are builders of the new state of Georgia."[134] The state-builder language kept recurring as I talked to others in the new administration. Saakashvili's inner circle didn't see themselves as democrats; they saw themselves as crafting a stronger, more efficient, more functional state from the hollowed-out hulk left at the end of Shevardnadze's era. It was a distinction that would haunt them soon enough.

On a rainy Tbilisi day, I talked with Kaha Hizanishvili over a pot of tea. He had been in charge of training Georgia's new intelligence and police services during Saakashvili's first years in office after 2004, and I wanted to know how he had started the turnaround. Like most people Saakashvili hired, Hizanishvili was educated in America. He had gotten his master's degree from the Fletcher School, a part of Tufts University in Boston that specializes in security studies. He and his

American wife landed plum jobs in Georgia for international companies but were about to return to the United States in the waning days of the Shevardnadze era. Educated, able, and in their late twenties, they were convinced their country had no future. Then the Rose Revolution occurred. Friends told Kaha that his country needed him. One former classmate was working for the newly appointed minister of the interior, Vano Merabishvili. "Come in for an interview," she said. Interior Ministries generally house police and domestic spying operations, and there, not the Defense Department, is where the real muscle lies in most post-Soviet countries. Frequently, they are run by tough characters, and Vano Merabishvili had such a reputation.[135]

Yet Kaha insisted on appointing the people he chose and having the freedom to talk to whomever he wanted—European countries, the CIA, Israel's Mossad, and others—to learn how they ran their systems. "I had so much independence I can't even describe it to you. I was twenty-nine when I started, and I was not the youngest by a long shot among people in similar roles. But they recycled people pretty fast. If the people I trained weren't worth their salt, then I could have lost my job."

He got to work, testing and refining as he went. "They gave me a wing in the intelligence building," he said, but "it looked like crap, and the budget was very small." He got rid of elementary-school-style desks with connected tables and outfitted the rooms from his memory of the Fletcher School. The physical changes were intended to alter the psychology of the department by treating officers as if they were in a Western university classroom, not the facility that had previously trained the KGB. He knew that training needed to include shooting skills, but to prevent a military mind-set from seeping into domestic security, he didn't want to use the military's firing range. With no budget for a proper range, he found a room in the basement and rigged a moving-target apparatus using a hand drill and some ingenious hardware. It looked so good that foreign donors began to visit, netting Kaha extra money in donations. Even more important, the heads of other departments liked the facility so much that they began to ask him to train their people and remade their offices in a similar fashion. He persuaded the United States to take the academy's two best students for a study tour of the CIA and FBI headquarters each year, then published weekly class rankings to ensure a transparent, merit-based system.

After about two years, the ministries for police and intelligence merged. Hizanishvili had shown so much ability that he was promoted to train the entire police force. His boss wanted officers in the field immediately, but Kaha insisted on at least six weeks of training, and even that seemed paltry; he extended the trainings to eight weeks after his boss left. To devise an entire program from scratch, he and his team spent late nights focusing the curriculum on the most common jobs police engaged in each day. The instructors hired were not full-time professors but people from the field, and interactive verisimilitude improved their teaching.[136] "We'd say, 'Okay, it's a domestic violence call, a kid is crying in the background, the lady is crying, the guy is drunk, and the neighbor is drunk'—go," explained Kaha.[137] As with the intelligence academy, he wanted the police academy to feel modern and inspire professionalism. "I wanted the police to respect themselves, and they would do that if they knew that this institution is respecting them," he explained. The EU, the United States, and other international agencies donated fax machines, paintball equipment, and other useful items. They offered to build a new academy, but the process would have taken too long. Instead of aid, Kaha reduced the staff that had bloated under Shevardnadze's patronage, then used the savings to fix classrooms.

ENERGY AND INITIATIVE

When the police, much of the civil service, and many local government posts all disappear nearly overnight, as they did in Georgia, criminals lose their "protection." Before they could regroup, Saakashvili passed a slew of new laws, modeled after statutes in the United States and Italy, which allowed Georgia's Mafia to be arrested for taking part in a criminal organization. Thieves-in-law were so surprised that anyone would arrest them that they started shooting when police arrived at their doors, not thinking through the consequences. Dozens of police officers died in the line of duty.[138] But within weeks, most of the major mafiosi were in jail or had fled the country. Reformers were taking initiative, and criminal groups were forced into a reactive crouch.

Thomas de Waal, an expert on the Caucasus and another colleague of mine, described Saakashvili's hyperactivity: "Saakashvili would offer wave after wave of ideas. Some were real; some were PR. Every speech would have ten new initiatives and a string of foreign visitors coming to bless the project, and it would just keep everyone off balance."[139] More than one person told me that they thought Saakashvili was manic-depressive, or worse. Maybe so. But there was an upside. The tumult kept opponents like the Mafia off guard, and convinced citizens that something was changing.

Reformers have to log immense hours to keep up the momentum. The successful leaders I found shared stunning levels of energy. Senator Hubert Humphrey compared Lyndon Johnson to "a tidal wave. . . . He went through the walls. He'd come through a door, and he'd take the whole room over."[140] Mayor Orlando of Palermo was renowned for meetings stretching into the night. Uribe was a workaholic whose frenetic pace began before dawn.[141] Saakashvili was famous for daily cabinet sessions that began after the workday ended—at midnight. He met with a *New Yorker* reporter at 2:00 a.m., and his Secret Service detail in New York called him "the Energizer Bunny."[142]

ACCOUNTABILITY

As minister of justice in 2000, Saakashvili had tried to revive the judiciary by hiring new, non-Soviet judges, only to watch them degenerate into corruption. As president, he knew that accountability was crucial to making his changes stick.[143]

In a country with so few jobs, Georgia's new police recruits and civil service hires were thrilled to be employed. They were also warned that corruption or rudeness to citizens would get them fired. To reduce opportunities for bribery, fines and municipal fees were paid at banks rather than on the spot. The administration created private bank windows within municipal offices to make direct payment simple and erected kiosks to enable easy electronic payments at bus stops and other convenient locations. To reduce opportunities for bribery in exchange for faster service, most departments were forced to issue paperwork and permits in twenty to thirty days. If the applicant hadn't received papers at the end of the time, the license or permit was deemed granted.[144] The government installed video cameras around the country and in police cars and opened a hotline to take citizen complaints. Plainclothesmen posing as regular citizens caught malefactors in the police and bureaucracy. If a customs officer was found taking bribes, the entire shift would be punished, with no distinction made between small misappropriations and major offenses.[145] Police caught taking bribes were humiliated in front of colleagues. "We didn't fire them one by one," said Hizanishvili. "Instead, their boss would have a staff meeting. And all [the corrupt cops'] friends are sitting in the same room. That is when the inspector general would come in and walk them out and make them take off their insignia and everything right there."[146]

Accountability cost political capital and required tough choices. In Georgia, politicians had to override unions and civil service rules in order to eliminate large numbers of employees. Mayor Mockus did the same in Bogotá when he fired the entire body of transit police and the secretariat for public works—nearly six thousand people. He let five thousand more state employees go the following year.[147] To avoid civil service rules that obstructed such mass firing, Mockus simply eliminated entire agencies. Bogotá's legislature, which had used police and government posts for patronage, fought back. But unlike partisan meddling with the civil service, these mass purges of the corrupt had overwhelming public support, allowing Mockus to push the changes through over the heads of a recalcitrant city council.[148]

More than any particular configuration of programs, accountability let a broken state work well enough to fight violence quickly. Bogotá's police had long assumed that the city's violence was caused by criminals killing other criminals, so despite a murder rate of 80 per 100,000 when Mayor Mockus took office, they barely bothered to brief the new mayor on homicides. Mockus forced the police to present him with statistics. They showed what Mayor Guerrero had found in Cali a decade before: big spikes on weekends near bar districts suggested that ordinary Colombians were both victims and perpetrators. Hugo Acero Velásquez, who ran the police reform program for Mockus, told me, "When we started working, we had meetings monthly, then biweekly, weekly, then daily."[149] Mockus forced the police to address all deaths, not just those of people deemed "worthy." He demanded a culture that respected the dignity of all life—criminal or otherwise. Against the will of his city council, he abandoned SWAT-team-style tactics that alienated communities in favor of community policing to gain trust. His efforts worked: homicides dropped 70 percent from 1993 to 2004, a period spanning his two terms in office.[150]

In Medellín, Mayor Fajardo created a homicide statistics bureau independent of the government so bureaucrats couldn't cook the books. He released statistics at a big press conference at the end of each month, using the public pressure to deepen accountability within law enforcement and his bureaucracy. In Bihar, Nitish Kumar traveled around the country holding meetings with citizens. The carefully orchestrated symbolism mimicked a lord hearing his people's grievances. But Kumar handed out his ministers' cell phone numbers and demanded that they perform. Then he followed up. His police chief, Abhyanand, called each of the forty police superintendents every night between 9:00 and midnight for an update on cases registered, problems, and progress on their trials. Myles Frechette, the former American ambassador to Colombia, recounted that Uribe "gets up early in the morning, [and] calls his ministers. He calls the generals, something that was never done before, telling them, 'You screwed up, why didn't you do this, why didn't you do that?'"[151] The end of impunity started at the top and trickled down.

Eventually, oversight boards and systems for hiring and firing had to be institutionalized within functional government agencies to avoid a new form of personalistic despotism. But personal accountability could begin immediately, even in the most broken states. Swift, strong accountability set a different tone within the first weeks of a new administration, alerting government workers that a new sheriff was in town.

USING THE MEDIA TO TELL A NEW STORY

The rest of the country also needs to know change is afoot. In Medellín, Mayor Fajardo wanted his name in the papers connected to a positive activity every day.[152] He required his staff to search for a "good news" story to publicize every news cycle. This was self-serving. But the headlines convinced jaded citizens that their city could be reborn. President Saakashvili was similarly adept at publicity. Many of the people I interviewed mentioned his administration's television program, the most popular in the country. "They had this show where they would play an audio of someone paying a bribe, and they would send someone to this guy's house and then—live on TV! They would arrest the person and throw him in prison. It would scare the crap out of people," one lawyer told me. Saakashvili copied the idea from Hong Kong, which had started running a "true crime" miniseries in 1975 that depicted real cases from its new Independent Commission Against Corruption. The commission was so successful in fighting the endemic corruption that once bedeviled the city, and the show was so popular, that new series are still produced and aired four decades later.

Constant media attention is distasteful to many who witness the relentless PR on display. Theodore Roosevelt, who did more than any other politician to overturn America's corrupt, Gilded Age politics, signed a book deal to write about his heroics in the Spanish-American War . . . *before* he went into battle.[153] But whether strategic or the result of a deep personality flaw, the constant courting of the media made these governments effective. It wooed foreign businesses and aid donors to provide additional investment. Far more important, media stunts caught the attention of a cynical public. The stories convinced citizens that reform was possible and that they now had a government that was acting, constantly, on their behalf. People struggling against violence in their neighborhoods or trying to lead honest lives in the face of corruption saw their new governments as allies. The good news in the media made reform seem achievable, something everyone could participate in. It magnified politicians' efforts by helping people believe there was a fight that they could join, a leader they could rally behind. Astute politicians used the media to give people a new sense of what was possible, inspiring their populations to change themselves.

8

RECIVILIZATION

[The] fight against the Mafia was [like] a cart with two wheels, one law enforcement and the other culture. If one wheel turned without the other, the cart would go in circles. If both turned together, the cart would go forward.

—LEOLUCA ORLANDO, MAYOR OF PALERMO[1]

Antanas Mockus was the unlikely mayor who tackled violence in Bogotá. He burst into the public eye in 1993, when, as president of the National University of Colombia, he dropped his trousers and mooned an auditorium of rowdy students. A forty-something professor with an Amish beard and tendency to quote the philosopher Jürgen Habermas and the economist Douglass North, he was an unlikely politician. But the constitutional reform of 1991 empowered independents to run. Frustrated by Bogotá's gangs of pickpockets, rampant disrespect for ordinary laws, and a yearly homicide rate twenty times that of the United States, Mockus launched a campaign in 1994. Equally frustrated, nearly two-thirds of Bogotans elected him mayor, bestowing the kind of mandate that cows opposition.[2]

Mockus showed a flair for publicity. He hired more than four hundred mimes to patrol the city's streets, using humor to shock people into obeying traffic laws. He had government workers paint stars on the asphalt wherever pedestrians were killed by traffic to publicize more careful driving and walking. He walked Bogotá's neighborhoods in a Superman costume, proclaiming himself a "super citizen."

He asked men to stay at home and watch the kids while he hosted a massive party of 700,000 women throughout Bogotá to publicize safer public spaces. Every stunt brought Mockus more media adoration. The math professor turned mayor became a local and international sensation.

Jaime Castro, Mockus's predecessor, had been a political heavyweight in Colombia. A charming man with a slim physique, silver hair, and an affable but aristocratic mien, Castro was also a reformer. As a delegate to Colombia's constitutional assembly in 1991, he slipped a few words into the constitution requiring a new governing law for the capital. The following year, when he became the capital's first directly elected mayor, he began collecting ideas for what would make the city more governable. At the end of the year, he crafted his notes into two hundred articles for the mandated legislation, providing Bogotá's future mayors with greater powers vis-à-vis the federal government and corrupt city council.[3] Castro adopted the management techniques that make politicians successful in combating Privilege Violence. He assembled a team of smart, competent, apolitical technocrats. He refused to engage in patronage with the city council, forcing them to fill out appointment cards noting the exact nature of their meeting with him to create transparency in city government.[4] He focused his time in office on the most substantive problems, such as writing the governing law and collecting taxes so that the city could have a budget for public services.[5] Mockus credits Castro's reforms with enabling him to reduce Bogotá's immense murder rate.

But when Castro left office in 1994, though Bogotá's fundamentals had been transformed, no one knew it. The downtown was still run by drug gangs and paramilitaries. Slums riddled the city center, and the peripheries remained at the mercy of guerrillas. Violence peaked a year into Castro's term, in 1993, and was hardly lower when he left office. Fairer taxation, fighting corruption, and the core improvements to how the city operated had no visible effect. Castro was such an unpopular mayor that he was nearly impeached. Despite his lifetime of public service and years spent authoring a regular newspaper column, he has few media profiles and, as far as I could find, no puff pieces touting his reforms. The memoir of his mayorship was titled, aptly, *Three Years of Solitude*.

The contrast between the two mayors matters, because, though Castro was the more serious policy maker, Mockus discerned a more salient insight. Privilege Violence can't be fought through government policy alone. Once violence and corruption have woven themselves into the civic fabric, the fight also requires change within society itself.

Politicians who pull their countries out of immense violence have to combat a vast public normalization of everyday criminality and a sense that with the state absent, people must look after their interests by any means necessary. No other politician would do so much to lay the infrastructure for reform in Bogotá as Castro. Yet if the public was not engaged, change couldn't extend beyond what one man could manage. Conversely, none of Mockus's stunts directly altered the city's crime rate, according to one of Colombia's premier anti-violence think tanks.[6] But they created a new mood that would be even more vital, by jump-starting social change far broader than anything Mockus could control directly.

Fighting illegal parking and littering seems petty when confronted with massive homicide, but enforcing these everyday laws exercised civic muscles. It let people know that the government was back in charge and that citizens had a role to play in making their societies work. Instead of fighting crime with zero-tolerance policies that criminalized large swaths of the population, Mockus invited citizens to self-police their behavior and take on the responsibilities of citizenship.[7] Bogotans rose to the challenge.

Governments cannot directly end social violence without resorting to mammoth, totalitarian repression. They need society to reassert morality. That isn't hard for traffic rules and litterbugs, but when it comes to endemic violence, it's an enormous and unrealistic request. People need to trust that calling the police to report a murder or telling a drug dealer to get off their stoop won't get them killed, when everything in their experience tells them it could. Such a leap of faith is too much to ask of most people. So few populations can heal by themselves.

To rebuild social trust, governments must prove they are serious about governing inclusively, retake the monopoly on force, and enforce the laws equally. They need to make these changes all at once to keep entrenched interests off balance and unable to twist the new order to their benefit. Only then can people regain enough agency and trust to fight violence in their neighborhoods. Governments and societies recover in tandem, propelling each other forward like two wheels on a cart.

BUILDING COLLECTIVE EFFICACY AND SOCIAL TRUST

Jane Jacobs, a New York journalist, self-taught expert in urban design, and personal hero of mine, first identified the role communities play in policing themselves. In the 1960s, Jacobs pitted herself against Robert Moses, a powerful city planner who had ruled New York City for three decades. Moses had a vision of a New York composed of tall apartment buildings surrounded by ample parking, separated by parks, and connected by highways.[8] When he threatened to ram an expressway through the West Village in lower Manhattan, Jacobs organized angry neighbors and decried the plan at public meetings. To save her neighborhood, she wrote her groundbreaking 1961 work, *The Death and Life of Great American Cities*. In it, she explained that "no amount of police can enforce civilization when the normal, casual enforcement of it has broken down."[9]

An urban planner's dream city may look orderly on paper, but it can leave streets dangerously devoid of life. Absent a community of eyes on the streets, people are vulnerable. The men playing dominoes on the street corner, the storekeepers, and the pedestrians walking their dogs deter crime long before police enter the picture. Jacobs wrote about a man trying to lead a little girl off a West Village street. As the girl protested, neighbors gathered in doorways, shopkeepers poked their heads out of stores, customers stopped shopping and cocked their ears. Unbeknownst to him, the man was quickly surrounded. He turned out to be the girl's father, but the point was made: crime and violence are less likely when people feel ownership over their neighborhoods. "The public peace . . . of cities is not kept primarily by the police, necessary as police are. It is kept primarily by an intricate, almost unconscious, network of voluntary controls and standards among the people themselves, and enforced by the people themselves," Jacobs wrote.[10] Cities whose physical structures encourage chance run-ins and loose relationships among neighbors are safer. Regular interactions help communities create norms and uphold implicit rules like "don't litter" and "don't pee in the street"— the sorts of inhibitions that Norbert Elias's civilization theory suggests also keeps violence down.[11]

Jacobs wasn't a scholar. She didn't hold a doctorate or even a college degree. But she was a uniquely astute observer.[12] Research has since confirmed her observations. A few years after Jacobs published her groundbreaking book, an academic named Felton James Earls locked himself in a soundproof room for thirty-six hours to map the effects of various sounds on a cat's brain. When he emerged, he found Chicago engulfed in riots: Martin Luther King Jr. had been shot the night before. Earls decided he couldn't spend his life in a lab and instead became an acclaimed scholar of criminality.[13] In the violent 1990s, Earls led a group of researchers conducting one of the largest and most expensive criminological studies in America. They tried to gain a holistic understanding of life in various Chicago neighborhoods. A decade and $51 million in grant money later, they wrote up their conclusions.[14] One of their strongest findings is the importance of what they called "collective efficacy."

Violence in America, as in most countries, clusters in places that are poor, where minorities live and opportunities are rare. A few Chicago neighborhoods, however, had every characteristic predictive of high rates of crime but were surprisingly safe. Earls and his team found that the communities with less violence were those where neighbors felt connected to one another, trusted each other, and were willing to uphold informal social norms.[15] It was just as Jane Jacobs had observed.

In these neighborhoods, Earls discovered, people felt individual efficacy, or a sense of control over their own lives. They also believed that together they could affect their communities. That collective efficacy depends on trust. Low levels of social trust are correlated with more poverty and more murder.[16] Greater trust allows communities to fight problems before they grow and enables the informal social controls that keep violence down.[17] Trust is a society's immune system.

The Harvard political scientist Robert Putnam, author of the acclaimed book *Bowling Alone*, studies social trust, particularly the trust among people with loose ties to one another such as shopkeepers and regular customers.[18] His landmark study of Italy argues that greater trust and the many loose relationships it fostered made northern Italy richer and its democracy more functional than the South of the country.[19] As the Sicilian prosecutor Paolo Borsellino said before he was killed by the mob, the existence of the Mafia in Sicily was "not the price of poverty, but the cost of distrust."[20]

While Putnam treated trust as something rooted in centuries of history and culture, Borsellino was right.[21] Violence could destroy even deep cultures of trust quite quickly. Putnam found that the region of Piedmont, in northern Italy near the borders of France and Switzerland, had some of the highest rates of social trust in the country, while Sicily ranked among the lowest.[22] But when the 'Ndràngheta Mafia moved to the Piedmont town of Bardonecchia during a construction boom in the late 1960s and early 1970s, social trust waned. At first, construction trades tried to organize anti-Mafia union rallies. Intimidation and a few murders stopped workers from attending. Judges received threatening calls. A police officer was transferred after writing a report on one of the mafiosi. A lawyer in charge of building applications had his house set on fire. By the 1990s, the local city council was firmly in the pocket of the mob. Fear pervaded the once friendly construction industry.[23] In a few decades, the Mafia had destroyed trust in a locale more culturally similar to Switzerland than to Sicily.

Jane and Peter Schneider studied the Mafia while living in Sicily for more than a decade during the height of Cosa Nostra's violence and its downfall. They found that the Mafia entangled people in social relationships, then used a sense of obligation to weasel favors that embroiled regular people in Mafia business. To reduce their chances of accidental contact with the Mafia, many Sicilians avoided forming relationships with strangers.[24] In Mexico, as murder rose in Ciudad Juárez, families stopped holding weddings, birthdays, and *quinceañeras*. They stuck to themselves, because shirttail relations and loose friendships could inadvertently lead to connections with the drug trade and thus to violence.[25] Some cultures might begin with higher levels of trust, as Putnam claimed, but violent criminals could quickly destroy that reservoir of resilience, irrespective of culture. Yet this more malleable understanding of social trust had a positive side. As Earls found in Chicago, trust can also emerge in the most inhospitable of circumstances.

How can a society build the trust and collective efficacy needed to eradicate violence when violence chips away at these very qualities? Communities could, theoretically, bootstrap their way to greater trust. The brave souls who started the programs in my "Happy Stories" folder could catalyze this process. But under an inimical government, these efforts often fail. Neighbors who build a community garden, only to have the government appropriate the land for a crony-connected casino, will feel disempowered and cynical. Eating spaghetti with police after a Sunday soccer match, only to face brutality and billy clubs on Monday, will unite people over shared distrust of the government.

Governments are essential to building social trust, according to Bo Rothstein, a political scientist who spent years running the Quality of Government Institute. Based in Sweden, his institute collected thousands of data points on the quality of government across Europe, comparing the data with the levels of social trust people claimed in surveys. He found that social trust grows when people trust their governments, particularly when they believe in the fairness of the courts and police.[26] When governments enforce laws equally so people know that merit will be rewarded and those who break laws will be punished, it becomes easier for people to cooperate and trust each other.[27] These two kinds of trust—in governments and in fellow citizens—were just what Randy Roth, Gary LaFree, and the other violence researchers had discovered brought homicide rates down.

A BIG BANG: GOVERNMENTS JUMP-START RECIVILIZATION

How can a new, reform-minded government prove that it is enforcing the law, after years of popular cynicism? When police are corrupt, bureaucracy is broken, judges have no books, and soldiers have no bullets, where should reform begin?

Everywhere at once. Countries caught in Privilege Violence are stuck in a vicious but interconnected system. They need a major disruption to alter the foundations of power and prove to society that change is real and likely to last.

When my older daughter was a baby, I would sit on the floor with her building towers of blocks. I would add the yellow rectangle to the blue square, put the red triangle on top, and—BAM!—she would knock the tower down. Like all infants, Cimarron was a miniature tyrant. We occasionally referred to her as "Cim" Jong Un after the baby-faced North Korean dictator. In countries with a few problematic pockets in need of reform, small incremental steps can lead to big improvements, each block building one atop the other.[28] But in countries that have a predatory elite who have constructed a structure of power to keep themselves on top, the incremental model doesn't work. Small reforms will be allowed to progress within bounds. But threaten the actual structure upholding power, and those who stand to lose will knock everything down. If systemic change occurs piecemeal or pauses, those who benefited from the old system figure out how to twist the new order to their advantage. It takes massive change on many fronts simultaneously to disarm entrenched interests long enough for reformers to gain a foothold.[29]

Alina Mungiu-Pippidi, a Romanian anticorruption activist turned academic, manages some of the largest studies on corruption in Europe. With Bo Rothstein, she documented modern and historical cases of countries that beat severe corruption, a common counterpart to Privilege Violence.[30] Incremental change worked, they discovered, in historical instances where monarchies forced gradual reforms from the top. But in the few cases where democracies substantially improved, positive reforms happened fast and on many fronts, simultaneously.[31]

Popular mandates sour if they aren't acted upon quickly. In Colombia, Uribe explained that "one of the most important strategies at the beginning of my presidency was to focus on 'early victories,' quick, tangible signs of progress that would demonstrate to Colombians that our government's policies were feasible."[32] In Georgia, a leading figure in the revolutionary administration, David Bakradze, told me, "Our team knew that we had to do the most painful things ... in the first two years, so that the most painful part of the job was done when we still had that wave of revolutionary support behind us." Foreign donors begged the new Georgian administration to slow down. "Europeans, they wanted a gradual, slower process, with planning, development of strategies, action plans, and piloting of reforms," explained Eka Tkeshelashvili, the deputy minister of the interior who oversaw security service reform. "We had no luxury of wasting time. We had to seize the momentum and deliver rather than plan. The accelerated pace was essential for us to implement game-changing, transformational reforms."[33] Staffers and bureaucrats were expected to make change quickly, collect data, and iterate until they got a program right, more Silicon Valley than central planning.

Media coverage, and reforms chosen for their symbolism as well as their concrete impact, let citizens know that something new was afoot.

UNITING COMMUNITIES

In Medellín, change was embodied by the city's gondolas. Medellín is nestled in a river valley and surrounded by mountains. Its business and industry are in the flatlands, while the poor live in slums careening up the steep hillsides and melting into the surrounding jungle. For slum dwellers, getting to work could take hours navigating hundreds of stairs cut into the hills or a long, stomach-churning bus ride along switchback roads. In the early 2000s article after article touted Mayor Fajardo's gondolas, which connected the slums to the subway system. Gondolas united the city. Gondolas ended the violence.[34] Every foreign delegation to Medellín rode in one. On my first morning in the city, I hopped on the subway to see them for myself. The gondolas *were* a wonder. Swathed in sunlight and free from graffiti, they united the city in a single view and cut commutes from what were then the most violent parts of town from hours to minutes.

But I was skeptical. Medellín's homicide rate had begun its decline in 2003. The first gondola didn't start running until a year later.[35] It's possible that the gondolas could have accelerated the trend. One study claimed that homicides in gondola-connected neighborhoods had declined 66 percent more than in non-connected areas, an astounding number if true.[36] But this was correlation and could have resulted from a variety of causes.[37] The gondolas were one of many reforms Mayor Fajardo enacted simultaneously. And even if the gondolas reduced crime where they existed, they didn't actually connect many people. In 2008, when the drop in violence was well along, Medellín had only one gondola line, with few stops.[38] The majority of Medellín's poor still faced long uphill walks to reach a station. Only 10 percent of the poor even rode the gondolas, according to another study.[39]

Searching for insights into Medellín's rebirth, I met with the former private secretary to Mayor Fajardo, David Escobar Arango, in a Medellín pizza parlor. David was smart, idealistic, and with black hair curling down his neck, a younger version of his former boss. Having spent years publicizing Fajardo's successes, he had his patter down. When he started to tell me the heroic story of an old lady who finally got to see the city she had lived in her whole life thanks to the gondola, I grew a little impatient. "Sure," I said. "Gondolas are great. But I used to work in a poor part of the Bronx with kids who never came into Manhattan. There was a subway, it cost a buck, and it only took fifteen minutes. They had the money. But few ever got on the train. Manhattan was a different world; those kids were cut off by a lot more than just transportation."

"It's not enough to build a gondola," David agreed. "But it opens the door, gives the opportunity for the rest of the intervention." He was co-authoring a book about "social urbanism," he explained, and he shared its thesis with me. "Symbolic changes to the physical fabric of a city help people feel more connected to each other, and give them a chance to meet the 'other.'"[40] It wasn't just the gondolas, he explained. Fajardo also cleaned up graffiti-covered parks and opened libraries built by star architects in the slums. Together, these efforts offered people dignity. The quality of the programs, he said, was important. "It gets people to cross boundaries and go to areas they wouldn't otherwise go, to take a new look at areas they had written off," David explained. The goal was to inspire people from all social classes to leave their comfort zones and become part of the same civic fabric. Fajardo's administration held a set of free public concerts in 2006. The police chief wanted to stop the shows, convinced there would be violence. There wasn't. The concerts encouraged all types of citizens to travel to areas in which they had never previously set foot. The city put Christmas lights along the river, an area of bus stations, casinos, and bars that had been beset by homicides at the beginning of Fajardo's administration. "We used these as symbols to show ourselves that we could coexist peacefully."

The construction projects themselves were just the vehicle, David was saying. They connected people across social boundaries and rebuilt trust among citizens and between previously marginalized citizens and their government. "In the area where formerly the corpses were dropped and where the women's prison is, we built a school, library, and park. In the area that was the trash dump, where a slum has formed, we reclaimed land and built the best community cultural center. It's not just the buildings. It's a change in narrative, a change in the way people feel about the place," he told me. Earls had proven that increasing social trust among people in the same community (known as "bonding social capital") deepens collective efficacy and reduces neighborhood violence. David was explaining that encouraging loose relationships among people from different communities (or "bridging social capital") was equally important for building trust and reducing violence across a city, or country.[41] Highly visible public works, when combined with deeper institutional reforms that brought communities together, were one way to build these bridges and reestablish the social contract. The concrete assertion through symbols, public works, and government programs that different groups are part of the same civic community helps people understand their role in society—who they are, who their fellow citizens are, what is expected of those who govern, and what is expected of them as citizens.

In Medellín, Mayor Fajardo allocated 40 percent of his budget for education in 2007. In 2002, only 20 percent of Medellín's students met national averages; by 2009, 80 percent of those tested did.[42] In Bogotá, Mayor Mockus incorporated 316 illegal slums into a new urban plan, providing them with water, sewers, electricity, and roads.[43] In Palermo, Mayor Orlando fixed streetlights, collected trash, and reopened the blighted Teatro Massimo, a huge theater in the center of the city that had been closed for decades thanks to Mafia-construction delays.[44] He renamed streets and piazzas for anti-Mafia fighters, persuaded elementary schools to teach a "culture of lawfulness" curriculum, and inspired students to clean up monuments defaced by years of neglect. In Georgia, Saakashvili transformed Tbilisi by putting up stunningly modern buildings and bridges. They grabbed attention in a land of nineteenth-century architecture and Soviet apartment blocks. Clear glass awnings and translucent walls in the Houses of Justice and police stations were practical and symbolic: nothing could be hidden. In Bihar, Nitish Kumar built 17,003 kilometers of roads and 336 bridges that literally connected the state, cutting travel time by hours.[45] His administration gave away tens of thousands of bicycles to schoolgirls with good grades. Each weekday, they filled the streets with blue uniforms and flying white scarves, living symbols that the state was investing in all its people.

ENFORCING THE LAWS

Programs that help the poor and create a more inclusive society are usually the purview of the Left. Law and order is generally favored by the Right. Rebuilding social trust so that society can pull itself out of violence requires both. In Naples, Mayor Borsellino had tried to pedestrianize piazzas without tightening law enforcement, and the mob soon took them over once again. Mexico's Ciudad Juárez brought in reformers from Bogotá and Medellín to try to re-create the magical urban planning solutions championed by those cities. And violence did come down in Juárez, but the drop was temporary. The governments of Armenia and Azerbaijan worried that the honest cops in neighboring Georgia would encourage their citizens to expect the same. They bought new uniforms and cars for their police but then allowed law enforcement to remain just as corrupt as ever.[46]

Compassion, flashy public works, and more serious initiatives to create a sense of shared civic community are essential, but not enough to jump-start recivilization. Encouraging society to self-police requires governments to enforce the laws. The state has to show that impunity is over. In Bihar, Kumar's administration arrested multiple notorious criminal politicians within weeks of taking office, including members of the ruling party such as Anand Mohan Singh. "When the *bahubalis* started getting convicted ... it was a game changer," explained Shaibal Gupta, who founded one of Bihar's most well-regarded think tanks. Singh's conviction was particularly symbolic. Gupta declared: "There was one *bahubali* who started crying in the courts. He was a very big *bahubali*, and he got a death sentence."[47] Not all the *bahubalis* were removed, but the arrests and long sentences for a few were enough for people to feel that the state was beginning to take charge.[48] Kumar also reopened a notorious case concerning anti-Muslim riots in Bhagalpur fifteen years before, when twelve hundred Muslims had been murdered and no one was brought to justice.

In Georgia, the minister of energy was arrested. So was the minister of transport and communication, the chief of the railway company, and the head of the Civil Aviation Administration. The president of the football federation and multiple other oligarchs met the same fate.[49] "These dramatic arrests, people ate it up, people loved it because for so many years they had seen these fat cats taking everything they weren't supposed to, and seeing these guys get arrested buoyed the mood of the country. It was empowering," a journalist in Tbilisi told me.[50]

"Once you change how people view their lives, their lives can change too. When people started to believe it, then people felt there was this possibility. People were not going to pay the doctor this bribe, because they don't have to; there's a police officer here, and these people will go to jail." She brought up the reality-TV show that depicted mafiosi being captured at night in their underwear. The images of mobsters stumbling out of bed, bleary-eyed, their flaccid bellies hanging over tighty-whities, defused fear.

Symbols are a shorthand that citizens use to judge whether their country is on the right track, and so symbolism is a crucial language for politicians to convey that they are breaking with the past. Vano Merabishvili, Georgia's former interior minister and Kaha's boss, explained, "Before the Rose Revolution, the best car was the criminal's car—better than the state official's car—and the best houses were the criminals' houses. Now it is absolutely different. They are sitting in prison. No one is listening to them, and businessmen and state servants have the good cars and houses."[51] Georgian schoolchildren stopped telling pollsters that their career ambition was to join the Mafia.

TAXATION AND REPRESENTATION

For years, researchers have asked people around the world to play the "Public Goods Game" to test a theory. In the game, players place money into a central fund, which is then doubled. Just like governments with tax revenue, students then get to redistribute the money among participants. When played in countries like Russia, Ukraine, Greece, and Saudi Arabia, where people feel it is okay to cheat on taxes, skip subway fares, and otherwise skirt the rules, players were less equitable, refusing to give back what people put in the pot.[52] The game mirrors real life. Robert Putnam found that when people think their fellow citizens are evading the law, they do the same.[53] In states where people feel a greater degree of trust and connection, they are more likely to pay their taxes. In her pioneering study of taxation and legitimacy, the Stanford political scientist Margaret Levi found that citizens pay their share when they trust in the fairness of their government.[54]

In other words, governments that enforce their laws and increase social trust make more money. Taxes, in turn, help strengthen deliberately weakened states by providing funds to buy cars for police, equipment for militaries, and streetlights for cities, as well as funding programs that create a more inclusive society.

Taxation does far more than just provide cash. Governments can also earn money by selling oil and collecting foreign aid. Yet there is still a bit of the stationary bandit in state building. Regimes that are able to profit without relying on citizens to work have less incentive to build economies that provide jobs. Extractive wealth from oil and minerals is highly correlated with repressive government. Countries that depend on oil exports for most of their GDP are almost entirely autocracies.[55] Public officials who skim wealth also benefit from keeping people too poor and ignorant to challenge their rule. Foreign aid can similarly "sever the bonds of accountability between rulers and ruled," cautions renowned democracy scholar Larry Diamond.[56] Additionally, it often arrives in feast-or-famine clumps that make planning difficult and force funds to be spent on foreign governments' timelines.[57] Moreover, aid makes governments address the priorities of outsiders, which may not coincide with common sense or with the desires of local people.[58]

Taxes, on the other hand, establish a direct and accountable relationship between a government and its citizenry. Of course, taxes can be misappropriated by corrupt officials. But they also provide a self-corrective mechanism.[59] When people pay taxes, they expect their governments to deliver, and they hold government institutions to account.[60] I spoke with a security guard in Albania in 2000, three years after government corruption and the collapse of a massive pyramid scheme caused an economic implosion, prison breaks, riots, and the looting of armories. "I wish the government collected taxes," he mused wistfully, "because if we had taxation, we would have representation."

In each country that successfully fought violence, as the government showed its commitment to governing for all people, and enforced the rules, tax revenues increased so that politicians could rebuild the state.

Colombia, for instance, received $9.4 billion from the United States between 1999 and 2016 in military equipment and development aid under Plan Colombia. Yet even such massive amounts of aid accounted for only about 5 percent of the total spent on security and governance; the vast majority came from Colombians.[61] President Uribe coaxed local businessmen to pay a security tax to fight the FARC guerrillas. Taxing the wealthy is rarely the strategy adopted by conservative security leaders, but it was essential to Colombia's rebirth.

After the Rose Revolution in Georgia, a series of foreign governments and foundations provided aid to top up salaries so that the government could hire competitively with private sector firms. The aid was crucial and timely: reform might have been impossible if such fast and flexible funding wasn't there to get the best people into position quickly. But Saakashvili also collected taxes, and within a year Georgia had enough money in the bank to pay back its foreign donors.[62] In Palermo, Orlando gained the funds to remake his city by collecting past-due taxes. People started to pay up during his term, thanks to a mix of bureaucratic improvements and greater trust. By 2002, Bogotá was collecting three times the revenue it had collected in 1990. When Mayor Mockus asked Bogotans to *voluntarily* give 10 percent more in extra taxes, over sixty-three thousand people complied.[63]

Societies and governments propel each other to recivilize. As governments enforce the laws and demonstrate their commitment to serve all their citizens, society increases its trust and gains a sense of collective efficacy. Stronger institutions, aided by increased tax revenue, enable governments to further fight violence. Each wheel on the cart drives the other forward—but as the state strengthens, the virtuous cycle can turn vicious. Sometimes society has to put on the brakes.

9

CENTRALIZATION AND SURVEILLANCE

The solution to the problem of the Mafia is to make the State work.

—ANTI-MAFIA PROSECUTOR PAOLO BORSELLINO[1]

For a Mafia man, Tommaso Buscetta was not very good at staying out of jail. He began his career in Sicily's black market after World War II and then became a Mafia assassin. In 1963, he planted a car bomb to kill a rival Mafia family. It exploded early as suspicious police crowded around the vehicle. Seven policemen and two bystanders were killed. Buscetta fled to New York, where he connected with the Gambino mob and ran drug operations up and down the East Coast. He was arrested and flew to Brazil upon his release, where he ran another Mafia operation moving drugs from Latin America to Europe. In 1972, Brazilian police found 132 pounds of heroin on his estate, and he was jailed again, tortured, then extradited to Italy, where he had been convicted in absentia for the murders he committed decades before.[2]

Buscetta was sentenced to Ucciardone, a prison on Palermo's waterfront and the notorious home of Sicily's Mafia for over a century. He moved into its hospital wing for the next four years. He didn't need nursing. Instead, he used the more permissive environment to conduct business. Expensive long-distance calls let him manage his global drug empire. He saw friends and family (by then he had managed to marry three wives simultaneously in Sicily, Mexico, and Brazil and had fathered seven children) and often dined on delivery from good restaurants, complete with wine and champagne. The prison authorities knew, but they didn't mind. The Mafia helped them police the jail, keeping the more violent prisoners in check. "Men of honor" were seen as polite and gentlemanly, unlike the left-wing terrorists and political prisoners who filled cells during the 1970s, trying to indoctrinate fellow inmates, riling them up with hunger strikes, and annoying their jailers. Prison authorities considered the Mafia members guests and treated them that way.

In 1980, Buscetta secured a day release from Ucciardone. Instead of returning that evening, he simply flew back to Brazil. He was in South America when the Corleone clan slaughtered his family—killing thirty-three people, nearly everyone he was close to—to gain control of Sicily's drug market as part of a rampage known as the second Mafia war.[3] When Brazilian police arrested Buscetta again in 1984, he tried to commit suicide on the plane back to Italy. The Corleones had powerful influence over Ucciardone, and Buscetta knew the fate in store for him was worse than mere death.

To save his life, Buscetta became the first Italian mafioso to turn state's witness. (Actually, he was the second, but speaking out was so vast a breach of the Mafia's tradition of silence that the police ignored the first turncoat, assuming he was mentally ill.[4]) Buscetta's testimony gave Giovanni Falcone, the soon-to-be-famous Mafia prosecutor, his first big break. Buscetta offered insights into how the Mafia functioned that enabled Falcone, Paolo Borsellino, and their prosecutorial colleagues to try hundreds of mafiosi in a high-security chamber underneath Ucciardone built strong enough to withstand a rocket attack. In 1985, 474 defendants stood in cages along the walls as anti-aircraft planes protected the grounds.[5] The judges listened to testimony for nearly two years—three judges, a precaution in case anything unfortunate happened to the presiding magistrate during proceedings.

The maxi-trial, as it was known, convicted 360 mafiosi in December 1987. It seemed like a major turning point in the fight against Sicily's mob. But Italy's government was still committed to maintaining power through Privilege Violence. Three years later, only 60 defendants remained behind bars. Most had gotten off on minor technicalities, while those still jailed operated their enterprises from prison and in cushy hospital wards, as Buscetta had done. A few crusading prosecutors couldn't change much—at first.

A new boss transferred Falcone and Borsellino and broke up the pool of prosecutors who shared information. It was a death sentence; the lawmen knew that their cohesion and collective knowledge protected each from Mafia murder. Falcone was kicked up to the Ministry of Justice in Rome, where the Mafia and its government protectors hoped he would no longer meddle in Sicilian affairs. In his new post, however, Falcone crafted laws to catch mobsters. He nudged aside Judge Corrado Carnevale—the Mafia's favorite magistrate, known as "the Sentence Killer" for his ability to get cases thrown out on technicalities—from hearing maxi-trial appeals. An honest judge confirmed the sentences and overturned many previous acquittals. Retrials held the next year sentenced a host of mafiosi to lives in prison. But the gains were fragile. The Mafia's political protectors were still in place. Anger over these retrials was what drove the Corleone clan to murder Falcone and Borsellino.

A few days after Borsellino's assassination, a flock of helicopters pulled alongside military transport planes on Ucciardone's prison grounds. A set of vans drove up and disgorged their prisoners. Four hundred inmates, all Mafia men, shuffled toward the aircraft en route to more secure locations, including a prison standing alone on an otherwise uninhabited island. From now on, each would be held in solitary confinement. Their letters would be read and censored. They were forbidden telephone contact with the outside world. There would be no association with other prisoners. No packages. No space for recreation or sports. No meetings with anyone other than family members, and those were permitted only once per month. The people of Palermo were in the streets protesting the murders of Falcone and Borsellino, and the Italian state needed to demonstrate that it was taking action. The prisoners were feeling the effects of 41-bis, a new provision Italy's government had just incorporated into its penal code.

In 2001, the European Court of Human Rights declared 41-bis a violation of the European Convention on Human Rights.[6] In 2007, a judge in Los Angeles ruled that it was tantamount to torture.[7] The penalties have been relaxed slightly. But Italy's top mafiosi are still subject to 41-bis. It's the only way Italy has found to prevent mafiosi from ordering assassinations through gestures to family members or running their enterprises through consigliere lawyers. It's a problem shared by other countries facing organized crime. In the United States in 2001, the FBI used thousands of hours of surveillance to indict forty-five members of the Genovese crime family. The wiretaps found that the operation was controlled by Vincent Gigante, a seventy-three-year-old man serving a twelve-year sentence for racketeering. He was running the family from the medical ward of a prison in Fort Worth, Texas.[8]

THE TOOLS TO FIGHT VIOLENCE

Only when a government is in place that actually wants to fight violence does it make sense to look at what policies work. In each successful case, I found governments turned to three tools: intelligence and surveillance, informants who can offer inside information (with witness protection programs to keep them alive), and asset seizure. These were the three ingredients the United States baked into legislation as America tackled its Mafia in the 1970s. That is no coincidence. Privilege Violence is a form of collusion between violent groups and members of government. Rooting it out requires the tools used to fight criminal conspiracy, along with one additional requirement specific to deliberately weakened, criminalized states: centralizing power. These instruments are essential to recovery. Yet wielding them to just the right degree is difficult. Politicians who get it wrong send their countries veering away from the path of security toward a new round of violence—this time, from the state.

RICO: Beating Organized Crime

The snack bar at the University of Notre Dame Law School once offered a sandwich called the RICO, advertised by the slogan: "Everything comes under it."[9] The joke is an allusion to a piece of legislation known as the Racketeer Influenced and Corrupt Organizations Act (RICO) written by Robert Blakey, a former student and current professor at the university. The act provided U.S. law enforcement with a new way of thinking about and combating crime, one that captured the far-reaching and protean nature of criminal organizations. Key provisions of the RICO law would spread from the United States to Sicily, Georgia, and around the world, providing ammunition to enable law enforcement to finally tackle violent groups entrenched within legitimate politics and business.

As a child growing up in the 1940s, Blakey was fascinated by gangster movies.[10] At Notre Dame Law School, he edited an article about a failed attempt to prosecute a Mafia plot after a 1957 conference in Apalachin, New York, brought together approximately seventy-five criminals involved in businesses ranging from grocery stores to funeral homes, coal companies, and construction. After graduating, Blakey joined the Department of Justice honors program. It put him in the Organized Crime and Racketeering Section, which had been created just six years before. Yet on a rather deflating first day of work in August 1960, his boss took him out to lunch and told him that the Mafia didn't exist. It was a common view at the time. J. Edgar Hoover, then director of the FBI, asked his head of intelligence to determine if the Mafia was real after the Apalachin meeting. The department concluded that it was. Hoover rejected the report as "baloney." He believed that while there were small bands of organized criminals and gangsters across the country, no central structure tied them together.[11]

President John F. Kennedy and his brother Robert, who became attorney general in 1961, disagreed. In *The Enemy Within*, Robert Kennedy wrote, "If we do not on a national scale attack organized criminals . . . they will destroy us."[12] The Kennedys invigorated Blakey's department, but after JFK's assassination Robert Kennedy left his post to run for Senate, and the fight against the Mafia cooled. The department emptied out. Blakey moved back to Indiana and became a professor. From Notre Dame Law School, he taught about organized crime and spent the middle of the 1960s consulting part-time to President Johnson's Commission on Crime and then to the National Commission on Reform of Federal Criminal Laws.[13] Reflecting on how inadequate U.S. law was to fighting the Mafia, he drafted much of the Racketeer Influenced and Corrupt Organizations Act, a piece of legislation that Senator John McClellan would steward until it passed both houses of Congress nearly unanimously in 1970.

The RICO Act addressed a huge stumbling block to tackling orga-nized crime in America. As in other countries whose legal system descends from England, U.S. criminal law is designed to prosecute one criminal for one crime committed at one time. That makes it easy to convict a person for murder, but very difficult to convict an orga-nized crime boss who presides over a business conglomerate engaged in many crimes over a long period, almost none of them committed directly by the top don.

The RICO Act tackled this problem. First, it recognized that ongoing criminal enterprises could exist—from the Mafia to drug cartels, street gangs, and looser conspiracies.[14] It covered crimes rang-ing from violence to the distribution of illegal goods; corruption in government, labor, and management relations; and extortion. Thus, it captured the white-collar crimes that proliferate during periods of false peace as well as the murders that spike in eras of violence. The RICO Act mandated that if a group could be proven to be involved in a pattern of crime, any person who was knowingly part of the orga-nization could be charged with those crimes and sentenced for up to twenty years. It didn't matter that the cartel leader didn't kill anyone personally; under the RICO Act he could be prosecuted for murder.

Blakey thought the law was handing law enforcement the keys to unlock their hardest cases. But laws do little, on their own. Mexico adopted a law against organized crime in November 1996, but drug violence has only grown over the last two decades. In the United States, RICO was such a radical departure from standard procedures that no one used it. Blakey began offering summer seminars at Cornell Law School to show law enforcement its worth.[15] Between sessions on how to use the new provisions, he tried to inspire his students with screenings of the gangster flick Little Caesar, which had sparked his own devotion to crime fighting. Blakey claimed that the RICO law was drafted to change the end of the movie, when the protagonist (not coincidentally named Rico) is shot in an alley by the police while Big Boy, the wealthy man behind the mob, escapes justice.

Prosecuting organized crime the RICO way, however, required a great deal of investigative policing. The painstaking detective work that seems de rigueur to anyone who watches police procedurals on television today was almost unimaginable in the 1970s. A decade passed before two iconoclastic lawmen first used the law in a prosecution.[16] By 1992, however, RICO had helped bring the entire New York mob to justice.[17]

Intelligence and Surveillance

Blakey also wrote Title III of the 1968 Omnibus Crime Control and Safe Streets Act, which authorized electronic surveillance at the federal and state levels with the approval of a court.[18] The FBI had used surveillance occasionally, but 1960s-era technology was poor and given to static, so common practice was to use wiretaps or bugs to gain information on a single individual committing a single crime, then begin prosecution. Eventually, the FBI began to surveil multiple phones over longer periods to build complex cases against interlocking criminal conspiracies.[19]

But wiretaps were exotic. Most law-enforcement officers had never used one. Police and prosecutors were evaluated on their numbers of arrests, so there was no incentive to spend months piecing together a single case, no matter how big the target. Giovanni Falcone himself was chastised by his department for "not making statistics," because he devoted his time to unraveling Cosa Nostra rather than solving a multitude of fast, routine cases.[20] Police departments worldwide generally consider detectives too cerebral. Their slow investigative work is often underfunded, disrespected, and ignored, particularly the work of detectives investigating violence in high-crime neighborhoods, where it is assumed most of the dead are criminals themselves.[21]

In addition to being uncommon, surveillance and domestic spying were, and continue to be, controversial. Three years before Blakey wrote the Crime Control Act, President Johnson signed an order canceling all electronic surveillance except when national security was at stake.[22] In 1972, President Nixon further discredited surveillance when he bugged the offices of political opponents during the Watergate scandal. The storm surrounding Edward Snowden's 2013 revelations regarding the massive National Security Agency surveillance program shows that the controversy has not dissipated with time. Surveillance has often been misused, as with the FBI's intelligence gathering on Martin Luther King Jr. and other civil rights leaders.

When used too broadly, with poor oversight, it can abrogate demo-cratic rights. In the United States, the courts in charge of approving surveillance on U.S. and foreign citizens denied just 8 of 1,485 appli-cations and 2 wiretap requests out of 3,170 in 2016.[23] Of course, law enforcement tries to bring cases likely to pass muster with the courts, but numbers this lopsided suggest that oversight may be thin.

Nevertheless, painstaking intelligence gleaned through surveil-lance is essential to tackling the violent criminal conspiracies that proliferate in countries caught in Privilege Violence. In places where witnesses are murdered, people are afraid to talk, and police are often corrupt or complicit in crime, surveillance is indispensable. In the early 2000s, at least seven witnesses were murdered each year in Southeast Los Angeles. By 2008, a lack of witness cooperation was impeding 40 percent of all homicide cases across the city where wit-nesses played a role.[24] In 2009, a witness in Watts who had seen a man murdered across the street spent three nights sleeping on the kitchen floor alongside his family to avoid the men who parked outside and threw rocks at his house with guns by their side.[25] Another witness refused to enter the courthouse in Compton, rolling himself into a ball and crying as police carried him in.[26] High rates of homicide and impunity frighten potential witnesses, enabling greater impunity and homicide. Surveillance can provide evidence without endanger-ing witnesses. It can also allow a government to gain informants by helping to build a case against minor members of an organization, thereby convincing them to turn on their superiors. Finally, intelli-gence gleaned from wiretaps, bugs, or hidden cameras is often the only way to incriminate kingpins who don't carry out violent crimes themselves.

In each country that recovered from violence, surveillance was crucial. In Bihar, police legally tapped twenty thousand phones.[27] They built cell phone towers in rural areas, then traced calls to eaves-drop on Maoist communication. They surveilled prisoners' phone calls to break extortion rings run from jail.[28] In Sicily, members of the special police unit in charge of capturing mafiosi showed me reams of raw surveillance footage of undercover operations. The wiretaps were crucial, the officers explained. They were needed to gather information, because the mob killed or otherwise silenced witnesses.

The physical distance protected police, too, from ambush and from the temptation of creating a relationship with their quarry.[29] In the Republic of Georgia, surveillance was used to keep the newly hired police honest. Cameras on police cars and undercover operatives were used to end petty corruption among municipal workers. The Georgian phone company allowed wiretaps to catch thieves-in-law. Video and audio surveillance fueled Saakashvili's hit TV show. In Colombia, Pablo Escobar was caught thanks to a wiretap on his phone that allowed a team of law enforcement to track him as he talked to his son. U.S.-provided intelligence assistance and surveillance equipment allowed President Uribe to effectively fight FARC guerrillas.

The importance of intelligence is not new.[30] President Theodore Roosevelt employed undercover agents to investigate land, postal, and timber fraud perpetuated by local politicians working with their congressmen. Fearing exposure, Congress prohibited the president from using the Secret Service for his investigations. So Roosevelt created a special force within the Department of Justice. This force eventually became the Federal Bureau of Investigation.[31]

Informants and Witness Protection

Technology has its limits. Without evidence of probable cause, it is illegal for police in some parts of the United States and many other countries to surveil phones or suspects. Inside informants provide essential information for law enforcement to choose their surveillance targets and (since conspiracies often include codes and jargon) to understand what they are seeing and hearing. Cooperation agreements—a form of plea bargaining in which criminals are offered more lenient sentences, and often witness protection, in exchange for information and testimony against other criminals—are thus crucial to fighting organized crime.

Like surveillance, plea bargains are rightly controversial. In much of Latin America, southern Europe, and elsewhere, legal systems are rooted in the ancient Roman tradition, which was influenced by the Catholic Inquisition. In these "inquisitorial" systems, the judge is also the prosecutor and detective, charged with discovering the truth. Bargaining with an alleged criminal has no place in such a system. In the adversarial trials of the United States and other former British colonies, where two lawyers argue over their versions of truth, plea bargains at least make sense. Until the early nineteenth century, however, the sentence for any felony conviction in Britain was death. Because allowing defendants to plead guilty was tantamount to allowing them to commit suicide, British and U.S. courts discouraged criminals from guilty pleas.[32]

Trading a guilty verdict for a more lenient sentence originated in the United States after the Civil War and became more frequent around the turn of the century.[33] Plea bargains helped clogged courts move cases more quickly. They were frequently used, however, in Prohibition cases, then the chief cause for court congestion. Political fixers were often anxious to finish the cases speedily, since guilty pleas and out-of-court settlements meant they could avoid publicizing ties between mobsters, saloon keepers, and politicians.[34] Corruption and plea bargaining were thus intertwined from birth. As of 2017, 94 percent of U.S. cases are settled through plea bargains. Most do not unravel complex criminal conspiracies. Instead, plea bargaining has become a routine and often coercive way to get defendants to plead guilty. The technique also traps people who are innocent but fear long mandatory sentences.[35] Some countries limit cooperation agreements to the least culpable parties within a criminal conspiracy so that small fry can be used to catch bigger criminals. The United States allows plea bargains with major criminals to catch smaller ones—a serious mistake that can make police an extension of criminal empires. Whitey Bulger, for instance, the notorious Boston mobster, turned informant and then used the information he fed to the FBI to get law enforcement to destroy his rival Italian mob for him.[36]

Yet with all these caveats, limited use of cooperation agreements that offer lenient sentences in exchange for inside information on criminal conspiracies is crucial to fighting Privilege Violence. Information provided by the security adviser to the Cali cartel, for example, allowed the U.S. Drug Enforcement Administration to capture the cartel's leadership.[37] It also cracked open one of the most significant criminal cases that tied the U.S. and Italian mobs.

In the precomputer era of the late 1970s, Giovanni Falcone was reconstructing Mafia relationships by laboriously tracing individual checks and connected bank accounts from Italy to France, Belgium, Switzerland, the United States, and Turkey. He contacted police and prosecutors across the globe for help. In December 1980, he made the first of many trips to the United States to better understand the relationships he was uncovering between New York's Gambino family and the Sicilian Mafia.[38] U.S. law enforcement introduced Falcone to the RICO laws. Falcone was so impressed that he translated them into Italian.

In those years, heroin addiction had started to skyrocket in Western Europe and North America. Falcone's relationship with U.S. police broke open the case known as the Pizza Connection, which traced America's heroin problem to Sicily and exposed that the drug was being distributed alongside cocaine from a series of pizza parlors along the East Coast. The case, which ran from 1984 to 1987, became the longest federal criminal trial ever to be held in front of a U.S. jury to that date. The court found that $1.6 billion worth of heroin had entered the United States through this route alone from 1975 to the spring of 1984.[39]

The trial turned on hundreds of hours of wiretapped conversations and video surveillance, much of it obtained by the undercover FBI agent Joseph Pistone (better known as Donnie Brasco for his alias). But undercover work was dangerous and bore the risk of corruption and forced criminality. Informants such as Tommaso Buscetta, brought to the United States to testify about his part in the conspiracy, were therefore equally important.[40]

When Falcone was promoted to the Ministry of Justice to get him out of Cosa Nostra's business in Sicily, he crafted a slew of regulations mimicking U.S. RICO legislation. They would get passed into Italian law over the next seven years each time the Mafia killed a lawmaker, a general, and finally Falcone himself. It took Falcone's murder for Italy's then prime minister, Giuliano Amato, to institute a witness protection program. The program increased the number of Italian prisoners who sought to become state informants from about two dozen in early 1992 to over two hundred by the end of that year.[41]

Internal informants aren't only of use against criminals. Following a core counterinsurgency technique, Bihar's military relied on intelligence from Dalit village informants to fight Maoist guerrillas.

In Colombia, authorities estimate that 50 percent of Uribe's military operations against the FARC were guided by intelligence gleaned from demobilized fighters who surrendered under Uribe's amnesty plan.[42] While Uribe is more often remembered for his use of military force or for his lenient demobilization agreement with right-wing paramilitaries, that bargain followed an equally controversial program to defang Marxist guerrillas with similarly easy terms. In his first year in office, Uribe launched the Program for Humanitarian Care for the Demobilized Combatant (Programa de Atención Humanitaria al Desmovilizado, or PAHD).[43] It offered guerrillas who had not committed crimes against humanity reduced sentences and sometimes a full amnesty, as well as free medical care, mental health treatment, housing, clothing, education, and vocational training. It was a lenient and controversial program, a dirty deal offered to Stalinists who kidnapped children, murdered policemen, and massacred uncooperative peasants, and it was criticized by the head of Colombia's armed forces and much of Colombian society.

Yet from 2002 to 2014, over seventeen thousand former guerrillas entered PAHD.[44] Defectors provided Colombia's armed forces with knowledge of the financing, drug-trafficking activities, and internal organization of the FARC. The informants also aided the guerrillas' disintegration from within. As word trickled back that demobilized fighters were not arrested or killed, but received the benefits promised, greater numbers of guerrillas deserted. Fearful that fighters would turn informants, multiple soldiers were executed by their commanders, which reduced trust within their ranks.[45] The amnesty was so devastating to the FARC that in 2015 it requested the program end for peace talks to continue.[46]

Criminal cooperation agreements and guerrilla amnesty programs can look (and be) unjust. They are a real challenge to countries trying to rebuild trust with their citizens.[47] A group of Serbian and Croatian judges and prosecutors met me in Washington to discuss U.S.-sponsored "rule of law" programs in their countries. The United States was pushing plea bargaining to address their organized crime, and the visitors hated the laws. "People already think we're corrupt," they explained. "Now we're supposed to make deals with criminals? It will confirm their fears." In pursuing cooperation agreements, countries need to limit their use to the most serious cases and even then take public opinion into account. In Italy, for instance, an informant is called a *penitento* to recall the Catholic ritual of penance and forgiveness. In the program's early days, they were forced to recount their crimes to schoolchildren to reinforce the confessional imagery. The public symbolism helped these dirty deals buttress the moral order, rather than undermine it (as began to occur when newspapers leaked photographs of Tommaso Buscetta mamboing on a yacht after turning state's witness).

Seizing Assets

Twenty years after Falcone employed the legislation copied from RICO, the Republic of Georgia did the same. During Mayor Orlando's first term governing Palermo, he received a call from Italy's minister of the interior. "You're a mob target," the minister said. "You need to take a long holiday—preferably abroad."[48] Orlando's political mentor and first boss had been Piersanti Mattarella, a Sicilian president killed by a Mafia bullet in 1980. So Orlando took the threat seriously. A few months before, the mayor had come across a set of old papers in an odd alphabet while riffling through city archives. He discovered it was Georgian grammar, written by a monk from Palermo whose journal described Georgia as a beautiful and exotic land. Tickled by the discovery, Mayor Orlando called Tbilisi and the two towns became sister cities.[49] Visiting a sister city seemed appropriately mayoral and above suspicion. So Orlando took his family to what proved to be the last gasp of Soviet-controlled Georgia.

Thus began a relationship that blossomed after the Rose Revolution. The new Georgian government needed help fighting its powerful Mafia. "We almost copied our legislation from the Italian anti-Mafia legislation," explained David Bakradze, one of the new government's senior leaders.[50] It was this legislation that made it criminal to knowingly participate in the thieves-in-law, which enabled the Georgians to break their Mafia before the mob understood the new rules.[51]

Another important aspect of the RICO legislation was the ability to seize assets used in criminal offenses. Temuri Yakobashvili, the former Georgian ambassador to the United States, told me that this was their key weapon. "Our president was friends with the mayor from Sicily. He asked, 'What do you do with Mafia bosses, do you jail them?' And Mayor Orlando said, 'No. The boss can run things from prison. His money is his power, so take that.'"[52]

When I spoke to a leading Italian prosecutor in Rome in the spring of 2015, he explained, "When I meet with mafiosi, they bring just one lawyer if the outcome is prison. They expect prison. The Mafia even has arrangements to pay for wives and children while a member is jailed. But when I threaten their assets, they bring four lawyers. It's their money that lets them be big men, run their criminal enterprises. Take away the money, and they are nothing."[53] In Bihar, India, similar provisions in the Prevention of Money Laundering Act, which came into force in 2005, were used to seize the assets of Maoist guerrillas. The former director of police Abhyanand said, "I got a feeling that they were hassled more by this law's implementation than by the sound of a gun."[54]

Blakey's years investigating the Mafia in the United States prompted similar conclusions. Cutting off money was key. But before RICO passed in 1970, U.S. criminal law offered no way to confiscate a criminal's assets.[55] Activities like theft and murder are crimes committed "against society," whose penalties can include imprisonment. Civil law applies to wrongs against other people, for which the sanction involves paying damages. So confiscating assets required a separate civil action, where a lesser "preponderance of evidence" was sufficient for conviction because civil sanctions are only monetary.[56]

Blakey's RICO law crossed civil and criminal boundaries by allowing courts to seize the assets used in criminal conspiracies without a separate civil suit, but with the tougher due process requirements of criminal law. This was instrumental to breaking the Cali cartel in Colombia, whose cocaine was feeding violence in American cities. In September 1995, under the RICO Act, the Clinton administration blocked the assets of nearly four hundred Cali-affiliated enterprises in the United States.[57] The government tightened the financial noose until the cartel could no longer pay its people or cover its mortgages.[58]

Giovanni Falcone began his career in the bankruptcy department, so he understood the importance of cutting off money to fight the mob. When Italy adopted RICO laws, it allowed assets to be frozen before a defendant was convicted—a controversial provision if the person proved innocent, but important in Italy, where a case might take a decade to make its way through the many levels of appeals.

Italian law also provides poetic justice by handing confiscated Mafia assets to anti-Mafia organizations. In Rome, I visited the head-quarters of one of the country's oldest and most significant anti-Mafia groups, Libera.[59] Nonprofit organizations usually fall into one of two categories: rich and venerable or small and scrappy. Libera straddles an odd middle ground. Located just steps from the famed Piazza Venezia, its offices occupied some of the most prime real estate in the city. Yet its elevator was hardly large enough for two. Each floor opened onto two or three tiny offices, so small they were barely func-tional. The director, a wiry man named Franco La Torre, grinned at my confusion. "This was a former brothel," he explained. "It was used by the Mafia to entertain politicians and to incriminate them. It was confiscated, and now it's ours."[60]

La Torre failed to mention that his father was responsible for the unique confiscation law. Pio La Torre had been a famous Commu-nist Party leader. The son of Corleone peasants, he was a construction worker who entered politics in 1948 when the Mafia killed one of his mentors. He rose through the party, becoming a member of parlia-ment in 1972 and joining its anti-Mafia commission.[61] In 1976, when parliament offered a watered-down account of the causes of the first Mafia war, La Torre and a judge wrote a minority report that linked the Mafia to a number of politicians. On March 31, 1980, Pio La Torre introduced legislation that, among other provisions, allowed courts to confiscate the goods of people belonging to a Mafia conspiracy. Although La Torre's legislation moldered, the Mafia sensed the threat. On a spring day in 1982, assassins boxed Pio La Torre's car into a one-way street and opened fire. A few months later when the Mafia killed the revered general Carlo Alberto Dalla Chiesa, who ended Italy's terrorist wave in the 1970s, parliament passed the law La Torre had championed and named it after him.[62]

Seizing assets is effective for decimating criminal empires, but it leaves a lot of hard-to-dispose-of goods in government hands. Colombia's government had passed a similar law, and when I asked Daniel Rico, then a member of Colombia's National Security Council, how it was working, he threw up his hands in exasperation. "We've confiscated apartments, cars, an entire zoo!" he exclaimed. "We can't dispose of these things."[63] The Colombian government was indeed ill-suited to maintaining Pablo Escobar's tigers and alligators. Italy's inefficient bureaucracy held scores of confiscated apartments, which sometimes left whole blocks empty, blighting neighborhoods while the government tried to figure out how to unload them.[64]

Asset seizure can also have far darker consequences. Criminal forfeiture law under RICO requires full criminal due process, such as the right to a lawyer and privileges against self-incrimination. Distinct from this, the United States has a civil forfeiture law left over from the Middle Ages, when sins were attributed to the items used to commit them.[65] A car transporting stolen goods, for example, is itself guilty of theft, even if the person driving is unaware of what is in her trunk. Thus, modern civil forfeiture law allows police to seize potentially "guilty" assets with no judicial ruling, even if no person has ever been accused of a crime. In 1970, Congress expanded those rules in the Comprehensive Drug Abuse Prevention and Control Act, allowing the government to seize drugs, drug equipment, and vehicles used to move drugs without a trial. In 1984, harsh War on Drugs legislation allowed federal law-enforcement agencies to keep the proceeds from such forfeitures, awarding state and local police up to 80 percent of the assets' value.[66] Intended to spur police to fight drugs, it instead incentivized legal government theft. Police departments across America have abused the law to steal money, cars, and goods from innocent Americans, knowing that most people lack the resources to press a civil suit and get them back.

Between 1988 and 1992, the Department of Justice reported that drug task forces had seized over a billion dollars' worth of assets.[67] A *Washington Post* investigation found that since 2001, 61,998 cash seizures of $2.5 billion in assets had occurred, from which state and local authorities kept over $1.7 billion. While some of those assets were undoubtedly related to crimes, cash was returned 41 percent of the time when citizens went through the effort and expense of mounting a case.[68] A journalist noted that in Louisiana confiscated money was spent on ski trips and other non-job-related uses, while in Los Angeles a whistle-blower in the Sheriff's Department claimed that deputies planted drugs and falsified reports to seize money.[69] There's no excuse for poorly written legislation that turns law-enforcement agents into de facto, and sometimes de jure, criminals. In India, an asset-seizure law for corrupt public officials mandates that if the officials prove their innocence, the state must return double the value of the assets taken. But Congress's attempt to reform U.S. laws in 2000 failed to remove incentives to steal in the name of policing.[70] These civil law injustices aren't a failure of RICO's criminal asset seizure and its variants abroad, but they serve as an important warning.

Criminal asset seizure is valuable not only because it removes the fuel from criminal conspiracies but also because it can free society from the fear that criminals will return. In Sicily, the former mafioso Giovanni Brusca owned a cottage amid the island's picturesque hills. Brusca was the man who had pushed the detonator that killed Falcone. He was known as "the Pig" and "the People-Slayer" for his brutality (he had murdered one or two hundred people; he claimed not to remember how many).[71] When his cottage was given to Libera Terra, an anti-Mafia farming operation, the townspeople knew his reign of terror was really over. "If you are eating the criminal boss, then you are the boss," explained Georgia's former U.S. ambassador Yakobashvili. "It is voodoo cannibalism. . . . You take on their power in the minds of people. Now *we* are the boss because we ate the powerful actors in the country."[72]

But power can be used for good or ill.

Centralizing Power

Countries facing Privilege Violence have an enemy within. By definition, some people working in the government protect violent groups, and many of the relationships remain in place even after a new leader takes the helm. In Bihar, where 67 percent of the winning state legislative candidates faced criminal charges in 2015, 38 percent of those cases involved serious crimes such as murder, kidnapping, and extortion.[73] In Colombia in the early years of the twenty-first century, a third of parliament ran campaigns financed by paramilitaries.[74]

Centralizing power to sideline corrupt legislators, bureaucrats, and judges is thus crucial to fighting Privilege Violence.[75] Two weeks after being elected president of Georgia, Saakashvili rushed a series of constitutional amendments through parliament that enabled him to dissolve the legislature, purge local politicians, and otherwise central-ize control. The new laws enabled parliamentarians to be investigated for corruption without parliamentary approval, a catch-22 require-ment that had previously made it impossible to prosecute criminal legislators.[76] Mayor Orlando of Palermo declared a state of emergency so that he could take over city planning from a corrupt city council and avoid handing over more city contracts to Mafia-tied construc-tion firms.[77] The U.S. Supreme Court revoked the South's ability to run elections without oversight for nearly fifty years, forcing every election law alteration to be federally approved. Theodore Roosevelt, who served with a politician he described as having been elected "while his hair was still short" from a term in state prison, wrote "What is normally needed" to make change against such entrenched interests "is the concentration in the hands of one man, or of a very small body of men, of ample power to enable him or them to do the work that is necessary."[78]

But Roosevelt added a crucial corollary. Countries also needed to devise "means to hold these men fully responsible for the exercise of that power by the people."[79]

COUNTRIES TURN TOWARD REPRESSION

It is possible to wield a stronger state security apparatus, surveillance, intelligence, and asset seizure to just the right degree, centralizing power enough to root out entrenched violence and corruption with-out becoming authoritarian. But it is easy to slip.

In December 2005, Saakashvili pruned local government posts, which had ballooned into the thousands thanks to Shevardnadze-era patronage and sinecure appointments. Georgia is a small country, so it made sense to consolidate 1,110 localities into 67.[80] Shrinking gov-ernment reduced corruption and waste. It also allowed Saakashvili to personally vet and control the leaders of all localities. Soon, even local soccer leagues in regional hinterlands were connected with Saa-kashvili's party.[81]

A year earlier, just a few weeks after his oath of office, Saakashvili passed a plea-bargaining law. He also revised the tax code, claiming that a simpler tax would be harder to evade. By January 1, 2005, the code was 95 percent shorter, and all Georgians owed an easy-to-calculate flat tax of 12 percent on their income.[82] Georgia's financial police visited various shady businessmen who had profited from the dirty Shevardnadze era. "You owe $5 million in back taxes," they'd explain. Then they would offer their version of a plea bargain: give the money to the government immediately, invest it in a government-approved project (often a building development in a poorer part of the country), or face prosecution and jail. In the middle of the night, with no lawyer, due process, or recourse, business owners signed away deeds to their properties and businesses.[83]

At first, Georgians cheered the tax collectors. It was rough justice, a little above the law, but clear moral retribution after years of public theft. But the administration kept changing the tax code. Constant alterations made it nearly impossible for anyone to stay legally compliant.[84] Financial police began to demand money from people who were not obviously corrupt. The tax police stepped up their efforts whenever the government needed funds. That meant harassment increased after Georgia's disastrous war with Russia in 2008, when skirmishes over the breakaway territory of South Ossetia led Georgia to fire on a Russian peacekeeping barracks. In a coordinated, devastating retaliatory attack, Russia's air force bombed Georgian pipelines, military installations, and civilian cities, its navy sank multiple Georgian ships in the Black Sea, and its army invaded across the northern border.[85] Although the Russians withdrew after four days, the war left Georgia with twenty thousand refugees, and the cost of rebuilding broke Georgia's fragile economy.

Tax authorities stepped up their efforts. The current head of the Georgian Young Lawyers' Association recounted the shtick of the financial police: "You know we can arrest you and put drugs in your pocket. And because of the judiciary's lack of independence, you'll go to prison, and you know what will happen to you in prison."[86] Tina Khidasheli, head of an opposition party and a future minister of defense, filled in the dots for me. "Everyone believed they would go to jail and be raped and tortured," she explained.[87]

By 2010, more than 95 percent of Tbilisians reported to pollsters that they felt safe at all times, an astounding reversal of the near anarchy that prevailed in the early 1990s.[88] But mandatory sentences and zero-tolerance policing policies instituted by Saakashvili in 2006 increased prison populations by 300 percent in just four years, until Georgia's convict population was, per capita, the largest in eastern Europe.[89] By 2011, nearly nine in ten people accused of a crime pleaded guilty and accepted a plea bargain.[90] It was a rate that would normally raise eyebrows in the international community but that the United States, a major source of aid to bolster the rule of law in Georgia, could hardly dispute given its similar plea-bargaining rates.[91] Saakashvili managed to reduce corruption in the judiciary, only to destroy its independence. Courts convicted 99 percent of criminal defendants. Judges were cowed. The few remaining independent voices claimed that courts were doling out the "telephone justice" of Soviet days, so called because government officials would call judges to tell them how to decide their cases.

Saakashvili also cracked down on the media. Independent stations that had once trumpeted his revolution were placed under state control, their ownership mysteriously transferred to shady shell companies with ties to government cronies.[92] In 2007, over 100,000 Georgians protested in the streets, galvanized by the ugly murder of a young banker in a bar carried out by members of the Interior Ministry.[93] Saakashvili's government fired on demonstrators and took control of what had been the last remaining opposition television station.

Nitish Kumar might have been moving in a similar direction in Bihar, though he didn't go nearly so far. Journalists trumpeted Kumar's many accomplishments. But Kumar's government bought so many advertisements that it had become the major financial backer of most media.[94] Papers that didn't toe the line found their ad revenue drying up.[95] Meanwhile, the number of *bahubalis* in Kumar's party list facing serious criminal charges grew from 22 percent to 35 percent between his 2005 and his 2010 elections.[96]

A series of revelations undermined Uribe's legacy in Colombia. In 2005, courts uncovered the "parapolitics" scandal, discovering that prior to their demobilization, paramilitaries had been using bribes and threats of violence to ensure that scores of friendly parliamentarians got elected. Don Berna's paramilitary consortium alone probably assisted the elections of 9 governors, 251 mayors, and more than 4,000 city council members.[97] A single paramilitary commander had paid $15 million each month in bribes to 890 politicians, security officers, and other informants.[98] Uribe's director of intelligence was found to have created counterfeit ballots that allowed paramilitary candidates to win by theft when money and intimidation failed.[99]

In 2008, a group of mothers from Soacha, a working-class suburb of Bogotá, unearthed more terrible complicity. Their sons had all mysteriously disappeared while searching for work. After meeting each other over months during visits to the local police headquarters, the mothers turned to investigative journalists for help locating the missing men. Their boys, the journalists discovered, had been lured away by a man posing as a job recruiter. The young men were then handed to military units that dressed them in guerrilla garb, killed them, and passed them off as guerrilla fighters killed in action. While military brutality was a long-standing problem, statistical analysis suggested that these murders had increased by 84 percent to 101 percent while President Uribe was in power. They particularly grew after the military issued a directive to use body counts to determine success in the guerrilla war.[100]

"Democracy happens in the council, in the parliament, not with an elected prince," Paul Bromberg, Mayor Mockus's handpicked successor in Bogotá, admonished his predecessor.[101] In Palermo, Mayor Orlando faced accusations that his cultish followers, known as Orlandiani, made decisions outside democratic processes. People muttered about the "men in black" running the city, a conspiracy of judges, Jesuit priests, and Orlando's cronies. Nitish Kumar was declared "dictatorial" and accused of running a one-man show.[102] President Uribe tried to amend the constitution to run for a third term, wiretapped judges, and floated the idea of allowing politicians connected with paramilitaries to avoid prison sentences.

Centralizing power was essential to disempower corrupt and complicit parts of government. Retaking the monopoly on force, and some use of force by the state, were needed to fight endemic violence. As president-elect, Saakashvili took an oath on the tomb of King David the Builder, a legendary Georgian king who tamed the feudal lords, brought order to the Caucasus, and presided over the Georgian golden age in 1100. "Today Georgia is split and humiliated. . . . Georgia will become a united, strong country," he promised.[103] Were these leaders heroic state builders or sweet-talking autocrats? The question split local citizens and foreign leaders.

In retrospect, it is easy to see that these countries were flirting with authoritarianism. But in the midst of reform, the line is less clear. Early on, detractors appeared to be self-interested. In Georgia, tens of thousands of corrupt police, bureaucrats, teachers, and judges who had lost their jobs under Saakashvili's purges swelled protesters' ranks.[104] In Sicily, there were likely only 5,000 or 6,000 made men, but scholars estimated that 100,000 to 200,000 Sicilians depended on Mafia-based business for their livelihoods, and many more needed Mafia money to capitalize their otherwise legitimate enterprises.[105] In 1988, during Orlando's first term as mayor, labor unions went on strike, carrying coffins and wielding signs: "With the mafia we work, without it, no!" and "If struggling for the workers signifies being Mafiosi, then long live mafia!"[106]

Clashes between classes also obscured what was happening. Many of the Georgians who had lost their jobs were playing by the rules of the old system and resented the young Western-educated elites. In Italy, banning Mafia-connected enterprises from government procurement meant Sicilian construction workers, electricians, and bricklayers lost work.[107] Civil service reform in the United States reduced corruption but handed government posts from poor immigrants to educated middle-class functionaries who could pass the civil service exams.[108] The Rose Revolutionaries, Italian anti-Mafia groups, and U.S. reformers were heroes to many, but they could all be painted, with some truth, as movements that sought to shift power to the middle class at the expense of the workingman.[109]

Gradually, however, opponents fueled by criminal money or mobilized by self-interest were joined by more idealistic voices, like the bereaved mothers of Soacha who clearly had no political agenda. Society realized it must apply the brakes to halt leaders whose confidence had curdled into arrogance and whose reforms now shaded into self-interest.

To bring violence under control, governments must wield the tools of a strong state. They need to centralize power to sideline bureaucrats and legislators complicit with violence. Breaking criminal conspiracies and insurgencies requires surveillance, informants, and asset seizure. But these are dangerous tools. Politicians convinced they are saving their countries can end up building a more repressive state. Thus, the leaders who pull their countries out of violence often become reformers and transgressors, Dr. Jekyll and Mr. Hyde. Their ends do not justify anti-democratic means. If democracies fail to wield the powers of a strong state carefully, they not only transgress ethically but also place citizen trust and the process of recivilization in jeopardy. It is up to societies to reverse course and hold their governments accountable, making their leaders tread the thin, difficult line that enables their countries to move forward out of violence.

PART III

NEXT STEPS

10

SOCIETY MAINTAINS THE PEACE

The memory of the path we have followed and the victories that were achieved should remain very much alive as proof of the fact that one can win ... that so many efforts, and so many sacrifices—even of human lives—count for something. I would not like to see us return to cultivating the paralyzing myth of a mafia not only invincible but indeed untouchable.

—SALVATORE LUPO, SICILIAN HISTORIAN[1]

Countries do not exit Privilege Violence smoothly. They lurch backward and sideways as citizens opt for repression or governments lean toward authoritarianism. Successful reforms spur opponents to regroup. Dirty deals can lead to another round of bloodshed. The places chronicled in this book have far to go. Yet despite their convoluted trajectories, each has made real progress in fostering a state that is less violent, in a sustainable way. Just as ignoring ongoing problems would be naïve, understating how much each country has improved would be equally blind to reality.

The usual way to tell whether a country is beating violence is by looking at the statistics. But violence data is so poor that numbers are often misleading, making them worse than useless—garbage in, garbage out.[2] Moreover, countries facing Privilege Violence tend to have spikes of death followed by lulls, making it difficult to judge whether one is seeing sustainable success or just measuring at a trough that might soon rise. To determine lasting progress, one should look for patterns over time that indicate a change in phase space—what complexity theorists call "the space of the possible."[3]

Complexity theory is an interdisciplinary science used to study phenomena where cause and effect are interdependent, affecting each other and changing the entire system. For example, when guerrilla violence catalyzes paramilitary violence, it yields reprisal from both sides. It also increases state violence, creating a rising spiral of death that feeds on itself. Complexity theorists have determined a way to measure change in situations that feature such interdependent interactions. Consider a dripping faucet. It turns out it is mathematically impossible to predict exactly where each drop will fall around the faucet's opening. But as anyone who has had a dripping faucet knows, it's very possible to know the space in which *all* the drops will fall; you can see it in the brown rusted oval left in the bottom of the sink. That oval is the "phase space" or the space where all possible drops can land. A country facing Privilege Violence will see death ebb and flow. But the numbers are all within a single phase space, the area of all possible violent outcomes given the power structure that prevails in the country at that moment in time. Imagine that the faucet gets pushed to one side. That brown oval in the bottom of the sink will shift too. That is what has occurred in each of the places that pulled themselves out of Privilege Violence.

Maintaining this improvement falls to society. Governments are always at risk of overstepping, and politicians can always play on past fissures to fracture communities. It is regular people who have the final word in determining whether their societies get away with murder or sustain security. The United States took a wrong turn after the civil rights movement, thrusting it backward into decades of increased violence before it pulled out of the downward spiral. Countries like Italy teeter on the edge. This chapter chronicles the last steps each state took to sustain success and where these places are now.

THE UNITED STATES DECIVILIZES, 1960s–1990s

The United States almost turned a corner in 1965. The civil rights movement opened the door for a more fully realized democracy across all fifty states. But America did not seize the moment; instead, the U.S. homicide rate began a long rise in the mid-1960s and didn't fall until the 1990s, because the United States failed to recivilize.

After the Supreme Court's *Brown v. Board of Education* decision of 1954, tens of thousands of segregationist Citizens' Councils spread across the South. They were composed of "bankers, doctors, lawyers, engineers, newspaper editors, and publishers: a few are preachers; some are powerful industrialists," according to southern writer Lillian Smith.[4] These community leaders agitated to get white and black integrationists fired if they worked for local businesses or government. Local banks cut off credit for business owners who supported integration and forced them to withdraw their money. Insurance companies canceled the policies of blacks trying to vote and whites trying to help them.[5]

"It's a quite well-bred mob," Smith continued. "Its members speak in cultivated voices, have courteous manners, some have university degrees, and a few wear Brooks Brothers suits. They are a mob nevertheless. For they ... protect the rabble, and tolerate its violence."[6] More than simply tolerate violence, the public language of these middle-class scions made violence more acceptable. There would be no "nigger voting," the defense attorney for Emmett Till's killers explained. "If any more pressure is put on us, the Tallahatchie River won't hold all the niggers that'll be thrown in it."[7] The president of the Mississippi Bar Association gave a speech suggesting that "the gun and the torch" were useful for deterring integration.[8] A state legislator felt that "a few killings would be the best thing for the state," to prevent the mayhem that would ensue if black southerners gained rights.[9] In the early 1960s, when the NAACP organizer Medgar Evers was murdered by a Citizens' Council member, three bank presidents in Greenwood, Mississippi, created the White Citizens Legal Fund to support the killer's legal costs.[10] The Klan violence of the era was thereby normalized, while the councils themselves were seen as "eminently respectable," according to the historian Charles Payne. In states like Mississippi, they were "hard to distinguish from the state government," which provided them with funding.[11]

Nonviolence is hard to sustain in the face of such blowback. A 1959 documentary titled *The Hate That Hate Produced* chronicled the rise of Elijah Muhammad, then the leader of the Nation of Islam. Muhammad had been born in 1897, among the South's most violent years. He saw his first lynching when he was ten years old.[12] In 1965, he published a book preaching a virulently antiwhite form of black power. Malcolm X, a follower of Muhammad's until just before his assassination at the hands of Muhammad's Nation of Islam, declared,

> Concerning nonviolence: It is criminal to teach a man not to defend himself when he is the constant victim of brutal attacks. It is legal and lawful to own a shotgun or rifle. We believe in obeying the law.... In areas where our people are the constant victims of brutality, and the government seems unable or unwilling to protect them, we should form rifle clubs that can be used to defend our lives and our property in times of emergency, such as happened last year in Birmingham; Plaquemine, Louisiana; Cambridge, Maryland; and Danville, Virginia.[13]

The brutality of southern police, politicians, and ordinary citizens pushed the once nonviolent civil rights movement toward its fringes, just as repression tends to do everywhere. Among radicalizing college students, Martin Luther King Jr. was passé; militancy became au courant. SNCC, the organization that had organized the Freedom Rides, denied its white members a vote in 1966, then evicted whites from the organization in 1967.[14] What was once an effective and broad movement narrowed and lost support.

While southern police used Klan violence against blacks, northern police were more guilty of indifference. Speaking to a government commission, a journalist explained, "For decades, little if any law enforcement has prevailed among Negroes in America.... If a black man kills a black man, the law is generally enforced at its minimum."[15] Left to police themselves, America's inner cities developed gangs, vigilantes, and the other pathologies seen the world over when the state refuses to enforce the law and uphold its monopoly on violence.[16] Black-on-black violence, which grew in the South under Jim Crow when police rarely entered black neighborhoods, deepened in northern cities to which southern blacks had flocked during the Great Migration.[17]

Riots broke out across black slums in the North: Harlem faced four days of burning storefronts and Molotov cocktails in 1964. In the Watts neighborhood of Los Angeles in 1965, thirteen thousand National Guardsmen were brought in to restore order after thirty-four people were killed. Twenty-three more died in Newark two years later, and the riots continued in Minneapolis, Chicago, Baltimore, and Washington, D.C., after the assassination of Martin Luther King Jr. in 1968. Black trust in government fell to a post–World War II low between 1971 and 1974, and black homicides peaked.[18]

American violence is inextricably related to race. Yet that was far from the only cause making people question the justice of the social order (a process that, whether for causes just or unjust, is highly correlated with increased violence). Women were demanding power, the Stonewall riots for gay rights occurred in 1969, and over the domestic tumult hung the daily roll call of deaths from the Vietnam War. Increasingly militant activists united their homegrown revolutions with the anticolonial wars overseas. America's invasion of Vietnam led Vietnam to "invade America," in the words of Tom Hayden, a leading white radical.[19]

Meanwhile, young Americans were letting go of their inhibitions. Breasts dangled braless; drugs and sex came into the open. Long-haired men and short-haired women wore jeans and sandals, not suits and heels. Some of this was liberating. But as Norbert Elias had noted, inhibitions also control impulsive behavior. As a buttoned-up society suddenly let it all hang out, decivilization, already well under way among the right-wing defenders of segregation, spread throughout the Far Left. By 1968, America faced threats from homegrown terrorists such as the Weathermen and the Symbionese Liberation Army, as well as vigilante groups like the Black Panthers. Hippies mingled with armed biker gangs.[20] A rally on the New Haven Green in 1972 to free the arrested Black Panther leader Bobby Seale featured "skinny twenty-somethings . . . carrying armloads of shotguns and M-1s."[21]

There was a dominant culture and a counterculture. Half the population had become the "other." Distrust grew, society polarized, and the security services picked a side.[22] America's police had professionalized since the turn-of-the-century era of machine politics and patronage appointments.[23] Yet as they became a distinct caste, they also grew distant from the people they policed and allied with one side of the polarized public.[24]

Police shootings and brutality rose across the country. The police killed someone in the line of duty every four days in New York City alone.[25] As disorder and riots spread, significant portions of the middle class backed repressive policies in response. In 1968, a Gallup poll found that 81 percent of respondents agreed that "law and order has broken down in this country," with most blaming "Negroes who start riots" and Communists.[26] The next year, 30 percent of Americans polled said that "police beating students" wasn't violence at all and felt the same about "police shooting looters."[27] A Gallup poll taken in 1970 after the National Guard shot four students at Kent State found 58 percent of respondents supported the guard and only 11 percent the students (many had no opinion).[28]

By the late 1960s, fears of increasing disorder merged with political and racial identity. "Choose the way of [the Johnson] Administration and you have the way of mobs in the street," Barry Goldwater expounded.[29] Richard Nixon and the segregationist George Wallace both ran on law-and-order platforms in the 1968 presidential election.[30] Polarization made it easy to dismiss each side's arguments for addressing violence as mere partisanship.

Police violence peaked in 1971. Yet even as policing improved, distrust of law enforcement was emblazoned in the minds of the largest generation of Americans in history, with its bulge of young men, the most criminogenic part of any population. Fueled by distrust of the state and polarization among the population, the homicide rate crept up to 5.6 per 100,000 in 1966.[31] As heroin poured in from Sicily, then cocaine from Colombia, murder continued its upward climb for a quarter century. It crested in 1991 at 9.8 per 100,000, a rate just shy of epidemic.[32]

THE UNITED STATES RECIVILIZES, 1993–2014

Crack cocaine is the most likely cause for the sudden spike in violence in the late 1980s and early 1990s at the end of this long upward trajectory.[33] Crack junkies willing to kill for a fix haunted American cities, while young drug dealers protecting their turf left neighborhoods soaked in blood. Children whose parents had been hollowed out of their humanity, overdosed, or jailed during the crack era refused to face the same fate. They abandoned hard drug use in droves. As users fell, so did violent crime. The fastest, greatest reductions were in the poor black neighborhoods that had been hit the hardest.[34] Across the United States, measures of delinquency, from smoking to teen pregnancy rates, plummeted. From 1993 to 2003, there was a 77 percent decline in juveniles arrested for murder, including an 83 percent decline for black youths.[35] Communities retook public spaces that had been open-air crack markets and "shooting galleries" for heroin, working with civic groups to build community gardens, revamp playgrounds, and goad the government into destroying drug-dealer-controlled high-rise public housing. Society was recivilizing.

Communities could help themselves because the state had spent two decades becoming better at enforcing the laws and governing inclusively. After 1971, Police Commissioner Patrick Murphy of New York City led other police chiefs in establishing guidelines that forbade the use of firearms except as a last resort against people who posed a serious threat, and established the Firearms Discharge Review Board to investigate police shootings. Murphy also created an early intervention program to identify and counsel officers prone to violent behavior. He trained officers in simulations so they could learn how to react to dangerous situations without the use of force. Similar changes, replicated in police departments across the country, led to a dramatic drop in police use of deadly force from the 1970s to the 1990s.[36] The fight against the Mafia in the 1970s bled into inquests that rooted out police corruption.[37] Trust in the government grew.[38]

Citizens—including those in the urban minority communities who suffered the most from police brutality and common crime—demanded that the government enforce law and order, fairly.[39] Police departments experimented with new techniques. Some much bally-hooed, media-friendly initiatives like zero tolerance and broken windows policing had mixed results or backfired.[40] But as the government poured funds into studies like Earls's Chicago research to discover what worked, police departments began working with communities to solve the problems that mattered most to locals. They instituted data systems that enabled hot-spot policing to target the few places in all cities where most crimes are committed. These personnel-intensive programs were possible because of federal legislation in 1994 that vastly increased the number of police officers across the country. Yet the fall in U.S. violence in the 1990s was so dramatic and unexpected that it remains a topic of debate.

The authors of *Freakonomics* grabbed headlines when they included in their best-selling book research by Steven Levitt and John Donohue hypothesizing that violence fell because abortion was legalized, reducing future generations of unwanted, under-parented teenagers.[41] The argument is eye-catching but poor social science—like all mono-causal explanations for phenomena that occur when many things are happening at once. It overgeneralizes (New York legalized abortion across the state, for instance, but homicide fell sharply only in New York City) and also cherry-picks data: Ireland and Poland remained peaceful despite having extreme restrictions on abortion. Violence has risen in South Africa despite abortion becoming legal in 1997.[42] A host of scholars have questioned the authors' reading of homicide statistics, computer errors, and other basic technical failures obscured in the name of a good story.[43]

Some scholars argue that a portion of the fall in crime resulted from phasing out lead in gasoline and home plumbing, essentially attributing the early 1990s crime wave to a massive case of country-wide lead poisoning. Lead interferes with the prefrontal cortex that regulates impulsive, violent behavior, so mass lead exposure could cause a widespread, Elias-style impulse reduction effect. Researchers have found that in U.S. counties with high air lead in 1990, murder rates were four times higher than in counties with lower air lead, and that 90 percent of the variation in violent crime across the United States from 1964 to 1998 could be explained by leaded gasoline use.[44] Studies on lead poisoning show strong correlations between lead abatement and the reduction in violence state by state and city by city.[45] The theory is intriguing and may account for some portion of the growth of U.S. violence and its reduction, but it doesn't explain why violence didn't face similar trajectories in other countries. France and Ireland, for instance, phased out leaded gasoline in 2000 while

Australia and Greece didn't leave it behind until 2002, but none of these countries experienced a violence spike or ensuing diminishment as a result.

Most criminologists believe that tougher law enforcement was responsible for perhaps a quarter of the violence reduction.[46] After 1985, when War on Drugs–era laws took effect requiring long mandatory sentences for a variety of offenses, the incarceration rate for violent offenders grew by 86 percent. With just 188,000 people in prison across the United States in 1968, getting violent people off the street was important at first.[47] The government, which felt absent to many city dwellers during these violent decades, needed to prove it wanted to protect its people. Greater certainty that wrongdoers would be sentenced also probably played a role in reducing police brutality: researchers in the 1970s found that when U.S. police of that era were convinced that courts would let criminals go free, they sometimes resorted to brutality as a way of extracting personal justice.[48]

Yet while initially helpful, the trajectory of mass incarceration and long sentences has long since become counterproductive.[49] Incarceration rates that have grown 600 percent between 1965 and 2000 are unlikely to still be affecting violence levels. While half of state prisoners and around 8 percent of federal prisoners are violent offenders (though that category includes people the police deem to have resisted arrest and people caught with illegal pepper spray, not just murderers), many of these prisoners are serving long sentences and were arrested years ago.[50] In the past decade, homicide convictions have accounted for just 0.4 percent of federal prison growth and less than 3 percent of new state convicts.[51] Nonviolent prisoners compose 478 percent of the increase in imprisonment. The most aggressive surge has been in arrests of juveniles, women, and low-level drug abusers.[52] The extent of these arrests—particularly of juveniles—is likely to increase violence, because recidivism levels in the United States are so high and because imprisonment on this scale is causing vast social disruption. In my state of New Mexico, for instance, 10 percent of all children have a parent who has served time.[53] By 2015, 2.3 million people were behind bars in America, a number greater than the combined populations of Boston, San Francisco, and Washington, D.C.

VIOLENCE IN THE UNITED STATES TODAY

The United States today doesn't seem peaceful. Thanks to the constant news cycle and the rise of social media, every gun massacre, police killing, and reprisal is made known to the public, shared, and shared again. As I started writing this chapter, another young black boy, Jordan Edwards, was murdered in the United States. He was fifteen years old and a straight-A student. He was killed by police in Texas while he sat in a car with friends, driving away from a party a classmate had thrown when his parents went out of town. The murders of black men at the hands of police have incited protests and riots across the country since the 2013 acquittal of George Zimmerman, the Hispanic man who shot seventeen-year-old Trayvon Martin in Florida. "Say his name. Emmett Till," they chant. "How many black boys will you kill?" An angry sniper shot five police officers in Dallas in reprisal. Embattled police units are letting enforcement in some black areas slip. As Chicago faces a sharp spike in homicides, the city's top police officer claims that Black Lives Matter protests are resulting in more black deaths because officers are less able to do their jobs. Meanwhile, southerners still kill each other at twice the national rate.[54] The states with the highest numbers of historical lynchings had the highest levels of incarceration and death sentences in the 1990s, a correlation that strengthens when only black death penalty cases are considered.[55]

This is not the vision of progress we expect from success stories. The racial turmoil and police killings in the United States, military murders and paramilitary collusion in Colombia, and government repression in Georgia suggest that we are trapped in an endless loop, not an upward trajectory. The trail out of Privilege Violence is so lurching that it can seem as if countries will never recover. Have any of the places in this book really made much progress?

Actually, yes. In 1991, homicide peaked for all Americans at 9.8 per 100,000. By 2014, murder was at an all-time modern low of 4.4 per 100,000. America had been that safe in only two other years—1954 and 1957—since 1900.[56] In New York City, as police officers use less deadly force and make fewer arrests than ever before, violence has declined for twenty-seven straight years.[57] Its murders are down 85 percent since 1991. L.A.'s homicide rate is on par with Lithuania's.[58] Though there was a slight uptick in homicide in 2015 and 2016, if just three outliers—Chicago, Baltimore, and Washington, D.C.—were removed from the statistics, homicides nationwide would still be at 1950s levels.[59]

All kinds of violence have fallen. In the 1970s, America faced nearly fifteen hundred terrorist incidents that killed 184 people. By the middle of that decade, fifty to sixty bombs went off around America each year.[60] But in the fifteen years since 9/11, only 103 Americans have died in terrorist attacks, nearly half of them in the single devastating June 2016 massacre in a gay nightclub in Orlando.[61] While school shootings terrify parents across the nation, children are far safer than they were in previous decades. Homicides of school-age children have fallen by more than half, from 7.72 per 100,000 in 1993 to 3.34 in 2016.[62] These are stunning improvements.

It's important to break U.S. statistics down by race. From 1993 to 2008, homicides of black male teens fell by more than half, from 79 to 31 per 100,000.[63] That number is still appallingly high, but it is an improvement. Young men are the most likely to die violently everywhere, and for black Americans of all ages homicides also halved from 39 to 19 per 100,000 between 1991 and 2015.[64] These numbers are still unacceptable. Since the 1980s, black Americans have been murdered at five to eight times the rate of white Americans, a measure of state injustice as well as the internal violence that has lodged in these communities after years of bearing the double burden of repressive policing and under-policing typical of Privilege Violence.[65] But in cities like Los Angeles, as caseloads fell, detectives could focus more time on each murder. Impunity diminished. Cold cases are being solved.[66] As the crime wave of the 1990s ebbed, black Americans became more likely than other racial groups to report nonfatal violent crime to the police, and police responded slightly faster than they did for whites—numbers that improved from the 1990s to the early years of the twenty-first century.[67]

In Chicago, bombings were "a nightly occurrence" in 1954 when an African American family moved into a white neighborhood, according to a Chicago Housing Authority report.[68] That is unimaginable today. The Ku Klux Klan and white supremacists are enjoying an ugly revival, but they are also reviled by a substantial and vocal portion of the population. Rather than being embraced by local business leaders, Richard Spencer, the man who coined the term "alt-right" to add respectability to the white supremacist movement he helps lead, was kicked out of his gym after being confronted by another member.[69]

It is impossible to know whether police violence and racial profiling are getting worse because national historical statistics don't exist.[70] Certainly, the statistics from New York City suggest improvements from the early 1970s. Moreover, now Americans are paying attention. High levels of violence against blacks and the problems of police brutality, long swept under the carpet, have erupted on the national stage. Issues of criminal justice, solitary confinement, long prison sentences for drug offenses, military-style policing, and civil asset seizure are garnering national press and bipartisan agreement. This is a sign of success. Ideas that would have seemed too radical to speak of publicly during the crime wave of the 1990s are mainstream. We are no longer a society where criminal justice is an esoteric topic. Police killings in the line of duty no longer go unrecorded. U.S. society, like all countries that have fallen into Privilege Violence, retains a dark, ugly undercurrent. The inequities in America remain pervasive and horrific. Acknowledging how far we've come is not an invitation to complacency. It is a recognition that progress is possible, and thus calls all of us to ongoing effort.

In 2018, violence is at one of the lowest points ever in modern American history. Yet it is ticking up slightly, especially in a handful of cities.[71] Police in some jurisdictions have moved away from proven techniques and increasingly rely on SWAT-style military tactics.[72] In 1972, America had a few hundred SWAT raids per year. In 2001, SWAT teams were deployed forty thousand times.[73] In New York City, where crime rates are at astonishing lows, recruitment ads in the subway show smiling multiracial cops in T-shirts. But in the thirty-five-thousand-person town of Hobbs, New Mexico, where three former police officers are suing the city for forcing them to target minorities, police recruitment videos feature SWAT team raids using battering rams and armored vehicles.[74]

Social trust among U.S. citizens and in government has been falling over the last decade, though because the fall has been concentrated among wealthier, older whites, who are at low risk for committing homicides, it has not yet contributed to a rise in violence.[75] Intense political polarization, however, could spread distrust to more criminogenic demographics.[76] So could the increase in economic inequality, which is the strongest predictor of general social trust across nations and is also linked to increased violent crime.[77] Well-publicized police violence is generating a renewed sense of illegitimacy, and interracial homicides are growing.[78] Three weeks before the 2016 election, 51 percent of the country's likely voters reported to pollsters that they were worried about violence on Election Day or soon after. One in five were not confident the United States would "have a peaceful transfer of power after the election."[79]

The United States now stands on a precipice. Do we continue to polarize politically and culturally or can we find a way to rebuild trust and a sense of shared nationhood across our differences? Can our political leaders enforce the laws equally and prove that they are governing for all citizens, or will they continue to concentrate privilege? U.S. violence has rarely been lower, but the future of America's story depends on what voters and the leaders they elect choose next.

WHERE ARE THE OTHER SUCCESS STORIES?

Sicily

Italy is also at a juncture. Corruption scandals in 1992 led voters to oust nearly the entire political class across all parties. But no reformist politician filled the void. Mayor Orlando formed a new anti-corruption party known as La Rete that won favor in Sicily, but it lacked national reach. Other parties also attracted regional support that split the vote, such as northern Italy's breakaway secessionist movement. The media baron Silvio Berlusconi capitalized on public anger and painted himself as the candidate of change. His easy populism won. Mayor Orlando was replaced by Diego Cammarata, who brought back mass patronage and corruption before leaving Sicily to become Berlusconi's top aide.

Berlusconi worried that the policies used to fight the Mafia would harm his business empire, which was bedeviled with conflicts of interest and ties to individuals linked with organized crime.[80] He skewered the judiciary, calling judges and other anti-Mafia reformers elitists and Communists.[81] He pushed through new laws that increased impunity, eased corruption, and benefited his businesses.[82] In 2008, the State Audit Board raised the alarm about the number of political amnesties granted to politicians charged with corruption, while the anticorruption high commissioner claimed that the statistics on corruption's decline were not a sign of success but instead reflected greater tolerance for bribes and kickbacks, especially among professionals and the private sector. Government payments for construction work that never began or was left incomplete rose.[83]

But while Berlusconi was reelected nationally multiple times, Sicilians pushed back. Lawyers connected to Mafia interests were elected to Italy's national parliament during the Berlusconi era, but popular pressure prevented them from overturning most anti-Mafia policies.[84] In the spring of 2000, jailed members of Cosa Nostra and other imprisoned mafiosi offered to repudiate the Mafia and confess their crimes—if the state left the rest of the mob intact. Berlusconi's TV stations welcomed the deal, and his minister of justice removed a magistrate who opposed it. But investigative journalists uncovered the dirty details of the offer, and more magistrates fought to kill the idea. It died in the light of public attention. In 2011, Berlusconi stepped down. He has since been convicted of corruption, tax evasion, and various other crimes in multiple trials.

A slew of arrests have decimated Sicily's crime families, and in 2018 Cosa Nostra is a shadow of its past self.[85] Anti-Mafia magistrates remain underpaid and understaffed, but Mafia impunity is now rare. Mafiosi have their meetings bugged. They get arrested, convicted, and sentenced.[86] Crime continues, of course, but the new criminal groups are smaller, less violent, and usually composed of immigrants to Italy whose scams are ephemeral, not deeply rooted in political connections and support.[87] Organized crime is still a significant presence on

Italy's mainland where society has not fought back: Rome, Naples, Apulia. It has also spread to other parts of the EU, benefiting from Europe's historically lax laws against money laundering and refusal to make participation in an ongoing criminal organization a crime. Yet Sicily has managed to maintain its successes.

Society continues to organize. One measure of increased social trust is that southern Italians have now formed as many private associations as northerners.[88] One of these is Addiopizzo—a movement begun in 2004 by young Italians to end the extortion that fueled the Mafia's social control. The Palermo Chamber of Commerce soon joined Addiopizzo and refused to admit members that paid the extortion tax. Eight years later, Roberto Helg, the leader of the chamber and director of the company that manages the Palermo airport, was revealed to be using threats of violence to extort €100,000 from a popular airport pastry shop.[89] Helg was caught, tried, and publicly humiliated for behavior once seen as normal.

After another national corruption scandal broke out in 2010, society rose up. A famous comedian founded the Five Star Movement. It is a party that echoes the populist, anti-elite desire for radical political change that fueled Berlusconi's popularity, and some pundits paint it with the same brush. That is a mistake. Like all political efforts, it is an imperfect vehicle that calls for some dubious policies, but they are not anti-democratic. Although the ill-considered statements of its founder gain attention, he holds no power. Instead Five Stars' grassroots leaders have channeled populist impulses into fighting corruption, its politicians take pledges to live within their means, and the party has taken up the anti-Mafia banner. Much of its popularity is fueled by this commitment to honesty, and it has attracted many middle-class Italians who want to change the structure of power and reduce the cozy cronyism that has held back their lives for so long. In 2018, the Five Star Movement won Italy's elections. Their path to governing, however, required forming a government with unsavory partners: either a right-wing coalition centered around Berlusconi's revived party or a far-right nationalist and populist movement. They chose the latter, creating a government whose first month in office has yielded policies crafted toward two entirely different constituencies rather than a coherent path forward for Italy. How this untested experiment in pleasing the Far Left and Far Right affects polarization and violence is anyone's guess.

Bihar

Nitish Kumar wanted to make a run for national political office on the ticket of the BJP, the powerful national political party with which he had partnered. But the BJP instead anointed Narendra Modi, now prime minister of India. Scorned, Kumar broke his ties with the party and, in doing so, lost the support of its upper-caste members. To rally a new set of voters, he ran in coalition with his old nemesis, Lalu Yadav. Together they won the election in 2015. Middle-class Biharis feared that the crime, violence, and corruption of Yadav's era would return. So far, however, that has not occurred. Instead, Kumar retained control over criminal justice and works to keep *bahubalis* on the run and prevent criminal politicians from getting out of jail.[90] Anand Mohan Singh remains behind bars, and Pappu Yadav has been in and out of prison since 2008. Mohammad Shahabuddin was convicted on multiple charges including murder and is now serving time in a New Delhi jail secured by police from the south of India who do not speak his language. After two years of governing in uneasy coalition, new accusations of Yadav family corruption enabled Kumar to force Yadav out of government altogether. While ensuing political drama has prevented Bihar from making the stunning progress it made under Kumar's previous terms in office, and clashes between Muslims and Hindus have returned (though far less frequently and violently than before), Bihar has maintained its security gains.[91]

Meanwhile, the Common Man Party, a new political organization that grew out of India's national anticorruption movement, is gaining power. It hasn't yet had the success of Italy's Five Star Movement, but it offers Indians of all classes a place to direct their aspirations for a more legitimate, effective government.

Colombia

After links between the paramilitaries and Colombia's parliament were uncovered, the Department of Administrative Security that had

Low-income housing built by drug kingpin Pablo Escobar, whose cultivated Robin Hood image and charitable activities bought him popularity. He was elected to Medellín's city council and then gained a seat in the national parliament in 1982. *(Getty Images)*

A peasant rides past two AUC paramilitary soldiers in rural Antioquia, the region surrounding Medellín plagued by significant drug activity. *(Shutterstock)*

Paramilitary fighters from the Catatumbo Bloc, a subsection of Don Berna's AUC, demobilize on December 10, 2004, following the agreement with President Uribe. (*Shutterstock*)

Relatives of victims of the "False Positives" scandal. The spring 2009 marchers demanded the dismissal of hundreds of military members for killing poor men to pass off as guerrillas. (*Shutterstock*)

A girl rides her bicycle in 2013 through Medellín's once-notorious Comuna 13. One of the gondolas built by the Fajardo administration rises in the background, connecting the hillside neighborhood to the city subway system. (*Shutterstock*)

The warlord Jaba Ioseliani, center, walking with an armed entourage in Tbilisi during Georgia's civil war of the early 1990s. (*Alamy*)

Just outside the parliament building in Tbilisi, the aftermath of the attempted car bomb intended to assassinate Georgian president Eduard Shevardnadze, August 29, 1995. (*AP Images*)

One of the many new police stations constructed under Georgian president Mikheil Saakashvili. Many of these stations were built entirely of glass, a symbolic indicator that corruption and other illegal activities would no longer be hidden or tolerated among the police. *(Shutterstock)*

Protesters walk down Rustaveli Avenue in Tbilisi, which runs in front of parliament, April 9, 2009. Protests became more frequent in the aftermath of Saakashvili's war with Russia in 2008 as he grew increasingly repressive and misused the justice system to silence his opponents and entrench his rule. *(Gipajournos Creative Commons)*

The aftermath of the car bomb that killed Italian anti-Mafia prosecutor Giovanni Falcone, his wife, and eight police escorts on the main highway from Palermo's airport, May 23, 1992. Two months later, a second bomb killed prosecutor Paolo Borsellino and five police escorts as Borsellino rang the doorbell to his mother's apartment. *(Shutterstock)*

Anti-Mafia protests began on July 24, 1992, during the funeral procession for assassinated Italian prosecutors Falcone and Borsellino. *(Getty Images)*

The Sicilian anti-Mafia organization Addiopizzo creates a NO MAFIA billboard on the side of the highway where Falcone was murdered. (*Addiopizzo*)

A French vision of the racial violence in the United States after the Atlanta riot of September 1906. Gubernatorial candidates exacerbated racial fears during the election season, leading to a multi-day riot in which dozens of black men were murdered as law enforcement stood by. Two years later, Georgia disenfranchised its black citizens. (*Courtesy of the National Library of France*)

The FBI poster of three civil rights workers who went missing during Mississippi's Freedom Summer after being pulled over for speeding. (*Courtesy of the Archives and Records Services Division, Mississippi Department of Archives and History*)

Sarju Devi, a Dalit woman, separates wheat under graffiti calling on Dalits to fight the upper-caste militia known as the Ranvir Sena. February 7, 1998. (*Shutterstock*)

Armed men prevent Dalits from leaving their village to vote in February 2005. The Bihar elections were so flawed, the federal government took control. A new election held that fall voted in Nitish Kumar as chief minister of Bihar. (*Shutterstock*)

Nitish Kumar and his tainted predecessor Lalu Prasad Yadav share a dais after campaigning together in the fall of 2014. Their alliance of convenience lasted barely two years before ongoing corruption allegations against Lalu Yadav led Kumar to return to his previous coalition with the BJP and regain the chief ministership on his own terms. *(Getty Images)*

Girls bike to their high school on the red bicycles distributed by Nitish Kumar's government. May 27, 2010. *(Getty Images)*

illegally tapped the phones of Uribe's opponents was disbanded. Several of its members are in jail. The gangs that grew out of the remnants of the demobilized paramilitaries still retain ties to some local politicians and security agents, but they have no national reach. The systemic relationship of violence and corruption throughout Colombian politics has ended.[92] With politicians and security leaders no longer preventing law enforcement from fighting criminals, Colombia dismantled over seven hundred gangs in 2012.[93] As the state has learned to fight more effectively, the average life-span of the leaders of each of these violent post-paramilitary groups has grown shorter. While the Cali cartel's leadership remained in control of its enterprise for nearly seventeen years, the head of a post-paramilitary gang can expect to be in prison within a year or two of taking control.[94]

The paramilitaries themselves are gone, and so is most guerrilla warfare in the country. President Juan Manuel Santos, Uribe's successor, opened historic peace negotiations with the FARC guerrillas in 2012. After the Colombian people, goaded by former president Uribe, rejected a peace agreement that contained too much impunity for the FARC, the guerrillas accepted a deal that offered far less. The new bargain allowed members of the Colombian military and some paramilitary members to escape responsibility for their crimes.[95] Entrenched interests are trying to twist the peace to their benefit by directing resources meant for the poor toward wealthy rural elites.[96] But on November 24, 2016, Colombia ended one of the world's longest-running wars. While Colombia's homicide rate is still high thanks to the long effects of decivilization and poor criminal justice, rates are down by more than three-quarters from their peak.

Georgia

In Georgia, the supposedly ancient culture of corruption and Mafia aggrandizement disappeared within a generation. Less than twenty-five years after being racked by civil war, gangs, militias, Mafia, and warlords, Georgia had a homicide rate of 2.7 per 100,000, just slightly higher than that of Finland.[97] In 2004, 97 percent of Georgians believed that the civil registry was among the most corrupt agencies in the country. Three years later, 97 percent of Georgians believed there was no corruption in the agency.[98] Only 2 percent of Georgians reported paying a bribe over the past year, and only 1 percent reported bribing a policeman. Finland, again, was the only country with a more honest force.[99] By 2010, Transparency International ranked the country as first in the world at reducing corruption. In the fall of 2014, when I spoke with Tina Khidasheli, leader of the Republican opposition party, she claimed that grand corruption had increased and ties between businesses and the state had grown. A booklet produced by Transparency International laying out the evidence of such grand corruption in several sectors is convincing.[100] But these instances are not endemic. The connection between the state and organized crime has fallen to among the lowest levels in Europe.[101] By 2007, 93 percent of society viewed the Mafia unfavorably.[102] In 2017, the World Justice Project's Rule of Law Index gave Georgia the top rule-of-law score among all countries in its income bracket worldwide.

Georgia's public, meanwhile, maintained pressure on the government. Saakashvili's final years in office were dogged by frequent citizen demonstrations. In 2009, Georgians filled the main street in Tbilisi with makeshift prison cells to protest Saakashvili's police state. On the eve of elections in 2012, a video broke that appeared to depict the prison rape of thieves-in-law by government agents. Georgians voted Saakashvili out and handed power to the Georgian Dream party.[103] At first a vehicle for a wealthy businessman who self-financed his campaign against Saakashvili but retained murky ties to Russia, by 2016 Georgian Dream united a coalition of centrists, businessmen, pro-Europeans, and social conservatives. Georgians had fought for safety and refused to believe they needed to surrender their democracy to achieve it.

PHASE SPACE HAS SHIFTED

Each of the countries I've described has seen a major shift in phase space. Violence at the levels of the past is now unthinkable. That is not misplaced optimism or a naïve sense of hope. In a bookstore in Tbilisi, I spoke with a German governance expert who had lived through the highs and lows of Georgia's recent history. "This is not a case of someone who came, tried, and failed," he said. "That's not the story line. The story isn't that there is no way to leave history behind. It's not like that; things are better. Things can get better."[104] Everyone I interviewed agreed.

Georgia had been buffeted by anarchy, civil war, a criminal state, and authoritarianism. But it consistently grew less violent and less corrupt. Another interviewee, highly critical of Saakashvili, admitted that after the Rose Revolution "you didn't have to put bars on your window on the third floor; you didn't have to worry about where you parked your car. Georgia was a dark, dim place before he came, and afterward there was electricity and police officers that people trusted."[105] "I'm optimistic," said an anticorruption researcher and academic. "Over twenty years, there's been huge progress. We've moved from civil war to real elections where the president stepped down."[106] General Chachibaia summed up the sentiment. "In the 1990s, we had mass kidnappings," he explained. "But now we are upset by just a little uptick in crime. Society demands that leadership takes measures if someone's car is stolen."[107]

Similarly, Sicily's Mafia has been thoroughly decimated. Over twelve hundred Mafia fugitives were arrested between 1992 and 2005, including the Corleone bosses such as Totò Riina, who had been in hiding for twenty-two years, and his successor, Bernardo Provenzano.[108] Asset seizure and confiscation have virtually bankrupted the major Mafia groups, so that by the late 1990s Cosa Nostra had to stop paying monthly salaries to support the families of convicted mafiosi, destroying their credibility with their foot soldiers.[109] Giovanni Falcone once said that his goal was not to eliminate the Mafia, which was impossible, but to reduce it to a normal criminal phenomenon. In 2012, Giovanna Fiume, an anti-Mafia activist and professor of history at the University of Palermo, believed that goal had been accomplished. "There are no murders of public officials or large-scale killings. The Mafia has not disappeared, but has become more like generalized political corruption, which is rising in Italy. And there's no more silence."[110] In 2001, Palermo's crime rate was lower than that of the famously "cleaner" northern Italian cities of Milan and Bologna.[111]

In Colombia, kidnappings for ransom fell by 87 percent from 2002 to 2007, assassinations by 45 percent, and terrorist attacks by 77 percent.[112] Homicides were cut almost in half from 2002 to 2008, and by 2017 they had fallen to between 22 and 24 per 100,000, rates not seen for more than four decades.[113] Until the Syrian war, internal displacement was higher in Colombia than anywhere else in the world. It, too, has fallen steadily since 2007.[114] The state is also less repressive. Extrajudicial killings by the police and military, though not entirely eliminated, fell dramatically after 2007, when the Colombian military shifted from counting guerrilla deaths as its metric of success to incentivizing captures and demobilizations.[115] Impunity has also fallen. Colombia retired twenty-seven army officers, including three generals and the army commander.[116] By June 2012, over eighteen hundred members of the security forces had been charged for murders in the line of duty.[117] Meanwhile, a series of institutional reforms, such as legal advisers, investigative commissions, and a complaints desk for civilians within every military unit, have been instituted to change military culture and institutionalize accountability.[118] The Supreme Court is investigating over 120 members of Congress and twenty departmental governors for links to paramilitaries, while twenty-seven prosecutions are pending against other politicians and officials for links to the FARC guerrillas.[119]

Bihar has sustained similar successes. Maoist terror as well as caste-based militia massacres had virtually ended in the state by 2010, because both Maoists and militias had largely disbanded.[120] Kidnapping for ransom was down 83 percent by the end of Kumar's first term, and murder had fallen 13 percent. Violent crime fell across India during this period, but it fell almost twice as fast in Bihar as the national average.[121] In 2005, having a new car was an invitation to theft, so perhaps the most telling statistic is that people began buying cars again. From 2005 to 2010, registered vehicles increased fourfold, from just 80,000 to 319,000.[122] Some argue that reports of rape and crimes against Dalits have risen, but while total reports are higher, the incidence is lower per capita, because of the state's high population growth.[123] Perversely, the increased reporting could also be a sign of success. Rape statistics are notoriously unreliable, and many experts believe rapes are not actually more frequent; if they were, families wouldn't continue sending girls to school on their bicycles. They believe that greater political representation of women and Dalits is instead leading more women to report rape and violence and that police are now filing reports on these crimes, something they had previously failed to do.[124]

Altering phase space is not just about changing laws, though they often play an important role. Nor does it just require a better government, since fresh faces can turn fetid over time. It also requires a fundamental change in what a society can imagine, what people believe is acceptable and what they dream is possible. "Society is maturing," explained General Chachibaia in Georgia. "It's always about society."[125]

This book is a series of success stories. But it is also a tragedy, in the ancient Greek sense. The protagonists are heroes, but they carry within them the seeds of their own undoing. Idealistic social leaders can mobilize societies to save themselves but need to make compromises and concessions that will alienate some of their most ardent supporters. The egos politicians need to save their countries drive those leaders to arrogance and overreach. Flawed human beings must do their best to walk a tightrope too narrow for most stumbling feet. The ethics of reform are so fraught that few who work to help their countries escape Privilege Violence can avoid soiling their hands. Nor is the path a simple teleology of forward progress. A straight line cannot be forged out of the crooked timber of humanity. Instead, societies are composed of fragile beings who are easily polarized. Places where violence has been normalized once are always at greater risk of fissure. Individuals must constantly be on guard to prevent a return to violence from both their fellow citizens and the state.

Yet in each society I chronicle, ordinary people have learned that they have power. Having risen up, they know that their voices matter. They work to reduce violence. They demand better from their governments. They force justice, and they make peace.

11

WHAT CAN WE DO?

The burden belongs to the nation, and the hands of none of us are clean if we bend not our energies to righting these great wrongs.

—W. E. B. DU BOIS[1]

"Tell me about these Progressives," he said.

I was in Ghana interviewing a high-ranking police officer. The force he served was one of the least corrupt in Africa, but bribes and kickbacks still had to be passed up the chain. No one could tell me who was at the top. Some claimed that the new inspector general, the head of the police, was honest, but it was still unclear where his loyalties lay. The officer I was talking to was one of a small clutch of reformers who were pushing for change. It was dangerous work. One of his close colleagues had been court-martialed for insubordination.

The officer sat next to me in a university faculty lounge in northern Accra, a location he had picked to be far from the prying eyes of police headquarters. The scent of fried plantains and groundnut stew wafted over from the nearby canteen. The room was filled with overstuffed chairs. A lazy fan barely turned overhead. Surrounded by professors reading newspapers, the scene felt far removed from the dangers of violence and corruption. When we started talking about this book, the officer wanted answers. "How did the Progressives clean up the corruption among America's politicians and police at the turn of the twentieth century?" he wanted to know.

"It took fifty years," I told him. The middle class organized, with concrete actions that could attract people who weren't particularly political but wanted to get playgrounds for their kids or safe food for their families. Progressives mastered using the press to popularize their cause. They got financial support from local businesses that were also hurt by corruption, and they brought in as broad a coalition as they could, including unsavory supporters who believed in eugenics and the inferiority of immigrants. The politics of success was ugly. Electorally, they teamed up with southern segregationists on one side of the aisle, while infiltrating the Republican Party on the other. They persuaded honest people to run for office at the state level and mobilized to get them elected. They identified police reformers, started law-enforcement journals, and held conferences to spread criminal justice reform. They persuaded police chiefs to see themselves as part of a profession, not just clocking time at a job they would lose whenever a new party came to power. And, of course, all this didn't end corruption. It's no longer systemic, but real problems persist. As I spoke, I realized how daunting and academic this sounded, how far removed from his daily life.

"Uh-huh, um-hm, okay," he murmured, "we can start this now."

In 1970, nearly 380,000 people around the world died in combat.[2] In forty-five years, battle deaths fell by two-thirds, to under 100,000 in 2016.[3] We now know that it is possible to prevent large numbers of violent deaths from war and other causes. That knowledge engenders responsibility.

In 2016, nearly 560,000 people, about one person every minute, died from homicide, organized crime, terrorism, state brutality, and conflict.[4] Every evening for the past several months, I put down this manuscript, pick my three-year-old daughter up from day care, and play with her until bedtime. What do I, who have written this, and you, who are reading it, owe to the families who can never do that because violence has torn them apart?

So far, this book has distilled lessons for those fighting violence in their own countries. Now it's time to consider the supporting role outsiders can play. There are scores of ideas that could help countries out of violence. Three are pivotal. First, the middle class, the people with power and voice, must choose to act on their democracies' problems. Power structures can be changed only when a broad, diverse movement anchored in the middle class devotes its energies to improvement. How can outsiders help the middle class within violent countries awaken and organize? Second, bargains that buy off violent groups are essential to pausing bloodshed, but they don't bring peace. How can states transition from dirty deals to more open, just governments? Finally, it's easy to criticize venal leaders of other countries. It's difficult to admit that our own policies and personal choices assist their predation. I'll delve into what we can do domestically in the United States, Europe and other parts of the world to help reformers working under perilous circumstances improve their own democracies.

Before jumping into solutions, the people and governments of relatively safe, strong countries need to radically rethink their role vis-à-vis change. Ending Privilege Violence requires altering a country's power structure, a charged political issue in any country. Imagine if the German government, concerned over U.S. violence, funded efforts to persuade Congress to rewrite U.S. criminal justice laws so that they resembled Germany's. Its prison system features shorter sentences, focuses on rehabilitation, involves far less dehumanization, and has an enviable recidivism rate for murderers of just 18 percent.[5] That means it is also cheaper. The Germans might be onto something. But would they get a majority of congressmen to listen? Should they?

Trying to directly influence legislation or policy—a common practice of development aid and international diplomacy—often fails even when it's successful. Alina Mungiu-Pippidi's team of good-governance researchers have found that when laws to improve government accountability are passed because of international pressure, they go unused. Only when they are pushed by local citizens do they get taken up by domestic pressure groups as tools for better governance.[6]

Outsiders can make a difference, but they need to be more savvy about their roles. Foreign governments, philanthropists, activists, and experts are supporting actors. The lead characters are a country's citizens. The question is not "what can we do?" It is "how can we help people in violent countries help themselves?"

MOBILIZING THE MIDDLE CLASS

We focus too much on fighting criminals and insurgents and too little on empowering citizens to make their states run accountably so that they can reduce demand for violence. Most antiviolence interventions, such as putting more police on the street, are intended to stop perpetrators. Another set of programs, such as after-school activities in crime-ridden neighborhoods, help victims. In countries with Privilege Violence, the former will work only once a government is in place that wants to govern inclusively and fight violence. The latter are important but palliative (and should be evaluated with these more humble expectations in mind). Reform requires focusing on the fulcrum of change: the middle class.

Building Better Leaders

It takes unique individuals to decide they are going to lead reform against seemingly hopeless odds, then persuade others to come together to make change. Such people are rare everywhere, but a sense of efficacy is one of the particular casualties of endemic violence. While many people desire a different system, most won't create a movement for change where none exists. They need something to plug into, an effort to put their energies toward. As Jacob Riis said of Theodore Roosevelt's struggle against New York's corrupt machine politics, "We had all the ammunition for the fight, the law and all, but there was none who dared begin it till he came."[7]

What can broaden the pool and improve the efficacy of potential leaders against violence? Philanthropists played a crucial role in supporting early U.S. civil rights organizations by spending decades supporting the slow, steady organizing that built leadership and laid the groundwork for change. Aid agencies spent years bringing together Medellín's middle class in workshops and conferences that crossed partisan boundaries, with no measurable outcomes except talk. Ultimately, they birthed a civic movement and independent political party that brought Mayor Fajardo to power.

Many "leadership development programs" exist today. Yet they don't look like these earlier efforts. Government programs choose emerging leaders from around the globe and take them on study tours across the United States or Europe, flitting from city to city to glean new ideas and make foreign connections. Academic programs engage (English-speaking-only) rising stars, and invite them to month- or yearlong university programs in which some of the most highly accomplished, engaged, active people in the world are made to sit as passive students before a variety of experts. I've taken part in some of these programs and have observed others. Participants usually enjoy them, learn a lot, and take a break from their exhausting and stressful lives. These programs offer significant insight that could be useful to reform. But how effective are they at catalyzing improvements in governance abroad? There is little research on which of these programs work, which fail to have lasting effects, and which may even backfire by inspiring leaders to emigrate, for instance, and remove their skills from their own countries.[8]

Leadership of a broad-based movement, by definition, isn't solitary. While social reform can be taught to some extent, it must also be lived. People become leaders by leading. If outsiders want to develop local leadership against violence, their efforts would not look like these existing programs. They would, instead, resemble start-up accelerators.

Accelerators and their cousins, business incubators, began to take off with the tech revolution in the United States in the early years of the twenty-first century. Their purpose is to give entrepreneurs with a good idea a turbo-boost so they can move interesting notions into marketable realities. Some incubators are run by nonprofit organizations that help particular populations, such as veterans, get businesses off the ground. But many accelerators, like Y Combinator or Techstars, are run by investors and are not charitable. If they work, the investors plan to put their money into nascent companies that could become wildly profitable. That market focus grants the model rigor.

They bring together business teams with a high potential for success. They provide them with space, time, and money to get their ideas off the ground. They arm them with useful skills and relationships. They offer mentorship from previously successful entrepreneurs. And for those deemed most likely to succeed, a pot of funding often lies at the end of the rainbow.

An accelerator to fight violence would follow a similar model. Instead of focusing on promising individuals, it could identify groups of leaders from across diverse communities within the same country. People with supporters among the middle class would get to know leaders among more marginalized citizens, organizers from rural and urban areas, policy thinkers, journalists, future politicians, law enforcement, and the military. The time spent together would forge crucial relationships across networks so that a rising politician could gain the trust and email addresses of top bloggers, future technocrats, and organizers with ties to different parts of the country.[9] It would also help the group learn proven skills needed to make change—gaining legitimacy, avoiding partisanship, working with the media, building a broad movement, managing for accountability. It would offer mentorship from successful social and political leaders inside and outside the country who had been in similar positions and were willing to provide continuing, real-time help at tough moments in the future fight. A few organizations with vaguely similar strategies exist to help movements fight authoritarian regimes—but little exists to help leaders build something better and more viable after a regime is ousted, or in place with flawed but democratic power structures.

Finally, like successful accelerators, such a program would offer some time, space, and funding for creating a joint strategy. Rather than building a marketable product, the leaders would forge a campaign for reform while determining whether they could work together as a team.[10] But as with business incubators, there could be a pot of fast, flexible money at the end of the program that could help cover anything from printing costs to legal fees, along with donors who could get to know the leaders, judge for themselves their potential, and support clean political campaigns or policy ideas they like. Funding to help impoverished, reform-oriented governments make change quickly and hire technocrats at competitive salaries with the private sector (as occurred in Georgia thanks to the Open Society Institute) could be part of the package.

It's hard to predict who will end up making societies better. The life paths of people who spark change are often atypical. Some are late bloomers; others who appear destined for greatness get derailed along the way. The process of picking leaders is like venture capital. One assumes a decent amount of risk that any single investment will bear fruit and tries to mitigate that risk with a portfolio, assuming that most bets won't make it.[11] Yet like venture capital, if one such investment pays off, the return on investment could be life changing to an entire country.

Education

Leaders need followers. It takes an educated citizenry to organize and outwit the forces of Privilege Violence in their own society. Some people who read early versions of this book asked whether it was possible for change to occur in countries that lacked a middle class. I can't say. But I found no case of a democracy successfully exiting Privilege Violence and remaining democratic without one. Education is therefore also a crucial first step for countries at this earlier developmental stage or countries whose professionals are too tied to the ruling regime to lead reform.

While education sounds remote from the processes needed to change power structures, it is, in fact, strongly predictive. Scholars attribute the rise of democracy in the twentieth century in part to the growth of education the century before.[12] In their studies on global corruption, Bo Rothstein and Alina Mungiu-Pippidi found that education and literacy are two of the most significant variables correlated with the control of corruption. They are so important that a population's average years of schooling in 1900 can explain 70 percent of the variation in corruption today (though length of schooling also, of course, correlates to the strength of these states' bureaucracies a century ago).[13] Supporting an educated citizenry can expand a middle class with the confidence and sense of personal efficacy required to demand more from their governments. These character traits are augmented when education increases job opportunities so that people are not reliant on favors and nepotism for their livelihoods.

Funding and improving mass education from pre-K onward through philanthropy, online courses, nonprofit and for-profit schools, and other means are all ways to build a citizenry with the wherewithal to stand up to the entrenched power structures preventing their countries from moving forward.

Liberal arts universities in the West also have an important role to play. Western education doesn't make anyone a reformer; if it did, scores of dictators' children wouldn't use their Ivy League and Oxbridge degrees to become more effectively corrupt princelings. Nor is Western education essential to making change. Many of the world's reformers, like Abhyanand, Bihar's police chief, are brilliant, creative, and effective without it. But at least one study suggests that a Western liberal education can jump-start the careers of foreign reformers.[14] It appears to be particularly useful for inculcating new norms for understanding what it means to be an elite and what one's responsibilities are to society. Some of my Colombian interviewees, for example, claimed that one factor behind the movement for a new constitution was that the children of Colombia's elite attended top Western schools and afterward aspired to be more like schoolmates who earned their way through systems that reward merit, not cronyism. El Tiempo, the leading newspaper in Colombia, published more balanced coverage after a generation educated in America and Europe took charge of its ownership.[15] In Mexico, elites have traditionally supported government policies, but some of their children who have been schooled in the United States are beginning to question their country's power structure. Moreover, by taking jobs outside government, they are liberated to criticize government mistakes.[16]

Not all education is equal. The study describing the benefits of Western education found that engineering and science don't have the same effect as the humanities and social sciences (including graduate subjects such as law) in inculcating new norms. So universities that are matriculating large numbers of foreign students should emphasize the value of merit and ensure students receive a well-rounded liberal arts and humanities education, despite the pull of tech jobs and STEM subjects. Meanwhile, as highly educated and wealthy parents

provide greater opportunities to their children and thereby monopolize spots in elite schools, universities will need to do more to ensure
that they remain meritocratic, or risk having foreign elites see the U.S.
system, particularly, as quite similar to their own rather than inspir-
ingly different.

Top universities could go one step further. They could use their
considerable leverage to deny admission to the children of a small
subset of the world's bloodiest oligarchs.[17] Policy makers have learned
that smart sanctions targeting a few individual leaders' pocketbooks
and travel prospects are far more effective ways to pressure foreign
governments than broad embargoes that impoverish entire countries. While the sins of the fathers should not fall on their children, the
threat of having their kids barred from the world's best universities
could be one of the few incentives that persuade some of the globe's
bloodiest warlords and drug lords to hold their fire.

TRANSFORMING DIRTY DEALS
INTO LEGITIMATE GOVERNMENTS

No left-wing protests would be complete without a "No justice, no
peace" placard. "We don't negotiate with terrorists" is a common
claim of the Right. Both views bear responsibility for continuing
cycles of violence.

It's smart policy to avoid bargaining over individual incidents of
terror that simply incentivize further mayhem. Yet in countries beset
by violence, forging agreements with terrorists, militias, and criminals to put down their weapons is the only way weak states can gain
enough time to rebuild. Strong demands for justice and restitution
from organized groups within society are useful for forcing more
concessions at the bargaining table and creating a more just peace.
But ultimately, to reduce violence in the short term, a deal must be
made, and it will, inevitably, entail some impunity and injustice, more
if the state is too corrupt and weakened to prevail on the battlefield.
Why else would the violent agree to disarm?

So the real issue is not this loud, stale debate over justice versus
peace. Instead, it is the thorny task of crafting agreements that violent individuals are willing to sign, which also include future-oriented

provisions that will slowly reduce their political and economic power over time. Such provisions can increase the chances that a short-term deal doesn't result in the long-term degradation of the state.

My conversations with veteran peace negotiators have offered insights into how to structure such trip wires.[18] Perpetrators of violence want immunity and impunity: they want to stay out of jail, and they want to retain as much ill-gotten money as possible. By tying provisions that accommodate these desires to reforms that enable a more level economic and political playing field, it is possible to create trip wires that kick in after a few years that could render a power structure less likely to devolve into Privilege Violence. Of course, negotiating parties will notice this fine print. But they may not take it seriously. Violent actors tend to be concerned with the immediate future, the interim structures created between the signing of an agreement and the resumption of normal government. If trip-wire provisions kick in after three or four years, violent groups are likely to assume that by then they will have enough power to remain untouchable. Most warlords, crime lords, and state perpetrators of abuse do not take long-term institutional and legal provisions very seriously, because they are used to being above the law and don't believe that such provisions will apply to them.[19]

Trip wires could take myriad forms, but wherever possible they should be red-line rules, requirements so obvious that they do not need strong institutions to oversee or enforce them.[20] They should focus on two overarching goals, which can be combined in actual provisions. First, they should ensure that politics is as open to new entrants as possible. It should become easier, over time, for those without preexisting wealth and power to gain appointed and elected office. It should also become gradually harder for corrupt leaders to attain office, and increasingly difficult to make money off government positions. Second, violent groups maintain power through wealth. Trip-wire provisions should reduce their ill-gotten assets over time. Ensuring that the economy is increasingly open, decentralized, and less reliant on the government reduces both opportunities for corruption and incentives to seek political office for self-enrichment.

Creating an economy in which small- and medium-sized enterprises can thrive helps build a middle class independent of the government while reducing the power of a predatory state.

Provisions that address these goals might include regulations that exclude formerly violent actors from owning or sitting on the boards of banks and other financial institutions, to prevent money laundering. They could reduce regulations on trade, opening businesses, and receiving professional certifications to make various ministry positions less lucrative. Asset disclosure laws for public officials should be required and should place the burden of proof on the official. Recidivist violence or corruption following an amnesty agreement could each be criteria that automatically bars a candidate from holding office. Electoral laws could ensure that independent candidates can run and help equalize their chances at voter recognition.

In some cases, it may be possible to persuade governments to turn certain powers over to independent national or international bodies. Mauritius, the small island off the coast of Madagascar, for example, has tried to attract greater investment by naming the Privy Council in the U.K. as its own court of final appeal, tying its hands in some matters of justice. In other cases, foreign aid and development organizations, a common presence in countries with Privilege Violence, can use their financial leverage alongside domestic pressure to extract similar organizationally hefty requirements. For example, foreign and security aid could be subject to external, independent audit, while a percentage of all aid to the country could be allocated to building independent, internationally accredited, domestic financial bodies with the responsibility of auditing government budgets within five years. Donors could also support processes to build domestic support for locally based institutions that could play useful roles in fighting violence. Where a public demands them, for instance, independent bodies that collect homicide statistics on violent deaths could be insisted upon in peace deals, and initial funds could be provided through outside donations. While many institutions founded to fight corruption fail, a few that have built strong bases of local support, such as Ghana's Commission on Human Rights and Administrative Justice and Romania's National Anticorruption Directorate, have been more effective.[21] To increase the chances of success, foreign supporters should not simply replicate institutions that work elsewhere, but help locals devise solutions to their problems, then use their leverage in peace treaties to buttress the solutions devised—such as providing ongoing funding earmarked as a percentage of tax revenue.

Another way outsiders can play a useful role is by increasing the pressure on violent groups so that governments can get a better deal at the negotiating table. For example, the U.S. decision to put Colombia's AUC paramilitary consortium on its list of terrorist organizations and then make demands for extradition undoubtedly assisted President Uribe in persuading the paramilitaries to disarm. Had he been so inclined, he could likely have worked with the United States to use America's threats as negotiating leverage.

In many cases, of course, governments presiding over Privilege Violence make deals to temporarily alleviate pressure. They have no intention of altering their power structures. In these countries, outsiders must tread carefully. If fears of corruption lead them to cut foreign aid, and that impending largesse was the carrot encouraging violent groups to sign a peace agreement, donors could unintentionally spur new bloodshed.[22] Instead, foreign governments and donors should work on reducing the prize to be gained from controlling the government. Reducing ministerial or bureaucratic powers, as Georgia did when it simply granted licenses if they weren't issued in a timely fashion, is one such creative solution. Cash-on-delivery aid programs make a country deliver on some developmental goal before reimbursing for costs, ensuring that even if money is skimmed, the project is completed. An even more robust example comes from Guatemala. In 2006, several honest members of the government invited the United Nations into the country to create the International Commission Against Impunity. The few hundred staff members who work at the agency have since forced out a former president, brought down the nation's two top law-enforcement officials, and started an overhaul of the entire criminal justice system. Thanks to UN pressure, prosecutors gained the powers proven elsewhere to be crucial to fighting crime: wiretaps, the ability to strike plea bargains, even an asset-seizure law.[23] International donors and governments can work to bolster such international bodies and organizations that empower reform contingents within otherwise problematic governments.

PHYSICIAN, HEAL THYSELF

Of course, the United States and Europe are not neutral bystanders to the phenomenon of Privilege Violence. They sometimes abet it, and often impede the improvement of some of the most violent countries in the world. Tightening the banking sector; reforming security assistance, development aid, and trade; and crafting creative systems to ensure that tourist dollars aren't funneled to violent groups are all domestic reforms to our own systems that would help other countries help themselves.

Finance

Efforts to fight violence abroad should begin in our hottest housing markets, stock markets, and financial hubs, because Privilege Violence is often motivated by money.[24] Most criminal gain is laundered not in Medellín or Palermo but in London and New York.[25]

Real estate is a particularly popular way to turn dirty money into a lavish house or apartment complex that can eventually be sold so that the profit turns up clean. Approximately 30 percent of all high-end, all-cash real estate transactions in six major U.S. cities involve shell companies that have been flagged with suspicious activity reports, according to the U.S. Department of the Treasury.[26] Miami has the largest number of houses bought with cash in the nation—more than 70 percent in 2012, a number that has remained high for years.[27] Some of these sales are perfectly legal. Some are not. Britain's National Crime Agency has said that London's property prices are being artificially inflated by criminals laundering money and hiding assets, and the U.K. government has found evidence of terrorist financing as well.[28] At One Hyde Park, a luxury building in central London just across from the Knightsbridge tube station, apartments have panic rooms with surveillance and protection technology and feature bulletproof glass, in a country where even police rarely carry guns. Of the seventy-six apartments that had been sold at the time of one journalist's investigation (at a top price, reportedly, of $214 million), a few were registered to individuals such as a senior Kazakh politician, while almost 80 percent were bought through anonymous companies registered in tax havens and shrouded by complex shell organizations intended to hide their identities.[29] In 2013, just before it was dissolved, the U.K.'s Financial Services Authority estimated that between £23 billion and £57 billion were being laundered through the U.K. each year—or somewhere between 1.4 and 3.6 percent of the national GDP.[30]

Today, British island dependencies and territories, such as the British Virgin Islands and the Caymans, form a legal Bermuda triangle where money can enter and never be found again—at least not by anyone legitimate. Switzerland has also vociferously fought to protect its banking secrecy laws, which have enabled some of the globe's most predatory government officials and violent criminals to steal from their countries.[31] The cousin of Syria's president, believed to be the president's "bagman" who launders his family's money, has Swiss and Panamanian accounts. The United States is also a leading destination for registering shell companies, thanks in part to Delaware's easy corporate registration laws.[32] Canada is another unexpected haven.

The U.K., however, stands out for taking the greatest steps to address this problem. As I write this, the British government is crafting a series of programs that would support investigative journalists working to uncover money laundering, then follow up on their discoveries with targeted regulatory and banking interventions. In October 2016, Britain passed a criminal finances bill that enables the government to seize assets from lawbreakers and to criminally prosecute banks and accounting firms whose staff are found to be aiding tax evaders. The government also created a listing of the real owners behind shell companies and is working on a property register, though some politicians are delaying its implementation. The European Union recently passed legislation to keep lists of the true owners of beneficial corporations (though the proof will be in its implementation). In the United States, both the House and the Senate have introduced bipartisan bills to tighten the U.S. financial system as well. The legislation is a long way from being passed, but the efforts mark the beginning of the kind of change that could make a difference to countries facing Privilege Violence.

Other reforms could entail public transparency regarding the private banking of public officials and their families. Information on such officials' accounts could be held on blockchain (a sexy name for what is, essentially, double-entry bookkeeping kept simultaneously across a network of computers to make it impossible to alter without leaving a trace). The financial industry could then use artificial intelligence to flag aberrations between publicly transparent assets and actual assets held by "politically exposed persons," a category of accounts already maintained by global banks. Countries could craft legislation similar to Britain's criminal finances bill that would enable the prosecution of the lawyers, accountants, bankers, and other professionals who knowingly assist violent criminals. These are known by law enforcement as the "third tier," alongside the "first tier" of violent criminals and the "second tier" of complicit politicians. Of course, such laws would require careful drafting; no one wants to deny anyone a defense lawyer by criminalizing the ability to represent, and it can be difficult to distinguish between legitimate advice to a company that made a mistake and serving as a consigliere to a criminal enterprise. But in the United States, a crime and fraud exception to attorney-client privilege already exists. It provides secrecy for the disclosure of past wrongs, but prevents lawyers from helping clients commit ongoing or future criminal acts. Stronger enforcement of regulations such as these to curb the banks, lawyers, and accountants who abet violence and corruption is possible.

Security Assistance, Development Aid, and Trade

The main way more peaceful countries fuel Privilege Violence abroad is through ill-considered security cooperation, security assistance, and development efforts. The first step to improving these programs is to see places caught in Privilege Violence for what they are. To many policy experts, Mexico is seen as a middle-income but embattled country, while Niger is so fragile it verges on failed. Yet the two share an underlying pattern. The vast majority of places beset by pervasive violence are not led by well-meaning but weak governments overwhelmed by violent forces. They don't just need a little outside expertise and a few helicopters to win the fight. These are countries in which many political and security leaders are locked in collusive relationships with violent groups. Their levels of complicity, not their supposed strength, should be the most salient feature in determining how foreign countries engage.

This does not mean, of course, that everyone working in these governments is in league with violent forces. Even in the most broken systems, honest people remain. These individuals are battling tough odds and deserve respect and support. But they rarely have the power to change the system. Security sector assistance and aid should not be predicated on the pretense that they do.[33]

Because bureaus that provide security cooperation and economic assistance are often rated on how quickly they get their money out the door, it can be easy for bureaucrats to cherry-pick facts that convince themselves otherwise. Mexico, for instance, has a history of extraditing a few criminals to the United States as sacrificial lambs in the weeks prior to U.S. congressional certification processes.[34]

In the 1890s, when New York passed early prohibition laws on alcohol, the police commissioner, Theodore Roosevelt, wrote,

> The law was very actively enforced, but it was enforced with corrupt discrimination. . . . [M]any of the men responsible for putting the law on the statute-books in order to please one element of their constituents, also connived at or even profited by the corrupt and partial non-enforcement of the law in order to please another set of their constituents, or to secure profit for themselves.[35]

If the skeptical eye that Roosevelt cast on his hometown's political order were to become a more common way of analyzing other countries' political structures, it is hard to overstate what a sea change it would be for international security and development assistance.

Security Sector Assistance

Security cooperation and assistance is by far the most significant way that the U.S. government props up states ruling through Privilege Violence. The United States currently spends about $18 billion a year in over 130 countries, about two-thirds of all countries on the planet.

This means that the United States doles out funds in amounts that are small within America's budget, and usually too minimal to do much in terms of providing security, but are enough to skew priorities and feed corruption within receiving states.[36] In fiscal year 2016, Mexico received $111 million, while the Department of Defense provided Kenya with $98 million and the Philippines (whose president has threatened to extrajudicially kill drug dealers and journalists) with $61 million.[37] Security budgets are one of the easiest places for governments to hide corruption, because they are legitimately somewhat opaque. Sensitive procurement—such as a communications network for Kenya's prison system, a secure server for its police department, or a military surveillance system—rarely requires that bidding requirements be made public, for understandable reasons. Yet that also makes security services easy places to conceal kickback schemes and other irregularities, which in Kenya amounted to the theft of 5 percent of its total GDP.[38]

It is far past time for the U.S. Congress and European oversight bodies to demand independent monitoring to determine what their security aid is buying and whether it is effective. When such monitoring has been required, as in Afghanistan, the results have suggested that corruption and diversion are causing the U.S. government to inadvertently support the very insurgents it is trying to fight.[39]

In countries beset by Privilege Violence, the goal of security assistance should be to build a functional relationship between the government and its citizens, because lasting security will not prevail until that goal is met.[40] Thus, a percentage of security sector assistance should be allocated to independent citizen monitoring and oversight within the country, to ensure funds are not misspent. Foreign assistance can also help a country expand security expertise among legislators and civilians so that there are independent local experts who understand where funds should be going and what equipment may be needed.

Meanwhile, democracies receiving security aid should be triaged by their levels of Privilege Violence and their desire to improve.[41] Based on an accepted scale of state-supported non-state violence, countries that score in the lowest tercile, implying significant collusion with non-state violent groups, should simply not be sent aid.

Where political realities preclude cutting assistance—as in a country like Iraq—strong auditing and oversight procedures should be funded at levels commensurate with the amount of aid, and governments should not be provided with equipment and training that could easily be turned against their citizens.

Countries in the middle tier should be offered defense and law-enforcement institution-building programs that assist Ministries of Defense and Interior with stronger budgeting, procurement, and other internal processes, organizational skills such as human resources improvements, and professional training.[42] These programs can alter professional cultures and create a cadre of skilled mid-tier bureaucrats. More symbolic practices, such as encouraging security services to swear an oath to serve their country's people—not the regime—can have deep effects on professional cultures over time. These efforts can position security agencies to do their jobs when a government allows them to do so.

Kinetic training within this middle group of countries should be reserved for elite, handpicked units that are closely monitored. Among other things, they should be inculcated with norms such as not shooting civilians, to enable the sort of security service defection from Privilege Violence that allowed the Rose Revolution to occur in the Republic of Georgia. Fungible money and equipment should be subject to audit and should be provided sparingly, largely as a sweetener to persuade a government to allow these deeper reforms.

Serious effort to build the capacity of other governments to fight should be reserved for countries in the top tier. Their commitment to govern inclusively suggests that here security aid can make a real difference. With less money wasted on the first group, more would be available for larger-scale, Plan Colombia–style programming within this set of states. Fast, flexible funding arrangements should be available to help this group of governments in their early months after taking office, when they need to show concrete change to their citizens and demonstrate that a new order is afoot. In many cases, speedy disbursement of relatively small amounts of money is far more important than large amounts of funding that arrive too late. Meanwhile, the professionalization efforts, oversight training, and citizen monitoring offered to the more complicit countries should also be provided as part of a standard package, in recognition that reform-minded governments rarely stay that way forever.

Development Aid

Development aid is crucial to help governments that are honestly working to fight violence. In Bihar, as Nitish Kumar improved the state, donors piled in to help. The United Nations, the Gates Foundation, the Asian Development Bank, the World Bank, and Britain's aid agency, the Department for International Development (DFID), all started providing support for police training, government administration, and accountability monitoring.[43] In Georgia, donors poured in money after the Rose Revolution, and in Colombia the United States and international funders also delivered billions.[44] But Georgia had taken over a billion dollars from the United States, the EU, and the World Bank before Saakashvili's government came to power, and the funds made little difference.[45] Colombia had received multiple aid packages worth nearly a billion dollars prior to Plan Colombia, with little to show for it. When changes are already well under way, philanthropic help makes speedier improvement possible. But it doesn't drive reform.

Meanwhile, thoughtless development aid can do active harm in countries whose governments are not committed to change. In Sicily after World War II and Naples after the 1980 earthquake, Italian government funding to assist poor and devastated regions increased Mafia power, leading the Sicilian prosecutor Giovanni Falcone to claim, "We have reached the point where any economic intervention on the part of the state only runs the risk of offering the Mafia further opportunities for speculation."[46] A sudden influx of international aid can lead to violence as different factions fight over the pot. Multiple studies have found that high levels of food aid, for instance, actually increase the risk of conflict and that the risk is significant enough that it offsets any positive effects of aid on economic growth and poverty reduction.[47] Highly factionalized democracies and so-called neopatrimonial countries with the kind of corrupt power structure that often leads to Privilege Violence are likely to have the lowest quality of governance when aid is highest, suggesting that assistance to these countries might inadvertently be buttressing inimical power structures.[48] As Ugandan journalist Andrew Mwenda argues, not only do high levels of aid provide a source of rents that make it less necessary for governments to enrich their own people to profit themselves, but they can tie the professional class to the government.[49] If the best jobs—or the only jobs—for professionals are state-supported, it becomes harder to mobilize a middle class to challenge Privilege Violence.

A popular theory promulgated during the early years of the U.S. and allied nations' war in Afghanistan posited that development aid can curb violence by enabling government services and generating income, thereby convincing people that their government is working for them and thus is more legitimate.[50] But as scholars began to study these programs, it became clear that this theory fell apart in practice. Some parts of the country must get programs first. Some places and people are going to gain more than others. If service delivery improves in a way that is inequitable, as is inevitable, and if those inequities fall along existing regional, ethnic, or religious fissures, the job programs, wells, court buildings, and other aid can create more grievances than they solve. Meanwhile, research suggests that receiving more and better services can just raise expectations, so even as the state is able to deliver more, people become more and more upset at the corruption and inefficiency that remain.[51] Finally, programs intended to buy the hearts and minds of aggrieved populations assume that people supporting violent insurgents will begin trusting the government if it provides goods such as electricity, water, roads, schools, and hospitals. But people who are angry at their governments for immense discrimination, supporting violent paramilitaries, or stealing their national assets are liable to have mixed feelings, at best, when foreign money helps politicians open a token health clinic in their district. While they may appreciate the ability to get vaccinations, they might still live in fear of an unaccountable power structure that steals their money or threatens their families.

The goal of development aid in places of Privilege Violence must be to build social momentum for change, rather than infusing money into a criminal state. In corrupt, violent contexts, economic development to increase GDP has been proven to fail. Only when aid is directed at improving governance, fighting corruption, and helping regular people hold their government to account does it seem to help.[52] Before an administration is in power that is committed to altering the power structure, development aid to fight violence should be directed almost entirely at citizens, not the government.[53] This is increasingly tricky in scores of countries that are erecting obstacles to foreign contributions reaching local groups.[54] Even without these obstacles, there is far to go. The United States is currently the largest foreign funder of civil society programs in the world. It devotes less than 0.2 percent of official assistance to civil society.[55]

Some aid seems so essential that it is hard to imagine stopping it until a decent government comes to power. The health community is on the verge of conquering a variety of horrible tropical diseases. Should this effort stop in countries whose governments impoverish their populations by skimming money to keep rapacious elites in power? It's a tough moral calculus—one that should not be ours to make. Instead, what if fungible aid given directly to a government budget—both security and development assistance—was put to a vote of the recipient country's public? The idea sounds outlandish. But what if the vote was not a national referendum, with all the expense and gamesmanship that would likely ensue, but a program of deliberative democracy in which a representative group of citizens was pulled aside for a few days, paid for their time, educated on the facts, and asked to vote up or down on each line item? Such public deliberation exercises have become commonplace in hundreds of governmental decisions worldwide, from determining local budget allocations in Paris to rebuilding New Orleans after Hurricane Katrina.[56]

Journalists could cover the deliberations so that the amounts of aid as well as the terms of debate are made clear to the broader public. The process would force foreign governments to let the citizens of a country know how much money is being given to their countries and to which sectors. It would also allow citizens to determine whether helicopters and ammunition for their security services, or an influx of funds into a corrupt health ministry, was desirable. Finally, it would be far more obvious if the money citizens voted for did not, in fact, materialize as expected.

In the metric-driven world of modern aid, what gets measured is what gets done. Despite challenges to the basic operating model, development assistance still uses GDP growth as its metric of success. But a rising GDP can hide an increasingly inequitable distribution of wealth that consolidates economic power at the top of society, keeps those at the very bottom alive, but does nothing to build the group in the middle. Rwanda, for instance, has been a developmental darling because its GDP has grown an average of 8 percent per year from 2001 to 2015. But income inequality has skyrocketed over the same period so that Rwanda's Gini coefficient, which measures inequalities of wealth, was 50.8 in 2013—among the twenty highest in the world.[57] Development funds in countries wrestling with Privilege Violence should be focused on and evaluated by their ability to build a middle class whose incomes are not linked to their governments. Aid that measures success should be based not on overall growth but on how well the economy increases the middle class (determined by quantifiable metrics such as education, income, and consumption). This middle-class growth would empower societies to create their own reforms.

Trade and Business

To break free from Privilege Violence, countries must have economies that are not controlled by their political and economic elites or unduly twisted to benefit the privileged. Small businesses and entrepreneurs are essential to create a middle class that is independent of the government and able to speak out against it without fear of losing livelihoods. Local businesses can also fuel domestic movements that alter power structures. Leonardo Arriola of Berkeley has found that opposition movements in Africa succeeded in places where they could amass financial support from businesses not affiliated with the ruling party.[58] Cities where businesses depend on international markets are incentivized to consider how the safety of their cities affects their bottom line. The political scientist Eduardo Moncada theorized that one reason Medellín's improvements have lasted longer than those of

Cali, even though both cities had dynamic, crime-fighting mayors, is that Medellín's business community was internationally focused and felt the effects of international fear and opprobrium more than Cali's inwardly focused, agriculturally based economy.[59] Getting small- and medium-sized businesses to support the fight against corruption and a trust-busting agenda was also essential to the Progressives' fight in Gilded Age America.

The business sector is not monolithic. Not all business is helpful. Agriculture and extractive industries with significant, immobile infrastructure investments can abet violent, oligarchic power structures. Companies like Chiquita are stuck farming their tropical fruits in Central America. Oil companies must pull black gold from countries like Nigeria. That often forces such companies into complicit relationships with paramilitaries, militias, and state security services.[60] Unable to leave the region and tied to particular pieces of land, they are prime targets for violent extortion. Businesses with immobile infrastructure in dangerous places also need to protect their workers. Often, the only security available for hire is connected to an existing violent group. Dropping foreign direct investment (or development aid workers) into a country beset by Privilege Violence often requires hiring private security companies owned by warlords or staffed by gangs and militias.

Chiquita, for example, admitted in court that it made over a hundred payments totaling $1.7 million to Don Berna's paramilitary consortium in Colombia for protection, continuing the payments for two years after the U.S. government declared Don Berna's group a terrorist organization.[61] Chiquita executives claimed that they were forced to do so, under threat of extortion from both guerrillas and paramilitaries. The claim is highly plausible. Yet multiple Colombian paramilitary leaders testified under oath to their country's Truth and Reconciliation Commission that some companies also used them as corporate assassins to eliminate union leaders, environmental activists, and others who threatened corporate interests.[62] These accusations are difficult to prove but are too common to be dismissed.

Finally, investors whose mission is not purely driven by profit, but involves social impact, often prefer to make investments in large enterprises. Such investments are easier to monitor and are justi-fied on the grounds that they could provide large numbers of jobs in poor or post-conflict countries. But an economy built around a handful of large businesses owned by a small number of people can abet Privilege Violence. Such big businesses are easily captured by oligarchs and venal governments. Government agencies such as the Overseas Private Investment Corporation, development banks, and impact investment institutions should consider how economic struc-tures can abet Privilege Violence. To create economies that contrib-ute to better governance, socially minded investors and banks should instead provide funds that encourage many small- and medium-sized firms. For instance, investments may educate or augment local bank-ing infrastructure, which often prefers making large loans to favored enterprises and can be resistant to the additional work and risk incurred in small- and medium-sized lending.[63] Assistance for local lending capacity, encouraging peer-to-peer lending platforms, assist-ing the insurance market, reducing regulatory hurdles for companies with fewer than fifty employees, and a host of other measures could assist in building a self-perpetuating economy that supports demo-cratic governance.

Stop Funding Violence with Tourist Dollars

It's easy to condemn the financial sector, government policies, and big businesses. But they are not alone in supporting Privilege Vio-lence. Before I traveled to Sicily to research this book, a family friend who adores Italian vacations shared stories from her own jaunts to the island. Once, she said, she had left some very valuable jewelry in a hotel safe in Palermo. Only when she was long checked out and hours away over winding mountain roads did she realize her mistake. But, she smiled—the hotel was run by the Mafia. What luck! They put her jewelry into a hotel car and sent it to her. Not a piece was missing.

It's a popular myth that the Mafia keeps crime down for ordinary people. Compared with places where many violent groups are in competition, a dominant organized criminal force does exert a pax mafioso.[64] But when measured against places without Privilege Violence, a criminally led peace enables far greater bloodshed. In 1990, just before it got its Mafia under control, Sicily had only 9 percent of Italy's population but 24 percent of the country's robberies, while the four southern regions with the greatest Mafia penetration (Campania, Calabria, Apulia, and Sicily) accounted for a third of the Italian population but two-thirds of robberies. Naples, where the Camorra mob is still active, has thirteen times the murder rate of the whole of Italy.[65]

My friend's attitude toward the Mafia is not unusual. In the United States, many see the mob as quaint. We joke about concrete shoes and cite *The Godfather* as one of the best films of all time (which, of course, it is). The common attitude seems to be that the Mafia may do some substandard construction work but is otherwise a relatively harmless artifact, sort of an elderly Italian Elks Lodge.

Few would feel this way about a drug cartel. Yet that, of course, is a significant aspect of the Mafia enterprise. In 1876, a visitor from Tuscany found Sicily gorgeous and enchanting. He might have returned home thinking it was one of the most pleasant places on earth. But as he learned more, he explained, "the perfume of orange and lemon blossom begins to smell like corpses."[66] Italian organizations like Addiopizzo—"Good-bye, Extortion!"—valiantly try to persuade tourists to frequent hotels and businesses that have turned their backs on Mafia ties and resist payoffs. They deserve our patronage.

The role of foreign tourists, investors, businesses, and philanthropists inadvertently supporting violence elsewhere is not confined to Italy. Jamaica and the Bahamas have some of the most violence per capita in the world. More adventurous travel destinations are adventurous for a reason: Myanmar's hotel chains and nicer restaurants are often owned by members of the military who have overseen breathtaking abuses. When I traveled to Myanmar, it was fairly simple to spend an hour on the internet learning which hotels and tour companies were connected to generals with blood on their hands. But it's easy to forget, while deciding where to eat lunch or which hotel looks enticing, that your choice of where to shop or stay might be fueling murders, kidnappings, and a brutal structure of power. Whether traveling for pleasure or investing for work, people putting money into places where violence is rife have an obligation to spend their money in ways that do not enrich the perpetrators of murder. We owe the people struggling against Privilege Violence this small but potent measure of human solidarity.

It would be easier, of course, if the travel industry took this problem to heart. Demanding consumers have persuaded industries from diamonds to rugs to certify their products and tighten their supply-chain partnerships so that consumers do not unwittingly contribute to actions they find morally noxious, such as insurgency and child labor. On travel websites, a violence rating system could be placed right next to the dollar sign icons for cost and the pictographs depicting whether a given locale is child-friendly. One could envision one to five tiny rifle icons to quickly depict the links between a given high-end resort and organized crime, warlords, or state security. Such a system could be used in the world's fifty most violent countries, as well as the three most violent countries in any given region (to include places such as Italy). A consortium of investigative journalists could work with such a travel service to craft the rating, which could be subject to the now-ubiquitous process of open peer review to avoid anyone being accused of libel. In addition to a steady base of income from travel sites such as TripAdvisor, a certification entity (based in the United States, again, out of libel concerns) could also create additional income streams by packaging its information for other interested parties, such as businesses wishing to mitigate investment risk.

Finally, like policy makers, we ordinary people must alter some fundamental attitudes. First, we must give politicians some respect. Democracies, by definition, cannot be run without elected leaders. It's easy to keep one's hands clean and denounce the messy process of politics. Yet someone has to walk the morally murky path of compromise that is required to forge a nation out of many people with vastly different value sets. Denouncing all politicians as corrupt and venal makes it far less likely that good people will want to run for office. Warts and all, politicians with their unique skill set are essential to pull their countries out of Privilege Violence.

Second, the common conceit that it is okay, even preferable, to let criminals kill criminals is profoundly dangerous. That is the thinking that enables the decivilizing spiral to begin, taking an entire country down with it until massive numbers of ordinary people are dying in violence erroneously dismissed as criminal turf wars or insurgent infighting. Even when a person is guilty of horrific acts of brutality, that individual requires justice and not an extrajudicial death sentence from the state or vigilante justice. I have no doubt that evil people exist: my father was a judge, and I spent years of my childhood sitting in the back of my father's courtroom, watching people guilty of immense depravity. Yet reducing violence begins with an acceptance of the sanctity of every life—because it is right, and because only by prizing each life as one of inherent worth can we create societies where the lives of innocents are protected.

CONCLUSION

There is nothing inevitable about a country caught in Privilege Violence finding its way to relative security. It's a stumbling, staggering journey, not an elevator ride. Many countries have yet to take the first steps. Courageous leaders and equally brave followers have to decide that they are willing to put themselves in danger to seek better lives for themselves and their countrymen. Pragmatic movements must team up with flawed, self-interested politicians. Savvy politicians with vision and skill must show society that change is possible. Then they need to craft carefully calculated deals with terrible, violent individuals, bargains that are necessary and yet leave blood on their hands. Where governments grow repressive, a new round of citizen protests are needed to right the ship. We each must decide to make positive change and then put in the long, hard work.

"A nation is a choice," wrote the historian Lerone Bennett Jr. "It chooses itself at fateful forks in the road. . . . And ever afterwards, the nation and the people who make up the nation are defined by the fork and by the decision that was made there, as well as by the decision that was not made there."

When people stand up and say "Enough," we whose lives are less endangered can help them. The lives we transform are not just those of the people caught in the cross fire, but our own. Economists expect talent to be equally distributed across the world. The fact that it seems so concentrated in a few safe countries suggests that we are losing the contributions of thousands of people who could have improved all of our lives but whose own lives have instead been stunted by bloodshed. There are seven billion people on our planet. We are losing the talents of one in six of them to violence.[67]

In 2016, for the first time in over a decade, global deaths from homicide ticked upward.[68] Every minute you have spent reading this book, another life has been lost. We now have a road map of what must be done. It is time to begin.

ACKNOWLEDGMENTS

While I lay in the hospital watching my vital organs shut down one by one, I considered the irony of having just spent months in tricky parts of the world researching violent death, only to potentially meet my end thanks to eating some *Listeria*-laden goody while six months pregnant. To Dr. Harpal S. Harrar, Dr. Kumar Kunde, and the many other doctors and ingenious nurses at St. Thomas' Hospital in London who saved my life and thereby enabled both my baby and this book to come into the world, my gratitude is unbounded and beyond words.

I've been blessed to be able to work at the Carnegie Endowment for International Peace. No finer colleague exists than Thomas Carothers, who shielded me from many duties to allow this work to proceed and then didn't show me the door after reading a far-too-early draft. Saskia Brechenmacher, Jeremy Weinstein, and my old friend Loren Griffith also read drafts and provided excellent advice at a stage far too nascent to ask of any reasonable person. My Carnegie Endowment colleagues Milan Vaishnav and Tom de Waal provided essential insight into India and Georgia, respectively, while Sarah Chayes offered crucial framing to the "Dirty Deals" chapter. Carnegie's graphics impresarios, particularly Courtney Griffith and David Grauel, created beautiful graphs out of complex data. Carnegie's junior fellows Yusuf Ahmad, Chayenne Polimedio, Julu Katticaran, and Gustavo Berrizbeitia provided invaluable research throughout this process; Caroline Kiernan added her abilities at a crucial stage; and Elena Barham became a true partner who deepened the theory behind this work. Many colleagues at DFID offered intellectual as well as years of essential financial support.

During a semester spent at Stanford University's Center for Advanced Study in the Behavioral Sciences (CASBS), I gained a beautiful space to work on this manuscript and an astounding group of interdisciplinary colleagues with which to discuss the ideas. I am particularly grateful to Dan Rodgers for his gentle assistance in bridging the historical and political science portions of this work. Margaret Levi, director of CASBS, served as guardian angel, not only reading an early draft at a book workshop she hosted, but taking me aside and, in about fifteen minutes while I waited for my taxi, reformulating the entire volume. I am immensely grateful for her time and guidance, as well as that of other colleagues who engaged with an early draft at a book workshop: Tino Cuéllar, James Fearon, Francis Fukuyama, Jorge González, Erik Jensen, Salar Kamangar, Aila Matanock, Ari Ratner, Stephen Stedman, and Barry Weingast. A CASBS workshop also facilitated the discovery of my agent, Max Brockman, whose cool guidance has been of immense assistance in my first foray into publishing with a trade press.

In addition to multiple CASBS forums, other venues that allowed me to test ideas at early stages included Stanford's Center on Democracy, Development, and the Rule of Law, the Clingendael Institute in the Netherlands, Loyola University's PROLAW program in Rome, the Austria Study Center for Peace and Conflict Resolution, CalCon at the University of San Diego's Joan B. Kroc School of Peace Studies, and the University of Maryland.

A particular thanks to Alejandro Ponce, Juan Botero, William Neukom, and other friends at the World Justice Project (WJP) who helped launch this research with an international conference they helped me coordinate with Beatriz Magaloni bringing together global experts on gangs, organized crime, and electoral violence to draw connections between separate fields. The WJP's Rule of Law Research Consortium meetings at Stanford and the University of Chicago also helped me deepen and develop these ideas.

Many of the best suggestions for how to stop admiring the problem and begin solving it stemmed from a workshop Zvika Krieger hosted for me at the World Economic Forum's Fourth Industrial

Revolution headquarters. Sarah Holewinski, Salar Kamangar, Paul Klingenstein, Tom Malinowski, Tomicah Tillemann, Jeremy Weinstein, and Catherine Wiesner all spent valuable hours reading an early version and offering ideas that have improved nearly every page of this book, particularly the final chapter. Ari Ratner has my particular gratitude for not only offering excellent thoughts in multiple workshops but providing me with his magic title-creation guide that led to *A Savage Order*.

I have never allowed anyone to do fieldwork for me, but being stuck in the hospital for two months prevented me from returning to India for interviews. Rushda Majeed worked with me to draft questions, craft an interview list, and discuss each meeting before and after. Our interviewing process in Bihar was as close as possible to being there myself—with the added benefit that Rushda speaks Hindi. I could not have addressed the Bihar case without her ability and acumen. The core of this book is drawn from fieldwork and interviews conducted between January 2014 and March 2015. Wagner University students conducted extra interviews in Mexico in the spring of 2017. I thank their professor Natasha Iskander, as well as Jessica Cardenas, Glynnis McIntyre, Sherylynn Sealy, and Isabel Vicentini de Armas for their hard work. I also thank the vast numbers of people in Georgia, Italy, Ghana, and Colombia who gave of their time for interviews, whether they are named in these pages or prefer to be anonymous. Their generosity and insight formed the foundation for my ideas.

Certain colleagues went above and beyond any reasonable duty. In particular, Randy Roth, whom I had never met, responded to emails with reams of unpublished research to help me dissect thorny questions regarding violence modeling and trust. A missive to Robert Blakey led him to read the entirety of chapter 9 and offer detailed thoughts on the RICO law that he drafted. Larry Diamond and Mike McFaul both have served as guiding lights in highlighting the worth of democracy in even the most inhospitable of circumstances. Gary Milante and Robert Muggah deserve particular appreciation for their collegial discussion of many of these ideas and for their own work in improving our understanding of violence. Meanwhile, like Michelangelo finding the sculpture in the stone, my editor, Maria Goldverg, managed to cull from a collection of underwhelming pages far in excess of my allotted word count a book of which we can both be proud.

I owe special appreciation to my parents for their libertarian child rearing. With no note of irony intended, their choice to raise me amid trigger-happy neighbors in Alaska led to multiple encounters with the wrong end of a rifle before I headed off to college, habituating me to a certain comfort level around violence. Their willingness to let their sixteen-year-old daughter fly off to a disintegrating Soviet Union sparked a lifetime of curiosity about the parts of the world that were falling down (and how to build them back up). My brother, Daniel, pulled me into that fateful St. Petersburg journey a quarter century ago and more recently answered a Hail Mary call to read the entire manuscript in three days and offer last-minute, invaluable drafting thoughts.

In this list of important people and places, I would be remiss not to add Ozo Coffee and Seeds Library Café in Boulder, Colorado, and Iconik in Santa Fe, whose pots of tea fueled countless hours of writing and revision. Thank you for never asking what I was doing or why I had made the high tables in your businesses into de facto standing desks for my "office."

This book had its genesis in a fateful walk in Aspen, Colorado, with Richard Danzig, who, upon finding out I did not like Westerns and had never read *Lonesome Dove*, pulled me into a bookstore, purchased a copy, and immediately wrote on the frontispiece, thereby ensuring I could not return it. Days spent at the Aspen Security Forum discussing the conflicts in Pakistan and Afghanistan, and evenings spent reading about cattle drives in America's Wild West, sparked the earliest questions into how some places got better after endemic violence.

I began field research for this book while pregnant with my first daughter and am finishing it while the second makes her presence felt forcefully below my rib cage. To Cimarron and Saskia Roan, I hope this book is one small step toward handing you a better world. Finally, to Will, my love and my true partner, there are not words enough to express all you are to me. Thank you for all your support in bringing this third baby to fruition.

NOTES

INTRODUCTION

1. Yolanda Figueroa, *El capo del golfo* (Mexico, D.F.: Grijalbo, 1997), 71, cited in Pimentel, "Nexus of Organized Crime and Politics in Mexico," 48.

2. Arce, "Dad Seeks Justice for Son Killed in Broken Honduras."

3. This description is drawn from ibid. and Arce and Mendoza, "Tragic Killing of Honduran Teen." I was senior adviser to a review of Honduran criminal justice conducted for a U.S. government agency to determine where aid might best be given to help the government combat violence. Our blunt report was instantly classified, and I cannot cite an official copy.

4. Miroff, "When the Police Are Part of the Problem."

5. Many countries have been involved in training Afghanistan's police since the U.S. and allied war began in 2001, but Germany was given the lead role under the Bonn Agreement. The United States eventually began its own training program, which became larger than that of the Germans (whose role was later taken over by the European Union). None of these efforts have created a trusted and well-functioning force. See Perito, *Afghanistan's Police.*

6. Numbers are drawn from the civil war data sets kept by Uppsala University and the Centre for the Study of Civil War, Peace Research Institute Oslo (PRIO).

7. Widmer and Pavesi, "Monitoring Trends in Violent Deaths." For more on why the statistics are all to be taken with caution, see Kleinfeld, *Reducing All Violent Deaths;* and Kleinfeld, "Why Is It So Difficult to Count Dead People?"

8. The Brazilian Forum of Public Safety reported 58,383 violent deaths in 2015, a year in which the Syrian Observatory for Human Rights documented 55,219 deaths in Syria.

9. Data from *Global Burden of Armed Violence 2015,* 3. The Uppsala/PRIO data set, "UCDP One-Sided Violence Dataset v1.4-2016," as seen in Melander,

Pettersson, and Themnér, "Organized Violence," covers state, terrorist, and insurgent violence from 1989 to 2015. Wars kill more people through indirect means—starvation, lack of access to medical facilities that have been bombed, and so forth. However, modeling these indirect deaths has as much to do with issues such as the level of country development and medical prowess as the virulence of violence. See Kleinfeld, "Why Is It So Difficult to Count Dead People?"

10. McEvoy and Hideg, "Global Violent Deaths 2017."

11. Numbers on one-sided violence and non-state armed violence only began to be collected internationally when the Human Security Report Project commissioned UCDP/PRIO to collect these numbers in 2003; as a result, while they have attempted to code backward in time where possible, data is far more lacking than for conflict violence. Moreover, the small-scale nature of these deaths and the intimidation of journalists means that UCDP/PRIO's methods of tracking English-language media to collect statistics may undercount such deaths more severely than war deaths.

12. Nigeria reported nearly 2,000 homicides in 2008—the only time in twenty-seven years it has reported homicide statistics—but had an additional 857 deaths from police killings in the line of duty that did not appear in homicide data. These numbers are drawn from the CLEEN Foundation, a Nigerian justice-sector reform organization, and are cited in *Small Arms Survey 2015*.

13. Breslow, "Staggering Death Toll." Mexican government statistics from the Instituto Nacional de Estadística, Geografía e Informática indicate 164,000 victims of homicide in the country between 2007 and 2014. During the same period, the United Nations found 21,415 civilian deaths in Afghanistan, and Iraq Body Count cites 81,636 Iraqi civilians murdered, for a total of fewer than 104,000.

14. Homicide, war deaths, and security service killings are drawn from McEvoy and Hideg, "Global Violent Deaths 2017." The latter category represents people killed by security services in the course of their duties and, due to the small number of countries reporting, vastly undercounts such deaths; in 2016, the United States alone was responsible for approximately 963 police killings according to the *Washington Post* data set; while in Brazil, police killed 4,224 people in the line of duty. Generally, law enforcement is more violent when countries are more violent—U.S. police "are 36 times more deadly than German police officers, but also 35 times likelier to be killed on the job," according to "Global Patterns," *Economist*. Terrorism data comes from the Global Terrorism Index 2017. UNODC numbers were used for the loose circle of organized criminal violence, but because they are extrapolations from a different year, I did not attribute a number.

15. One reason these findings may appear surprising is that war deaths are reported per war, not per year, so they add up over time. Conversely, absolute

numbers of homicides are rarely reported. If they are, they are annual counts, so are rarely as large. More frequently, homicides are given as per capita rates, which gives a more accurate sense of comparison between countries but obscures overall deaths. India, for instance, has the second-largest absolute number of murders most years—generally around 32,000 to 35,000 a year over the last decade, or more in any given year than the total deaths from war in Yemen and Ukraine combined. But with a population of well over a billion people, India's homicide *rate* is remarkably low: just 3.5 per 100,000, or half the world's average, according to the UN Office on Drugs and Crime, the body tasked with maintaining global counts. The Igarapé Institute, which begins with UNODC's numbers but then cross-checks with local police, morgues, and think tanks for greater accuracy, puts India's rate at an even lower 2.8 per 100,000, below Latvia's.

16. Dowdney, *Neither War nor Peace,* 70.

17. Villagran, "Victims' Movement in Mexico," 125.

18. The first five years of life are when children develop the prefrontal-lobe connections in their brains that regulate self-control. Violent environments disrupt those connections, leading many less-resilient children who witness violence to have reduced impulse control and increasing their likelihood of perpetrating violence as teenagers. Sharkey et al., "Effect of Local Violence," 2,287–93. The possibility that violence affects DNA is still under development. For more on neuroscience, see Mill, "Dynamic Epigenetic Responses."

19. New Orleans's 2011 homicide rate of 57.6 per 100,000 almost exactly matched Afghanistan's rate of violent death from war, homicide, and other causes, as measured by Alvazzi del Frate, Kraus, and Nowak, *Global Burden of Armed Violence 2015,* 66.

20. Consejo Ciudadano, "World's 50 Most Violent Cities."

21. Centers for Disease Control, "Rates of Homicide, Suicide."

22. Murphy, Karimi, and Shoichet, "Mother and Son's Deportation Pits Senator Against Homeland Security."

23. Mack and Serif, "Sie können es nicht lassen!"

24. I must admit I was skeptical of this fact when I started this book. I was convinced, however, by the masterly work of Pinker in *The Better Angels of Our Nature.* For further, see Eisner, "Modernization, Self-Control, and Lethal Violence"; Gurr, "Historical Trends in Violent Crime: A Critical Review"; and Gurr, "Historical Trends in Violent Crime: Europe and the United States."

25. Compare modern wars to World War II. As of October 2016, after fifteen years of war in Afghanistan, the U.S. military had lost 1,200 civilian contractors and just under 2,400 service members—nearly 600 of them dead from causes other than battle, such as suicide and illness. On D-day alone, approximately 2,000 Allied soldiers lost their lives. At the Battle of the Bulge, 19,000

troops died between December 1944 and January 1945. The Battle of Monte Cassino featured 50,000 Allied casualties. In May 1942, at the Second Battle of Kharkov, around 250,000 Russian troops were killed, injured, or captured. The Battle of Luzon, from January to August 1945, killed over 200,000 Japanese forces.

26. "Human Security Report 2009–2010," 21.

27. Erikkson, Wallensteen, and Stollenberg, "Armed Conflict," 594.

28. Hironaka, *Neverending Wars*, 106, 124; "Human Security Report, 2009–2010," 41–42, which claims that the end of the Cold War contributed to the end of the wars in Mozambique, Guatemala, El Salvador, Yemen, and Ethiopia.

29. "Human Security Report 2009–2010," 22–23.

30. Walter, "Conflict Relapse," 1. Statistics come from PRIO in 2014, the latest comparable data available.

31. "Human Security Report 2009–2010," 36, 157. There had been a 79 percent reduction from 1984 to 2008. Ibid., 157. Battle deaths include both troops killed in battle and civilians killed by cross fire. While I am counting violent deaths, indirect deaths from disease, famine, and non-war-related injuries are actually the biggest killers in war. However, these have also fallen as medicine and general levels of economic development and infrastructure have improved.

32. McEvoy and Hideg, "Global Violent Deaths 2017," 10.

33. Data from the PRIO database.

34. Pinker, *Better Angels of Our Nature*. Accurate cross-country counts of violence are stunningly problematic because of underreporting, incompatible reporting, manipulation, and other issues. See Kleinfeld, "Why the Data Must Improve."

35. Data sourced from Eisner, "Long-Term Historical Trends"; and UNODC for 2010, graph reproduced from Max Roser at www.OurWorldinData.org, licensed under a Creative Commons CC-BY-SA license.

36. Fearon and Hoeffler, "Conflict and Violence Assessment," 3. For further, see Eisner, "Modernization, Self-Control, and Lethal Violence"; Gurr, "Historical Trends in Violent Crime: A Critical Review"; and Gurr, "Historical Trends in Violent Crime: Europe and the United States."

37. "Homicide in the United States, 1950–1964," 2, and recent CDC statistics. The 2014 U.S. homicide rate was 4.4 per 100,000. From 1955 to 1958, homicide in the United States fell to approximately 4.5 per 100,000, which was itself a local low; prior to the 1950s, it had not been so peaceful in the United States since 1910.

38. Numbers are drawn from Centers for Disease Control data, which is considered more reliable than FBI statistics because the CDC counts bodies after

an autopsy at a local morgue that appear to have been killed intentionally. Police reports can be politicized, and in many countries, police count murders only when cases are closed, leading to significant undercounts.

39. Darby and MacGinty, *Contemporary Peacemaking.*

40. "Human Security Report 2009–2010," 66–67, 69, drawing in part on the work of Regan, Frank, and Aydin, "Diplomatic Interventions and Civil War," 135–46.

41. Walter, *Committing to Peace.*

42. While further work is needed to disentangle causation from correlation, research suggests that including community organizations in peace talks decreases the likelihood of a re-outbreak of violence by up to 64 percent, and another study of 156 peace agreements found that including women made it 35 percent more likely that peace would last fifteen years or longer. See Nilsson, "Anchoring the Peace"; and Stone, "Quantitative Analysis of Women's Participation."

43. Today, for all their many flaws, peacekeeping missions are 75–85 percent more likely to prevent civil wars from reoccurring than places with no such missions, especially where peacekeepers have strong rules of engagement and real funding. In fact, two-thirds of UN peacekeeping missions were successful, and they contributed to the fact that since the early 1990s civil wars have been cut in half, and from 1993 to 2003 deaths in civil wars reduced by fivefold. UN peacekeeping is also cheap. In 2005, the UN's seventeen peacekeeping operations, involving seventy thousand troops, cost less than one month of U.S.-led operations in Iraq. See Dobbins et al., "The UN's Role in Nation-Building." See also Kleinfeld, "The United States and the Future of Humanitarian Intervention"; Gilligan and Sergenti, "Do UN Interventions Cause Peace?"; Fortna, *Does Peacekeeping Work?,* 125; Doyle and Sambanis, "International Peacebuilding"; and Beardsley, "Peacekeeping and the Contagion of Conflict," which finds that peacekeeping had little effect during the Cold War but strong positive effects afterward, suggesting that a renewed Cold War–style geopolitics might reduce peacekeeping's worth. Additionally, see Hultman et al., "Beyond Keeping Peace"; and Kreps and Wallace, "Just How Humanitarian Are Interventions?," which finds that peacekeeping forces with strong mandates and high capacity can also reduce violence against civilians and fighting more generally, though this may come at the cost of prolonging war. Lastly, see Kathman and Wood, "Managing Threat, Cost, and Incentive to Kill"; and Gleditsch, *All International Politics Is Local,* which suggest that peacekeepers also reduce the spread of conflict.

44. Elizabeth Ferris, "Changing Times: The International Response to Internal Displacement in Colombia," Brookings Institution, 2014.

45. In 1991, Medellín had 6,349 killings, or more than 17 murders a day, for a homicide rate of 381 per 100,000. All homicide numbers are from the UNODC

unless otherwise noted. New York City had fewer than 300 murders in 2017; to match Medellín's rate per capita, it would have to have had 32,000.

46. Nell McShane Wulfhart, "36 Hours in Medellín, Colombia," *New York Times,* May 13, 2015.

47. Nitish Kumar, interview by Rushda Majeed, July 3, 2015, in conjunction with author. See also Aiyar, "Bihar," 47; and Chakrabarti, *Bihar Breakthrough,* 12, 45–46.

48. Raghwesh Ranjan, interview by Rushda Majeed, July 15, 2015, in conjunction with author.

49. Pascale, Sternin, and Sternin, *Power of Positive Deviance.*

50. Because international relations scholars can't put countries in a petri dish and inflict different levels of violence on them, naturally occurring experiments, where two locations face nearly the same initial conditions and one alters for an external, exogenous reason, are the closest we can come.

51. In academia, the methodological pitfall I am avoiding is known as picking on the dependent variable.

52. Casey and Herrero, "How a Politician Accused of Drug Trafficking Became Venezuela's Vice President"; Mele, "2 Nephews of Venezuela's First Lady Convicted of Drug Charges."

53. "Customs Agents Find Cocaine on Colombian Air Force Plane," CNN, Nov. 10, 1998.

54. Jain, "Criminals as Leaders—Yet Again?"; and Vaishnav, *When Crime Pays.*

55. "Brazil's Political Crisis," *Economist,* March 26, 2016.

56. "Crime in Brazil," *Economist,* March 24, 2018.

57. Schneider and Schneider, *Reversible Destiny,* 34.

58. World Bank, "World Development Report 2011," 1.

1: VIOLENCE TODAY

1. T. S. Eliot, *Murder in the Cathedral* (New York: Harcourt Brace Jovanovich, 1935), 43. The play is about King Henry II's murder of Thomas Becket, the archbishop of Canterbury, in 1170, an era of ubiquitous violence and an act committed to deny any check on the king's power, including that of religious authority.

2. Violence statistics are highly unreliable. See Kleinfeld, "Why Is It So Difficult to Count Dead People?" However, they must be used, so this book takes the path used by most violence scholars and looks for patterns over time, rather

than relying on any single statistic as definitive. For more on the methodology, see chapter 10's discussion of phase space.

3. In Libya, for instance, the United Arab Emirates and Qatar finance rival warlords.

4. Reprinted with permission of the Geneva Declaration Secretariat. From Alvazzi del Frate, Krause, and Nowak, *Every Body Counts*, 56.

5. McEvoy and Hideg, "Global Burden of Armed Violence 2017," 18.

6. The Brazilian Forum of Public Safety reported 58,383 homicides in Brazil in 2015, a year in which the Syrian Observatory for Human Rights counted 55,219 deaths in the Syrian war.

7. World Bank, "Gross Domestic Product 2016."

8. Widmer and Pavesi, "Monitoring Trends in Violent Deaths," 4.

9. "Global Terrorism Index 2017," 4. The Global Terrorism Index is based on data from the Global Terrorism Database, which is contracted by the U.S. Department of State as its terrorism data provider.

10. Ibid.

11. McEvoy and Hideg, "Global Violent Deaths 2017," 24–25. The twenty-three countries, in order, are Syria, El Salvador, Venezuela, Honduras, Afghanistan, Jamaica, Iraq, Libya, Somalia, South Sudan, Belize, Trinidad and Tobago, South Africa, the Bahamas, Lesotho, Brazil, Guatemala, Colombia, Central African Republic, Guyana, Dominican Republic, Namibia, and Yemen. Only nine of these countries were at war.

12. For instance, researchers in Georgia found that "Georgian guerrillas have two often-conflicting identities: a political one that makes them fight against Abkhaz separatism, and a criminal role that creates an incentive for them to cooperate with Abkhaz militia and criminal groups in smuggling." Kukhianidze, Kupatadze, and Gotsiridze, "Smuggling in Abkhazia," 80.

13. Perito, *Afghanistan's Police*, 7, details the drug connections and corruption of both the Taliban and the Interior Ministry and police forces in Afghanistan.

14. Dawson, "Social Determinants of the Rule of Law," 319.

15. While academics have been more reluctant to decamp from their silos, the community of security practitioners recognize this change in the nature of violence. The edited volume by Michael Miklaucic and Jacqueline Brewer, *Convergence: Illicit Networks and National Security in the Age of Globalization*, is one of a few recent works to highlight this scholarship.

16. "Global Terrorism Index 2017," 68.

17. This is true of both insurgents and pro-government militias and paramilitaries in modern forms of warfare. Naylor, "Insurgent Economy."

18. Stanley McChrystal, "COMISAF's Initial Assessment," Memorandum to Secretary of Defense Robert Gates, Aug. 30, 2009, 2–9, 2–10, cited in "Corruption in Conflict," 35.

19. Huntington, *Clash of Civilizations*, 217.

20. Gleditsch and Rudolfsen, "Are Muslim Countries More Prone to Violence?"

21. Indonesia has the world's largest Muslim population as of 2015; India has the third largest, just a few million behind Pakistan. Pakistan has played host to extreme violence, but it is also an example of the pattern of governance that leads to violence that I describe within this chapter.

22. Charles de Secondat Montesquieu, *Persian Letters* (Oxford: Oxford University Press, 2008), 39.

23. May, *The Mongol Conquests in World History*.

24. Aya Batrawy, Paisley Dodds, and Lori Hinnant, "Islam for Dummies: IS Recruits Have Poor Grasp of Faith," AP, Aug. 15, 2016.

25. Atran, "ISIS Is a Revolution." Richard Danzig, former secretary of the U.S. Navy, found a similar compulsion among Aum Shinrikyo terrorists in Japan. Among the most educated and potentially successful members of Japanese society, they had turned to a cult preaching murder out of a desire to stand out and be heroic, "like Luke Skywalker," in a culture where conformity was the norm. Personal discussion with the author.

26. Young men often fuse these high-minded motives with a desire for personal dignity, elevating individual indignation by wrapping it in a grander cause. See Scott Atran's testimony before the UN Security Council in Atran, "Scott Atran on Youth, Violent Extremism."

27. In Europe particularly, many violent jihadists are being recruited from convicted criminals with violent backgrounds who are then converted to Islam. The religious justification cloaks violent proclivities in grandiose rationalization. See Basra, Neumann, and Brunner, "Criminal Pasts, Terrorist Futures"; and Roy, *Jihad and Death*.

28. Walter, "New New Civil Wars." A deeper reading suggests that the repression and authoritarianism common to so many Arab states stems from the Mamluk period, when leaders relied on slave armies rather than aristocrats to protect their territories. That choice meant that private property rules never gained as much strength in the Middle East as in Europe, where feudal lords demanded stronger protections. It also meant that sultanistic, corrupt rulers were fought not by feudal armies but by religious leaders, who therefore gained significant moral authority (unlike the Roman Catholic Church, whose internal moral contradictions led to dissatisfaction and eventually challenge). Authoritarian governance in much of today's Middle East comes not from Islam itself but from this historical happenstance that forced political elites to

meld with religious leaders for legitimacy, creating an absence of a mediating class. For more on this history, see Blaydes and Chaney, "Political Economy Legacy"; and Blaydes and Chaney, "Feudal Revolution."

29. Journalists such as Kaplan and scholars such as Huntington also advocated variants of the argument that primordial ethnic differences make for violent instability. See Kaplan, "Coming Anarchy"; and Huntington, *Clash of Civilizations*. However, multiple scholars have found no relationship between ethnic fissures and civil war. For examples of such work, see Fearon and Laitin, "Ethnicity, Insurgency, and Civil War"; Collier and Hoeffler, "Greed and Grievance in Civil War"; Montalvo and Reynal-Querol, "Fractionalization, Polarization, and Economic Development"; and Lake and Rothchild, "Spreading Fear."

30. While CNN launched in 1980, the first Gulf War in 1991 was a watershed event that vastly increased viewership and propelled the small enterprise into the ranks of global media players.

31. For further, see Collier and Hoeffler, "Greed and Grievance in Civil War."

32. Most historians and a multitude of other scholars jumped on the other side of the debate, offering a series of more complex stories of causation, until, ultimately, many scholars felt the debate had petered out because the causes were intertwined. See, for instance, Stewart, *Horizontal Inequalities and Conflict*; Bowen, "Myth of Global Ethnic Conflict"; Collier and Hoeffler, "Greed and Grievance in Civil War"; and Cederman and Girardin, "Beyond Fractionalization."

33. See Gurr, "People Against States"; and Gurr, "Ethnic Warfare on the Wane."

34. Around 150,000 people died in the various conflicts precipitated by Yugoslavia's demise. Estimates for the Rwandan genocide range from 500,000 to 2 million. Uppsala University puts the death toll at around 800,000, and scholarship suggests that between 600,000 and 800,000 Tutsis and perhaps an additional 60,000 Hutus lost their lives in 1994. See Verpoorten, "Death Toll of the Rwandan Genocide." Numbers on the Congo's deaths are highly contested. Like many African civil wars, most victims of the protracted civil conflict in the Democratic Republic of the Congo (DRC) (1998–2003) died not because of the fighting but because of the higher vulnerability to diseases during a conflict that obstructed access to food and medicine. A November 2002 study by the International Rescue Committee (IRC) corroborated this thesis. Yet a few years later, IRC researchers thought that they had underestimated mortality because of empty households and security conditions, which impeded access to the worst areas. Consequently, they extrapolated findings from war zones to the whole country, speaking about the "First African World War"—a conflict that, according to the IRC, claimed 5.4 million victims in ten years (1998–2008), totaling 8 percent of the total population of the DRC. These figures were

never validated by experts, and the IRC never provided confidence estimates. Moreover, the IRC found child mortality rates that were twice as high as those of different credible estimates. See Pérouse de Montclos, Minor, and Sinha, *Violence, Statistics, and the Politics of Accounting for the Dead.*

35. Lieven, *Chechnya*, 351.

36. Kukhianidze, "Corruption and Organized Crime in Georgia," 217–18.

37. See Restrepo, Spagat, and Vargas, "Dynamics of the Colombian Civil Conflict." Some got more specific with their cultural explanations, touting the glamorization of the *paisa* in Medellín culture, an unrefined hustler skilled at making money regardless of the cause, a belief set that had long linked the region to smuggling and set it up for drug running when the cocaine binge of the 1980s hit. Yet Cali and Bogotá had their share of violence, although they didn't have the folklore of the *paisa*. For the scholarly take on the cultural argument, see Vargas, "State, Esprit Mafioso, and Armed Conflict in Colombia." For a similar take in popular culture, see Bowden, *Killing Pablo*. Barry Latzer, a U.S. criminologist and author of *The Rise and Fall of Violent Crime in America*, is also a proponent of the cultural theory of crime to explain why the "honor culture" of the Scotch-Irish in the U.S. South and the transferal of that culture to African Americans in the South and, through the Great Migration, to the North, has led to greater violence within those subcultures.

38. For scholarship on Latin American masculinity and violence, see Baird, "Violent Gang and the Construction of Masculinity." Or, more popularly, "A Lethal Culture: Drugs and Machismo Are a Dangerous Mix," *Economist*, Dec. 11, 2014.

39. The Venezuelan Violence Observatory, a nonpartisan organization composed of researchers from seven of the country's universities, found the 2015 homicide rate across Venezuela to be 90 per 100,000; in 2011, it was 67 per 100,000 in what was then the worst year on record. In 2016, Venezuela dropped to dead last in the World Justice Project's annual Rule of Law Index.

40. Kleinfeld, *Advancing the Rule of Law*, 98–107.

41. Smith, "Changing an Organisation's Culture."

42. Moore, *Social Origins*, 486.

43. See Thompson, "America's Culture of Violence"; "Mass Shootings and Gun Control: A Culture of Violence," *Economist*, June 22, 2015; and Frum, "Cultural Roots of Crime."

44. *Chicago Tribune*, Nov. 22, 1875, quoted in Chevigny, *Edge of the Knife*, 125–26.

45. Leovy, *Ghettoside*, 48, citing, "Screen Writer Bandit Killed," *Los Angeles Times*, June 17, 1925.

46. Known as the "Subway Vigilante," Bernhard Goetz seriously wounded his four alleged muggers but did not kill any of them. He served eight months in jail for carrying an unlicensed firearm but was found not guilty of attempted murder, assault, and other charges, although a later civil case awarded one of the shot men who was left paraplegic and brain damaged $43 million in damages.

47. Santaella-Tenorio et al., "What Do We Know About the Association Between Firearm Legislation and Firearm-Related Injuries?," is a literature review of such studies and found that, on average, homicide rises by 6.8 percent in places where Stand Your Ground laws have passed, driven largely by an increase among white males.

48. In fact, DNA is a good analogy. Scientists now know that many genetic traits are heritable but not inevitable. Instead, people may carry genes that predispose them toward an illness or a type of behavior, but those genes are activated only if the person is exposed to particular conditions, such as stress in the womb, a particular environment, or a virus. Culture is like the genetic predisposition. A culture may incline a society toward some level of violence, but whether and how that violence is expressed has a lot more to do with how the country is governed and the institutions it has created.

49. See U.S. National Security Strategy 2002, 10–11, and opening letter by George W. Bush.

50. Fearon, "Governance and Civil War Onset," 80. See also Fearon and Laitin, "Ethnicity, Insurgency, and Civil War."

51. For just a sampling of the most prominent of the research findings on the correlation between weak states and violence, see Fearon and Laitin, "Ethnicity, Insurgency, and Civil War"; Goldstone et al., "Global Model for Forecasting Political Instability"; King and Zeng, "Improving Forecasts of State Failure"; and Hegre et al., "Toward a Democratic Civil Peace." Case studies also offer causal connections between weak states and violence, such as Goodwin, *No Other Way Out*; Skocpol, *States and Social Revolutions*; and Goldstone, *Revolutions and Rebellions in the Early Modern World*.

52. For one example and a listing of others, see Rice and Stewart, "Index of State Weakness in the Development World."

53. A fierce terminology battle is under way between the U.S. Department of Defense, which engages in security cooperation, and the State Department, which insists it undertakes security assistance. The European Union prefers the term "security sector reform." While nuances between these exist, I am using the terms interchangeably here to imply funds that help train and equip security forces in other countries. Funding numbers are drawn from the Security Assistance Monitor.

54. Security Assistance Monitor. For more on the strategy of working by, with, and through foreign militaries, see Brown and Karlin, "Friends with Benefits."

55. A joint communication from the EU high representative for foreign affairs and security policy lists the EU budget line for security sector reform as €253,506,177 in 2016; see *Definitive Adoption (EU, Euratom) 2016/150*, 1,263. The UN number is a lowball figure because it integrates security sector reform with peacekeeping missions, but a 2012 article separates out $95 million in the UN Peacebuilding Fund for security sector reform work. See Cheng-Hopkins, afterword, 52.

56. For more on how the United States and Europe use aid to attempt to build functional police, courts, prisons, and other rule-of-law institutions in scores of countries around the world, see Kleinfeld, *Advancing the Rule of Law*.

57. Ibid.; Kleinfeld, "Fragility and Security Sector Reform."

58. Perito, *Afghanistan's Police*, 7.

59. "The Capture of Mosul: Terror's New Headquarters," *Economist*, June 14, 2014.

60. The early members of the Zetas were recruited from the Grupo Aeromóvil de Fuerzas Especiales. Turbiville, "Firefights, Raids, and Assassinations," 124, 128–32.

61. McInnis and Lucas, "What Is 'Building Partner Capacity'?"; Skorupski and Serafino, "DOD Security Cooperation."

62. McNerney et al., *Assessing Security Cooperation*, xv, 70; Taw, "Effectiveness of Training International Military Students in Internal Defense and Development"; Watts, *Countering Others' Insurgencies*, 39–44. Not a single case of effectiveness was found in all of Africa and the Middle East.

63. Cliffe and Roberts, *World Development Report 2011*; Fearon and Laitin, "Ethnicity, Insurgency, and Civil War"; Collier and Hoeffler, "Greed and Grievance in Civil War"; Elbadawi and Sambanis, "Why Are There So Many Civil Wars in Africa?"

64. Low-level violence tends to precede civil war and lowers income, as demonstrated by Sambanis, *Using Case Studies to Expand the Theory of Civil War*, 307. Because 90 percent of countries facing civil war are actually facing recurrent civil war, their incomes have already been lowered by the first civil war, and the ongoing effect of war is causing poverty, not necessarily the other way around. Fearon and Laitin hold that poverty causes state weakness, which invites challengers to the government such as insurgents and civil war. This correlation holds yet does not explain why so many of the poorest states have remained peaceful—such as Malawi and Burkina Faso. Nor does it explain the weakness

of middle-income states such as Syria, Iraq, Libya, Colombia, and others that have been beset by civil war and insurgencies.

65. UNODC, Homicide Statistics. In *American Homicide,* Randy Roth estimates that world homicide rates are 13.6 per 100,000 in middle-income countries, compared with 8.8 per 100,000 in low-income countries and 4 per 100,000 in high-income countries (274–313). These numbers are largely driven by Latin America, but not entirely.

66. Of course, anger at surrounding poverty could cause international terrorism even if terrorists themselves were not poor. But in fact citizens of the poorest countries in the Middle East are the least likely to commit suicide attacks. For further discussion, see Krueger, *What Makes a Terrorist?* See also Benmelech, Berrebi, and Klor, "Economic Conditions and the Quality of Suicide Terrorism."

67. See Abadie, "Poverty, Political Freedom, and the Roots of Terrorism." A study looking at terrorism across ninety-six countries from 1986 to 2002 found no correlation between poverty and terror. See Piazza, "Rooted in Poverty?" Krueger and Maleckova, in "Education, Poverty, and Terrorism," also found no relationship between poverty and terror. Unemployment and poverty might have been linked to domestic terrorism in the case of the Provisional Irish Republican Army and the Spanish terrorist group the ETA, but domestic terror is different from international.

68. For a review of this literature, see Maxwell and Stone, "Nexus Between Economics and Family Violence."

69. Monkkonen, *Murder in New York City,* 8.

70. There are many definitions of the Mafia and organized crime, but most scholars now tend to agree that organized crime arises when economies are modernizing or transitioning to market economies but the state is unable or unwilling to protect property rights or reliably settle business disputes. See Gambetta, *Sicilian Mafia,* 86–92. See also Abadinsky, *Organized Crime;* Hess, *Mafia and Mafiosi.* So organized criminals become market protectors and entrepreneurs, and thus they tend to thrive when markets grow.

71. The graph consists of democracies and anocracies (regimes with democratic and autocratic features) after the Cold War (1992–2015). We created our universe of cases by dropping country-year observations from the Polity IV data set that scored −6 or lower on the Polity2 indicator, a standard cutoff point to eliminate autocracies. We then overlaid the remaining democracies and anocracies with country-year pairings of public goods provision and evaluations on World Bank project performances by the bank's Independent Evaluation Group (IEG). The indicator for public goods provisions creates an average across access to electricity, improved water supply, and improved san-

itation variables, created from World Bank annual-level data. We calculated project performance evaluation data as an average of IEG evaluations assessing the borrowing government's implementation and project management performance over the time period. Significant variations in project length, differences between evaluation dates and project end dates, and inconsistent project activity levels in a given year made it impossible to construct comparable annual-level data.

72. The data from the Committee to Protect Journalists omits journalists killed as a direct result of an ongoing conflict in which death occurred in cross fire. While the magnitude of murders and frequency both matter, given varied population sizes and the generally tight community of reporters who know one another and know the meaning of an assassination of one of their own, frequency is more salient. In at least fifteen years out of twenty-three, Colombia, Brazil, Mexico, and Russia had at least one murdered journalist, a consistency mirrored in Pakistan and the Philippines (thirteen years) and to a lesser extent Sri Lanka, Thailand, Turkey, Ukraine, and Venezuela (five to eight years with murdered journalists). Magnitude and frequency appear related: in the Philippines in 2009, there were thirty-three known murdered journalists; in Turkey in 1992, there were nine; in Pakistan, there were seven murdered each year from 2010 through 2012; and in most years this set of countries witnessed at least two to four journalists killed in years in which any were murdered.

73. The Minorities at Risk Data measures both violence against peaceful civilians and nonviolent minority group organizations between 2004 and 2006.

74. In fact, we found that countries scoring well on World Bank projects were particularly correlated with repression, perhaps suggesting that countries could deliver controversial programs more easily by violently suppressing democratic dissent. See Kleinfeld, *Improving Development Measurement and Evaluation*, for an explanation of why development metrics favor authoritarianism.

75. This trend was catalyzed by two academics who claimed to have overturned the idea of the "democratic peace theory" by uncovering a relationship between democratic transitions and war. See Mansfield and Snyder, "Democratization and the Danger of War." The high correlation between anocracy—or regimes with features of both autocracy and democracy—and civil war was taken as a given until James Raymond Vreeland published an article showing that among the variables for coding a country as an anocracy was political violence, high levels of factionalization, and, in the case of Freedom House, civil war itself. See Vreeland, "Effect of Political Regime on Civil War"; and Hill and Jones, "Empirical Evaluation of Explanations," 677.

76. Fearon, "Homicide Data, Third Revision."

77. See Walter, "Why Bad Governance Leads to Repeat Civil War." I mention "recurring" civil wars because Walter had already found that 90 percent of modern civil wars are re-outbreaks of prior civil wars.

78. Marshall, "Global Trends in Democratization," 17.

79. Goldstone et al., "Global Model."

80. According to the research and advocacy group Death Penalty Worldwide, based at Cornell Law School, China executed at least 2,400 people in 2015, or one execution for every 562,000 people. The next-largest number was Iran, which had 966, and then the numbers fall to a few hundred in Pakistan and fewer throughout the rest of the world. Before a 2007 legal reform, China is believed to have executed over 10,000 people a year, according to Amnesty International.

81. It is following a long tradition. Soviet officials used to insist that homicide did not occur in a country where the people ruled. Lysova and Shchitov, "What Is Russia's Real Homicide Rate?"

82. Kleinfeld, *Reducing All Violent Deaths*. Egypt, for example, claims to have had 990 homicides and 31 conflict-related deaths in 2011, the year of the Arab Awakening protests and crackdowns. Yet according to the media, in January and February of 2011 alone, at least 841 people were killed in unrest.

83. There were 192 fully sovereign countries not subject to sovereignty claims in 2007, but counting countries is not simple, given disputed territories like Taiwan and country-like bodies such as Vatican City. Classifying democracies is more difficult, particularly given this creeping authoritarianism. I follow the classification of Larry Diamond in "Facing Up to the Democratic Recession"; Freedom House found 123 democracies that year.

84. Diamond also notes that the failure rates for democracies grew following the year 2000 and had been growing each decade since 1980. Steven Levitsky and Lucan Way claim that a number of these democracies are illiberal and more authoritarian in character. I am concerned with violence, so am looking at a subset of democracies, whether liberal or illiberal, that had increasing corruption and declining rule of law as charted in ibid., 149. See also Levitsky and Way, *Competitive Authoritarianism*.

85. The eight coups were in Fiji, Guinea-Bissau, Nepal, Thailand, Bangladesh, Honduras, Mali, and Turkey. See Diamond, "Facing Up to the Democratic Recession," 145. Levitsky and Way's book, *Competitive Authoritarianism*, 4, studies thirty-five cases that occurred between 1990 and 1995 and notes that others, such as Venezuela and Nigeria, arose after 1995. There is no agreed-upon list among scholars for which countries fall into this category. Diamond, Levitsky, and Way all have slightly different interpretations, as do surveys such as Freedom House, but the order of magnitude is similar even if the precise country count differs.

86. LaFree and Tseloni, "Democracy and Crime"; Wantchekon and Yehoue, "Crime in New Democracies"; Piccone, "Democracy and Violent Crime." While Latin America's high levels of violence affect these indicators, the find-

ing that newer democracies were more violent than other political regimes held even when Latin American data were excluded from analysis. When I wrote an article defining the rule of law in 2005, I made the point that the concept contained different end goods that were not reducible to one another, human rights, civil liberties, and security among them. It was an unusual view in an era when the rule of law was seen to contain all of these goods, which were assumed to move up and down in lockstep. See Kleinfeld, "Competing Definitions of the Rule of Law."

87. Latinobarómetro opinion poll, 2015. See also "El declive de la democracia," Latinobarómetro, 2016.

88. Between 1989 and 2013, the number of anocracies, as coded in the Polity IV data set, grew from thirty to fifty-three. While Polity IV is highly imperfect, the trend is mirrored in other common data sets measuring regime type. See Marshall, "Polity IV Project."

89. The bad Mexican restaurant is on the Democratic side of the street. Republican members of Congress have a privately owned town house nearby that is slightly more conducive to meetings.

90. In 1976, the Supreme Court ruled in *Buckley v. Valeo* that spending money to influence elections was a form of constitutionally protected free speech, in a case that pitted two presidential candidates against the Federal Election Commission campaign finance regulations. In a 1978 decision, *First National Bank of Boston v. Bellotti*, the Court struck down attempts to regulate corporate campaign expenditures for the same reason. Later decisions have followed on these precedents.

91. Walzer, *Spheres of Justice*.

92. In 2010, Steven Levitsky and Lucan Way coined the term "competitive authoritarianism," but it has not caught on in popular or policy circles. They distinguish competitive authoritarian regimes from constitutional oligarchies that deny suffrage to a significant portion of the population by law, tutelary regimes in which nonelected military or religious leaders constrain elected leaders, and semi-competitive democracies in which elections are free but a major party is banned. For my purposes of understanding violence within countries that hold elections, these distinctions are less useful; the salient distinction is whether regimes manage to restrict suffrage in nonviolent ways or turn to violence to maintain power.

93. For decades, the idea of oligarchy was a conceptual muddle. Because democracy entailed a large segment of the population having the right to vote, scholars believed that democracies ipso facto could not be oligarchies, since the idea had degenerated into simply the idea of "rule by a few." Yet Aristotle explicitly says that the fact that the wealthy tend to be few is happenstance to oligarchy. His version of oligarchy was the degeneration of aristocratic government so that rule by the noble few who deserved to rule by virtue of their aris-

tocratic birth became rule by the wealthy few with no such legitimate claim. Jeffrey Winters in *Oligarchy* has done modern scholars a service by reclaiming the idea that oligarchy can occur in any political system where a small group maintains its grip on power through access to wealth and where the political system is distorted by that group to focus on protecting existing wealth and income. See Aristotle, *Politics*, bks. 4 and 5, 1,205–64; and Winters, *Oligarchy*, 4–6, 11. See also Mungiu-Pippidi, *Quest for Good Governance*, 97.

94. Aristotle, *Politics*, bk. 5, chap. 12, 1,264.

95. Theodore Roosevelt, "The Industrial Problems of Peace," cited in Dalton, *Strenuous Life*, 519.

96. The decrease in judicial quality scores outpaces that of their corruption scores, indicating some heterogeneity in institutional dysfunction.

97. Interestingly, World Bank project outcomes improve with increased levels of violence—one of many variables suggesting why development banks often prefer to work with more authoritarian countries.

98. Pimentel, "Nexus of Organized Crime and Politics in Mexico," 37.

99. Ibid., 46; Astorga and Shirk, "Drug Trafficking Organizations," 6–9.

100. Pimentel, "Nexus of Organized Crime and Politics in Mexico," 8; Astorga and Shirk, "Drug Trafficking Organizations"; Bailey and Godson, *Organized Crime;* Davis, "Undermining the Rule of Law"; Pimentel, "Mexico's Legacy of Corruption"; Paternostro, "Mexico as a Narco-democracy"; Andreas, "Political Economy of Narco-corruption in Mexico."

101. Pimentel, "Nexus of Organized Crime and Politics in Mexico," 45; Corchado, *Midnight in Mexico*, 42; Bailey and Godson, *Organized Crime*, 19. DFS allegedly decided to work with criminals in order to fight leftist guerrilla groups in the 1970s.

102. Rafael Aguilar Guajardo, in particular, would become a cartel leader in Juárez until his murder in 1993. Pimentel, "Nexus of Organized Crime and Politics in Mexico," 46.

103. Ibid., 44.

104. Eventually, the former commander of the Fifth Military Region and former commissioner of the National Institute to Combat Drugs was charged with working with the Juárez cartel. Benítez Manaut, "Role of the Military," 147.

105. Pimentel, "Nexus of Organized Crime and Politics in Mexico," 37–38.

106. Bailey and Godson, *Organized Crime*, 12–13.

107. Andres Oppenheimer, *Bordering on Chaos*, 301, cited in Pimentel, "Nexus of Organized Crime and Politics in Mexico," 52.

108. Bailey and Godson, *Organized Crime*, 13.

109. Rios Contreras, "How Government Structure Encourages Criminal Violence," 99.

110. Ibid., 99–101.

111. Ibid., 19, 21, 24.

112. Latinobarómetro opinion survey 2015.

113. Citizens of Mexico City and Monterrey, interviews by Wagner master's degree students, Jan. 2017, on behalf of author.

114. Acemoglu and Robinson, *Economic Origins of Dictatorship and Democracy;* and North, Wallis, and Weingast, *Violence and Social Orders,* are among the many scholars who explicate the tight relationship between economic control and political openness.

115. The United States does not seem to be quite at this point, though scholars disagree. The Princeton professor Martin Gilens found that policy makers respond far more to the preferences of the affluent and of organized pressure groups. Where policy desires of lower- and middle-income Americans diverge from those of the upper class, Gilens found that they have zero statistical influence on policy making. See Gilens, *Affluence and Influence.* His findings are disputed by Enns, "Relative Policy Support and Coincidental Repression"; Bashir, "Testing Inferences About American Politics"; and Branham et al., "When Do the Rich Win?," who argue that most of the time (on 89.6 percent of the bills studied, to be precise), the middle class agree with the rich—perhaps because Gilens's "rich" cutoff of a household income of $190,000 per year included many people who consider themselves upper middle class. Of the 185 bills on which they disagreed, the differences were usually small, and even then the middle class got their preferences 47 percent of the time. Nor do the breakdowns fall on strictly partisan or ideological lines.

2: PRIVILEGE VIOLENCE

1. W. E. Gladstone, *Two Letters to the Earl of Aberdeen on the State Prosecutions of the Neapolitan Government* (New York: J. S. Nichols, 1851).

2. Wellman, *Dynasty of Western Outlaws,* 70–71.

3. The Civil War mustered over a million men in the Union army, but demobilization was so rapid that a year later there were only eleven thousand volunteers left. Congress voted to rebuild the military to a peak of fifty-seven thousand in September 1867 but then cut the authorization steadily until by 1876 the total force was limited to fewer than twenty-eight thousand, a number that remained until the Spanish-American War in 1898.

4. Skowronek, *Building a New American State.*

5. William O. Stoddard, *Abraham Lincoln: The True Story of a Great Life* (New York: Fords, Howard & Hulbert, 1885), 215, cited in Carman and Luthin, *Lincoln and the Patronage.*

6. Even at the height of the Civil War when the nation was at stake, corruption dogged the Union war effort. "For sugar the government often got sand; for coffee, rye; for leather, something no better than brown paper; for sound horses and mules, spavined beasts and dying donkeys; and for serviceable muskets and pistols, the experimental failures of sanguine inventors, or the refuse of shops and foreign armories." Robert Tomes, *Harper's Monthly,* July 1864.

7. Shirley, *Law West of Fort Smith,* 23.

8. Ibid., ix, 47.

9. This Louis L'Amour version of the Wild West was challenged by revisionist historians who claimed that the West in these decades was far less violent than previously imagined, because the numbers of dead were quite small. Violence historians such as Roth have since noted that murder is counted not on an absolute basis but per capita, and when the number of murders was divided by the very small number of people, the original version of a tremendously violent western frontier was reinstated.

10. In May 1862, the Homestead Act allowed any American who had not taken up arms against the United States to claim up to 160 free acres of federal land. Multiple acts were passed over the years, ending only in 1976. Alaska, where I grew up, granted an extension, and people continued to homestead throughout my childhood.

11. The Johnson County War was one of many such feuds throughout the West in these years. A similar set of battles between farmers and ranchers is currently being fought across Africa's Sahel, exacerbated by altering climactic conditions that require moving the cattle off traditional ranges and by urban elites who launder money through cattle, arm the pastoralists to keep their herds safe, and ensure the state does little to prosecute violence.

12. Bommersbach, "Dead Wrong About Cattle Kate."

13. Pfeifer, *Rough Justice,* 55.

14. In the cattle town murders in Kansas during these Wild West years, 40 percent of assailants and 15 percent of victims were law-enforcement officers. Most were Republicans in hostile Democratic environments, according to Roth, *American Homicide,* 382–84.

15. Roosevelt, *Ranch Life and the Hunting Trail,* 114–29.

16. For Bodie numbers, see McGrath, "Violence and Lawlessness," 133; Leadville numbers come from Courtwright, *Violent Land;* Dodge City and New

Mexico statistics come from Roth, "Homicide Rates in the American West"; and Roth, *American Homicide*, 354. Arizona numbers are drawn from McKanna, *Homicide, Race, and Justice*, 39. McKanna separates homicide rates by race: the white homicide rate for Gila was 152 per 100,000, the Apache was 178.

17. See Roth, *American Homicide*, 360, 385, and 403. According to his account, in Los Angeles County homicide fell from 198 per 100,000 in the late 1860s and the 1870s to 23 per 100,000 in the 1880s and 1890s.

18. Across California on the eve of World War I, homicide rates had fallen to 12 per 100,000 in California, 15 per 100,000 in Colorado. For these statistics, see ibid., 403–11. The frontier was defined as a point beyond which there were fewer than two people per square mile. In 1893, Frederick Jackson Turner published his famous frontier thesis, forever linking the U.S. national character to its experience of this frontier.

19. Wayne Gard's *Chisholm Trail* is the standard scholarly history. For something more fun, I recommend Larry McMurtry's 1985 book, *Lonesome Dove*, which is not billed as a historical novel but in fact hews disturbingly close to actual events.

20. Oshinsky, *Worse Than Slavery*, 12.

21. Disenfranchisement was a complex matter. Confederates were required to take a loyalty oath or be personally pardoned by President Johnson—who, as a southerner himself, pardoned most Confederates within a year before Congress had met. A frustrated Congress passed Reconstruction Acts in 1867 that barred some Confederate leaders from voting until southern states ratified new constitutions. That meant enfranchisement was decided state by state, and solid numbers are difficult to come by for the entire region, particularly because disenfranchisement was often carried out by military order. In Louisiana in 1867, for example, General Philip Sheridan had disenfranchised nearly half the white population the year before the state voted on a new constitution. See Tunnell, *Crucible of Reconstruction*, 134.

22. Kousser, "Voting Rights Act," 135, 141.

23. Foner, *Freedom's Lawmakers*; Kousser, "Voting Rights Act," 135, 141.

24. Rable, *But There Was No Peace*, 62.

25. Richardson, *West from Appomattox*, 104, citing *New-York Tribune*, May 12, 1871, 2.

26. Tunnell, *Crucible of Reconstruction*, 153.

27. Moneyhon, *Texas After the Civil War*, 176.

28. Bartoletti, *KKK*, 103–4.

29. Tunnell, *Crucible of Reconstruction*, 153.

30. Ibid., 102.

31. Foner, *Reconstruction*, 110.

32. Lane, *Day Freedom Died*, 3.

33. Oshinsky, *Worse Than Slavery*, 26, 28.

34. Tunnell, *Crucible of Reconstruction*, 154, 156.

35. Moneyhon, *Texas After the Civil War*, 95–96.

36. Kenneth M. Stampp, *The Era of Reconstruction, 1865–1877* (New York: Vintage, 1965), 78, cited in Tunnell, *Crucible of Reconstruction*, 6.

37. U.S. Congress, *Report of the Select Committee on the New Orleans Riots*, 370.

38. Tunnell, *Crucible of Reconstruction*, 104–6.

39. In Memphis, for instance, local policemen began arguing with a northern regiment of black soldiers who had been mustered in the city, and the ensuing police-backed mob killed forty-six people. See Ash, *Massacre in Memphis*.

40. Trelease, *White Terror*, 14.

41. Tunnell, *Crucible of Reconstruction*, 157. See also Barnes and Connolly, "Repression, the Judicial System, and Political Opportunities for Civil Rights Advocacy During Reconstruction," 331; Bryant, "Ku Klux Klan in the Reconstruction Era"; and Christensen, "1868 St. Landry Massacre."

42. Redding and James, "Estimating Levels and Modeling Determinants," 157.

43. J. David Hacker, the most convincing demographic historian of the Civil War, concludes that approximately 22.6 percent of southern white men between twenty and twenty-four and about 13 percent of southern white males between the ages of ten and forty-four in 1860 lost their lives to wartime killing and disease. See Hacker, "Census-Based Count."

44. Hagen, Makovi, and Bearman, "Influence of Political Dynamics."

45. Governor Davis had asked local leaders to submit the names of their most wanted and received 2,790 names. Moneyhon, *Texas After the Civil War*, 140–41; Perkinson, *Texas Tough*, 97.

46. Perkinson, *Texas Tough*, 91.

47. Moneyhon, *Texas After the Civil War*, 189.

48. Roth, *American Homicide*, 425–26.

49. Lincoln anticipated local resistance and established the Freedmen's Bureau to help former slaves learn to read and write, vote, get fair wages, and claim their rights. But after his assassination, Johnson rehabilitated seven thousand Confederates in the months after the war's end before Congress came into session. Born and bred in Tennessee, he vetoed funding for the Freedmen's Bureau on the grounds that it would make newly independent slaves overly dependent on government largesse. Some local bureau offices shuttered for lack of funds.

Others upheld new laws forcing black men and women to work for whatever wages were on offer or risk being jailed as indigents. The bureau hobbled along for a few years, its budget slashed and many of its personnel laid off.

50. In *Barren v. Baltimore* in 1833, the Supreme Court ruled that the Bill of Rights applied only to the national government; states did not have to abide by its rules. The Civil Rights Act was a first step toward mandating national rights, using the constitutional clause that guaranteed each state a republican form of government. Kutler, *Supreme Court and the Constitution.*

51. Lane, *Day Freedom Died,* 4.

52. Pildes, "Democracy, Anti-democracy, and the Canon," 309. See Tunnell, *Crucible of Reconstruction,* 173–218, for more on violence.

53. Bartoletti, *KKK,* 142.

54. Ibid., 101–2.

55. The event is known as the Colfax massacre, and the killings are estimated at anywhere from 60 to 150.

56. The Supreme Court ruled that under the Fourteenth and Fifteenth Amendments, Congress could prohibit state governments from infringing on rights of citizens but had no jurisdiction over the actions of private individuals. Thus, the verdict overturned the Enforcement Act and the Ku Klux Klan Act by saying that the federal government couldn't legislate against murder, which was a state crime. Attacks by armed men increased in the daytime as southern mobs quickly understood the implication of the ruling. Rable, *But There Was No Peace,* 129; Gibson, *Boundary Control,* 55–56. In 1883, the Court held the Civil Rights Act unconstitutional.

57. Calhoun, *Bloody Shirt,* 54.

58. Epperly et al., "Rule by Violence, Rule by Law," 15.

59. They were also contested in Oregon.

60. University of Missouri Kansas City Law School, "Lynchings by Year and Race," law2.umkc.edu. Lynching statistics are generally sourced from contemporary accounts and are thus disputed; other sources include Bailey and Tolnay, "Lynched"; and Equal Justice Initiative, *Lynching in America.*

61. By the 1880s, most lynchings, which had previously taken place in the West, had moved to the South.

62. Makovi, Hagen, and Bearman, "The Course of Law," 868–70.

63. New Orleans *Daily Picayune,* July 23, 1903, cited in Makovi, Hagen, and Bearman, "The Course of Law," 860.

64. Tolnay, Beck, and Massey, "Black Competition and White Vengeance," 628, data from 1880 to 1935.

65. Beck and Tolnay, "Killing Fields of the Deep South," 526–39.

66. We know this story because in 1871, the U.S. Congress sent an investigative mission to the South and recorded testimony, and Hannah and Samuel were brave enough to travel across the state to testify. 42nd Cong., 2nd Sess., House of Representatives Report 22, pt. 13, "Testimony Taken by the Joint Select Committee to Inquire into the Condition of Affairs in the Late Insurrection States—Florida," testimony taken by the subcommittee, Nov. 10, 1871, Jacksonville, Fla. (Washington, D.C.: Government Printing Office, 1872), 54–64.

67. Epperly et al., "Rule by Violence, Rule by Law," calculated lynching dates and correlations with elections from 1876 to 1952.

68. For years, scholars had followed Beck in considering lynchings a largely economic phenomenon. More recently, researchers realized that Beck's numbers included only successful lynchings and thus skewed the statistics. Moveover, because Republican districts had less lynching success, the statistics were skewed in a particularly political manner. Reexamining attempted and completed lynchings, Hagen, Makovi, and Bearman, "Influence of Political Dynamics on Southern Lynch Mob Formation and Lethality," 761, found, as Epperly et al. did, that they had a political character.

69. The political scientists Robert Mickey and Edward Gibson call the South of this period an "authoritarian enclave," a repressive, one-party state within a broader democracy. See Mickey, *Paths out of Dixie;* and Gibson, *Boundary Control.*

70. "As long as poor whites directed their hatred and frustration against the black competitor, the planters were relieved of class hostility directed against them." Wilson, *Declining Significance of Race,* 54.

71. Perkinson, *Texas Tough,* 142. Child rapists are not sympathetic figures, but in addition to allowing mob justice rather than courts to rule, lynching made it impossible to know if the accused was guilty. If the mob murdered the wrong man, then a child rapist was still free.

72. Ginzburg, *100 Years of Lynching,* 20, 46. See Allen's *Without Sanctuary* for depictions of lynching postcards. Leon Litwack's commentary within that book describes the carnival atmosphere.

73. See also Makovi, Hagen, and Bearman, "The Course of Law," 880.

74. Kousser, *Southern Politics,* 238–65; Redding and James, "Estimating Levels and Modeling Determinants."

75. In 1889, North Carolina passed a law that "books shall not be interchangeable between the white and colored schools, but shall continue to be used by the race first using them." Mickey, *Paths out of Dixie,* describes how southerners considered ending all public higher education in some states rather than open up to blacks when the Supreme Court legally declared integration in the 1940s through the 1960s.

76. Wilkerson, *Warmth of Other Suns,* 39.

77. John Hope Franklin, *Reconstruction After the Civil War*, 3rd ed. (Chicago: University of Chicago Press, 2012), cited in Gibson, *Boundary Control*, 51–52.

78. They also built two or three thousand Union Leagues across the former Confederacy to support Republicans.

79. Kousser, "Voting Rights Act," 135, 141; Foner, *Reconstruction*, 537–39.

80. Kousser, *Southern Politics*, 241.

81. Perkinson, *Texas Tough*, 141.

82. Epperly et al., "Rule by Violence, Rule by Law," 19.

83. Pildes, "Democracy, Anti-democracy, and the Canon," 12, 27.

84. Redding and James, "Estimating Levels and Modeling Determinants," 157–58.

85. Intergroup contact theory is one of the foundational ideas in social psychology. Decades of research, starting in 1954 with Gordon W. Allport's book *The Nature of Prejudice* (Cambridge, Mass.: Addison-Wesley), suggest that prejudice can be reduced through positive interpersonal contact. See Page-Gould, Mendoza-Denton, and Tropp, "With a Little Help from My Cross-Group Friend." Meta-tests also bear it out; see Pettigrew and Tropp, "Meta-analytic Test."

86. Pilgrim, "What Was Jim Crow." In 1920, Mississippi passed a law abrogating free speech, saying that "printed, typewritten or written matter urging or presenting for public acceptance or general information, arguments or suggestions in favor of social equality or of intermarriage between whites and Negroes, shall be guilty of a misdemeanor and subject to fine not exceeding five hundred (500.00) dollars or imprisonment not exceeding six (6) months or both." For the law itself, see *Codes, Hemingway's 1921 Supp.* S1103; Laws, 1920, chap. 214. For a more complete bibliography of these laws, see CivilPolitics .org.

87. For those who didn't get the point, one of the few registered voters in 1955 received an unsigned letter: "Last warning. If you are tired of living, vote and die." The NAACP sent a photocopy of the note to the Senate Judiciary Committee. Tyson, *Emmett Till*, 110.

88. The recent growth of scholarship into "authoritarian enclaves" within democratic countries has greatly enriched the study of democracy and owes its origins to Mickey, *Paths out of Dixie;* and Gibson, *Boundary Control*.

89. Makovi, Kagen, and Bearman, "The Course of Law," 883.

90. Epperly et al., "Rule by Violence, Rule by Law," 33–34.

91. "We of the South have never recognized the right of the negro to govern white men and we never will," he explained. Quoted in Davidson and Grofman, *Quiet Revolution in the South*, 194.

92. Ibid., 29. The graph shows lynchings per county-month.

93. Multiple studies have found that rather than substitute nongovernmental for state violence, governments that support pro-government militias are also more violent themselves. Cohen and Nordas, "Do States Delegate Shameful Violence to Militias?"; Mitchell, Carey, and Butler, "Impact of Pro-government Militias"; Stanton, "Regulating Militias." Carey, Colaresi, and Mitchell, "Governments, Informal Links to Militias," 852.

94. Alvarez, "Militias and Genocide"; Ahram, Proxy Warriors; Kirschke, "Informal Repression, Zero-Sum Politics"; Byman and Kreps, "Agents of Destruction"; Carey, Colaresi, and Mitchell, "Governments, Informal Links to Militias"; Staniland, "States, Insurgents."

95. Carey, Mitchell, and Lowe, "States, the Security Sector, and the Monopoly of Violence," 250; Carey, Colaresi, and Mitchell, "Governments, Informal Links to Militias," 852; Cohen, States of Denial, 62. While some literature claims that these organizations are also used to provide logistical advantages during wartime (Eck, "Repression by Proxy") or as a force multiplier (Alvarez, "Militias and Genocide"; Jentzsch et al., "Militias in Civil Wars"), this does not illuminate their frequent use during periods of peace.

96. Grare, "Reforming the Intelligence Agencies in Pakistan's Transitional Democracy," 28.

97. The Bakassi Boys of southern Nigeria, for instance, emerged in response to violent crime but were subsequently backed by state governors who used them for electoral violence (Harnischfeger, "Bakassi Boys"). The gangs of Pakistan's Karachi are similarly supported by political parties who offer impunity (Gayer, "Guns, Slums"). Staniland, "Militias, Ideology, and the State"; Anderson, "Vigilantes, Violence, and the Politics of Public Order in Kenya"; International Crisis Group, Bangladesh; Jaffrelot, Hindu Nationalist Movement; Klopp, "'Ethnic Clashes'"; Le Bas, "Violence and Urban Order in Nairobi"; Paden, "Midterm Challenges in Nigeria"; Wilkinson, Votes and Violence; Yusuf, Conflict Dynamics in Karachi.

98. Francis in his introduction to Civil Militia argues that such violent, non-state fighters are a low-cost form of security employed by weak states. Yet Campbell and Brenner's study of such groups, Death Squads in Global Perspective, in capable countries from Weimar Germany to apartheid South Africa and elsewhere leads them to argue that weakness is an inadequate explanation. The Pro-government Militia database created by Carey, Mitchell, and Lowe ("States, the Security Sector") finds that both weak and strong states use violent non-state proxies that encompass more formalized relationships such as civil defense forces and informal, deniable relationships with groups such as death squads and vigilantes, findings supported by Klare ("Deadly Connection") and Reno (Warlord Politics and African States).

99. "Rise and Fall of 'False Positive' Killings in Colombia," 4, 11. See also HRW, "The Sixth Division: Military-Paramilitary Ties and U.S. Policy in Colombia" (2001), 93, 95, 99.

100. Acemoglu, Robinson, and Santos, "Monopoly of Violence," 21.

101. Paul and Vivekananda, "Knowing Our Legislators."

102. Vaishnav, *When Crime Pays*, 147, citing an Oct. 2010 interview.

103. For Colombia, see Porch and Rasmussen, "Demobilization of Paramilitaries"; Andreu-Guzmán, "Criminal Justice and Forced Displacement," 4–6; Saab and Taylor, "Criminality and Armed Groups"; and Dudley, *Walking Ghosts*, 99. For Bihar, see Kumar, *Community Warriors*, 69–70; and Human Rights Watch, *These Fellows Must Be Eliminated*. For the United States, see Beck and Tolnay, "Killing Fields." For Sicily, see Stille, "All the Prime Minister's Men."

104. Benítez Manaut, "Role of the Military," 156.

105. In Colombia, for instance, various public advocates spoke against the paramilitaries, and the Human Rights Unit and the Technical Investigation Unit of the Attorney General's Office vigorously prosecuted paramilitaries for violence. But the human rights defenders were not power players within governments where more powerful factions supported the paramilitaries. They paid for their internal dissent with their lives; from 1998 to 1999 alone, a dozen officials from the unit investigating paramilitary violence were killed or forced to leave their jobs because of threats, and seven more were kidnapped. HRW, "Sixth Division," 3, 75.

106. Across the 150 countries cataloged, lynching and ethnic riots tended to decline when law enforcement starts prosecuting them. See Horowitz, *Deadly Ethnic Riot*, 518–21.

107. India National Police Commission, "Third Report, 22.6–22.7."

108. O'Grady, "In Nigeria, $2 Billion in Stolen Funds."

109. "Nigerian Military: Some Officers Selling Arms to Boko Haram," Associated Press, Sept. 4, 2016.

110. Stanley McChrystal, "COMISAF's Initial Assessment," Memorandum to Secretary of Defense Robert Gates, Aug. 30, 2009, 2–9, 2–10, cited in "Corruption in Conflict," 35.

111. The aptly named New York police sergeant "Clubber" Williams explained to the Lexow Commission investigating corruption in 1895, "Now, let me tell you something. They may beat you in court, the complainant may not show up, they may jump their bail, politicians may interfere, there are several ways they can beat you, but this [he pointed to the marks and bruises on someone worked over by the police] they've got, and make no damned mistake about it."

Jeffers, *Commissioner Roosevelt,* 9. Williams was later found to own property in Connecticut and a yacht, both of which would have been impossible to afford on his police salary. See "Farewell to Williams," *New York Times,* May 25, 1895. Hans Toch found that cops of the 1970s mixed corruption and brutality as a sort of vigilante justice that allowed police to exert punishment in places where they were convinced that the courts would let criminals go free. See Toch, Grant, and Galvin, *Agents of Change,* 78–79.

112. Jauregui, *Shadows of the State, Subalterns of the State,* 176–77. Chevigny, in *The Edge of the Knife,* 161, found similar dynamics in his study of modern Brazilian police engaged in extrajudicial killings.

113. "Crime in Brazil," *Economist;* Human Rights Watch, "Good Cops Are Afraid."

114. Human Rights Watch, "Good Cops Are Afraid."

115. "Global Patterns," *Economist.*

116. Lohmuller and Dudley, "Appraising Violence in Honduras."

117. Dudley, "Homicides in Guatemala."

118. Ibid. A UN study found that in 2000, only about 14 percent of El Salvador's killings could be attributed to gangs; see UNODC, *Crime and Development in Central America.*

119. Global Witness, "New Data on the Murder Rate," finds that at least 109 activists opposed to dam, mining, logging, and infrastructure projects were murdered in Honduras between 2010 and 2015. It is unclear who perpetrated the murders, but they happened far from gang-related turf.

120. Edmonds-Poli, "Effects of Drug-War Related Violence," 147, 148.

121. Unsurprisingly, the Philippines has the highest rate of impunity for journalist killings of any country after the failed state of Somalia and war-torn Iraq and Syria. Brazil, Nigeria, Mexico, Pakistan, India, Russia, and Bangladesh are the other non-warring countries at the top of the list. See Committee to Protect Journalists, "2016 Impunity Index."

122. Luiz Eduardo Soares, a former federal secretary of public security in Brazil, claimed that "There's practically no serious crime in Rio without police participation" see "Crime in Brazil," *Economist.* The strategies of obfuscation used by criminal police have stayed remarkably stable over time. In New York City, during the era of machine politics and state-level Prohibition restrictions, the future president Theodore Roosevelt wrote, "The police used the partial and spasmodic enforcement of the law as a means of collecting blackmail. The result was that the officers of the law, the politicians, and the saloon-keepers became inextricably tangled in a network of crime and connivance at crime. The most powerful saloon-keepers controlled the politicians and the

police, while the latter in turn terrorized and blackmailed all the other saloon-keepers. It was not a case of non-enforcement of the law. The law was very actively enforced, but it was enforced with corrupt discrimination." Roosevelt, *Autobiography*, 189.

123. Robles, "Honduras Becomes the Murder Capital."

124. Ibid. To help with these problems, the UN subsequently sent the Support Mission Against Corruption and Impunity in Honduras (Misión de Apoyo Contra la Corrupción y la Impunidad en Honduras); the commission members have received so many death threats that they were forced to move their families out of the country.

125. Perkinson, *Texas Tough*, 143. White convicts by this time were sent to different laboring sites from blacks, and owing to prison reforms those sites failed to turn a profit, while black prison labor remained valuable.

126. Perkinson, *Texas Tough*, 105; Armes, *Story of Coal and Iron in Alabama*. In full disclosure, given my employment at the Carnegie Endowment for International Peace, this company later merged with Andrew Carnegie's U.S. Steel. Perkinson notes that recorded mortality rates of over 20 percent put U.S. Steel in the same category as German and Japanese companies that used slave labor in World War II. See Blackmon, "Hard Time."

127. Perkinson, *Texas Tough*, 102.

128. New laws known as "Black Codes" criminalized loitering, owing debts, breaking curfew, and vagrancy (which was defined as working fewer than six days a week, excepting the Sabbath). Stealing food, a rampant problem in an era where blacks were hardly paid, could earn years in prison. Just after the end of the Civil War, nine southern states passed versions of such Black Codes to effectively reinstate slavery, and eight of those states had also created convict laws to hire out prisoners to plantations and private companies, but they had been overturned by congressional fiat a few years later when Republicans gained control during Reconstruction. As Congress changed hands in the late 1800s, southern politicians successfully reinstated the laws.

129. Perkinson, *Texas Tough*, 105.

130. Oshinsky, *Worse than Slavery*, 51, 56, 59, 60; Ayers, *Promise of a New South*; Novak, *Wheel of Servitude*. Railroads, frustrated by the wage demands, brawls, and low-quality work of free labor, seized the opportunity for convict labor. "We cannot get free men to do the same kind of labor for, say, six times as much as the convict costs," explained a railroad official. "And if [a convict] dies it is a small loss." With rental labor, there was no incentive to minimize death, as there was under slavery, when people were owned. Thus researchers believe the leasing system was more deadly than slavery itself.

131. In Texas, black imprisonment shot up by 500 percent from 1871 to 1880, compared with 60 percent for whites (Perkinson, *Texas Tough*, 97). In South

Carolina by 1880, there were only 25 white prisoners out of 431 convicts; in Georgia, there were 1,200 prisoners, nearly 1,100 of whom were black. In Alabama, 97 percent of county convicts were black. Oshinsky, *Worse Than Slavery*, 63.

132. Oshinsky, *Worse Than Slavery*, 60; the years were between 1877 and 1879.

133. Perkinson, *Texas Tough*, 148, 151–76.

134. For further, see Novak, *Wheel of Servitude*. South Carolina's numbers from Oshinsky, *Worse Than Slavery*, 60. Mississippi's overall convict mortality rate was 15 percent in 1887, compared with less than 1 percent in states like Ohio and Illinois. The former attorney general Frank Johnston explained that convict leasing had produced an "epidemic death rate without the epidemic." Oshinsky, *Worse Than Slavery*, 50, 51.

135. After police raped and killed a young girl in a Bogotá police station in 1993, Colombian public confidence in police fell to 21 percent. Police involvement in drug cartels was also well known. Polling was from the Universidad de Antioquia in 1994, 53, as cited in Llorente, "Demilitarization in a War Zone," 117–18.

136. Corchado, *Midnight in Mexico*, 74.

137. Stille, *Excellent Cadavers*, 20. Gaspare Pisciotta was murdered in 1954 in Ucciardone Prison in Sicily after providing information crucial to his cousin's capture. Given that the criminals roamed freely throughout Sicily giving newspaper interviews and meeting with politicians and even a prosecutor, it is no surprise that a court sentence included the line "The only people unable to find Giuliano [the bandit] were the police."

138. Levi, *Consent, Dissent, and Patriotism*, 16.

139. Self-defense vigilantism in response to unpoliced violence has been documented in Mexico, South Africa, India, Indonesia, Pakistan, Guatemala, Nicaragua, Kenya, Nigeria, and the United States. See Pratten, "Politics of Protection"; Pratten and Sen, *Global Vigilantes*; Burr and Jensen, "Introduction"; Harnischfeger, "Bakassi Boys"; Asfura-Heim and Espach, "Rise of Mexico's Self-Defense Forces"; and Lindsey, "Criminal State."

140. "Jungle Justice: Trial by Fire," *Economist*, Dec. 24, 2016, 74. Vigilantes in Nigeria favor wrapping suspects in tires soaked in gasoline and setting them ablaze, a penalty for minor theft as well as more serious crimes like rape.

141. John Lester, a founder of the Klan, claimed that it was created "to protect property and preserve law and order." Richardson, *West from Appomattox*, 91. In Brazil, 30 percent of the population in 1990 claimed to support vigilante assassins, many of whom were off-duty or former police (see Toch, Grant, and Galvin, *Agents of Change*, 147; Chevigny, *Edge of the Knife*, 146; and Bayley, *Patterns of Policing*, 160).

142. Vigilantes have become self-serving violent gangs for hundreds of years, from Afghan enforcers of order in the Middle Ages to western posses. In the United States, some abolitionist Jayhawks and Confederate militias both devolved into criminal gangs. See Tierney, *Chasing Ghosts*, 63–65. Theodore Roosevelt noted the same tendency in the late nineteenth century, when he was a young rancher in Montana: "About this time there had been much horse-stealing and cattle-killing in our Territory and in Montana, and under the direction of some of the big cattle-growers a committee of vigilantes had been organized to take action against the rustlers, as the horse thieves and cattle thieves were called. The vigilantes, or stranglers, as they were locally known, did their work thoroughly; but, as always happens with bodies of the kind, toward the end they grew reckless in their actions, paid off private grudges, and hung men on slight provocation." Roosevelt, *Autobiography*, 112.

143. Hume, "Armed Violence and Poverty," 15.

144. Leovy, *Ghettoside*, 234.

145. Gambetta, *Sicilian Mafia*; Kukhianidze, "Corruption and Organized Crime in Georgia."

146. Felbab-Brown, *Aspiration and Ambivalence*.

147. Bartoletti, *KKK*, 57.

148. Felbab-Brown, Trinkunas, and Hamid, *Militants, Criminals, and Warlords*, 25.

149. Cooke and Sanderson, "Militancy and the Arc of Instability," 20.

150. Ibid., 15.

151. Amnesty International, *Stars on Their Shoulders, Blood on Their Hands*.

152. This is not to claim any good for Boko Haram. They have inflicted immense harm on their society, including acts of depravity such as sending five-year-old children as suicide bombers back into their own homes. UNICEF, "Silent Shame."

153. Brooke, "Drug Lord Is Buried as a Folk Hero."

154. The cross-European policing agency Europol explained that mafiosi controlled votes in southern Italy, which let them buy elections. They diverted public funds, rigged tenders, and bloated the public sector with patronage appointees. By abetting the breakdown of public services, the Mafia was able to juxtapose the image of "an inefficient, cumbersome and distant public bureaucracy" with the "more brisk and efficient management" of the Mafia clans. Europol, "Threat Assessment on Italian Organized Crime," 7.

155. Rakove, *Don't Make No Waves*, 112.

156. Lamb, "Microdynamics of Illegitimacy," 52; Chepesiuk, *Drug Lords*, 71.

157. Varese, "Secret History of Japanese Cinema."

158. Slade, *Reorganizing Crime*, 157; Felbab-Brown, Trinkunas, and Hamid, *Militants, Criminals, and Warlords*, 24.

159. Earlier, Pinkerton detectives had come close to capturing the gang. But they threw a bomb into the family home, killing James's eight-year-old half brother. The Missouri state legislature, sympathizing with the "Confederate" gang against the northern forces of law and order, passed a bill granting them amnesty for their crimes during the Civil War, but it passed only with a simple majority, not the two-thirds vote needed to make it into law.

160. I owe this wording to Leovy, *Ghettoside*, 80.

161. For instance, when Brazilian politicians tried to disrupt the leadership structure of two major gangs who had taken over the prisons, both organizations retaliated with violence in middle-class neighborhoods to force the government to stop. Felbab-Brown, Trinkunas, and Hamid, *Militants, Criminals, and Warlords*, 109.

162. Ibid., 111–12. While the then president, Calderón, denies any favoritism, a 2010 investigative report by National Public Radio found that the Mexican government arrests Sinaloa cartel (the largest in Mexico) members at a rate of one-quarter of Zeta members, and uncovered collusion between the Mexican army and the Sinaloa cartel in Juárez. Burnett, Peñaloza, and Benincasa, "Mexico Seems to Favor Sinaloa Cartel in Drug War."

163. Schuberth, "Challenge of Community-Based Armed Groups."

164. Benítez Manaut, "Role of a Military," 153; Melara Minero, "Los servicios de seguridad privada en El Salvador."

165. "Crime and Development in Central America," 81–82. Many of these companies are owned by former police and security services, creating some obvious conflicts of interest.

166. Pachico, "98% of Mexico's 2012 Murder Cases Unsolved"; Rubio, "Impunidad en el Triángulo Norte"; Murtagh, "How to Fix Latin America's Homicide Problem."

167. Fellman, *Inside War*, xvi.

3: DECIVILIZATION

1. Nicolay and Hay, *Abraham Lincoln*, 420.

2. Davis, "Bogotazo."

3. By October 2016, just over eighteen hundred U.S. service members had died fighting in Afghanistan (600 more had died from causes other than battle, such as suicide).

4. Dudley, *Walking Ghosts*, 5–7. This cloaking of personal vendetta and homicide within political violence is common to many civil wars. See Kalyvas, *Logic of Violence in Civil War*.

5. Colombia did not allow direct local elections until constitutional reforms occurred in 1991. Peeler, "Elite Settlements and Democratic Consolidation," 95.

6. Balcázar, interview by author, Bogotá, Feb. 5, 2015.

7. Landazábal, spoken to Dudley, *Walking Ghosts*, 37.

8. Porch and Rasmussen, "Demobilization," 522–23; Bowden, *Killing Pablo*, 13–15, 18.

9. Rempe, "Guerrillas, Bandits," 305.

10. In 1965, the Colombian president decreed that all Colombians could be drafted to reestablish order; in 1968, the executive decree was enshrined into legislation through Law 48, which allowed the creation of self-defense militias by private groups. It was not declared unconstitutional until 1989, when paramilitary groups murdered a commission of judges sent to investigate other paramilitary murders. In 1989, Presidential Decree 1194 criminalized private armed groups and forbade military and police personnel to arm or train such groups. Yet while paramilitary groups technically remained illegal, they came back under a 1994 program known as CONVIVIR, when a more liberal government attempted to copy a "neighborhood watch" model used in Chile. In 1997, the Constitutional Court declared it unconstitutional to arm civilian groups, but paramilitaries continued in underground form with significant government collusion. See Porch and Rasmussen, "Demobilization."

11. Weber, "Politics as a Vocation." It's this supposed "legitimacy" of state violence that accounts for the strange blindness international relations scholars tend to show toward violence emanating from the state, and why state violence is rarely counted in scholarship looking at violence by regime type.

12. In Japan, the process of building a centralized state with control over force took place largely under the Tokugawa shogunate from 1600 to 1868. The Meiji Restoration period, which began in 1868, curbed the right of samurai to wear swords, the final step in centralizing the use of force. See Grindle, *Jobs for the Boys*, 45–46.

13. The context for Jefferson's famous 1787 letter from France in which he wrote that "the tree of liberty must be refreshed from time to time with the blood of patriots and tyrants" was his concern that the proposals for the Constitution were creating an overly strong executive, in part due to a backlash among the elite classes following Shays's Rebellion.

14. Laws that determine when it is legal to use deadly force, however, do matter to overall violence. For instance, after Florida passed a law in 2005 giving citizens the right to use deadly force if they "reasonably believed" their lives

were threatened, the state saw a 24 percent rise in the homicide rate, which has been sustained. States that lacked the law continued the general decrease in homicides occurring across the United States. See Humphreys, Gasparrini, and Wiebe, "Evaluating the Impact." Countries with the highest rates of deadly violence also tend to have a greater percentage of firearm-related killings than less deadly countries (50 percent to 12 percent). See McEvoy and Hideg, "Global Violent Deaths 2017," 49.

15. The piece of doggerel is sadly anonymous.

16. See George Orwell, "As I Please," *Tribune*, Aug. 18, 1944. Colombia's land was held in a hodgepodge of land grants and structures left over from Spanish rule. The *encomienda* system relied on indigenous Indians, who owned the land, paying tribute to Spanish overseers. The *concierto* system required forced labor by indigenous people, while the mining *mita* system relied on Indian and African slaves. These were replaced in the eighteenth and nineteenth centuries by the hacienda system, which partially privatized land but further complicated the mess: for instance, the Spanish crown would grant a favored member of the elite a large tract of land in the "New World" covering already settled property—making it unclear whose ownership rights prevailed. A moderate president, Alfonso López Pumarejo, attempted to strike a compromise that would clarify land laws while upholding private property in the late 1930s, but his attempts were undermined by growing radicalization of both the peasants and the landlords. The latter often acted in conjunction with local land judges, setting the stage for *La Violencia* three years after Pumarejo's resignation. See Richani, *Systems of Violence*, 12–23.

17. This is about the same time allotted for most assessments to determine U.S. aid priorities today, and if it strikes you as ridiculously limited to understand a country as large and complex as Colombia, you are correct.

18. Rempe, "Guerrillas, Bandits," 313–14.

19. Hadley and Kleinfeld, "Fostering a State-Society Compact"; Rempe, "Guerrillas, Bandits," 312–14.

20. Rempe, "Guerrillas, Bandits," 321.

21. Dudley, *Walking Ghosts*, 31, 49.

22. Goodwin, *No Other Way Out*, 48, 143, 162, 178, for how repression encourages insurgency. Repression's radicalizing effects are also found in research on the Irish Republican Army in O'Leary and Silke, "Understanding and Ending Persistent Conflicts." For Central American conflicts, see Booth and Walker, *Understanding Latin America*; and Walton, *Reluctant Rebels*. For the Philippines, see Kerkvliet, *Huk Rebellion*, 192–93, 240–41, 227, 238. And more generally, see Mason and Krane, "Political Economy of Death Squads"; Gurr, "Political Origins of State Violence and Terror." In the United States, similar dynamics have been discovered by Lipset, "Radicalism or Reformism"; and Bendix, *Nation*

Building and Citizenship, which found that political repression, rather than just inequality or exploitation, tended to radicalize workers to join revolutionary groups. In general, see Tilly, *From Mobilization to Revolution*, 101–6. Barbara Walter, "Conflict Relapse," 82, finds that higher numbers of political prisoners and extrajudicial killings make the renewal of civil war two to three times more likely.

23. "Journeys to Extremism in Africa," United Nations, 5. The study interviewed 495 individuals who had joined violent extremist groups, another 78 who were recruited by force, and a control group of 145 individuals. Interviewees were spread across Kenya, Nigeria, Somalia, and Sudan, as well as a smaller number in Cameroon and Niger.

24. Fearon, "Governance and Civil War Onset," 25. Of course, correlation is not causation, and increased human rights abuse might be an early manifestation of a government-sponsored dirty war.

25. Collier finds that poor democracies have a greater propensity to civil war than wealthier democracies. For autocracies, greater wealth yields a far slighter reduction in the probability of war, according to Hegre and Nome. See Collier and Hoeffler, "Greed and Grievance"; and Hegre and Nome, "Democracy, Development, and Armed Conflict."

26. Martin Luther King Jr., interview by Etta Moten Barnett, Accra, Ghana, March 6, 1957, in King, *Papers of Martin Luther King Jr.*, 4:146. While in Accra for the country's first presidential inauguration, he pulled aside the U.S. vice president, Richard Nixon, and told him, "I want you to come visit us down in Alabama where we are seeking the same kind of freedom the Gold Coast is celebrating." Cited in Carson et al., *Martin Luther King Jr. Encyclopedia*, 113.

27. Corruption began under British colonial rule; subsequent African leaders simply continued the tradition. See Victor T. LeVine, *Political Corruption: The Ghana Case* (Stanford, Calif.: Hoover Institution Press, 1975).

28. The closest they came was when a low-level lieutenant, Jerry Rawlings, launched a coup and became president in 1979. He encouraged people's justice to replace the elite courts. But class fissures weren't strong in Ghana, and little violence ensued.

29. Ray, "Rural Local Governance and Traditional Leadership in Africa and the Afro-Caribbean," 6–7.

30. Goodwin, *No Other Way Out*, 143–78.

31. Ibid., 234.

32. The administration of Alfonso López Michelsen also allowed unlimited U.S. dollars to be converted into pesos in this era. Bowden, *Killing Pablo*, 25; Richani, *Systems of Violence*, 98.

33. Chepesiuk, *Drug Lords*, 61.

34. Lee and Thoumi, "Criminal-Political Nexus," 59. It is difficult, of course, to estimate the actual value of an illegal export, and scholars have come to differing conclusions. The amount of $4 billion a year in the mid-1980s is common to a number of data sets and would be about 10 percent of Colombia's GDP in that era. See Steiner, "Colombia's Income from the Drug Trade"; and Rocha, "Aspectos económicos de las drogas."

35. Rempel, *At the Devil's Table*, 25.

36. The Cali cartel was following a well-trod path in buying its way into social prominence. In turn-of-the-century America, Robert Gans, a prominent member of Los Angeles's corrupt political machine, gave vast amounts to Jewish charities in order to gain high-profile roles in that community. In both cases, outing the criminals would harm respectable reputations, giving those community leaders a stake in whitewashing criminal reputations. See Woods, "Progressives and the Police," 111.

37. Maclean, *Social Urbanism and the Politics of Violence*, 36.

38. Bowden, *Killing Pablo*, 21.

39. Rempel, *At the Devil's Table*, 58; Felbab-Brown, "Violent Drug Market," 16n38.

40. Gugliotta and Leen, *Kings of Cocaine*, 407.

41. Goldsmith, "Police Accountability Reform in Colombia," 172.

42. The FARC initially opposed the drug trade on moral grounds, seeing drugs as incompatible with the Communist utopia it advocated. That stance put it at odds with the local population of peasants, who wanted the money coca growing could provide. So the FARC altered its strategy to retain peasant support, as described in its 1982 Seventh Conference conclusions. See Felbab-Brown, Trinkunas, and Hamid, *Militants, Criminals, and Warlords*, 80.

43. Hristov, *Blood and Capital*, 70–71.

44. It is hard to overstate the importance of land as a driver in the violence and displacement in Colombia. Ranchers, drug cartels, and businesses use violence to clear land, while guerrillas seek control over land to tax the people living there, to use them as forced soldiers, and for coca farms. Colombia's ombudsman declared the paramilitary strategy of violent displacement of peasants under the rubric of fighting guerrillas a "reverse land-reform taking place at gunpoint." Andreu-Guzmán, "Criminal Justice and Forced Displacement," 4–6; Dudley, *Walking Ghosts*, 99.

45. Hristov, *Blood and Capital*, 65.

46. Dudley, *Walking Ghosts*, 42–43.

47. The National Center of Historical Memory, a victims' group, documented massacres from 1982 to 2013 and found that 347 had been committed by the FARC or other guerrillas, 158 had been conducted by Colombia's military and police, and 1,166 were committed by paramilitaries. Just over 300 additional massacres had been committed by unidentified groups and other actors. Castro, "Trail of Death."

48. Gutiérrez Sanin and Jaramillo, "Crime, (Counter-)insurgency," 20–22.

49. Statistics from Colombia's Medical Examiner's Office.

50. Felbab-Brown, "Violent Drug Market," 15–16.

51. An after-action report on the siege says that the protection given to the Palace of Justice was "untimely" withdrawn in late October. The document offers four hypotheses as to why this occurred but concludes that "multiple testimony received by the Truth Commission agree that the withdrawal of protection could have been planned." See Gómez Gallego, Herrera Vergara, and Pinilla Pinilla, *Informe Final*, 66. The same bodyguard reduction tactic led to the conviction of General Miguel Maza Márquez, who received thirty years in prison in 2016 for reducing the state-provided contingent of bodyguards on the day of the presidential candidate Luis Galán's assassination in 1989. "Colombian General Jailed for 30 Years Over Galan Death," BBC News, November 25, 2016.

52. Dudley, *Walking Ghosts*, 45.

53. Elias offers an overwhelming number of examples of impulsive violence and sadism that were viewed as amusing at the time. Elias, *Civilizing Process*, 162–63. The general tenor of the times was not confined to Europeans. Mongol historians talk of the mass enjoyment of rape and ingenious forms of murder, such as when Mongol generals inching toward Ukraine after the Battle of the Kalka River in 1223 built a wooden platform of tree trunks, under which they placed three bound princes of Kiev whom they had just conquered. It wasn't just that one military killed the leaders of the other. The Mongol army officers feasted, drank, and caroused atop the platform, actions that crushed the Kievans to death beneath their feet. Curtin, *Mongols*, 135.

54. Elias, *Civilizing Process*, 169, citing A. Luchaire, *La société française au temps de Philippe-Auguste* (Paris, 1909), 278.

55. Atran, "ISIS Is a Revolution."

56. Elias, *Civilizing Process*, 334–40.

57. Ibid., 341.

58. Prest, "Dancing King."

59. Interestingly, some portions of society held on to the duel through the early twentieth century, but it became highly ritualized and something that

was restricted to upper classes, while murders over slights often recur in modern subsections of societies that have decivilized.

60. Kahneman, *Thinking, Fast and Slow.*

61. Kleider, Parrott, and King, "Shooting Behavior."

62. See Kohlberg, "State and Sequence."

63. Haidt, "Emotional Dog and Its Rational Tail"; Haidt and Joseph, "Intuitive Ethics"; Pizarro and Bloom, "Intelligence of Moral Intuitions."

64. Greene et al., "fMRI Investigation of Emotional Engagement."

65. Eisner, "Interpersonal Violence in the British Isles."

66. Lane, "On the Social Meaning of Homicide Trends," 59.

67. Elias, *Civilizing Process,* 445.

68. Roth, "Measuring Feelings and Beliefs," 211–13. Roth finds that violence declined prior to this civilizing, but given that U.S. colonists had emerged from an already-civilized England and had likely reverted to more primitive activity by necessity in the New World, I don't see the earlier reduction in violence as undermining Elias's thesis, though Roth adds explanatory power for violence in the modern, post-civilized age.

69. Roth, *American Homicide,* 17–18, 450–51, citing Virginia Sapiro and Steven J. Rosenstone, "American National Election Study: 1998 Pilot Study (ICPSR 2693)" (ICPSR, 2005), www.icpsr.umich.edu.

70. Roth, "Measuring Feelings and Beliefs," 199. The precise criteria Roth correlated with violence were "1. The belief that government is stable and that its legal and judicial institutions are unbiased and will redress wrongs and protect lives and property; 2. A feeling of trust in government and the officials who run it, and a belief in their legitimacy; 3. Patriotism, empathy, and fellow feeling arising from racial, religious, or political solidarity; and 4. The belief that the social hierarchy is legitimate, that one's position in society is or can be satisfactory and that one can command the respect of others without resorting to violence."

71. Roth, *American Homicide;* Eisner, "Modernization, Self-Control, and Lethal Violence." Gary LaFree, in *Losing Legitimacy,* found that crime grew with political distrust, economic stress, and family disintegration. Roger V. Gould in *Collision of Wills* sees concerns about the social order at the heart of violence.

72. Della Porta, *Social Movements,* 173.

73. Medellín's Gini coefficient was 51; the national average was 46. Roldán, *Blood and Fire.*

74. Colombia Medical Examiner's Office data.

75. Violence jumped somewhat in 2008 when President Uribe broke his promise to Don Berna and extradited him to the United States, leaving a vacuum of power in Medellín that set off a turf war among remaining criminals. But as the government regained control, it fell again, and reached 21 per 100,000 by 2016. Statistics are all from ibid.

76. Rosenberg, "Colombia's Data-Driven Fight Against Homicide."

77. While the government statistics are slightly higher at 24 per 100,000, this figure comes from the Igarape Institute Homicide Monitor, which is more accurate.

78. Franco et al., "The Effects of the Armed Conflict," 351–53.

79. In a single apartment complex in Naples, there were so many paid assassins by the 1990s that the going price for a hit was just $3,300.

80. Oshinsky, Worse than Slavery, 24. The coarsening of language Elias described is also prevalent. A local paper, for instance, discussed a lynching as "another Negro barbecue," and a New Orleans paper described a lynching as "artistic" while considering it amusing that another victim was named "Will Steak." Hair, Kingfish and His Realm, 67.

81. Oshinsky, Worse Than Slavery, 24.

82. Ayers, Vengeance and Justice, 17; Lane, Murder in America, 350.

83. Egley, Logan, and McDaniel, "Gang Homicides, Five U.S. Cities, 2003–2008."

84. Leovy, Ghettoside, 81.

85. Ibid., 40.

86. Monkkonen, "Diverging Homicide Rates," 81.

87. Frederick Law Olmsted traveled through the violent South in the 1850s and wrote Journeys and Explorations in the Cotton Kingdom, explaining frontier origins for the violence. David Hackett Fischer claims that Scotch-Irish culture catalyzed violence; Bertram Wyatt-Brown blamed an "honor culture," which Richard Nisbett tried to quantify in the modern South through psychological tests. The cultural explanations also make little sense when one remembers that Australia, settled by convicts entering an equally sparsely governed territory, has had a homicide rate hovering at less than half that of America for the last twenty-five years.

88. Monkkonen, "Diverging Homicide Rates," 81.

89. Lane, Murder in America.

4: DIRTY DEALS

1. "Mexican Cartels United Against the 'Z,'" Borderland Beat: Reporting on the Mexican Cartel Drug War, March 5, 2010.

2. Tilly, *Coercion, Capital, and European States.*

3. Olson, "Dictatorship, Democracy, and Development," 567–76.

4. Their terminology discussed "limited-access" versus "open-access" orders, but I believe the "extractive state" language used by Daron Acemoglu and James Robinson is more evocative and describes a relatively similar phenomenon.

5. Goldsmith, "Police Accountability Reform in Colombia," 172.

6. Bowden, *Killing Pablo,* 70–85.

7. Gerstel, "Andean Drug Strategy a Failure."

8. Chepesiuk, *Drug Lords.*

9. Marroquín, *Pablo Escobar;* Bowden, *Killing Pablo.*

10. Daniel Rico, interview by author, Jan. 26, 2015, and author's email correspondence with Escobar's son, Feb.–March 2017.

11. According to the journalistic account by Mark Bowden, the U.S. State Department opposed working with Los Pepes while the Drug Enforcement Administration was willing to do so. While no U.S. government agency admits to assisting Los Pepes, intelligence somehow passed hands. See Bowden, *Killing Pablo,* 180–200.

12. Ibid. A more sanitized account is in Felbab-Brown, "Violent Drug Market," 16. See also Woody, "'Nobody Is Ever Going to Tell You.'"

13. Homicide data for Georgia, as with most countries, is incomplete. However, it appears that by 2010, the last year data was reported internationally under the Saakashvili government, the rate was 4.40, which is on par with the U.S. homicide rate at its lowest points in the 1950s and today. In 2014, the Georgian Dream government reported a rate of 2.68, which matches tiny European Liechtenstein.

14. De Waal, *Caucasus,* 131, 152.

15. Ibid., 132.

16. "April 9, 1989, Soviet Crackdown in Tbilisi," Radio Free Europe/Radio Liberty Photo blog, April 7, 2014, www.rferl.org.

17. De Waal, *Caucasus,* 132.

18. Ibid., 133.

19. Kukhianidze, "Corruption and Organized Crime in Georgia," 219.

20. Driscoll, *Warlords and Coalition Politics,* 77; Jones, *Georgia,* 83.

21. Nodia, "Putting the State Back Together," 417.

22. Jones, *Georgia,* 76.

23. Ibid., 34.

24. Driscoll, *Warlords and Coalition Politics*, 6–7.

25. Ibid., 47–49.

26. Technically, Shevardnadze was prime minister during this time, but Georgians universally saw him and refer to him as president, which is sensible because he did not have a party that held seats in the parliament.

27. De Waal, *Caucasus*, 142.

28. This incident occurred in 1992; see ibid., 143.

29. In a brilliant book about violence in former Soviet republics, Jesse Driscoll puts some color into the relatively bloodless theory of North, Wallis, and Weingast: "Warlords understood perfectly that great powers could not send much money or guarantee regime support until *after* strong local clients had emerged, via a violent process of sorting and attrition on the streets. They bargained among each other and ultimately backed the ascendency of a civilian figurehead. The president rehabilitated warlords and granted them ministry positions in exchange for security." See Driscoll, *Warlords and Coalition Politics*, 8.

30. Ibid., 91.

31. Jones, *Georgia*, 83, 95.

32. It's not clear if Kitovani moved into Abkhazia under Shevardnadze's orders or his own volition. De Waal, *Caucasus*, 157–59.

33. Admiral Baltin, the commander of Russia's fleet in the Black Sea, moved his artillery into position, as if he were preparing to fire on the Zviadist who remained loyal to their ousted president. For further detail, see Driscoll, *Warlords and Coalition Politics*, 185, footnote 261.

34. Japaridze, interview by author, Dec. 4, 2014.

35. Russians had long joked, combining the delectable Georgian cuisine with their denigration of the country's sovereignty, "Georgia? That's not a country; it's a restaurant!" In fairness, my favorite restaurant in St. Petersburg in 1992 and 1993 was, indeed, the "Georgian."

36. On June 24, 1992, Shevardnadze and Yeltsin met in the Black Sea resort of Dagomys and signed what was intended as a temporary peace treaty to end the escalation in South Ossetia. It became a long-term bandage. The Abkhazia cease-fire was broken that fall by the Abkhaz, who routed the Georgians and blocked the roads, forcing thousands to cross the Caucasus Mountains on foot in winter. The local Svans further robbed and terrorized the refugees. Where I was interviewing militia members, children's drawings along the walls commemorated this mountainous flight, the guns and weaponry wielded against them, and the freezing cold. For over a decade, a landmark hotel in the center of Georgia held hundreds of refugees whose web of clotheslines reminded the

city that Georgia still had hundreds of thousands of internally displaced persons who constituted more than 5 percent of the population, a number that grew by forty thousand out of the renewed war over South Ossetia in 2008. De Waal, *Caucasus*, 165.

37. Jones, *Georgia*, 99–100.

38. Usupashvili, interview by author, Dec. 4, 2014.

39. Alexandre Kukhianidze, interview by author, Dec. 6, 2014.

40. Driscoll, *Warlords and Coalition Politics*, 13.

41. Ibid., 97.

42. Ibid., 87.

43. Di John and Putzel, "Political Settlements"; and North, Wallis, and Weingast, *Violence and Social Orders*, argue that the success of a bargain has more to do with the satisfaction of elites than fulfilling wider interests of society.

44. Fukuyama, *State-Building*; Ghani and Lockhart, *Fixing Failed States*; Chesterman, Ignatieff, and Thakur, *Making States Work*; Call, "Knowing Peace When You See It"; Barnett, "Building a Republican Peace"; Stewart, "Social Exclusion and Conflict"; Keating and Knight, *Building Sustainable Peace*; Burton and Higley, "Political Crises and Elite Settlements"; Hartzell and Hoddie, "Institutionalizing Peace."

45. The good news is that reoccurrences of violence following peace agreements are generally less deadly than the first round. Human Security Report Project, *Sexual Violence, Education, and War*, 178–79. Thus, the 2011 World Development Report found that an important component of peace was "an 'inclusive enough' political settlement."

46. The Stanford scholar Stephen Stedman, in "Spoiler Problems in Peace Processes," finds that these deals need to address the problem of potential spoilers and hard-liners and sometimes bring in civil society groups that can represent such interests. Stedman, Rothschild, and Cousens, in *Ending Civil Wars*, speak to the importance of power sharing between previously warring groups and international commitment to convince all of those with weapons that the agreement will be kept.

47. For example, the United States spent years brokering negotiations to enable South Sudan to peacefully break away from the rest of Sudan in 2011. But just two years later, the new president fired his vice president; then both took up separate armies and started a war over who would control the state's money. For further, see Spears, "Understanding Inclusive Peace Agreements in Africa."

48. Rothchild and Roeder, *Power Sharing*, 29–50; Horowitz, "Making Moderation Pay," 9.

49. Driscoll, *Warlords and Coalition Politics,* 9.

50. Tull and Mehler, "Hidden Costs of Power-Sharing"; DeWaal, "Political Marketplace."

51. Tattersall, "Nigerian Rebel Leaders."

52. *Small Arms Survey 2013: Everyday Dangers,* 119. For further, see Peel, *Swamp Full of Dollars.*

53. Jarstaad and Nilson, "From Words to Deeds"; Wallensteen and Eriksson, "Negotiating Peace," 33–34. In Liberia, for instance, a series of peace agreements rewarded warring parties with government posts and varying percentages of state agencies. Parties used their negotiating positions to acquire political power that could be translated into economic power. During implementation of the most recent, and most sustained, peace deal, fighting factions demanded that disarmament and demobilization be halted until "posts in the government and public corporations had been distributed 'properly.'" A few months later, former fighters obstructed the deployment of peacekeeping troops, demanding the right to appoint eighty-four assistant ministerial positions. See *First Progress Report,* 6, and *Second Progress Report,* 1.

54. Knight, "Corruption in Twentieth Century Mexico," 223.

55. This is particularly the case with dirty deals made among criminal or insurgent groups themselves. In Italy, for instance, the first modern Mafia war broke out in the early 1960s. A police crackdown led to historically low murder rates, so that in 1968 just sixteen people were killed in Palermo. But when a second Mafia war started in the early 1980s, thousands died. The police made hundreds of arrests, though many mafiosi were quickly released on appeal. Violence fell again until the early 1990s, when the third Mafia war broke out, and the number of deaths increased again. Dickie, *Cosa Nostra,* 250–52; Jamieson, *Antimafia,* 18.

56. "Rivers of Blood," *Economist,* Oct. 10, 2015, 35.

57. El Salvador's much-heralded truce between its violent gangs was brokered in 2012, in exchange for moving gang leaders to lower-security jails where they could have cell phones and be nearer to their families. Death rates plummeted. But by 2013, the truce began to falter. Homicides had fallen, but kidnappings and disappearances were rising. Critics claimed that gangs were rearming and had simply shifted operations. In 2015, a few days before midterm elections, a new government broke the agreement and moved the gang leaders back to maximum-security prisons. The next month, violence skyrocketed, and by the end of the year death rates were higher than before the agreement, giving El Salvador the highest homicide rate in the world.

58. Wells, "'Rising Extortion.'"

59. In El Salvador, only about 10 percent of extortion attempts were reported, according to ibid.

60. Wilson, "Chronicle of a Massacre."

61. Forced displacement rose from 221,638 newly displaced in 2006 to 380,863 in 2008, according to the Consultoría para los Derechos Humanos y el Desplazamiento; International Crisis Group, "Virtuous Twins," 4.

62. Alex Rondeli, interview by author, Dec. 5, 2014.

63. Schneider and Schneider, *Reversible Destiny*, 224.

64. Behan, *Camorra*, 150–51.

65. Nadeau, "How the Mafia Murdered the Townspeople of Amatrice."

66. *States of Security*, 23. The civil war ran from 1960, when the population was 4.1 million, to 1996, when it was 10.21 million. Thus, adjusted for population, Guatemala faced 44 homicides per 100,000 in 2009, an even greater per capita rate of death post–civil war than the raw numbers suggest.

67. Jones, *Georgia*, 100–101.

68. Engvall, "Against the Grain," 16; World Bank, *Fighting Corruption in Public Services*, 7.

69. Kukhianidze, "Corruption and Organized Crime in Georgia," 217–18.

70. In fact, state legislators would often propose legislation harmful to a company just to be bribed to kill it. Dalton, *Strenuous Life*, 139.

71. Benson, *Political Corruption in America*, 60.

72. Baker, "Courthouse That Graft Built."

73. The warden at Sing Sing in the 1840s reportedly let prisoners escape in exchange for bribes. He deliberately underfed his prisoners and sold the food—something military officers did in Georgia 150 years later to their own troops. See Curie, *Crime and Punishment in America*, 50.

74. In Colombia in 1986, a prisoner being held for the murder of a U.S. DEA agent spent $2 million bribing the guards and warden, then simply walked out of a Bogotá prison. But the prison authorities weren't simply greedy. A prior warden had been killed for refusing to cooperate with an earlier plot to release the same prisoner. Gugliotta and Leen, *Kings of Cocaine*, 427.

75. Cearley, "Cop Marked for Death."

76. Ibid.

77. Sabet, *Police Reform in Mexico*, 2–4.

78. Statistically, the majority of countries where corruption is a problem are weak electoral democracies, although many autocracies are in the bottom third of all countries in controlling corruption, with just 10 percent in the upper tercile. Autocratic anticorruption drives also tend to be both repressive and discriminatory so that corruption can be allowed among favorites and

prevented among lower-level officials and those who have fallen out of favor. Mungiu-Pippidi, *Quest for Good Governance*, 62, 96.

79. Pranab Bardhan, in "Corruption and Development," calls corruption a "frequency dependent phenomenon": the more people who are corrupt, the less reason any individual has not to engage in corruption. Mishra, "Persistence of Corruption," similarly finds that when corruption is the norm, it is the way the system functions and forms its own mode of social organization. So the entire system must be re-created; it cannot be "cleaned up."

80. Colin Powell, the former U.S. secretary of state and defense, once said, "Nigerians as a group, frankly, are marvelous scammers. . . . I mean, it's in their national culture." Yet the very idea of a Nigerian people is fairly new. The state's borders were drawn by nineteenth-century colonialism, and its people see themselves as having such different ethnic and religious cultures that parts of the country have tried to violently secede. Corruption in Nigeria is endemic but has been baked into everyday life thanks to a power structure, not a single culture.

81. This situation is what economists call a globally inferior Nash equilibrium, a stable state that is, nevertheless, worse than other possible stable states. It is perhaps most easily understood from a snippet of Joseph Heller's *Catch-22*. An American pilot explains to his officer that he will not be flying any more missions, because "from now on I'm thinking only of me." "But Yossarian, suppose everyone felt that way?" responded his officer. "Then I'd certainly be a damned fool to feel any other way, wouldn't I?" Heller, *Catch-22* (New York: Simon & Schuster, 1961), 409.

82. As Frank Serpico, the New York City police officer who exposed endemic corruption on his force in 1970, claimed, "Ten percent of the cops in New York City are absolutely corrupt, 10 percent are absolutely honest, and the other 80 percent—they wish they were honest." Armstrong, *They Wished They Were Honest*, viii.

83. Mishra, "Persistence of Corruption." My colleague Sarah Chayes also used this phrase in her report "Honduras."

84. Rothstein, *Quality of Government*, 100–101.

85. Hash-Gonzalez, *Mobilization and Empowerment*, 35.

86. Behan, *Camorra*, 155–56.

87. Roosevelt, *Autobiography*, 489.

88. Perceptions of inequity in service delivery upset citizens' notions of state legitimacy in a multitude of empirical cases drawn from Africa, Asia, and Latin America. See Ndaruhutse, *State-Building, Peace-Building, and Service*. See also Dix, Hussmann, and Walton, *Risks of Corruption to State Legitimacy*.

89. The literature on what are known as "ultimatum games" suggests that offers of less than 30 percent of a given amount are typically rejected, a finding that has held across vastly different cultures studied, with only a few exceptions. Chimpanzees have also been found to exhibit such "non-rational" preferences for equity, giving up a potential reward to prevent someone else from receiving what is perceived to be an unfairly large benefit. For a sampling of this literature, see Colin Camerer and Richard Thaler, "Ultimatums, Dictators, and Manners," *Journal of Economic Perspectives* 9 (1995): 209–19; Alvin E. Roth, "Bargaining Experiments," in *Handbook of Experimental Economics*, ed. J. Kagel and A. Roth (Princeton, N.J.: Princeton University Press, 1995); and David G. Rand et al., "Evolution of Fairness in the One-Shot Anonymous Ultimatum Game," *Proceedings of the National Academy of Sciences of the United States of America* 110, no. 7 (2013): 2,581–86. For animal players, see Darby Proctor, Sarah F. Brosnan, and Frans B. M. de Waal, "How Fairly Do Chimpanzees Play the Ultimatum Game?," *Communicative and Integrative Biology* 6, no. 3 (2013).

90. Wiktorowicz, "Why Trump's Speech on Terrorism Was Such a Missed Opportunity."

91. Data from 2010–2012 COMISAF Reports from the Afghanistan Nationwide Quarterly Assessment Research Survey Data drawn from the International Security Assistance Force, the international forces that have been prosecuting the war in Afghanistan. A 2009 report from the British government assistance agency, DFID, had similar findings. See Ladbury, "Testing Hypotheses on Radicalisation in Afghanistan," cited in SIGAR, "Corruption in Conflict," 10.

92. Carothers and Carothers, "Seeking Political Stability Abroad?"

93. Shelley, introduction to *Organized Crime and Corruption in Georgia*, 4–5.

94. Hash-Gonzalez, *Mobilization and Empowerment*, 37.

95. Shelley, introduction to *Organized Crime and Corruption in Georgia*, 4–5.

96. Hash-Gonzalez, *Mobilization and Empowerment*, 36.

97. Ginty, "Hybrid Governance," 450. The World Bank, the IMF, the Council of Europe, the Conference on Security and Cooperation in Europe, the EU, and the United States, among others, provided aid to Georgia.

98. Driscoll, *Warlords and Coalition Politics*, 95.

99. Jones, *Georgia*, 197.

100. Ginty, "Hybrid Governance," 450.

101. Jones, *Georgia*, 264.

102. Hash-Gonzalez, *Mobilization and Empowerment*, 37.

103. Marten, *Warlords*, 73.

104. De Waal, *Caucasus*, 145.

105. Marten, *Warlords*, 90.

106. Shelley, introduction to *Organized Crime and Corruption in Georgia*, 4–5.

107. Jones, *Criminology*, 98.

108. Political party official, interview by author, Dec. 2014.

109. Serio and Razinkin, "Thieves Professing the Code," 76. Godson et al. note similar cultural alterations in "Building Societal Support for the Rule of Law in Georgia."

110. Usupashvili, interview by author, Dec. 5, 2014.

5: THE MIDDLE CLASS

1. Schneider and Schneider, *Reversible Destiny*, 210.

2. Kleinfeld, "Improving Development Aid Design and Evaluation."

3. Aristotle, *Politics*, book 4, chap. 11, 1,221, writes "This is the class of citizens which is most secure in a state, for they do not, like the poor, covet their neighbours' goods; nor do others covet theirs . . . and as they neither plot against others, nor are they themselves plotted against, they pass through life safely."

4. Economists have gravitated toward $10 a day as a middle-class threshold for income, but a single number yields vastly different consumption abilities, so it makes more sense to adjust for purchasing power. See Kharas, "Unprecedented Expansion of the Global Middle Class."

5. Max Weber's full definition in *Economy and Society* is the most useful: "A class situation is one in which there is a shared typical probability of procuring goods, gaining a position in life, and finding inner satisfaction." Weber also divides the working and the middle classes by the fact that the former have only their labor to offer, while the latter also hold educational credentials. On autonomy of work, see Lipset, "Some Social Requisites for Democracy." On middle-class values, see López-Calva, Rigolini, and Torche, "Is There Such a Thing as Middle Class Values?"

6. Riedel, "Homicide in Los Angeles County," 55.

7. Leovy, *Ghettoside*, 333. Leovy draws her Iraq mortality data from Preston and Buzzell, "Service in Iraq," which calculated a rate of 392 per 100,000 among troops deployed in 2003–2006. Factoring in just the combat deaths makes a rate of 309 per 100,000. For twenty- to twenty-four-year-old black males, death from homicide in Los Angeles County hit a high of 368 per 100,000 in 1993.

8. Leovy, *Ghettoside*, 305–6. Given that black Americans are killed at five to eight times the rate of whites, that perception is often, sadly, correct.

9. Papachristos and Wildeman, "Network Exposure and Homicide Victimization."

10. Green, Horel, and Papachristos, "Modeling Contagion Through Social Networks."

11. Pinheiro, "The Rule of Law," 4–5.

12. Leovy, *Ghettoside*, 38.

13. Ibid., 34, 37.

14. The African American journalist Ida Wells, for instance, likely did more than any other individual to focus national attention on the problem of southern lynching. But for years, she accepted the dominant belief voiced by the black professional class that living lawfully and comporting oneself in an orderly manner would keep her safe. Only after a white mob murdered the father of her godchild along with two other middle-class black entrepreneurs in a dispute that pitted a white grocery store against their black "People's Grocery" did Wells accept that lynching could happen to law-abiding people like her. Silkey, *Black Woman Reformer*, 53–54.

15. Leovy, *Ghettoside*, 65, 270. Leovy recounts how wrong this assumption of guilt is, noting that in one August week in 2009 five males were killed in Southeast L.A. They included a thirteen-year-old boy with no tattoos, implying that he had no gang affiliation; a sixteen-year-old with no criminal background who happened to be the cousin of another homicide victim who was in a gang; a twenty-one-year-old working man, also with no gang connections; and a forty-nine-year-old man, who had formerly been a bank robber but had no recent criminal history.

16. I tell this story in chapter 7. See Pollack, "'They Could Have Killed Me Easily.'"

17. Corchado, *Midnight in Mexico*, 19.

18. Villagran, "Victims' Movement in Mexico," 129.

19. Ibid., 121, 129, citing a telephone interview with Juan Carlos of Ciudad Juárez in Aug. 2012.

20. Ibid., 123, 128–29.

21. Ibid., 130–33. In 2002, the organization Justice for Our Daughters took up the cause of these poor women. The mothers were working-class women whose cause was eventually folded into Mexico United Against Crime. It is hard to say whether the effort to find justice for these poor women would have gained much attention had the drug war not led the middle-class group to join forces with their cause.

22. Sicily's Cosa Nostra is organized into groups that cooperate and occasionally compete known as *cosche*, usually translated into English as "families." These families may include blood relatives, but unlike the 'Ndràngheta Mafia located in the toe of Italy's boot, a *cosca* is rarely an actual family unit.

23. Dickie, *Cosa Nostra*, 140.

24. These internal stressors can be caused by competition among groups, or other threats—as with the withdrawal of funding in the post-Soviet era. In Italy in the 1970s, left-wing terrorist groups under threat from the state increased activities that were needed to gain funds, avoid arrest, and maintain loyalty. Yet bank robberies made political activists look like criminals, killing police entailed innocent victims, and the murder of fellow activists who broke the rules alienated others within the group. Della Porta, *Social Movements*, 123–24.

25. Cronin, *How Terrorism Ends*; Abrahms, "Why Terrorism Does Not Work."

26. Felbab-Brown, Trinkunas, and Hamid, *Militants, Criminals, and Warlords*, 25, 86, 88.

27. Saviano, *Gomorrah*, 119–20.

28. Behan, *Camorra*, 137–38.

29. Pasotti, *Political Branding in Cities*, 35.

30. Ibid. From 1985 to 1990, only 15 percent of public sector contracts in Naples were competitive public tenders, and the national audit office in 1990 found that more than two-thirds of all tenders had violated government contracting rules. Behan, *Camorra*, 121. I interviewed an Italian professor who had recently moved to Naples. Although she researched organized crime, even she was shocked by how deep Mafia patronage networks reached into the university faculty. Monica Massari, interview by author, March 4, 2015.

31. In some ways, the Camorra were a more difficult problem than Sicily's Cosa Nostra because they were so decentralized. Jailing one group would simply increase turf wars rather than reduce violence. But the many warring factions also offered more avenues for turning disgruntled members into informants, which is how Colombia fought the many criminal gangs it faced after demobilizing its paramilitaries. So the Camorra's structure doesn't decisively explain Naples's difficulties.

32. Bassolino became mayor because of a quirk of national politics. The year before, a group of magistrates known as the *mani pulite*, or "clean hands," judges had launched a series of investigations into corruption that implicated all the existing parties. In Naples, the investigations prevented the entire local political class from serving. The moderate wing of the local Communist Party recalled Antonio Bassolino from his parliamentary post in Rome to help rebuild the party. With the political field suddenly emptied and a new law allowing direct

elections of city leaders (previously they were appointed by parties), he was elected mayor.

33. Pasotti, *Political Branding in Cities*, 106–7.

34. The council dissolutions happened from 1991 to 2010.

35. Ibid., 114–15.

36. Behan, *Camorra*, 139–40.

37. Ibid., 135.

38. Ibid., 6.

39. Direzione Investigativa Antimafia, "Camorra," 166.

40. In 1997, over six hundred police officers were found to be on the Camorra payroll, faking investigations into some factions while arresting rival clans. An internal informant claimed that each Camorra clan had a political sponsor and that together the mob and the politician would determine who would be elected for major political roles. While informant laws were crucial to fighting Sicily's Mafia, the Camorra used Naples's corrupted police force to murder the relatives of mafiosi turned informers, disabling that tool of investigation. Allum and Allum, "Revisiting Naples," 195; McCarthy, *Crisis of the Italian State*, 151; Vannucci, "Politicians and Godfathers"; Jamieson, *Antimafia*, 85. Global Security, "Camorra."

41. Global Security, "Camorra."

42. Paternostro, interview by author, Feb. 26, 2015.

43. Dickie, *Cosa Nostra*, 60.

44. Ibid., 40.

45. Ibid., 39–40.

46. Some Sicilians also rebelled against a united Italy but were quashed by military troops and martial law in 1866.

47. Revisit the historical homicide chart on page 9 to see the spike in Italian homicides in that era.

48. Under the Bourbon empire, all land was owned by the king. Kings would grant estates to lords, but the monarch could always take them back if a lord lost favor.

49. Schneider and Schneider, *Culture and Political Economy in Modern Sicily*, 119.

50. After centuries of stagnation, former feudal lords who had been stuck with fixed landholdings after feudalism was abolished could now purchase additional land and do with it what they pleased. A parliamentary inquiry in 1878 found that 93 percent of the church lands were bought by those "who were already rich." See Schneider and Schneider, *Reversible Destiny*, 26.

51. The story of Sicily's Mafia is unique, but it bears a common thread with those of the *yakuza* in Japan, the Russian Mafia, and the Chinese triads. Organized crime tends to arise when an economy is modernizing but the state is unable to protect property rights or reliably settle business disputes, so organized crime steps in to provide this service. While weak states allow organized criminal groups to arise, that origin explains little regarding why Mafias continue to thrive for decades after a state has strengthened. For discussion, see Gambetta, *Sicilian Mafia;* Abadinsky, *Organized Crime;* and Hess, *Mafia and Mafiosi.*

52. Schneider and Schneider, *Reversible Destiny,* 31.

53. The connection between Sicily's violence and local politics was clear from the start. As early as June 1875, a left-wing senator named Diego Tajani, a former member of Palermo's Appeals Court, spoke from the chamber floor. "Gentlemen of the Government. . . . The mafia in Sicily is not dangerous or invincible in itself. It is dangerous and invincible because it is an instrument of local government." Dainotto, *Mafia,* 29.

54. This understanding of the growth of the Sicilian Mafia is based on the meticulous research of a new generation of Mafia historians, among them Fiume, "Bandits, Violence, and the Organization of Power in Sicily"; Lupo, *Storia della Mafia;* Pezzino, *Mafia;* and Riall, *Sicily and the Unification of Italy.*

55. Schneider and Schneider, *Reversible Destiny,* 29.

56. Lupo, *Storia della Mafia;* Pezzino, *Mafia.*

57. The rate was 1 homicide for every 3,194 Sicilians, versus 1 in every 44,674 persons in Lombardy in the north of the country. Dainotto, *Mafia,* 28.

58. Dickie, *Cosa Nostra,* 91. This document could have been witness testimony in the Mafia trials of the 1990s, so similar are the modern Mafia practices to those of a century before.

59. Ibid., 132.

60. Ibid., 134.

61. Ibid., 159.

62. Ibid., 150–58, tells the story of Mussolini, Mori, and the Mafia in full.

63. Duggan, *Fascism and the Mafia.*

64. Dickie, *Cosa Nostra,* 158.

65. It is unclear how knowledgeable the Allies were about what they were doing. Some claim that the U.S. war effort was directly working with Lucky Luciano, a famous mobster, to recapture the island. Others claim that Italian mafiosi who fled during Mussolini's crackdown infiltrated U.S. armed forces and became interpreters during the recapturing of the island, then used their

positions to help the Mafia. While I can't find any proof of these stories, I also can't find anything to disprove them, and both might well have occurred.

66. Schneider and Schneider, *Reversible Destiny*, 49–52.

67. For further, see Judt, *Postwar.*

68. Ginsborg, *History of Contemporary Italy*, 100–101, 146–52; McCarthy, *Crisis of the Italian State*, 44; Schneider and Schneider, "Mafia, Anti-Mafia," 505–6.

69. Schneider and Schneider, *Reversible Destiny*, 53.

70. Ginsborg, *History of Contemporary Italy*, 100–101, 146–52. Italy had fifty-four governments in fifty years, from the end of World War II through 1994, but in Sicily the Christian Democrats were always the large party in a coalition of smaller parties. The smaller parties were unwilling to denounce corruption because they were better off becoming part of the government and thus sharing in the spoils. On the mainland, the Communist Party was similarly hobbled, though it did win Naples under Mayor Bassolino and sometimes controlled the university town of Bologna in the North.

71. Stille, "All the Prime Minister's Men."

72. A similar situation occurred in turn-of-the-century America, where the Republican and Democratic machines colluded to rid themselves of Theodore Roosevelt, who was interfering with their graft. Jeffers, *Commissioner Roosevelt*, 218.

73. McCarthy, *Crisis of the Italian State*, 44–45.

74. Pino Arlacchi, *Men of Dishonor: An Account of Antonio Calderone*, trans. Marc Romano (New York: William Morrow, 1993), 182–84, quoted in Dickie, *Cosa Nostra*, 71–73.

75. After World War II, the Christian Democrats refused to demilitarize the police, and the force kept the mission bequeathed by Mussolini: to preserve the internal security of the state, rather than to protect citizens. Donatella Della Porta, a political scientist, interviewed militants in Germany and Italy, studying each step of their violence to determine why terrorism in Italy had been worse than in Germany. She found that at every juncture Italian police used more violent tactics. Della Porta, *Social Movements*, 60, 73, 190.

76. Ibid., 159.

77. When these neo-Fascist plants set off a bomb in Milan that killed sixteen and left dozens wounded, the police arrested an innocent anarchist who later "fell from a window" during police questioning. Dickie, *Cosa Nostra*, 268.

78. Della Porta, *Social Movements*, 18–19, 31, 60–65.

79. *Small Arms Survey 2013*, 84. The IRA killed approximately 1,800 people during its thirty-year campaign, about 650 of them civilians unconnected to the conflict. Lavery, "I.R.A. Apologizes for Civilian Deaths in Its 30-Year Campaign."

80. One of the most famous of these is Peppino Impastato, the son of a mafi-oso who turned against the family business and became an anti-Mafia activ-ist in Sicily. He ran for city council in 1978, and the Mafia murdered him by tying dynamite to his stomach and placing him on a railroad track, framing his death as that of a left-wing terrorist killed by his own bomb. Close ties between the police and the Mafia kept the truth from emerging until 1997. The level of political polarization emerged a few years later. In 1981, the banking empire built by Michele Sindona, one of the world's wealthiest international financiers and a funder of the Christian Democratic Party, began to crash amid fraud alle-gations. In an attempt to save himself, Sindona provided information to the state on a scandal that became known as P2. Sindona had been a member of a Masonic lodge, common among elite Italians. Throughout the 1970s, his lodge had used blackmail, bribes, and intimidation to strategically undermine Italy's Left and keep it out of government. Of the Masonic lodge's 950 members, 52 were high-level officials in Italy's national police force, 37 were members of the Treasury police, and 11 were police chiefs. There were 50 army officers, 5 current and former government ministers, 38 members of parliament, and the principal owner and editor of Italy's largest paper. See Schneider and Schnei-der, *Reversible Destiny*, 75.

81. The role of the media in perpetuating the status quo was significant in Italy, though outside the scope of this story. I suggest Gundle and O'Sullivan's "Mass Media and the Political Crisis," 206–20.

82. Many centuries later, La Boétie's points would be proven quantitatively by social scientists. From 1900 to 2006, nonviolent movements succeeded 53 per-cent of the time, compared with 26 percent of the time for violent movements. Terrorism fares even worse, succeeding only about 7 percent of the time. See Chenoweth and Stephan, *Why Civil Resistance Works*; and Abrahms, "Why Ter-rorism Does Not Work," 42.

83. For further, see Carothers and Youngs, "Complexities of Global Protests."

84. Scordato, interview by author, Feb. 27, 2015.

85. In the 1960s, Vito Ciancimino, who began as public works commissioner, then mayor of Palermo, caused what was known as "the sack of Palermo" by issuing thousands of illegal building permits to Cosa Nostra fronts. The Mafia replaced ancient palazzi and historic monuments with shoddy concrete apart-ment blocks and chopped down the lemon groves ringing the city to build suburban tract housing. The city center became a ghetto, crowded, dangerous, and owned by the Mafia. Ciancimino issued school contracts to mafiosi, who forced schools to lease space from their apartment buildings, leaving hundreds of students to share bathrooms built for a single family, with no outdoor areas for recess or proper space for classrooms. See Orlando, *Fighting the Mafia and Renewing Sicilian Culture.*

86. Bowden, *Killing Pablo,* 91–100.

87. General Miguel Maza Márquez was sentenced to thirty years in prison in 2016 for his role in the murder. Santofimio, who wanted to eliminate a political rival, received a twenty-four-year sentence.

88. On August 22, 1989, strikes that had begun around Poland were taken up by the Gdansk shipyard. On August 26, the government agreed to negotiation, heralding the beginning of the end of the U.S.S.R.'s breakup. Reflecting twenty-five years later on the changes he wrought, Fernando Carrillo discussed the role of Eastern Europe's fight against the Soviet Union in inspiring Colombia's students. Carrillo Flórez, "La séptima papeleta."

89. Fox, Gallón-Giraldo, and Stetson, "Lessons of the Colombian Constitutional Reform of 1991," 470–71.

90. Ibid. As with most off-season elections, turnout was low, but those who did choose to vote clearly had a strong preference.

91. Ibid.

92. Ibid., 476–77.

93. Prior to official ballots, party bosses provided voters with party ballots that were often colored and thus easy to discern, and public voting made it impossible to vote secretly.

94. Ibid., 470–72.

95. The direct election of mayors had mixed effects. It helped reduce violence in the big cities but probably contributed to violence in smaller rural areas without a middle class. In places where the professional class was too small to create a public outcry, existing politicians and paramilitary forces who were often connected to drug cartels used direct elections to gain control. Others believe that the change led to the fracturing of politics into local clientelist networks. For more on the constitutional changes, see Bejarano, "Constitution of 1991."

96. Some guerrillas were undoubtedly using the party as a front to further their war, but for others who saw their funding drying up with the end of the Soviet Union, the move into politics was a genuine attempt to abandon fighting for the ballot box. In 1988, the head of the FARC's political party, the UP, traveled to Eastern Europe and was surprised to learn that real socialism was dead. He began to date a bourgeois lawyer and tried to open up a perestroika within the FARC to break the UP from doctrinaire Communism and guerrilla warfare. Dudley, *Walking Ghosts,* 135.

97. Ibid., 170–71.

98. Pereira and Ungar, "Persistence of the 'Mano Dura.'" Buchanan et al., "Mano Dura in the Americas," 1, 5, finds that Mano Dura policies attract

strong pluralities of support from more than a third of the public—though not majorities—in ten Latin American countries. However, policies need win only a majority of voters, not entire publics. Interestingly, corruption was more linked to support than crime victimization. In the Philippines, where somewhere between six thousand and twelve thousand people have been murdered in extrajudicial killings in just two years since President Duterte took office and issued his call for vigilante justice, more than three-quarters of the population approve of the approach. "Global Patterns," *Economist*.

99. The Bhagalpur blinding case is infamous, as is the population's support after facing years of brutal crime. See Ahmed and Bobb, "Bhagalpur."

100. Holland, "Right on Crime"; Wolf, "Policing Crime in El Salvador." In various parts of Latin America, the military has a history of conducting vaccination campaigns, building roads, and constructing other public works in rural areas to boost its public image and build intelligence networks to fight insurgencies. Different recruitment patterns mean that militaries are also often seen as more educated, competent, and trustworthy than low-paid, low-status police. Citizens also tend to trust the military because they have less interaction with its forces compared to police forces they know all too well. Benítez Manaut, "Role of the Military," 128–29; Pereira and Ungar, "Persistence of the 'Mano Dura.'"

101. O'Leary and Silke, "Understanding and Ending Persistent Conflicts."

102. Wilson, "Trump Draws Criticism for Ad He Ran."

103. Luttwak, "Dead End."

104. Driscoll, *Warlords and Coalition Politics*, 65.

105. Czerniecka and Heathershaw, "Security and Border Management," 86.

106. Security Assistance Monitor, "Security Aid Pivot Table—Tajikistan," shows $34,677,461 in aid in 2014. See also Goodman and Drager, "Military Aid Dependency."

107. Czerniecka and Heathershaw, "Security and Border Management," 87–88.

108. Standish, "How Tajikistan's President Extended His Term—for Life."

109. Tynan, "Tajikistan."

110. In a YouTube video, the colonel called on fellow Tajiks to join him, then taunted his old colleagues: "Listen, you dogs, the president and ministers. If only you knew how many boys, our brothers are here, waiting and yearning to return to reestablish Sharia [Islamic] law [in Tajikistan]. . . . We are coming to you, God willing, we are coming to you with slaughter. . . . Listen, you American pigs, I've been to America three times, and I saw how you train fighters to kill Muslims. God willing, I will come with this weapon to your cities, your homes, and we will kill you." See Tynan, "Tajikistan"; International Crisis

Group, "Crisis Watch: Tajikistan"; and Dyner, Legiec, and Rekawek, "Ready to Go."

111. Abadie, "Poverty, Political Freedom, and the Roots of Terrorism."

112. The Global Terrorism Index, 2015, 70.

113. See chapter 1, note 34 for statistical citations. Belgian colonists had placed the minority Tutsi ethnic group in charge of Rwanda, and the mismatch between Tutsi power and a larger Hutu population had led to decades of fighting since the late 1950s, which was less over ethnicity per se than economic and political control. Just prior to the 1994 genocide, the country had fought a civil war and was negotiating a truce when a plane carrying the Hutu presidents of Rwanda and neighboring Burundi was shot down. The Hutu government accused the Tutsis of the crash and started the genocide within hours. However, the significant preparation for the genocide (the government had drawn up lists of Tutsis house by house and had distributed them to armed party wings and radio hosts) suggests a less-than-spontaneous catalyst.

114. Unlike in most countries with plastic-bag bans, the penalty for violating Rwanda's law can entail months in jail. De Freytas-Tamura, "Public Shaming and Even Prison for Plastic Bag Use in Rwanda."

115. For excellent reporting on the successes and failures of President Kagame's Rwanda, see Gettleman, "Global Elite's Favorite Strongman"; and Reyntjens, "Rwanda," 22–27. For an evenhanded but positive take, see Tepperman, Fix, 87–104.

116. Office of the UN High Commissioner for Human Rights, Report of the Mapping Exercise, para. 31; Reyntjens, "Rwanda," 25–27.

117. While the DRC's war has resulted from incursions by multiple neighboring countries as well as internal fighting, Rwanda's military has played a significant role in keeping M23 rebels an active part of the conflict. Charbonneau and Nichols, "Exclusive: Rwanda Army Officers Aiding M23 Rebels in Congo."

118. Gerald Gahima, the former chief of staff and attorney general under Kagame, explained that Rwanda has no natural resources, so it is rather absurd that it could become a major exporter of gold, diamonds, and other minerals without anyone asking about the provenance of the resources. See the UN Security Council, Addendum to the Group of Experts on the DRC's Interim Report.

119. Counting war deaths in the DRC is fraught. Indirect deaths from disease and malnutrition are greater than direct violent deaths. The International Rescue Committee published a study claiming 5.4 million direct and indirect deaths in the conflict and has called it the world's deadliest war since World War II. In "The Shrinking Costs of War," the Human Security Report Project, which collects excellent conflict statistics, believes that the extrapolation rate used by the IRC is unreliable and claims a lesser number of around 900,000. However, even with the diminished number, the war in the Congo (which has

continued following this 2010 debate, yielding further casualties) surpasses the deaths in Rwanda's own genocide.

120. The field of international relations is grounded in the Westphalian settlement of the Thirty Years' War, when deadly warfare between Catholics and Protestants ended with an agreement that to stop the bloodshed, sovereigns could pick their people's religion. The settlement was interpreted to hold that what states did to their own people within their own borders was their own business. This pragmatic decision, intended to reduce overall bloodshed when states were weak and international wars bloody, began to unravel in the 1990s thanks to the human rights movement. Yet state violence is still considered by many realist international relations scholars as part of the state's "legitimate" monopoly on violence, despite the modern reality that states now kill far more of their own people than interstate wars. Dane and Gartner, *Violence and Crime*, 63.

121. The finding that established democracies almost never go to war with one another is one of the few strongly verified proofs of international relations. Although democracies do wage war on non-democracies, the prevalence of democratic peace means that autocracy certainly does not reduce international war. However, the prevalence of mixed or middling democratic regimes launching international wars is muddied, because the answer depends on their youth, the prevalence of other democracies in the neighborhood, and the levels of independence of the executive. See the excellent review of this research in Lee, "Lakatosian View of the Democratic Peace Research Program." Thus, rather than put international war into the repressive or non-repressive side of this equation, it makes more sense to set it aside.

122. The PRIO data set, which begins in 1946, finds total war deaths to be 9,112,363; colonial/imperial war deaths, 714,899; interstate war deaths, 3,355,964; civil war deaths without foreign intervention, 3,422,013; civil war deaths with foreign intervention, 1,619,487.

123. For more on the problems of the existing data sets, see Kleinfeld, *Reducing All Violent Deaths*.

124. Rough estimates of war deaths, erroring on the high side, include: Russian Civil War (10,000,000, including famine); Chinese Civil War (10,000,000, including famine); Mexican Revolution (2,150,000); Spanish Civil War (350,000); Libyan resistance to Italian colonization (125,000); Second Italo-Ethiopian War (800,000); China's warlord era (7,000,000, including famine); various smaller civil wars (under 500,000).

125. Homicide statistics are drawn from the Geneva Declaration data set.

126. Rummel, *Statistics of Democide*, vii, found 170 million deaths from democide but subsequently updated these numbers online to 264 million. See Rummel, "Statistics of Democide." Rummel unfortunately died before I could

obtain his full database. His numbers tend to overestimate democides by total-itarian regimes and underestimate those of authoritarian regimes compared to other scholars, but those two biases largely cancel each other out in this overall count.

127. While war deaths are always difficult to ascertain, the Syrian Observa-tory for Human Rights, which operates on the ground, is considered the best source. It reports 346,612 deaths on Syrian territory from March 15, 2011, until December 10, 2017, including Syrian rebel forces, government soldiers, militia members, and various Islamist groups. In addition to war deaths, it attributes 14,739 killings in government detention. Civilian murders also include 6,328 from Russian bombings, 2,775 from the international coalition, 552 from Turkish forces, and 7,475 by rebel factions. It also estimates an addi-tional 90,000 deaths it cannot ascertain precisely, including about 5,200 civil-ians abducted by Islamic State and perhaps 45,000 killed in Syrian detention centers through torture. See Syrian Observatory for Human Rights, "About 500,000 Persons Were Killed in Syria During 81 Months After the Syrian Revo-lution."

128. The two cases were in Turkey from 1984 to 1999 and in Croatia from 1992 to 1995. Paul, Clarke, and Grill, *Victory Has a Thousand Fathers*, xxi, 97.

129. Goodwin, *No Other Way Out*, 245.

130. Wood, *Insurgent Collective Action and Civil War in El Salvador*, 234.

131. In the United States, the Campbell Collaboration, seeded with funds from the conservative-leaning Smith Richardson Foundation, unites the world's top social scientists to canvass existing research for answers to various policy questions. Over thirty-five Campbell systematic reviews considered criminal justice policies and found that many popular tough-on-crime tactics actu-ally worsen criminality. See the website for the Campbell Collaboration for a complete and updated set of reviews: www.campbellcollaboration.org. For full disclosure, the Smith Richardson Foundation also supported my first book. Its peer review process is one of the most rigorous I have ever undergone.

132. "Global Patterns," *Economist*.

133. Skarbek, "Governance and Prison Gangs," details this phenomenon among Los Angeles prison gangs; Lessing, "Inside Out," has done the same in Brazil.

134. Felbab-Brown, Trinkunas, and Hamid, *Militants, Criminals, and Warlords*, 104; Dudley, "How Mano Dura Is Strengthening Gangs"; Rivera, "Discipline and Punish."

135. Behan, *Camorra*, 114.

136. Dowdney, *Neither War nor Peace*, 35. The full set of countries were the United States, El Salvador, Ecuador, Colombia, Brazil, Jamaica, Nigeria, South Africa, the Philippines, and Northern Ireland.

137. See Farrington, "Effects of Public Labeling"; and Klein, "Labeling Theory and Delinquency Policy."

138. See, for example, Farrington, "Key Results from the First Forty Years of the Cambridge Study"; Laub and Sampson, *Crime in the Making*; and Laub and Sampson, *Shared Beginnings, Divergent Lives*.

139. See Le Blanc and Fréchette, *Male Criminal Activity from Childhood Through Youth*.

140. As with all research, there are caveats. In this case, while most studies showed that entering the criminal system increased delinquency, one study that looked at first-time offenders found that arrest diverted youth from re-offending. See Petrosino, Turpin-Petrosino, and Guckenburg, "Formal System Processing of Juveniles," 32–33.

141. In the United States, transferring juveniles to the adult justice system increases their likelihood to be rearrested for violence and other crimes, according to a review of studies by McGowan et al., "Effects on Violence of Laws and Policies Facilitating the Transfer of Juveniles," 14; and Tonry, "Treating Juveniles as Adult Criminals," 3–4.

142. Irwin, *Prisons in Turmoil*; Nagin, Cullen, and Johnson, "Imprisonment and Reoffending."

143. For a fuller exploration of this dynamic, see Rivera, "Discipline and Punish"; Jutersonke, Muggah, and Rogers, "Gangs, Urban Violence, and Security Interventions"; Seelke, *Gangs in Central America*; Meyer and Seelke, *Central America Regional Security Initiative*; Gledhill, "La mala administración de la seguridad pública"; and Osorio, "Hobbes on Drugs."

144. An American commander explained that because detainees were forming relationships and sharing combat information while in confinement, "Abu Ghraib is a graduate-level training ground for insurgency" (Shanker, "Abu Ghraib Called Incubator for Terrorists"). The internment camp known as Camp Bucca in Iraq has been blamed for training terrorist recruits who later formed part of the core of the Islamic State, the same role played by Long Kesh in the history of the Irish Republican Army (Dingley, *IRA*, 102). For positive social movements, jail can also be a university. Activists in the U.S. civil rights movement found that "the bonds formed in southern jails were among the foundations of the new social movement," according to the 1960s activist Tom Hayden. Quoting Charles Sherrod of the Student Nonviolent Coordinating Committee, Hayden wrote, "You got ideas in jail. . . . We're up all night sharing creativity, planning action." Hayden, *Long Sixties*, 23.

145. This insight was the basis of the police chief William Bratton's CompStat system, in which he had the NYPD map each criminal incident, convened a police meeting each day to review the data, and then sent police to flood those areas most beset by violence, a technique that has subsequently spread world-

wide. It has been proven effective in numerous studies. See Anthony Braga and David Weisburd, *Policing Problem Places: Crime Hot Spots and Effective Prevention* (New York: Oxford University Press, 2010); David Weisburd et al., "Trajectories of Crime at Places: A Longitudinal Study of Street Segments in the City of Seattle," *Criminology* 42 (2004): 283–321; Anthony Braga, *The Effects of Hot Spot Policing on Crime* (Oslo: Campbell Systematic Reviews, 2007); Lawrence Sherman, Patrick Gartin, and Michael Buerger, "Hot Spots of Predatory Crime: Routine Activities and the Criminology of Place," *Criminology* 27 (1989): 27–55; Lawrence Sherman and David Weisburd, "General Deterrent Effects of Police Patrol in Crime 'Hot Spots': A Randomized Controlled Trial," *Justice Quarterly* 12, no. 4 (1995): 625–48; and Dennis Rosenbaum, "The Limits of Hot Spot Policing," in *Police Innovation: Contrasting Perspectives*, ed. David Weisburd and Anthony Braga (New York: Cambridge University Press, 2006), 245–63.

146. These effective policing policies are difficult to implement, because police tend to dislike paperwork and these techniques require entering police reports and crime data into computers to generate statistics that can be compared across neighborhoods to see where patterns of crime are building. By elevating the role of analysis, they also place a greater premium on the work of detectives, who are often viewed as desk jockeys within a force. So when police departments try to implement these proven strategies, they are sometimes stymied by recalcitrant rank and file.

147. For more on Violent Crime Abatement Teams, Repeat Offender Units, and the Code 6 Program, see studies by Martin and Sherman, "Selective Apprehension"; and Allan F. Abrahamse et al., "An Experimental Evaluation of the Phoenix Repeat Offender Program," *Justice Quarterly* 8, no. 2 (1991).

148. See Sherman et al., "Preventing Crime"; "Effectiveness of Police Activity in Reducing Crime, Disorder, and Fear"; and Braga and Weisburd, "Pulling Levers."

6: POLITICAL MOVEMENTS

1. The counts of lynchings vary. The NAACP claims that there were 4,743 lynchings from 1882 to 1968, with 3,446 of these against blacks. See chapter 2, note 60 for other cites.

2. A mob cut off the boys' penises, pulled off chunks of skin, and shoved a screwdriver through the neck of one boy until it stuck through the other side. See Tyson, *Emmett Till*, 68–69, 112, 119, 120.

3. The man was leaving the courthouse with absentee ballots to bring to blacks who wanted to vote. The murder occurred so close to the sheriff that he could recognize one of the killers and describe the shirt of another. Ibid., 68–69, 112, 119, 120.

4. Scholars of social movements consider the role of what are called political opportunity structures in gaining success. Movements blocked through one structure can try another. For example, activists may make use of the courts to get around the problem of being locked out of electoral politics because of voting restrictions. See Tilly and Tarrow, *Contentious Politics*, 49.

5. NAACP Legal Department, "NAACP Legal History."

6. In *Giles v. Harris* (1903) and *Giles v. Teasley* (1904), the Supreme Court upheld the state constitutional amendments and laws that banned blacks from having an equal right to vote. Justice Oliver Wendell Holmes Jr. explained that if the Court decided the other way, it would simply be "an empty form" because if "the great mass of the white population intends to keep the blacks from voting . . . a piece of paper won't defeat them." Instead, he offered his theory of judicial restraint. Relief "from a great political wrong, if done, as alleged, by the people of a state and the State itself, must be given by them or by the legislative and political department of the United States." See Pildes, "Democracy, Anti-democracy, and the Canon," 306.

7. *Brown* was really a series of cases brought in Kansas, South Carolina, Virginia, the District of Columbia, and Delaware but is known as *Brown v. Board* because Oliver Brown's name appeared as the first plaintiff in court filings. Pildes, "Democracy, Anti-democracy, and the Canon."

8. For an account of life in the Jim Crow South and the supposedly integrated North during these years, I recommend Wilkerson's *Warmth of Other Suns*.

9. Alexander, *New Jim Crow*, 37.

10. From 1954 to 1963, no black schoolchild attended an integrated school in South Carolina, Alabama, or Mississippi. See Klarman, "*Brown*, Racial Change," 7, 9.

11. Wilkerson, *Warmth of Other Suns*, 436.

12. It took President Eisenhower sending the 101st Airborne to Little Rock, Arkansas, in 1957 to enforce the Court's desegregation order. It was the first time federal troops had stepped on southern soil since Reconstruction. It would not be the last.

13. Alexander, *New Jim Crow*, 37.

14. Lincoln, "First Debate with Douglas" (1858). For the role of public sentiment, see Agnone, "Amplifying Public Opinion."

15. Tyson, *Emmett Till*, 201.

16. Ibid., 74, 131.

17. The speech was given at the Dexter Avenue Baptist Church, where Martin Luther King preached—one of the many organizations that worked in parallel to create an effective movement. Ibid., 211.

18. The women were only the first wave. After the arrests, Montgomery's African Americans boycotted the city's bus system for over a year. Because they accounted for 75 percent of bus ridership, the loss of forty thousand customers for 381 days was a powerful weapon as well as a potent statement. Cohen, "Why the Woolworth's Sit-In Worked."

19. Sicilians would later mimic this technique by holding summer work programs for northern Italian students to farm on the land confiscated from Sicilian mafiosi.

20. Eisenhower, "President's News Conference of March 16, 1960," 294.

21. International Civil Rights Center and Museum, "Greensboro Chronology."

22. The same logic now fuels some groups pressing for primary elections in the United States, which are paid for by taxpayers, to open themselves to independent voters who have not affiliated with a party. As independent voters grow to nearly 44 percent of the electorate, primaries that do not allow them to vote effectively disenfranchise much of America, particularly since the majority of congressional districts and a plurality of state legislative districts are effectively held by a single party. See Kleinfeld et al., "Renewing U.S. Political Representation," 4.

23. The Mississippi voter drive, for instance, enabled many lower-class black citizens to vote for the first time in their lives, but it was an action done for them, not by them. Hayden, *Long Sixties*, 35.

24. The pioneering study was conducted by Freedman and Fraser, "Compliance Without Pressure."

25. One study of the civil rights movement suggests that diverse tactics unified around a single goal are the most likely to garner a positive political response. See Olzak and Ryo, "Organizational Diversity, Vitality."

26. Alexander, *New Jim Crow*, 37; Hayden, *Long Sixties*, 23. Jailers would comment on the "damn singing," which built solidarity in jails while driving guards crazy. See also chapter 5, note 144.

27. Civil Rights Movement Veterans, "Sit-Ins."

28. From 1900 to 2006, nonviolent movements succeeded 53 percent of the time, compared with 26 percent of the time for violent movements. Chenoweth and Stephan, *Why Civil Resistance Works*.

29. Martin Luther King Jr. somehow learned what Connor was planning and met the bus in Georgia to warn them about a conspiracy brewing in Alabama. Arsenault, *Freedom Riders*, 99–101, xi.

30. Ibid., 143.

31. Ibid., 145, 146.

32. Ibid., 150–59.

33. Ibid., 4–6.

34. Ibid., 234–35.

35. Ibid., 4.

36. Organizers would succeed in registering over 250,000 people by 1968, half the eligible black voters in Mississippi.

37. The moniker was a conscious echo of the "Republican summer" immediately after the Civil War when slaves were first registered to vote.

38. Johnson, State of the Union address, Jan. 8, 1964, www.lbjlibrary.org.

39. McAdam, *Freedom Summer.*

40. The longest-serving senator in U.S. history, Byrd continued to serve West Virginia in the Senate until 2010. Byrd, *Classic Speeches, 1830–1993*, 701–7.

41. Niven, *Politics of Injustice.*

42. Caro, *Means of Ascent.* Caro's assessment of Johnson's remarkable turn-around was that Johnson was, in fact, committed to helping blacks, the poor, and the marginalized but was also ambitious, and that as a politician from Texas, he was doing what he needed to do to gain power.

43. Because of the timing of decolonization (Ghana was the first country to win independence in 1957; a spate of other countries followed in 1960 but often took some time to organize their diplomatic representation), African diplomats began arriving and driving along Highway 40 in Maryland only in the early 1960s.

44. In 1963, security leaders such as Secretary of State Dean Rusk would testify that a public accommodations bill to end segregation in restaurants and hotels along Highway 40 in Maryland was "crucial to the nation's ability to win the Cold War with the Soviet Union." Romano, "No Diplomatic Immunity."

45. Dudziak, *Cold War Civil Rights*, 95.

46. Dreier, "Little Known Story of 'We Shall Overcome.'"

47. Tyson, *Emmett Till*, 133, 194.

48. The concept emerged from Evelyn Brooks Higginbotham, *Righteous Discontent: The Women's Movement in the Black Baptist Church, 1880–1920* (Cambridge, Mass.: Harvard University Press, 1994), when embedding activism in a "politics of respectability" was seen as a useful technique for women to increase their relative power by distancing themselves from more socially disreputable behavior within their community. The Black Lives Matter movement, along with other modern protesters, has claimed that because people deserve rights regardless of non-respectable behavior, movements should enlarge the concept of respectability rather than respect existing norms. While perhaps mor-

ally justified, particularly given the potential mental stressors attributed to the need for African Americans to "pass" in white society, abandoning middle-class morality is psychologically ill informed and likely to reduce movement effectiveness.

49. One of the early studies of social protest found that mainstream acceptance was the currency by which protests gained success. See Gamson, *Strategy of Social Protest*. This trend of requiring mainstream acceptance and thus working within middle-class opinion still holds: an analysis on the marriage rights movement in the United States found that its success was aided by using the "politics of respectability" and connecting to mainstream cultural and political tropes. See Woodly, *Politics of Common Sense*.

50. It is difficult to overstate what a success it was to bring these groups together. Unions were widely believed to be supporting guerrilla fighters. Businessmen in Antioquia were suspected of funding paramilitaries. To work together was to collaborate with people whom friends and colleagues believed were personally supporting murder. But the tremendous level of violence in the city pushed some to overcome their political prejudices. The business community, facing a crippling financial crisis sparked by a global recession, was also looking for new solutions. Credit goes to many seminars held for years by international development banks, aid agencies, and the then president of Colombia's $155 million Presidential Program for Medellín, which brought professionals together for years until they built trust. The program cost very little but took significant time—precisely the sort of program that is very difficult for development groups to justify today. Maclean, *Social Urbanism and the Politics of Violence*, 34–36.

51. Kurtz-Phelan, "Q&A: Medellín Mayor Turns City Around." Moises Naím, in *The End of Power*, also recognizes that because politics is how political change occurs, social-media-fueled protests that get people into the streets but don't engage people in sustained political activity fail.

52. For instance, in Sinaloa, Mexico, in 2012, thousands of citizens arrived in caravans to take back a popular beach that had become the site of a number of drug massacres. After driving out the criminals, they rebuilt local businesses using micro-credit, public-private partnerships, and volunteers. See the Joan B. Kroc School of Peace Studies' Trans-Border Institute at the University of San Diego, where they are documenting this and other efforts at ground-up revitalization.

53. North, Wallis, and Weingast, *Violence and Social Orders*, 27.

54. World Bank, *World Development Report 2011*, 11.

55. The Gilded Age flirted with Privilege Violence but did not succumb. Theodore Roosevelt would campaign for president by fighting what he called "law-defying" and "predatory" wealth and corruption on both sides of the aisle. Election Days were violent affairs, fueled by liquor, with gangs roam-

ing to ensure votes went their way. The Supreme Court accepted company-controlled militias using force to block labor unrest. Thomas A. Scott, who ran the Pennsylvania Railroad during its great strike of 1877, reportedly suggested that the strikers be given "a rifle diet for a few days" to "see how they like that kind of bread." In New York City, the wealthy donated immense sums to build the ornate Seventh Avenue Armory, in case class warfare broke out. Under-class movements of violent anarchists had begun to bomb cities. But while the police in many towns were politicized, corrupt pawns of political machines, the U.S. military did not resort to brutality, and police violence was confined. The changes to America's political economy brought about by the Progressive movement prevented class from joining race as a violent fissure in the United States. See Burrows and Wallace, *Gotham*, 1,008; Dalton, *Theodore Roosevelt*, 60, 139, 204, 265, 377, 386; Benson, *Political Corruption in America*, 49, 60, 71, 170; and Fogelson, *Big City Police*, 17–19, 20, 33.

56. While Theodore Roosevelt's father had been a forerunner of the Progressive movement, founding a multitude of "good government" clubs to denounce corruption from leather armchairs in wood-paneled libraries, the Roosevelts found young Theodore's interest in fighting for votes alongside men who were "rough and brutal and unpleasant" unacceptable. Morris, *Rise of Theodore Roosevelt*, 125.

57. This style has been described favorably by Carne Ross in *The Leaderless Revolution: How Ordinary People Will Take Power and Change Politics in the 21st Century* (New York: Plume, 2013).

58. Initiative for Policy Dialogue and Friedrich-Ebert-Stiftung, *World Protests, 2006–2013*. A similar study found that about a third of recent protests led to improvements in democratic quality. See Brancati, *Democracy Protests*.

59. Chenoweth, "How Social Media Helps Dictators."

60. This phenomenon, known as "closing space for civil society," now affects more than a hundred countries, including established democracies such as India and Israel. In addition to laws banning foreign donations or making it more difficult to get protest permits, some countries are using innocuous regulations on health and safety, fire codes, and tax laws to harass those who threaten to hold them to account, while others use violence. See Carothers and Brechenmacher, "Closing Space"; Rutzen, "Civil Society Under Assault"; and Wolff and Poppe, *From Closing Space to Contested Spaces*.

61. See Taber and Lodge, "Motivated Skepticism in the Evaluation of Political Beliefs"; Lord, Ross, and Lepper, "Biased Assimilation and Attitude Polarization"; Munro et al., "Biased Assimilation of Sociopolitical Arguments"; and Westen et al., "Neural Bases of Motivated Reasoning."

62. Westen et al., "Neural Bases of Motivated Reasoning."

63. Dunning and Balcetis, "Wishful Seeing."

64. The research on confirmation bias is extensive. For a popular portrayal, see Haidt, *Righteous Mind*, 91–103. For original research, see, for instance, Nickerson, "Confirmation Bias"; Lord, Ross, and Lepper, "Biased Assimilation and Attitude Polarization"; Edwards and Smith, "Disconfirmation Bias"; Taber and Lodge, "Motivated Skepticism in the Evaluation of Political Beliefs"; Redlawsk, "Hot Cognition or Cool Consideration"; and Lodge and Taber, *Rationalizing Voter*.

65. Westen et al., "Neural Bases of Motivated Reasoning."

66. Levendusky, *Partisan Sort*. Levendusky's work is put in context by Barber and McCarty, "Causes and Consequences of Polarization," 22–24.

67. In fact, in the United States right-wing views on these three issues conflate two areas where government should have less of a regulatory role and a third where it should have more; left-wing views are the opposite, but equally inconsistent. On the growing role of identity politics, see Mason, *Uncivil Agreement*. The implications are extreme. Since the terms "Republican" and "Democratic" now represent an entire cluster of identity characteristics, citizens expect someone from the other party to hold views that differ on core values, not just policies. So those citizens who identify with a party increasingly report disliking each other, and the majority report that, for instance, they would be less comfortable with their child marrying someone of the opposite party than of another race, a significant change from the 1960s.

68. Mason, "'I Disrespectfully Agree.'"

69. Haidt, *Righteous Mind*; Westen et al., "Neural Bases of Motivated Reasoning."

70. For more, see Amenta et al., "Political Consequences of Social Movements"; Amenta and Caren, "Legislative, Organizational, and Beneficiary Consequences of State-Oriented Challengers"; Chenoweth and Stephan, *Why Civil Resistance Works*; and Polletta and Ho, "Frames and Their Consequences."

71. In their study of regime change, Chenoweth and Stephan found that broad membership increases the probability of success, particularly when participants represent diverse sectors of society. *Why Civil Resistance Works*, 30, 39.

72. Alexis de Tocqueville, *Recollections of Alexis de Tocqueville* (New York: Macmillan, 1896), 71.

73. Aristotle, *The Politics*, bk. 5, chap. 12, 1,263.

74. India's Common Man party took this course, and so did the U.S. civil rights movement in 1964, when it attempted to form a Mississippi Democratic Party that would be separate from the segregationist Democrats of the South. Progressives had previously tried this technique, forming a party that could win at state and local levels and that provided a vehicle for Theodore Roo-

sevelt's presidential campaign when he broke with the Republican Party and tried to run in 1912 on the Progressive Party ticket. While he lost, the campaign elevated and brought into the mainstream a series of Progressive causes, many of which later succeeded.

75. Kinzer, "Tbilisi Journal."

76. Steavenson, "Marching Through Georgia."

77. Kinzer, "Tbilisi Journal."

78. For an overview of the critical junctures concept, see Capoccia and Kelemen, "Study of Critical Junctures."

79. Jones, "Rose Revolution."

80. Hash-Gonzalez, *Mobilization and Empowerment*, 46.

81. Sometimes these organizations benefited from the financial and training support from the West and sometimes they succeeded in spite of Western donors' restrictions.

82. Ibid., 45.

83. These students had formerly organized successfully to fight corruption in their universities, one example of how a social change organization can serve as a breeding ground for leaders who later become more political.

84. Ibid., 51–52.

85. Ibid., 37.

86. Esadze, "Georgia's Rose Revolution," 112.

87. Hash-Gonzalez, *Mobilization and Empowerment*, 61–63.

88. Ibid., 57.

89. Ibid., 63–65.

90. Sharp, *From Dictatorship to Democracy*, 63–64.

91. Chachibaia, interview by author, Dec. 10, 2014. Chachibaia's response was critical: Chenoweth and Stephan's work suggests that security force defections increased the probability of a campaign's success by 60 percent. *Why Civil Resistance Works*, 46–50, 58.

92. Hash-Gonzalez, *Mobilization and Empowerment*, 102.

93. Ibid., 61.

94. President Clinton provided $70 million in aid to the new state of Georgia, which included a policy directive for the CIA to train and equip a special bodyguard unit for the president. Driscoll, *Warlords and Coalition Politics*, 99.

95. Steavenson, "Marching Through Georgia."

96. Mydans, "Georgian Leader Agrees to Resign, Ending Standoff."

97. Zhvania died naked in the home of another man. The heating system appeared to be leaking carbon monoxide. Some claimed it was a homosexual tryst that resulted in tragedy thanks to post-Soviet heating problems, others that the entire scene had been doctored to besmirch the political leader's reputation while getting rid of him.

98. ODIHR, "Georgia: Extraordinary Presidential Election."

99. Lamb, "Microdynamics of Illegitimacy," 252.

100. Devlin and Chaskel, "From Fear to Hope in Colombia," 4.

101. Majeed and Bacon, "Palermo Renaissance Part 2," 7, 20.

7: POLITICIANS

1. Harry Truman, impromptu remarks to the Reciprocity Club in Washington, D.C., on April 11, 1958, as reported in the *New York World-Telegram and Sun*, April 12, 1958, 4.

2. Caro, *Path to Power*, 5.

3. In modern Palermo, the Mafia-connected Salvo cousins collected all taxes in return for a 10 percent share of all that they gave to the state—three times the going rate in the rest of Italy. But when Mayor Orlando fired them and put in place state inspectors, state breakdown and the level of corruption were so advanced that evasion dramatically increased. Gambetta, *Sicilian Mafia*, 160, 163.

4. Devlin and Chaskel, "Conjuring and Consolidating a Turnaround," 5.

5. Ibid.

6. Devlin and Chaskel, "From Fear to Hope in Colombia," 5.

7. David Escobar Arango, interview by author, Feb. 3, 2015.

8. Wallace, "Colombia's Mayor Fights Cali's Murder Rate with Science."

9. In New York City at the turn of the twentieth century, for instance, voters ousted the corrupt incumbent favored by Tammany Hall's machine bosses and elected the reform candidate Mayor William L. Strong. *The New York Times* crowed, "The Tammany Tiger has been flayed alive." But Mayor Strong was a novice, and the Tammany machine knew that it could simply stop the city from running until voters demanded an administration that could fix potholes and pick up garbage. Tammany Hall's Boss Croker admitted that "people could not stand the rotten police corruption." But he wasn't worried. Putting his arm around a reporter's shoulder, he explained, "They'll be back at the next election. They can't stand reform either." Jeffers, *Commissioner Roosevelt*, 55.

10. Forero, "Explosions Rattle Colombian Capital During Inaugural."

11. Balcázar, interview by author, Feb. 5, 2015.

12. Bouvier, "Colombia's Crossroads." The FARC also used kidnappings of high-profile people to gain negotiating leverage, while all the guerrilla groups and the paramilitaries kidnapped for economic gain.

13. Cited in Lamb, "Microdynamics," 180.

14. Pardo, "Colombia's Two-Front War."

15. Arias, interview by author, Feb. 9, 2015.

16. This amount was spent over the duration of Plan Colombia from 1999 to 2016.

17. Felbab-Brown, Trinkunas, and Hamid, *Militants, Criminals, and Warlords,* 88. While the navy, air force, and army had a combined total of 131,000 men, most were conscripts, more effective at logistics and administration than fighting. The 22,000 professional troops were rarely used for offensive actions.

18. Felbab-Brown, "Violent Drug Market," 9.

19. International Crisis Group, "Colombia: Peace at Last?," 2–3.

20. Johnson and Johnson, "Colombia: Ending the Forever War," 72.

21. General Edgar Vale, interview by author, Feb. 2, 2015.

22. From 1954 to 1964, the U.S. government trained approximately 250 Colombian military each year in counterinsurgency (Dudley, *Walking Ghosts,* 34–35) and then launched Plan Lazo, which backfired as described earlier. In 1989, at the height of the U.S. drug war, President George H. W. Bush provided Colombia with military equipment and training. Some of the intelligence assisted the fight against Pablo Escobar. However, decapitating one cartel without addressing the deeper causes of violence simply allowed other groups to fill the vacuum until violence again began rising. See statistics from Restrepo, Spagat, and Vargas, "Dynamics of the Colombian Civil Conflict," 414.

23. In 1999, Colombia Libre held the largest peace demonstration ever seen in Colombia, and pressure for peace was high, although the territorial giveaway was extremely unpopular. Only after the peace negotiations failed did the Colombian people believe that fighting was the only way to end the guerrilla movement. See Korn, "Assessing Victory," 14.

24. For more on the FARC's move toward drug dealing, see Yagoub, "Colombia Busts Over 100 FARC Cocaine Labs"; and Lamb, "Microdynamics," 213.

25. Gallup polling cited by Lamb, "Microdynamics," 213.

26. Invamer-Gallup polling. Since these polls rely on phone calls, they underrepresent the most marginalized members of Colombia who don't have phones and tend to be most affected by violence, and they should thus be taken with a grain of salt. Nevertheless, these polling results allow for comparison across presidencies, and Uribe's continued popularity during his two terms is extremely high and unusual in the context of other Colombian presidencies.

27. International Crisis Group, "Colombia: Peace at Last?," 3.

28. Colombia had 1,100 municipalities at this time. International Crisis Group, "Peace at Last?," 3.

29. Llorente and McDermott, "Colombia's Lessons," 9–11.

30. Kidnapping statistics from Colombia's Ministry of Defense show a high of approximately thirty-five hundred in 2000, dropping to just below three thousand through 2002, after which they drop quickly until they are down to just a few hundred a year by 2009.

31. International Crisis Group, "Colombia: Peace at Last?," 3.

32. Colombia's courts have been investigating General Montoya since at least 2015 for his potential role in killing civilians and for the military's practice under his leadership of killing innocent Colombians and passing them off as guerrilla fighters. Interview by author, Feb. 4, 2015.

33. The Inter-American Commission recommended that cases regarding the incursion and aftermath be taken up by the Inter-American Court of Human Rights, such as *Caso Yarce y Otras vs. Colombia*, 65.

34. An indicative story from this era emerged from my interview with a Colombian government official who was flying into the jungle with a military pilot around this time. He told me that a VIP military pilot was "a plum job and usually goes to people well along in their careers or who have people pulling strings for them—the son or cousin of a general." So over a beer, he asked the pilot, "Who is your cousin?" The pilot smiled and said, "No, I have no god-father. I was named the best lieutenant in my class, and so I got this job. I was given an area of Medellín that was really bad with homicides and car thefts and so on, and by end of my term crime was zero and I was rated the best lieutenant." The government official was impressed and asked the pilot what he had done to accomplish such a feat. "Nothing," the pilot replied. "The military top command made this agreement with Don Berna. He agreed to keep citizens secure and deal with crimes like car theft, and the military promised to leave him alone. And I benefited." Colombian government official, interview by author, Jan. 26, 2015.

35. The Colombian courts eventually rolled back some elements of this agreement, forcing full statements to the Truth and Reconciliation Commission upon threat of further jail time outside the amnesty agreement, and adding other elements to increase justice. A few groups then balked at demobilizing, but the AUC, the largest consortium of paramilitaries, had already signed by that time and continued the demobilization process despite the changes to the agreement.

36. Human Rights Watch, "Breaking the Grip?"

37. Daniel Millares and William Quintero (Organization of American States demobilization experts with MAPP), interview by author, Jan. 27, 2015.

38. Uribe might have encouraged paramilitary formation from 1995 to 1997 as governor as a means of fighting the FARC. Porch and Rasmussen, "Demobilization of Paramilitaries in Colombia," 526.

39. Carpenter, "Justice, Interrupted"; Rohter, "Colombians Tell of Massacre."

40. Human Rights Watch, "Smoke and Mirrors"; Porch and Rasmussen, "Demobilization of Paramilitaries in Colombia," 529.

41. Porch and Rasmussen, "Demobilization of Paramilitaries in Colombia," 530–31; Millares and Quintero, interview by author, Jan. 27, 2015.

42. The U.S. Department of Justice relies on an extensive study by Durose, Cooper, and Snyder, *Recidivism of Prisoners Released in 30 States in 2005*. In this study of 404,638 prisoners in thirty states, researchers found that 71.6 percent of violent offenders were likely to be rearrested within five years in modern America.

43. By 2002, approximately 80 percent of all the conflict deaths in Colombia were carried out by the paramilitaries. Despite the many flaws in the demobilization process, it yielded an immediate drop in homicides of about 13 percent and a more significant drop over time as the criminal bands were themselves fought. See Restrepo and Muggah, "Colombia's Quiet Demobilization," 43; see also Saab and Taylor, "Criminality and Armed Groups," 462. Percentage declines in deaths and assaults varied by region across Colombia; these are countrywide averages. See Porch and Rasmussen, "Demobilization of Paramilitaries in Colombia," 530nn71 and 72.

44. Lamb, "Microdynamics," 218.

45. New Orleans's rate in 2007 was approximately 76.4 per 100,000, as calculated in Van Landingham, "2007 Murder Rates in New Orleans, Louisiana," 5, 776. Medellín's rate that year was 38 per 100,000. It rose in 2008 after the extradition of the paramilitary leader Don Berna set off a turf war within the remaining drug and criminal gangs, then returned to its previous declining trajectory. In 2017, murder rates per 100,000 were Detroit, 45.8; Baltimore, 45.2; St. Louis, 39.6.

46. Data from CINEP and Colombia's National Institute of Legal Medicine and Forensics.

47. Chakrabarti, *Bihar Breakthrough*, 2.

48. Aiyar, "Bihar," 50–51.

49. Sankarshan Thakur, interview by Rushda Majeed, July 13, 2015, on behalf of and in conjunction with author.

50. Chakrabarti, *Bihar Breakthrough*, 13.

51. Ibid.; Witsoe, "A View from the States—Bihar," 9.

52. Aiyar, "Bihar," 51.

53. Statistics drawn from "Crime in India 1990," "Crime in India 1999," and "Crime in India 2000," all produced by India's National Crime Records Bureau, as cited in Witsoe, "View from the States," 303–4. Population statistics are approximate, based on the 2001 Indian census showing Bihar with 8.1 percent of the total population in the country.

54. Kohli, *Democracy and Discontent*, 225.

55. Ironically, this was actually a reform of the previous system when the British taxed directly. After the British demanded so much in taxes that they forced Bihar into a famine with mass starvation, the system was reformed to create fixed taxes collected by local landlords. The idea was to give local landlords an incentive to reinvest in their holdings.

56. In 1994, Bihar had reached only 8 percent of its own target for land redistribution (Kumar, "Violence and Political Culture," 4,978). Whether one agrees with land redistribution as an effective solution to Bihar's endemic poverty and social exclusion or doesn't (I do not see mass subsistence agriculture on tiny plots as a path toward enrichment), the state's failure to keep this promise to the poor was radicalizing for many and continues to be a rallying cry for the dispossessed.

57. Parishad, "Landlessness and Social Justice," 16.

58. Emergency rule was a period of martial law declared by Indira Gandhi in which state repression skyrocketed. In addition to mass arrests of people suspected of political crimes, India engaged in population control by forcing sterilization on millions of unwilling men and women throughout rural India. When India restored the vote, voters overwhelmingly rejected Gandhi's Congress Party.

59. Sometimes entire subcastes will make a bid for greater social status. Often, these attempts are achieved by mimicking some of the social mores of those with higher status—one of them being purdah, or the practice of keeping women at home and out of the public eye, or, literally, under cover. So, ironically, if a caste is trying to gain higher social standing, women's freedom and rights tend to fall.

60. Sharma, "Rise of the Rest of India."

61. Debt bondage was also used to re-enslave former slaves in the U.S. South after Reconstruction and into the early twentieth century. Southern courts refused to act against the practice, so Theodore Roosevelt fought through the Department of Justice, fifty years after the Civil War's end.

62. Monkkonen, "Diverging Homicide Rates," 157.

63. For further, see Mathew and Moore, "State Incapacity by Design." Population and income statistics are from Indian National Census data.

64. Farooquee, "In Bihar Village."

65. Chakrabarti, *Bihar Breakthrough*, 14.

66. The Bhagalpur riots of 1989 happened, not coincidentally, in the same district where police brutality and rampant crime had led to the Bhagalpur blindings (mentioned in chapter 5) a decade before. Clearly, the police repression had not reduced violence in the district.

67. In the late 1940s, some of the worst violence in India took place in Bihar during the partitioning of the British Raj between Indian and Pakistan. Wilkinson, "Why Is Violence," 5.

68. Chaudhart, "Where Booth Capturing Was Born." The most recent census to 1967 was in 1961, when Bihar had a population of 46,555,610. At this same time, India had a population of 458.6 million, according to the World Bank, making Bihar approximately 10 percent of the population.

69. Vaishnav, *When Crime Pays*, 88.

70. Ibid., 87.

71. Kumar, "Illegitimacy of the State," 8.

72. Heinz, "Bihar," 31.

73. Anish Ankur, interview by Rushda Majeed, July 9, 2015, on behalf of and in conjunction with author.

74. Jha, "Brahmeshwar Singh."

75. Narula, *Broken People*, 5.

76. Bihar's politicians are generally known by their first names, because last names are shared by all members of a subcaste.

77. Kumar, "Violence and Political Culture," 4,978.

78. Aiyar, "Bihar," 47.

79. Chakrabarti, *Bihar Breakthrough*, 14.

80. In 2002, only 7 of Bihar's 244 police cadre officers came from the largest lowest-caste groups, according to Jeff Witsoe's research, as cited in Mathew and Moore, "State Incapacity by Design," 6. Many police favored their caste over the law; in well-known cases, they would stand aside or even abet militias as they burned Dalit homes and raped Dalit girls. Narula, "Broken People," 8. Meanwhile, police stations in most villages were on the upper-caste side of town, where Dalits couldn't safely tread without risking a beating from an upper-caste villager. Aiyar, "Economic Freedom of the State," 46.

81. Jha and Pushpendra, "Governing Caste," 17–18.

82. Ibid., 14.

83. Ibid., 16–19.

84. Devi's government was dismissed on February 12, 1999, by the central government, but then reinstated on March 8, 1999, when the Indian legislature would not back the dissolution. She served as chief minister between March 8, 1999, and March 2, 2000, her party was reelected with a slight majority in the 2000 elections, and she continued to serve until President's Rule overturned the next set of elections and ushered in Nitish Kumar.

85. Chakrabarti, *Bihar Breakthrough,* 29, 45–46.

86. Thottam, "Breaking Free."

87. Ramakrishnan, "History of Massacres."

88. Narula, "Broken People," 8.

89. "Annual Report 2003–2004." These massacres were often portrayed as caste antagonism run amok or guerrilla violence, but Bihar's top policeman told a different story. "What was surprising to me," he explained, "was that whichever caste chose to commit a massacre, the place of violence would normally be just at the boundary of two regions and not very deep inside." If the goal was to intimidate another caste, it would be easier to do it deep inside one's own territory. "Caste riots were a means of extending the area of control of certain militias at the cost of rival militias," explained the policeman. "And when I say area of control, I mean control over the revenue and economic activity of the people of that area." Abhyanand, interview with Rushda Majeed, June 29, 2015, in conjunction with author.

90. Kumar, *Matter of Rats,* xvii–xviii.

91. Bhatia, "Naxalite Movement," 1,540–41.

92. Kumar, *Matter of Rats,* 69.

93. Quraishi, *Documented Wonder;* S. Y. Quraishi, interview by author, Sept. 24, 2014.

94. Abhyanand, interview by Rushda Majeed, June 29, 2015, on behalf of and in conjunction with author. Abhyanand claimed they actually found three million fraudulent names but were allowed to remove only two million of them.

95. Vaishnav, *When Crime Pays,* 202–4.

96. Witsoe, "Territorial Democracy," 65.

97. Vaishnav, *When Crime Pays,* 201–2.

98. Ibid., 189–90.

99. Ibid., 188.

100. Chakrabarti, *Bihar Breakthrough,* 221.

101. In 2010, it was 35 percent. Vaishnav, *When Crime Pays,* 181.

102. Ibid., 158–59.

103. This course of events was explained in an off-the-record interview with a professor of Bihari history, conducted by Rushda Majeed, July 9, 2015, in collaboration with author, and is corroborated in Chakrabarti, *Bihar Breakthrough*, 82; and Aiyar, "Bihar," 52.

104. Kumar recruited top Biharis from across the Indian Civil Service who had left their state in frustration, asking the best among them to return.

105. Abhyanand, interview by Rushda Majeed, June 29, 2015, on behalf of and in conjunction with author.

106. "86 Policemen Killed by Naxals in Bihar Since 2005: Statistics," *Economic Times*, Sept. 5, 2010.

107. Chakrabarti, *Bihar Breakthrough*, 59.

108. Shahabuddin had used a classic Robin Hood strategy to build a base of support among constituents by constructing two wings for the local hospital, erecting a stadium, and creating three colleges—one for girls, one for medicine, and one for engineering—as well as issuing a fatwa that doctors should not charge more than 50 rupees for an appointment and should set aside a day each week to serve the poor. As one villager said, before Shahabuddin "we had only potholes in the name of a road here. Colleges had closed because there was no money . . . doctors never turned up on time . . . but now everything works." See Singh, "Jail No Bar for Bihar Candidates"; and Chakrabarti, *Bihar Breakthrough*, 72.

109. Extrajudicial murders known as "encounter killings" had been a significant problem. Police often captured and murdered guerrillas—as well as innocent civilians—without trial, then faked crime scenes to make it appear that suspects had been killed in battle. For further, see Kleinfeld and Majeed, "Fighting Insurgency with Politics."

110. Ibid., 5.

111. Gates and Kaushik, *Unconventional Warfare*, 76.

112. Dey, "Naxalites in Noida."

113. Shrivastava, "Jungle Gangs." Information gathered from a Public Interest Litigation request lodged in Dec. 2014.

114. Jha, "Nazalite Movement in Bihar and Jharkhand."

115. Shrivastava, "Jungle Gangs."

116. Indian National Police statistics on deaths and incidents of left-wing extremist violence.

117. Shrivastava, "Jungle Gangs."

118. Accurate newspaper accounts on Bihar can be hard to come by, particularly given the penchant for "paid news" in the state. This account is composed of contemporary news accounts from Balchand, "Naxalites Lay Siege to Jehanabad," 1; "Maoists Storm Jehanabad Jail," *Rediff News*, Nov. 14, 2005; Bhatia, "Jailbreak and the Maoist Movement"; and Singh, "Tactical Retreat by the Maoists."

119. Given the paucity of electricity in most of Bihar at this time, cutting off electricity was more a show of rebel ability than a necessary measure.

120. Anandi, "Bihar."

121. "Amir Das Commission Probing Politician-Sena Nexus Disbanded," *Outlook*, April 8, 2006.

122. Kumar, interview by Rushda Majeed, July 6, 2015, on behalf of and in conjunction with author.

123. *Indira Sawhney v. Union of India*, on the Mandal Commission, 1992.

124. Sinha, *Nitish Kumar*, 342.

125. Mukherjee, "Coalition Building," 8.

126. Aiyar, "Bihar," 57.

127. Ibid., 55.

128. Ibid.

129. Mukherji and Mukherji, "Bihar," 37–38. However, under Lalu Yadav, staff absentee rates of 58 percent in primary health centers topped the nation, and more than a quarter of primary schoolteachers were always absent—the third-worst rate in the country. See Chakrabarti, *Bihar Breakthrough*, 14.

130. "Quality Education Still a Challenge, Says Nitish Kumar," *Press Trust of India—News 18*, July 16, 2015.

131. In a second natural experiment, Chhattisgarh, another state facing Maoist violence, built schools for impoverished tribal children that quickly brought attendance up from less than 50 percent of six-to-fourteen-year-olds to nearly 90 percent. That program might have done far more for education and development. But it did not redistribute power, and it does not seem to have affected the state's insurgency. See Kleinfeld and Majeed, "Fighting Insurgency with Politics," 10–11.

132. Arun Kumar, interview by Rushda Majeed, July 3, 2015, on behalf of and in conjunction with author; Shaibal Gupta, interview by Rushda Majeed, July 7, 2015, on behalf of and in conjunction with author.

133. According to police records, assembled in Aiyar, "Bihar," 57, violent incidents fell from 1,309 during the last five years of Yadav's reign to 514 from

2006 to 2010; civilian deaths dropped from 760 to 214; and Maoist arrests grew from 1,437 to 2,250.

134. Bakradze, interview by author, Dec. 5, 2014.

135. Merabishvili was arrested in 2013 and charged with abuse of office and bribery, charges that some claim were politically motivated. In 2016, he was sentenced to a further six and a half years for ordering the beating of a member of parliament.

136. The part-time instructors were also cheap in comparison to full-time teaching staff. However, their hourly wage was high, making the teaching posts a perk that could be awarded to the best police rather than treating a full-time instructional role as a sop for the worst officers, as occurs in many countries.

137. Hizanishvili, interview by author, Dec. 11, 2014.

138. Ibid.

139. De Waal, conversation with author, Sept. 22, 2014.

140. Caro, *Master of the Senate*, 452.

141. Forero, "For Colombia's Ascetic Leader."

142. Steavenson, "Marching Through Georgia."

143. As minister of justice under Shevardnadze, Saakashvili had spearheaded the mass firing of Soviet-era judges who understood their jobs to be taking orders from the top and putting people in jail, rather than interpreting the law. After hiring more Westernized judges who saw the law as a separate branch of government, he was dismayed to see the judiciary turn itself into a corrupt, self-serving guild.

144. World Bank, *Fighting Corruption in Public Services*, 59.

145. Ibid., 39–40.

146. Hizanishvili, interview by author, Dec. 11, 2014.

147. Pasotti, *Political Branding in Cities*, 166.

148. Moncada, "Toward Democratic Policing," 436.

149. Acero Velásquez, interview by author, Feb. 2, 2015.

150. Mockus served two terms as mayor, from 1995 to 1997 and again from 2001 to 2003, both prior to most of Uribe's efforts at the national level. From 1993 to 2004, homicide rates fell from 80 to 28 per 100,000. World Bank, *World Development Report 2011*, 113.

151. Forero, "For Colombia's Ascetic Leader."

152. David Escobar Arango, interview by author, Feb. 3, 2015.

153. Morris, *Rise of Theodore Roosevelt*, 669.

8: RECIVILIZATION

1. Orlando, *Fighting the Mafia and Renewing Sicilian Culture*.

2. In 1994, Mockus won with 64 percent of the city's vote and took office on January 1, 1995.

3. Castro, interview by Matthew Devlin and Sebastian Chaskel, Princeton University, Innovations for Successful Societies, Oct. 6, 2009, 3, 6.

4. Devlin and Chaskel, "Conjuring and Consolidating a Turnaround," 2.

5. When Castro took office in 1992, Bogotá owed U.S.$2.6 billion, and the national government would not pay any further city debts. Meanwhile, Bogotans were paying the same in taxes as they had paid thirty years earlier. Ibid.

6. An interesting study attempted to disaggregate the myriad measures used in Bogotá by Mayor Mockus to determine which had the strongest effect on reducing violence. The study is rigorous, but it misses the way in which measures are interrelated and the role played by some measures in catalyzing society itself to bring down its own violence. See Sánchez, Espinosa, and Rivas, *¿Garrote o zanahoria?*

7. Mockus, a philosophy professor, was the most articulate in espousing these ideas of recivilization, but he was inspired by Cali's mayor who had tried the ideas earlier, and the notions were implemented in Sicily, Georgia, and Medellín as well. For a deeper description of Mockus's thought, see Gutiérrez Sanín et al., "Politics and Security in Three Colombian Cities."

8. Moses held over a dozen titles in New York government, none of which fully captured the extent of his power over urban planning from the 1930s to the 1960s. While his positions largely allowed him to build highways and parks alongside them as well as public housing, the best examples of his vision coming to fruition are Stuyvesant Town and Peter Cooper Village in Manhattan. Moses was inspired by Le Corbusier, and his vision was common for urban planners at the time.

9. Jacobs, *Death and Life*, 32.

10. Ibid.

11. In fact, the actual broken windows theory, so well popularized but distorted in New York City, was about fighting the sorts of disorders that make people feel the social order is breaking down, even if the neighborhood is not particularly violent. See chapter 10, note 40.

12. Jacobs's arguments transformed urban planning, starting a movement known as New Urbanism that returned features like sidewalks and front porches to neighborhoods where homes once turned their garages to the street, and encouraged cities to build areas that mixed housing, shops, and offices to encourage people to walk around and get to know their neighbors.

13. Hurley, "Scientist at Work."

14. Ibid.

15. A multitude of fascinating research has emerged from the Project on Human Development in Chicago Neighborhoods. These findings on collective efficacy appear in Sampson, Raudenbush, and Earls, "Neighborhoods and Violent Crime." The types of social relationships built within neighborhoods are known as "bonding social capital" among academics, because they bond similar people together.

16. Putnam, "Social Capital."

17. For one of the more thorough explications of the various forms of trust and their relative efficacy, see Uslaner, *Moral Foundations*, especially 219–30. Uslaner sees trust as a cultural variable, based in part on his analysis of various regime types' trust levels. However, he fails to distinguish between titular democracies, power structures, and institutions, so I see Bo Rothstein's work as more applicable.

18. Putnam's analysis of social trust was soon transformed into a blunt way of recording social capital: development agencies began to simply count the number of people's relationships or the number of social organizations in existence. In *Ghettoside*, Jill Leovy's book about the unchecked violence in marginalized parts of Los Angeles, the author makes the point that those living in the Watts and Compton neighborhoods had plenty of interconnection and interaction. Far from helping residents find their collective voice, the enforced interdependence of poor, marginal lives led to distrust, arguments, and violence. A study of Weimar Germany (Berman, "Civil Society and the Collapse of the Weimar Republic") noted that the country had a multitude of civil groups, and it descended into Nazi violence by exploiting these associations and networks. The sheer number of social relationships doesn't reduce violence; in fact, the growing network understanding of violence suggests that the wrong relationships can put one much more at risk. Increasing trust reduces violence.

19. See Putnam, *Making Democracy Work*.

20. Jamieson, *Antimafia*, xxi.

21. Putnam claimed, for example, that Southern Italy's low-trust society began in the Middle Ages with the conquest of the Norman mercenaries and grew under centuries of further invasion and feudal rule. Putnam, *Making Democracy Work*, 121, 149. He also found that Scandinavians had more trust, crediting a Scandinavian culture that continued even after they had been living in the United States for generations. Putnam, "E Pluribus Unum."

22. Putnam, *Making Democracy Work*, 97, 149–50.

23. Varese, "How Mafias Migrate," 430, 433.

24. Schneider and Schneider, *Reversible Destiny*, 125.

25. Corchado, *Midnight in Mexico*, 227.

26. See Rothstein and Stolle, "State and Social Capital"; Kumlin and Rothstein, "Questioning the New Liberal Dilemma"; and Rothstein, *Quality of Government*, 151. The highest correlation with social trust is trust in police and courts, according to Rothstein, but that does not indicate the direction of causation.

27. The converse is also clearly true: where institutions fail, they provide room for other forces to exercise power. In Italy, for instance, the World Bank ranked the judiciary just three steps higher than that in Afghanistan in 2011 at enforcing contracts. With institutions so slow and broken, the Mafia can step in as a means of making contracts stick. Gambetta, *Sicilian Mafia*; Dickie, *Blood Brotherhoods*, 658–59.

28. Levy, in *Working with the Grain*, argues for enclaves of excellence and incremental change.

29. For example, when the Republic of Georgia managed to break the bribery required to get into college and made university admissions merit based, the families who had scraped together the bribe money were unhappy. They weren't necessarily dishonest people; they had managed at great personal cost to scramble to the top of the old system and now faced a new set of rules that put them at a disadvantage.

30. Mungiu-Pippidi, *Quest for Good Governance*; Rothstein, *Quality of Government*.

31. Mungiu-Pippidi, *Quest for Good Governance*, 156.

32. Glenn, *Rethinking Western Approaches*, 189.

33. Tkeshelashvili, interview by author, Dec. 8, 2014.

34. To be fair, many of these journalists' stories are more thoughtful and nuanced than their titles suggest—more so, in fact, than the academic study of the gondolas whose numbers are often cited. Nonetheless, no one can resist the causal allure of the gondolas. See, for example, Eberlein, "How Gondolas and Hip Hop Transformed the Most Dangerous City in the World"; Parkinson, "Medellín's Strategy for Driving Down Crime"; "How Giant Outdoor Escalators Transformed a Colombian Neighborhood," CNN, Dec. 14, 2015; and Cerdá et al., "Reducing Violence by Transforming Neighborhoods."

35. According to Colombia Reports, Medellín's homicide rate was 177 per 100,000 in 2002, 107 per 100,000 in 2003, and 56 per 100,000 in 2004—the year the gondola opened. By 2005, it was 37 per 100,000. Today it is 21.6 per 100,000, below the national average. The second gondola opened in 2008, just as violence temporarily rose again following the paramilitary leader Don Berna's extradition. See Alsema, "Fact Sheets: Medellín Crime Statistics"; and Llorente, Garzon, and Ramirez, "Asi Se Concentra El Homicidio en las Ciudades."

36. Cerdá et al., "Reducing Violence by Transforming Neighborhoods," 1,050–51.

37. For instance, researchers assumed the gondolas had been randomly placed in different regions when in fact their sites had been carefully chosen.

38. After 2008, there were only two lines with just a few stops and another short gondola that continued to a park at the top of a hill rather than a slum neighborhood.

39. For more, see Brand and Dávila, "Mobility Innovation at the Urban Margins."

40. Medellín's miracle was also assisted by a unique public utility—Empresas Públicas de Medellín (EPM), which provides water, sewer, trash, and other utility services to the city. Its financial resources enabled the municipality to finance Fajardo's infrastructure projects. Amid a sea of corruption, EPM's mandate and its unique leadership (it was run by one honest man for over fifteen years, and there was a tacit agreement among the city's elites not to interfere in this company) enabled its success. The few times politicians tried to interfere with it, "it was like messing with someone's mom," I was told; society immediately responded and saved its utility, which was the pride of the region. Daniel Arango, interview by author, Feb. 3, 2015.

41. Baron et al., *Social Capital: Critical Perspectives.*

42. Kimmelman, "City Rises, Along with Its Hopes."

43. Pasotti, *Political Branding in Cities,* 173 n6.

44. Bacon and Majeed, "Palermo Renaissance Part 1."

45. Aiyar, "Bihar," 63.

46. Shahnazarian, "Police Reform."

47. Gupta, interview by Rushda Majeed, July 7, 2015, on behalf of and in conjunction with author.

48. Chakrabarti, *Bihar Breakthrough,* 34–35.

49. World Bank, *Fighting Corruption in Public Services,* 27–28.

50. Molly Corso, interview by author, Dec. 10, 2014.

51. Ibid., 19.

52. Pinker, *Better Angels of Our Nature,* 540–41.

53. Putnam, "Social Capital," 12. In Central America, a Latinobarómetro poll in 2005 found that 80 percent of those polled believed their fellow citizens evaded the law—a statistic that leads to widespread tax avoidance, among other pathologies. "Crime and Development in Central America," 83.

54. Levi, *Of Rule and Revenue.* Levi found that even in Australia, when a single Supreme Court justice began to create loopholes that allowed the upper class to pay less, the country faced a tax revolt until the system was reconstituted to become more fair. She calls this "ethical reciprocity." Levi, *Trust and Governance,* 86–88.

55. As Diamond explains, when oil becomes a country's dominant export, the state makes money without the people. The people become clients, not citizens, and when a middle class emerges, it is one not of independent entrepreneurs but of professionals dependent on the state. States based on oil may gain revenue, but it is not based on a relationship with their own people, who can induce accountability. Diamond, *Spirit of Democracy*, 74–79.

56. Ibid., 247.

57. The literature on this problem has been growing since 2003, when Buliř and Hamann published an IMF paper on the empirical effects of aid volatility. See Buliř and Hamann, "Volatility of Development Aid"; and Celasun and Walliser, "Predictability of Aid."

58. For instance, the United States provided Afghanistan with new police cars following the incursion into that country in 2001. "Buy U.S." rules forced the United States to provide American-made cars for Afghanistan's police, but their high-end electronics could not be serviced in Afghanistan. The GPS chips inserted into the cars betrayed that the cars were simply driven to Pakistan and sold. U.S. government official in charge of this aid program, interview by author, May 3, 2014.

59. In places where officials pocket funds, citizens tend to be resentful and evade payment. Tilley, *War Making*, also discusses how popular resistance to a state that was too extractive could yield concessions that created a fairer and more equitable state.

60. As Albert Hirschman wrote in his seminal book, *Exit, Voice, and Loyalty*, members of a group have two options when they perceive that an entity to which they belong, whether a nation or a business, is in decline. They can voice grievance and attempt to improve things, or they can leave. In the case of a country on the decline, it is easy for the middle class to choose the exit option, through emigration or simply by putting children in private schools, moving to gated communities, stashing their money in foreign banks, and so on. When loyalty is increased to the point where citizens pay taxes, more citizens move toward the "voice" option and try to improve the situation instead.

61. White House, "Fact Sheet: Peace Colombia."

62. Bennett, "Delivering on the Hope of the Rose Revolution," 9; Dadalauri, "Political Corruption," 15.

63. Pasotti, *Political Branding in Cities*, 164–65.

9: CENTRALIZATION AND SURVEILLANCE

1. Jamieson, *Antimafia*, xxi.

2. "Mobster Tommaso Buscetta Talks, and the Mafia's Worldwide Drug Ring Starts to Crumble," *People*, Oct. 22, 1984.

3. "Tommaso Buscetta," *Economist*, April 20, 2000.

4. In fairness, he had also turned to a self-harming form of extreme Catholicism as penance for the sins he had committed while a member of the Mafia, increasing law enforcement's skepticism regarding his sanity.

5. In an attempt to move the state away from fascist practices such as Mussolini's discretionary prosecutions, Italian law mandates speedy indictment after a finding of probable cause, leading to mass trials such as this.

6. "La Corte Europea per i Diritti Umani."

7. Gorman, "Judge Rules in Favor of Trafficker."

8. Hays, "FBI: Gigante Still Runs Crime Family."

9. The short-lived sandwich was the result of a student cooking competition, an occasional feature of Notre Dame life.

10. Blakey's story is drawn largely from Blakey, "RICO: The Genesis of an Idea," although Blakey was generous enough to read this chapter and verify facts.

11. Schlesinger, *Robert Kennedy*, 264.

12. Robert Kennedy had just finished a three-year stint as chief counsel to the McClellan Commission, a Senate inquiry into labor union racketeering and connections with organized crime. Both Kennedys had heard enough of Jimmy Hoffa's testimony to convince them that the threat the Mafia posed was great. Kennedy, *Enemy Within*, 265; Blakey, "RICO: The Genesis of an Idea," 24n25.

13. The students dubbed his class Gang Busters.

14. The RICO Act is written broadly enough that lawyers have even attempted to apply it to companies guilty of ongoing human rights violations in foreign countries. I first encountered the law as an undergraduate in the mid-1990s working with a team of law students at Yale Law School's Lowenstein International Human Rights Clinic. We were attempting to use the RICO statute to bring a case against oil companies that were complicit with the Burmese government in murders and torture to protect their pipelines.

15. Blakey directed the Cornell Institute on Organized Crime.

16. After spending three June days in Blakey's class, Jules Bonavolonta, an iconoclastic former Green Beret, exclaimed, "My eyes just flashed with the beauty of it all." Then he and his colleague James Kossler raced back to New York, bringing Blakey with them to explain to colleagues how to fight the Mafia and transform the way the FBI did business. Blum, *Gangland*, 28–29.

17. Ibid.

18. Senator McClellan shepherded this legislation as well.

19. Sophisticated criminal organizations use throwaway cell phones and encrypted messages to render wiretaps useless, so bugs can be more effective to evade such countermeasures.

20. Stille, *Excellent Cadavers*, 43.

21. Detectives also tend to work in silos, so people working robbery, homicide, and drug beats may never put a full picture together.

22. Calder, *Intelligence, Espionage, and Related Topics*.

23. These numbers are reported by the FISC and Article III Courts. See Empty Wheel, "Confirmed: The FISA Court Is Less of a Rubber Stamp than Article III Courts," June 28, 2017.

24. Leovy, *Ghettoside*, 74, 76.

25. Ibid., 78.

26. Ibid., 247.

27. Chakrabarti, *Bihar Breakthrough*, 66.

28. Ibid.

29. Francesco Sanfilippo, interview by author, Feb. 25, 2015.

30. In the 1870s, President Grant used intelligence to infiltrate the Ku Klux Klan. The findings of these early detectives fueled the drafting of the Enforcement Act and the Ku Klux Klan Act and led the Justice Department to authorize a bipartisan committee to hear more evidence about the Klan throughout many southern states. The committee collected testimony like that of Samuel and Hannah Tutson, quoted in chapter 2. Bartoletti, *KKK*, 131.

31. Dalton, *Strenuous Life*, 341–42; Jeffers, *Commissioner Roosevelt*, 263. Congress's fear of exposure is, ironically, the reason that the FBI operates without a charter today, giving it ambiguous powers that have become controversial in the presidential investigation of Donald Trump.

32. Alschuler, "Plea Bargaining and Its History."

33. Ibid., 28n151; and Fisher, *Plea Bargaining's Triumph*.

34. Alschuler, "Plea Bargaining and Its History."

35. Dripps, "Guilt, Innocence, and Due Process."

36. Bulger and the corrupt FBI agent were later found guilty on RICO charges. For a description of the breadth of the problem, see Strong, "Plea Bargaining, Cooperation Agreements, and Immunity Orders," 32, 34; and the testimony in the U.S. House of Representatives, *Everything Secret Degenerates*. For a comprehensive set of plea-bargaining arrangements around the world, see Stephen C. Thaman, "Plea-Bargaining, Negotiating Confessions, and Consensual Resolution of Criminal Cases," *Electronic Journal of Comparative Law* 11, no. 3 (Dec. 2007).

37. Chepesiuk, *Drug Lords*, 226.

38. Stille, *Excellent Cadavers*, 36, 43, 46.

39. For more on the historic case, see ibid. and Shana Alexander, *The Pizza Connection: Lawyers, Drugs, and the Mafia* (New York: Diane, 1988). The prosecutor of this trial later ended up head of the FBI.

40. Falcone's close ties to U.S. prosecutors allowed him to get Buscetta and another Sicilian mafioso, Salvatore Contorno, into the U.S. witness protection program before Italy created its own. Cracking the case led Italy and the United States to sign treaties to cooperate on extradition and legal assistance.

41. Stille, "All the Prime Minister's Men."

42. Porch and Rasmussen, "Demobilization of Paramilitaries in Colombia," 530n67. Guerrilla deserters occasionally abetted highly violent operations such as the Comuna 13 incursion.

43. The Colombian Reintegration Agency is widely viewed as one of the most effective fighter reintegration programs in the world, and the FARC hated it as a result. The U.S. government assisted it financially and morally when it was under fire from various quarters.

44. Glenn, *Rethinking Western Approaches to Counterinsurgency*, 188. The campaign was run with a private ad agency whose astute marketing tactics recognized that guerrilla fighters were both perpetrators and victims. After meeting with demobilized guerrillas, the advertisers noted that their main motivation for leaving was that they missed their mothers and that the most common time to defect was at Christmas. So they placed huge, lit Christmas trees in the jungle with the message "If Christmas can come to the jungle, you can come home. Demobilize. At Christmas everything is possible." Because more guerrillas traveled by river than by land, they went to villages along waterways and asked acquaintances of the guerrillas to send the fighters messages. They collected notes, crosses, toys, and jewelry and put them in floating, lit balls they sent down the river at night before Christmas—generating a defection every six hours. Later, they recorded mothers asking their children to come home, holding up childhood photographs recognizable to the guerrillas but not to their commanders. Another agency made ads for demobilization that played before soccer games—Colombia's second religion.

45. Ramírez de Rincón, "Drug Trafficking," 83.

46. U.S. participant in the negotiations, conversation with the author, Jan. 19, 2018.

47. Even in the United States, the First Circuit Court of Appeals noted that cooperation agreements "lessen public confidence in the law's insistence on just deserts." *United States v. Milo*, 506 F.3d 71, 77 (2007). See Richman, "Cooperating Defendants," 293n23.

48. Orlando, *Fighting the Mafia and Renewing Sicilian Culture*.

49. Ibid.

50. Bakradze, interview by author, Dec. 5, 2014.

51. Because the code of the thieves (the internal "law" from which they derived their name) prohibited members from denying membership, many were caught before they knew the new law even existed. Slade, *Reorganizing Crime*, 88.

52. Yakobashvili, interview by author, Aug. 20, 2014.

53. Italian anti-Mafia prosecutor, off-the-record interview by author, Feb. 27, 2015.

54. Abhyanand, interview by Rushda Majeed, June 29, 2015, on behalf of and in conjunction with author.

55. Like all legislation, the law required administrative rules to be written before it could take effect. The Federal Rules of Criminal Procedure enabled this provision in 1972. Maxeiner, "Bane of American Forfeiture Law," 769.

56. This distinction applies to most common-law countries whose laws derive from Britain. It doesn't hold for countries whose legal systems have French, Roman, or other roots.

57. Reina, "Drug Trafficking and the National Economy," 90.

58. Chepesiuk, *Drug Lords*, 228–29, 250–52.

59. Its full name is Libera Associazioni, Nomi e Numeri Contro le Mafie.

60. It's not just organized criminals who use brothels to lure lawmakers. In the twentieth century, Mutual Life Company maintained a "House of Mirth" in Albany to influence state legislators. Benson, *Corruption in America*, 62.

61. Parliament was forced to create the commission after the first anti-Mafia war, but it was uninterested in a strong anti-Mafia body, so those on the commission who wished to give it teeth had to fight colleagues on the commission as well as in the broader parliament.

62. The day after La Torre's murder, Carlo Alberto Dalla Chiesa, a general esteemed for ending the Red Brigades' terrorism in the 1970s, was appointed to stop the violence of what was shaping up to be the second Mafia war. Four months later, Chiesa was driving with his wife when the Mafia forced him off the road and killed them both, along with their driver.

63. Rico, interview by author, Jan. 26, 2015.

64. Schneider and Schneider, *Reversible Destiny*, 238.

65. The property itself is the "defendant," and it's unnecessary to lodge any criminal charge against the owner. These are known as civil *in rem* (against

the property) proceedings. In the United States, administrative forfeiture banning the import of various goods and drugs is another *in rem* action against the property itself, which allows the federal government to seize property without judicial involvement, based on the Tariff Act of 1930.

66. Alexander, *New Jim Crow*, 78–79.

67. Ibid., 79.

68. Sallah et al., "Stop and Seize."

69. Alexander, *New Jim Crow*, 80–81; Stillman, "Rise of Civil Forfeiture"; Eric D. Blumenson and Eva S. Nilsen, "Policing for Profit: The Drug War's Hidden Economic Agenda," *University of Chicago Law Review* 65 (1998): 35, 45.

70. The Civil Asset Forfeiture Reform Act of 2000 creates the possibility of an "innocent owner," but owners must prove that they did everything they could to protect their property from being used in a crime. Because civil cases do not require court-appointed attorneys for poor plaintiffs, however, people must pay for a lawyer or represent themselves—after having their property or money taken. Alexander, *New Jim Crow*, 82–83.

71. Brusca once kidnapped the eleven-year-old son of another mobster, tortured him in a tiny room for over two years, then strangled him. He dropped the boy's body into a vat of acid so that his family would not even be able to bury their son's corpse.

72. Yakobashvili, interview by author, Aug. 20, 2014.

73. Association for Democratic Reforms, *Analysis of Background Details*, which provides annual statistics on criminality among Indian politicians. The numbers presented here are not out of the ordinary.

74. Acemoglu, Robinson, and Santos, "Monopoly on Violence," 21.

75. Nitish Kumar empowered bureaucrats over multiple ministers who were incompetent or criminal. Bureaucrats would have to come to him every few weeks with full, detailed reports. Ministers, their bosses, could either rise to the occasion and lead the meeting or step aside. Chakrabarti, *Bihar Breakthrough*, 236–39.

76. World Bank, *Fighting Corruption in Public Services*, 93–94.

77. Bacon and Majeed, "Palermo Renaissance Part 1," 20.

78. Roosevelt, *American Ideals*, 143; Roosevelt, *Autobiography*, 171.

79. Roosevelt, *Autobiography*, 171.

80. Geographically, Georgia is just a bit larger than West Virginia, and in 2005 its population of 4.3 million was on par with Kentucky's. The organic law on local self-government was adopted in December 2005. In 2005, a con-

stitutional amendment also reduced the number of parliamentarians from 235 to 150, effective in 2008.

81. Timm, "Neopatrimonialism," 7, 11–13.

82. Rabushka, "Flat Tax Spreads to Georgia."

83. Muskhelishvili, "Institutional Change," 324. The financial police might also have supported grand corruption. Throughout my interviews, Davit Kezerashvili's name kept arising as the young leader of the Financial Police, who then became defense minister at the age of twenty-nine and eventually fled the country to France with far more money than was normal for a public servant. But other than a handful of such examples, few interviewees mentioned personal enrichment; instead, the money seems to have funded Saakashvili's party itself. Transparency International, "Who Owns Georgia."

84. I was told a particularly pitiful story about an ice rink owner who became a favorite of Saakashvili's. As a magnanimous gesture, Saakashvili's government opened ice rinks around the country—often temporary, traveling rinks owned by a single company. The company repeatedly wrote to the tax authorities to try to pay local taxes each time Saakashvili suddenly determined he wanted to open a new rink. But the tax authorities never wrote back. Eventually, the company was hit with such a large tax bill that the owner was jailed after being unable to pay. Tina Khidasheli, interview by author, Dec. 4, 2014.

85. At the time, world leaders blamed President Saakashvili for sparking an unwinnable conflict with his northern neighbor. Saakashvili claims the war was defensive, which resonates more following Russia's similarly murky incursion into Ukraine's Crimea six years later. From what can be pieced together regarding the events that sparked the war, it appears that in August 2008, rebels in South Ossetia began shelling Georgian villages. On August 7, Saakashvili called for a cease-fire, but mortars continued to fall. That night, Georgian troops opened fire, hitting civilian housing blocks, government buildings, and the Russian peacekeeping barracks. Georgian troops moved into South Ossetia the next day, after which Russia attacked. Steavenson, "Marching Through Georgia."

86. Georgian Young Lawyers' Association, interview by author, Dec. 16, 2014.

87. Khidasheli, interview by author, Dec. 4, 2014.

88. World Bank, *Fighting Corruption in Public Services*, 21.

89. Slade, "No Country for Made Men," 627.

90. Slade, "Politics of Punishment." The exact number is 87.5 percent.

91. The German aid agency GIZ, the UN Children's Fund, the Council of Europe, the American Bar Association, the Norwegian Mission of Rule of Law

388   Notes to Pages 240-242

Advisors, DPK Consulting, the Organization for Security and Co-operation in Europe, and the U.S. Agency for International Development all provided training and aid for the courts during these years.

92. Robakidze, "Georgia," 8–9; Transparency International, "Georgian Advertising Market."

93. Jones, *Georgia*, 112.

94. Chakrabarti, *Bihar Breakthrough*, 208.

95. Rushda Majeed, off-the-record interview with Bihari journalist on behalf of and in conjunction with author, July 9, 2015.

96. Vaishnav, *When Crime Pays*, 181, 328.

97. Pachico, "Ties Binding Crime."

98. "Colombia: Peace at Last?," 6.

99. To pressure voters into voting for the paramilitary's preferred candidate, the paramilitary leader in one town put the names of city councillors in a bag, pulled out two, and explained that he would kill them and other randomly chosen people if his preferred candidate did not win. Acemoglu, Robinson, and Santos, "Monopoly on Violence," 22.

100. "Rise and Fall of 'False Positive' Killings," 14, 26.

101. Pasotti, *Political Branding in Cities*, 213.

102. Chakrabarti, *Bihar Breakthrough*, 203.

103. "Saakashvili Takes Oath on Tomb of King David the Builder," *Caucasian Knot*, Jan. 24, 2004.

104. Saakashvili had reduced the Ministry of Interior alone from forty thousand to seventeen thousand, firing over fifteen thousand police officers, among other personnel. Slade, "State on the Streets," 6.

105. Stille, *Excellent Cadavers*, 157–58.

106. Schneider and Schneider, *Reversible Destiny*, 88.

107. Tighter procurement rules made many Sicilian firms noncompetitive, so work went to northern Italian firms. Ibid., 3.

108. John M. Allswang's *Bosses, Machines, and Urban Voters*, for instance, suggests that the personal relationships between bosses and their clients were better for the poor than impersonal civil service exams and the bureaucracy touted by better-educated progressives. On an individual level, this may well be correct. But the former system created stasis; individual poor people might be served, but the system kept them poor and uneducated, while the progressive system eventually led to public education, forty-hour workweeks that allowed parents to spend more time raising their children, safety rules that prevented early

death and child labor, and other reforms that reduced poverty and moved the United States from a developing to a developed nation. See Thelen, "Review: Urban Politics," 408.

109. In Progressive Era America, many Irish and Italian immigrants didn't like the paternalistic, "WASP" Progressives who lectured them on how to act and whose Prohibition laws denied them their right to drink. To them, reducing patronage meant taking jobs from working-class immigrants who couldn't speak much English and handing them to people who could pass tests—in other words, the educated middle class. Dalton, *Strenuous Life*, 153.

10: SOCIETY MAINTAINS THE PEACE

1. "Una risposta alla mafia invisible," *Segno* 30, no. 251 (2004): 15, cited in Schneider and Schneider, "Mafia, Antimafia," 509.

2. As of July 2017, ninety-six countries—about half the world—could not provide one data point per year on homicides from 2010 to 2015. Africa is particularly underrepresented, with forty-five countries offering few statistics, as well as eighteen countries in the Americas and seven in Oceania, two regions that are generally the most violent in the world. McEvoy and Hideg, "Global Violence Deaths 2017," 15. Different definitions make numbers hard to compare internationally; for instance, Mexico counts auto accidents in its homicide statistics. Police may report a homicide only once it's been solved or charges have been filed, so even within the same city the statistics of law enforcement and morgues often differ. Manipulation is widespread from Chicago to Russia. A U.S. presidential task force wrote in 1967 that "in some respects, the present [U.S.] system is not as good as that used in some European countries 100 years ago." *Task Force Report: Crime and Its Impact*, 123. For more on these problems, see Kleinfeld, "Why Is It So Difficult to Count Dead People?"; and Kleinfeld, *Reducing All Violent Deaths*.

3. Serious scholars of violence generally follow an approach of looking at patterns over time for this reason. See Roth, "Homicide Trends"; Eisner, "Modernization, Self-Control, and Lethal Violence"; Spierenburg, "History of Murder"; and McMahon, Eibach, and Roth, "Introduction: Making Sense of Violence." For a thorough description of how complexity theory can be applied to understanding the dynamics of violent countries, see Kleinfeld, "Improving Development Aid Design and Evaluation."

4. Tyson, *Emmett Till*, 97, citing Smith.

5. Ibid., 101, 105.

6. Ibid., 97, citing Smith.

7. Ibid., 106.

8. Ibid., 107.

9. Ibid.

10. Ibid., 102.

11. Ibid., 98, citing Charles Payne, *I've Got the Light of Freedom: The Organizing Tradition and the Mississippi Freedom Struggle* (Berkeley: University of California Press, 1995), 431.

12. Muhammad was carrying a load of firewood across town when he stumbled upon an eighteen-year-old he knew hanging lifeless from a tree, surrounded by a crowd of white men. Clegg, *Original Man*, 10.

13. Malcom X, *Malcom X Speaks*, 22.

14. Forman, *Making of Black Revolutionaries*, xv–xvi.

15. *Report of the National Advisory Commission on Civil Disorders*, 308, better known as the Kerner Commission. Sociologists who studied the Jim Crow South, from which most northern blacks had emigrated, noted the high levels of crime emanating from abandonment by the state. In the 1940s, John Dollard, *Caste and Class in a Southern Town*, 274, found that "the formal machinery of the law takes care of the Negroes' grievances much less adequately than of the whites', and to a much higher degree the Negro is compelled to make and enforce his own law with other Negroes." A decade earlier, the anthropologist Hortense Powdermaker found that "since no Negro can expect to find justice by due process of law, the 'lawlessness' sometimes ascribed to the Negro may be viewed as being rather his private, individual 'law enforcement.'" *After Freedom*, 126.

16. Gunnar Myrdal, a Swedish social scientist, found in *An American Dilemma* that despite all their problems with the police, black southerners wanted *more* law enforcement to protect themselves from both blacks and whites.

17. Before the Jim Crow era, there was little difference between black and white violence in the United States. Eric Monkkonen, *Murder in New York City*, 164, traces the beginnings of the discrepancy to the 1880s, when Jim Crow began and southern states (where most African Americans lived) abandoned policing black neighborhoods. These findings were corroborated by Lane, *Roots of Violence*. A fuller discussion of this phenomenon and the high levels of southern African American violence are included in Leovy, *Ghettoside*, 155, citing "Mortality Statistics Reports, 1921 and 1920, Twenty-First Annual Report," U.S. Department of the Census. During the Great Migration, many African Americans moved from these conditions to northern cities and had children, many of whom were young men in age groups correlated with violence across races by the 1960s.

18. Black trust in government faced a sudden spike in the mid-1960s thanks to the civil rights successes but was still low when more finely grained questions were asked, such as whether those surveyed believed many government officials were crooked. Roth, "It's No Mystery"; Roth, "Homicide Trends."

19. Hayden, *Long Sixties,* 58.

20. This mix had deadly effects at California's Altamont Speedway Free Festival in 1969 at what was intended as Woodstock West. Hippies who had idealized Hells Angels as "fellow outlaws" in the counterculture had hired the bikers to police the venue, leading to violence and a murder.

21. Hayden, *Long Sixties,* 74.

22. After the Kent State killings in 1970, law enforcement killed two protesters in Mississippi, and the National Guard turned its bayonets on protesters at the University of New Mexico. With over a million students protesting across the country, some of them violently, President Nixon was removed to Camp David for two days for his safety, while the Eighty-Second Airborne occupied the basement of the White House Executive Office Building.

23. U.S. police professionalization was thanks largely to one man—August Vollmer. As head of Berkeley's police force, president of the California Chiefs of Police, and eventually leader of the International Association of Chiefs of Police, Vollmer transformed policing from a partisan patronage job into a profession. He invented polygraph testing, elevated detective work, and partnered with universities to train forces in ideas like criminal modus operandi, a concept he brought to the United States from Europe. By the 1940s, he had established the national model of depoliticized, professional police forces.

24. Fyfe and Skolnick, *Above the Law,* xi–xv, 95–97.

25. Sources agree that 1971 was the peak year for police violence but disagree on the numbers, which were not required to be reported nationally. For instance, the New York Police Department killed between eighty-seven and ninety-three people in the line of duty in 1971; the higher number comes from Roth, *American Homicide,* 455; the lower from Toch, *Agents of Change,* 66. According to *The Washington Post* database, police across the nation killed 82 people a month in 2017.

26. Cited in Alexander, *New Jim Crow,* 46.

27. Blumenthal et al., *Justifying Violence,* xvi, 28, 228.

28. "A Newsweek Poll: Mr. Nixon Holds Up," *Newsweek,* May 25, 1970. Letters to the editor in *Life* magazine the following week included thoughts such as "One might just as well say that a Marxist, shot while robbing a gas station of money with which to further his cause, was killed for his political beliefs. —Ralph Milerton, Memphis, Tenn." Reeves, *President Nixon,* 226.

29. Goldwater, "Peace Through Strength," 744.

30. In 2017, it seems inevitable that America is polarized into a Right that supports more aggressive law enforcement and a Left that leans antiwar and anti-force. But in the lead-up to World War II, pacifism was mainstream as hundreds of thousands of Americans united behind a nonpartisan antiwar

movement led by Republican and Democratic senators, businesspeople, and mainstream national celebrities such as Charles Lindbergh. The America First Committee's merger of isolationism, pacifism, and anti-Semitism, though hardly a laudable mix, appealed across party lines.

31. See LaFree, *Losing Legitimacy*, 100–104; Roth, *American Homicide*, 435–68; and American National Election Studies' Cumulative Data File, variables VCF0604 and VCF0608. From 1958 through 2004, the relationship between the homicide rate and trust in government was remarkably strong, with an r^2 of 0.65. The r^2 for the relationship between the belief that many politicians are crooked and the homicide rate, 1958–2004, was 0.60. Roth, "Homicide Trends."

32. "Crime in the United States," in *FBI Uniform Crime Reports*. The World Health Organization describes a homicide epidemic at 10 per 100,000. The white homicide rate peaked in 1980 as trust in government fell to a post–World War II low under the Carter administration. Roth, *American Homicide*, 452–64.

33. Roth, "Homicide Trends."

34. Johnson, Golub, and Dunlap, "Rise and Decline of Hard Drugs," conducted an exhaustive study following thirteen thousand drug users arrested in Manhattan between 1987 and 1997 that shows the move away from crack began with young people altering their behavior. Johnson describes a similar effect in Washington, D.C., when crack use declined during a period when the capital "had fewer officers on the street, the police made fewer arrests for drugs, and the mayor himself was indicted for smoking crack.... Something clearly happened to change the attitude among youths.... They deserve a lot of the credit." Egan, "Crack's Legacy." The ethnography of Curtis, "Improbable Transformation of Inner-City Neighborhoods," 1,259, 1,263, echoes the same phenomenon, describing how young people in Brooklyn neighborhoods devastated by drugs "shared a conviction that they would not succumb to the same fate that nearly erased the preceding generation." The criminologist Latzer traces the same phenomenon in *Rise and Fall of Violent Crime in America*, 250–53. I share with Latzer, Johnson, Golub, and Dunlap a belief that improved policing as well as cultural change among these subcultures together altered violence; Curtis is more dubious about the effectiveness of policing strategies during the crack era.

35. Office of Juvenile Justice and Delinquency Prevention, *Statistical Briefing Book*.

36. Crucially, as the number of civilians shot dropped, there was no adverse effect on the crime rate. Today, New York City has one of the lowest rates of both police violence and homicide of any city in the United States. When the U.S. Supreme Court decided in 1985 that shooting a felon who presented no threat of physical injury was unconstitutional, several police authorities

argued in court *on behalf* of the stricter rules on deadly force. Fyfe and Skolnick, *Above the Law*, 134–35.

37. The Knapp Commission, for example, began under New York City's Mayor Lindsay to investigate corruption in that city's police force. The counsel to the commission and later chairman of New York's Commission to Combat Police Corruption noted in 2012 that "the attitude throughout the department seems fundamentally hostile to the kind of systematized graft that had been a way of life almost forty years ago." Armstrong, *They Wished They Were Honest*.

38. In 1994, 19 percent of respondents to a Pew survey said they trusted the government to do what is right; this number steadily increased to a peak of 54 percent in October 2001, directly after the 9/11 attacks. Pew Research Center, "Public Trust in Government: 1958–2017." Other measures suggest that trust in the government continued growing until 2004. Roth, "Homicide Trends."

39. Alexander, *New Jim Crow*, 42.

40. The broken windows theory advocates mass arrests for minor quality-of-life infringements such as turnstile jumping and vandalism, based on a hypothesis by George Kelling and James Q. Wilson that disorder was frightening in itself and invited crime (see Kelling and Wilson, "Broken Windows"). When researchers studied the tactic, they found that targeting petty infractions reduces petty infractions, but there was little correlation between violence and disorder: most graffiti artists are not murderers. Zero-tolerance policies occasionally reduce property crime, but most studies agree that they have no clear effect on violent crime. Among these studies are Pollard, "Zero Tolerance"; Jang, Hoover, and Lawton, "Effect of Broken Windows Enforcement"; and Sampson and Raudenbush, "Systematic Social Observation." Two studies did find links between minor crimes and broken windows theory; see Kelling and Sousa, "Do Police Matter?"; and Corman and Mocan, "Carrots, Sticks, and Broken Windows." One reason for the lack of efficacy may be implementation. Kelling and Wilson's article suggested that increased policing by neighborhood cops on foot patrol would uphold norms of behavior, in keeping with the recivilizing ideal. But what occurred in practice was militarized policing and mass arrests, which had the opposite effect, turning neighborhoods against police and depriving law enforcement of important intelligence on more serious wrongdoers. See Hinkle and Wiesburd, "Irony of Broken Windows Policing"; and Sherman, "Communities and Crime Prevention."

41. Levitt co-wrote *Freakonomics* with journalist Stephen Dubner, and includes an uncritical description of his own research with Donohue from their joint article "Legalized Abortion and Crime," despite the fact that it had already been cast into doubt by other scholars. Donohue and Levitt support their argument with the curious fact that the homicide rate of Canada—which legalized abortion a few years before the United States—rose and fell alongside that of the United States, though at a much lower level. The similarity between

rises and falls in crime in America and Canada led one of the greats of American criminology, Frank Zimring, to cast a critical eye on whether government
policy made any difference at all, though he eschews a simple demographic
explanation and believes many social factors played a role. For further detail,
see Zimring, *Great American Crime Decline*, 108, 121–25. Looking at the numbers myself, they seem more easily explained by similar baby booms in Canada and the United States, leading to a rise in violence starting in the 1960s,
but Canada's drop from around 3 to 2 per 100,000 is so much less dramatic
than the United States' that it seems to me entirely possible to explain through
demographics and civilizing. In fact, even Canadian criminologists point to
the recivilizing processes of moderation and self-restraint, as well as economic
factors, as being crucial to their own country's violence reduction. See Marc
Ouimet in "Explaining the American and Canadian Crime Drop in the 1990s."

42. The Choice on Termination of Pregnancy Act was passed in 1996 but
came into force on February 1, 1997. Drawn from Barclay and Tavares, "International Comparisons of Criminal Justice Statistics 2001."

43. A series of researchers have questioned Levitt and Donohue's analysis,
finding statistical errors as well as failures to carefully read homicide statistics
(for instance, if abortion was causing homicide to fall, the youngest perpetrators should have been eliminated first, but, in fact, the opposite was occurring
as the crime wave ebbed). See, for instance, Theodore Joyce, "Did Legalized
Abortion Lower Crime?" *Journal of Human Resources* 38 no. 1 (2003): 1–37; and
Christopher Foote and Christopher Goetz, "The Impact of Legalized Abortion
on Crime: Comment," Federal Reserve Bank of Boston, January 31, 2008.

44. The researchers used the 1990 time period as an extrapolation of higher
pollutants in the 1970s that lingered through old facilities. Stretesky and Lynch,
"Relationship Between Lead Exposure and Homicide," 155. See also Nevin,
"How Lead Exposure Relates to Temporal Changes in IQ, Violent Crime, and
Unwed Pregnancy."

45. For further exploration, see James J. Feigenbaum and Christopher Muller,
"Lead Exposure and Violent Crime in the Early Twentieth Century," *Explorations
in Economic History* 62 (Oct. 2016): 51–86; and Jessica Wolpaw Reyes, "Environmental Policy as Social Policy? The Impact of Childhood Lead Exposure on
Crime," *B.E. Journal of Economic Analysis and Policy* 7, no. 1 (2007).

46. Spelman, "Limited Importance of Prison Expansion"; Zimring, *Great
American Crime Decline*.

47. This number includes state and federal prisoners. It does not include
people in jail awaiting trial or those serving sentences of less than six months.
Minor-Harper, "State and Federal Prisoners, 1925–85," 2.

48. Toch, Grant, and Galvin, *Agents of Change*, 78–79.

49. Perkinson, *Texas Tough*, 1, 6; Alexander, *New Jim Crow*, 93. Or to consider
the numbers per capita, in 1972 in the United States, 161 Americans were

incarcerated per 100,000 in population, a rate that had stayed fairly steady since the early twentieth century, with the exception of a Prohibition spike in the late 1930s. The numbers started rising the following year, and by the peak, in 2007, imprisonment had hit 767 per 100,000. See *Growth of Incarceration in the United States*, 33–35.

50. These numbers are greater than the number of new homicide convictions because people convicted of murder tend to serve long sentences, so these inmates have often been behind bars for many years.

51. The United States uses prison for people who have been convicted of crimes. However, approximately 740,000 people are in jail as of 2016, most of them awaiting trial rather than having been found guilty of any crime, though some are serving short sentences. About half a million of these simply cannot afford to post bail and may spend months behind bars, which can cost them jobs, relationships, and the custody of children. Zeng, "Jail Inmates in 2016."

52. Perkinson, *Texas Tough*, 21.

53. Linthicum, "Sad State for Children."

54. Ayers, *Vengeance and Justice*, 17; Lane, *Murder in America*, 350.

55. Jacobs, Carmichael, and Kent, "Vigilantism, Current Racial Threat, and Death Sentences," using national lynching data from the NAACP and comparing it with Tolnay and Beck data on the South. Jacobs, Malone, and Iles, "Race Relations and Prison Admissions."

56. Eckberg, "Table Ec-190–198: Reported Homicides and Homicide Rates."

57. Southall, "Crime in New York City Plunges to a Level Not Seen Since the 1950s."

58. The homicide rate in Lithuania is approximately 6.7 per 100,000, while Los Angeles had a rate of 6.8 in 2017, according to the Brennan Center for Justice, "Crime in 2017 Updated Analysis."

59. In 2016, the FBI listed a homicide rate of 5.34 per 100,000; without the population and murders in those three cities, the rate would have dropped to 5 per 100,000. For comparison, it was 5.2 per 100,000 in 1950. Eckberg, "Table Ec-190–198: Reported Homicides and Homicide Rates."

60. Jenkins, "1970s."

61. Bergen et al., "Terrorism in America After 9/11."

62. Centers for Disease Control and Prevention statistics, looking at homicide and legal intervention killings by police for children ages five to nineteen: webappa.cdc.gov. Of course, school shootings feel different to many Americans because they are affecting a middle-class demographic used to safety, while juvenile homicides of the 1990s disproportionately affected minority children in inner cities. In 1997, 85 percent of U.S. counties had no juvenile homicides, while five counties had a quarter of all juvenile killings. In 1997, the

rate of juvenile murder for African American youth was 9.1 per 100,000; for whites, 1.8. See Finkelhor and Ormrod, "Homicides of Children and Youth," 2. Reports of missing children are down 40 percent from 1997, while the U.S. population has grown by 30 percent. See Ingraham, "There's Never Been a Safer Time to Be a Kid in America."

63. Cooper and Smith, "Homicide Trends in the United States," 14. In Los Angeles, the rate was 368 per 100,000, similar to the death rate of soldiers deployed to the Iraq War and in the vicinity of Medellín; by 2010, it had fallen to about 158 per 100,000. Leovy, *Ghettoside*, 316.

64. Leovy, *Ghettoside*, 11; Centers for Disease Control data, 2015.

65. Fox and Zawitz, "Homicide Trends in the United States." In 1980, 2000, and 2005, the black rate was six times as high as the white rate, in 1985 it was five times as high, in 1990 and 1995 it was seven times as high, and though the official statistics are not available at the time of writing, according to Nate Silver on his website 538, it was eight times as high in 2015. Silver, "Black Americans Are Killed at 12 Times the Rate of People in Other Developed Countries."

66. Leovy, *Ghettoside*, 316.

67. According to the National Crime Victimization Survey, from 2001 to 2005, 55 percent of blacks reported nonfatal violent crime to the police compared with 48 percent of whites, and police response times were slightly faster for African Americans, with 91 percent of calls getting a response within an hour. Those numbers are improving: from 1992 to 2000, blacks reported nonfatal violent crime 48 percent of the time compared with whites doing so 42 percent of the time. Harrell, "Black Victims of Violent Crime," 7–8. More recent numbers are not available.

68. Tyson, *Emmett Till*, 20, citing the Chicago Housing Authority.

69. Kunzelman, "'Alt-Right' Leader Loses Gym Membership."

70. Despite new Department of Justice regulations that are intended to increase police reporting of homicides to a national body, *The Washington Post's* counts of police shootings continue to identify nearly twice as many killings as the FBI's official tracking, and local forces have an incentive to treat police shootings as justifiable homicides, because these need not be included in homicide statistics at all. McEvoy and Hideg, "Global Violent Deaths 2017," 29; Zimring, *When Police Kill*, 29.

71. Friedman, Grawert, and Cullen, "Crime Trends."

72. Rodney Balko provides an excellent, evenhanded history of the growth of militarized policing in *Rise of the Warrior Cop*.

73. SWAT teams were first introduced in the 1960s for prison riots and hostage negotiations, but they were rare until the 1980s War on Drugs. At that

time, Congress decided to allow police departments to take surplus military gear (the program was known as Section 1208 and then renamed Section 1033). At first, allocations of military equipment were fairly small, and departments largely gained innocuous goods such as fax machines, cold-weather clothing, and ammunition for their existing weapons. But over time, the program grew, and as the wars in Iraq and Afghanistan continued, there was more surplus military equipment. After 2011, serious military hardware such as armored vehicles starts to appear on the allocation charts. See Skorup and O'Sullivan, "Breaking Down Department of Defense Grants." For SWAT team numbers, see Alexander, *New Jim Crow*, 75. Two recent studies contend that military gear transfers have reduced crimes and assaults on officers. However, both papers find that the equipment of most value is not weapons but back-office IT equipment, uniforms, and gear such as surveillance equipment, which compose about two-fifths of the 1033 program's giveaways. Bove and Gavrilova, "Police Officer"; Harris et al., "Peacekeeping Force."

74. Kent, "Former Hobbs Officers Sue HPD for Racial Discrimination." Similar ads aired in Florida, Texas, Arkansas, Georgia, California, and even Vermont. Parascandola, "NYPD Campaign Wants New Recruits"; Balko, "Disturbing Messages in Police Recruiting Videos."

75. By the mid-1980s, trends in social trust and homicide in the United States became more difficult to correlate, because homicide and trust began to diverge significantly by demographic. Since 2004, trust in government has fallen by nearly half, but homicides have also continued to fall. Unpacking the statistics, however, shows that the fall in trust in government has been far higher among older, wealthier white Americans—the group least at risk of committing homicide. Among African Americans, belief in the legitimacy of the social hierarchy, trust in the federal government, and hope that they can do better have been rising since the 1990s, and the poor have also been more confident than the wealthy. Meanwhile, mass incarceration, ironically, probably reduced homicides among men over twenty-five, because many of the men who would have been killed on the streets were in jail. Roth, "Trends in Homicide."

76. Paxton, "Is Social Capital Declining in the United States?"

77. Fajnzylber and Loayza, "Inequality and Violent Crime," 18. Inequality seems to significantly reduce social solidarity among citizens of different groups while increasing it within the same group (except in formerly Communist countries, where equality has a very different history). In other words, it breaks bridging capital although it deepens bonding capital. Corruption is a more powerful predictor of governmental legitimacy. Uslaner, *Moral Foundations*, 210, 220, 232, 244–45; Rothstein and Uslaner, *All for All*. For an overview of income and wealth inequality in the United States, see Bachman, "Income Inequality."

398 Notes to Pages 259–263

78. The last year for which the comprehensive FBI report *Crime in the United States* is available, 2016, shows that the number of interracial killings increased 13 percent from 2014. Cella and Neuhauser, "Race and Homicide in America."

79. Page and Shedrofsky, "Poll: Clinton Builds Lead in Divided Nation Worried About Election Day Violence."

80. For decades, Berlusconi denied rumors about such Mafia ties. In 2014, however, Italy's highest Supreme Court of Cassation ruled that the former senator Marcello Dell'Utri was a member of the Mafia and served as Berlusconi's link with Cosa Nostra for eighteen years. Forty members of the Mafia testified in the trial. Berlusconi cannot be tried for mob ties because of the statute of limitations. Day, "Silvio Berlusconi's Links with Organised Crime Confirmed."

81. Sberna and Vannucci, "It's the Politics."

82. Berlusconi's government oversaw a series of laws that took a step back, such as law 234/1997, which decriminalized abuse of office; laws 140/2003 and 124/2008, which gave senior officeholders immunity; law 140/2003, which required parliamentary approval to collect evidence against MPs; law 251/2005, which strengthened the statute of limitations for corruption crimes; law 61/2002, which enabled fishy accounting; and law 102/2009, which provided an amnesty for people to repatriate and regularize assets that had been hidden abroad.

83. Ruggiero, "Who Corrupts Whom?," 92, 97.

84. Ibid., 26.

85. Dickie, *Blood Brotherhoods*, 616.

86. Ibid., 659–60.

87. Paoli, "Decline of the Italian Mafia," 15–16.

88. Jamieson, *Antimafia*, 152.

89. "Chamber of Commerce Head Arrested for Bribery in S. Italy," *Global Times*, March 4, 2015.

90. Srivastava, "Nitish Kumar Is Ruining Powerful Criminals of Bihar's Happiness."

91. Singh, "Now Bihar Simmers."

92. International Crisis Group, "Colombia: Peace at Last?," 22–23; McDermott, "Peace Initiatives," 68.

93. Bargent, "Colombia Police."

94. Lamb, "Microdynamics," 281, citing a chart published by *Semana* magazine with the number of years different traffickers had spent leading their organizations, with the Cali cartel leadership lasting fifteen to seventeen years and the post-paramilitary groups lasting one to two years. See also Rico, "Criminal Diaspora," 9.

95. The final peace agreement allows Colombian military commanders to evade war crimes responsibility, so long as they claim ignorance of their subordinates' wrongdoing. The clause may violate Article 28 of the Rome Statute (the founding document of the International Criminal Court, to which Colombia is a signatory), which requires states to hold accountable commanders who "knew or, owing to the circumstances at the time, should have known" about subordinates' war crimes. It also allows civilians to participate in justice tribunals voluntarily, so despite the massive cooperation between government and paramilitary forces, unless the court has evidence of particular individuals committing particular crimes, paramilitary commanders and members can evade responsibility for horrific past violence.

96. Álvaro Balcázar, interview by author, Feb. 5, 2015.

97. Finland's rate was 2.0 per 100,000; both numbers are from 2014 statistics drawn from UNODC and the Centers for Disease Control.

98. World Bank, *Fighting Corruption in Public Services*, 72.

99. Ibid., 20–21.

100. "Who Owns Georgia?" Transparency International 2013.

101. Transparency International, Global Corruption Barometer, 2010.

102. Slade, *Reorganizing Crime*, 164.

103. Saakashvili had tried to manipulate electoral processes and tighten campaign financing so opposition forces couldn't run against him without having their donors harassed by the tax police and their campaigns hobbled by regulatory obstacles. Bidzina Ivanishvili's personal wealth allowed him to circumvent this obstacle.

104. Hans Gutbrod, interview by author, Dec. 9, 2014.

105. Molly Corso, interview by author, Dec. 10, 2014.

106. Alexandre Kukhianidze, interview by author, Dec. 6, 2014.

107. Chachibaia, interview by author, Dec. 10, 2014.

108. Paoli, "Decline of the Italian Mafia," 15–16.

109. Ibid., 23. The Mafia was also no longer able to direct mass public money into its own coffers. Maria Loi, "In carcere il Gotha di Cosa Nostra: I pizzini di Provenzano svelano i nuovi capi," *Antimafia Duemila* 6, no. 3 (2006): 2–6, cited in Paoli, "Decline of the Italian Mafia," 2–6.

110. Bacon and Majeed, "Palermo Renaissance Part 1," 16.

111. Ibid., 18.

112. Government of Colombia, "Examen periódico universal," 5.

113. International Crisis Group, "Virtuous Twins," 4. The Colombian government listed a rate of 24.4, but the Igarape Institute, whose statistics are more thorough, found a lower rate of 22.1 per 100,000.

114. International Crisis Group, "Colombia: Peace at Last?," 6.

115. Ibid., 6–7; "Rise and Fall of 'False Positive' Killings in Colombia," 26.

116. "Colombian Government Dismisses 27 Top Army Officers," McClatchy, Oct. 30, 2008.

117. International Crisis Group, "Colombia: Peace at Last?," 6–7.

118. International Crisis Group, "Virtuous Twins," 9; International Crisis Group, "Colombia: Peace at Last?," 9.

119. International Crisis Group, "Colombia: Peace at Last?," 6.

120. Chakrabarti, *Bihar Breakthrough*, 85; Mukherji and Mukherji, "Bihar," 84; Aiyar, "Bihar," 63–65; Kleinfeld and Majeed, "Fighting Insurgency with Politics," 4. Some of the statistics in Bihar are disputed, largely because those who cite less positive numbers have not adjusted for population growth. Bihar's population increased by 11 percent from 2006 to 2010. Kidnapping actually increased in Bihar in this era, which sounds discordant until it becomes clear that marriages by elopement, rather than traditionally arranged marriages, are often reported as kidnappings by family members. Violent kidnappings are generally kidnappings for ransom, which fell.

121. Aiyar, "Bihar," 64.

122. Mukherji and Mukherji, "Bihar," 35.

123. Gupta, "Unraveling Bihar's 'Growth Miracle,'" 56.

124. For more on the issue of crimes against women in Bihar, see Iyer et al., "Power of Political Voice."

125. Chachibaia, interview by author, Dec. 10, 2014.

11: WHAT CAN WE DO?

1. W. E. B. Du Bois, *The Souls of Black Folk: Essays and Sketches* (New York: A. C. McClurg, 1903), 58.

2. PRIO Battle Deaths Dataset 3.0. The exact number they list is 379,410.

3. In 2016, the number of battle deaths worldwide was approximately 99,000, and the decline continues. Small Arms Survey 2017, 1.

4. McEvoy and Hideg, "Global Violent Deaths 2017," 1.

5. "Von drei Straftätern wird einer rückfällig," *Spiegel Online*, Feb. 14, 2014.

6. See Kocaoglu, Figari, and Darbishire, *Using the Right to Information as an Anti-corruption Tool*.

7. Jeffers, *Commissioner Roosevelt*, 172.

8. There is some research, for instance, that suggests donor funding perversely tamps down the willingness of recipients to engage in street protests,

perhaps because of the increasingly technical turn in international support that requires similarly more technocratic practices on behalf of grantees. Elgin-Cossart, Jones, and Esberg, "Pathways to Change," 51.

9. See Canales, *From Ideas to Institutions;* and Johnson, *Where Good Ideas Come From,* for the importance of networks that cross lines for innovation.

10. Given the importance of trust, an accelerator would best be structured to run in multiple sessions over time, so that strategy formation could take place after a trusting team had cohered.

11. I owe this important insight and comparison to conversations with Tomicah Tillemann.

12. Educated citizens had helped end monarchies across Europe by the 1920s, creating a statistically significant trend by the twentieth century. Glaeser, Ponzetto, and Shleifer, "Why Does Democracy Need Education?"

13. Mungiu-Pippidi, *Quest for Good Governance,* 88.

14. See Gift and Krcmaric, "Who Democratizes?"

15. Pasotti, *Political Branding in Cities,* 49–50.

16. Carlos Vilalta (a professor of criminology at CIDE), interview by a team of master's students at New York University's Wagner School working under my supervision, Jan. 19, 2017.

17. Universities could work in tandem with entities such as the U.S. Department of State's Magnitsky sanctions task force to determine when such a sanction would be appropriate and useful.

18. Peace negotiators in Angola, Guatemala, Syria, Colombia, Afghanistan, Mozambique, Myanmar, and other states, interviews by author, Oct. 3; Nov. 16, 20, 30; Dec. 11, 2017.

19. Paul Williams, interview by author, Oct. 3, 2017.

20. Messick and Kleinfeld, "Writing an Effective Anti-corruption Law."

21. For Ghana, Emile Short, interview by author, Feb. 28, 2014; and Kwabena Oteng, interview by author, March 2, 2014. In Romania, the government passed an emergency decree on January 31, 2017, to effectively decriminalize any governmental corruption under $47,600. Within hours, hundreds of thousands of protesters had taken to the streets, and the government was forced to roll back the law. They were emboldened by years of strong leadership from the National Anticorruption Directorate, which is one of the most trusted institutions in the country. The fact that the army and gendarmerie are slightly more trusted is a key reason that while Romania has endemic corruption, it does not have Privilege Violence. "Corruption in Romania: People v Pilferers," *Economist,* Feb. 11, 2017, 39.

22. Driscoll, *Warlords,* 10.

23. "Reaching the Untouchables," *Economist*, March 13, 2010.

24. Of course, not all corruption leads to the sort of violence detailed here. The violence in Syria today, and before that in Algeria, seems to be helping multiple monarchies in the Middle East keep a lid on their countries, despite corruption. But when corruption is part of the Privilege Violence equation, it is an important aspect to tackle.

25. As Detective Lester Freamon of *The Wire* explained prior to issuing subpoenas against a number of Baltimore politicians, "You follow drugs, you get drug addicts and drug dealers, but you start to follow the money and you don't know where the fuck it's going to take you."

26. Cited in Vittori, "How Anonymous Shell Companies Finance Insurgents, Criminals."

27. Prah, "Share of Homebuyers Paying Cash Reaches New High."

28. Evans, "How Laundered Money Shapes London's Property Market."

29. The facts of this case come from Shaxson, "Tale of Two Londons."

30. "Money Laundering: FAQs," Financial Services Authority.

31. "The Whistleblower's Story."

32. "Keeping Foreign Corruption out of the United States." For a more popular account, see Michel, "U.S. Is a Good Place for Bad People to Stash Their Money."

33. Terminology in this field is fraught. I use the internationally common term "security sector assistance" to encompass the broad range of government efforts to interact with foreign entities that use force to protect the state and citizens. However, the U.S. Department of Defense prefers the term "security cooperation," while U.S. civilian agencies prefer "security assistance."

34. Pimentel, "Nexus of Organized Crime and Politics in Mexico," 49.

35. Roosevelt, *Autobiography*, 189.

36. Many of these programs understand that the funding is too little to accomplish any security goals; it is instead intended to build relationships with other militaries. There is worth to such relationships, but where relationships are the goal, there are better ways to forge them than with fungible equipment, and it is important to ensure that the Rolodexes are maintained. See Hadley and Kleinfeld, "Fostering a State-Society Compact."

37. Epstein and Rosen, "U.S. Security Assistance," 6, 15.

38. These are all examples from Kenya's Anglo-Leasing scandal. The American ambassador calculated that the money could have supplied every HIV-positive Kenyan with ten years of antiretroviral treatment. Wrong, *It's Our Turn to Eat*, 166.

39. Riechmann and Lardner, "$360 Million Lost"; DeYoung, "U.S. Trucking Funds Reach Taliban"; SIGAR, "Quarterly Report," opening letter.

40. Hadley and Kleinfeld, "Fostering a State-Society Compact."

41. In some cases, this is impossible, as with Israel and Egypt, where treaty obligations require a certain amount of assistance. However, it could be achieved across most countries.

42. These programs are discussed in *Effective, Legitimate, Secure: Insights for Defense Institution Building*, eds. Alexander Kerr and Michael Miklaucic, National Defense University (Washington, D.C.: Center for Complex Operations, Institute for National Strategic Studies, National Defense University, 2017).

43. Raghwesh Ranjan, interview by Rushda Majeed, July 15, 2015, on behalf of and in conjunction with author.

44. In 2004, the EU and the World Bank provided a billion dollars to Georgia's new government, while the United States awarded $295.3 million through the Millennium Challenge Account and further money through military assistance and the U.S. Agency for International Development (Dadalauri, "Political Corruption," 14). The OSCE, ICITAP, the UNOMIC, the EU THEMIS program, the Council of Europe, IOM, and France, Germany, and America all provided funds for police reform in Georgia (Slade, "State on the Streets," 6); and British, Turkish, and German assistance all helped transform the border guards from a military to a civilian police structure in the late 1990s, but it did little good until after the Rose Revolution (Dadalauri, "Political Corruption," 12–13), after which the Germans and Americans helped train the border police and coast guard (Kukhianidze, "Corruption and Organized Crime," 228). The United States also supported Georgia's work with NATO's Partnership for Peace and trained four Georgian battalions between 2002 and 2004, providing $64 million, about four times Georgia's annual defense budget at the time (Miller, "Is the Road in Georgia Too Perilous?," 47). I discuss the U.S. aid package to Colombia, Plan Colombia, in chapter 7.

45. Jones, *Georgia*, 138, 253. Georgia received $1.8 billion from the United States from 1992 to 2009, another billion from the World Bank, and half a billion from the EU between 1992 and 2007.

46. Behan, *Camorra*, 187; Falcone and Padovani, *Men of Honour*, 135.

47. Humphreys and Varshney, "Violent Conflict and the Millennium Development Goals." Other scholars have found that food aid increased insurgent-based conflict in the Philippines, such as Crost, Felter, and Johnston, "Aid Under Fire." Meanwhile, Nathan Nunn of Harvard and Nancy Qian of Yale found that U.S. food aid generally increased the length of conflict. See "U.S. Food Aid and Civil Conflict."

48. See Alesina and Weder, "Do Corrupt Governments Receive Less Foreign Aid?" Scholars such as Bräutigam and Knack, in "Foreign Aid, Institutions,

and Governance in Sub-Saharan Africa," actually show that foreign aid makes corruption, the rule of law, and bureaucratic quality worse, in part because it reduces the need for governments to collect taxes from their people. Tavares, "Does Foreign Aid Corrupt?," suggests that foreign aid does reduce corruption, but that the effect is greater in less corrupt countries and some donors are better than others. Countries caught in a false peace with clientelistic relationships—known to scholars as neopatrimonial countries—and those that have highly partisan democracies seem to be at greatest risk of having lower-quality governance when aid is highest. See Knack, "Does Foreign Aid Promote Democracy?" For the Naples and Sicily cases, see Pasotti, *Political Branding in Cities*, 7.

49. Mwenda has made these points in much of his journalism, but they are best summarized in his TED talk, "Aid for Africa? No Thanks," www.ted.com.

50. Kleinfeld and Bader, "Extreme Violence and the Rule of Law," 7.

51. For further, see McLoughlin, "When Does Service Delivery Improve the Legitimacy of a Fragile or Conflict-Affected State?"

52. Mungiu-Pippidi, *Quest for Good Governance*, 204.

53. There is a controversy within the aid field about providing money to unelected nonprofit organizations versus state budgets. Many development experts claim that by ignoring the state, aid weakens governments and fails to build local skill at managing services. Legitimate states do need to be strengthened to deliver for their people, and the critique of unelected and often equally biased nonprofits is a fair one. In areas such as education and health, providing assistance through the government, with monitoring and controls, may make sense to deliver services, though in more corrupt environments it is unlikely to change the basic problems that have led to the poor governance and could cause others.

54. See Carothers and Brechenmacher, *Closing Space*; and Rutzen, "Civil Society Under Assault."

55. In FY 2018, the total planned foreign budget according to the U.S. government is $27.3 billion (this includes security, the largest category at $7.7 billion). Of this figure, $261.55 million is earmarked for civil society, disbursed through State and USAID, which means that 0.96 percent of the foreign budget goes to civil society funding. Robinson, "Out of the Ivory Tower," 60.

56. In Paris, participatory budgeting was instituted by Mayor Anne Hidalgo in 2014. AmericaSpeaks organized over twenty-five hundred New Orleans residents who had dispersed following Hurricane Katrina into forty-eight deliberative rounds to plan for disaster recovery, a process that in addition to aiding planning, also fostered social trust. See Wilson, "Deliberative Planning."

57. Finoff, "Decomposing Inequality and Poverty in Post-war Rwanda," 209.

58. Arriola, *Multiethnic Coalitions in Africa*.

59. Moncada, "Business and the Politics of Urban Violence in Colombia."

60. Witold Henisz, in *Corporate Diplomacy*, suggests that extractive industries are faring less well economically than they could be because they are doing such a poor job of improving the social environments in which they work. As a board member of extractive companies such as Rio Tinto, he has the ability to have influence, but his ideas are not yet mainstream in the industry.

61. See the National Security Archive.

62. See the testimony of José Gregorio Mangones Lugo, a.k.a. Carlos Tijeras, former AUC commander, and Salvatore Mancuso, entered into the court record in cases against Chiquita and Dole.

63. Canales, "From Ideas to Institutions"; Kleinfeld, *Let There Be Light*.

64. Felbab-Brown, Trinkunas, and Hamid, *Militants, Criminals, and Warlords*, 107.

65. Gambetta, *Sicilian Mafia*, 32; Ministry of Interior data cited in *Repubblica*, 1991; and "Camorra-Neapolitan Mafia." If you think about it, this makes sense. The Mafia's primary business is extortion and the promise that it will protect transactions in the face of a broken state. So its incentive is to both allow more crime and break the state's ability to fight back so that its protection is more valuable and more people will turn to its services.

66. Leopoldo Franchetti's report on the Mafia in Sicily, cited and translated in Dickie, *Cosa Nostra*, 56.

67. World Bank, *World Development Report 2011*, 2.

68. McEvoy and Hideg, "Global Violent Deaths 2017," 1.

BIBLIOGRAPHY

Abadie, Alberto. "Poverty, Political Freedom, and the Roots of Terrorism." *American Economic Review* 96, no. 2 (2006): 50–56.

Abadinsky, Howard. *Organized Crime*. Boston: Cengage Learning, 1990.

Abbot, Edith. "The Civil War and the Crime Wave of 1865–70." *Social Service Review* 1 (1927): 212–34.

Abrahamse, Allan F., Patricia A. Ebener, and Peter W. Greenwood. "An Experimental Evaluation of the Phoenix Repeat Offender Program." *Justice Quarterly* 8 (1991): 141–68.

Abrahms, Max. "Why Terrorism Does Not Work." *International Security* 31 (2006): 42–78.

Acemoglu, Daron, and James A. Robinson. *The Economic Origins of Dictatorship and Democracy*. New York: Cambridge University Press, 2006.

Acemoglu, Daron, James A. Robinson, and Rafael J. Santos. "The Monopoly of Violence: Evidence from Colombia." *Journal of the European Economic Association* 11 (2013): 5–44.

Agnone, J. "Amplifying Public Opinion: The Policy Impact of the U.S. Environmental Movement." *Social Forces* 85, no. 4 (2007): 1,593–620.

Ahmad, Yusuf, Alyssa Dougherty, Rachel Kleinfeld, and Alejandro Ponce. *Reducing Violence and Improving the Rule of Law: Organized Crime, Marginalized Communities, and the Political Machine*. Washington, D.C.: Carnegie Endowment for International Peace and World Justice Project, 2014.

Ahmed, Farzand, and Dilip Bobb. "Bhagalpur: An Area of Darkness." *India Today*, Nov. 29, 2013.

Ahram, Ariel I. *Proxy Warriors: The Rise and Fall of State-Sponsored Militias*. Stanford, Calif.: Stanford University Press, 2011.

Aiyar, Swaminathan S. Anklesaria. "Bihar: How the Poorest, Worst Governed State Attained Double-Digit Growth and Became a Role Model." In *Economic Freedom of the State of India: 2013*, edited by Swaminathan S. Anklesaria Aiyar, Bibek Debroy, and Laveesh Bhandari. Washington, D.C.: Cato Institute, 2014.

Alesina, Alberto, and Beatrice Weder. "Do Corrupt Governments Receive Less Foreign Aid?" *American Economic Review* 92, no. 4 (2002): 1,126–37.

Alexander, Michelle. *The New Jim Crow*. New York: New Press, 2010.

Allen, James. *Without Sanctuary: Lynching Photography in America*. Santa Fe, N.M.: Twin Palms, 2000.

Allum, Felia, and Percy Allum. "Revisiting Naples: Clientelism and Organized Crime." In *Italy Today: The Sick Man of Europe*, edited by Andrea Mammone and Giuseppe A. Veltri. New York: Routledge, 2010.

Alschuler, Albert W. "Plea Bargaining and Its History." *Colombia Law Review* 79, no. 1 (1979).

Alsema, Adriaan. "Fact Sheets: Cali Crime Statistics." *Colombia Reports*, March 10, 2013.

Alvarez, Alex. "Militias and Genocide." *War Crimes, Genocide, and Crimes Against Humanity* 2 (2006): 1–33.

Alvazzi del Frate, Anna, Keith Krause, and Matthias Nowak, eds. *Global Burden of Armed Violence 2015: Every Body Counts*. Geneva: Geneva Declaration, 2015.

Amenta, Edwin, and Neal Caren. "The Legislative, Organizational, and Beneficiary Consequences of State-Oriented Challengers." In *The Blackwell Companion to Social Movements*, edited by David Snow, Sarah Soule, and Hanspeter Kriesi, 461–88. Malden, Mass.: Blackwell, 2004.

Amenta, Edwin, Neal Caren, Elizabeth Chiarello, and Yang Su. "The Political Consequences of Social Movements." *Annual Review of Sociology* 36, no. 1 (2010): 287–307.

American National Election Studies Cumulative Data File, 1948–2008. ICPSR08475—v14. Ann Arbor, Mich.: Inter-university Consortium for Political and Social Research, 2011. doi:10.3886/ICPSR08475.v14.

Amnesty International. *Stars on Their Shoulders, Blood on Their Hands: War Crimes Committed by the Nigerian Military*. London: Amnesty International, 2015.

"Analysis of Background Details of Winners in Bihar MLC Elections—2015." Delhi: Association for Democratic Reforms, 2015.

Anandi, Anisha. "Bihar: HC Acquits 26 Convicted of Laxmanpur-Bathe Carnage." *Times of India*, Oct. 10, 2013.

Anderson, D. M. "Vigilantes, Violence, and the Politics of Public Order in Kenya." *African Affairs* 101 (2002): 531–55.

Andreas, Peter. "The Political Economy of Narco-corruption in Mexico." *Current History* 97 (1998).

Andreas, Peter, Eva C. Bertram, Morris J. Blachman, and Kenneth E. Sharpe. "Dead-End Drug Wars." *Foreign Policy* 85 (1991).

Andreu-Guzmán, Federico. "Criminal Justice and Forced Displacement in Colombia." In *Case Studies in Transitional Justice and Displacement*. Brookings-LSE Project on Internal Displacement. New York: International Center on Transitional Justice, 2013.

"Annual Report 2003–2004." New Delhi: Ministry of Home Affairs, Government of India, 2005.

"Anti-Mafia Commission Report on the Camorra." Rome: Italian Parliament, 1993.

"April 9, 1989 Soviet Crackdown in Tbilisi." Radio Free Europe/Radio Liberty Photo Blog, April 7, 2014, http://www.rferl.org.

Arce, Alberto. "Dad Seeks Justice for Son Killed in Broken Honduras." *USA Today*, Nov. 12, 2012.

Arce, Alberto, and Martha Mendoza. "Tragic Killing of Honduran Teen Leaves Us Asking Questions." *Christian Science Monitor*, Nov. 14, 2012.

Archer, Dane, and Rosemary Gartner. *Violence and Crime in Cross-National Perspective.* New Haven, Conn.: Yale University Press, 1984.

Arias, Enrique Desmond. "A Cross-National Comparison." In *Maras: Gang Violence and Security in Central America*, edited by Thomas Bruneau, Lucia Dammert, and Elizabeth Skinner. Austin: University of Texas Press, 2011.

Aristotle, *The Basic Works of Aristotle.* New York: Random House, 1941.

Armes, Ethel. *The Story of Coal and Iron in Alabama.* Cambridge, Mass.: University Press, 1910.

Armstrong, Michael. *They Wished They Were Honest: The Knapp Commission and New York City Police Corruption.* New York: Columbia University Press, 2012.

Arriola, Leonardo R. *Multiethnic Coalitions in Africa: Business Financing of Opposition Election Campaigns.* Cambridge, U.K.: Cambridge University Press, 2012.

Arsenault, Raymond. *Freedom Riders: 1961 and the Struggle for Racial Justice.* Oxford: Oxford University Press, 2006.

Asfura-Heim, P., and R. Espach. "The Rise of Mexico's Self-Defense Forces: Vigilante Justice South of the Border." *Foreign Affairs* 92, no. 4 (2013): 143–50.

Ash, Stephen. *A Massacre in Memphis: The Race Riot That Shook the Nation One Year After the Civil War.* New York: Hill and Wang, 2014.

Association for Democratic Reforms. "Analysis of Background Details of Winners in Bihar MLC Elections—2015." Delhi: Association for Democratic Reforms, 2015.

Astorga, Luis, and David A. Shirk. *Drug Trafficking Organizations and Counter Drug Strategies in the U.S.–Mexican Context.* San Diego: Center for U.S.–Mexican Studies, University of California San Diego, 2010.

Atran, Scott. "ISIS Is a Revolution." *Aeon* (2015).

———. "Scott Atran on Youth, Violent Extremism, and Promoting Peace." blogs.plos.org.

Ayers, Edward L. *The Promise of the New South.* New York: Oxford University Press, 1992.

———. *Vengeance and Justice: Crime and Punishment in the 19th-Century American South.* Oxford: Oxford University Press, 1984.

Bachman, Daniel. "Income Inequality in the United States: What Do We Know and What Does It Mean?" *Deloitte Insights, Issues by the Numbers*, July 2017.

Bacon, Laura and Rushda Majeed. "Palermo Renaissance Part 1." In *Innovations for Successful Societies.* Princeton, N.J.: Princeton University, 2012.

Bailey, Amy Kate, and Stewart E. Tolnay. *Lynched: The Victims of Southern Mob Violence.* Chapel Hill: University of North Carolina Press, 2015.

Bailey, John J. "What Can Mexico Learn from Colombia to Combat Organized Crime?" In *One Goal, Two Struggles: Confronting Crime and Violence in Mexico and Colombia,* edited by Cynthia C. Arnson, Eric L. Olson, and Christine Zaino. Washington, D.C.: Wilson Center, 2014.

Bailey, John J., and Roy Godson, eds. *Organized Crime and Democratic Governability: Mexico and the U.S.–Mexican Borderlands.* Pittsburgh: University of Pittsburgh Press, 2001.

Baird, Adam. "The Violent Gang and the Construction of Masculinity Amongst Socially Excluded Young Men." *Safer Communities* 11, no. 4 (2012): 179–90.

Baker, Kevin. "The Courthouse That Graft Built." *New York Times,* March 23, 2002.

Balchand, K. "Naxalites Lay Siege to Jehanabad, Free Cadre from Jail." *Hindu,* Nov. 14, 2005.

———. "Rabri Sworn in CM, Given 10 Days to Prove Majority." *Hindu,* March 12, 2000.

Balko, Radley. "The Disturbing Messages in Police Recruiting Videos." *Washington Post,* April 16, 2014.

———. *Rise of the Warrior Cop: The Militarization of America's Police Forces.* New York: Public Affairs, 2014.

Barber, Michael, and Nolan McCarty. "Causes and Consequences of Polarization." In *Negotiating Agreement in Politics,* edited by Jane Mansbridge and Cathie Jo Martin, 19–53. Washington, D.C.: American Political Science Association, 2013.

Barclay, G., and C. Tavares. "International Comparisons of Criminal Justice Statistics 2001." London: U.K. Home Office, 2003.

Bardhan, Pranab. "Corruption and Development: A Review of the Issues." *Journal of Economic Literature* 35, no. 3 (1997): 1,331.

Bargent, James. "Colombia Police Dismantle Hundreds of Gangs in 2012." *InSight Crime,* June 21, 2013.

Barnes, Donna A., and Catherine Connolly. "Repression, the Judicial System, and Political Opportunities for Civil Rights Advocacy During Reconstruction." *Sociological Quarterly* 40, no. 2 (1999): 327–45.

Barnett, Michael. "Building a Republican Peace: Stabilizing States After War." *International Security* 30, no. 4 (Spring 2006): 87–112.

Baron, Stephen, John Field, and Tom Schuller. *Social Capital: Critical Perspectives.* Oxford: Oxford University Press, 2000.

Bartoletti, Susan Campbell. *They Called Themselves the KKK.* New York: Houghton Mifflin, 2010.

Bashir, Omar S. "Testing Inferences About American Politics: A Review of the 'Oligarchy' Result." *Research and Politics* 2, no. 4 (2015).

Basra, Rajah, Peter Neumann, and Claudia Brunner. "Criminal Pasts, Terrorist

Futures: European Jihadists and the New Crime-Terror Nexus." London: ICSR, Oct. 2016.

Bayley, David H. *Patterns of Policing: A Comparative International Analysis.* New Brunswick, N.J.: Rutgers University Press, 1990.

Beardsley, Kyle. "Peacekeeping and the Contagion of Conflict." *The Journal of Politics* 73, no. 4 (2011).

Beck, E. M., and Stewart E. Tolnay. "The Killing Fields of the Deep South: The Market for Cotton and the Lynching of Blacks." *American Sociological Review* 55, no. 4 (1990): 526–39.

Behan, Tom. *The Camorra.* London: Routledge, 1996.

Bejarano, Ana María. "The Constitution of 1991." In *Violence in Colombia, 1990–2000,* edited by Charles Bergquist, Ricardo Peñaranda, and Gonzalo Sánchez, 53–74. Wilmington, Del.: Scholarly Resources, 2001.

Bendix, Reinhard. *Nation Building and Citizenship.* Berkeley: University of California Press, 1977.

Benítez Manaut, Raúl. "Containing Armed Groups, Drug Trafficking, and Organized Crime in Mexico: The Role of the Military." In Bailey and Godson, *Organized Crime and Democratic Governability,* 126–58.

Benmelech, Efraim, Claude Berrebi, and Esteban F. Klor. "Economic Conditions and the Quality of Suicide Terrorism." Working paper, National Bureau of Economic Research, 2010.

Bennett, Richard. "Delivering on the Hope of the Rose Revolution: Public Sector Reform in Georgia, 2004–2009." In *Innovations for Successful Societies.* Princeton, N.J.: Princeton University, 2011.

Benson, George C. S., Alan Heslop, and Steven A. Maaranen. *Political Corruption in America.* Lexington, Mass.: Lexington Books, 1978.

Bergen, Peter, Albert Ford, Alyssa Sims, and David Sterman. "Terrorism in America After 9/11." New America, www.newamerica.org.

Berman, Sherri. "Civil Society and the Collapse of the Weimar Republic." *World Politics* 49 (April 1997).

Bhatia, Bela. "Jailbreak and the Maoist Movement." *Economic and Political Weekly* 40, no. 41 (2005): 5,369–71.

———. "The Naxalite Movement in Central Bihar." *Economic and Political Weekly* 40, no. 15 (2005): 1,536–49.

Blackmon, Douglas A. "Hard Time: From Alabama's Past, Capitalism and Racism in a Cruel Partnership." *Wall Street Journal,* July 16, 2001.

Blakey, Robert G. "RICO: The Genesis of an Idea." *Legal Studies Research Paper,* No. 08-18, University of Notre Dame Law School.

Blaydes, Lisa, and Eric Chaney. "The Feudal Revolution and Europe's Rise: Political Divergence of the Christian West and the Muslim World Before 1500 CE." *American Political Science Review* 17, no. 1 (2013): 16–34.

———. "Political Economy Legacy of Institutions from the Classical Period of Islam." In *The New Palgrave Dictionary of Economics,* edited by Palgrave Macmillan. London: Palgrave Macmillan, 2016.

Blum, Howard. *Gangland: How the FBI Broke the Mob.* New York: Simon & Schuster, 2009.

Blumenthal, M. D., R. I. Kahn, F. M. Andrews, and K. B. Head. *Justifying Violence.* Ann Arbor: University of Michigan Press, 1972.

Bommersbach, Jana. "Dead Wrong About Cattle Kate." *True West,* Oct. 9, 2014.

Booth, J. A., and T. W. Walker. *Understanding Latin America.* Boulder, Colo.: Westview, 1993.

Bouvier, Virginia M. "Colombia's Crossroads: The FARC and the Future of the Hostages." Washington, D.C.: U.S. Institute of Peace, 2008.

Bove, Vincenzo, and Evelina Gavrilova. "Police Officer on the Frontline or a Soldier? The Effect of Police Militarization on Crime." *American Economic Journal: Economic Policy* 9, no. 3 (Aug. 2017): 1–18.

Bowden, Mark. *Killing Pablo: The Hunt for the World's Greatest Outlaw.* New York: Penguin Books, 2001.

Bowen, John Richard. "The Myth of Global Ethnic Conflict." *Journal of Democracy* 7, no. 4 (1996): 3–14.

Braga, Anthony, and David Weisburd. "Pulling Levers: Focused Deterrence Strategies to Prevent Crime." *Crime Prevention Research Review* 6. Washington, D.C.: Department of Justice, Office of Community Oriented Policing Services, 2012.

Brancati, Dawn. *Democracy Protests.* Cambridge, U.K.: Cambridge University Press, 2016.

Brand, Peter, and Julio D. Dávila. "Mobility Innovation at the Urban Margins: Medellín's Metrocables." *City* 15, no. 6 (2011): 647–66.

Branham, Alexander, Stuart N. Soroka, and Christopher Wlezien. "When Do the Rich Win?" *Political Science Quarterly* 132, no. 1 (2017): 43–62.

Braütigam, Deborah A., and Stephen Knack. "Foreign Aid, Institutions, and Governance in Sub-Saharan Africa." *Economic Development and Cultural Change* 52, no. 2 (2004): 255–85.

"Brazil's Political Crisis." *Economist,* March 26, 2016.

"Breaking the Grip: Obstacles to Justice for Paramilitary Mafias in Colombia." Washington D.C.: Human Rights Watch, 2008.

Breslow, Jason M. "The Staggering Death Toll of Mexico's Drug War." *PBS Frontline* (2015). www.pbs.org.

Brooke, James. "A Drug Lord Is Buried as a Folk Hero." *New York Times,* Dec. 4, 1993.

Brown, Frances Z. and Mara Karlin. "Friends with Benefits: What the Reliance on Local Partners Means for U.S. Strategy." *Foreign Affairs.* May 8, 2018.

Bryant, Jonathan. "Ku Klux Klan in the Reconstruction Era." www.georgiaencyclopedia.org.

Buchanan, Cornelia, Liz DeAngelo, Ruidan Ma, and Chris Taylor. "Mano Dura in the Americas: Who Supports Iron Fist Rule?" *Americas Barometer Insights* 80 (2012).

Bulíř, Aleš, and A. Javier Hamann. "Volatility of Development Aid: From the Frying Pan into the Fire?" *World Development* 36, no. 10 (2008): 2,048–66.

Burnett, John, Marisa Peñaloza, and Robert Benincasa. "Mexico Seems to Favor Sinaloa Cartel in Drug War." NPR, May 19, 2010. www.npr.org.

Burnside, Craig, and David Dollar. "Aid, Policies, and Growth: Reply." *American Economic Review* 94, no. 3 (2004): 781–84.

Burr, L., and S. Jensen. "Introduction: Vigilantism and the Policing of Everyday Life in South Africa." *African Studies* 63, no. 2 (2004): 139–52.

Burrill, Donald R. *Servants of the Law: Judicial Politics on the California Frontier, 1849–89.* Lanham, Md.: University Press of America, 2011.

Burrows, Edwin, and Mike Wallace. *Gotham: A History of New York City to 1898.* Oxford: Oxford University Press, 1999.

Burton, Michael, and John Higley. "Political Crises and Elite Settlements." In *Elites, Crises, and the Origins of Regimes,* edited by Mattei Dogan and John Higley. Lanham, Md.: Rowman & Littlefield, 1998.

Bush, George W. "Opening Letter." In *U.S. National Security Strategy.* Washington, D.C.: White House, 2002.

Byman, D., and S. Kreps. "Agents of Destruction? Applying Principal-Agent Analysis to State-Sponsored Terrorism." *International Studies Quarterly* 11, no. 1 (2010): 1–18.

Byrd, Robert C. *The Senate, 1789–1989.* Vol. 3, *Classic Speeches, 1830–1993.* Courtesy of the U.S. Senate Historical Office.

Calder, James D. *Intelligence, Espionage, and Related Topics, 1844–1998.* Westport, Conn.: Greenwood Press, 1999.

Calhoun, Charles W. *From Bloody Shirt to Full Dinner Pail: The Transformation of Politics and Governance in the Gilded Age.* New York: Hill and Wang, 2011.

Call, Charles. "Knowing Peace When You See It: Setting Standards for Peacebuilding Success." *Civil Wars* 10, no. 2 (2008): 173–94.

"Camorra." Global Security, 2015. www.globalsecurity.org.

Campbell, B. B., and A. D. Brenner, eds. *Death Squads in Global Perspective: Murder with Deniability.* New York: Palgrave Macmillan, 2002.

Canales, Rodrigo. "From Ideals to Institutions: Institutional Entrepreneurship in Mexican Small Business Finance." *Organization Science* 27, no. 6 (2016): 1,548–73.

Capoccia, Giovanni, and R. Daniel Kelemen. "The Study of Critical Junctures: Theory, Narrative, and Counterfactuals in Historical Institutionalism." *World Politics* 59 (April 2007): 341–69.

Carey, Sabine C., Michael P. Colaresi, and Neil J. Mitchell. "Governments, Informal Links to Militias, and Accountability." *Journal of Conflict Resolution* 59, no. 5 (2015): 850–76.

Carey, Sabine C., Neil J. Mitchell, and W. Lowe. "States, the Security Sector, and the Monopoly of Violence: A New Database on Pro-government Militias." *Journal of Conflict Resolution* 50 (2013): 249–58.

Carman, Harry J., and Reinhard H. Luthin. *Lincoln and the Patronage.* New York: Columbia University Press, 1943.

Caro, Robert A. *Master of the Senate.* New York: Vintage Books, 2002.

———. *Means of Ascent.* New York: Alfred A. Knopf, 1990.

———. *The Path to Power.* New York: Alfred A. Knopf, 1982.

Carothers, Thomas, and Saskia Brechenmacher. "Closing Space: Democracy and Human Rights Support Under Fire." Washington, D.C.: Carnegie Endowment for International Peace, 2014.

Carothers, Thomas, and Christopher Carothers. "Seeking Political Stability Abroad? Fight Corruption." *National Interest,* Jan. 25, 2018.

Carothers, Thomas, and Richard Youngs. "The Complexities of Global Protests." Washington, D.C.: Carnegie Endowment, Oct. 8, 2015.

Carpenter, Murray. "Justice, Interrupted." *Pacific Standard,* March 15, 2016.

Carrillo Flórez, Fernando. "La séptima papeleta: El sueño estudiantil que cambió la historia." *El Tiempo,* July 3, 2016.

Carson, Clayborne, Tenisha H. Armstrong, Susan A. Carson, Erin K. Cook, and Susan Englander. *The Martin Luther King Jr. Encyclopedia.* Santa Barbara, Calif.: Greenwood Press, 2008.

Casey, Michel. "The U.S. Is a Good Place for Bad People to Stash Their Money." *Atlantic,* July 13, 2017.

Casey, Nicholas, and Ana Vanessa Herrero. "How a Politician Accused of Drug Trafficking Became Venezuela's Vice President." *New York Times,* Feb. 16, 2017.

Castro, Daniel. "The Trail of Death." *InSight Crime,* May 8, 2014.

Cearley, Anna. "A Cop Marked for Death." *San Diego Tribune,* March 13, 2005.

Cederman, Lars-Erik, and Luc Girardin. "Beyond Fractionalization: Mapping Ethnicity onto Nationalist Insurgencies." *American Political Science Review* 101, no. 1 (2007): 173–85.

Celasun, Oya, and Jan Walliser. "Predictability of Aid: Do Fickle Donors Undermine Aid Effectiveness?" *Economic Policy* 55 (2008): 546–94.

Cella, Matthew, and Alan Neuhauser. "Race and Homicide in America, by the Numbers." *U.S. News & World Report,* Sept. 29, 2016. www.usnews.com.

Cerdá, Magdalena, Jeffrey D. Morenoff, Ben B. Hansen, Kimberly J. Tessari Hicks, Luis F. Duque, Alexandra Restrepo, and Ana V. Diez-Roux. "Reducing Violence by Transforming Neighborhoods: A Natural Experiment in Medellín, Colombia." *American Journal of Epidemiology* 175, no. 10 (2012): 1,045–53.

Chakrabarti, Rajesh. *Bihar Breakthrough: The Turnaround of a Beleaguered State.* New Delhi: Rupa, 2013.

Charbonneau, Louis, and Michelle Nichols. "Exclusive: Rwanda Army Officers Aiding M23 Rebels in Congo—U.N. Experts." Reuters, June 28, 2013.

Chaudhart, Pranava K. "Where Booth Capturing Was Born." *Times of India,* Feb. 14, 2005.

Chayes, Sarah. *Honduras: Corruption as the Operating System.* Washington, D.C.: Carnegie Endowment for International Peace, 2017.

———. *The Punishment of Virtue: Inside Afghanistan After the Taliban.* London: Penguin, 2006.

Cheng-Hopkins, Judy. Afterword to *The United Nations SSR Perspective.* www.un .org.

Chenoweth, Erica. "Why Social Media Helps Dictators." *Foreign Policy,* Nov. 16, 2016.

Chenoweth, Erica, and Maria J. Stephan. *Why Civil Resistance Works: The Strategic Logic of Nonviolent Conflict.* New York: Columbia University Press, 2011.

Chepesiuk, Ron. *Drug Lords: The Rise and Fall of the Cali Cartel.* Wrea Green: Milo Books, 2005.

Chesterman, Simon, Michael Ignatieff, and Ramesh Thakur. *Making States Work: State Failure and the Crisis of Governance.* Tokyo: United Nations University Press, 2005.

Chevigny, Paul. *Edge of the Knife: Police Violence in the Americas.* New York: New Press, 1997.

Chilton, Martin. "Merle Haggard: 'Sometimes I Wish I Hadn't Written Okie from Muskogee.'" *Telegraph,* April 8, 2016.

Christensen, Matthew. "The 1868 St. Landry Massacre: Reconstruction's Deadliest Episode of Violence." *Theses and Dissertations* (2012): paper 190.

Civil Rights Movement Veterans. "The Sit-Ins: Off Campus and into Movement" photo archive. www.crmvet.org.

Clegg, Claude Andrew, III. *An Original Man: The Life and Times of Elijah Muhammad.* New York: St. Martin's Press, 1997.

Cliffe, Sarah, and Nigel Roberts. *World Development Report 2011.* Washington, D.C.: World Bank, 2011.

Cohen, D. K., and R. Nordas. "Do States Delegate Shameful Violence to Militias? Patterns of Sexual Violence in Recent Armed Conflicts." *Journal of Conflict Resolution* 59, no. 5 (2015): 877–98.

Cohen, Sascha. "Why the Woolworth's Sit-In Worked," *Time,* Feb. 2, 2015.

Cohen, Stanley. *States of Denial: Knowing About Atrocities and Suffering.* London: Polity, 2001.

Colazingari, Silvia, and Susan Rose-Ackerman. "Corruption in a Paternalistic Democracy: Lessons from Italy for Latin America." *Political Science Quarterly* 113, no. 3 (1998): 447–70.

Collier, Paul, and Anke Hoeffler. "Greed and Grievance in Civil War." *Oxford Economic Papers* 56, no. 4 (2004): 563–95.

"Colombia: Peace at Last?" International Crisis Group, 2012.

"Colombian Government Dismisses 27 Top Army Officers." McClatchy, October 30, 2008.

"Confirmed: The FISA Court Is Less of a Rubber Stamp Than Article III Courts." *Empty Wheel,* June 28, 2017. Available online at www.emptywheel.net.

"Corruption in Conflict: Lessons from the U.S. Experience in Afghanistan." Washington D.C.: Special Inspector General for Afghanistan Reconstruction, September 2016.

"Corruption in Romania: People v Pilferers." *Economist*, Feb. 11, 2017.

Committee to Protect Journalists. "2016 Impunity Index."

Conlin, Joseph Robert. *The American Past: A Survey of American History*. Boston: Wadsworth, Cengage, 2012.

Consejo Ciudadano para la Seguridad Pública y la Justicia Penal A.C. "World's 50 Most Violent Cities: 2015 Rankings." Mexico: Consejo Ciudadano para la Seguridad Pública y la Justicia Penal, 2015.

Cooke, Jennifer G., and Thomas M. Sanderson. "Militancy and the Arc of Instability." Washington, D.C.: Center for Strategic and International Studies, 2016.

Cooper, Alexia, and Erica L. Smith. "Homicide Trends in the United States, 1980–2008." Washington, D.C.: U.S. Department of Justice, Bureau of Justice Statistics, 2011.

Corchado, Alfredo. *Midnight in Mexico: A Reporter's Journey Through a Country's Descent into Darkness*. New York: Penguin Books, 2014.

Corman, Hope, and Naci Mocan. "Carrots, Sticks, and Broken Windows." NBER Working Paper No. 9061 (2002).

Cornish, W. "Legal Control over Cartels and Monopolisation, 1880–1914: A Comparison." In *Law and the Formation of Big Enterprises in the 19th and the Early 20th Centuries*, edited by N. Horn and J. Kocka. Göttingen: Vandenhoeck & Ruprecht, 1979.

"Corruption in Conflict: Lessons from the U.S. Experience in Afghanistan." Washington, D.C.: Special Inspector General for Afghanistan Reconstruction, Sept. 2016.

Courtwright, David T. *Violent Land: Single Men and Social Disorder from the Frontier to the Inner City*. Cambridge, Mass.: Harvard University Press, 2009.

"Crime and Development in Latin America." Vienna: United Nations Office of Drugs and Crime, 2007.

"Crime in Brazil: Mourning Marielle," *Economist*, March 24, 2018.

Criminal Justice Statistics Center. "Homicide in California, 1993–2004." State of California, Department of Justice. ag.ca.gov.

Cronin, Audrey Kurth. *How Terrorism Ends: Understanding the Decline and Demise of Terrorist Campaigns*. Princeton, N.J.: Princeton University Press, 2011.

Crost, Benjamin, Joseph Felter, and Patrick Johnston. "Aid Under Fire: Development Projects and Civil Conflict." *American Economic Review* 104, no. 6 (2014): 1,833–56.

Curie, Elliott. *Crime and Punishment in America*. New York: Macmillan, 1998.

Curtin, Jeremiah. *The Mongols: A History*. Cambridge, Mass.: Da Capo Press, 2003.

Curtis, Richard. "The Improbable Transformation of Inner-City Neighborhoods: Crime, Violence, Drugs, and Youth in the 1990s." *Journal of Criminal Law and Criminology* 88, no. 4 (1998).

Czerniecka, Katarzyna, and John Heathershaw. "Security and Border Management." In *The European Union and Central Asia*, edited by Alexander Warkotsch. New York: Routledge, 2010.

Dadalauri, Nina. "Political Corruption: The Case of Georgia." In *Corruption and Development: The Anti-corruption Campaigns*, edited by Sarah Bracking, 155–66. London: Palgrave Macmillan, 2007.

Dainotto, Roberto. *The Mafia: A Cultural History*. London: Reaktion Books, 2015.

Dalton, Kathleen. *Theodore Roosevelt: A Strenuous Life*. New York: Vintage Books, 2002.

Daly, Martin, and Margo Wilson. *Homicide*. New Brunswick, N.J.: Transaction, 1988.

Darby, J., and R. MacGinty, eds. *Contemporary Peacemaking: Conflict, Peace Processes, and Post-war Reconstruction*. 2nd ed. London: Palgrave Macmillan, 2008.

Davidson, Chandler, and Bernard Grofman, eds. *Quiet Revolution in the South*. Princeton, N.J.: Princeton University Press, 1994.

Davis, D. "Undermining the Rule of Law: Democratization and the Dark Side of Police Reform in Mexico." *Latin American Politics and Society* 48, no. 1 (2006): 55–86.

Davis, Jack. "The Bogotazo." Washington, D.C.: Center for the Study of Intelligence, 1996.

Dawson, Andrew. "The Social Determinants of the Rule of Law: A Comparison of Jamaica and Barbados." *World Development* 45 (2013): 314–24.

Day, Michael. "Silvio Berlusconi's Links to Organized Crime Confirmed." *Independent*, May 12, 2014.

Definitive Adoption (EU, Euratom) 2016/150 of the European Union's General Budget for the Financial Year 2016.

de Freytas-Tamura, Kimiko. "Public Shaming and Even Prison for Plastic Bag Use in Rwanda." *New York Times*, Oct. 28, 2017.

Della Porta, Donatella. *Social Movements, Political Violence, and the State*. Cambridge, U.K.: Cambridge University Press, 1995.

Della Porta, Donatella, and Mario Diani. *Social Movements: An Introduction*. Malden, Mass.: Blackwell, 2006.

Devlin, Matthew, and Sebastian Chaskel. "Conjuring and Consolidating a Turnaround: Governance in Bogotá, 1992–2003." In *Innovations for Successful Societies*. Princeton, N.J.: Princeton University, 2010.

———. "From Fear to Hope in Colombia: Sergio Fajardo and Medellín, 2004–2007." In *Innovations for Successful Societies*. Princeton, N.J.: Princeton University, 2011.

———. "Organizing the Return of Government to Conflict Zones: Colombia, 2004–2009." In *Innovations for Successful Societies*. Princeton, N.J.: Princeton University, 2010.

DeWaal, Alex. "The Political Marketplace: Analyzing Political Entrepreneurs and Political Bargaining with a Business Lens." In *Memorandum—World Peace Foundation Seminar,* 2014.

de Waal, Thomas. *The Caucasus: An Introduction.* Oxford: Oxford University Press, 2010.

Dey, Abhishek. "Naxalites in Noida: Have Maoist Splinter Groups Supported by the State Taken to Crime?" *Scroll.in,* Oct. 19, 2016.

DeYoung, Karen. "U.S. Trucking Funds Reach Taliban, Military-Led Investigation Concludes." *Washington Post,* July 24, 2011.

Diamond, Larry. "Facing Up to the Democratic Recession." *Journal of Democracy* 26, no. 1 (2015): 141–55.

———. *Spirit of Democracy: The Struggle to Build Free Societies Throughout the World.* New York: Hold and Company, 2008.

Dickie, John. *Blood Brotherhoods: A History of Italy's Three Mafias.* New York: Public Affairs, 2014.

———. *Cosa Nostra: A History of the Sicilian Mafia.* London: Palgrave Macmillan, 2004.

Di John, Jonathan, and James Putzel. "Political Settlements: Issues Paper." Governance and Social Development Resource Centre, 2009.

Dingley, James. *The IRA.* Santa Barbara, Calif.: Praeger, 2012.

Direzione Investigativa Antimafia. "Camorra." Semi-annual report, Italian Parliament Anti-Mafia Commission, Dec. 21, 1993. Rome: Ministry of the Interior, 1993.

Dix, Sarah, Karen Hussmann, and Grant Walton. *Risks of Corruption to State Legitimacy and Stability in Fragile Situations.* Bergen: U4 Anti-corruption Resource Centre, 2012.

Dobbins, Jaomes et al. *The UN's Role in Nation-Building.* Santa Monica: RAND Corporation, 2005.

Dobson, William J. *The Dictator's Learning Curve.* New York: Anchor Books, 2013.

Dollard, John. *Caste and Class in a Southern Town.* Garden City, N.Y.: Doubleday Anchor, 1949.

Donohue, John, and Steven Levitt. "Legalized Abortion and Crime." *Quarterly Journal of Economics* 116 (2001): 379–420.

Dowdney, Luke. *Neither War nor Peace: International Comparison of Children and Youth in Organized Armed Violence.* Rio de Janeiro: Viva Rio and COAV, 2005.

Doyle, Michael W., and Nicholas Sambanis. "International Peacebuilding: A Theoretical and Quantitative Analysis." *American Political Science Review* 94, no. 4 (2000): 779–801.

Dreier, Peter. "The Little Known Story of 'We Shall Overcome.'" *Huffington Post,* Aug. 29, 2013.

Dripps, Donald A. "Guilt, Innocence, and Due Process of Plea Bargaining." *William and Mary Law Review* 57, no. 4 (2016): 1,343–93.

Driscoll, Jesse. *Warlords and Coalition Politics in Post-Soviet States.* Cambridge, U.K.: Cambridge University Press, 2015.

Dudley, Steven. "Homicides in Guatemala: Introduction, Methodology, and Major Findings." *InSight Crime,* 2017. www.insightcrime.org.

———. "How 'Mano Dura' Is Strengthening Gangs." *InSight Crime,* 2010. www.insightcrime.org.

———. *Walking Ghosts: Murder and Guerrilla Politics in Colombia.* New York: Routledge, 2006.

Dudziak, Mary. *Cold War Civil Rights: Race and the Image of American Democracy.* Princeton, N.J.: Princeton University Press, 2011.

Duggan, Christopher. *Fascism and the Mafia.* New Haven, Conn.: Yale University Press, 1989.

Duke, Naomi N., Sandra L. Pettingell, Barbara J. McMorris, and Iris W. Borowsky. "Adolescent Violence Perpetration: Associations with Multiple Types of Adverse Childhood Experiences." *Pediatrics* 124, no. 4 (2010): e778–e86.

Dunning, David, and Emily Balcetis. "Wishful Seeing: How Preferences Shape Visual Perception." *Current Directions in Psychological Science* 22, no. 1 (2013): 33–37.

Durose, Matthew R., Alexia D. Cooper, and Howard N. Snyder. *Recidivism of Prisoners Released in 30 States in 2005: Patterns from 2005 to 2010.* Washington, D.C.: Bureau of Justice Statistics Special Report, 2014.

Dyner, Anna, Arkadiusz Legiec, and Kacper Rekawek. "Ready to Go? ISIS and Its Presumed Expansion into Central Asia." Policy Paper No. 19 (121), Polish Institute of International Affairs, 2015.

Eberlein, Sven. "How Gondolas and Hip Hop Transformed the Most Dangerous City in the World." *Yes! Magazine* 72 (Winter 2015).

Eck, K. "Repression by Proxy: How Military Purges and Insurgency Impact the Delegation of Coercion." *Journal of Conflict Resolution* 59, no. 5 (2015): 924–46.

Eckberg, Douglas. "Table Ec190–198: Reported Homicides and Homicide Rates, by Sex and Mode of Death, 1900–1997." In *Historical Statistics of the United States,* edited by Susan B. Carter, Scott Sigmund Gartner, Michael R. Haines, Alan L. Olmstead, Richard Sutch, and Gavin Wright. Cambridge, U.K.: Cambridge University Press, 2006.

Edmonds-Poli, Emily. "The Effects of Drug-War Related Violence on Mexico's Press and Democracy." In *Building Resilient Communities in Mexico: Civic Responses to Crime and Violence,* edited by David A. Shirk, Duncan Wood, and Eric L. Olson, 143–71. Washington, D.C.: Wilson Center, 2014.

Edwards, Kari, and Edward E. Smith. "A Disconfirmation Bias in the Evaluation of Arguments." *Journal of Personality and Social Psychology* 71, no. 1 (1996): 5–24.

"The Effectiveness of Police Activity in Reducing Crime, Disorder, and Fear." In *Fairness and Effectiveness in Policing: The Evidence,* edited by Wesley Skogan and Kathleen Frydl, 217–51. Washington, D.C.: National Academies Press, 2004.

Egan, Timothy. "Crack's Legacy: A Special Report; A Drug Ran Its Course, then Hid with Its Users," *New York Times*, Sept. 19, 1999.

Egley, Arlen, Jr., J. Logan, and Dawn McDaniel. "Gang Homicides, Five U.S. Cities, 2003–2008." *Morbidity and Mortality Weekly Report*, Jan. 27, 2012.

"86 Policemen Killed by Naxals in Bihar Since 2005: Statistics." *The Economic Times*, September 5, 2010.

Eisenhower, Dwight D. "The President's News Conference of March 16, 1960." In *The Public Papers of the Presidents of the United States: Dwight D. Eisenhower, January 1, 1960, to January 20, 1961.* Washington, D.C.: Office of the Federal Register, 1961.

Eisner, Manuel. "Interpersonal Violence in the British Isles, 1200–2016." In *Oxford Handbook of Criminology*, edited by Alison Liebling, Shadd Maruna, and Lesley McAra. Oxford: Oxford University Press, 2017.

———. "Long-Term Historical Trends in Violent Crime." *Crime and Justice* 30 (2003): 83–142.

———. "Modernization, Self-Control, and Lethal Violence: The Long-Term Dynamics of European Homicide Rates in Theoretical Perspective." *British Journal of Criminology* 41, no. 4 (2001): 618–36.

Elbadawi, E., and N. Sambanis. "Why Are There So Many Civil Wars in Africa?" *Journal of African Economics* 9, no. 3 (2000): 244–69.

Elgin-Cossart, Molly, Bruce Jones, and Jane Esberg. "Pathways to Change: Baseline Study to Identify Theories of Change on Political Settlements and Confidence Building." New York: Center for International Cooperation, New York University, 2012.

Elias, Norbert. *The Civilizing Process: Sociogenetic and Psychogenetic Investigations.* Rev. ed. Malden, Mass: Blackwell, 2000.

Engvall, Johan. "Against the Grain: How Georgia Fought Corruption and What It Means." Washington, D.C.: Central Asia–Caucasus Institute, 2012.

Enns, Peter K. "Relative Policy Support and Coincidental Repression." *Perspectives on Politics* 13, no. 4 (2015): 1,053–64.

Epperly, Brad, Ryan Strickler, Paul White, and Christopher Witko. "Rule by Violence, Rule by Law: Voter Suppression and the Rise and Fall of Lynching in the U.S. South." White paper, University of South Carolina, 2016.

Epstein, Susan B., and Liana W. Rosen. "U.S. Security Assistance and Security Cooperation Programs: Overview of Funding Trends." Congressional Research Service R45091, Feb. 1, 2018.

Equal Justice Initiative. *Lynching in America: Confronting the Legacy of Racial Terror.* 3rd ed. Montgomery, Ala.: Equal Justice Initiative, 2017.

Erikkson, Mikael, Peter Wallensteen, and Margareta Stollenberg. "Armed Conflict, 1989–2003." *Journal of Peace Research* 40, no. 5 (2004): 593–607.

Esadze, Londa. "Georgia's Rose Revolution: People's Anti-corruption Revolution?" In *Organized Crime and Corruption in Georgia*, edited by Louise Shelley, Erik R. Scott, and Anthony Latta, 111–19. Washington, D.C.: American University Transnational Crime and Corruption Center, 2007.

ET Bureau. "Can Growth Tame Maoists?" *India Times*, April 1, 2013.

European Union Agency for Law Enforcement Cooperation. "Threat Assessment on Italian Organized Crime." The Hague: European Union Agency for Law Enforcement Cooperation, 2013.

Evans, Judith. "How Laundered Money Shapes London's Property Market." *Financial Times*, April 6, 2016.

Evans, Michael. "The Andean Strategy: Attacking Drugs by Hitting the Insurgency." National Security Archive. nsarchive2.gwu.edu.

Fajnzylber, Pablo, Daniel Lederman, and Norman Loayza. "Inequality and Violent Crime." *Journal of Law and Economics* 45, no. 1 (April 2002): 1–39.

Falcone, Giovanni, and Marcelle Padovani. *Men of Honour: Truth About the Mafia*. London: Warner Books, 1993.

"Farewell to Williams." *New York Times*, May 25, 1895.

Farooquee, Neyaz. "In Bihar Village, an Enduring Love for Lalu Prasad Yadav." *New York Times*, Nov. 23, 2013.

Farrington, David P. "The Effects of Public Labeling." *British Journal of Criminology* 17 (1977): 112–25.

————. "Key Results from the First Forty Years of the Cambridge Study in Delinquent Development." In *Taking Stock of Delinquency: An Overview of Findings from Contemporary Longitudinal Studies*, edited by Terrence P. Thornberry and Marvin D. Krohn, 137–83. New York: Kluwer-Plenum, 2003.

Fearon, James D. "Governance and Civil War Onset." Washington, D.C.: World Bank, 2010.

————. "Homicide Data, Third Revision." Background paper prepared for the World Development Report 2011 team, World Bank Group, Washington, D.C., 2011.

Fearon, James D., and Hoeffler, Anke, "Conflict and Violence Assessment Paper: Benefits and Costs of the Conflict and Violence Targets for the Post-2015 Development Agenda." Copenhagen Consensus Center, August 22, 2014.

Fearon, James D., and David Laitin. "Ethnicity, Insurgency, and Civil War." *American Political Science Review* 97 (2003): 75–90.

Felbab-Brown, Vanda. *Aspiration and Ambivalence*. Washington, D.C.: Brookings Institution, 2012.

————. "The Violent Drug Market in Mexico and Lessons from Colombia." Washington, D.C.: Brookings Institution, 2009.

Felbab-Brown, Vanda, Harold Trinkunas, and Shadi Hamid. *Militants, Criminals, and Warlords: The Challenge of Local Governance in an Age of Disorder*. Washington, D.C.: Brookings Institution Press, 2018.

Fellman, Michael. *Inside War: The Guerrilla Conflict in Missouri During the American Civil War*. New York: Oxford University Press, 1989.

Finkelhor, David, and Richard Ormrod. "Homicides of Children and Youth." Office of Juvenile Justice and Delinquency Prevention, Oct. 2001.

Finkelhor, David, H. A. Turner, Richard Omrod, S. Hamby, and K. Kracke. "Children's Exposure to Violence: A Comprehensive National Survey." U.S. Department of Justice, 2009.

Finoff, Kade. "Decomposing Inequality and Poverty in Post-war Rwanda: The Roles of Gender, Education, Wealth, and Location." *Development Southern Africa* 31, no. 2 (2015): 209–28.

"First Progress Report of the Secretary-General on the United Nations' Mission to Liberia." New York: United Nations Security Council, 2003.

Fischer, Claude. "A Crime Puzzle: Violent Crime Declines in America." *Berkeley Blog*, June 16, 2010. blogs.berkeley.edu.

Fisher, George. *Plea Bargaining's Triumph: A History of Plea Bargaining in America.* Stanford, Calif.: Stanford University Press, 2003.

Fiume, Giovanna. "Bandits, Violence, and the Organization of Power in Sicily in the Early Nineteenth Century." In *Society and Politics in the Age of the Risorgimento: Essays in Honor of Denis Mack Smith*, edited by John Davis and Paul Ginsborg, 71–90. Cambridge, U.K.: Cambridge University Press, 1991.

Fogelson, Robert. *Big City Police.* Cambridge, Mass.: Harvard University Press, 1977.

Foner, Eric. *Reconstruction: America's Unfinished Revolution, 1863–1877.* New York: Harper Perennial, 2014.

———, ed. *Freedom's Lawmakers: A Directory of Black Officeholders During Reconstruction.* Rev. ed. Baton Rouge: Louisiana State University Press, 1996.

Forero, Juan. "For Colombia's Ascetic Leader, Signs That Violence Is Easing." *New York Times*, Nov. 10, 2003.

———. "Explosions Rattle Colombian Capital During Inaugural." *New York Times*, Aug. 8, 2002.

Forman, James. *The Making of Black Revolutionaries.* Seattle: University of Washington Press, 1972.

Fortna, Virginia Page. *Does Peacekeeping Work? Shaping Belligerents' Choices After Civil War.* Princeton, N.J.: Princeton University Press, 2008.

Fox, Donald T., Gustavo Gallón-Giraldo, and Anne Stetson. "Lessons of the Colombian Constitutional Reform of 1991: Toward the Securitizing of Peace and Reconciliation?" In *Framing the State in Times of Transition*, edited by Laurel E. Miller and Louis Aucoin. Washington, D.C.: U.S. Institute of Peace, 2010.

Fox, James Alan, and Marianne W. Zawitz. "Homicide Trends in the United States." White paper, Bureau of Justice Statistics, 2007.

Francis, David J. Introduction to *Civil Militia: Africa's Intractable Security Menace?*, edited by David J. Francis, 1–29. Burlington, Vt.: Ashgate, 2005.

Franco, Saúl, Clara Mercedes Suarez, Claudia Beatriz Naranjo, Liliana Carolina Báez, and Patricia Rozo. "The Effects of the Armed Conflict on the

Life and Health in Colombia." *Ciência & Saúde Coletiva* 11, no. 2 (2006): 349–61.

Freedman, J. L., and S. C. Fraser. "Compliance Without Pressure: The Foot-in-the-Door Technique." *Journal of Personality and Social Psychology*, no. 4 (1966): 196–202.

Friedman, Matthew, Ames C. Grawert, and James Cullen. "Crime Trends: 1990–2016." New York: Brennan Center for Justice, 2017.

Frum, David. "The Cultural Roots of Crime." *Atlantic*, June 19, 2016.

Fukuyama, Francis. *State-Building: Governance and World Order in the 21st Century.* Ithaca, N.Y.: Cornell University Press, 2004.

Gambetta, Diego. *The Sicilian Mafia.* Cambridge, Mass.: Harvard University Press, 1993.

Gamson, William. *The Strategy of Social Protest.* Homewood, Ill.: Dorsey Press, 1975.

Gard, Wayne. *The Chisholm Trail.* Oklahoma City: University of Oklahoma Press, 1979.

Gates, Scott, and Kaushik Roy. *Unconventional Warfare in South Asia: Shadow Warriors and Counterinsurgency.* New York: Routledge, 2014.

Gayer, L. "Guns, Slums, and 'Yellow Devils': A Genealogy of Urban Conflicts in Karachi, Pakistan." *Modern Asian Studies* 41, no. 3 (2007): 515–44.

Gerstel, Steve. "Andean Drug Strategy a Failure." UPI, Feb. 25, 1992. www.upi .com.

Gettleman, Jeffrey. "The Global Elite's Favorite Strongman." *New York Times Magazine*, Sept. 4, 2013.

Ghani, Ashraf, and Clare Lockhart. *Fixing Failed States: A Framework for Rebuilding a Fractured World.* Oxford: Oxford University Press, 2008.

Gibson, Edward L. *Boundary Control: Subnational Authoritarianism in Federal Democracies.* New York: Cambridge University Press, 2013.

Gift, Thomas, and Daniel Krcmaric. "Who Democratizes? Western-Educated Leaders and Regime Transitions." *Journal of Conflict Resolution* 61, no. 3 (2017): 671–701.

Gilens, Martin. *Affluence and Influence: Economic Inequality and Political Power in America.* Princeton, N.J.: Princeton University Press, 2014.

Gilligan, Michael J., and Ernest J. Sergenti. "Do UN Interventions Cause Peace? Using Matching to Improve Causal Inference." *Quarterly Journal of Political Science* 3 (2008): 89–122.

Ginsborg, Paul. *A History of Contemporary Italy: Society and Politics.* New York: St. Martin's Griffin, 1990.

Ginzburg, Ralph. *100 Years of Lynching.* New York: Black Classic Press, 1962.

Glaeser, Edward L., Giacomo A. M. Ponzetto, and Andrei Shleifer. "Why Does Democracy Need Education?" *Journal of Economic Growth* 12, no. 2 (2007): 77–99.

Gledhill, J. "La mala administración de la seguridad pública." *Revista de Antropología Social* 22 (2013): 25–57.

Gleditsch, Kristian Skrede. *All International Politics Is Local: The Diffusion of Conflict, Integration, and Democratization*. Ann Arbor: University of Michigan Press, 2002.

Gleditsch, Nils Petter, and Ida Rudolfsen. "Are Muslim Countries More Prone to Violence?" *Research and Politics* 3, no. 2 (April–June 2016): 1–9.

Glenn, Russell W. *Rethinking Western Approaches to Counterinsurgency*. New York: Routledge, 2015.

"Global Patterns: Why They Do It." *Economist*. March 10, 2018.

Global Security. "Camorra." Global Security, 2015. www.globalsecurity.org.

———. "Camorra—Neapolitan Mafia." www.globalsecurity.org.

"Global Terrorism Index 2017." Institute for Economics and Peace, Sydney, 2017.

Global Witness. "New Data on the Murder Rate of Environmental and Land Activists in Honduras." Press release, March 4, 2016.

Godson, Roy, Dennis Jay Kenney, Margaret Litvin, and Gigi Tevzadze. "Building Societal Support for the Rule of Law in Georgia." *Trends in Organized Crime* 8, no. 2 (2004): 5–27.

Goldsmith, Andrew J. "Police Accountability Reform in Colombia." In *Civilian Oversight of Policing: Governance, Democracy, and Human Rights*, edited by Andrew J. Goldsmith and Colleen Lewis. Oxford: Hart, 2000.

Goldstone, Jack A. *Revolution and Rebellion in the Early Modern World*. Berkeley: University of California Press, 1991.

Goldstone, Jack A., Robert H. Bates, David L. Epstein, Ted Robert Gurr, Michael B. Lustik, Monty G. Marshall, Jay Ulfelder, and Mark Woodward. "A Global Model for Forecasting Political Instability." *American Political Science Review* 54, no. 1 (2010): 190–208.

Goldwater, Barry. "Peace Through Strength." In *Vital Speeches of the Day*. Vol. 30. New York: City News, 1964.

Gómez Gallego, Jorge Aníbal, José Roberto Herrera Vergara, and Nilson Pinilla Pinilla. *Informe Final: Comisión de la Verdad sobre los hechos del Palacio de Justicia*. Colombia: Comisión de la Verdad Palacio de Justicia, 2010. imas2010.files.wordpress.com.

Goodman, Colby, and Michael Drager. "Military Aid Dependency: What Are the Major U.S. Risks Around the World?" Security Assistance Monitor, March 8, 2016. securityassistance.org.

Goodwin, Jeff. *No Other Way Out: States and Revolutionary Movements, 1945–1991*. Cambridge, U.K.: Cambridge University Press, 2001.

Gorman, Anna. "Judge Rules in Favor of Trafficker." *Los Angeles Times*, Oct. 15, 2007. articles.latimes.com.

Gould, Roger V. *Collision of Wills: How Ambiguity About Social Rank Breeds Conflict*. Chicago: University of Chicago Press, 2003.

Government of Colombia. "Examen periódico universal: Informe de Colombia."

Grare, Frédéric. "Reforming the Intelligence Agencies in Pakistan's Transitional Democracy." Washington, D.C.: Carnegie Endowment for International Peace, 2006.

Green, Ben, Thibaut Horel, and Andrew Papachristos. "Modeling Contagion Through Social Networks to Explain and Predict Gunshot Violence in Chicago, 2006 to 2014." *Journal of the American Medical Association*, Jan. 3, 2017, published online.

Greenberg, David. *Republic of Spin: An Inside History of the American Presidency.* New York: W. W. Norton, 2016.

Greene, J. D., R. B. Sommerville, L. E. Nystrom, J. M. Darley, and J. D. Cohen. "An fMRI Investigation of Emotional Engagement in Moral Judgment." *Science* 293, no. 5537 (2015): 2,105–8.

Grindle, Merilee. *Jobs for the Boys: Patronage and the State in Comparative Perspective.* Cambridge, Mass.: Harvard University Press, 2012.

The Growth of Incarceration in the United States: Causes and Consequences. Washington, D.C.: National Academy of Sciences, 2014.

Gugliotta, Guy, and Jeff Leen. *Kings of Cocaine: An Astonishing True Story of Murder, Money, and Corruption.* New York: Simon & Schuster, 2010.

Gundle, Stephen, and Noelleanne O'Sullivan. "The Mass Media and the Political Crisis." In *The New Italian Republic: From the Fall of the Berlin Wall to Berlusconi,* edited by Stephen Gundle and Simon Parker. London: Routledge, 1996.

Gupta, Chirashree Das. "Unravelling Bihar's 'Growth Miracle.'" *Economic and Political Weekly* 45, no. 2 (1981): 52–60.

Gurr, Ted Robert. "Ethnic Warfare on the Wane." *Foreign Affairs* 79, no. 3 (2000): 52–64.

———. "Historical Trends in Violent Crime: A Critical Review of the Evidence." *Crime and Justice* 3 (1981): 295–353.

———. "Historical Trends in Violent Crime: Europe and the United States." In *Violence in America, Volume 1: The History of Crime,* edited by Ted Robert Gurr, 21–54. Thousand Oaks, Calif.: Sage Publications, 1989.

———. "People Against States: Ethnopolitical Conflict and the Changing World System." *International Studies Quarterly* 38, no. 3 (1994): 347–77.

———. "The Political Origins of State Violence and Terror: A Theoretical Analysis." In *Government Violence and Repression: An Agenda for Research,* edited by Michael Stohl and George Lopez, 45–72. New York: Praeger, 1986.

———. *Rogues, Rebels, and Reformers: A Political History of Urban Crime and Conflict.* Beverly Hills, Calif.: Sage, 1976.

———, ed. *Violence in America: The History of Crime.* New York: Sage, 1989.

Gutiérrez Sanín, Francisco, and Ana María Jaramillo. "Crime, (Counter-)Insurgency, and the Privatization of Security—the Case of Medellín, Colombia." *Environment and Urbanization* 16, no. 2 (2004): 17–30.

Gutiérrez Sanín, Francisco, María Teresa Pinto, Juan Carlos Arenas, Tania

Guzmán, and Maria Teresa Gutiérrez. "Politics and Security in Three Colombian Cities." Working paper 44. Instituto de Estudios Políticos y Relaciones Internacionales, March 2009.

Hacker, J. David. "A Census-Based Count of the Civil War Dead." *Civil War History* 57, no. 4 (2011): 307–48.

Hadley, Stephen J., and Rachel Kleinfeld. "Fostering a State-Society Compact." Washington, D.C.: U.S. Institute of Peace, 2016.

Hagen, Ryan, Kinga Makovi, and Peter Bearman. "The Influence of Political Dynamics in Southern Lynch Mob Formation and Lethality." *Social Forces* 92, no. 2 (2013): 757–87.

Haidt, Jonathan. "The Emotional Dog and Its Rational Tail: A Social Intuitionist Approach to Moral Judgment." *Psychological Review* 108, no. 4 (2001): 814–34.

———. *The Righteous Mind: Why Good People Are Divided by Politics and Religion.* New York: Vintage, 2013.

Haidt, Jonathan, and Craig Joseph. "Intuitive Ethics: How Innately Prepared Intuitions Generate Culturally Variable Virtues." *Daedalus* 133, no. 4 (2004): 55–66.

Hair, William Ivy. *The Kingfish and His Realm: The Life and Times of Huey P. Long.* Baton Rouge: Louisiana State University Press, 1996.

Hanson, Stephanie. "FARC, ELN: Colombia's Left-Wing Guerrillas." *Washington Post*, March 12, 2008. www.washingtonpost.com.

Harnischfeger, J. "The Bakassi Boys: Fighting Crime in Nigeria." *Journal of Modern African Studies* 41, no. 23 (2003).

Harrell, Erika. "Black Victims of Violent Crime." Bureau of Justice Statistics Special Report, Aug. 2007, 7–8.

Harris, Matthew C., Jinseong Park, Donald J. Bruce, and Matthew N. Murray. "Peacekeeping Force: Effects of Providing Tactical Equipment to Local Law Enforcement." *American Economic Journal: Economic Policy* 9, no. 3 (2017): 291–313.

Hartzell, Caroline, and Matthew Hoddie. "Institutionalizing Peace: Power Sharing and Post–Civil War Conflict Management." *American Journal of Political Science* 47, no. 2 (April 2003): 318–32.

Hash-Gonzalez, Kelli. *Popular Mobilization and Empowerment in Georgia's Rose Revolution.* Lanham, Md.: Lexington Books, 2012.

Hayden, Tom. *The Long Sixties: From 1960 to Barack Obama.* Boulder, Colo.: Paradigm, 2009.

Hays, Tom. "FBI: Gigante Still Runs Crime Family." Associated Press, Jan. 22, 2002.

Healy, Gene. "Corrupt FBI Let Mobster Whitey Bulger Keep Killing." *Washington Examiner*, July 19, 2013. www.washingtonexaminer.com.

Hegre, Håvard, Tanja Ellingsen, Scott Gates, and Nils Petter Gleditsch. "Toward a Democratic Civil Peace? Democracy, Political Change, and Civil War, 1816–1992." *American Political Science Review* 95, no. 1 (2001): 33–48.

Heinz, Carolyn Brown. "Bihar: Caste, Class, and Violence." In *The Modern Anthropology of India: Ethnography, Themes, and Theory*, edited by Peter Berger and Frank Heidemann, 30–45. New York: Routledge, 2013.

Henisz, Witold J. *Corporate Diplomacy: Building Reputations and Relationships with External Stakeholders*. New York: Routledge, 2014.

Hess, Henner. *Mafia and Mafiosi: Origin, Power, and Myth*. New York: New York University Press, 1998.

"Hidden Menace: How Secret Companies Are Putting Troops at Risk and Harming American Taxpayers." Global Witness, July 2016.

High Representative of the European Union for Foreign Affairs and Security Policy. "Joint Communication to the European Parliament and the Council." News release, 2015, eur-lex.europa.eu.

Hill, D., and Z. Jones. "An Empirical Evaluation of Explanations for State Repression." *American Political Science Review* 108, no. 3 (2014): 661–87.

Hinkle, J. C., and D. Wiesburd. "Irony of Broken Windows Policing: A Microplace Study of the Relationship Between Disorder, Focused Police Crackdowns, and Fear of Crime." *Journal of Criminal Justice* 36, no. 6 (2008): 503–12.

Hironaka, Ann. *Neverending Wars: The International Community, Weak States, and the Perpetuation of Civil War*. Cambridge, Mass.: Harvard University Press, 2005.

Hirschman, Albert. *Exit, Voice, and Loyalty: Responses to Decline in Firms, Organizations, and States*. Cambridge, Mass.: Harvard University Press, 1970.

Holland, A. "Right on Crime? Conservative Party Politics and Mano Dura Policies in El Salvador." *Latin American Research Review* 48, no. 1 (2013): 44–67.

Horowitz, Donald L. *The Deadly Ethnic Riot*. Berkeley: University of California Press, 2013.

———. "Making Moderation Pay: The Comparative Politics of Ethnic Conflict Management." In *Conflict and Peace-Building in Multiethnic Societies*, edited by Joseph Montville, 421–73. Lanham, Md.: Lexington Books, 1990.

"How Giant Outdoor Escalators Transformed a Colombian Neighborhood." CNN, December 14, 2015.

Hristov, Jasmin. *Blood and Capital: The Paramilitarization of Colombia*. Athens: Ohio University Press, 2009.

Hultman, Lisa, Jacob Kathman, and Megan Shannon. "Beyond Keeping Peace: United Nations Effectiveness in the Midst of Fighting." *American Political Science Review* 108, no. 4 (2014): 737–53.

Human Rights Watch. "Breaking the Grip? Obstacles to Justice for Paramilitary Mafias in Colombia." Washington, D.C.: Human Rights Watch, 2008.

———. "Good Cops Are Afraid: The Toll of Unchecked Police Violence in Rio de Janeiro." New York: Human Rights Watch, 2016. www.hrw.org.

———. *Human Rights Watch World Report*. Washington, D.C.: Human Rights Watch, 2000.

———. "Smoke and Mirrors: Colombia's Demobilization of Paramilitary Groups." New York: Human Rights Watch, July 31, 2005.

————. *These Fellows Must Be Eliminated: Relentless Violence and Impunity in Mani-pur*. New York: Human Rights Watch, 2008.

Human Security Project. "The Shrinking Costs of War." Vancouver: Simon Fraser University, 2010.

Human Security Report Project. *Sexual Violence, Education, and War: Beyond the Mainstream Narrative*. Vancouver: Human Security Press, 2012.

"Human Security Report 2009–2010." Cambridge University, Human Security Project.

Hume, Mo. "Armed Violence and Poverty in El Salvador." Bradford: Centre for International Cooperation and Security, University of Bradford, 2004.

Humphreys, D. K., A. Gasparrini, and D. J. Wiebe. "Evaluating the Impact of Florida's 'Stand Your Ground' Self-Defense Law on Homicide and Suicide by Firearm." *JAMA Internal Medicine*, 177, no. 1 (2017).

Humphreys, Macartan, and Ashutosh Varshney. "Violent Conflict and the Millennium Development Goals: Diagnosis and Recommendations." Prepared for the meeting of the Millennium Development Goals Poverty Task Force Workshop, Bangkok, June 2004.

Huntington, Samuel. *The Clash of Civilizations and the Remaking of World Order*. New York: Simon & Schuster, 1996.

Hurley, Dan. "Scientists at Work, Felton Earls: On Crime as Science." *New York Times*, Jan. 6, 2004.

India National Police Commission. "Third Report, 22.6–22.7." New Delhi: India National Police Commission, 1980.

Ingraham, Christopher. "There's Never Been a Safer Time to Be a Kid in America." *Washington Post*, April 14, 2015.

Initiative for Policy Dialogue and Friedrich-Ebert-Stiftung. *World Protests, 2006–2013*. New York, Sept. 2013.

Inter-American Court of Human Rights. *Caso Yarce y Otras vs. Colombia*. earthrights.org.

International Civil Rights Center and Museum. "The Greensboro Chronology." www.sitinmovement.org.

International Crisis Group. "Bangladesh: Back to the Future." Report 226. 2012.

————. "Colombia: Peace at Last?" Latin American Report 45, Sept. 25, 2012.

————. "CrisisWatch Tajikistan," March 2017.

————. "The Virtuous Twins: Protecting Human Rights and Improving Security in Colombia." Brussels: International Crisis Group, 2009.

Irwin, J. *Prisons in Turmoil*. Boston: Little, Brown, 1980.

Iyer, Lakshmi, Anandi Mani, Prachi Mishra, and Petia Topalova. "The Power of Political Voice: Women's Political Representation and Crime in India." *American Economic Journal: Applied Economics* 4, no. 4 (2012): 165–93.

Jacobs, David, Jason T. Carmichael, and Stephanie L. Kent. "Vigilantism, Current Racial Threat, and Death Sentences." *American Sociological Review* 70, no. 4 (2005).

Jacobs, David, Chad Malone, and Gale Iles. "Race Relations and Prison Admissions: Lynching, Minority Threat, and Racial Politics." *Sociological Quarterly* 53 (2012): 166–87.

Jacobs, Jane. *The Death and Life of Great American Cities.* New York: Vintage, 1961.

Jaffrelot, C. *The Hindu Nationalist Movement in India.* New York: Columbia University Press, 1998.

Jain, Varupi. "Criminals As Leaders—Yet Again?" *India Together,* November 19, 2005.

Jamieson, Alison. *The Antimafia: Italy's Fight Against Organized Crime.* Basingstoke: Palgrave Macmillan, 2000.

Jang, H., L. T. Hoover, and B. A. Lawton. "Effect of Broken Windows Enforcement on Clearance Rates." *Journal of Criminal Justice* 36, no. 6 (2008): 529–38.

Jarstad, Anna K., and Desiree Nilson. "From Words to Deeds: The Implementation of Power-Sharing Pacts in Peace Accords." *Conflict Management and Peace Science* 25, no. 3 (2008): 206–23.

Jauregui, Beatrice. "Shadows of the State, Subalterns of the State: Police and Law and Order in Postcolonial India." Ph.D. diss., Chicago: University of Chicago, 2009.

Jeffers, H. Paul. *Commissioner Roosevelt: The Story of Theodore Roosevelt and the New York City Police, 1895–1897.* New York: John Wiley and Sons, 1994.

Jenkins, Brian Michael. "The 1970s and the Birth of Contemporary Terrorism." *Hill,* July 30, 2015.

Jentzsch, Corinna, Stathis N. Kalyvas, and Livia Isabella Schubiger. "Militias in Civil Wars." *Journal of Conflict Resolution* 59, no. 5 (2015): 755–69.

Jha, Giridhar. "Brahmeshwar Singh: The Butcher Behind the School Teacher-Like Looks." *India Today,* June 1, 2012.

Jha, Manish K., and Pushpendra. "Governing Caste and Managing Conflicts: Bihar, 1990–2011." Kolkata: Mahanirban Calcutta Research Group, 2012.

Jha, Sanjay K. "Naxalite Movement in Bihar and Jharkhand." *Dialogue* 6, no. 4 (April–June 2005).

Johnson, Bruce, Andrew Golub, and Eloise Dunlap. "The Rise and Decline of Hard Drugs, Drug Markets, and Violence in Inner-City New York." In *The Crime Drop in America,* edited by Alfred Blumstein and Joel Wallman. Cambridge, U.K.: Cambridge University Press, 2000.

Johnson, Kyle, and Michael Jonsson. "Colombia: Ending the Forever War?" *Survival: Global Politics and Strategy* 55, no. 1 (2013): 67–86.

Johnson, Lyndon. "State of the Union, 1964." www.lbjlibrary.org.

Johnson, Steven. *Where Good Ideas Come From: The Natural History of Innovation.* New York: Penguin, 2010.

Jones, Stephen. *Criminology.* Oxford: Oxford University Press, 2001.

Jones, Stephen F. *Georgia: A Political History Since Independence.* London: I. B. Tauris, 2013.

———. "The Rose Revolution: A Revolution Without Revolutionaries?" *Cambridge Review of International Relations* 19, no. 1 (2006): 33–48.

"Journey to Extremism in Africa: Drivers, Incentives and the Tipping Point for Recruitment." United Nations Development Programme (2017).

Judt, Tony. *Postwar: A History of Europe Since 1945*. New York: Penguin Books, 2006.

"Jungle Justice: Trial by Fire." *Economist*, December 24, 2016.

Jutersonke, O., Robert Muggah, and D. Rogers. "Gangs, Urban Violence, and Security Interventions in Central America." *Security Dialogue* 40, no. 4–5 (2009): 373–97.

Kahneman, Daniel. *Thinking, Fast and Slow*. New York: Farrar, Straus and Giroux, 2011.

Kalyvas, Stathis N. *The Logic of Violence in Civil War*. Cambridge, U.K.: Cambridge University Press, 2006.

Kaplan, Michael. "Syria's Civilian Death Toll: Number of Isis Victims in 2015 Is Much Less Than Assad Regime–Inflicted Casualties." *International Business Times*, Dec. 29, 2015. www.ibtimes.com.

Kaplan, Robert. "The Coming Anarchy." *Atlantic*, Feb. 1994.

Kathman, Jacob D. and Reed M. Wood. "Managing Threat, Cost, and Incentive to Kill: The Short- and Long-Term Effects of Intervention in Mass Killings." *Journal of Conflict Resolution* 55, no. 5 (2011): 735–60.

Keating, Thomas F., and W. Andy Knight. *Building Sustainable Peace*. Tokyo: United Nations University Press, 2004.

"Keeping Foreign Corruption out of the United States: Four Case Histories." U.S. Senate Permanent Subcommittee on Investigations Report, Feb. 4, 2010, and testimony. www.hsgac.senate.gov.

Kelling, George L., and William H. Sousa Jr. "Do Police Matter? An Analysis of the Impact of New York City's Police Reforms." New York: Manhattan Institute, Dec. 2001.

Kelling, George L., and James Q. Wilson. "Broken Windows: The Police and Neighborhood Safety." *Atlantic*, March 1982.

Kennedy, Robert. *The Enemy Within: The McClellan Committee's Crusade Against Jimmy Hoffa and Corrupt Labor Unions*. New York: Popular Library, 1960.

Kent, Jackie. "Former Hobbs Officers Sue HPD for Racial Discrimination." KRQE.com, Oct. 9, 2017.

Kerkvliet, John. *The Huk Rebellion: A Study of Peasant Revolt in the Philippines*. Berkeley: University of California Press, 1977.

Kharas, Homi. "The Unprecedented Expansion of the Global Middle Class." Washington, D.C.: Brookings Institution, Feb. 28, 2017.

Kimmelman, Michael. "A City Rises, Along with Its Hopes." *New York Times*, May 20, 2012.

Kindy, Kimberly, Marc Fisher, Julie Tate, and Jennifer Jenkins. "A Year of Reckoning: Police Fatally Shot Nearly 1,000." *Washington Post*, Dec. 26, 2015. www.washingtonpost.com.

King, Gary, and Langche Zeng. "Improving Forecasts of State Failure." *World Politics* 53, no. 4 (2001): 623–58.

King, Martin Luther, Jr. *The Papers of Martin Luther King Jr.*, Vol. 4, *Symbol of the Movement, January 1957–December 1958.* Edited by Clayborne Carson. Berkeley: University of California Press, 1992.

Kinzer, Stephen. "Tbilisi Journal: The 'Man of the Year' Just 29 and via Manhattan." *New York Times*, June 4, 1998.

Kirschke, L. "Informal Repression, Zero-Sum Politics and Late Third Wave Transitions." *Journal of Modern African Studies* 38, no. 3 (2000): 383–405.

Klare, M. T. "The Deadly Connection: Paramilitary Bands, Small Arms Diffusion, and State Failure." In *When States Fail: Causes and Consequences*, edited by R. I. Rotberg, 116–34. Princeton, N.J.: Princeton University Press, 2004.

Klarman, Michael. "*Brown*, Racial Change, and the Civil Rights Movement." *Virginia Law Review* 80 (1994).

Kleider, Heather M., Dominic J. Parrott, and Tricia Z. King. "Shooting Behavior: How Working Memory and Negative Emotionality Influence Police Officer Shoot Decisions." *Applied Cognitive Psychology* 24, no. 5 (2010): 707–17.

Klein, Malcolm. "Labeling Theory and Delinquency Policy: An Empirical Test." *Criminal Justice and Behavior* 13 (1986): 47–79.

Kleinfeld, Rachel. *Advancing the Rule of Law Abroad: Next Generation Reform.* Washington, D.C.: Carnegie Endowment for International Peace, 2012.

———. "Competing Definitions of the Rule of Law." In *Promoting the Rule of Law Abroad: In Search of Knowledge*, edited by Thomas Carothers. Washington, D.C.: Carnegie Endowment for International Peace, 2006.

———. "Fragility and Security Sector Reform." Washington, D.C.: U.S. Institute of Peace, 2016.

———. *Improving Development Aid Design and Evaluation: Plan for Sailboats, Not Trains.* Washington, D.C.: Carnegie Endowment for International Peace, 2014.

———. *Let There Be Light: Electrifying the Developing World with Markets and Distributed Energy.* Washington, D.C.: Truman National Security Institute, 2011.

———. *Reducing All Violent Deaths, Everywhere: Why the Data Must Improve.* Washington, D.C.: Carnegie Endowment for International Peace, 2017.

———. "The United States and the Future of Humanitarian Intervention." In *The Future of Human Rights: U.S. Policy for a New Era*, edited by William F. Schulz, 52–71. Philadelphia: University of Pennsylvania Press, 2008.

———. "Why Is It So Difficult to Count Dead People?" BBC News, Oct. 12, 2017. www.bbc.com.

Kleinfeld, Rachel, and Harry Bader. *Extreme Violence and the Rule of Law: Lessons from Eastern Afghanistan.* Washington, D.C.: Carnegie Endowment for International Peace, 2014.

Kleinfeld, Rachel, and Rushda Majeed. *Fighting Insurgency with Politics: The Case of Bihar.* Washington, D.C.: Carnegie Endowment for International Peace, 2016.

Kleinfeld, Rachel, with Richard Youngs and Jonah Belser. "Renewing U.S. Political Representation: Lessons from Europe and U.S. History." Washington, D.C.: Carnegie Endowment for International Peace, 2018.

Klopp, J. M. "'Ethnic Clashes' and Winning Elections: The Case of Kenya's Electoral Despotism." *Canadian Journal of African Studies* 35, no. 3 (2001): 473–518.

Knack, Stephen. "Does Foreign Aid Promote Democracy?" *International Studies* 48, no. 1 (2004): 251–66.

Knight, Alan. "Corruption in Twentieth Century Mexico." In Little and Posada-Carbó, *Political Corruption in Europe and Latin America.*

Kocaoglu, Nurhan, Andrea Figari, and Helen Darbishire, eds. *Using the Right to Information as an Anti-corruption Tool.* London: Transparency International, 2006.

Kohlberg, L. "State and Sequence: The Cognitive-Developmental Approach to Socialization." In *Handbook of Socialization Theory and Research,* edited by D. A. Goslin, 347–480. Chicago: Rand McNally, 1969.

Kohli, Atul. *Democracy and Discontent: India's Growing Crisis of Governability.* Princeton, N.J.: Princeton University Press, 1991.

Korn, Alexander B. "Assessing Victory: How to Identify the Correct Measures of Success in Counterinsurgency Welfare—the Case of the FARC in Colombia." Master's thesis, Naval Postgraduate School, 2013.

Kousser, Morgan. *The Shaping of Southern Politics.* New Haven, Conn.: Yale University Press, 1974.

———. "The Voting Rights Act and the Two Reconstructions." In *Controversies in Minority Voting: The Voting Rights Act in Perspective,* edited by Bernard Grofman and Chandler Davidson. Washington, D.C.: Brookings Institution, 1992.

Kreps, Sarah E., and Geoffrey L. Wallace. "Just How Humanitarian Are Interventions? Peacekeeping and the Prevention of Civilian Killings During and After Civil Wars." American Political Science Association, Toronto Meeting Paper (2009).

Krueger, Alan B. *What Makes a Terrorist? Economics and the Roots of Terrorism.* Princeton, N.J.: Princeton University Press, 2007.

Krueger, Alan B., and Jitka Maleckova. "Education, Poverty, and Terrorism: Is There a Causal Connection?" *Journal of Economic Perspectives* 17, no. 4 (Winter 2003): 119–44.

Kukhianidze, Alexandre. "Corruption and Organized Crime in Georgia Before and After the 'Rose Revolution.'" *Central Asian Survey* 28, no. 2 (2009): 215–34.

Kukhianidze, Alexandre, Alexander Kupatadze, and Roman Gotsiridze. "Smuggling in Abkhazia and the Tskhinvali Region in 2003–2004." In *Organized Crime and Corruption in Georgia,* edited by Louise Shelley, Erik R. Scott, and Anthony Latta, 69–92. New York: Routledge, 2007.

Kumar, Amitava. *A Matter of Rats: A Short Biography of Patna.* Durham, N.C.: Duke University Press, 2014.

Kumar, Arun. "Violence and Political Culture: Politics of the Ultra Left in Bihar." *Economic and Political Weekly* 38, no. 47 (2003): 4,977–83.

Kumar, Ashwani. *Community Warriors: State, Peasants, and Caste Armies in Bihar.* London: Anthem, 2008.

Kumar, Avinash. "Illegitimacy of the State in Bihar." *Economic and Political Weekly* 44, no. 44 (2009): 8–11.

Kumlin, Staffan, and Bo Rothstein. "Questioning the New Liberal Dilemma: Immigrants, Social Networks, and Institutional Fairness." *Comparative Politics* 43, no. 1 (2010): 63–80.

Kunzelman, Michael. "'Alt-Right' Leader Loses Gym Membership After Confrontation." *Washington Post*, May 22, 2017.

Kurtz-Phelan, Daniel. "Q&A: Medellín Mayor Turns City Around." *Newsweek*, Nov. 10, 2007.

Kutler, Stanley I. *The Supreme Court and the Constitution: Readings in American Constitutional History.* Boston: Houghton Mifflin, 1969.

"La Corte Europea per i Diritti Umani ha accolto il ricorso di un recluso a pianosa condanna per maltrattamenti in carcere." *Il Tirreno*, Oct. 20, 2001. ricerca.gelocal.it.

Ladbury, Sarah. "Testing Hypotheses on Radicalisation in Afghanistan: Why Do Men Join the Taliban and Hizb-i Islami? How Much Do Local Communities Support Them?" London: Department for International Development, 2009.

LaFree, Gary. *Losing Legitimacy: Street Crime and the Decline of Social Institutions in America.* New York: Routledge, 1999.

LaFree, Gary, and Andromachi Tseloni. "Democracy and Crime: A Multilevel Analysis of Homicide Trends in Forty-Four Countries, 1950–2000." *Annals of the American Academy of Political and Social Sciences* 605, no. 1 (2006).

Lake, David A., and Donald Rothchild. "Spreading Fear: The Genesis of Transnational Ethnic Conflict." In *The International Spread of Ethnic Conflict: Fear, Diffusion, and Escalation,* edited by David A. Lake and Donald Rothchild, 35–60. Princeton, N.J.: Princeton University Press, 1998.

Lamb, Robert Dale. "Microdynamics of Illegitimacy and Complex Urban Violence in Medellín, Colombia." Ph.D. diss., University of Maryland, 2010.

Lane, Charles. *The Day Freedom Died: The Colfax Massacre, the Supreme Court, and the Betrayal of Reconstruction.* New York: Macmillan, 2008.

Lane, Roger. *Murder in America: A History.* Columbus: Ohio State University Press, 1997.

———. "On the Social Meaning of Homicide Trends." In *Violence in America: The History of Crime.* Newbury Park, Calif.: Sage, 1989.

———. *Roots of Violence in Black Philadelphia, 1860–1900.* Cambridge, Mass.: Harvard University Press, 1986.

Latinobarómetro. Informe 2015. Santiago: Latinobarómetro, 2015. www.latinobarometro.org.

———. Informe 2016. Santiago: Latinobarómetro, 2016. www.latinobaro metro.org.

Latzer, Barry. *The Rise and Fall of Violent Crime in America.* New York: Encounter Books, 2016.

Laub, John H., and Robert J. Sampson. *Crime in the Making: Pathways and Turning Points Through Life.* Cambridge, Mass.: Harvard University Press, 1993.

———. *Shared Beginnings, Divergent Lives: Delinquent Boys to Age 70.* Cambridge, Mass.: Harvard University Press, 2003.

Lavery, Brian. "I.R.A. Apologizes for Civilian Deaths in Its 30-Year Campaign." *New York Times,* July 17, 2002.

Le Bas, Adrienne. "Violence and Urban Order in Nairobi, Kenya, and Lagos, Nigeria." *Studies in Comparative International Development* 48, no. 3 (2013): 240–62.

Le Blanc, Marc, and Marcel Fréchette. *Male Criminal Activity from Childhood Through Youth: Multilevel Developmental Perspectives.* New York: Springer, 1989.

Lee, James Ray. "A Lakatosian View of the Democratic Peace Research Program." In *Progress in International Relations Theory,* edited by Colin Elman and Miriam Fendius Elman. Cambridge, Mass.: MIT Press, 2003.

Lee, Rensselaer W., III, and Francisco E. Thoumi. "The Criminal-Political Nexus in Colombia." *Trends in Organized Crime* 5, no. 3 (1999).

Leovy, Jill. *Ghettoside: A True Story of Murder in America.* New York: Random House, 2015.

Lessing, Benjamin. "Inside Out: The Challenge of Prison-Based Criminal Organizations," Reconstituting Local Orders White Paper, Washington, D.C.: Brookings Institution.

Lester, John C., and D. L. Wilson. *Ku Klux Klan: Its Origin, Growth, and Disbandment.* New York: Neale, 1884.

"A Lethal Culture: Drugs and Machismo Are a Dangerous Mix." *Economist,* December 11, 2014.

Levendusky, Matthew. *The Partisan Sort: How Liberals Became Democrats and Conservatives Became Republicans.* Chicago: University of Chicago Press, 2009.

Levi, Margaret. *Consent, Dissent, and Patriotism.* Cambridge, U.K.: Cambridge University Press, 1997.

———. *Of Rule and Revenue.* Berkeley: University of California Press, 1989.

———. "A State of Trust." In *Trust and Governance,* edited by Margaret Levi and Valerie Braithwaite, 77–101. New York: Russell Sage Foundation, 2003.

Levitsky, Steven, and Lucan Ahmad Way. *Competitive Authoritarianism: Hybrid Regimes After the Cold War.* New York: Cambridge University Press, 2010.

Levy, Brian. *Working with the Grain.* Oxford: Oxford University Press, 2014.

Lieven, Anatol. *Chechnya: The Tombstone of Russian Power.* New Haven, Conn.: Yale University Press, 1999.

Lindsey, Tim. "The Criminal State: The Premanisme and the New Indonesia." In *Indonesia Today: Challenges of History,* edited by Grayson J. Lloyd and Shannon L. Smith, 283–97. Singapore: Institute of Southeast Asian Studies, 2001.

Linthicum, Leslie. "A Sad State for Children." *Santa Fe New Mexican*, Jan. 21, 2018.

Lipset, Seymour Martin. "Radicalism or Reformism: The Sources of Working Class Politics." *American Political Science Review* 77 (1983): 1–18.

———. "Some Social Requisites of Democracy: Economic Development and Political Legitimacy." *American Political Science Review* 53 (1959): 69–105.

Little, Walter, and Eduardo Posada-Carbó, eds. *Political Corruption in Europe and Latin America*. London: Palgrave Macmillan, 1996.

Llorente, María Victoria. "Demilitarization in a War Zone." In *Public Security and Police Reform in the Americas*, edited by John Bailey and Lucia Dammert. Pittsburgh: University of Pittsburgh Press, 2006.

Llorente, María Victoria, Juan Carlos Garzón, and Boris Ramírez, "Así Se Concentra El Homicidio en las Ciudades." *El Espectador*, April 2017.

Llorente, María Victoria, and Jeremy McDermott. "Colombia's Lessons to Mexico." In *One Goal, Two Struggles: Confronting Crime and Violence in Mexico and Colombia*, edited by Cynthia J. Arnson and Eric Olson. Washington, D.C.: Wilson Center, 2014.

Lodge, Milton, and Charles Taber. *The Rationalizing Voter*. New York: Cambridge University Press, 2013.

Lohmuller, Michael, and Steven Dudley. "Appraising Violence in Honduras: How Much Is 'Gang-Related'?" *InSight Crime*, May 18, 2016.

López-Calva, Luis F., Jamele Rigolini, and Florencia Torche. "Is There Such a Thing as Middle Class Values? Class Differences, Values, and Political Orientation in Latin America." Washington, D.C.: World Bank, Nov. 2011.

Lord, Charles G., Lee Ross, and Mark R. Lepper. "Biased Assimilation and Attitude Polarization: The Effects of Prior Theories on Subsequently Considered Evidence." *Journal of Personality and Social Psychology* 37 (1979): 2,098–109.

Lupo, Salvatore. *Storia della Mafia*. Rome: Donzelli, 1993.

Luttwak, Edward. "Dead End: Counterinsurgency Warfare as Military Malpractice." *Harper's Magazine*, Feb. 2007.

"Lynchings by Year and Race." University of Missouri Kansas City Law School, law2.umkc.edu.

Lysova, Alexandra, and Nikolay Schitov. "What Is Russia's Real Homicide Rate? Statistical Reconstruction and the 'Decivilizing Process.'" *Theoretical Criminology* 19, no. 2 (2015): 257–77.

MacGinty, R. "Hybrid Governance: The Case of Georgia." *Global Governance* 19, no. 3 (2013): 443–61.

Mack, Andrew. "Even Failed Peace Agreements Save Lives." *Political Violence @ a Glance*, Aug. 10, 2012.

Mack, Steffen, and Walter Serif. "'Sie können es nicht lassen!'" *Mannheimer Morgen*, Jan. 30, 2016.

Maclean, Kate. *Social Urbanism and the Politics of Violence: The Medellín Miracle.* New York: Palgrave, 2015.

Majeed, Rushda, and Laura Bacon. "Palermo Renaissance Part 2: Reforming City Hall, 1993–2000." In *Innovations for Successful Societies.* Princeton, N.J.: Princeton University, 2012.

Makovi, Kinga, Ryan Hagen, and Peter Bearman. "The Course of Law: State Intervention in Southern Lynch Mob Violence 1882–1930." *Sociological Science* 3 (2016): 860–88.

Mansfield, Edward D., and Jack Snyder. "Democratization and the Danger of War." *International Security* 20, no. 1 (1995): 5–38.

"Maoists Storm Jehanabad Jail." *Rediff News,* Nov. 14, 2005.

Margolin, Gayla, and Elana B. Gordis. "Children's Exposure to Violence in the Family and Community." *Current Directions in Psychological Science* 113, no. 4 (2004): 152–55.

Marroquín, Sebastián. *Pablo Escobar: My Father.* New York: Thomas Dunne Books, 2016.

Marshall, Monty G. "Global Trends in Democratization." In *Peace and Conflict 2005: A Global Survey of Armed Conflicts, Self-Determination Movements, and Democracy,* edited by Monty G. Marshall and Ted Robert Gurr. College Park, Md.: Center for International Development and Conflict Management, 2005.

———. "Polity IV Project: Political Regime Characteristics and Transitions, 1800–2013."

Marten, Kimberly. *Warlords: Strong-Arm Brokers in Weak States.* Ithaca, N.Y.: Cornell University Press, 2012.

Martin, Susan E., and Lawrence W. Sherman. "Selective Apprehension: A Police Strategy for Repeat Offenders." *Criminology* 24 (1986): 55–72.

Mason, Lilliana. "'I Disrespectfully Agree': The Differential Effects of Partisan Sorting on Social and Issue Polarization." *American Journal of Political Science* 59, no. 1 (2015): 128–45.

———. *Uncivil Agreement: How Politics Became Our Identity.* Chicago: University of Chicago Press, 2018.

Mason, T. David, and Dale A. Krane. "The Political Economy of Death Squads: Toward a Theory of the Impact of State-Sanctioned Terror." *International Studies Quarterly* 33, no. 2 (1989): 175–98.

"Mass Shootings and Gun Control: A Culture of Violence." *Economist,* June 22, 2015.

Mathew, Santhost, and Mick Moore. "State Incapacity by Design: Understanding the Bihar Story." Brighton: Institute of Development Studies, 2011.

Maxeiner, James R. "Bane of American Forfeiture Law Banished at Last." *Cornell Law Review* 62, no. 4 (1977).

Maxwell, Christopher D., and Rebecca J. G. Stone. "The Nexus Between Economics and Family Violence: The Expected Impact of Recent Economic

Declines on the Rates and Patterns of Intimate, Child, and Elder Abuse." Working paper, Department of Justice, Washington, D.C., 2010.

May, Timothy. *The Mongol Conquests in World History*. New York: Reaktion Books, 2012.

McAdam, Doug. *Freedom Summer*. New York: Oxford University Press, 1988.

McCarthy, Patrick. *The Crisis of the Italian State: From the Origins of the Cold War to the Fall of Berlusconi*. New York: St. Martin's Press, 1995.

McDermott, Jeremy. "Going Back to Crime: Drug Trafficking and Emerging Criminal Gangs." In *Peace Initiatives and Colombia's Armed Conflict*, edited by Cynthia J. Arnson and María Victoria Llorente. Fundación Ideas para la Paz and Woodrow Wilson International Center for Scholars, Dec. 2009.

McEvoy, Claire, and Gergely Hideg. "Global Violent Deaths 2017: Time to Decide." Geneva: Small Arms Survey, Dec. 2017.

McGowan, Angela et al. "Effects on Violence of Laws and Policies Facilitating the Transfer of Juveniles from the Juvenile Justice System to the Adult Justice System: A Systematic Review." *American Journal of Preventive Medicine* 32 (2007): 7–28.

McGrath, Roger D. "Violence and Lawlessness on the Western Frontier." In Gurr, *Violence in America*, 122–45.

McInnis, Kathleen J., and J. Lucas. "What Is 'Building Partner Capacity'? Issues for Congress." Congressional Research Service, paper R44313, 2015. fas .org.

McKanna, Clare V. *Homicide, Race, and Justice in the American West, 1880–1920*. Tucson: University of Arizona Press, 1997.

McLoughlin, Claire. "When Does Service Delivery Improve the Legitimacy of a Fragile or Conflict-Affected State?" *Governance* 28, no. 3 (2015): 341–56.

McMahon, Richard, Joachim Eibach, and Randolph Roth. "Making Sense of Violence? Reflections on the History of Interpersonal Violence in Europe." *Crime, History, and Societies* 17, no. 2 (2013): 5–26.

McNerney, Michael, Angela O'Mahony, Thomas S. Szayna, Derek Eaton, Caroline Baxter, Colin P. Clarke, and Emma Cutrufello. *Assessing Security Cooperation as a Preventive Tool*. Santa Monica, Calif.: Rand, 2014.

Melander, Erik, Thérése Pettersson, and Lotta Themnér. "Organized Violence, 1989–2015." *Journal of Peace Research* 53, no. 3 (2016): 617–31.

Melara Minero, L. M. "Los servicios de seguridad privada en El Salvador." *Estudios Centroamericanos* 56, no. 636 (2001): 907–32.

Mele, Christopher. "2 Nephews of Venezuela's First Lady Convicted of Drug Charges." *New York Times*, Nov. 18, 2016.

Messick, Richard E., and Rachel Kleinfeld. "Writing an Effective Anticorruption Law." *PREM Notes* 58. Washington, D.C.: World Bank, 2001.

Meyer, P. J., and C. R. Seelke. *Central America Regional Security Initiative: Background Policy Issues for Congress*. Washington, D.C.: Congressional Research Service, 2012.

Mickey, Robert. *Paths out of Dixie: The Democratization of Authoritarian Enclaves* in *America's Deep South, 1944–1972*. Princeton, N.J.: Princeton University Press, 2015.

Miklaucic, Michael and Jacqueline Brewer, eds. *Convergence: Illicit Networks and National Security in an Age of Globalization*. Washington, D.C.: Center for Complex Operations, National Defense University, 2013.

Mill, Jonathan. "Dynamic Epigenetic Responses to Childhood Exposure to Violence." Unpublished. March 2012.

Miller, Jake M. "Is the Road in Georgia Too Perilous?" *Military Intelligence* 29, no. 2 (April–June 2003): 44–47.

Minor-Harper, Stephanie. "State and Federal Prisoners, 1925–85," Bureau of Justice Statistics bulletin. Washington, D.C.: U.S. Department of Justice, Oct. 1986.

Miroff, Nick. "When the Police Are Part of the Problem." Public Radio International, Nov. 26, 2011. www.pri.org.

Mishra, Ajit. "Persistence of Corruption: Some Theoretical Perspectives." *World Development* 34, no. 2 (2006): 349–58.

Mitchell, Neil J. *Agents of Atrocity: Leaders, Followers, and the Violation of Human Rights in Civil War*. New York: Palgrave Macmillan, 2004.

Mitchell, Neil J., Sabine C. Carey, and C. K. Butler. "The Impact of Pro-government Militias on Human Rights Violations." *International Interactions* 40 (2014): 812–36.

"Mobster Tomasso Buscetta Talks, and the Mafia's Worldwide Drug Ring Starts to Crumble." *People*, October 22, 1984.

Moncada, Eduardo. "Business and the Politics of Urban Violence in Colombia." *Studies in Comparative Development* 48, no. 2 (Summer 2013).

———. "Toward Democratic Policing in Colombia? Institutional Accountability Through Lateral Reform." *Comparative Politics* 41, no. 4 (2009): 431–49.

Moneyhon, Carl H. *Texas After the Civil War: The Struggle of Reconstruction*. College Station: Texas A&M University Press, 2004.

"Money Laundering: FAQs." Financial Services Authority. www.fsa.gov.uk.

Monkkonen, Eric H. "Diverging Homicide Rates: England and the United States, 1850–1875." In Gurr, *Violence in America*, 80–101.

———. *Murder in New York City*. Berkeley: University of California Press, 2001.

Montalvo, José G., and Marta Reynal-Querol. "Fractionalization, Polarization, and Economic Development." *American Economic Review* 95, no. 3 (2005): 796–816.

Moore, Barrington. *Social Origins of Dictatorship and Democracy*. Princeton, N.J.: Princeton University Press, 1966.

Morris, Edmund. *The Rise of Theodore Roosevelt*. New York: Random House, 2010.

Morris, Loveday. "Investigation Finds 50,000 'Ghost' Soldiers in Iraqi Army, Prime Minister Says." *Washington Post*, Nov. 30, 2014.

Mukherjee, Rohan. "Coalition Building in a Divided Society: Bihar State, India, 2005–2009." In *Innovations for Successful Societies*. Princeton, N.J.: Princeton University, 2009.

Mukherji, Arnab, and Anjan Mukherji. "Bihar: What Went Wrong? And What Changed?" New Delhi: National Institute of Public Finance and Policy, 2012.

Mungiu-Pippidi, Alina. *The Quest for Good Governance: How Societies Develop Control of Corruption.* Cambridge, U.K.: Cambridge University Press, 2015.

Munro, Geoffrey D., Peter H. Ditto, Lisa K. Lockhart, Angela Fagerlin, Mitchell Gready, and Elizabeth Peterson. "Biased Assimilation of Sociopolitical Arguments: Evaluating the 1996 U.S. Presidential Debate." *Basic and Applied Social Psychology* 24 (2002): 15–26.

Murphy, Paul P., Faith Karimi, and Catherine E. Shoichet. "Mother and Son's Deportation Pits Senator Against Homeland Security." CNN, May 4, 2017. www.cnn.com.

Murtagh, Robert. "How to Fix Latin America's Homicide Problem." *U.S. News & World Report,* June 28, 2017. www.usnews.com.

Muskhelishvili, Marina. "Institutional Change and Social Stability in Georgia." *Southeast European and Black Sea Studies* 3 (2011): 317–32, 324.

Mydans, Seth. "Georgian Leader Agrees to Resign, Ending Standoff." *New York Times,* Nov. 24, 2003.

Myrdal, Gunnar. *An American Dilemma: The Negro Problem and Modern Democracy.* New York: Harper Brothers, 1944.

Nadeau, Barbie Latza. "How the Mafia Murdered the Townspeople of Amatrice." *Daily Beast,* Aug. 30, 2016.

Nagin, D. S., F. T. Cullen, and C. L. Johnson. "Imprisonment and Reoffending." *Crime and Justice* 38 (2009): 115–200.

Naím, Moisés. *The End of Power: From Boardrooms to Battlefields and Churches to States, Why Being in Charge Isn't What It Used to Be.* New York: Basic Books, 2014.

Narula, Smita. "Broken People: Caste Violence Against India's Untouchables." New York: Human Rights Watch, 1999.

National Advisory Commission on Civil Disorders (the Kerner Commission). *Report of the National Advisory Commission on Civil Disorders.* New York: Bantam Books, 1968.

National Association for the Advancement of Colored People. "NAACP Legal History." www.naacp.org.

National Crime Records Bureau and Ministry of Home Affairs. "Crime in India 2016: Statistics." ncrb.gov.in.

Naylor, R. T. "The Insurgent Economy: Black Market Operations of Guerrilla Groups." In *Wages of Crime: Black Markets, Illegal Finance, and the Underworld Economy.* Ithaca, N.Y.: Cornell University Press, 2002.

Ndaruhutse, Susy. *State-Building, Peace-Building, and Service Delivery in Fragile and Conflict-Affected States: Synthesis Research Report.* London: CFBT Education Trust, 2012.

Nevin, Rick. "How Lead Exposure Relates to Temporal Changes in IQ, Violent Crime, and Unwed Pregnancy." *Environmental Research* 83 (2000): 1–22.

Nickerson, Raymond S. "Confirmation Bias: A Ubiquitous Phenomenon in Many Guises." *Review of General Psychology* 2, no. 2 (1998): 175–220.

Nicolay, John, and John Hay. *Abraham Lincoln: Complete Works.* New York: Francis D. Tandy, 1905.

"Nigerian Military: Some Officers Selling Arms to Boko Haram." Associated Press. Sept. 4, 2016.

Niven, David. *The Politics of Injustice: The Kennedys, the Freedom Rides, and the Electoral Consequences of Moral Compromise.* Nashville: University of Tennessee Press, 2003.

Nodia, Ghia. "Putting the State Back Together in Post-Soviet Georgia." In *Beyond State Crisis? Postcolonial Africa and Post-Soviet Eurasia in Comparative Perspective,* edited by Mark R. Beissinger and Crawford Young. Washington, D.C.: Woodrow Wilson Center Press, 2002.

North, Douglass, John Joseph Wallis, and Barry Weingast. *Violence and Social Orders: A Conceptual Framework for Interpreting Recorded Human History.* Cambridge, U.K.: Cambridge University Press, 2009.

Novak, Daniel A. *The Wheel of Servitude: Black Forced Labor After Slavery.* Lexington: University Press of Kentucky, 1978.

Nunn, Nathan, and Nancy Qian. "U.S. Food Aid and Civil Conflict." *American Economic Review* 104, no. 6 (2014): 1,630–66.

Office for Democratic Institutions and Human Rights. "Georgia: Extraordinary Presidential Election, January 4, 2004." Warsaw: Office of Security and Cooperation in Europe, 2004.

O'Grady, Siobhan. "In Nigeria, $2 Billion in Stolen Funds Is Just a Drop in the Corruption Bucket." *Foreign Policy,* Nov. 18, 2015.

OJJDP Statistical Briefing Book. Office of Juvenile Justice and Delinquency Prevention, 2004.

O'Leary, Brendan, and Andrew Silke. "Understanding and Ending Persistent Conflicts: Bridging Research and Policy." In *Terror, Insurgency, and the State: Ending Protracted Conflicts,* edited by Marianne Heiberg, Brendan O'Leary, and John Tirman. Philadelphia: University of Pennsylvania Press, 2007.

Olson, Mancur. "Dictatorship, Democracy, and Development." *American Political Science Review* 87, no. 3 (1993): 567–76.

Olzak, S., and E. Ryo. "Organizational Diversity, Vitality, and Outcomes in the Civil Rights Movement." *Social Forces* 85, no. 4 (2007): 1,561–92.

Orlando, Leoluca. *Fighting the Mafia and Renewing Sicilian Culture.* New York: Encounter Books, 2001.

Oshinsky, David. *Worse than Slavery: Parchman Farm and the Ordeal of Jim Crow Justice.* New York: Free Press, 1996.

Osorio, Javier. "Hobbes on Drugs: Understanding Drug Violence in Mexico." Ph.D. diss., University of Notre Dame, 2013.

Ouimet, Marc. "Explaining the American and Canadian Crime Drop in the 1990s." *Champ Pénal* 1 (2004): 33–50.

Pachico, Elyssa. "98% of Mexico's 2012 Murder Cases Unsolved." *InSight Crime,* July 17, 2013. www.insightcrime.org.

———. "Ties Binding Crime to Politics in Colombia May Weaken." *InSight Crime,* Aug. 2011.

Paden, J. "Midterm Challenges in Nigeria: Elections, Parties, and Regional Conflict." Washington, D.C.: U.S. Institute of Peace, 2013.

Page, Susan, and Karina Shedrofsky. "Poll: Clinton Builds Lead in Divided Nation Worried About Election Day Violence." *USA Today,* Oct. 26, 2016.

Page-Gould, E., R. Mendoza-Denton, and L. R. Tropp. "With a Little Help from My Cross-Group Friend: Reducing Anxiety in Intergroup Contexts Through Cross-Group Friendships." *Journal of Personality and Social Psychology* 95 (2008): 1,080–94.

Paoli, Letizia. "The Decline of the Italian Mafia." In *Organized Crime: Culture, Markets, and Policies,* edited by Dana Siegel and Hans Nelen, 15–28. New York: Springer, 2008.

Papachristos, Andrew V., and Christopher Wildeman. "Network Exposure and Homicide Victimization in an African American Community." *American Journal of Public Health* 104, no. 1 (2014): 143–50.

Parascandola, Rocco. "NYPD Campaign Wants New Recruits to 'Bring Who You Are,' Stresses 'Compassionate' Policing." *New York Daily News,* Oct. 23, 2016.

Pardo, Rafael. "Colombia's Two-Front War." *Foreign Affairs,* July/Aug. 2000.

Parishad, Ekta, and PRAXIS. "Landlessness and Social Justice: An Assessment of Disparities in Land Distribution and Prospects of Land Reforms." Patna: Institute for Participatory Practices, 2009.

Parkinson, Charles. "Medellín's Strategy for Driving Down Crime: Add More Gondolas." *Next City,* Nov. 11, 2013.

Pascale, Richard, Jerry Sternin, and Monique Sternin. *The Power of Positive Deviance: How Unlikely Innovators Solve the World's Toughest Problems.* Boston: Harvard Business Press, 2010.

Pasotti, Eleonora. *Political Branding in Cities: The Decline of Machine Politics in Bogotá, Naples, and Chicago.* Cambridge, U.K.: Cambridge University Press, 2010.

Paternostro, Silvana. "Mexico as a Narco-democracy." *World Policy Journal* 12, no. 1 (1995): 41–47.

Paul, Christopher, Colin P. Clarke, and Beth Grill. *Victory Has a Thousand Fathers: Sources of Success in Counterinsurgency.* Santa Monica, Calif.: Rand, 2010.

Paul, Samuel, and M. Vivekananda. "Knowing Our Legislators." *India Together,* 2004. indiatogether.org.

Paxton, Pamela. "Is Social Capital Declining in the United States? A Multiple Indicator Assessment." *American Journal of Sociology* 105, no. 1 (July 1999): 88–127.

Peel, Michael. *A Swamp Full of Dollars: Pipelines and Paramilitaries at Nigeria's Oil Frontier.* London: I. B. Tauris, 2011.

Peeler, John A. "Elite Settlements and Democratic Consolidation: Colombia, Costa Rica, and Venezuela." In *Elites and Democratic Consolidation in Latin America and Southern Europe*, edited by John Higley and Richard Gunther. Cambridge, U.K.: Cambridge University Press, 1992.

Pereira, Anthony, and Mark Ungar. "The Persistence of the 'Mano Dura': Authoritarian Legacies and Policing in Brazil and the Southern Cone." In *Authoritarian Legacies and Democracy in Latin America and Southern Europe*, edited by Katherine Hite and Paola Cesarini. South Bend, Ind.: University of Notre Dame Press, 2004.

Perito, Robert. *Afghanistan's Police: The Weak Link in Security Sector Reform*. Washington, D.C.: U.S. Institute of Peace, 2009. www.usip.org.

Perkinson, Robert. *Texas Tough: The Rise of America's Prison Empire*. New York: Metropolitan Books, 2010.

Pérouse de Montclos, Marc-Antoine, Elizabeth Minor, and Samrat Sinha, eds. *Violence, Statistics, and the Politics of Accounting for the Dead*. Switzerland: Springer International, 2016.

Petrosino, Anthony, Carolyn Turpin-Petrosino, and Sarah Guckenburg. "Formal System Processing of Juveniles: Effects on Delinquency." *Campbell Systematic Reviews* (2010): 32–33.

Pettigrew, T. F., and I. R. Tropp. "A Meta-analytic Test of Intergroup Contact Theory." *Journal of Personality and Social Psychology* 90 (2006): 751–83.

Pew Research Center. "Public Trust in Government: 1958–2017." Pew Research Center, May 3, 2017. www.people-press.org.

Pezzino, Paolo. *Mafia: Industria della violencia*. Florence: La Nuova Italia, 1995.

Pfeifer, Michael J. *Rough Justice: Lynching and American Society, 1875–1947*. Urbana-Champaign: University of Illinois Press, 2006.

Piazza, James. "Rooted in Poverty? Terrorism, Poor Economic Development, and Social Cleavages." *Terrorism and Political Violence* 18 (2006): 159–77.

Piccone, Ted. "Democracy and Violent Crime." Washington, D.C.: Brookings Institution, 2017.

Pildes, Richard H. "Democracy, Anti-democracy, and the Canon." *Constitutional Commentary* 17, no. 295 (2000).

Pilgrim, David. "What Was Jim Crow." Jim Crow Museum of Racist Memorabilia, Ferris State University, 2012.

Pimentel, Stanley A. "Mexico's Legacy of Corruption." In *Menace to Society: Political-Criminal Cooperation Around the World*, edited by Roy Godson. London: Routledge, 2003.

———. "The Nexus of Organized Crime and Politics in Mexico." In Bailey and Godson, *Organized Crime and Democratic Governability*, 33–57.

Pinheiro, Paulo Sérgio. "The Rule of Law and the Underprivileged in Latin America." In *The (Un)Rule of Law and the Underprivileged in Latin America*, edited by Juan E. Méndes, Guillermo O'Donnell, and Paulo Sérgio Pinheiro, 1–5. Notre Dame, Ind.: University of Notre Dame Press, 1999.

Pinker, Steven. *The Better Angels of Our Nature: Why Violence Has Declined.* New York: Viking Press, 2011.

Pizarro, David A., and Paul Bloom. "The Intelligence of the Moral Intuitions: Comment on Haidt." *Psychological Review* 100, no. 1 (2003).

Pollack, Harold. "'They Could Have Killed Me Easily': One Colombian Mayor's Fight Against Homicide." *Washington Post*, June 13, 2003.

Pollard, C. "Zero Tolerance: Short-Term Fix, Long-Term Liability?" In *Zero Tolerance: Policing a Free Society*, edited by Norman Dennis, 44–61. London: IEA Health and Welfare Unit, 1998.

Polletta, Francesca, and M. Kai Ho. "Frames and Their Consequences." In *The Oxford Handbook of Contextual Political Analysis*, edited by Robert Goodin and Charles Tilly. New York: Oxford University Press, 2004.

Porch, Douglas, and María José Rasmussen. "Demobilization of Paramilitaries in Colombia: Transformation or Transition?" *Studies in Conflict and Terrorism* 31, no. 6 (2008): 520–40.

Powdermaker, Hortense. *After Freedom: A Cultural Study in the Deep South.* New York: Viking Press, 1939.

Prah, Pamela. "Share of Homebuyers Paying Cash Reaches New High." *USA Today*, May 29, 2014.

Pratten, D. "The Politics of Protection: Perspectives on Vigilantism in Nigeria." *Africa* 78, no. 1 (2008):1–15.

Pratten, D., and A. Sen. *Global Vigilantes.* London: Hurst, 2008.

Prest, Julia. "Dancing King: Louis XIV's Roles in Molière's *Comédies-Ballets*, from Court to Town." *Seventeenth Century* 16, no. 2 (2001): 283–98.

Preston, Samuel, and Emily Buzzell. "Service in Iraq: Just How Risky?" *Washington Post*, Aug. 26, 2006.

Putnam, Robert. "E Pluribus Unum: Diversity and Community in the Twenty-First Century, the 2006 Johan Skytte Prize Lecture." *Scandinavian Political Studies* 30, no. 2 (June 2007): 137–74.

———. *Making Democracy Work.* Princeton, N.J.: Princeton University Press, 1993.

———. "Social Capital: Measurement and Consequences." Presentation to the Organisation for Economic Co-operation and Development, 2001.

"Quarterly Report to the United States Congress." Special Inspector General of Afghanistan Reconstruction (SIGAR), July 30, 2013.

Quraishi, S. Y. *A Documented Wonder: The Making of the Great Indian Election.* New Delhi: Rain Light, 2014.

Rable, George C. *But There Was No Peace: The Role of Violence in the Politics of Reconstruction.* Athens: University of Georgia Press, 2007.

Rabushka, Alvin. "The Flat Tax Spreads to Georgia." Hoover Institution, Stanford University, Jan. 3, 2005.

Rakove, Milton. *Don't Make No Waves . . . Don't Back No Losers: An Insider's Analysis of the Daley Machine.* Bloomington: Indiana University Press, 1976.

Ramakrishnan, Venkitesh. "A History of Massacres." *Frontline Magazine,* March 12, 1999.

Ramírez de Rincón, Marta Lucía. "Drug Trafficking: A National Security Threat—Similarities Between Colombia and Mexico." In *One Goal, Two Struggles: Confronting Crime and Violence in Mexico and Colombia,* edited by Cynthia J. Arnson, Eric L. Olson, and Christine Zaino. Washington, D.C.: Wilson Center, 2014.

Ray, Donald I. "Rural Local Governance and Traditional Leadership in Africa and the Afro-Caribbean: Policy and Research Implications from Africa to the Americas and Australasia." In *Grassroots Governance? Chiefs in Africa and the Afro-Caribbean,* edited by Donald I. Ray and P. S. Reddy, 1–30. Calgary: University of Calgary Press, 2003.

"Reaching the Untouchables." *Economist,* March 13, 2010.

Redding, Kent, and David R. James. "Estimating Levels and Modeling Determinants of Black and White Voter Turnout in the South, 1880 to 1912." *Historical Methods* 34, no. 4 (2001): 141–58.

Redlawsk, David. "Hot Cognition or Cool Consideration? Testing the Effects of Motivated Reasoning on Political Decision Making." *Journal of Politics* 64, no. 4 (2002): 1,021–104.

Reeves, Richard. *President Nixon: Alone in the White House.* New York: Simon & Schuster, 2001.

Regan, Patrick M., Richard W. Frank, and Aysegul Aydin. "Diplomatic Interventions and Civil War: A New Dataset." *Journal of Peace Research* 46, no. 1 (2009): 135–46.

Reina, Mauricio. "Drug Trafficking and the National Economy." In *Violence in Colombia, 1990–2000: Waging War and Negotiating Peace,* edited by Charles Bergquist, Ricardo Peñaranda, and Gonzalo Sánchez. Wilmington, Del.: Scholarly Resources, 2001.

Rempe, Dennis M. "Guerrillas, Bandits, and Independent Republics: US Counter-insurgency Efforts in Colombia, 1959–1965." *Small Wars and Insurgencies* 6, no. 3 (1995): 304–27.

Rempel, William C. *At the Devil's Table: The Untold Story of the Insider Who Brought Down the Cali Cartel.* New York: Random House, 2011.

Reno, William. *Warlord Politics and African States.* Boulder, Colo.: Lynne Rienner, 1999.

Restrepo, Jorge, and Robert Muggah. "Colombia's Quiet Demobilization: A Security Dividend?" In *Security and Post-conflict Reconstruction: Dealing with Fighters in the Aftermath of War,* edited by Robert Muggah. New York: Routledge, 2009.

Restrepo, Jorge, Michael Spagat, and Juan Vargas. "The Dynamics of the Colombian Civil Conflict: A New Dataset." *Homo Oeconomicus* 21, no. 2 (2004): 296–328.

Reyntjens, Filip. "Rwanda: Progress or Powder Keg?" *Journal of Democracy* 26, no. 3 (2015): 19–33.

Riall, Lucy. *Sicily and the Unification of Italy: Liberal Policy and Local Power, 1859–1866.* Oxford: Oxford University Press, 1998.

Rice, Susan, and Stewart Patrick. "Index of State Weakness in the Developing World." Washington, D.C.: Brookings Institution, Feb. 26, 2008.

Richani, Nazih. *Systems of Violence: The Political Economy of War and Peace in Colombia.* Albany: State University of New York Press, 2002.

Richardson, Heather Cox. *West from Appomattox: The Reconstruction of America After the Civil War.* New Haven, Conn.: Yale University Press, 2007.

Richman, Daniel C. "Cooperating Defendants: The Costs and Benefits of Purchasing Information from Scoundrels." *Federal Sentencing Reporter* 8, no. 5 (April 1996): 292–95.

Rico, Daniel. "The Criminal Diaspora." Washington, D.C.: Woodrow Wilson International Center for Scholars, 2013.

Riechmann, Deb, and Richard Lardner. "$360 Million Lost to Insurgents, Criminals in Afghanistan." *Seattle Times*, Aug. 17, 2011.

Riedel, Marc. "Homicide in Los Angeles County: A Study of Latino Victimization." In *Violent Crime: Assessing Race and Ethnic Differences*, edited by Darnell F. Hawkins. New York: Cambridge University Press, 2003.

Rios Contreras, Viridiana. "How Government Structure Encourages Criminal Violence: The Causes of Mexico's Drug War." Ph.D. diss., Harvard University, 2012.

"The Rise and Fall of 'False Positive' Killings in Colombia: The Role of U.S. Military Assistance, 2000–2010." Nyack, N.Y.: Fellowship of Reconciliation and Colombia-Europe-U.S. Human Rights Observatory, 2014.

Rivera, L. G. "Discipline and Punish: Youth Gangs' Response to 'Zero-Tolerance' Policies in Honduras." *Bulletin of Latin American Research* 29, no. 4 (2010): 492–504.

"Rivers of Blood." *Economist*, Oct. 10, 2015.

Robakidze, Nino. "Georgia: Immature Media." *Caucasus Analytical Digest* 25, no. 18 (March 2011).

Robinson, Mark. "Out of the Ivory Tower: Civil Society and the Aid System." In *Civil Society and the Aid Industry*, edited by Alison van Rooy. Sterling, Va.: Earthscan, 2013.

Robles, Frances. "Honduras Becomes the Murder Capital of the World." *Miami Herald*, Jan. 23, 2012.

Rocha, R. "Aspectos económicos de las drogas ilegales en Colombia." In *Drogas ilícitas en Colombia: Su impacto económico, político y social*, edited by F. Thoumi. Bogotá: Dirección Nacional de Estupefacientes, United Nations Development Program, and Planeta, 1997.

Rodríguez-Garavito, César. "Toward a Sociology of the Global Rule of Law Field: Neoliberalism, Neoconstitutionalism, and the Contest over Judicial Reform in Latin America." In *Lawyers and the Rule of Law in the Age of Globalization*, edited by Yves Dezalay and Bryant Garth, 156–82. New York: Routledge, 2011.

Rohter, Larry. "Colombians Tell of Massacre, as Army Stood By." *New York Times,* July 14, 2000.

Roldan, M. *Blood and Fire: La Violencia in Antioquia, Colombia, 1946–1953.* Chapel Hill, N.C.: Duke University Press, 2002.

Romano, Renee. "No Diplomatic Immunity: African Diplomats, the State Department, and Civil Rights, 1961–1964." *Journal of American History* 87 (2000): 546–79.

Roosevelt, Theodore. *American Ideals, and Other Essays, Social and Political.* New York: Charles Scribner's Sons, 1906.

———. *An Autobiography.* New York: Macmillan, 1913.

———. *Ranch Life and the Hunting Trail.* New York: Century, 1888.

Rosenberg, Tina. "Colombia's Data-Driven Fight Against Homicide." *New York Times,* Nov. 20, 2014.

Roth, Randolph. *American Homicide.* Cambridge, Mass.: Harvard University Press, 2009.

———. "Homicide Rates in the American West." July 2010. cjrc.osu.edu.

———. "Homicide Trends in the United States over the Past Century: How Should We Describe and Explain Them?" Unpublished paper for National Academy of Sciences.

———. "It's No Mystery: Why Homicide Declined in American Cities During the First Six Months of 2009." Nov. 22, 2009, unpublished.

———. "Measuring Feelings and Beliefs That May Facilitate (or Deter) Homicide: A Research Note on the Causes of Historic Fluctuations in the United States." *Homicide Studies* 16, no. 2 (2012).

Rothchild, Donald, and Philip G. Roeder. "Power Sharing as an Impediment to Peace and Democracy." In *Sustainable Peace: Power and Democracy After Civil Wars,* edited by Philip G. Roeder and Donald Rothchild. Ithaca, N.Y.: Cornell University Press, 2005.

Rothstein, Bo. *The Quality of Government: Corruption, Social Trust, and Inequality in International Perspective.* Chicago: University of Chicago Press, 2011.

Rothstein, Bo, and Dietlind Stolle. "The State and Social Capital: An Institutional Theory of Generalized Trust." *Comparative Politics* 40, no. 4 (2008): 441–59.

Roy, Olivier. *Jihad and Death: The Global Appeal of Islamic State.* Oxford: Oxford University Press, 2017.

Rubio, Kenia, and La Prensa Gráfica. "Impunidad en el Triángulo Norte." *La Prensa Gráfica* (2014). mediacenter.laprensagrafica.com.

Ruggiero, Vincenzo. "Who Corrupts Whom? A Criminal Eco-system Made in Italy." *Crime, Law, and Social Change* 54, no. 1 (2010): 87–105.

Rummel, Rudolph. "Statistics of Democide: Genocide and Mass Murder Since 1900." www.hawaii.edu.

———. *Statistics of Democide: Genocide and Mass Murder Since 1900.* Charlottesville: Center for National Security Law, School of Law, University of Virginia, 1997.

Rutzen, Doug. "Authoritarianism Goes Global II: Civil Society Under Assault." *Journal of Democracy* 26, no. 4 (2015): 28–39.

Saab, Bilal Y., and Alexandra W. Taylor. "Criminality and Armed Groups: A Comparative Study of FARC and Paramilitary Groups in Colombia." *Studies in Conflict and Terrorism* 32, no. 6 (2009): 455–75.

"Saakashvili Takes Oath on Tomb of King David the Builder." *Caucasian Knot*, January 24, 2004.

Sabet, Daniel. *Police Reform in Mexico: Informal Politics and the Challenge of Institutional Change.* Stanford, Calif.: Stanford University Press, 2012.

Sallah, Michael, Robert O'Harrow Jr., Steven Rich, and Gabe Silverman. "Stop and Seize." *Washington Post*, Sept. 6, 2014.

Sambanis, Nicholas. *Using Case Studies to Expand the Theory of Civil War.* Environmentally and Socially Sustainable Development Network. CPR Working Papers, 2003.

Sampson, Robert J., and Stephen W. Raudenbush. "Systematic Social Observation of Public Places: A New Look at Disorder in Urban Neighborhoods." *American Journal of Sociology* 105 (2000): 637–38.

Sampson, Robert J., Stephen W. Raudenbush, and Felton Earls. "Neighborhoods and Violent Crime: A Multilevel Study of Collective Efficacy." *Science* 277, no. 5328 (1997): 918–24.

Sánchez, Fabio, Silvia Espinosa, and Ángela Rivas. *¿Garrote o zanahoria? Factores asociados a la disminución de la violencia homicida y el crimen en Bogotá, 1993–2002.* Bogotá: CEDE, 2003.

Santaella-Tenorio, J., Cerdá M., Villaveces A., et al. "What Do We Know About the Association Between Firearm Legislation and Firearm-Related Injuries?" *Epidemiologic Reviews*, 38, no. 1 (2016): 140–57.

Saviano, Roberto. *Gomorrah: A Personal Journey into the Violent International Empire of Naples' Organized Crime System.* New York: Picador, 2008.

Sberna, Salvatore, and Alberto Vannucci. "'It's the Politics, Stupid!' The Politicization of Anti-corruption in Italy." *Crime Law and Social Change* 60, no. 5 (2013): 565–93.

Schlesinger, Arthur M., Jr. *Robert Kennedy and His Times.* Boston: Houghton Mifflin, 1978.

Schneider, Jane, and Peter Schneider. *Culture and Political Economy in Western Sicily.* Amsterdam: Elsevier, 2013.

———. "Mafia, Anti-Mafia, and the Plural Cultures of Sicily." *Current Anthropology* 46, no. 4 (August–October 2005): 501–20.

———. *Reversible Destiny: Mafia, Antimafia, and the Struggle for Palermo.* Berkeley: University of California Press, 2003.

Schuberth, M. "The Challenge of Community-Based Armed Groups: Towards a Conceptualization of Militias, Gangs, and Vigilantes." *Contemporary Security Policy* 36 (2015): 296–320.

"Screen Writer Bandit Killed." *Los Angeles Times*, June 17, 1925.

Second Progress Report of the Secretary-General on the United Nations' Mission to Liberia. New York: Security Council, March 22, 2004.

Security Assistance Monitor. "Security Aid Pivot Table—Tajikistan." Security Assistance Monitor Online. securityassistance.org.

"Security Assistance Monitor." Security Assistance Monitor Online. security assistance.org.

Seelke, C. R. *Gangs in Central America.* Washington, D.C.: Congressional Research Service, 2014.

Serio, Joseph D., and Vyacheslav Stepanovich Razinkin. "Thieves Professing the Code: The Traditional Role of *Vory v Zakone* in Russia's Criminal World and Adaptations to a New Social Reality." Crime and Justice International, Crime & Justice Europe.

Shahnazarian, Nona. "Police Reform and Corruption in Georgia, Armenia, and Ngorno-Karabakh." Policy Memo No. 232. Washington, D.C.: PONARS Eurasia, Sept. 2012.

Shanker, Thom. "Abu Ghraib Called Incubator for Terrorists." *New York Times,* Feb. 15, 2006.

Sharkey, Patrick. "The Acute Effect of Local Homicides on Children's Cognitive Performance." *Proceedings of the National Academy of the Sciences* 107, no. 26 (2010): 11,733–38.

Sharkey, Patrick, Nicole Tirado-Strayer, Andrew V. Papachristos, and C. Cybele Raver. "The Effect of Local Violence on Children's Attention and Impulse Control." *American Journal of Public Health* 102, no. 12 (2012): 2,287–93.

Sharma, Ruchir. "The Rise of the Rest of India: How States Have Become the Engines of Growth." *Foreign Affairs,* Sept. 2013.

Sharp, Gene. *From Dictatorship to Democracy.* Boston: Albert Einstein Institution, 1994.

Shaxson, Nicholas. "A Tale of Two Londons." *Vanity Fair,* April 2013.

Shelley, Louise. Introduction to *Organized Crime and Corruption in Georgia,* edited by Louise Shelley, Erik R. Scott, and Anthony Latta. New York: Routledge, 2007.

Sherman, Lawrence, Denise Gottfredson, Doris MacKenzie, John Eck, Peter Reuter, and Shawn Bushway. "Communities and Crime Prevention." *Preventing Crime: What Works, What Doesn't, What's Promising: A Report to the United States Congress,* edited by Lawrence Sherman. Bethesda: University of Maryland Department of Criminal Justice and Criminology, 1997.

———. "Preventing Crime: What Works, What Doesn't, What's Promising." *Research in Brief.* Washington, D.C.: National Institute of Justice, July 1998.

Shirley, Glenn. *Law West of Fort Smith.* Lincoln: University of Nebraska Press, 1957.

Shrivastava, Kumar Sambhav. "The Jungle Gangs of Jharkand." *Hindustan Times,* Jan. 24, 2016.

Silkey, Sarah L. *Black Woman Reformer: Ida B. Wells, Lynching, and Transatlantic Activism.* Atlanta: University of Georgia Press, 2004.

Silver, Nate. "Black Americans Are Killed at 12 Times the Rate of People in Other Developed Countries." fivethirtyeight.com, June 18, 2015.

Singh, Ajit Kumar. "A Tactical Retreat by the Maoists." *South Asia Intelligence Review* 5, no. 29 (2007).

Singh, Jyotsna. "Jail No Bar for Bihar Candidates." BBC News, April 21, 2004.

Singh, Santosh. "Now Bihar Simmers: Communal Clashes Surge After BJP-JDU Split." *Indian Express,* Nov. 6, 2014.

Sinha, Arun. *Nitish Kumar and the Rise of Bihar.* New Delhi: Penguin Books, 2011.

Skarbek, David. "Governance and Prison Gangs." *American Political Science Review* 105, no. 4 (2011): 702–16.

Skocpol, Theda. *States and Social Revolutions.* Cambridge, U.K.: Cambridge University Press, 1979.

Skolnick, Jerome H., and James J. Fyfe. *Above the Law: Police and the Excessive Use of Force.* New York: Simon & Schuster, 2010.

Skorup, Brent, and Andrea O'Sullivan. "Breaking Down Department of Defense Grants to State and Local Law Enforcement." Washington, D.C.: George Mason University, Mercatus Center, 2014.

Skorupski, Bolko J., and Nina M. Serafino. "DOD Security Cooperation: An Overview of Authorities and Issues." Congressional Research Service, paper R44602. fas.org.

Skowronek, Stephen. *Building a New American State: The Expansion of National Administrative Capacities, 1877–1920.* Cambridge, U.K.: Cambridge University Press, 1982.

Slade, Gavin. "No Country for Made Men: The Decline of the Mafia in Post-Soviet Georgia." *Law and Society Review* 46, no. 3 (2012): 623–49.

———. *Reorganizing Crime: Mafia and Anti-Mafia in Post-Soviet Georgia.* Oxford: Oxford University Press, 2013.

———. "The State in the Streets: The Changing Landscape of Policing in Georgia." *Caucasus Analytical Digest,* April 2011, 5–8.

Small Arms Survey 2011: States of Security. Geneva: Small Arms Survey, 2011.

Small Arms Survey 2013: Everyday Dangers. Geneva: Small Arms Survey, 2013.

Smith, Martin E. "Changing an Organisation's Culture: Correlates of Success and Failure." *Leadership and Organization Development Journal* 24, no. 5 (2003): 249–61.

Southall, Ashley. "Crime in New York City Plunges to a Level Not Seen Since the 1950s." *New York Times,* Dec. 27, 2017.

Spears, Ian S. "Understanding Inclusive Peace Agreements in Africa: The Problems of Sharing Power." *Third World Quarterly* 21, no. 1 (2000): 105–18.

Spelman, William. "The Limited Importance of Prison Expansion." In *The Crime Drop in America,* edited by Alfred Blumstein and Joel Wallman, 97–129. New York: Cambridge University Press, 2000.

Spierenburg, Pieter. *A History of Murder: Personal Violence in Europe from the Middle Ages to the Present.* Cambridge, U.K.: Polity Press, 2008.

Srivastava, Amitabh. "Nitish Kumar Is Ruining Powerful Criminals of Bihar's Happiness." *Daily O*, March 21, 2017.

Standish, Reid. "How Tajikistan's President Extended His Term—for Life." *Foreign Policy*, May 25, 2016.

Staniland, Paul. "Militias, Ideology, and the State." *Journal of Conflict Resolution* 59, no. 5 (2015).

———. "States, Insurgents, and Wartime Political Orders." *Perspectives on Politics* 10 (2012): 243–64.

Stanton, Jessica A. "Regulating Militias: Governments, Militias, and Civilian Targeting in Civil Wars." *Journal of Conflict Resolution* 59, no. 5 (2015): 899–923.

Steavenson, Wendell. "Marching Through Georgia." *New Yorker*, Dec. 15, 2008.

Stedman, Stephen. "Spoiler Problems in Peace Processes." *International Security* 22, no. 2 (1997): 5–53.

Stedman, Stephen, Donald Rothschild, and Elizabeth Cousens, eds. *Ending Civil Wars: The Implementation of Peace Agreements.* Boulder, Colo.: Lynne Rienner, 2002.

Steiner, R. "Colombia's Income from the Drug Trade." *World Development* 26, no. 6 (1998): 1013–31.

Stewart, Frances. "Social Exclusion and Conflict: Analysis and Policy Implications." Oxford: Centre for Research on Inequality, Human Security, and Ethnicity, 2006.

———, ed. *Horizontal Inequalities and Conflict: Understanding Group Violence in Multiethnic Societies.* London: Palgrave Macmillan, 2008.

Stille, Alexander. "All the Prime Minister's Men." *Independent*, Sept. 23, 1995.

———. *Excellent Cadavers: The Mafia and the Death of the First Italian Republic.* New York: Pantheon Books, 1996.

Stillman, Sarah. "Taken: The Rise of Civil Forfeiture." *New Yorker*, Aug. 12–19, 2013.

Stretesky, Paul, and Michael Lynch. "The Relationship Between Lead Exposure and Homicide." *Archives of Pediatric Adolescent Medicine* 155, no. 5 (2001): 579–82.

Strong, Robert R. "Plea Bargaining, Cooperation Agreements, and Immunity Orders." 155th International Training Course Visiting Experts' Paper, Office of Overseas Prosecutorial Development Assistance, and Training, U.S. Department of Justice, Washington, D.C.

Syrian Observatory for Human Rights. "About 500000 Persons Were Killed in Syria During 81 Months After the Syrian Revolution Started." Syrian Observatory for Human Rights. www.syriahr.com.

Taber, Charles S., and Milton Lodge. "Motivated Skepticism in the Evaluation of Political Beliefs." *American Journal of Political Science* 50, no. 3 (2006): 755–69.

Task Force Report: Crime and Its Impact—an Assessment. Washington, D.C.: President's Commission on Law Enforcement and the Administration of Justice, 1967.

Tattersall, Nick. "Nigerian Rebel Leaders Give Up Arms in Amnesty Deal." Reuters, Oct. 3, 2009.

Tavares, José. "Does Foreign Aid Corrupt?" *Economic Letters* 79 (2003): 99–106.

Taw, Jennifer Morrison. "The Effectiveness of Training International Military Students in Internal Defense and Development." Santa Monica, Calif.: Rand, 1993.

Tepperman, Jonathan. *The Fix: How Nations Survive and Thrive in a World in Decline.* New York: Tim Duggan Books, 2016.

Testimony of William Mithoff, New Orleans, Jan. 1, 1867, from Report of the Select Committee on the New Orleans Riots, U.S. Congress. Washington, D.C.: Government Printing Office, 1867.

Thelen, David P. "Review: Urban Politics: Beyond Bosses and Reformers," *Reviews in American History* 7 no 3 (1979): 406–12.

Thompson, Nicholas. "America's Culture of Violence." *New Yorker*, Dec. 15, 2012.

Thottam, Jyoti. "Breaking Free: How Nitish Kumar Turned Bihar into a Model of Indian Reform." *Time*, Nov. 7, 2011.

Tierney, John J., Jr. *Chasing Ghosts: Unconventional Warfare in American History.* Dulles, Va.: Potomac Books, 2006.

Tilly, Charles. *Coercion, Capital, and European States, AD 990–1990.* New York: Wiley-Blackwell, 1992.

———. *From Mobilization to Revolution.* New York: Addison-Wesley, 1978.

———. "War Making and State Making as Organized Crime." In *Bringing the State Back In*, edited by Peter Evans, Dietrich Rueschemeyer, and Theda Skocpol, 169–87. Cambridge, U.K.: Cambridge University Press, 1985.

Tilly, Charles, and Sydney Tarrow. *Contentious Politics.* New York: Paradigm, 2007.

Timm, Christian. "Neopatrimonialism by Default. State Politics and domination in Georgia After the Rose Revolution," Paper presented at workshop "Neopatrimonialism in Various World Regions, German Institute of Global and Area Studies, 23 August 2010.

Toch, Hans, James Douglas Grant, and Raymond T. Galvin. *Agents of Change: A Study in Police Reform.* New York: Wiley, 1975.

Tolnay, Stewart E., E. M. Beck, and James L. Massey. "Black Competition and White Vengeance: Legal Execution of Blacks as Social Control in the Cotton South, 1890 to 1929." *Social Science Quarterly* 73, no. 3 (1992): 627–44.

"Tomasso Buscetta." *Economist*, April 20, 2000.

Tonry, Michael. "Treating Juveniles as Adult Criminals: An Iatrogenic Violence Prevention Strategy if Ever There Was One." *American Journal of Preventive Medicine* 32 (2007): 3–4.

Transparency International. "The Georgian Advertising Market." Tbilisi: Transparency International, Georgia, Dec. 2011.

———. Global Corruption Barometer, 2010.

———. "Who Owns Georgia: Meet David Iakovashvili, Now in Control of

Assets Formerly Owned by Dato Kezerashvili." Transparency International, Georgia, Sept. 10, 2013.

Trelease, Allen W. *White Terror: The Ku Klux Klan Conspiracy and Southern Reconstruction.* New York: Harper & Row, 1971.

Tunnell, Ted. *Crucible of Reconstruction: War, Radicalism, and Race in Louisiana, 1862–1877.* Baton Rouge: Louisiana State University Press, 1992.

Turbiville, Graham H., Jr. "Firefights, Raids, and Assassinations: Tactical Forms of Cartel Violence and Their Underpinnings." *Small Wars and Insurgencies* 21, no. 1 (2010): 123–44.

Tynan, Deirdre. "Tajikistan: An Ever More Fragile State in a Brittle Region." *New Eastern Europe,* Jan. 28, 2016.

Tyson, Timothy B. *The Blood of Emmett Till.* New York: Simon & Schuster, 2017.

United Nations Children's Fund (UNICEF). "Silent Shame: Bringing Out the Voices of Children Caught in the Lake Chad Crisis." April 12, 2017.

United Nations Economic and Social Council Commission on Crime Prevention and Criminal Justice. "World Crime Trends and Emerging Issues and Responses in the Field of Crime Prevention and Social Justice." Vienna: United Nations, 2014.

United Nations Office of the High Commissioner for Human Rights. "Report of the Mapping Exercise." New York: United Nations. www.ohchr.org.

United Nations Office on Drugs and Crime. "Crime and Development in Central America." Vienna: United Nations Office on Drugs and Crime, 2007.

United Nations Security Council. *Addendum to the Group of Experts on the DRC's Interim Report (S/2012/348).* June 26, 2012.

U.S. House of Representatives. Report 22 pt. 13. "Testimony Taken by the Joint Select Committee to Inquire into the Condition of Affairs in the Late Insurrection States—Florida." 42nd Congress, 2nd Session. Testimony taken by the subcommittee November 10, 1871, Jacksonville, Florida, Washington Printing Office, 1872, p. 54–64.

U.S. House of Representatives Committee on Government Reform. *Everything Secret Degenerates: The FBI's Use of Murderers as Informants.* 108th Cong., 2nd Sess., 2004. www.gpo.gov.

Uslaner, Eric M. *The Moral Foundations of Trust.* Cambridge, U.K.: Cambridge University Press, 2002.

Vaishnav, Milan. *When Crime Pays.* New Haven, Conn.: Yale University Press, 2017.

Van Landingham, Mark. "2007 Murder Rates in New Orleans, Louisiana." *American Journal of Public Health* 98 (May 2008).

Vannucci, Alberto. "Politicians and Godfathers: Mafia and Political Corruption in Italy." In *Democracy and Corruption in Europe,* edited by Donatella Della Porta and Yves Mény. London: Pinter, 1997.

Varese, Federico. "The Secret History of Japanese Cinema: The Yakuza Movies." *Global Crime* 7, no. 1 (2006): 105–24.

Vargas, Ricardo. "State, Esprit Mafioso, and Armed Conflict in Colombia."

In *Politics in the Andes: Identity, Conflict, Reform*, edited by Jo-Marie Burt and Philip Mauceri. Pittsburgh: University of Pittsburgh Press, 2004.

Verpoorten, Marijke. "The Death Toll of the Rwandan Genocide: A Detailed Analysis for Gikongoro Province." *Population* 60, no. 4 (2005): 401–39.

Villagran, Lauren. "The Victims' Movement in Mexico." In *Building Resilient Communities in Mexico: Civic Responses to Crime and Violence*, edited by David A. Shirk, Duncan Wood, and Eric L. Olson. Washington, D.C.: Wilson Center, 2014.

"The Virtuous Twins: Protecting Human Rights and Improving Security in Colombia." Brussels: International Crisis Group, 2009.

Vittori, Jodi. "How Anonymous Shell Companies Finance Insurgents, Criminals, and Dictators." Washington, D.C.: Council on Foreign Relations, Sept. 7, 2017.

"Von drei Straftätern wird einer rückfällig." *Spiegel Online* (2014). www .spiegel.de.

Vreeland, James. "The Effect of Political Regime on Civil War: Unpacking Anocracy." *Journal of Conflict Resolution* 52, no. 3 (2008): 401–25.

Wallace, Arturo. "Colombia's Mayor Fights Cali's Murder Rate with Science." BBC News, Oct. 14, 2014.

Wallensteen, Peter, and Mikael Eriksson. "Negotiating Peace: Lessons from Three Comprehensive Peace Agreements." Uppsala: Uppsala University, Department of Peace and Conflict Research, 2009.

Walt, Vivienne. "Chevron, Total Accused of Human Rights Abuses in Burma." *Time*, July 6, 2010.

Walter, Barbara F. *Committing to Peace: The Successful Settlement of Civil Wars.* Princeton, N.J.: Princeton University Press, 2002.

———. "Conflict Relapse and the Sustainability of Post-conflict Peace." In *Conflict, Security, and Development: World Development Report*. Washington, D.C.: World Bank Group, 2011.

———. "The New New Civil Wars." *Annual Review of Political Science* 20 (2017): 469–86.

———. "Why Bad Governance Leads to Repeat Civil War." *Journal of Conflict Resolution* 59, no. 7 (2014): 1,242–72.

Walton, John. *Reluctant Rebels: Comparative Studies of Revolutions and Underdevelopment.* New York: Columbia University Press, 1984.

Walzer, Michael. *Spheres of Justice: A Defense of Pluralism and Equality.* New York: Basic Books, 1984.

Wantchekon, Leonard, and Etienne Yehoue. "Crime in New Democracies." New York: New York University, 2002.

Watts, Stephen. *Countering Others' Insurgencies: Understanding US Small-Footprint Interventions in Local Context.* Santa Monica, Calif.: Rand, 2014.

Weber, Max. *Economy and Society.* Edited by Guenther Roth and Claus Wittich. Berkeley: University of California Press, 1978.

———. "Politics as a Vocation." July 1919.

Wellman, Paul I. *A Dynasty of Western Outlaws.* Lincoln: University of Nebraska Press, 1986.

Wells, Miriam. "'Rising Extortion' Signals Trouble for El Salvador's Gang Truce." *InSight Crime,* March 18, 2013.

Westen, Drew, Pavel S. Blagov, Keith Harenski, Clint Kilts, and Stephan Hamman. "Neural Bases of Motivated Reasoning: An fMRI Study of Emotional Constraints on Partisan Political Judgment in the 2004 U.S. Presidential Election." *Journal of Cognitive Neuroscience* 18 (2006): 1,947–58.

"The Whistleblower's Story: One Man's Fight Against the Swiss Offshore Banking System," *Economist,* Dec. 23, 2017.

White House, Office of the Press Secretary. "Fact Sheet: Peace Colombia— a New Era of Partnership Between the United States and Colombia." News release, Feb. 4, 2016.

Widmer, Mireille, and Irene Pavesi. "Monitoring Trends in Violent Deaths." In *Research Notes.* Geneva: Small Arms Survey, 2016.

Wiktorowicz, Quintan. "Why Trump's Speech on Terrorism Was Such a Missed Opportunity." *Washington Post,* May 21, 2017.

Wilkerson, Isabel. *The Warmth of Other Suns: The Epic Story of America's Great Migration.* New York: Vintage, 2011.

Wilkinson, Richard. "Why Is Violence More Common Where Inequality Is Greater?" *Annals of the New York Academy of Sciences* 1,036, no. 1 (2006): 1–12.

Wilkinson, Steven. *Votes and Violence: Electoral Competition and Ethnic Riots in India.* Cambridge, U.K.: Cambridge University Press, 2006.

Wilson, Michael. "Trump Draws Criticism for Ad He Ran After Jogger Attack." *New York Times,* Oct. 23, 2002.

Wilson, Patricia A. "Deliberative Planning for Disaster Recovery: Remembering New Orleans." *Journal of Public Deliberation* 5, no. 1 (Dec. 2008).

Wilson, Scott. "Chronicle of a Massacre." *Washington Post,* Jan. 28, 2001.

Wilson, William Julius. *The Declining Significance of Race: Blacks and Changing American Institutions.* Chicago: University of Chicago Press, 1978.

Winters, Jeffrey A. *Oligarchy.* Cambridge, U.K.: Cambridge University Press, 2011.

Witsoe, Jeffrey. "Territorial Democracy: Caste, Dominance and Electoral Practice in Postcolonial India." *Political and Legal Anthropology Review* 32, no. 1 (2009): 64–83.

———. "A View from the States—Bihar." In *Routledge Handbook of Indian Politics,* edited by Atul Kohli and Prerna Singh. London: Routledge, 2010.

Wolf, S. "Policing Crime in El Salvador." *NACLA Report on the Americas* 45, no. 1 (2012): 43–47.

Wolff, Jonas, and Annika Elena Poppe. *From Closing Space to Contested Spaces.* Frankfurt: Peace Research Institute Frankfurt, 2015.

Wood, Elisabeth Jean. *Insurgent Collective Action and Civil War in El Salvador.* Cambridge, U.K.: Cambridge University Press, 2003.

Woodly, D. R. *The Politics of Common Sense*. New York: Oxford University Press, 2015.

Woods, Joseph Gerald. "The Progressives and the Police: Urban Reform and the Professionalization of the Los Angeles Police Forces." Ph.D. diss., University of California Los Angeles, 1973.

Woody, Christopher. "'Nobody Is Ever Going to Tell You': 3 Theories Regarding Who Killed 'the King of Cocaine,' Pablo Escobar." *Business Insider*, Oct. 4, 2015.

World Bank. *Anticorruption in Transition: A Contribution to the Policy Debate*. Washington, D.C.: World Bank, 2000.

———. "Case Study: Reduction of Crime in Bogotá: A Decade of Citizens' Security Policies." Washington, D.C.: World Bank, 2005.

———. *Fighting Corruption in Public Services: Chronicling Georgia's Reforms*. Washington, D.C.: World Bank, 2012.

———. "GDP (Current US$)." data.worldbank.org.

———. "Gross Domestic Product 2016." databank.worldbank.org.

———. *World Development Report 2011: Conflict, Security, and Development*. Washington, D.C.: World Bank, 2011.

Wrong, Michela. *It's Our Turn to Eat: The Story of a Kenyan Whistle Blower*. New York: HarperCollins, 2009.

X, Malcolm. *Malcolm X Speaks: Selected Speeches and Statements*. Edited by George Breitman. New York: Grove Press, 1965.

Yagoub, Mimi. "Colombia Busts Over 100 FARC Cocaine Labs." *InSight Crime*, Aug. 3, 2006.

Yusuf, H. "Conflict Dynamics in Karachi." Washington, D.C.: United States Institute for Peace, 2012.

Zeng, Zhen. "Jail Inmates in 2016." Bureau of Justice Statistics, Feb. 22, 2018.

Zimring, Franklin E. *The Great American Crime Decline*. New York: Oxford University Press, 2008.

———. *When Police Kill*. Cambridge, Mass.: Harvard University Press, 2017.

Zinecker, Heidrun. "Violence in a Homeostatic System—the Case of Honduras." *PRIF Reports*, no. 83. Frankfurt: Peace Research Institute Frankfurt, 2008.

INDEX

Page numbers in *italics* refer to illustrations. Page numbers beginning with 301 refer to endnotes.

cooperation agreements, 229
Corleone, Italy, 127, 131–2, 235
Corleones, 222
corruption, 60, 277
in Africa, 334
in Colombia, 206
as counterpart to Privilege Violence,
212, 237–8, 286–7
decivilization and, 94–5
as frequency dependent phenomenon,
344
in Georgia, 115, 118–20, 263–4
and homicide rates, 91
in New York, 115–16, 271, 283, 327–8,
351
opposition to, 117–18
plea bargains and, 230
of police, 211
in Sicily, 259
states weakened by, 101, 115–17
and taxes, 219
in weak electoral democracies, 343–4
Cosa Nostra, 68, 127, 128–34, 227, 265
alignment with landed class, 136
imprisoned members of, 260
organization of, 348
origins of, 129–31
peaceful resistance to, 136–7
Council of Europe, 387
counterculture, 251–2
coups, 33, 37
in Ghana, 31
cow towns, 46
crack, 252–3
Crimea, 387
Crime Control Act, 227
crime hot spots, 13
Croker, Boss, 367
culture, 311
honor, 96, 310
violent, 28–30
culture of lawfulness, 215–16

Dalits, 182–3, 185, 186, 372, 373
informants among, 231
intelligence to law enforcement by,
196–7
Kumar's attempt to win over, 195

loss of support for Maoists by, 195
massacre of, 194
reports of crime against, 266–7
voting by, 196
wealth and education amassed by,
195
Dalla Chiesa, Carlo Alberto, 122, 235
deals, with violence groups, 101
Death and Life of Great American Cities, The
(Jacobs), 208–9
death penalty, 256, 315
debt bondage, 371
decivilization, 15, 91–2
in Colombia, 92–4
corruption and, 94–5
and normalization of violence, 95
in United States, 96
of U.S., 248–52
Defense Department, U.S., 311, 402
Defense Ministry, Georgia, 108–9
Delaware, 281
democide, 144–5
democracy
and "end of history," 37
faltering of, 37–8
transition to, 42
and violence, 11, 13–14, 23–4, 28, 35–7,
315
war and, 356
democratic peace theory, 314
Department for International
Development (DFID), 286
desegregation
of U.S. armed services, 158
see also Brown v. Board of Education
development aid, 280, 282–3, 286–9,
403–4
Devi, Rabri, 187, 373
Dirección Federal de Seguridad (DFS), 41
dirty deals, 101–21, 247, 342
in Bihar, 189, 194
in Colombia, 101–3, 110, 112, 113–14,
179–80, 194
in Georgia, 103–10, 111, 119
in Nigeria, 112
pitfalls to, 111–12
transformed into legitimate
governments, 276–7

Justice Ministry, Italian, 223
juvenile murder, 395–6

Kagame, Paul, 143–4
Kahneman, Daniel, 89
Kansas, 319
Kansas City Times, 70
Kennedy, John F., 156–7, 225
Kennedy, Robert, 156, 225, 382
Kent State, 252, 391
Kenya, 284, 402
  gangs hired by political parties in, 60–1
  vigilantism in, 329
Kerner Commission, 390
Kezerashvili, Davit, 387
KGB, 109, 199
Khidasheli, Tina, 166, 239
kidnappings
  in Bihar, 181, 187, 190, 400
  in Colombia, 177, 265
  in Mexico, 71
Kiev, 164, 336
King, Martin Luther, Jr., 81, 156, 158, 227,
  334, 361
  assassination of, 209, 251
  as passé among college students, 250
Kitovani, Tengiz, 105–7, 109
Kmara, 168
Knapp Commission, 393
Knights of the White Camellia, 49
Know-Nothing party, 50
Kodori Gorge, 119
Korean War, 7
Ku Klux Klan, 49–50, 52, 53, 66, 67, 152,
  154, 158, 250, 383
  civil rights workers killed by, 157
  founding of, 329
  freedom rides vs., 155–6
  normalization of, 249
  punishment for desertion from, 68
  revival in 1950s of, 258
Ku Klux Klan Act, 322
Kumar, Nitish, 172, 173, 181, 197, 286,
  373, 386
  accused of being dictator, 241
  anticrime reform by, 190
  Bihar miracle of, 187–8
  BJP's break with, 262

citizens' meetings with, 203
crime lords given positions by, 189
crime lords sentenced by, 191, 192, 195
criminal reforms of, 240
election of, 188, 189, 190
pledge to establish rule of law by, 181
roads and bridges built by, 216
social programs of, 195–6

La Boétie, Étienne de, 135–6, 352
labor unions, 363
  in Sicily, 242
LaFree, Gary, 211
Landazábal Reyes, Fernando, 75
landlords, 185
Lane, Roger, 90
Latin America, 37
  masculinity in, 310
  military projects in, 354
  as unsatisfied with governments, 38, 42
La Torre, Franco, 235
La Torre, Pio, 122, 235, 385
lead, 254–5
leaders, 271–4
leadership development programs, 272
Lehder, Carlos, 81–2
lemons, 130
Leovy, Jill, 95, 125, 347, 378
Lesotho, violent deaths in, 22
Lester, John, 329
"Letter from a Birmingham Jail" (King),
  156
Leviathan (Hobbes), 31
Levitt, Steven, 254, 393–4
Lexow Commission, 326–7
Liberal Party, Colombia, 72–3
Libera Terra, 237
Liberia, 342
  civil war in, 81
Liberia (anti-Mafia group), 235
Libya, 11
  death toll in, 21
  violent deaths in, 22
Lincoln, Abraham, 45, 49, 53, 72, 73, 321
  on slavery, 152
Lindbergh, Charles, 392
literacy, in Bihar, 196
Lithuania, 257

A Note About the Author

Rachel Kleinfeld advises governments, philanthropists, and activists on how democracies make major social change. As a senior fellow at the Carnegie Endowment for International Peace, she focuses on countries facing violence, corruption, injustice, and poor governance. In 2010, *Time* magazine named her one of the top 40 political leaders under 40 in America for her decade of work as the founding CEO of the Truman National Security Project, and she was named a Young Global Leader of the World Economic Forum in 2015. From 2011 to 2014 she served on the State Department's Foreign Affairs Policy Board, which advised the secretary of state quarterly. She is the author of two previous books on international policy and appears frequently in the media, from *The Wall Street Journal* and *The New York Times* to the BBC, *Fox & Friends*, and numerous radio stations. Kleinfeld received her B.A. from Yale University and her M.Phil. and D.Phil. from Oxford University, where she was a Rhodes scholar. She lives in New Mexico and works in Washington, D.C., but harkens back often to the log house on a dirt road where she was raised in her beloved Fairbanks, Alaska.

A Note on the Type

This book was set in Albertina, the best known of the typefaces designed by Chris Brand (b. 1921 in Utrecht, The Netherlands). Issued by The Monotype Corporation in 1965, Albertina was one of the first text fonts made solely for photocomposition. It was first used to catalog the work of Stanley Morison and was exhibited in Brussels at the Albertina Library in 1966.

Composed by North Market Street Graphics,
Lancaster, Pennsylvania

Printed and bound by Berryville Graphics,
Berryville, Virginia

Designed by Betty Lew